STONYHURST PHILOSOPHICAL SERIES

STONYHURST PHILOSOPHICAL SERIES

THEORIES OF KNOWLEDGE

ABSOLUTISM
PRAGMATISM
REALISM

16478

BY

LESLIE J. WALKER, S.J. M.A.

SOMETIME PROFESSOR OF PHILOSOPHY AT STONYHURST COLLEGE

BD161
W18

SECOND EDITION

LONGMANS, GREEN & CO.
39, PATERNOSTER ROW, LONDON
NEW YORK, BOMBAY, AND CALCUTTA

1911

Nihil obstat :

J. N. STRASSMAIER, S.J.

Censor deputatus

Imprimatur :

EDM : CANONICUS SURMONT

Vicarius Generalis

WESTMONASTERII
die 14 Martii 1910

ROEHAMPTON : PRINTED BY JOHN GRIFFIN

PREFACE

THE improvement in the position of Catholic philosophical literature which has manifested itself both in English and foreign languages during the past twenty years is of a most cheering character. It used to be not unfrequently remarked that the great majority of works on philosophy published during the last century by writers adhering to the Scholastic tradition were Latin manuals, compends and summaries, reproducing and repeating over and over again the same bare outlines of the philosophy of the Schoolmen, without any attempt to develop that system, or to bring its doctrines into living contact with modern thought. And we fear it has to be admitted that there was some justification for the complaint. Balmez, Kleutgen and a few other writers did indeed furnish most substantial and valuable contributions in which the principles of the great Catholic thinkers of the Middle Ages were brought to bear intelligently on modern problems. But the greater part of the Latin manuals which appeared during the nineteenth century exhibited little effort at an understanding or an enlightened criticism of the philosophers since Hume. Modern speculation was usually condemned *en masse*. There was rarely any attempt to discriminate the elements of truth which might be found in an erroneous system, or to look at an opponent's conclusions from his own standpoint. He taught some obviously wrong doctrines; and he was to be refuted. As the space of a text-book was very limited, the refutation was necessarily somewhat summary.

In the circumstances this was probably inevitable. Almost the only class of Catholic readers at all interested in philosophy were ecclesiastical students who needed instruction in the essentials of Scholastic philosophy, chiefly as a grammar to their subsequent Theology. The Latin compendia designed to meet their wants had to compress into the narrowest space an epitome of the Scholastic system, dwelling especially on those topics which prepare the way for theological doctrines to be subsequently studied. Modern philosophical speculations apart from their connections with religious dogma possessed little or no interest, whilst domestic disagreements on metaphysical issues of minor import absorbed much energy and space. At the same time it was more urgently needful that the student should be warned that the conclusions or the systems of heterodox thinkers were false than that he should be enabled to understand these systems or to see how these conclusions had been reached. Accordingly the representations of such opponents' views were often inadequate, and the refutations at times superficial. Still, on the whole, they sufficed fairly well for the purpose in hand.

But the situation has been steadily changing during the last thirty years. In addition to the clerical student, to whom a more liberal culture is now necessary, an increasing number of educated lay-Catholics have arisen who, finding themselves in the midst of a society in which philosophical problems and systems are keenly discussed, are inevitably themselves drawn to take an interest in such discussions. It is therefore no longer sufficient for present-day needs to furnish a brief outline of the Scholastic doctrine with a summary refutation in two or three syllogisms of leading adversaries. Indeed it begins to be a serious question whether such treatment is not calculated to do more harm than good. It is now extremely probable that the student will himself read the opponent's own presentation of his doctrine, and if the previous representations or refutation be unfair, then there will be an inevitable reaction and the student's sympathy will be enlisted on the side of the writer whom he believes to have been unjustly dealt with. A careful, patient and scrupulously fair considera-tion of an opponent's views, if they are discussed at all, is the only profitable course at the present day, whilst the most effective form of philosophical criticism is that which, instead of singling out particular flaws, takes a large view of a system as a whole, traces it back to its sources, examines its internal consistency, and then follows it out to its ultimate consequences. It is thus, and not by arguments deduced from summarily assumed principles, which our opponent will not admit, that an erroneous system is to be most fruitfully controverted.

Happily, as I have already observed, there is manifest in recent years a large and increasing improvement in this respect in Catholic philosophical literature, both in English and foreign languages ; and new works are constantly appearing which exhibit the genuine philosophical spirit. True fidelity to the teaching of St. Thomas involves not the mere repetition or translation of the phrases or arguments of the great Scholastic Doctor, but the evolution of his principles and their intelligent application to the problems raised by the advance of Science and the varied conditions of human life to-day. The great fundamental philosophical questions will indeed remain always with us. But even these are ever presenting new aspects and raising new issues, whilst sundry minor metaphysical controversies which once intensely agitated the keenest intellects of Europe now possess merely a historical interest. What we more particularly want in these circumstances are monographs or substantial works devoted to the special problems of the present time. In comprehensive treatises of this kind, it is possible to attempt to shed some new light on the problems which now face us.

It is, therefore, with the greatest pleasure that I welcome the present volume as, in my view, both a valuable addition to modern Catholic philosophical literature, and also peculiarly suitable to present needs. It deals with the problem which lies at the root of so many other philosophical questions,—the great problem of epistemology. The author in the course of his work undertakes primarily the examination of the two most keenly discussed theories of knowledge of the present day, Absolutism and Pragmatism. But in his study he is naturally led back to their sources in Criticism and Empiricism. He puts each system before us as expounded by its best representatives ; he keeps constantly in view their mutual relations, and their connections with Kant and Hume, and he contrasts the most important features of each theory with the Realism of Aristotle and Aquinas. It is this method of intelligent and judicious consideration of current philosophical opinions from the standpoint of Scholasticism that appears to me to be specially profitable to-day. The work has obviously involved a very thorough and painstaking study of the different phases of Neo-Kantianism and also of the various forms of anti-intellectual Voluntarism, whilst the criticisms bring out some of the best merits of the Scholastic doctrine. The reader possessed of an acquaintance with recent philosophical speculation will appreciate the knowledge and acuteness with which the diverse aspects of the central problem are handled. In its original form, from which the present differs only by a slight expansion of some parts, this essay was submitted to the University of London. The fact that it should have gained for its author the degree of Master of Arts with the mark of distinction for special merit from a body so little suspect of excessive sympathy with Scholasticism as the London University is a guarantee of the value of the work, as it is at the same time a creditable testimony to the high standard of fair-mindedness and impartiality of that Institution.

MICHAEL MAHER, S.J.

Stonyhurst,
March, 1910.

AUTHOR'S PREFACE

As the Introduction to this work sufficiently explains its scope and purpose, further remarks by way of Preface are hardly necessary. Suffice it to say that it has been my sincere endeavour throughout to present the views of opponents in as fair a light as possible and for the most part in their own words. In this I have been much assisted by the kindness of Dr. Schiller, who has read several of the Chapters dealing with Pragmatism, and has aided me with valuable suggestions. My thanks are also due to the Rev. P. Hobart and the Rev. M. M'Donald for their services in the laborious work of reading and correcting proofs; and to the Rev. J. H. Oldham and other friends who have assisted me to prepare the Index.

St. Beuno's College, March, 1910.

PREFACE TO THE SECOND EDITION

My attempt to outline and defend the general principles of a Scholastic theory of knowledge, and to determine precisely its relation to other theories, is, as not a few critics have pointed out, for the most part pioneer work in Epistemology. It was only to be expected, therefore, that my endeavours would meet with considerable adverse criticism. Yet so far is this from being the case that I have found it necessary to make but few alterations in the present edition. One or two obscure passages have been modified, and one or

two technical inaccuracies corrected. An Appendix
has also been added in which the extremely
important, though much misunderstood notion of
' independence ' is discussed. These are the only
changes that have been made.

To modify the general plan of my work, with
which some have found fault, has been of course
impossible. Nor does it seem to me desirable ; for
the arrangement I have chosen is at any rate logical
and consecutive. To discuss the criteria of truth
before we have decided what truth is, or to
decide what truth is before we examined the
working of our cognitive faculties and discovered
the nature of the terms between which the truth-
relation holds, would to my mind be the reverse
of sound logic. Some treatment of the psychological
and metaphysical problems which underlie and are
pre-supposed by any doctrine of truth is essential
to the right understanding of such a doctrine,
whatever it may be. As therefore the problems to
be discussed fall more or less clearly under these
heads—psychology, metaphysics, and epistemology
proper, I have taken this as the basis for dividing
up my work. For the benefit of those, however,
who would prefer some other arrangement, especially
in regard to my treatment of Pragmatism, I beg
to suggest that the chapters of my book be read in
the following order. *Absolutism*, Intro. §§ 4—9,
ch. iii., iv., viii.—x. (xvi.), xix. ; *Pragmatism*,
§§ 10—17, ch. v.—vii. (xvi.), xvii., xx.—xxii. ;
Realism, §§ 18—24, ch. i., ii., xiii.,—xv., xvi.,
xviii., xxiii., xxiv.

St. Beuno's College, January, 1911.

ANALYSIS OF CONTENTS.

___

INTRODUCTION.

ABSOLUTISM.

PRAGMATISM.

PART I.

THE PSYCHOLOGICAL ANALYSIS OF COGNITION.

CHAPTER I.
THE DATA OF EXPERIENCE.—SENSE-PERCEPTION.

CHAPTER III.

THE PSYCHOLOGY OF CRITICISM AND THE DISTINCTION OF SUBJECT AND OBJECT.

§ 49.   Criticism is not psychological in the Lockian sense ;

§ 50.   but Dr. Caird is mistaken in thinking that Criticism or any other epistemology can be independent of psychology.

§ 51.   The Criticism of Kant presupposes psychological data, and so do later Criticism and Absolutism.

§ 52.   Dr. Caird, in fact, takes too narrow a view of psychology, and wrongly identifies the psychologist's standpoint with that of Locke, though introspection certainly testifies to the distinction of subject and object.

§ 53.   Mr. Shadworth Hodgson and the pragmatists, however, deny that this distinction is ultimate, a statement which admits of more than one interpretation.

§ 54.   But if it mean that the distinction is not ultimate as a fact, as both pragmatists and absolutists at times assert, neither can explain how it has arisen in consciousness.   For Absolutism it is simply a mystery,

§ 55.   and in the pragmatic philosophy of ' Pure ' Experience, which explains it as in some strange and inconceivable fashion the evolutionary product of sentience,

§ 56.   it becomes more mysterious than ever.

§ 57.   The psychology of human experience, which is undoubtedly the basis of Kantian Criticism, is converted later on into a psychology of the Absolute ; and hence the problems of human cognition are neglected by the absolutist.

§ 58.   Otherwise the psychology of Absolutism—since it is the validity, not the existence of common-sense beliefs that are denied—is accurate so far as it goes ;

§ 59.   though it ignores for the most part the purposive character of human cognition,

§ 60.   and in this is distinctly inferior to the psychology of Kant.

CHAPTER IV.

REALITY AS SENTIENT EXPERIENCE.

§ 61.   Mr. Bradley's Absolutism differs from other Absolutisms both in method, and in his constant appeal to experience,

§ 62.   which, he admits, must provide the data upon which the metaphysician has to work.

§ 63.   This appeal to experience gives to his metaphysical theory a distinctly subjective tone,

§ 64.   and his position approximates to the *esse* is *percipi* of Hume ; though he explicitly rejects Subjective Idealism.

§ 65.   It is by an appeal to experience that he attempts to prove his thesis that reality is sentient experience.

§ 66.   But his proof breaks down, because (1) even granting

CHAPTER V.

POSTULATION AND THE EXPERIMENTAL THEORY OF KNOWLEDGE.

§ 82. The standpoint of both Pragmatism and Humanism is psychological.

§ 83. According to the pragmatist, all cognition takes the form of postulation, which is followed by purposive experiments and so leads to the satisfaction of human needs—

§ 84. a doctrine which, in a restricted form, is admitted by most philosophers, notably by Kant.

§ 85. Indeed, Pragmatism may be regarded as a development of Kant's *Second Critique*, just as Absolutism is a development of the *First* and the *Third*. Hence pragmatic scorn for Kant is hardly justified.

§ 86. Even in the *First Critique* there are traces of postulation, and in the *Second* the principle is fundamental.

§ 87. By Kant, however, postulation is restricted to objects of faith, while in Pragmatism it is the only source of knowledge ; but since, in neither theory can a postulate be completely verified, we may well ask why the pragmatist has generalised the principle.

§ 88. This generalisation may be accounted for in three ways— (1) by the undue emphasis which the pragmatist lays on the emotional and volitional tendencies of our nature, (2) by his fondness for the inductive method of the scientist, or (3) by erroneous psychological analysis.

§ 89. But neither by the first nor by the second method of arriving at the principle can its universality be established ;

§ 90. while the third fails to take account of ' facts ' which appear to be ' given,' and of axioms which appear to be self-evident.

§ 91. Professor Dewey, in his *Experimental Theory of Knowledge*, denies that factual experience is strictly cognitional.

§ 92. But his assertion that all knowledge involves actual remembrance is false, for it is not involved in knowledge *per modum habitus ;*

§ 93. nor do all cognitive acts necessarily imply memory,

§ 94. still less anticipation.

§ 95. Dr. Schiller attempts to bring axioms into harmony with the pragmatic theory of knowledge, by showing that they all began life as postulates.

§ 96. But the principle of Identity,

§ 97. and the principle of Contradiction, as enunciated by Dr. Schiller, are not the principles for which logicians claim self-evidence.

§ 98. His account of the origin of belief in the ' external world ' is also unsatisfactory ; for if the perception of the ' real ' and the ' external ' was not immediate at the outset, as it usually is in adult life, we could never have formed a notion of 'objective reality' at all.

§ 99.   The pragmatic method, in fact, breaks down when it comes to a question of origin, and is forced to seek completion either in Apriorism or in Aristotle.

§ 100.   In conclusion, then, while admitting that postulation and experiment have an important function in the economy of knowledge, we must deny that they are the only source of knowledge.   pp. 124—160

CHAPTER VI.

CONCEPTION AND THE COGNITIVE RELATION.

CHAPTER VII.

GENETIC PSYCHOLOGY AND THE FACULTIES.

PART II.

THE METAPHYSICAL CONDITIONS OF KNOWLEDGE.

CHAPTER VIII.
APRIORISM AND ABSOLUTISM.

§ 135. Apriorism was invented in order to explain how relations between 'ideas' can be universal and yet real.

§ 136. It postulates that in knowledge the object conforms to *a priori* mental forms :

§ 137. hence knowledge, though it presupposes experience, is not due wholly to experience.

§ 138. Kant divides knowledge into three kinds, empirical, *a priori*, and 'pure' *a priori*.

§ 139. Faith is not strictly knowledge, for it quits the field of possible experience ; hence the existence of objects of faith is merely postulated—

§ 140. an argument which presupposes Immanence, the fundamental doctrine of Absolutism.

§ 141. But Kant stops short of Absolutism, since he admits a *Ding-an-sich ;*

§ 142. and to this dualism are due the chief defects of his theory.

§ 143. His attempt to overcome it in the *Second Critique*, leads only to the further dualism of the 'pure' and 'practical' reasons ;

§ 144. and this necessitates a *Third Critique*, in which Kant approaches nearer to Absolutism, but never reaches it ;

§ 145. for to the end he appears to have remained a dualist.

§ 146. Fichte, however, at once abolished the *Ding-an-sich*, and so got rid of dualism ;

§ 147. but in his theory Nature is inadequately accounted for, and his Absolute is never realised ;

§ 148. while Schelling's Absolute is a mere abstraction.

§ 149. Hegel overcomes these defects by making the Absolute at once ground, organic unity, and final end or term.

§ 150. Absolutism, therefore, is a theory of knowledge transformed into a theory of reality ; and its differentiations depend largely upon the view which is taken of the Absolute Ground, which is, however, always some form of consciousness.

§ 151. Thus Green, starting from the data of human consciousness, finds that reality is always conceived by us as an unalterable order of relations,

CHAPTER IX.
CRITICISM OF APRIORISM.

CHAPTER X.

CRITICISM OF ABSOLUTISM.

relations are appearances, because they mutually presuppose one another, rests upon assumptions already rejected.

§ 184. In fact, to assert that related objects are not really 'isolated,' but presuppose unity of ground because they are united in one act of thought, involves an illicit transition from the psychological to the real order.

§ 185. Moreover, against the Aristotelian theory of relations Mr. Bradley's arguments break down, for (1) a relation of difference in that theory is easily accounted for,

§ 186. (2) a relation does not introduce diversity within quality, since it is but another aspect of its *fundamentum,*

§ 187. (3) a change of relation, if real, implies a change in one of the objects concerned, but not necessarily in both,

§ 188. and (4) Comparison is valid whether relations are 'real' or not.

§ 189. The theory of relations upon which Absolutism is based, therefore, is false ; though a world of related objects certainly implies a spiritual principle as the condition of its existence.

§ 190. But is the creative act of this principle an act of intelligence ; and is this principle immanent in, and one with, the universe ? This Green and others assume ; but without proof,

§ 191. and with the result that the personality, unity and humanity of man is destroyed ;

§ 192. while the growth and the actual nature of human knowledge is still unexplained.

§ 193. For though 'objectivity,' 'otherness' and the apparent independence of the external world can be accounted for in some sort of way by Absolutism,

§ 194. the explanations given are not satisfactory.

§ 195. In Green's theory there is also a contradiction, since the Absolute must be held responsible for both truth and error, good and evil ; and though Mr. Bradley declares that these appearances are reconciled in the Absolute, he cannot tell us *how ;*

§ 196. nor do his arguments prove that such a reconciliation is possible.

§ 197. Absolutism, therefore, is essentially incomplete, and this incompleteness is due to the predominance of certain ideas, viz.,

§ 198. Organic Whole,

§ 199. Immanence,

§ 200. and Unity in Difference, each of which is valid it applied to finite things, but invalid if applied to the universe at large.

§ 201. Absolutism, therefore, is unsatisfactory because it fails to take account of facts which are relevant, to reconcile itself with which it would have to undergo considerable modification.

pp. 256—295

CHAPTER XI.
THE PHILOSOPHY OF PURE EXPERIENCE.
I. EXPOSITION.

CHAPTER XII.
THE PHILOSOPHY OF PURE EXPERIENCE.
II. CRITICISM.

§ 220. To criticise the philosophy of Pure Experience in its as yet inchoate form, is no easy task,

§ 221. while to determine its precise relation to Humanism and Pragmatism is still more difficult.

§ 222. But, at any rate, Dr. Schiller's position approximates very closely to that of the philosophy of Pure Experience,

§ 223. and he certainly teaches and endeavours to prove that in knowing we ' make ' reality,

§ 224. and make it in a metaphysical sense ;

§ 225. though it is not clear whether we ' make ' it by knowledge alone, or by knowledge *plus* action.

§ 226. But, in any case, if the human ' making of reality ' extends to all that is real, the process could never have begun,

§ 227. and though the philosophy of Pure Experience *alias* Panpsychism solves this difficulty so far as reality is concerned, the origin of human knowledge still remains a mystery.

§ 228. Indeed, it would seem that it never could have arisen at all in a panpsychic universe, if our thoughts never terminate in other minds.

§ 229. Professor James appeals to space as a common medium between mind and mind ; but this, if it be treated in accordance with the principles of a philosophy of Pure Experience, leads to Monism ; and if interpreted realistically, it seems irrational to restrict the common *object* of perception to space.

§ 230. The disruptive tendency of the philosophy of Pure Experience is also illustrated by the ' possible experiences ' in which conceptual thought terminates, for these can never become actual for ' me ' unless different experiences possess something in common ;

§ 231. and, again, in the philosophy of Avenarius, in which experiences must be at bottom one, or else, if plural, causally interact.

§ 232. The self, too, as explained in a philosophy of Pure Experience, renders memory, purpose, conation, and experience itself unintelligible ;

§ 233. and so long as this philosophy refuses to admit that the self is a real unity, it is wholly incompatible with Personal Idealism.

§ 234. But Personal Idealism itself is unsatisfactory, since a multiplicity of rational psychic beings cannot be an ultimate fact, but presupposes either an Absolute ground or else a personal God.

§ 235. If the latter alternative be adopted, the idealistic assumption that the subject experiencing and the real object experienced are not distinct, alone bars the way to a complete return to Realism.

CHAPTER XIII.
THE CONDITIONS OF KNOWLEDGE
EX PARTE OBJECTI.

and sweet, or, identifying the thing with its unity of ground, say that it *has* these qualities ;

§ 251. and so may predicate of the ground what is different, without ascribing to the whole what it is not.

§ 252. Other objections raised by Mr. Bradley are due to misinterpretation or to the absolutist theory of relations ; but against causation he urges that it must be at once continuous and not continuous.

§ 253. Mr. Bradley, however, wrongly conceives a *continuum* as a series of unextended points, whereas it essentially implies extension, either in space or time ; and though to define the notion is not easy, yet its validity is presupposed by geometry ;

§ 254. and it may, at any rate, be illustrated by the continuity of consciousness, and, again, by the continuity of material things.

§ 255. In fine, if continuity be rightly understood, we must affirm that causation also is continuous, a fact which shows the imperfection, but does not destroy the reality of the finite world.

pp. 346—372

CHAPTER XIV.

THE CONDITIONS OF KNOWLEDGE
EX PARTE SUBJECTI.—I. THE SENSES.

§ 256. The condition of knowledge *ex parte subjecti*, in brief, is a sentient organism endowed with intellect and will, together with passive and active *potentiæ*.

§ 257. Man, however, does not first know his sensations or ideas and then infer objects to correspond : he thinks of objects by means of ideas : to know and to know how we know are quite different things.

§ 258. The knower and the known are brought together by interaction ; for the causal action of the object produces in the sentient organism an ' impression ' like in form to itself.

§ 259. And the ' correspondence ' here asserted, so far from being absurd, not only follows from general metaphysical principles, but is confirmed by physiology and physics.

§ 260. For, in the first place, the ' quality ' of the nervous impulse does not depend upon the ' specific energy of the nerves,'

§ 261. but would seem to be determined ultimately by physical stimuli ;

§ 262. while, in regard to the ' quality ' of sensation itself, its primary function is to enable us to distinguish object from object, which it does with remarkable accuracy ; and if it tells us nothing of the nature of objects, it, at any rate, does not deceive us in that respect.

§ 263. In regard to the *sensibilia communia*, there is correspondence between configuration in space and retinal or tactual impressions ;

§ 264. and in the perception of a third dimension the combination of intensively and extensively graduated series of sensations is objectively determined.

§ 265. To this it may be objected that the alleged correspondence is merely peripheral, whereas sensation is exclusively cerebral ; but neither of these statements can be proved.

§ 266. Moreover, the scholastic theory is confirmed by 'localisation,' in which sensations are 'projected' back into their causes. PP. 373—391

CHAPTER XV.

THE CONDITIONS OF KNOWLEDGE
EX PARTE SUBJECTI.—II. THE INTELLECT.

§ 267. The intellect is passive in that it is determined by *species* derived from the phantasm ; but has also many active functions.

§ 268. It apprehends or abstracts the universal implicit in the sense-impression,

§ 269. and thus we get notions which have real significance, because they correspond to, and are ultimately determined by, their objects ;

§ 270. for in sense-perception intellect and sensation function in unity.

§ 271. The notions of Substance, Causality and Purpose are not only contained implicitly in, but also presupposed by, the data of consciousness.

§ 272. Thus causality is implied in change ;

§ 273. and substance is presupposed as the ground of a complexus of accidents or activities ; though it is for the physicist to draw the line between substantial unities in the concrete.

§ 274. Many notions are so simple that they cannot be strictly defined ;

§ 275. except that inasmuch as they form part of the rational plan of the universe they may be defined by the relations to which they give rise.

§ 276. Thus geometrical notions once determined, their relations also are determined, any one of which may be used to ' define ' the notion.

§ 277. The aim of all science, in fact, is to reconstruct the rational plan of the universe in some one of its aspects ; and their method is one, in that they seek to synthesise a complexity of relations under a few simple principles.

§ 278. But some sciences are more complete, because more abstract than others, which presuppose them, and on account of the complexity of their objects, are developed later.

§ 279. And for a similar reason, while the abstract sciences are based on axioms, *i.e.*, self-evident truths expressing relations between simple entities, physical science has no axioms.

§ 280. The laws of nature themselves, in fact, are necessary, only given the existence of the objects which *de facto* constitute the physical universe.

§ 281.   Thus the first and second of Newton's laws are not axioms ; but general principles which have been verified in experience,

§ 282.   for the notion of ' force ' which they employ, although it cannot be defined, is certainly not a mere ' ratio.'

§ 283.   Again, the third law of motion, and the principle of Conservation of Energy are but particular cases of Spinoza's axiom ; but since this so-called axiom, as a *physical* principle, is not self-evident, they require to be verified in experience.

§ 284.   And in this verification process the functions of the intellect—apprehension, judgment and reasoning—are further illustrated.

§ 285.   Summary of the conditions of knowledge in the Aristotelico-Scholastic or Causal Theory.

§ 286.   Truth, cognition, knowledge, and error defined.

PP. 391—418

PART III.

THE EPISTEMOLOGICAL VALUE OF COGNITION.

CHAPTER XVI.
DEVELOPMENT AND VALIDITY.

§ 287.   The third problem of cognition is intimately connected with the first and the second.

§ 288.   It is useless, however, to discuss the validity of knowledge, unless we possess it ; yet there is a tendency in modern philosophy to deny that we know anything for certain.

§ 289.   This tendency is due in Absolutism to a preconceived doctrine of development, and in Pragmatism to the alleged facts of development.

§ 290.   All development, according to the disciples of Kant, takes the form of a ' reconciliation of antitheses in a higher synthesis '—

§ 291.   a principle which is generally recognised in its psychological form as Apperception ; though for the pragmatist the ' mediating idea ' is the leading characteristic in the process.

§ 292.   This latter point is not of great importance ; but it is important to note that, as the case of radio-activity shows, development does not necessarily involve the negation of previous hypotheses.

§ 293.   Yet this the Hegelian affirms ; and hence in his view our present knowledge is subject to *indefinite* modification, so that it is not strictly knowledge at all.

§ 294. Synechism teaches that the growth of knowledge is continuous, and will never be completed, and hence the pragmatist infers that our truest formulæ are only human devices conducive to more efficient action.

§ 295. But the variety of conflicting hypotheses in modern speculation does not justify this sceptical attitude.

§ 296. Common-sense knowledge has increased, but, apart from religious superstition, has not undergone any radical change.

§ 297. True, it is the 'factual' element in it that has survived ; but facts are knowledge, and we are justified in excluding superstitions and conjectural interpretations of phenomena, which were by no means universally accepted.

§ 298. In regard to theory, we are at the present day in a position quite different from that of the ancients, whose speculations for the most part were tentative.

§ 299. The Copernican revolution is the only reversal of importance that has occurred in what was generally accepted as certain ; and even this has left many truths intact.

§ 300. The discovery of the law of Gravitation was not a reversal but a new truth,

§ 301. and modern theories of the elements and of the constitution of matter do not reverse, but rather include and develop the essential characteristics of older views.

§ 302. The same may be said of the modern theories of light and of heat.

§ 303. Again, *our* space would seem to be Euclidian in spite of the geometry of a fourth dimension.

§ 304. While meta-geometries, so far from disproving, rather presuppose and confirm the validity of Euclid's geometry.

§ 305. Hence we may conclude that a sceptical attitude in regard to our present knowledge is justified neither by a study of its history,

§ 306. nor by the Hegelian theory of development, which proves to be inconsistent with the facts.   pp. 419—448

CHAPTER XVII.
PRAGMATISM AND PHYSICAL SCIENCE.

§ 307. It is not possible to keep philosophy altogether distinct from science, and as some scientists have taken up a definite metaphysical standpoint, the philosopher cannot be blamed for criticising them.

§ 308. Fifty years ago the scientist started from the standpoint of common-sense Realism, but now many adopt the attitude of Empirical Idealism or Pragmatic Sensationalism.

§ 309. Mach (and Poincaré) distinguish three stages in scientific procedure.

§ 310. In the first, the experimental stage, science according to Mach has to deal with reality, *i.e.*, with sensations, grouped together under names according to the principle of Thought-economy.

§ 311. Thus psychology and physical science treat of the same objects, but from different points of view.

§ 312. M. Le Roy goes further and affirms that, since in the formation of our percepts and concepts practical utility and even caprice may enter, scientific laws are 'contingent' and unverifiable.

§ 313. M. Poincaré rejects this view ; yet it seems to be a necessary consequence of the Sensationalism, the Pragmatism, and the doctrine of Thought-economy, adopted by Mach and other scientists.

§ 314. This philosophical position, however, must not be confused with the scientific Pragmatism of M. Duhem, which is quite compatible with Realism in metaphysics.

§ 315. For M. Duhem's Pragmatism is restricted to the 'mathematical' stage of physics, whereas that of Mach extends also to the experimental stage, and is really a metaphysic.

§ 316. A further difference also exists : M. Poincaré admits quasi-axiomatic principles which are beyond the control of experience, whereas M. Duhem holds that all physical laws must in the end be verifiable *à peu près*.

§ 317. And though these views can to some extent be reconciled,

§ 318. their divergence seems to have a deeper root in the philosophical standpoints of their respective advocates.

§ 319. M. Poincaré and the French pragmatists regard as objectively true that which is normal enough to be accepted by anyone of sound mind.

§ 320. And this 'normal objectivity' belongs only to what is generally recognised as useful or ' *commode*.'

§ 321. Such doctrines as these clearly belong to philosophy, though apparently they have developed from a purely scientific Pragmatism,—

§ 322. an attitude which has arisen from the prevalence of conflicting theories in science.

§ 323. But a physicist who is a pragmatist in science, may be a realist in philosophy ; and it is legitimate to ask whether he ought not also to be a realist in science.   pp. 449—473

CHAPTER XVIII.

REALISM AND PHYSICAL SCIENCE.

§ 324. Truth in Realism is determined by its object,

§ 325. and in general it is the *aim* of the scientist that his concepts, laws, and truths should be so determined.

§ 326. But is this *de facto* the case ? M. Duhem thinks

CHAPTER XIX.
ABSOLUTE TRUTH.

§ 347. Absolute truth is 'the systematic coherence of a significant whole,' and human truth is the partial manifestation of this absolute truth in finite centres of experience.

§ 348. This doctrine presupposes (1) that relations intrinsically modify their terms.

§ 349. (ii.) that all parts get their meaning from the whole to which they belong, and

§ 350. (iii.) that the 'real' and the 'mental' factor in truth are not independent.

§ 351. And from it follows the corollary (1) that there are no truths which are intrinsically necessary, and

§ 352. (ii.) that truth cannot be predicated of isolated judgments.

§ 353. Hence Absolute truth is an ideal, toward which human truth 'approximates' in varying degrees, but always at a distance.

§ 354. *Criticism :* The assumptions upon which this theory is based are unwarranted ; and 'coherence' as a criterion of truth is useless.

§ 355. Professor Bosanquet's view of axioms leads to a Sceptical Subjectivism, and Mr. Bradley's view, when examined, turns out to be but little better.

§ 356. The doctrine that isolated judgments are not true, is merely an inference drawn from the assumption that truth is coherence, for such judgments have meaning, and are not necessarily subject to intrinsic modification as knowledge grows.

§ 357. Again, it is not true that there are no judgments which are false *per se*, or that such judgments are meaningless.

§ 358. Nor can it be proved that our present knowledge is subject to indefinite modification.

§ 359. Finally, the metaphysical difficulties inherent in the Absolutist theory are fatal to it.   pp. 506—526

CHAPTER XX.
THE NATURE OF PRAGMATIC TRUTH.

§ 360. The most systematic account of Truth from the pragmatic point of view is given by Herr Simmel in his *Philosophie des Geldes.*

§ 361. In the organisation of our experience, he says, we look for absolute values, but later on discover that all truth is relative and that it is impossible to find any axiom which is self-sufficing.

§ 362. Thus 'reciprocity of mutual proof' is the fundamental form of all thought ; and hence of the *whole* of knowledge truth is not predicable.

CHAPTER XXI.
THE VALUE OF PRAGMATIC TRUTH.

§ 381.   Nor is the definition justifiable unless the ' copy-view ' be wholly untenable.

§ 382.   But, even granting this, is the pragmatic view justified by its consequences ?

§ 383.   The habitual, corroborative and reciprocal character of some truths may be granted ; but in emphasising relative to the neglect of positive value, and utility to the neglect of real significance, Herr Simmel has set at nought his own doctrine.

§ 384.   The pragmatic theory, in fact, leads to a Sceptical Subjectivism ; for in that theory:

§ 385.   (1) all knowledge is tinged by idiosyncrasy,

§ 386.   (2) all facts are ' transfigured ' by human interests, and verified by a process which itself is largely subjective,

§ 387.   (3) the data to which truth corresponds, and (4) the ' objectivity,' and ' independence ' (etc.) of truth are subjectively interpreted.

§ 388.   In short, human truth always bears the mark of human fabrication which can neither be got rid of nor abstracted from.

§ 389.   All attempts to escape this Subjectivism are in vain, for (1) an appeal to ' objective control ' does not get rid of the subjective element,

§ 390.   (2) the ' normal objectivity ' which is said to arise when truths become generally accepted, is not *real* objectivity,

§ 391.   (3) to declare that facts are 'immanent ' (whence the doctrine that reality cannot be known as it is in itself) implies the philosophy of Pure Experience, which is untenable,

§ 392.   and (4) the claim that pragmatic truth is all we need is false, for we desire to know reality.   pp. 550—588

CHAPTER XXII.

PRAGMATIC CRITERIA OF TRUTH.

§ 393.   ' Truth must make a difference to action.'—This criterion is too narrow, if understood literally, and too wide if it mean ' difference to experience.'

§ 394.   ' Truth must satisfy emotional needs.'—But the emotions are too variable to afford a sure criterion, and would only lead to contradictory beliefs.

§ 395.   The emotions, however, may be taken as expressive of the fundamental demands of our nature, an appeal to which is not irrational, and in *some* cases may be of service.

§ 396.   ' Truth must be useful, *i.e.*, it must satisfy our practical needs.'—But many *facts* are quite useless and even harmful, yet we do not regard them as false or unreal.

§ 397.   ' It must also determine our expectations rightly.'— This criterion is of value in scientific research, but must not be confused with the practically useful consequences to which a theory may lead.

§ 398.   ' Truth must stand the test of verification by the

CHAPTER XXIII.

CRITERIA OF ERROR IN REALISM.

as purpose, does not necessarily lead to error, and the pragmatist's contention that fact is distorted by purpose, confuses the intent with the content of thought.

§ 415. Abstraction, judgment, and reasoning are all *per se* reliable, *in so far as they compel our assent ;* but they do not always do so,

§ 416. and hence leave room for an *influxus voluntatis.*

§ 417. This may operate in various ways, and would seem to be the only cause of formal error.

§ 418. For the realist therefore the ultimate criterion of truth is objective evidence, or the evident determination of the mind by the object about which it is thinking.

§ 419. Thus, human testimony in regard to fact is credible, provided we have no reason to distrust it ; but theories must be judged by their *intrinsic* evidence.

§ 420. This does not mean that the evidence need be complete, but that theory be self-consistent and coincide with fact at least approximately.

§ 421. Similarly in metaphysics ' evidence ' is the criterion by which we judge of principles, processes, and facts ; and is quite sufficient to give certainty in regard to some of the doctrines of metaphysics.

§ 422. Regarded psychologically ' evidence ' is identical with what Newman calls the ' sanction of the Illative sense.'

§ 423. Newman fully admits the human character of the ' making ' of truth ; but he is not a pragmatist.

§ 424. For to him, as to the realist, there is but one final criterion of truth, *viz.*, ' objective evidence.'

pp. 620—650

CONCLUDING CHAPTER.

§ 425. Absolutism and Pragmatism are differentiations of Criticism which have developed in opposite directions, but which both tend toward a more realistic attitude.

§ 426. The psychology of Absolutism is scanty, lifeless, and non-human ; that of Pragmatism is genetic and human to such an extent that it leads to Subjectivism.

§ 427. Realism, on the other hand, while recognising the functions of purpose and action, subordinates them to cognition proper, and while allowing that axioms are regulative insists that in their objective aspect they are also constitutive.

§ 428. Though there are striking resemblances between the metaphysics of Pragmatism and certain forms of Absolutism, Absolutism is a Monism, Pragmatism a Pluralism.

§ 429. But the assumptions upon which Absolutism is based and the conclusions to which it leads are incompatible with the data of human experience ;

§ 430. while its theory of relations, being at bottom psychological, inevitably results in contradiction.

THEORIES OF KNOWLEDGE

COGNITION

THE PSYCHOLOGICAL ANALYSIS—ITS METAPHYSICAL CONDITIONS, AND ITS EPISTEMOLOGICAL VALUE

INTRODUCTION

§ 1. Cognition is an act of the mind, one of the three primary functions into which modern psychology divides all psychical activity. But it is more than this ; it implies a *relatio ad extra*, a reference to something other than itself, a something we call an object, in contradistinction from the subject, which is the mind itself that knows. To discover the nature of this relation is the aim of a theory of knowledge. Hence its problem is three-fold. We have to analyse psychologically the nature and function of those mental activities by which knowledge is acquired and to discuss the influence which they have upon one another ; we have to enquire into the conditions of knowledge, to ask what precisely is to be understood by subject and object,

B

and how far knowledge is due to the activity of the one, how far to that of the other ; and we have to examine the notions of validity, truth, objectivity, and to determine the criterion by which we may decide when these notions are applicable to an act of cognition, and when they are not. No one of these aspects of the problem can be left out if our treatment of the subject is to be adequate. A theory of knowledge which fails to define its position in regard to any one of them is incomplete. At the same time the scope of the theory of knowledge is so vast, the terms which an epistemologist uses are capable of so many different shades of meaning, the analysis of mental processes which he institutes have given apparently such divergent results, and the relations which he finds to exist between mind on the one hand and objective reality on the other admit of so many different interpretations, that some division of the subject must perforce be made ; and the obvious division is that which I have indicated above.   Accordingly, we shall discuss first the psychology of cognition ; secondly, its meta-physical conditions ; and, lastly, its epistemological value, *i.e.*, the objectivity and validity of cognitive acts and the criteria by which we distinguish the true from the false.

§ 2. Various solutions of the problem of knowledge have been offered at different times as philosophy has developed ; but just as that problem is three-fold, so curiously enough there are three solutions, each of them characteristic of a distinctive line in modern philosophic thought, which especially claim the attention of the philosopher of to-day.   Were

I writing a history of the theory of knowledge, it would be possible, I think, to show that modern theories are but developments of older views ; but this is not my present purpose. Suffice it to say, that in discussing modern attitudes in respect to the theory of knowledge, we are in reality discussing the solutions of a bygone age stripped of their antique ornaments and peculiar old-fashioned dress, and decked, instead, in the rich and flowing robes with which the fashion of the day contrives to obscure the outlines of the form that is hid beneath. If it be true that " there is nothing new under the sun," it is also true in philosophy that there is nothing that grows old. Pragmatism, that strange mushroom growth which sprang up in a night and has spread itself on the morning breeze throughout the continents of Europe and America, does but revive the human standpoint of Protagoras and the perpetual evolution of Heraclitus' flux. The critical Apriorism of Kant, developing through Hegel and his off-spring, the Neo-Hegelians, has culminated in an Absolute Idealism which recalls at once the Platonic theory of a world of εἴδη and the doctrine of Parmenides that the universe is one, plurality and difference mere seeming, while at the same time imparting to both a dynamic impulse more con-sistent with our modern conception of organic life and growth. The third solution is that of the realist. Realism, if we may argue from outward expression to inward thought, dates back at least to the time when man first began to record his thoughts in writing. Finding at length systematic formulation in the philosophy of Aristotle, it became the central feature of the Scholasticism of the Middle Ages. Since the Renaissance and the Reformation, however, the influence of the Aristotelian scholastic has been restricted for the most part to seminaries and to some few catholic universities, most of the great centres of learning preferring the Idealism of some thinker more modern and more daring in his speculations than either Aristotle or Aquinas. Realism is indeed characteristic of the Scottish School, and there are signs that a " new " Realism is gaining ground in the philosophic world at large ; nevertheless, if we wish to study it as a system, we must study it either in Aristotle himself or in the philosophy of Modern Scholasticism which takes Aristotle as its base.

§ 3. Pragmatism, Absolutism and Scholastic Realism contain amongst them at least in germ the only possible solutions which can be given to the problem of knowledge. Psychologically, knowledge may be regarded either as a function of the intellect or as a function of the will ; or else we may hold that, while both intellect and will co-operate, their functions are distinct. Metaphysically, the universe is either one or many, the origin of knowledge either subjective or objective, the distinction of subject and object either relative or absolute. And, epistemologically, truth is either theoretical or practical, and depends for its acceptance either upon its power to satisfy the intellect or upon its power to satisfy our practical needs and our will, or, it may be, upon both. Again, our present knowledge is either a mere moment in the process of evolution, capable of indefinite modification in the future ;

or there are some truths which are axiomatic and self-evident and thus form a foundation upon which a system of validated truth may be built. Each of these alternatives may be said to characterise one or other of the three Epistemologies we are about to consider. As, however, on the one hand a theory of knowledge should be considered as a whole and judged as a whole, while, on the other hand, owing to the vastness of the subject, we are forced to make arbitrary divisions, and to treat it part by part, it will be better perhaps for us to give a preliminary sketch of the general character and standpoint of each of these theories before proceeding to compare their positions in regard to psychology, metaphysics and the criteria and nature of truth.

§ 4. A theory of knowledge is implicitly a refutation of scepticism ; and when any development in that theory takes place, it is usually preceded and conditioned by the sceptical tendencies of the day, from which it seeks an escape. Scepticism was especially repugnant to the mind of Kant, at once synthetical, critical and religious. He saw that it contained its own refutation, and refused to believe that "human reason lures us on by false hopes only to deceive us in the end." The prolific fruitfulness of philosophic minds in the age which preceded his own had led to many conflicting doctrines. Geulincx, Malebranche and Spinoza had drawn from Cartesian premises conclusions inconsistent with each other. Leibnitz had been succeeded by the semi-scholastic Wolff. Each philosopher attempted to solve the problem of

Reality in a different way, and the Sceptic, watching this conflict of intellect with intellect, used the arguments of one side only to refute those of the other. Cartesianism, Occasionalism, the *Vision en Dieu*, Spinozism, the *Monadology*, and the School of Wolff were by him alike repudiated. To the Sceptic the confusion of dogmatic Rationalism signified the bankruptcy of reason. Kant, whose education in the School of Wolff pre-disposed him to take the Intellectualist side against the Sensationalism of Locke and Hume, admitted, while bemoaning, the controversies and differences which prevailed among Rationalists ; but at the same time blamed the Sceptic for "ignoring points of agreement and finding only opposition, where they should have sought the pre-suppositions between which conflicting dogmas rest." "Scepticism," he says, "might have been a useful regress had it gone back over the ground traversed by the dogmatists to the point where their wanderings began."[1] But to deny the validity of reason could lead only to philosophic despair. The theories of Descartes, Leibnitz, and Spinoza were incompatible and their incompatibility demanded explanation, but it did not justify sceptical doubt. Their divergencies undoubtedly concealed much that was true. To declare with the Sceptic that metaphysical reasoning could lead to nought but inconsistency was to ignore the difference between what is complementary and what is contradictory. Divergence and conflict by no means justified such despair ; for it might be possible, by re-examining the fundamental principles

[1] *Kritik der reinen Vernunft.* Preface to Second Edition.

of all philosophy and all cognition, to find a common ground by means of which all differences might be reconciled or explained, and in this way to re-establish on a surer basis the metaphysical notions of God, of Immortality and of Freedom.

§ 5. Here, implicit even in the Introduction to the *Critique of Pure Reason*, are two principles which characterise all Critical Philosophy : the principle of Unity in difference, and the principle of the reconciliation of antitheses in a higher synthesis. Both principles in Kant are logical rather than metaphysical ; and logically understood they form the basis of Hegel's famous Dialectic, as well as of more modern works such as the *Logic* of Professor Bosanquet and Dr Joachim's *Nature of Truth*. Truth, as ' Unity in Difference,' becomes a system, an organism, in which no judgment has meaning if taken by itself, but each is essentially relative, and can be understood only if taken in conjunction with others, while these again form together but a partial aspect of the whole. The Whole alone is self-evident, absolutely intelligible and consistent ; and until we know it as it is, with all its differences, our knowledge will be imperfect and incomplete. Hence all truth is an approximation, subject to modifications which may transform it almost beyond recognition. Every theory in science or philosophy is a thesis which admits of an antithesis with which it can be completely reconciled only when the Whole is known. All knowledge is organic ; but human knowledge is an organism which is but partially developed. It is ever evolving, ever getting modi-fied, ever growing, yet never seeming to approach much nearer to the Ideal which alone can give it truth by making it perfect and complete.

§ 6. Though Kant in the *Critique of Judgment* speaks of the universe as an organic whole which, as Ground, determines the form and combination of the parts in systematic unity, the metaphysical import of the doctrine of Unity in difference and of its corollary—or perhaps its presupposition—the doctrine of Immanence was but imperfectly realised by its author. The conception of the universe as Unity of Ground amid structural difference is characteristic rather of the Fichtean and Hegelian development of Criticism, and constitutes the central feature of Absolute Idealism. But we must return to Kant in order to seek yet another principle which is even more characteristic of his own philosophy, and which has lived on after him as another distinguishing mark by which we may recognise the Critical philosopher.

Kant proposed to repel the attacks of scepticism and to re-establish the authority of reason by a *new method.* The rationalist had failed hitherto because he had based his reasoning upon principles and postulates which he had never examined. His philosophy was too objective. Absorbed in the work of construction, he forgot to enquire into the conditions which rendered his constructions possible. His method was essentially dogmatic, for he reasoned without first criticising the faculty of reason. Systems built upon such uncritical foundations inevitably resulted in inconsistency, for ignorant of the sphere within which their conceptions were valid, some gave to one principle universal application, while others denied it altogether, and substituted another in its stead. This fundamental error Kant proposed to remedy by enquiring critically into the presuppositions of knowledge itself, especially of metaphysical knowledge, by what he calls a " critical examination of the faculty of reason in general in so far as it seeks for knowledge that is independent of all experience."[1]

§ 7. It was what he understood to be the methods of science that suggested to Kant his new method of Critical Philosophy. Struck by the contrast between the insecurity of metaphysics and the harmonious results which had been attained in physics and mathematics since the days of Bacon, he asked himself why it was that metaphysics "had never been so fortunate as to hit upon the sure path of science, but had kept groping about, and groping, too, among the same ideas."[2]

The intellectual revolution by which at a bound mathematics and physics became what they are now, is [he says] so remarkable that we are called upon to ask what was the essential feature of the change that proved so advantageous to them, and to try at least to apply to metaphysics as far as possible a method that has been successful in other rational sciences.[3]

As a result of this enquiry, Kant found that in physics and mathematics reason forces nature to conform to a preconceived plan. The scientist forms his conceptions and his definitions *a priori*, and in the light of these he interprets nature, forcing its data to conform to his preconceived ideas. Nature is intelligible only by means of that which

[1] *loc. cit.*, p. xxxv.   [2] *loc. cit.*, p. xiv.   [3] *loc. cit.*, p. xvi.

reason itself has put into Nature. The possibility of science depends upon *a priori* categories to which experience is compelled to conform. Generalising this principle, Kant postulated that in *all* knowledge the object conforms to the mind and not the mind to the object; and thereby he hoped to get rid of the contradictions of rational and dogmatic metaphysics.

In this purpose, as judged by the opinion of his successors, Kant failed; for he separated subject and object in such a way that they could never be brought together in knowledge. Yet the principle of *a priori* synthesis remains. For Critical Philosophy the mind, by its activity, does not merely acquire, but constitutes knowledge. Every man, as the late Dr. Caird puts it, " has within him the general plan for a self-consistent natural system,"[1] by means of which he arranges synthesises, categorises and brings to unity the manifold of sense. The categories of Kant were no mere empty forms, but real syntheses; no mere receptacles into which matter is poured like molten lead into a mould, but active functionings of the mind. The ' combining ' activity of the understanding converts the chaotic manifold of sense into the world of experience, and the mind, observing a sequence, by its own act makes it a causal connection. Even the ' Transcendental Unity of Apperception ' is not merely the abstract presupposition of all knowledge, but implies at bottom the self-activity of the subject.

§ 8. But though Kant analysed the structure of

[1] *Critical Philosophy of Kant*, vol. i., p. 18.

the human mind and discovered the various forms of synthesis by which it combines and integrates the data of experience, he did not treat of the development of these categories, nor of their relations *inter se*. He endowed his categories with activity indeed, but not with life. It was Hegel who organised the categories and imparted to them dynamic force. It was Hegel who made them relative and declared that, apart from one another, they are nothing at all. Yet if pure affirmation is its own negation, affirmative and negative as opposites are reconciled in a higher unity which expresses their correlativity as parts of a significant whole. And combining this idea with the Fichtean revolution which had abolished the noumenal thing-in-itself, we are led to the notion of Reality as a rational and organic system, in which all differences are relative and presuppose identity of ground. Of this the final unity, the category of categories, for Hegel is self-consciousness which transcends even the fundamental difference of the self and the not-self and recognises that objective reality is posited by itself, in itself, and for itself, in order that it may realise and know itself. This is the final stage in the development of knowledge, absolute knowledge ; but it exists merely as an Idea, a term toward which as mind we are ever approaching but which we never reach.

Thus Absolutism is Criticism self-realised. Finding that thought and being are one, from a Theory of Knowledge Criticism has grown into a Theory of Reality. The categories are no longer regarded as constitutive of a phenomenal, but of a real world ;

and that last condition of all knowledge—the
Transcendental Unity of Apperception—is hypos-
tatised, becoming the real Subject of an universal
consciousness, an Absolute which is the Ground of
all things, and yet is nothing in abstraction from
that of which it is the Ground. A logical presupposition is henceforth transformed into an
ontological principle. The unknown thing-in-itself
—that bug-bear of all philosophers—is banished for
ever. Thought and Reality are identified in the
living knowledge of a concrete organic whole.
Kant declared that he was concerned "not with
objects, but with the way in which the knowledge
of objects may be gained, so far as that is possible
a priori." Criticism, for him, was " not a doctrine,
but a criticism of pure reason, and its special value
is entirely negative, because it does not enlarge our
knowledge, but only casts light upon the nature of
reason and enables us to keep it free from error."
But Criticism, in examining its own presuppositions,
discovered that the ultimate metaphysical conditions of knowledge, subject and object, are
essentially relative, immanent and ultimately
identical in the Ground of Knowledge itself. From
a Method Criticism grew into a Theory of Knowledge,
and from a Theory of Knowledge it has developed
into a Metaphysic.

§ 9. " The essential feature of the method of
Neo-Kantianism," says Professor Veitch, " is its
analysis of knowing and its consequent determination of what is meant by being ; and, indeed, of
Being itself."[1] And though we may decline to

[1] *Knowing and Being,* p. 12.

designate as Kantian writers of such divergent views
as Fichte, Schelling, Hegel, Renouvier, Green, the
brothers Caird, or Messrs. Wallace, McTaggart,
Bradley, Joachim and Bosanquet, the fact remains
that the fundamental principles of their philosophical positions are the same as those of Kant.
All adopt the principles of Immanence and of
identity of ground amid structural difference. All
maintain, with Renouvier, that "the nature of mind
is such that no knowledge can be acquired or
expressed, and consequently no real existence
conceived, except by means of relation and as a
system of relations."[1] All acknowledge, with Mr.
Bradley, that Reality cannot be vitiated by self-
discrepancy, "and that since Reality is one, and
must own and cannot be less than appearance,"[2]
we must somehow reconcile discrepant appearances
in higher syntheses. In this way knowledge is
evolved, but its evolution for us is incomplete; and,
therefore, as all allow, with Dr. Joachim, *our* knowledge is only an approximation and may have to
undergo indefinite modification in every part before
it attains to the Ideal of a significant and systematic
Whole. Finally, all grant the *a priori* structure
and the constructive activity of mind, in virtue
of which, as Professor Bosanquet puts it, "intelligence creates and sustains our real world," so that
"logical science is the analysis, not of individual
real objects, but of the intellectual structure of
reality."[3]

---

[1] *Les dilemmes de la Metaphysique*, p. 11
[2] *Appearance and Reality*, p. 105.
[3] *Logic*, vol. ii., p. 236.

These considerations justify us, I think, in classing those idealist philosophers who identify being and thought, and affirm the universe to be a rational and systematic whole, comprising a ground and its multiform differences, as members of one great school in which, amid much divergence and variety of opinion, the main principles of Criticism still survive. Absolutism or Objective Idealism—if we may give the doctrines of this school a common name—is thus a thesis in the organic development of philosophic thought ; and according to Hegelian principles we should look for an antithesis : that antithesis is Pragmatism.

§ 10. In its origin there is a remarkable resemblance between Pragmatism and Absolutism. So manifold were the differentiations of Critical Philosophy, so vague and mystical many of its ideas, so non-human and difficult to grasp its interpretation of the Universe, that at length a protest was evolved, accompanied by a demand for greater clearness and greater simplicity of thought. This demand was first voiced by Mr. C. S. Peirce (1879) who suggested a new kind of Occam's razor by means of which we might distinguish useful from useless metaphysical notions. Only those notions which had ' practical bearings ' on human life were worthy of discussion ; the rest might be consigned to oblivion. Metaphysics, he says, " has hitherto been a piece of amusement for idle minds, a sort of game at chess ; and the *ratio essendi* of Pragmatism is to make a clean sweep of most of the propositions of ontology, nearly all of which are senseless rubbish, where words are defined by words and so on without ever reaching any real concept." [1]

Mr. Peirce's ideas did not take root immediately ; but after an interval of several years they reappeared in the writings of Professor James and Dr. Schiller, and, backed up by vigorous polemics from the pens of both these writers, have developed into that many-sided Theory of Knowledge, which we now know under the name of Pragmatism. Professor James and Dr. Schiller both thought that Metaphysics once again needed to be " re-established on a surer basis " in order to defend it from the attacks of Scepticism. Dr. Schiller was convinced that " the vague and meaningless abstractions," " the gorgeous cloudland " and " the philosophic extravagance " of Absolutism

must have generated an unavowed but deep-rooted and widespread distrust of and disgust with the *methods* which have starved philosophy in the midst of plenty, and condemned it to sterility and decay in the very midst of the unparalleled progress of all other branches of knowledge. [2]

§ 11.   As in the days of Kant, so now, one of the branches of knowledge in which progress is most rapid and most marked is that of Science. Accordingly we once more find the philosopher asking the scientist to teach him how to philosophise. The revolution in philosophy which Mr. Peirce inaugurated was significant.   If metaphysical ideas are to be valued according to their practical bearings and if our conception of such bearings or effects is

---

[1] *The Monist,* Apr. 1905, p. 171.
[2] *Riddles of the Sphinx,* p. 94.

the whole of our conception of an object, then truth will be determined in part at least by purposes and needs, and our evaluations will depend largely upon the emotions and the will. The thesis which Professor James defends in his *Will to Believe* is precisely this, that our emotions not only do, but ought, in some cases at any rate, to act as determinants of choice in regard to rival theories. This is of the very essence of Pragmatism ; but at the time when the *Will to Believe* was written Pragmatism was still in the embryonic stage. What it needed was a principle, more precise and more scientific than the practical maxim of Peirce, yet at the same time no less human, a principle which should sum up in a few words the universal characteristics of the act of cognition. Already in his pre-pragmatic *Riddles* Dr. Schiller had suggested that it might be possible to provide food for the starving philosopher, " simply by basing our Metaphysics on our Science," and eventually the required principle was found in the method of Science, which is now discovered to consist, not, as Kant said, in forcing nature to conform to *a priori* forms *already existing* in the mind, but in *framing* hypotheses with a view to controlling nature and in verifying those hypotheses in experience by means of their practical results.

Pragmatism claims that this is the universal form which all cognition takes. " All mental life is purposive." [1] Cognition is due to the *exigencies of human nature* which awaken in us the desire to organise the crude material of experience and

[1] Schiller, *Studies in Humanism*, p. 10.

" transmute it into palatable, manageable, and liveable forms."[1] Hence Pragmatism is "a systematic protest against all ignoring of the purposive character of actual knowing,"[2] or "a thorough recognition that the purposive character of mental life generally must influence and pervade our most remotely cognitive activities."[3] In order to mould experience to suit our needs, we *frame hypotheses* or 'make guesses,' in which we *postulate* that whenever we perform any determinate action nature will respond in a certain way. We then *experiment*, that is, we carry into execution the proposed action and await results. If nature, *as modified by our action*, responds on all occasions in the way we desire, our postulate is validated and is so far true. If nature does not respond as we desire, we frame a new hypothesis and experiment again.

Thus for the pragmatists ' experience ' is experiment in the concrete. In the acquisition of knowledge we always begin with a hypothesis which we doubt and wish to verify. It presents a claim to truth, but is not yet ' true.' Action follows, and if its consequences harmonise with our preconceptions, our hypothesis is confirmed and validated.[4] Hence all truths are logical values. They are hypotheses *framed so as to satisfy our needs* and verified in experience. They are *worth* something to us for they enable us to adapt ourselves to our environment, or rather to adapt that environ-

---

[1] Schiller, *'Axioms as Postulates' in Personal Idealism*, § 1.
[2] *Studies in Humanism*, p. 11.
[3] Schiller, *Humanism*, p. 8.
[4] Peirce, " What Pragmatism is," *Monist*, Apr. 1905, p. 173.

Ç

ment to the exigencies of our nature. That is *true* which, by its consequences, satisfies human needs ; and the pragmatic criterion of truth, though it may be expressed in many ways, is ultimately reducible to this power of consequences to satisfy our needs, not indeed any particular need, but the needs of our whole nature and personality.

§ 12. This is Pragmatism, which, from an examination of " the actual ways in which discrimination between the true and the false is effected," professes to have discovered a general method of determining the nature of truth. Dr. Schiller, however, in his *Axioms as Postulates* extends the pragmatic doctrine of Postulation to the genesis of knowledge in the past history of the race. We seem to be *given* an external world, but this is an illusion ; it has really been formed by the validated postulates of our ancestors, and in so far as it seems to be given to us in ready-made concepts and axioms, we are really living on our capital, inherited or acquired, not helping to carve or ' create ' the cosmos, but enjoying the fruit of our labours or those of others.[1] This application of pragmatic principles to the genesis of knowledge in the race is known as Humanism. It is an extension and a generalisation of Mr. Peirce's maxim that the idea of a thing is the idea of its consequences for us. All truths, no matter whether they appear as axioms or as *a priori* concepts, are at bottom man-made truths, values determined by human needs. Humanism, says Professor James, " is the doctrine that, to an unascertainable extent, our truths are

[1] *'Axioms as Postulates,'* § 5.

man-made products. Human nature shapes all our questions, human satisfaction lurks in all our answers, all our formulas have a human twist."[1]

§ 13. The terms 'Pragmatism' and 'Humanism' are usually applied to the latest development of *Anglo-American* Philosophy; but M. Blondel originally called his *Philosophie de l'Action* by the name of Pragmatism; while French writers such as MM. Le Roy, Wilbois, Milhaud, and German writers such as Mach, Avenarius, and Simmel, are frequently claimed as humanists, and even "the great Poincaré," says Professor James, "misses it only by the breadth of a hair."[2]

M. Blondel's philosophy, however, is hardly pragmatic. Still, inasmuch as his philosophic proof of great religious truths is based on the 'Ideals' which are revealed in purposive human action, there is a certain resemblance in their religious aspect between the two doctrines. The pragmatism of Le Roy, Mach and other French and German writers, on the other hand, is very similar to the Anglo-American production, though it appears to have originated quite independently of Professor James and Dr. Schiller. It began as a Critique of Science; and to Science it is still, for the most part, restricted. The Neo-Criticism of Renouvier marked a return to the point of view of the Practical Reason. In emphasising the antithesis between scientific categories and the postulate of Freedom, he gave preference to the latter and pronounced Science incapable of solving the problem of Reality except on the basis of Freedom. The French *Philosophie de la Contingence* takes a similarly restricted view

[1] *Pragmatism,* p. 242.   [2] *Mind,* N.S. 52, p. 46.

of the applicability of scientific laws ; but goes
further, and to a large extent reverses the Kantian
Revolution. Nature, in this theory, is not determined by any *a priori* forms, but is an independent
and even a free agency. We try to reconstruct it
mentally, but it refuses to conform exactly to the
categories we force upon it. We seek to explain it
by universal and necessary laws ; but they are
found to be inapplicable in many cases, for the simple
reason that their necessity and their universality is
due to our abstraction, and not to Nature itself,
which is concrete and contingent. M. Boutroux,
in his work entitled *De la Contingence des Lois de la
Nature,* definitely introduces freedom into the
hitherto sacred realm of Physical Science.[1] No
physical law is absolutely exact, but only *à peu
près*, because it expresses merely a quantitative
relation between phenomena, whereas, in reality,
over and above the phenomenon there is the substance ; over and above quantity, quality ; and
over and above the law, the real cause. Real
causes, moreover, though striving to attain a
definite end, are in some degree free in respect of
the means which they use. Consequently the
future is contingent ; natural laws are not necessary,
and their universality is weakened by an element
of chance.

§ 14. The connection between this *Philosophie
de la Contingence*—or as it is sometimes called ' The
New Philosophy of France '—and Anglo-American
Pragmatism lies in this, that both protest against

---

[1] cf. *Humanism*, pp. 12 (note), 15, and *Studies in Humanism*,
pp. 411 et seq. 427.

the view that in knowledge we copy reality. Science, they say, has no right to hypostatise her laws, for they are mere abstractions. Still less has she any right to regard them as constitutive, for they are merely methodological. From the time of Montaigne onwards Scepticism had withheld its destructive hand from the creations of the scientist, but now the Scientific Methods in which Kant had so firm a belief, are once more called in question. Science and Metaphysics are reduced to the same level of certainty or uncertainty. Both are constructions and must stand or fall together according as they behave under the rigorous test of practical consequences for man. Both work by means of hypotheses which can only as a rule be partially verified ; and so are never certain, but only more or less probable, more or less convenient, workable, prolific, satisfactory. The 'true' is the expedient, the hypothesis that is useful and will work. But 'what will work to-day may not work to-morrow,' so that truth for the Pragmatist as for the Absolutist is never more than an approximation, provisionally true but subject to indefinite modification. "When we discover the place which is held by hypotheses in the Sciences," says M. Poincaré, "we ask ourselves if all their constructions are well-founded, and we believe that a breath would destroy them."[1] Scientific laws, M. Le Roy declares, are merely symbols, convenient formulæ, *discours*, which, the more systematic they become, the further are they removed from concrete reality. Similarly, Professor James asserts that scientific definitions are only

[1] Pref. to *La Science et L'Hypothèse.*

'man-made formulæ,' which exist in verbal and conceptual quarters, and lead to useful, sensible termini, but which cannot be said to correspond with them.

§ 15. There is a growing tendency, too, in both French and Anglo-American Pragmatism to take a social view of Truth ; and to regard it as satisfying the *common* needs of the race rather than those which are peculiar to the individual. Truth has what M. Milhaud calls a "*normal objectivity*." Or as M. Poincaré expresses it, " Nothing is objective but that which is true for all."[1] Professor James likewise affirms that " true ideas lead to consistency, stability, and flowing human intercourse, and lead away from eccentricity and isolation."[2] Even Dr. Schiller, who believes that our metaphysics must always have a personal tinge,[3] yet admits that the latter tends to disappear through the interaction of human minds, which gradually learn to impose the same, or at least very similar, forms on the plastic receptivity of matter.[4] Clearly, then, the 'new' Philosophy of France forms part of the pragmatic movement, though, like the German edition of Pragmatism, it is confined, for the most part, to the Philosophy of Science, and neglects that religious and emotional aspect of Pragmatism which is set forth in the *Will to Believe* and in *The Ethical Basis of Metaphysics* with which Dr. Schiller introduces us to his work on *Humanism*.

§ 16. In Germany, Pragmatism has found a

[1] *La Valeur de la Science*, p. 265.
[2] *Pragmatism*, p. 215.
[3] '*Axioms as Postulates*,' § 1.
[4] *Ibid :* §§ 1 to 5, and cf. *Studies in Humanism*, pp. 16, 17 and 428.

friend in Herr Simmel, who, in his *Philosophie des Geldes*, treats incidentally of the nature of truth. Herr Simmel regards truth as a value determined by our needs, of which economical values are only a particular case ; but though his standpoint and the general form of his arguments is different from that usually adopted by Pragmatism, his claim to rank as a pragmatist can hardly be questioned. Professor Mach also is undoubtedly a pragmatist ; and his Pragmatism is much more thorough-going even than that of the *Philosophie de la Contingence*, though, like the latter, it is chiefly concerned with Science. For Professor Mach, as for M. Poincaré, the data of Science are sensations, and its aim is to organise, classify and systematise the latter by means of symbolic formulæ. All cognition is governed by the principle of Thought-economy, which expresses a primary need of our nature and demands, among other things, that when experience fails to confirm our expectations, a minimum of modification must be introduced into the ideas by which it is symbolised, and that both ideas and formulæ must always be expressed in the simplest possible way.

Avenarius has given to the scientific theory of Energetics, of which Professors Mach and Ostwald are among the chief representatives, a philosophical setting in his *Kritik der reinen Erfahrung* (1890). His point of view is biological. Knowledge is only one form of a *vital series*—pain, striving, satisfaction ; and, as with Professor Mach, the principle of Thought-economy dominates all cognitive activities. As knowledge develops, the useless representations

which characterise popular religions and realistic
philosophies will be eliminated. True philosophy
must return to pure experience, in which all knowledge is descriptive, and in which quantitative
rather than qualitative relations and laws prevail.

§ 17. Whether or not there is any metaphysic
which can be called pragmatic may be disputed.
Indeed, Professor James expressly declares that
Pragmatism is compatible with *any* metaphysic, and
the Corridor-Theory of the Italian pragmatist,
Papini, seems to confirm this view. On the other
hand, we are informed that the primary aim of
Pragmatism is to re-establish metaphysics on a
scientific basis ; and Mr. Peirce's test of ' practical
bearings ' was intended especially for the elimination
of ' useless ' metaphysical notions, a purpose to
which both Professor James and Dr. Schiller are
accustomed to apply it. Moreover, every theory of
knowledge has to discuss the metaphysical conditions
of knowledge, and so is forced, *nolens volens*, to take
up some metaphysical attitude. Pragmatism, then,
cannot help being to some extent metaphysical.

This is admitted by Professor James, who tells us
that Pragmatism has at any rate ' metaphysical
affinities ;' and if we may judge by his own metaphysical writings, the tendency of Pragmatism is
toward a Philosophy of Pure Experience, in which
no trans-experiential agents of unification, substances, intellectual categories and powers, or selves,
are needed.[1] Dr. Schiller, on the other hand, has
defined Pragmatism in one place as " a conscious

---

[1] " A World of Pure Experience " (James), *Journ. of Phil.
Psy. and Sc. Methods,* 1904, p. 534.

application to epistemology (or logic) of a teleological psychology which ultimately implies a voluntaristic metaphysic." [1] Now for a voluntaristic metaphysic, " actual realities are always relative to the ends of practical life, and human valuations exercise their sway over every region of our experience." [2] Hence, regarded from this aspect, Pragmatism would seem to tend toward Personal Idealism, since that practical life in regard to which reality is relative, and that active process of evaluation in which truth is said to consist, seems to imply a real personal agent. In any case, Pragmatism certainly has pronounced metaphysical affinities, and these we must discuss in their proper place, and shall then see how far the Philosophy of Pure Experience and Personal Idealism are presupposed by and how far they serve to complete Pragmatism itself.

§ 18. The term Realism, in its original signification, is applied to the doctrine that universals have, at any rate, some kind of objective existence and are not mere creations of the mind ; but the term has acquired a wider signification and may now be applied to any philosophy which adopts the standpoint of common-sense, and attempts to interpret and systematise its beliefs without explaining them away. Now, the ordinary man believes in real objects, real houses, windows, doors, stones, trees, animals and men, which exist and act and thrive and are acted upon quite independently of himself. He does not confuse things with his own sensations, nor does he ever dream that it is he himself or his

[1] *Studies in Humanism*, p. 12.   [2] *Humanism*, p. 8.

ancestors, or both, who have constructed and built up the world he sees about him by the action of their minds. He regards his own thoughts and feelings as somewhat flimsy and extremely transient acts or qualities which belong to himself, whereas the existence of *real things* is something quite different. Real things have their own qualities, colours, shapes, sizes, weights. Some of them move about, others remain still. Some of them grow, others do not. But all of them have properties by which we are able to distinguish one from another, to recognise them and to get to know them. The plain man knows something about himself, too. He, like the rest, is a ' thing,' but a thing which thinks and feels and wills, besides being able to move, to act and to be acted upon. He believes, also, that there are many other beings which have ideas, emotions, passions like to his own, to which they give expression in much the same way that he does. Finally, he usually believes also in a supreme Being, far more perfect than all the rest of the world put together—a Being by whom all these things have been made, who watches over them, and by whom he and other human beings will be rewarded or punished according to their deserts.

Such, in brief, are the beliefs of common-sense, and with these as his data, the realist begins to philosophise. He does not assume the validity of *all* these beliefs as a datum. The validity of belief in the existence of God, for instance, has to be proved. Nevertheless that, in general, there are real things which have an existence and nature of their own, and are in this respect both independent of and external to himself, he regards as a self-evident truth, as he does also the possibility of knowing them. Or, to put the matter in another way, to the realist it is self-evident that knowledge is possible. Hence he infers that the faculties by means of which knowledge is acquired must, in general, be trustworthy, and their deliverances objectively valid. Now, one of the deliverances of our human faculties which is not only normal, but absolutely universal, and, one might almost say, instinctive, is that there does exist an objective real world ; hence this also the realist accepts as a self-evident truth. Similarly, in regard to those other beliefs of common-sense, the belief in real substances, causes, activities, purposes, the aim of the realist is to explain without explaining away. Somehow such beliefs have arisen, and it is the business of the philosopher to account for them, to discuss their origin, to show how far they are valid, and, if invalid, to show how far they err, and how it comes about that what seems to be a natural and normal function of the human mind should lead us astray. In this enquiry the guiding principle of the realist is as follows. Hold fast to what you know, and do not doubt what you seem to have arrived at by an immediate judgment and a natural process of reasoning unless you are forced so to do. The beliefs of spontaneous common-sense may, in the end, turn out to be false ; but do not begin by assuming them to be false. Rather accept them as true, and then see whether, on this basis, it is not possible to give a rational and consistent account of the universe—an account which shall explain both the nature and the possibility of knowledge and truth, and which shall also provide us with useful criteria for distinguishing truth from error.

§ 19. The realist, then, begins to philosophise from the point of view of common-sense. Accordingly he understands by knowledge a psychical act or state in which somehow the nature of objective reality is revealed to the human mind, and by truth the correspondence of knowledge with objective fact. We observe, perceive, apprehend, judge and reason correctly in so far as our observation, perception, concepts, judgments and conclusions have an objective counterpart to which they correspond. Truth is an *adaequatio*. But there can be no question of truth, unless in perceiving, conceiving, and judging, our thoughts have objective reference. Sensations as such are neither true nor false, but only become so when integrated into percepts and referred to objective reality. Objective reference, however, is a function of the intellect, and as it is this which gives to our thoughts and ideas their claim to truth, truth is defined, not as an *adaequatio sensus*, but as an *adaequatio intellectus et rei*.

§ How is this *adaequatio* or correspondence possible ? Common-sense believes that objects act upon the senses, and it is upon this assumption and upon the principle that every effect must resemble its cause, that the realist—or at any rate the scholastic realist—bases his explanation of correspondence. External and material objects affect our senses and thus directly or indirectly determine the content of thought; *i.e.*, determine what we think

as opposed to thought itself considered as a form of
mental activity. The metaphysical conditions of
knowledge in Realism, therefore, are on the part
of the object (1) activity (*omne ens agit secundum
suam naturam*) and (2) intelligibility (*omne ens non
solum est unum* (individuum) *et bonum* (appetibile),
sed etiam verum (intelligibile) ; while on the part of
the subject there is required both passivity (*omnis
cognitio fit secundum similitudinem cogniti et cognoscentis*) and activity of a psychical and conscious
order (*cognitum est in cognoscente secundum modum
cognoscentis*). Further, owing to the fact that all
intellectual activity is conditioned by that of the
nervous system, which alone is directly affected by
material objects, cognition is mediated by sense-
perception, and all knowledge is ultimately derived
from sense-data. (*Nihil est in intellectu nisi quod
fuerit in sensu*). This latter condition, however,
does not exclude the possibility of our knowing
objects other than those of which we have direct
experience, as Kant maintained. On the contrary,
we know many things of which we have had no
direct experience ; for just as from the existence of
knowledge we may infer the existence of whatever
is presupposed by knowledge as its condition, so
from the fact that certain objects exist and are
directly experienced, we may infer the existence of
others as their conditions or causes.

§ 21. The ultimate criterion of truth for Realism
follows from its theory of the nature of truth. It
is objective evidence ; we give our assent only when
we believe that the object and not any other cause
has determined the content of our thoughts. Other

criteria there are, of course, for contradiction, illicit inference, the influence of prejudice, preconceived ideas and illusions due to the abnormal state of the mind, must be excluded ; but these are mostly negative, and in the end assent is given, or should be given, only when it is evident that the object about which we are thinking, and that alone, has determined the content of our thoughts.

§ 22. The theory of knowledge which I have briefly outlined above and to which I have given the name of Realism, is, in principle, the same as that of Aristotle and Aquinas, though neither of these philosophers wrote what we should call an Epistemology. There are other Realisms. Reid, Hamilton, and the Scottish school of Common-Sense base their Realism solely on Intuition, and consequently their treatment of the subject is far less systematic than that of Aristotle or the Scholastics. There is also a ' new ' Realism which has found many exponents in England and America, notably Professor Bertrand Russell and Mr. Moore. The ' new ' realists distinguish consciousness from the objects about which we are conscious not only in external sense-perception and ideal thought, but in all perception and in all thought. Hunger, pain and pleasure are not identical with the feeling or consciousness of hunger, of pain and of pleasure. Doubtless there is something to be said in favour of this opinion, though it may easily be misunderstood, and suggests the ultra-Realism of certain Mediæval philosophers. In any case as yet the ' new ' Realism is not sufficiently explicit on the larger question of metaphysics to admit of our taking it as an alternative to the more fully developed Pragmatism and Absolutism.

§ 23. Accordingly, when I speak of Realism in the course of this study, I shall refer to Realism as interpreted by Aristotle and the Scholastics, for this is the only systematic and fully developed Realism. Moreover, there has been of late, as Professor Case has pointed out, a marked tendency to return to the Aristotelian standpoint in philosophy, and it is the justification of this tendency which I wish to discuss. Materialism and Positivism, though still plausible to superficial minds, have proved themselves incapable of giving an interpretation of the Universe which can satisfy the philosopher. Absolutism, Pragmatism and Realism are the only alternatives between which the philosopher can make a rational choice. Pragmatism is the antithesis of Absolutism, and at present is contending with the latter for supremacy in the philosophic world. Realism, in regard to these two extremes, occupies a *via media*, and it is as a *via media* that I wish here to present it. Aristotle has said that virtue lies in the mean ; and we may say the same, perhaps, of philosophic truth. But by a *via media* I understand not an eclectic philosophy, nor yet a compromise, but rather what Hegelians would call a ' higher ' synthesis. The true way in philosophy is that which, by a critical examination of the very foundation upon which philosophy is built, shall discover at what point precisely divergence has arisen, shall show how far the divergence on either side is due to exaggeration or to a one-sided view, and hence shall be able to reconcile the two antitheses by distinguishing in them that which is true and well-founded, from that which is false.

§ 24. At the root of every philosophy, moreover, lies its theory of knowledge Hence, no surer test of the strength of a philosophic position can be applied than an examination of the theory of knowledge upon which it is based. The conditions which that theory must satisfy are, as I have already indicated, three-fold. First of all, its psychological analyses of cognition must be exact ; it must not generalise for theory's sake unless such generalisations are warranted by introspective fact. Secondly, metaphysical conditions must be assigned which show the possibility of knowledge and of truth, while yet retaining for these terms their full and real significance ; for to mutilate the notion of truth in order to explain it is irrational, and to assign to knowledge a sense altogether foreign to that which is commonly accepted, is to explain, not knowledge, but something else for which it would have been better to coin a new term. And, in the third place, the validity of cognitive processes must be examined, and criteria of truth assigned by means of which to test their validity. How far Absolutism, Pragmatism and Realism satisfy these conditions remains to be seen ; but in so far as either fails, it is incomplete, and must contain somewhere an element of error. A final judgment cannot be passed, however, until we have studied each theory in all its bearings, psychological, metaphysical, and epistemological, since each theory forms a whole, and as a whole it should be judged.

PART I.

THE PSYCHOLOGICAL ANALYSIS OF COGNITION.

CHAPTER I.

THE DATA OF EXPERIENCE.

SENSE-PERCEPTION.

§ 25. It is impossible to examine the truth of theory with any hope of success, unless first we know where fact ends and where theory begins. Theory itself may be, and often, indeed, it claims to be, merely a description of facts, more accurate, more ultimate, and more systematic than that of the data with which we started. Hence the distinction between theory and fact, it may be said, is relative to our point of view. Be that as it may, it is necessary to start somewhere, and it is necessary also clearly to realise where we do start. For, in order to discuss the validity of explanation or theoretical description—if the latter term be preferred—it is essential to know precisely what it is we are trying to explain. Philosophers, scientists, all theorists do *de facto* take for granted certain data which they think will be clear, obvious, ' given ' to everybody alike, and will therefore be admitted

D

by all. Much philosophic confusion, however, might have been avoided in the past had theorists taken the trouble at the outset to tell us precisely what their data were, instead of leaving it to critics to discover this for themselves.

§ 26. What, then, are the data upon which the Theory of Knowledge is built ? What the facts which an epistemologist may take for granted without being guilty of a *petitio principii ?* The philosopher will reply ' the data of experience ;' and of late, philosophising scientists also have taken up this convenient formula. But what are the data of experience ? The phrase is a familiar one, yet I doubt if any two persons would interpret it exactly in the same way. Does it mean the data of *our* experience, or the data of ' pure ' experience ? If the data of *our* experience, by what means are we to distinguish what is a datum from what is not, *i.e.*, from what is due to interpretation, to preconceived ideas, to a background of theory ? And if the data of ' pure ' experience is meant, how are these data to be discovered, and where are they to be found ?

Mr. Shadworth Hodgson holds that all philosophy should start from the data of pure experience.[1] The distinctions of subject and object, of things and their appearances, of mind and matter, are to be excluded from the realm of the given. They are not data, but accretions with which the pure

---

[1] cf. *Studies in Humanism,* p. 187, where Dr. Schiller tells us that ' Fact,' in the wider sense of the term, which includes imaginings, illusions, errors, and which is anterior to the distinction of appearance and reality, is " the starting point and final touchstone of all our theories about reality,"

data of experience have been distorted and defiled.

Although [he says] the ultimate data of experience without which all further or more complex forms of it would be impossible, consists of states or process-contents of consciousness, this by no means implies that they consist of states or process-contents of consciousness *as distinguished from realities.*[1]

To regard them as such is to adopt the psychological point of view, and hence to introduce into philosophy an assumption which is wholly unfounded in the data of pure experience.

Now, it is a very easy matter to tell us that we must begin to philosophise merely upon the data of ' pure ' experience ; but it is quite a different matter to attempt to carry this principle out in practice. For, from what source, may I ask, are such data to be obtained ? To whose experience do they belong ? To that of the amoeba, the savage, the new-born babe, perhaps. But we are neither amoebae, nor savages, nor yet new-born babes ; nor can we imagine what is the state of mind of such interesting beings. We cannot even construct it hypothetically, no matter how powerful our imagination may be, or how apt we may be at making guesses, unless we first study the data of our own experience, and base our fanciful guess-work upon these. Personally, though I have tried hard, I must confess that I have found myself quite unable to get rid of the subject-object distinction in any of my conscious acts. Either I think of things as part of myself, or else as something other

[1] *The Metaphysics of Experience,* vol. i., p. 116.

than myself. Even when basking idly in the sun
or passively enduring the pleasures of a warm bath,
or gazing with absent mind at what is before me,
there still seems to be in my mind some faint distinguishing of subject and object. It may be said
that I *put* the distinction there when I reflect.
Possibly; but such a statement, at any rate, is not
a datum of experience. I seem to be able to intro-
spect a psychical act, even while it is taking place ;
and there I find the distinction sure enough. But
even if all introspection is retrospection it still seems
to be true that in any act of cognition which is just
going, or which is retained in memory, objects are
regarded as something other than myself. Indeed,
if introspection is incompatible with direct objective
experience, it ought also to be incompatible with
retained or remembered experiences, and so to be
impossible altogether.

In no case, however, is my argument affected.
For unless memory invariably plays us false, the
distinction of subject and object, which appears
when we reflect, must have been there originally,
though it may have belonged to the ' fringe ' of consciousness to which we do not directly attend. That
all developed human consciousness is noetic, and
that in all noetic consciousness subject and object
are distinct, is, in fact, admitted now by almost all
psychologists. *Our* experience is certainly not *pure*
experience. It may have been ' pure ' when we
started life, but of this we neither have nor can have
any certain knowledge, for no one remembers what
he was like when first he emerged from his mother's
womb. It is absurd, then, to base philosophy on

data of which we have no certain knowledge, and about which no two philosophers can be found to agree. Our only course, therefore, is to start with knowledge as we have it, with human knowledge, which is the only knowledge common to us all, and upon which each may reflect when he wills.

§ 27. The *data* of *our* experience, then, are the data from which the epistemologist must start and which he must seek to explain.[1] These data, thanks to introspection, are readily accessible to all. Our minds are always more or less cognitive. We are always observing, listening, reading, thinking. Even when actively engaged we are not wholly unconscious of what is going on around us, and we certainly think, as a rule, about what we are doing. Each one of us has already acquired a stock of knowledge of greater or less extent, and to this he adds daily by perception, by inference, and by means of information gained from others. Thus it is possible for us to study, not only knowledge as a habit or state of mind, but also knowledge in the making.

There is clearly a difficulty, however, in taking as our starting point the data of *our* experience. Our experience is certainly not what it was in infancy, and it may be objected that the beliefs which now accompany our cognitive acts and seem to be spontaneous are not so in reality. The data of our experience, it may be said, are so hopelessly intermingled with interpretations due to the process by

---

[1] cf. *Studies in Humanism*, p. 184, where we are told that we must start with " immediate experience, with the actual knowing just as we find it in our own adult minds ; " but contrast p. 187 cited above § 26 where a contradictory assertion is made.

which knowledge has been acquired in the individual
or in the race, that it is impossible to distinguish
what is a datum from what is not.   The possibility
of such an admixture of interpretation with primitive
data cannot be denied.   But it must be remembered
that we do not claim to start with primitive data.
It is one thing to say that we have in our experience
such and such data, and quite another thing to
pretend that these data are the data of ' pure '
or original experience.   The data of our experience,
our beliefs about ourselves and objective reality and
the judgments in which such beliefs are acquired,
confirmed and expressed, these we know for certain.
Of these we are directly conscious, and can discover
by introspection, not, indeed, how they arose in
the first instance, but how we add to them by the
actual cognitive processes which are constantly
taking place in our own minds.   Such beliefs may or
may not be illusory, but it is certain that we have
them.   They may or may not be ' impure ; ' they
may or may not be due to interpretation and illicit
inference ; that remains to be proved and can neither
be assumed nor straightway denied.   But it is
certain that at present belief in our own existence,
spiritual and corporeal, in an objective and material
world, and in other minds and bodies like to our
own, *appears* to be spontaneous and natural.   Of
the data of ' pure ' experience no one can tell us
anything for certain.   Their very existence is little
more than a hypothesis.   But the data of our
experience are simply the beliefs of the plain man
before he begins to philosophise, and the cognitive
processes by which fresh beliefs are day by day

generated in his mind—beliefs and processes which, I allow, are not what they were when the man was a child, and which may be illusory and false, but beliefs and processes which, provided we make no assumption as to their objective validity, are certainly obvious to all and disputed by none, and so may be taken as data for a theory of knowledge. From these data every epistemologist, whether Kantian, Pragmatist, or Realist, has begun, and must always begin, for these are the only *data* that exist *for us*. Having philosophised already, it may be somewhat difficult, perhaps, to eliminate the influence of one's own philosophic standpoint from one's introspective readings. However, we can but make the attempt, and endeavour to correct the errors of one's own introspection by the assistance of those who are still in the happy state of unsophisticated common-sense; and we may well begin with sense-perception, which, as the primary source from which all knowledge is derived, naturally has the first claim upon our attention.

§ 28. ' At the present moment there is a little tit upon my window-sill picking up crumbs of bread.' This statement implies a judgment on my part. I perceived a tit in a certain environment, and have expressed my act of perception in the form of a judgment to the truth of which I give my assent. What is involved in this act of cognition ? Was there any activity on my part ? Apparently there was, for I refer the act of perception to myself and say that *I* perceived. I seem to have been conscious, even during the act of perception itself, of my own psychical operation. True, my self-consciousness was very slight. It was with the perceived objects that my attention was chiefly, if not wholly, engrossed. Yet I certainly did not confuse the tit, the window, and the garden which I saw through the window, with myself, nor yet again with one another. To me they at once appeared as things, objective, real, distinct. I saw the little tit with its yellow breast, its greenish-blue wings and the black and white markings of its back. I heard the rattle of its claws and the tapping of its beak. I observed how it threw crumb after crumb aside before it found one to suit its taste. Then, when it flew away and my attention passed to the window and the garden, I recognised them at once. Hedges and trees and plants and soil were clearly distinguished. I was conscious that they were the same as they were a moment ago, the same as they were yesterday and the day before ; and to this judgment also I gave my assent. To me, at any rate, my judgment did not present merely a 'claim to truth ; ' it was a truth, immediate, factual, self-evident.

Now, all this, the psychologist will tell me, implies that I had sensations of colour, of yellow and black and white, and sensations of sound by means of which I distinguished one object from another, and muscular sensations by means of which I assigned them to their respective distances, and universal ideas under which the different objects were subsumed. This, however, is theory pure and simple. No doubt it is well-founded and true. Nevertheless, sensations were not given as data in the series of perceptions which occurred. Sensations and ideas may have been involved in each of my acts of perception, but I was not aware of it at the time. I did not perceive my sensations nor yet my ideas. What I perceived were external objects. Nor was I conscious either in the act of perception itself or in the reflective act which followed, that I perceived by means of sensations and ideas ; though, as a psychologist, I believe this to be actually the case. The colours which I observed, belonged as qualities to the tit ; the distances were given as part of what I perceived ; the tit, the window, and the garden were objects, things, having the qualities and performing the actions which I have described. All *I* did was to perceive. It was the objects themselves which possessed qualities, were stationary or moved about, were active or passive, underwent changes, or, again, did not change at all.

§ 29. Nor do I seem to have been responsible in any way for what occurred, except in so far as I was conscious of it. I say that I distinguished object from object ; yet this seems to be a figure of speech rather than an accurate description of fact. I was not aware of any distinguishing or of any synthesis on my part. What I perceived was not perceived as one whole. The tit was a whole and so were the other objects, but each whole was individual and distinct from the rest. From the outset the tit was clearly distinguished from the window and the garden ; and though the trees and hedges of the latter were not distinguished from one another till my attention was directed to them after the tit had gone, they were certainly neither perceived nor felt as a whole. There was, indeed, a certain *togetherness* about what I perceived. I saw a-tit-through-a-window-overlooking-the-garden. But this simply means that I took in the scene at a single glance, not that the different objects which I perceived were merged in any felt-whole or were in any sense a unity. The only real wholes which I seem to perceive are individual objects. The perception of these doubtless implies the synthesis of qualities distinguished one by one in the past and re-united to form my percept of (*v.g.*) the tit. But these qualities do not constitute a *felt* whole. The whole itself, as well as its unity and the different qualities it comprises, seems to be something objective, something distinct from me and independent of any activity on my part, something the parts of which I believe to have been there all along, whether distinguished and again synthesised by me or not. Both analysis and synthesis, in a sense, are mine, since it is I who make them. But in making them I cannot help myself. The object seems to force me to make them, and in so doing to reveal to my mind its own nature, its own objective, real, and individual unity in difference.

§ 30. Again, I can find no trace of purpose in the acts of perception I have described. They seemed to occur quite accidentally, and to have nothing to do either with my purposes or with my needs. If you ask me what it was made me perceive what I did perceive, I should say it was just the objects which were there when I looked up. Perhaps I looked up to see what was there? It may be that I did; but I do not see how this affects what I saw, or how it can possibly be said to modify the facts which I observed. If facts are modified or muti-lated by purposes, it is certainly not a datum of experience. To the plain man, even when he *selects* his facts, as when he goes out to look for a golf-ball which he lost the day before, or when he digs in British *tumuli* in the hope of finding traces of a bygone age, or when he works in the laboratory, arranging apparatus, weighing chemicals, pouring out acids—in a word, preparing his experiments—it does not seem that his purposive and selective actions alter what he finds, in the sense of making it less real or less objective. They are still facts, though it was he himself who placed the conditions which brought those facts to light. Perception may often be purposive, but purpose determines the intent, not the content, of thought ; it determines what we look for, not what we find. Perception may also be selective, for there are many things which we might observe but do not, because such things are irrelevant to our purpose and so fail to attract our attention. Nevertheless, what we do observe even under circumstances which we our-selves have brought about, we believe to be as objectively true and real as the facts which force themselves upon our notice independently of any pre-formed purpose or pre-conceived idea. Experi-mental observations seem to be as valid objectively as those which are made by the comparatively passive observer. In neither case is assent deter-mined by purpose or by the power of facts to satisfy our needs ; for whether we find what we want or discover something else, whether our experiments turn out as desired or otherwise, we accept as given what we perceive to take place.

§ 31. Ordinarily, too, assent is absolute. Either we assent or we doubt. And if the plain man assents to a fact perceived by himself, rarely can you get him to own that he has made a mistake. Should you succeed, however, a judicious use of the Socratic method will lead to interesting results. The plain man will probably qualify his admission of error by some such phrase as " Well ! it looked like that at any rate." By which he means that though things in reality were not as he perceived them, yet they appeared to be so at the time. If, however, you press the point you will probably succeed in convincing him that his mistake was due, not to false appearance, but to false inference or to a false interpretation of sense-data. And by this means you will be able to prove to him that in perception we not only use the senses but also subsume objects under universal ideas, and that errors of perception are often due to the subsumption of a perceived object under the wrong idea. Indeed, that he has what logicians call universal ideas, he will readily admit. For he knows what is meant (*v.g.*) by a man. It is a being with a body more or less like his own and performing actions very much in the same way that he does. And there are many objects of this kind to which his idea of ' man ' is applicable. Of colours, sizes and shapes he can tell you little perhaps, but he knows that they are qualities which may belong to the same or to different objects. Of honesty, virtue and truth he can tell you more since these concern him more closely and he ha

probably thought more about them and often
heard them discussed. In any case, he may
easily be convinced that of such qualities he
has universal ideas and also that these ideas are
abstract, for he knows very well that colours
are never found without something coloured,
and that honesty does not exist except in an
honest man.

§ 32. Now, suppose you call the attention of
this victim of your philosophic zeal to a dirty,
unkempt, and ill-clad object lying by the road-side,
and ask him what he takes it to be. Suppose also
he replies that ' it may be either a gipsy or a tramp,
more probably the latter.' You may then point
out that here an inference has been made, and that
though this inference is based upon perceptual data,
the predicates ' gipsy ' and ' tramp ' are not actually
contained therein as objects of sense-perception.
Hence you may show that in many cases of what
seems to be immediate perception, inference is
involved. For instance, the minds of other men
are not perceived directly, but inferred from the
perception of their bodies. In the universal idea
' man,' therefore, certain characteristics or ' notes '
are not objects of sense-perception, but of inference.
And the same may be said of many other universal
ideas. At the same time, though we can distinguish
in a universal idea, especially when we hesitate in
applying it, elements which are not given in sense-
data from those which are, both what we perceive
and what we infer belongs to the object, and belongs
to it, not on account of our way of looking at it or
thinking about it, but on account of its own nature,

which we seem to be able, by means of perception and inference, to get to know.

Whether we perceive directly or whether we infer, we believe that it is the object itself whose nature is revealed to our intelligence.

§ 33. Thus both universal ideas and inferences are involved in perception, as even the plain man may be forced to admit. Strictly, however, and as applied to perception in general, this is not a datum of perceptual experience, but belongs to theory. Ordinarily, what we perceive, whether it be natural objects, or their qualities, colours, shapes and distances, we perceive immediately. Our subsumption is not deliberate. Our universal ideas function unconsciously. The assertion that *all* perception involves subsumption under universal ideas and is really inferential in character is itself an inference based on particular cases in which perception halts and stumbles. That universal ideas exist, and function in sense-perception can readily be verified in experience ; but whether or not *all* perception is inferential is quite another matter. Indeed, if it were, it would be difficult to conceive how perception could begin.

§ 34. Similarly, all questions as to the functioning of sensation-complexes and of *a priori* categories or forms, the synthetic and constructive activity of the mind, the modification of fact owing to selection, purposes and needs, *so far as perception in general is concerned*, pertain to theory. In some cases hypotheses of this kind explain very well how we perceive, but fail to satisfy other conditions, and are often in contradiction with common-sense belief, as, for instance, the theory that universals are *a priori* forms of the mind; while the hypothesis that the objects of perception are sensations is even worse off, for it explains nothing. It does not even explain how we perceive, still less how we come to believe in an objective and real world consisting of numberless individual objects, quite independent of ourselves, except when directly or indirectly we operate upon them by physical movements or when *vice versa* they operate upon us. It may be true, after all, that what we perceive are at bottom nothing but our own sensations, but this, at any rate, is not a datum of experience nor a common-sense belief. It is a theory ; nay, more, a meta-physical theory, for which, personally, I can find no adequate foundation in the data of experience, and the value of which for epistemology seems to me to be evanescent. To introspection, what we perceive does not appear as something determined by us, and we certainly believe it to be determined *ab extra*. The object of perception appears, not as a sensation, nor yet as a synthesis of sense-data under *a priori* forms, but as a thing having qualities and performing operations, and sometimes *in addition to this, but never instead of this*, serving certain purposes which we wish to realise. Colour appears, not as a sensation, but as a quality of real things ; and a thing is something which has qualities but is not itself merely a quality. The plain man knows little of the nature of things and their qualities. He cannot define them. None the less qualities appear to him as distinct from one another, and distinct from himself. He does not say that he has sensations of hardness or roughness, but that things feel hard or soft, rough or smooth. Sounds, too, and even smells, are perceived, not as sensations, but as the qualities of things. We say that we hear a sound or perceive a smell, not that we have an auditory or an olfactory sensation ; and this holds even when we fail to localise the sound or the smell.

The object of strictly external perception, then, is always something real and independent[1] of ourselves, and though it implies the functioning of universal ideas, we are not ordinarily conscious of this fact ; still less are we aware that our perceptions are due to *a priori* forms of synthesis, or that their content is determined in any way by human purposes and needs.

§ 35. The perception of our own body and its various qualities and states furnishes us with further and different data. We still perceive objects, indeed ; for the distinction of subject and object is never entirely lost as long as we are in any way conscious. But the object of perception is now some part of ourselves. By means of sight we perceive the shape of our limbs, and by means of touch the smoothness and softness of our skin. Perceiver and perceived are, in this case, only relatively distinct, for we recognise that in reality they are one.

Moreover, although what we perceive in this way is usually a state or quality belonging to some part

[1] By this I do not mean, of course, that the object of perception is unrelated to consciousness, or that *quâ* the content of perception it is not *in* consciousness ; but that *quâ* real we believe it to be other than, outside of, and not dependent on ourselves, and to have a nature of its own which as such is not affected by the fact of its becoming known. See Appendix.

of our bodies in the same way that colour and shape, hardness and softness, belong as qualities to external things, sometimes the object of what may be called perhaps ' internal ' perception, is more vague and ill-defined. We *feel* warm or cold all over. We feel hungry or thirsty, but we cannot say precisely *where*. We have pains, aches, feelings of discomfort or of healthy exuberance. Sometimes such feelings are, more or less, located ; sometimes they are not located at all. But in either case we recognise them not only as states of our body, but as *feelings* or *sensations*.

There are cases, therefore, in which the object of perception is a sensation. There is, in fact, a kind of gradation between what we perceive as the qualities of objects—of external things or of our own bodies—and what we perceive as sensations. On the one hand, colours, shapes, sounds, hardness and other properties perceived by actual contact, are perceived as qualities of objects and not as sensations. On the other hand, the ' voluminous ' feelings we get in the body as a whole, as well as various pains and aches and muscular sensations, are certainly recognised to be of the nature of sensation ; while temperature and taste seem to form a half-way house. Sometimes we perceive with the tongue the flavour of meat, wine, fruit, or peppermint, with the hand the warmth of water, and with the face the coolness of the breeze. Sometimes we merely ' get a taste,' a *sensation* of bitterness or sweetness localised loosely in the mouth, or we feel hot from the effects of violent exercise or cold on account of a chill.

E

§ 36. This gradation between what is perceived as sensation and what is perceived as the quality of objects has led to the theory that sensations are always the means by which we perceive (*id quo percipitur*), and also to the more questionable theory that the object of perception (*id quod percipitur*) is at bottom sensation. Both theories may also appeal to the fact that even in external perception we can often distinguish sensation, provided we look for it. For instance, the muscular sensation in the organ of sight may be detected when we change the convergence of the eyes. In touch-contact, too, sensation may be perceived and located in the tips of the fingers, if we attend to *them* and not to the object touched. Even colour may appear as a sensation when the eyes are almost closed and all variation in tone, tint, and outline are, as far as possible, eliminated. It must be noted, however, that these latter are abnormal and exceptional cases, and in no way render false what has been said about the object of external perception in general, viz., that that object is normally not a sensation but the quality of a real thing.

The data of perceptual experience are not as such sensations, and if the *id quod percipitur* theory be expressed in this form it is certainly false. That the qualities of objects are ultimately reducible to sensations may or may not admit of proof ; but for external perception, in the strict sense of the term, the object perceived does not appear as a sensation. Possibly, it might so appear if our experience were ' pure,' which it is not ; but, more probably, as Mr. Shadworth Hodgson says, for ' pure ' experience there is no distinction of subject and object, and consequently what is perceived would appear, if it appeared at all, *neither* as a quality of an object *nor* as a sensation. And under such conditions perception proper would not exist, for there would be neither subjective nor objective reference. Hence, as introspection fails to reveal to us the data of pure experience, we must be content to take experience as we find it ; and, this being so, we are forced to admit that for us in our present stage of development the data of experience include what we believe to be the qualities of external objects.

CHAPTER II.

THE DATA OF EXPERIENCE—*Continued.*

CONCEPTUAL THOUGHT.

§ 37. Unable to analyse an act of perception directly, psychologists are accustomed to ' analyse ' it by the aid of data extrinsic to the act itself. These data are obtained either by experiment or by direct introspection in which attention is concentrated on processes that usually pass unnoticed ; and in this way an act of perception is ' analysed into a complex of sensations.' But of the ' sensations ' which are said to have functioned in the act of perception thus analysed, we were quite unconscious when we perceived. Strictly speaking, sensations when functioning in a percept are not sensations at all, but merely nervous processes. Nor is the

percept itself in any way comparable with the sum
of the sensations it is said to involve. When I
perceive a picture there hanging on my wall at
about six yards distance from where I sit, not only
am I unconscious of the focussing of my eyes, of
their movement in their sockets, of the variation in
convexity of their lenses, and of the revived images
of the movements necessary to reach and to handle
the picture, but the sum of these sensations,
immediate and revived, is something different from
and quite inadequate to represent what I mean
when I say that I perceive the picture six yards
away. The sensation-complex involved is not
equivalent to the percept ; nor yet is the sum of
the individual sensations equivalent to the complex
in which they are said to be fused. The fusion of
the sensations destroys altogether their individuality, while the sensation-complex which results
qua a complex of sensations, is altogether obliterated
for consciousness by the percept to which it gives
rise.

Moreover, *a percept has meaning*. It is not merely
a sensation-complex, nor merely the *appearance* of
a certain arrangement of colour localised in a certain
way. What I mean when I say that I perceive a
picture hanging on a wall at six yards distance, is
something more than what I feel, and something
more than what is apparent to my senses. The
object of perception is not merely clear, distinct,
and apparently external, but it has definite
objective meaning and significance. Whence it
follows that some other mental function is involved
in perception besides that of sensation. That

function would seem to belong to universal ideas under which, as we have seen, perceived objects are subsumed. Now universal ideas correspond to *names*. They function whenever names are used, and it is by this means that we understand what we hear or what we read. Hence, by examining introspectively what takes place in our minds when we listen to or read the words of another, we may be able to arrive at a clearer notion of the nature of an idea as opposed to an image or a sensation.

§ 38. Suppose that I call at the house of a friend, and, on enquiring for him, am told that ' he has already gone to his office.' Such an answer is no mere string of words. Its significance is perfectly definite, and the objects to which the words refer are brought clearly before my mind. I say ' before my mind,' yet the objects signified are not perceived by me, nor do I imagine or picture them. They are ' present ' only in idea, which means nothing more than that I am able to think about them ; that, knowing my friend and knowing what is meant by ' going to an office,' I am able to understand the answer I received. But it is of real objects and not of ideas that we think. Ideas are the instruments by means of which we think of objects. Our thoughts, impelled by the words which we hear or which we read, are directed to objects about which we think, and which are therefore said to be present to our minds. We call this ' presence-in-idea ' to distinguish it from the real presence of the object in sense-perception. Yet ideas as such are not objects, but rather functions of the mind which enable us to think of absent objects.

Moreover, what we think about the object, what
the object means to us, is itself something objective
and real. When thinking of real objects thought
does not, so we believe, create the object, but
merely causes it to be ideally present. The content
of our ideas is thought as part of the object itself.
This is true even when the object is not a concrete
thing, but something abstract—a moral whole, a
system of relations, such, for instance, as 'the
British Policy in Egypt.' However relations are
to be explained, we believe that somehow or other
they are real.

The apparent reality of objects of thought may
be an illusion, but our belief in it is none the less
a datum. By this belief thought about reality is
distinguished from thought about fictitious or
imaginary beings, the products of our own or of
another's constructive ingenuity. In the latter
case, what we think about is still objective, but
not real. The object is present to our thoughts as
before, but we no longer believe in its reality.
Thought has always an objective reference ; it is
thought about objects. But there are different
kinds of objectivity. The objects about which we
think may be real or ideal. If real, they may be
present before us in the concrete or present only
to our thoughts. If ideal, they may be the
creations of our own or of another's fancy. When
created by another, they are independent of ourselves, and our knowledge of them may possess
the quality of truth, but they are not real. When
created by our own imagination, they are neither real
nor independent. It is with real objects, however,

that we are concerned, and, before proceeding further, we must discuss the meaning of our belief in ' objective reality.'

§ 39. Belief in the reality of the objects about which we think is not confined to those ideas which Professor James describes as ' truncated experiences, leading to sense-termini.' For the functioning of an idea in our minds to be accompanied by belief in the reality of that which it signifies, it is not necessary that the idea should ' terminate ' in a sense-percept. ' The British Policy of Egypt ' and ' The American Constitution ' are both ideas of real objects, yet in neither case is that object perceived by the senses. Again, no working-man has ever seen, or heard, or felt a Trades Union, yet he knows very well what the term means, and firmly believes in its reality. If you attempt to define a Trades Union you must introduce the notion of purpose, and say, (*v.g.*) with Professor Nicholson, that a Trades Union is ' a voluntary association of labour for mutual assistance, protection and benefit.' Now, it is possible that Professor James, who is able to feel ' buts ' and ' ifs ' and ' ands ' and ' ors,' may be able also to feel causes and purposes, even when they are not his own. Hence it may be possible for Professor James to build up some complex feeling which corresponds, or which he imagines must correspond, with a Trades Union or a British Policy. But the plain man will tell you that he gets no such feelings, and with him I quite agree. I feel eagerness, anxiety, longing, hope, fear, when I think of something which I hope to do or which I hope will be done ; but I experience no such

emotion when it is a question of the purpose of
somebody else, except in so far as I make it my
own. Nor do I identify such feelings with the objects
towards which they are directed. I know what
these feelings are, and therefore I understand what
is meant when somebody tells me he desires happiness or is anxious about his health ; but my
knowledge is not a feeling nor is it necessarily
accompanied by any feeling that I can detect.
Purposes, in fact, are not feelings at all, but ideas
which, when present to the mind, arouse feelings
or emotions. Nor is the idea or knowledge of a
feeling itself a feeling, but rather something intellectual. I am also quite at a loss when I attempt
to distinguish the feelings which are supposed to
accompany conjunctive and disjunctive relations.
I cannot realise the feeling which accompanies a
' but ' or an ' if.' When I perceive a difference
between two things, I certainly ' feel ' the contrast.
But my perception of difference is not the mere
feeling. I know what ' difference ' means, and it
does not mean the feeling which I get when I
perceive a contrast which pleases or annoys me.

It seems to me, then, that it is quite impossible
to reduce the definition of a ' Trades Union ' or of
any other notion of the kind to feelings, images
or sense-termini. No feeling and no percept is
adequate to represent or express the notion of a
common purpose, such as that of ' labouring
for mutual assistance, protection and benefit.'
' Labour ' itself can hardly be pictured or perceived.
I can perceive hop-pickers at work in a field, but
that is not what I mean by ' labour.' It is only a

concrete example which expresses at once too much and too little, when I compare it with my idea of 'labour.' Universal ideas are contained within the individual cases to which they apply, and to this they may be said to 'lead.' But that common 'something,' though it is realised there in each individual example, cannot be perceived by the senses. We perceive men, trees, books, colours, concrete and particular motions and changes, but we do not perceive humanity, tree-ness, book-nature, colouredness, or change and motion in general. We cannot lay hold of these things, so to speak, by sight or by touch or by hearing. Yet somehow or other we do lay hold of the universal characters which are realised in particular cases, and when such and such a case (S) presents itself, we recognise in it the universal character (P) at once, and affirm in consequence that S is P.

Apart altogether from theory, therefore, the mental function by means of which universal ideas are formed and by means of which they are recognised in concrete cases, is, even for introspection, something quite different from feeling and sensation ; though it is from sense-experience that such ideas are obtained, and the function by which they are formed is included in what we call an act of perception. There seem to be no sense-termini to which the causes, purposes, and logical conventions signified by the conjunctions 'since,' 'because,' 'in order to,' 'so that,' 'in as much as,' correspond, or for which they can be substituted. Causes, purposes, and abstract universal ideas are as objective and real as the concrete things in which they are revealed, but they seem to belong to the rational structure or plan of the universe rather than to anything which can be felt by the senses. Belief in objective reality does not mean, therefore, that objects have been or are capable of being experienced as sensations, but merely that their nature and their existence has been determined independently of our thoughts about them. They exist somehow in the concrete; though, if relational or abstract, they do not exist in isolation or as individual things. And when we know such objects, we believe that our knowledge somehow or other comes from the object and is determined by the object; otherwise it would not be knowledge. How it comes, or how it is determined, neither introspection nor common-sense belief can say: that is a matter which the plain man leaves to the philosopher.

§ 40. Logicians tell us that our ideas have content, and that they may be analysed into simpler ideas or notes. If you were to ask me, however, what was the content of the ideas which came to my mind when I was told that my friend had gone to his office, I should find it very difficult to answer you. I could tell you, perhaps, a good deal about the person in question, what he looks like, and what he has done. Yet even of this I was not conscious when his name was mentioned. My knowledge of persons or things, however comprehensive, is certainly not called to mind at the sound of their names. But although the idea of my friend was vague in that I did not think of any one of his characteristics in particular, it was perfectly definite in that I knew at the time what object the name signified, and should have hesitated to believe, even if I did not immediately reject, any answer incompatible with his habits or character. In the same way, the other objects of which I thought were similarly vague, and yet in like manner sufficiently definite for me to understand clearly the import of the answer I received. I did not picture to myself an office, nor did I imagine my friend perambulating the streets. Yet I knew what an ' office ' meant, and I knew what was intended when I was told that my friend had gone there. And this I knew in spite of the fact that I had never been to his office and did not know what it was like, and was ignorant also as to *how* he went, whether on foot, by motor, or by train.

Definite significance is perfectly compatible with unanalysed content, and both are characteristic of all continuous discourse. Through frequently thinking of the same thing, we build up a concept of it, and thus seem to grasp in idea its nature as a whole. Hence, whenever a name is mentioned, we think of the object signified by means of a preformed idea, which then and there begins to function in our minds. Yet such an idea is seldom realised in the fulness of its content. In continuous conversation or reading, though each phrase has definite significance, the idea which it awakens in the mind is supplanted by another and yet another before it has time to develop. If, therefore, we wish to analyse an idea, we must stop talking or reading and allow the idea to unfold itself in consciousness.

§ 41. Let us experiment in this way with the idea expressed in the phrase 'going to an office,' and see what happens. Immediately I fix my attention upon what these words signify, and allow the idea to 'work,' other ideas and images awaken in my mind in rapid succession. I picture people leaving their dwellings after an early breakfast in haste to catch a train ; I imagine others who, having partaken of their morning meal at a later hour, stroll leisurely to the station or are whisked off in an automobile. I see an office peopled with clerks who sit upon high stools, and, with pens behind their ears, stare vigorously at day-books and ledgers which lie open before them. I think of the purposes for which offices exist, of commerce, of the Stock Exchange, and of Government Departments. All these things about which I think, are to me, things objective, real, and independent of myself, whether I can picture them or not. Commerce, for instance, and a Government Department, is to me just as objectively real as more concrete things, such as a ledger, a clerk or a desk.

Reflecting, however, on these ideas which have been brought to consciousness by the phrase 'going to the office,' I find that they are not essential to the meaning of that phrase. They are all connected with the original idea, and must have been somehow mentally associated with it, otherwise they would not have become conscious. But they are not what a logician would call the essential 'notes' of the idea 'going to an office.' Rather they are particular, and in some instances alternative cases, to which that notion, as a whole, or the office part of it, would apply. There is, moreover, an indefinite number of other cases in which the ideas in question are realised. One may go to an office in other ways besides those which occurred to my mind. The office might contain clerks, or it might contain only my friend, their employer, or again, it might be empty. While, to the clerks, if there, one might assign a great variety of attitudes and occupations. The office, again, might neither be that of a merchant, nor of a stockbroker, nor yet of a Government official ; it might belong to a newspaper editor, or it might be in a railway depôt.

I have not analysed logically the idea ' going to an office,' but have allowed it to develop by means of its associations ; and the products of that association-process are equivalent to the original idea neither individually nor as a sum, nor yet as a system. They signify at once too much and too little, just as we found to be the case when we tried to represent the notion of ' labour ' by an image of hop-pickers working in a field. Nevertheless, the associated ideas illustrate or exemplify the original notion; and from them one might, by abstraction, form a definition more or less adequate. One might say, for instance, that ' to go to an office ' is ' to proceed from any place whatever and by any means whatever to a building adapted for business purposes.' Doubtless Socrates would be able to pick holes in this definition. That does not matter. Suffice it that I have a more or less accurate notion of what ' going to an office ' means.

§ 42. Hence, although our ideas in continuous

discourse have *explicitly for consciousness* very little
content indeed, yet the fact that they are capable
of giving rise to associations intimately connected
with the original idea and containing implicitly its
definition, shows that they are no mere words.
Latent or implicit within the original idea are all
those subordinate ideas which exemplify and define
its meaning, and which psychologically form its
content. Only on this hypothesis can the facts be
explained. For clearly when an idea is analysed
psychologically by means of its associations, that
idea functions throughout, controlling the whole
process and preventing irrelevant ideas from
arising, or causing them to be dismissed at once
if they do arise. And, again, in discourse ideas
exercise a similar function or controlling power.
Ideas are aroused by their corresponding terms,
and by them we understand what we hear or what
we read, though they may seem to have no content
except that which the speaker or writer chooses to
develop for us.

This process goes on smoothly enough so long as
the statements made harmonise with the ideas that
are awakened in our minds. But should some
assertion fail so to harmonise, should some new
attribute be predicated which seems to us incompatible with the object to which it is assigned, at
once thought hesitates, and if it fails to assimilate
the new predicate, will, in the end, reject it as false.
Unless, then, we hold that an idea contains potentially, implicitly, schematically, the particular cases
which have already been subsumed and systematised
under it on previous occasions and which virtually

include its definition, I fail to see how we are to explain the controlling power which is exercised by the idea, both in discourse and in an associative process. Unquestionably, cerebral conditions account, in part at least, for the associations which arise in the latter case, and the suggestions of the speaker or writer for those which arise in the former ; but no brain-processes and no mere words can account for the objective significance of our thoughts, or for the accepting or rejecting of associated ideas, or for the assent or dissent which accompanies cognition when we listen or read.

An idea, therefore, is a function of the mind by means of which, somehow or other, we apprehend the nature of objects ; and its content, even though unconscious, functions in the mind whenever that idea is recalled, and so controls both association and assent.

§ 43. Ideas have also another function—they influence action. Their objective reference is, as we have seen, not always to something real or existing. They may refer to something which we should like to exist, to some change which we desire to bring about. Regarded from this point of view, ideas are called purposes.

A purpose is nothing more than an idea signifying an object not yet real, but which we seek to realise by action. Suppose that we enter a room which is in darkness with the intention of consulting some book. The idea of consulting this book is a purpose, and till that purpose is realised this idea controls all our operations, mental and physical. We remember having seen the book in a particular room ; hence we go there. The darkness of the room suggests the need of lighting the gas ; hence we grope about for matches. The idea of matches suggests the mantelshelf, and thither we make our way. Finally, having secured the matches and lit the gas, we take down the book that we need from the library shelves. It was the idea of consulting this book which controlled the various operations performed in order to realise it. And here, again, as in the former case of cognition, the idea which guided the process need not have been explicit or fully developed as to its content. We may have had, to begin with, a picture of the book, of its size, the colour of its binding and the plates with which it may have been illustrated, or we may have thought merely of its title or of the name of its author, or of the subject in general of which it treated. Again, the more immediate purpose of obtaining a light may have obliterated for con-sciousness the original purpose, just as when cognition is directed to theoretical purposes, the general idea of the subject in hand may be obscured by more immediate points of interest which occupy us. Nevertheless, in practice as in theory, the original idea or purpose is operative throughout, and to it other ideas and purposes are subordinate, though it is always possible that one purpose may be displaced by another more attractive, and that one idea may be superseded by another to which it has led by association in the course of its own development.

§ 44. The question now arises how far purpose governs even 'our most remotely cognitive

activities. "All thought is purposive," we are
told ; and this would seem to be true in general,
for we always intend either to gain knowledge by
the development of our ideas and by sense-
experience, or else to bring about some practical
result. But *how far* and *in what sense* is thought
purposive ? How far, for instance, is what I have
written in this chapter due to the purpose with
which I began it, viz., that of ascertaining the data
of experience in order to distinguish them from the
theories by which absolutists, pragmatists, and
realists seek to explain them ?

Just as when I attempted to describe the processes of sense-perception and of rational discourse,
so now, when I attempt to describe the development
of my own thoughts, I find that idea after idea
emerges above the threshold of consciousness, only
to be rejected, until at last some one is evolved
which suits my purpose. Similarly, the verbal
forms in which, first mentally, and apparently by
means of auditory images, and then in writing I
seek to express these ideas, are rejected or modified
again and again until they seem to give more or
less adequate expression to that which I wish to
say. Why do I reject some ideas and accept others ?
Why do I continually change the verbal forms
which come spontaneously to mind ? One does not
think of it at the time ; the process is automatic,
as it were. Yet, now that I reflect, I recognise
that at the outset I had a general notion of different
forms of cognition on the one hand, and of the
various theories by which cognition is explained
on the other. Under each of these ideas innumer-

F

able others have been systematically subsumed in the past ; and though of the full content of no one of them was I more than implicitly or schematically conscious at any given moment, yet they seem to have controlled throughout the development of my thoughts, and to have caused me to select and to set down in writing only those data of experience which seemed to bear upon the problems—again only schematically apprehended—which are to be discussed in future chapters. My thought has all along been purposive in that all irrelevant ideas have been rejected and only those which concern the fundamental problems of the psychology of cognition have been allowed to develop in consciousness.

§ 45. But how are we to account for the succession of our thoughts ? Clearly they are not due wholly to the general purpose or problem we have in hand, for though this may contain them schematically, it does not determine their order. Nor can they be due merely to verbal association : for though verbal expressions accompany our ideas in the form of images, they have nothing to do with the evolution of the general purpose. On the contrary, they are subordinate to each individual idea which they attempt to express. The verbal form which thought takes is quite a secondary matter. We modify a verbal expression at will. We cross out or correct the written sentence without scruple, if it fails to express the thought which lies, as it were, at the back of the words. Thought seems to anticipate the words in which it is expressed, and to control them in such a way that while the sentence is yet inchoate, and long before it has completed itself, it is often rejected as inadequate. Moreover, at times one seems to have thoughts without words, an intuition of wide extent, not clear in detail and yet not vague, a general grasp of the problem in hand, a thought which in a flash seems to make clear the solution and to reveal the problem and solution as a whole. Clearly the succession of our thoughts cannot be accounted for by verbal expressions. Nor can it be accounted for wholly by physiological habit. For physiological habit conditions only images, and but few images are involved in abstract thought as a rule, while in regard to verbal images we have already seen that they are, for the most part, if not wholly, both subordinate and subsequent to thought. It would seem, then, that in order to account for the succession of ideas in conceptual and constructive thought, we must call in another factor, viz., intellectual habit. Cerebral processes undoubtedly underlie, and in some sense condition all thought and all ideas, however abstract. But between abstract ideas there is a logical as well as a physiological connection ; and it seems to me that this logical connection—which is a *datum* of experience, whereas the physiological connection is not—has more to do with the association of ideas in many cases than purely physiological habits in which the passage of the nervous impulse is governed solely by the law of least resistance.

§ 46. Habit, however, is not the ultimate explanation of the order and sequence of our ideas ; for we may still ask how has habit itself been formed ?   And to answer this we are forced back once more upon objective experience.   All ideas are conditioned by sense-experience.   However abstract and complex they may be, if real as well as objective, there must be some object or system of objects in which they are realised.   It is in objective experience that ideas are formed, and to some extent the order and sequence of those ideas is determined by our environment itself.   Yet indirectly purposes and needs also play a part in determining this order. We perceive first those attributes of objects which have practical value as satisfying our needs. Others again are perceived because curiosity or the desire to know prompts us to observe and examine.   Our needs also, in a higher stage of development, prompt us to seek to solve social, moral and religious problems on the one hand, and historical, scientific and philosophical problems on the other.   Thus what we enquire about and what we neglect, and hence the order in which knowledge is acquired, is determined in part by our environment, but in part also by our purposes and needs.   Guided partly by subjective interests and partly by the accidental circumstances in which we find ourselves, we form ideas of objective realities, ideas which from the beginning are connected with one another, but are gradually grouped together in systems and subsumed under more general notions.   As we think these ideas again and again and pass from one to another, habits of thought are formed, logical connections between ideas are discovered, and other and larger groupings of them are made.   When, therefore, we wish to solve some ·problem, to develop and examine the bearings of some complex and general notion, some principle, hypothesis or law, these preformed habits of thought begin to function. Ideas already conceived and connections already discovered, force one another in rapid succession above the threshold of consciousness. And all this takes place under the guidance of a purpose, which, itself an idea, assumes for the time control of our habits of thought. The purpose which dominates all our mental energies is, in this case, a theoretical one ; it is prompted not by practical needs, but by the need which we feel of somehow solving the problems that the universe presents to us.

Hence my final answer to the question 'what is it determines the succession of our thoughts when we reflect?' is that the succession is due partly to physiological and partly to intellectual habits, both of which presuppose and have been built up by objective experience, the strength of these habits depending, other conditions being the same, upon the intensity and the frequency of repetition of those experiences or of our reflections upon them. Purposes which in constructive thought consist in a general grasp of the problem in hand have little to do with the succession of ideas as such, though they control it throughout. By them the relevancy of associated ideas is determined, but not the particular order in which they arise. On the other hand, the building up of the habits by which the sequence of ideas in association is determined is again largely due to purposive selection.

§ 47. Need-prompted purposes, then, are clearly

of the greatest importance as determining factors
in the acquisition of knowledge. Thought is
selective, and selection implies purpose. Purposes,
however, are themselves ideas which we seek to
realise, and are themselves derived ultimately from
experience ; nor does purposive selection destroy
our belief in the objective validity of knowledge.
In ideal thought of absent objects, as in perception
itself, the result of our purposive strivings after
knowledge is that objects become known to us as
they really are in themselves. Our knowledge is
not adequate, but none the less it may be true so
far as it goes. Purposive selection is compatible
with objective validity, because while purposes
determine what objects we observe, they do not, as
a rule, determine the result of our observations. On
the contrary, the content as opposed to the intent
of perception and thought seems to be determined
by the object itself. Similarly, in the knowledge
which we gain from others, interest determines
what questions we ask, what lectures we attend, and
what books we read ; but the information gained
comes in all cases from without. Whether we admit
it as true or reject it as false, assent or dissent
depends upon whether or not we believe that we
have acquired knowledge of real objects which have
manifested themselves to us through the words of
another. If our purpose is, as I suppose, to acquire
knowledge, and if we approach the subject with a
mind open to conviction, assent or conviction will
arise either from the known credibility of our
informant in regard to matters of fact, or, if it is a
question of theory, from the intrinsic reasonableness

or self-evidence of its presentment, and from its consistency with knowledge already acquired. If, on the other hand, one approaches a particular subject upon which one's own mind is already made up, one's purpose can only be to ascertain the opinions of others; and here, again, when we assent, to the proposition that ' X.Y.'s opinion is so and so,' our assent is determined, not by purpose, but by what we have heard him say.

§ 48. I do not wish to deny, of course, that purpose may affect assent. All I assert here is that wherever assent is given it does not appear *at the time* to be determined by purposes, needs, emotions or will, or by anything other than the object about which we think. Subsequently we may discover that subjective conditions and interests have influenced us ; but, at the time, that influence is unconscious, otherwise we could not give our assent. I regard it as a psychological fact that assent is possible only in so far as we are unaware of the influence of subjective conditions, emotional and voluntary. On the other hand, it cannot be denied that it is also a psychological fact that purposes and other subjective influences are some-times found to have influenced assent and to have caused it to be given where it should not have been given. In the case above cited, that one does not give one's assent to XY's opinion as opposed to the fact that such an opinion is his, may be due to a preformed will-*not*-to-believe, or, in other words, to the conviction that we are right and that, therefore, he must be wrong. Undoubtedly assent is often withheld on account of prejudice ; and, similarly, prejudices may cause assent to be given where it ought to be withheld, as we sometimes discover afterwards to our cost. Ordinarily, however, we are not influenced by these subjective conditions—at least such is our belief—and when their influence is discovered, at once we withdraw our assent and begin to doubt. The honest seeker after truth, knowing the possibility of his being unduly influenced by subjective interests and the will to believe or not to believe, is particularly careful to eliminate such a possibility as far as he can, and will only give his full assent when it is clear to him that all subjective conditions have been excluded, and that his knowledge is determined solely by objective evidence. The assertion that the *content* of thought is modified directly by human purposes and needs and that truth depends upon the satisfaction of these needs is, therefore, not a datum of experience, but a theory, and a theory which it is not easy to reconcile with what is an introspective datum, viz., that we believe our ideas and our judgments to be determined by their objects, and that, on this account, we give our assent to their objective validity.

CHAPTER III.

THE PSYCHOLOGY OF CRITICISM AND THE DISTINCTION OF SUBJECT AND OBJECT.

§ 49. Two diametrically opposite opinions are prevalent in regard to the psychological basis of Criticism, and of the Absolutism to which it has given rise. The late Dr. Caird wished to exclude psychology altogether from Criticism. Professor James, Mr. Shadworth Hodgson, and other non-critical writers consider the Kantian and Hegelian standpoint, on the other hand, to be essentially psychological, and reject it precisely because, in their opinion, it is vitiated by a psychological fallacy. Professor James accuses Green and Caird of what he calls the psychologist's fallacy, *i.e.*, the fallacy of reading into psychological states *before analysis* all that the psychologist finds in them when that analysis is complete. Attempts have also been made to treat the *Criticism* of Kant on the same lines as the *Enquiry* of Locke, since both Kant and Locke held that an examination of the faculty of cognition was necessary by way of introduction to a study of philosophy.

The latter view is certainly wrong; for though there is a *prima facie* resemblance between the Lockian and the Kantian enquiries, the standpoint of Locke is essentially different from that of Kant. As Dr. Caird has pointed out, Locke examines the understanding " very much as we might examine

a telescope to discover whether there was a flaw
in its construction which might distort our vision of
the objects seen through it;"[1] while Kant examines
the nature of mind with a view to discover in it
the *a priori* forms which are presupposed by
knowledge, without which knowledge is impossible,
and by which in this sense it is limited. The
position of Kant is, therefore, very different from
that of Locke.

§ 50. On the other hand, Dr. Caird seems to
me to carry his dislike of the psychological position
too far when he endeavours to dispense with the
psychologist's aid altogether in epistemology, on
the ground that the knowledge of mind presupposes
a knowledge of matter. Mind, he says, presupposes
matter, both as its organ, and as the environment
about which it thinks. Without matter there would
be no objects, and therefore no knowledge. Hence,
"to understand mind in the sense in which we
contrast it with matter" (*i.e.*, in the psychological
sense) "implies that we already understand the
material world, and to base our knowledge on our
psychology would, therefore, be to base it on what
is the latest and most complex result."[2] Thus, for
Dr. Caird, there is a distinction between the relation
of subject and object as presupposed by the
possibility of knowledge, and the relation of mind
and matter as *objects* of knowledge; and it is with
the former, and not with the latter, that Criticism
is concerned. "Criticism has to deal with the
knowledge of mind only in so far as mind is presupposed in everything known or knowable; *i.e.*, in

[1] *Critical Philosophy of Kant,* p. 10.   [2] *Ibid.*

so far as the principles which are involved in the relations of objects to a conscious self are the latent presuppositions of all knowledge, the principles through which everything else must be known, and by means of which, therefore, every other kind of knowledge must be tried." [1]

But can psychology and epistemology be separated from one another so completely as this ? As sciences treating of different topics, the one of knowledge and truth, the other of psychical processes as such, they are undoubtedly distinct ; yet the subject which is treated of in epistemology and the 'mind' with which psychology is concerned are surely one and the same. Again, if *a priori* forms and 'latent presuppositions' and principles of a psychological order are involved in all knowledge, how are we to examine them unless we know what they are; and how are we to know what they are unless our 'Criticism' is preceded by an introspective examination and a psychological analysis of our own acts of cognition ? Whence does Criticism learn the functions of its categories, of substance, causality, reciprocity and the like, if not from its reflection on human thought-processes ? Granted that there is in consciousness an *a priori* element, that each self-conscious being "has within him the general plan for a self-consistent natural system," and that this plan is a kind of framework upon which all knowledge is built, which is common to all minds, and constitutes the general form of all knowledge ; granted all this, how, may I ask, does it come about that Criticism

[1] *Ibid*, p. 11.

has learnt the nature of this framework? How, indeed, does it know that such a framework exists except by a study of cognition as it actually takes place in human minds? It may be that this ' scheme which we carry about with us ' is, in a sense, unconscious, *i.e.*, " it may never be reflected on (by the ordinary man) or made the object of attention for itself," and few, perhaps, may " know that they have it in their minds at all, and fewer still be able to define and describe it."[1] Yet, if such exists, it must at times have been reflected on, since Criticism claims to have analysed it and bases its theory of the constructive and constitutive activity of thought largely on the results of that analysis.

To understand mind in the sense in which it is opposed to matter does imply that we already understand the material world, to some extent at least ; but it does not follow from this that our knowledge of matter is prior to our knowledge of mind, still less that our knowledge of mind and matter in opposition is prior to all cognitive experience. Internal and external perception, consciousness of our own mental acts, and of changes in our environment develop side by side, and only through the continual contrasting of subject and object is knowledge possible. We cannot discuss the conditions of knowledge unless we know what knowledge is, and this we cannot know except in our own experience. The epistemologist must start from certain data, and the data which he needs for his purpose are clearly those of empirical

[1] *Ibid*, pp. 18, 19.

psychology, which is merely an orderly and classified arrangement of the functionings of the human mind which may be verified by anyone who will reflect.

§ 51. The psychological aspect of Criticism was recognised by Kant, who distinguished two questions which Criticism has to answer, the *psychological* question as to the existence in the mind of the forms which we use in Cognition, and the *transcendental* question as to the validity of these forms. The discussion of the first question Dr. Vaihinger calls a *Transcendental Psychology*. It is a psychology inasmuch as it is an analysis and a classification of the processes of cognition ; and it is transcendental in that the classification is made with a view to discussing the relations of the forms, thus classified, to phenomena or to the object of knowledge. The latter problem is of course of primary importance in Criticism, since its aim is to discover the conditions of the possibility of knowledge. But, though Criticism is thus primarily and essentially an epistemology, it may in truth be said to have a psychological basis, since it presupposes a psychological analysis of cognition.

Later Criticism seems to borrow even more from the psychologist. It attempts to trace the development of mind from a state of vague consciousness in which discrimination and distinction are at a minimum, through a consciousness of objects posited by itself to a consciousness of itself as mind. And this process, though attributed by later critical philosophers to the Absolute, is at bottom a general, if somewhat mystical, account of the development of individual human minds ; and therefore may be said to lean upon psychology.

§ 52.   How, then, can we account for Dr. Caird's refusal to admit that Criticism involves psychology ? It would seem to be due, in the first place, to the narrow view which he takes of the latter science. Not only does he describe it as ' the latest and most complex product ' of knowledge ; but he defines it as a science which treats only of the knowledge which man has of himself " as a human being, distinguished from other human beings, from the animals and from nature in general, and standing in definite relations to each of them." Yet psychology is more than this.   It is not merely comparative, it is introspective : it is a study of mind and of mental operations in general.   It treats not only of man's relations to other conscious beings, but also of his knowledge of himself as a thinking, willing,   and   self-conscious   subject.   Hence   it includes a knowledge of man, " regarded simply as a self, the thinking subject which is implied in all objects of knowledge." [1]

Another reason why Dr. Caird excludes psychology from Criticism is that he wrongly identifies the psychological with the Lockian standpoint in regard to knowledge.   He complains that in the psychological or Lockian view of knowledge, consciousness of objects is reduced to consciousness of the states of our own minds.   We are thus involved in a closed cycle.   The mind is imprisoned within itself and knows nothing of the world without.   Hence psychology becomes the sum-total of all possible

[1] *Critical Philosophy of Kant*, p. 11.

knowledge. This error Criticism claims to have remedied by substituting for the closed cycle of our own ideas the closed cycle of the intelligible world ; and by insisting that though we cannot know objects except in relation to a conscious self, yet knowledge must always be knowledge of objects.[1] The argument here used is valid, and the Lockian view is certainly an error which needs correction ; but it is curious that Dr. Caird should have refused to admit psychology as the basis of the Critical Theory of Knowledge because psychology, in his opinion, does not recognise the distinction of subject and object ; for it is precisely because Criticism recognises this distinction as fundamental in knowledge that Professor James and Mr. Shadworth Hodgson maintain that " Kantian philosophy, and those philosophies which have, as it were, sprung from its loins, *never get beyond the psychological* point of view." [2] At any rate, all psychology is not Lockian psychology ; and that objective reference which Locke seems to deny to our ideas is by the introspective psychologist fully admitted. True, the latter takes as the object of his present thinking his own thought-processes and ideas. But introspection, so far from implying a confusion between thought-processes and their objects, on the contrary, reveals the psychological fact that all ideas have objective reference; and not only is the object of thought, whether internal or external, always regarded by us as distinct from our thoughts about it, but in most cases it is regarded as distinct

---

[1] *Ibid,* pp. 12—15.
[2] *The Metaphysics of Experience,* vol. i., p. ix,

from and external to ourselves. And whatever metaphysicians may have to say about the validity of this distinction, if any distinction is psychological, certainly the distinction of subject and object is such, for it appears as the universal characteristic of all human cognition and indeed of all consciousness of which we have any experience.

§ 53. This will, I take it, be generally admitted so far as *our* experience goes ; but the pragmatist denies that the distinction is ultimate, and hence, with Mr. Hodgson, accuses Kantian philosophies of never transcending the psychological point of view. All philosophies of ' *pure* ' experience regard the distinction of subject and object as the product of mental development either in the individual or in the race. It is a datum of *our* experience, but not of pure experience. The ultimate data of experience consist of process-contents of consciousness, but not of process-contents of consciousness as distinguished from realities. Consciousness and perception cannot themselves be perceived except in contradistinction from reality, and therefore not until reality and real existence have a meaning for us. Mr. Hodgson therefore concludes that the distinction of subject and object belongs to a more complex kind of knowledge from which it is possible to abstract.[1]

In considering this objection we may remark, in the first place, that it is not quite clear what Mr. Hodgson means by saying that consciousness can only be recognised as such in distinction from reality, for surely consciousness itself is a reality.

[1] *The Metaphysics of Experience,* vol. i., p. 116.

He may mean that consciousness can only be recognised as such in distinction from what is non-conscious, or he may be referring to the distinction of the conscious self from all that is not the conscious self, or to the distinction between the self, psychical and corporeal, and the rest of the universe, or, again, merely to the distinction between thought and its object, whatever that object may be. In the latter case the distinction is certainly fundamental for thought, since thought, without objective reference, is not thought at all, and it would seem that the distinction arises in consciousness as soon as we begin to reflect. But in neither case is the distinction ultimate, if by ' ultimate ' is meant that it appears at the dawn of conscious life, for to mere sentient experience there is doubtless no such distinction. Hence, in regard to those absolutists who identify being and thought, the objection that they never transcend the psychological point of view has some foundation, since, asserting, as they do, that the relation of objects to a conscious self, or, in other words, the subject-object distinction, is the latent presupposition of all knowledge, they are unable to explain the apparent evolution of self-consciousness in the individual. For if there is nothing but thought, and if for thought the subject-object distinction is ultimate, how is it that it is not for several years that an infant is able to make this distinction ?

§ 54. The statement that the subject-object distinction is not ultimate may mean, however, not that it is not ultimate for all forms of consciousness, but that it is not ultimate as a *fact*. And in this

G

sense the statement would be endorsed, not only by
pragmatic philosophers of 'pure' experience, but
also by many philosophers who adopt the standpoint
of Absolutism, who admit Immanence as a fundamental principle, and whose method is that of a
critical regress, but who, nevertheless, prefer to
regard being, not as thought, but rather, with
Fichte, as an Indifference-point, with Mr. Wallace,
as 'potential consciousness' in which ego and
non-ego are not distinguished, or, with Mr. Bradley,
as Sentient Experience.   Yet to all alike the doctrine
opens the way to difficulties, not only metaphysical,
but also psychological.   If the subject-object distinction is not a fact, how does such a distinction
arise in consciousness ?   If ego and non-ego are
ultimately one, how is it that they appear to be
distinct ?

The genetic psychologist can trace the genesis of
the ideas of 'self' and of an 'external world,' but
his skill is of no avail to Absolutism.   The ordinary
solution, *scil.*, that the distinction of ego and non-ego
arises from the contrast between the active and
passive aspects of consciousness, apart from the
difficulties inherent in such an explanation, is of
no use to the absolutist.   For why should passivity
appear as a limitation of the ego by a non-ego?
If it be due to something outside us, the non-ego
itself is (according to the doctrine of Immanence)
outside knowledge ; and if it arise from within, and
be due to the nature of mind, its origin is every bit
as much a mystery as the distinction which it is said
to explain.   Mr. Bradley gives the problem up, as
he does so many other problems of interest and

importance, on the ground that he is not bound to explain everything so long as he is consistent in what he does explain. But though the reply *refugio in mysterium*, like that of a *Deus ex machina*, is convenient and may be acceptable from the point of view of thought-economy, it can hardly be satisfactory to the true philosopher. The inability of absolutists to account for the origin of the subject-object distinction must count heavily, therefore, against their interpretation of reality, and especially against the doctrine of Immanence, to which that inability is due. For if Immanence is false, the difficulty vanishes, since subject and object, ego and non-ego, are then distinct, not only for thought, but in reality; while that the intellect is capable of understanding the meaning and implication of the data of experience, or, in other words, of apprehending in them the nature of real objects, is presupposed as the condition of the possibility of knowledge.

§ 55. The same difficulty also confronts the pragmatist, if, in addition to his Pragmatism, he adopt a philosophy of pure experience, as most would seem to do. In attempting to answer the difficulty, however, he takes a somewhat different line from that of the Absolutist. Assuming, with a singularly whole-hearted enthusiasm, the doctrine of Evolution, he replies, with Dr. Schiller, that the distinction of subject and object is the product of an evolutionary process, and assigns its origin to just that moment when the human mind passed from the sentient to the intelligent level of con-sciousness. Or, to put the matter in another way :

the subject-object distinction is due to thought,
and thought is but a higher (*i.e.*, a more useful)
form of sentience. But in the first place evolution,
as a general doctrine, is not yet established; and
even if it were, that thought should, by some
mysterious process, evolve itself from sentience, is
wholly incomprehensible. They are, indeed, intimately connected, and in perception seem to act
together as a functional unit; but, taken in
abstraction—as we must take them when, as
psychologists, we are treating scientifically of their
relations one to another—feeling is essentially
different from thought. By thought we break up
the unity of the presented object; we distinguish
it from ourselves and from other things; we abstract
from it characteristics which are common to a class;
we apprehend the relations of these characteristics
one to another; and we join them together to
form concepts of the most varied and intricate
complexity. The senses, on the other hand, do
none of these things. By them we get feelings and
frame pictures; but for sentience there are no
universals, no relations, no conscious analysing and
synthesising of characteristics, no distinguishing of
subject and object, and no unities in difference
which we apprehend as such. Hence the doctrine
that thought has been, or is, evolved from mere
sentient experience is untenable, unless we suppose
that the being, in which this evolution takes place,
has already *in potentia* the faculty of thought.
From 'pure' experience, as such, the power of
rational thought cannot have been evolved, nor yet
the distinction of subject and object. Granted an

embryonic human mind, in which intellectual powers are latent, it is conceivable that intellectual functions should appear in the course of its development. It is conceivable also that the distinction of subject and object should, in this sense, have been ' evolved,' given real subjects and real objects and the power of the former to apprehend the significance of certain sense-data. But the evolution of intellect from a lower form of consciousness in which it was not even present *in potentia* is a sheer impossibility.

§ 56. Granted, however, for the sake of argument, that this is not so, it is still impossible for the pragmatic philosopher of pure experience to account for the subject-object distinction. It is a fact that at some time or other we begin to distinguish objects from ourselves and to regard the latter as external and independent of both body and mind. And the usual explanation of this is that it is our way of distinguishing between states of consciousness in which we feel resistance but ourselves are comparatively passive, and states of consciousness in which we are aware of our own activity. For, in the former, what is experienced is beyond our control, and so independent, while, in the latter, we can modify the content of consciousness pretty much as we please. Again, what is comparatively permanent in consciousness we regard as part of ourselves, and what is transient, changing from moment to moment, we regard as external. But, even granted that our belief in an external world is valid, this account of its origin presents many difficulties. For instance, it is not only in the perception of what we call 'external' objects that we are passive, but also when enduring a pain in any part of the body, and as such pains are also, as a rule, independent of our control, they ought to appear external. Again, the bodily 'tone' can afford but a meagre basis for the distinction in question, since it is only in a very broad sense that it can be said to be constant, comprising, as it does, sensations which arise from ever-varying bodily conditions and emotions and moods, the inconstancy of which is notorious. Hence, unless it be admitted that the mind can, by some sort of intuition, apprehend the significance of these and other sense-data—a significance which does not exist in a philosophy of 'pure' experience—our explanation breaks down. Doubtless certain experiences of the sentient order are succeeded by belief in an external world, but to identify these psychological antecedents of belief, which are revealed only by psychological analysis, with the belief itself is to be guilty of the psychologist's fallacy. For belief in an external world and the sensation-complexes which are supposed to give rise to it are not the same thing ; and, as M. Boutroux says, " we have no more right to identify belief in external reality with the sense experiences which, so the psychologist says, result in such a belief, than we have to identify man with the chemical elements of which his body is composed."

The distinction of subject and object, self and not-self, internal and external, can be *explained*, then, neither by the pragmatic philosopher of 'pure' experience, nor by the absolutist, no matter whether

the latter identifies reality with thought or with
sentient-experience, or with any other of its manifold
characteristics. Yet such distinctions, whether
ultimate or not, are among the data of our
experience. And if ' to get beyond the psychological
point of view ' means to deny the validity of these
distinctions, it were better to stay where we are
rather than to adopt a doctrine which declares such
glaring facts to be so hopeless a mystery.

§ 57. To return, however, to the psychology of
Criticism. Psychological data are presupposed by
Criticism, no less than by other theories of knowledge ; nor do I think that this could have been
called in question by the late Dr. Caird had he
rightly understood the standpoint of the psychologist. A knowledge of the processes of cognition
is necessary in order to construct a theory of
knowledge, and that knowledge must be gained by
an introspective study of perception and thought
as it takes place in the human mind. Yet it is
false to say that Criticism never gets beyond the
psychological point of view, for its enquiry is in
regard to the conditions and presuppositions of
knowledge. Indeed, we may say of Criticism, what
Fichte said of his own philosophy, that, in essence,
it is neither a psychology, nor a political science,
nor yet a theory of morals, but a *Wissenschaftslehre*,
a theory of knowledge.

For this theory of knowledge *human* psychology
provides the data ; and the human character of
the problem was recognised by Kant, who never
confuses human with divine knowledge. But,
unfortunately, later Criticism, beginning with Fichte

himself, lost sight of this significant distinction.
The metaphysical and critical aspects of the theory
became more and more prominent, till at last the
real basis of Kant's Apriorism was forgotten, and
a human psychology was converted into a
psychology of the Absolute. In Absolutism, so
all-absorbing has the idea of Absolute knowledge
and Absolute truth become, that the more pressing
problems of human knowledge and human truth
are neglected, and absolutists content themselves
with the assertion that somehow or other, but in
a very imperfect way, the knowledge which belongs
to the Absolute is reproduced in finite centres of
experience, more commonly known as human minds.
Absolutism forgets that to assign the metaphysical
conditions of knowledge is but a means to an end,
and that the primary question for the epistemologist
is to determine how far human cognition is valid
and objective. This is unfortunate, for, as the
pragmatist says, what we are most concerned with
is human truth, not Absolute truth ; human knowledge, not knowledge in general. To ascertain the
conditions which make knowledge possible is but
part of the problem of epistemology, which should
also apply these conditions in the concrete in order
to ascertain the nature, extent and validity of
human claims to truth. That human knowledge
is not simply experiencing without something
experienced and a somebody who experiences it,
that it implies a metaphysic, and without a metaphysic cannot be understood, I fully agree ; but
a metaphysic of the Absolute or of the Universe in
general is not the final aim of the theory of know-

ledge. Absolutism is right in regarding psychology
as of secondary importance, since its function is
merely to furnish us with data. But the function
of a metaphysic of the Absolute is also of secondary
importance in a *Wissenschaftslehre*, and should not
be allowed to obscure the end and purpose of the
latter, which is to discover the conditions of *human*
knowledge and to ascertain the criterion of *human*
truth. Kant's view of the function of epistemology
was sound, and whatever we may think of his
metaphysics or of the solution which he gives to
the problem of knowledge, it must be granted that
he was faithful to the true instinct of an epistemologist. Throughout his three *Critiques*, it is the
solution of the problems of human knowledge that
is ever before his mind. From beginning to end
it is with human knowledge alone that he is concerned, and his final purpose to determine the extent
and sense in which that knowledge is valid, is ever
kept in view.

§ 58. In regard to the psychological data of
which Absolutism makes use, there is, for the most
part, nothing peculiar or distinctive. It has not a
psychology of its own, but accepts in general the
data which are revealed by introspection, though
the latter, when described by a believer in the
Absolute, are often tinged by the Absolute point
of view. The different objects and qualities which
we perceive, for instance, and which belong
apparently to an outside world, are described as
differences which break out within the unity of a
felt or experienced whole. Of this, more later; but,
for the present, it is sufficient that in the main

Absolutism is careful to distinguish between what
is a datum of experience and what is not. It does
not claim that its *a priori* forms and categories are
experienced as such in our cognitive acts. They
are implied therein, for without them knowledge
would be impossible ; but they are not introspective
data. On this point no fault can be found with
Absolutism. The exigencies of a satisfactory
theory of knowledge and of the universe at large
may necessitate the assertion that the objects of
knowledge are not material and independent objects,
but rather ideas immanent within the universal
mind by whose thought-activity they are posited
or produced. But such an assertion clearly belongs
to theory, and is not an experimental fact ; nor
does it pretend to be other than what it is. Material,
concrete and individual things are interpreted as
appearances, and common-sense belief in the reality
of such things is declared to be invalid. But the
existence of such beliefs is not denied. They are
rejected because they are said to be full of contradictions, and because they are inconsistent with
the only theory which seems to be able—in the
opinion of many—to give a consistent and satisfactory explanation of the universe, of which human
knowledge is but an aspect or a part.

§ 59. On the other hand, there is some truth in
the pragmatist's statement that Absolutism neglects
many of the characteristics of human cognition.
In spite of the prominent place assigned in Hegel's
philosophy to the Idea which is at once the Ground
and *telos* of the Universe, purposes and needs are
much neglected by Absolutism, and their relation to

Cognition is not adequately discussed. Absolutism is inclined to take a purely intellectual or rational view of the universe, and to subordinate Will to Thought. That a theory of the universe must satisfy our whole nature in its intellectual, emotional, and volitional sides alike, is not denied ; but practically in the construction of the metaphysics of Absolutism mention is seldom made of emotional needs or of the purposes which express themselves in the strivings of our will. The reason of this omission is obvious. *The Second Critique* of Kant does not form part of the foundation upon which Absolutism has been built, and it was in this *Critique* that Kant treated of the value of human ideals. Moreover, when Reality and Thought are regarded as one, and when, in place of human knowledge is substituted the knowledge which pertains to the Absolute, it is but natural that human purposes and human needs, whose force is felt by us largely because we are finite beings, should be overlooked in the absorbing interest of that one Being who is all-perfect and all-complete, who embraces and realises in himself all that exists; and who, consequently, has neither needs nor postulates, since his nature is not finite. Cognition in the Absolute is prompted, not by purposes and needs which seek their realisation in something outside; but exists because the Absolute realises itself in itself and for itself.

§ 60. In the Criticism of Kant, on the other hand, where knowledge is, as I have said, regarded not from the Absolute, but from the human point of view, neither is the function of purposes and

needs obscured by intellectualism, nor does Kant
go to the other extreme and make the principle of
postulation universal, as do the pragmatists; though
he assigns to it a function, the scope of which is
sufficiently, if not too great. For him, as for
Professor James, all metaphysical theories are
postulates, based on ideals which human purposes
and needs prompt us to strive to realise. Metaphysics is matter, not of knowledge, but of faith.
Nor can it be said that Kant makes the mind as
passive in its acts of cognition as it is supposed to
be in the theory which treats it as a *tabula rasa.*
His categories are not merely receptacles into which
phenomena are poured like molten liquid into a
mould. Doubtless Kant's treatment of Space and
Time and his table of Categories lend themselves
somewhat to this view; but to limit thus his
conception of the function of mind is to distort
his meaning. For he insists again and again upon
the constructive activity of thought. Thought, both
speculative and practical, is essentially active,
imposing its forms on nature; as speculative it
constructs from confused perceptive data its world
of experience, and as practical it moulds the
rebellious impulses of the sensuous order into
harmony with the autonomous dictates of reason.

The psychology of Kant, therefore, seems to me
to be far more complete than the psychology
of Absolutism. Its chief defect is that Kant
isolates too much the functions of the various
cognitive faculties, and neglects to treat of their
relations one to another. Sense-data are synthesised under the forms of Space and Time, and again

under the categories ; but of the relation of the
forms of Space and Time to the categories, or to
the schemata of the imagination under which,
provisionally, they are grouped, or, yet again, to
the principles of reason, Kant has nothing to tell
us. He assumes that all these faculties function
in harmony, but how this harmony is brought about
he does not say, nor does he assign any sufficient
reason for the necessity of the many and varied
functions, which, for him, are involved in an act of
cognition. Neither does the absolutist throw any light
upon these unsolved Kantian problems. Instead,
neglecting what Kant did insist upon—the purposive
nature of human thought, he has become a pure
intellectualist and so has evoked a pragmatic
reaction.

CHAPTER IV.

REALITY AS SENTIENT EXPERIENCE.

§ 61. At first sight it may appear somewhat out
of place to begin to discuss *Appearance and Reality*
while yet we are in the psychological part of our
subject, especially as its author has expressly
warned us that to attempt to base metaphysics on
psychology can only lead to " a disastrous hybrid
which possesses the merits of neither science."[1]
Mr. Bradley's method, however, differs considerably
from that of other objective idealists. In Book I.
he endeavours to show that our ordinary philo-

---

[1] *Appearance and Reality*, p. 76.

sophical notions, such as qualities, things, substance and accident, space, time, causality, are riddled with contradictions; and, hence, infers that all these are merely appearances which, taken as they stand, cannot be true of the real, and which yet, since they indubitably exist, must somehow belong to Reality.[1] In Book II. the 'general character of Reality' is first laid down, and then follows a discussion of ' the way in which appearances can belong to Reality,' or rather an attempt to prove that in predicating appearances of Reality no contradiction is involved. The positive result of *Appearance and Reality* may be summed up in two theses, " *Reality is One* " and " *Reality is Sentient-Experience.*" The first of these is essential to all forms of Absolutism ; the second is peculiar to Mr. Bradley.

But there is yet another difference between Mr. Bradley's standpoint and that of other Absolutists. In support of his assertions, and particularly in support of these two fundamental theses, he makes constant appeals to the psychological data of experience. His philosophy, in fact, may be regarded from two points of view. It may be treated as a theory which must be considered and judged as a whole according as it renders or fails to render a satisfactory and rational account of the Universe : or we may select principles which are fundamental in Mr. Bradley's position and inquire what foundation these have in the data of experience. Regarded from the first point of view, I shall discuss Mr. Bradley's position, together with

[1] For a discussion of some of Mr. Bradley's arguments see chap. xii.

that of other forms of Absolutism, in the chapter dealing with the Metaphysics of Absolutism ; but as the author of *Appearance and Reality*, in order to establish the above-mentioned theses, himself makes appeal to the data of experience, his psychological standpoint must be dealt with at once.

§ 62. In regard to the function of psychology in the theory of knowledge, or rather in metaphysics (for Mr. Bradley says there is really no such science as the theory of cognition),[1] my own opinion is practically the same as Mr. Bradley's. The theory of knowledge is not *based* wholly on psychology, *i.e.*, it cannot be proved merely by psychological analysis. Still less can metaphysics be established in this way. Yet, as Mr. Bradley says, the metaphysician is forced to trespass inside the limits of psychology. Consequently, "the metaphysician who is no psychologist, runs great dangers. For he must take up, and must work upon the facts about the soul; and, if he has not tried to learn what they are, the risk is very serious."[2] This is precisely my own view of the matter. Psychology must provide the data upon which the epistemologist works, and his theories must be confirmed or verified in the experiences which he seeks to explain, but nothing more.

§ 63. Theoretically, then, Mr. Bradley and I are at one in regard to the function of psychology in metaphysics ; yet I cannot help but think that Mr. Bradley's philosophy has been very largely influ-

---

[1] *loc. cit.* p. 76. This statement is not explained by Mr. Bradley, but it refers, I take it, to a *purely psychological* theory of cognition.

[2] *Ibid.*

enced by, even if it is not wholly due to, his
psychological views. Nor do I stand alone in this
opinion. In an article entitled " The New Realism
and the Old Idealism," which appeared in *Mind* for
July, 1906, the following passage occurs :—

The more recent system of Mr. Bradley has in some
respects a more objective aspect (than that of Green).
His repudiation of the ballot of bloodless categories is
familiar to everyone ; and his criticism of the Self goes
far to destroy subjectivity. Yet, on the other hand,
he is in some fundamental points far more decidedly
subjective than Green, or perhaps than any other
prominent representative of idealism. Certainly by
his constant appeal to ' experience,' as at once the
standpoint and the goal in the search for reality, he
gives to his philosophy a subjective turn from which
he is never quite able to free it. The world for Mr.
Bradley is a straightened-out experience, but still it
is an experience, and nothing more ; and, indeed, the
most purely subjective aspect of experience—mere
feeling—seems in the end to be for Mr. Bradley its
most important and significant aspect.[1] [Professor
Mackenzie's advice to idealists, therefore, is :] ' Close
thy Berkeley—open thy Plato ; close thy Bradley—
open thy Hegel.' [2]

§ 64. There is a great deal of truth in these
remarks. Mr. Bradley is not a subjective idealist,
and Phenomenalism he expressly rejects ; yet, for
all that, his position approximates very closely to
the *esse* is *percipi* of Hume. Objects, if abstracted
from our perception of them, are nothing, said
Hume : they exist only when they are perceived.
But perception is a state of the mind. Hence
objects are really states of the mind, and their

[1] *loc. cit.*, p. 313.   [2] *Ibid*, p. 327.

esse is *percipi.* Compare this argument with the statements which Mr. Bradley makes in support of, if not in proof of, his thesis that Reality is Sentient Experience. He thus introduces the subject in his second Chapter on *The General Nature of Reality*.[1]

We perceive, on reflection, that to be real, or even barely to exist, must be to fall within sentience. Sentient experience, in short, is reality, and what is not this is not real. We may say, in other words, that there is no being or fact outside of that which is commonly called psychical existence. Feeling, thought, and volition (any groups under which we class psychical phenomena) are all the material of existence, and there is no other material, actual or even possible.

This position does not involve Subjectivism, for Mr. Bradley does not first " divide the percipient subject from the universe ; and then, resting on that subject, as on a thing actual by itself," urge " that it cannot transcend its own states." " To sum up the subject as real independently of the whole, and to make the whole into experience in the sense of an objective of that subject,"[2] seems to him indefensible. " The universe and its objects must not be called states of my soul."[3] It is the whole itself which is experience, and there is no subject which exists independently of this whole. The philosophy of *Appearance and Reality* is, therefore, not subjective but objective Idealism or Absolutism.

On the other hand, the passage quoted above is characteristic of Mr. Bradley's standpoint, and seems to approximate so closely to the Humeian doctrine that Professor Mackenzie's protest is hardly

---

[1] *Appearance and Reality,* chap. xiv., p. 144.
[2] *Ibid.* p. 145.   [3] *Ibid.* p. 301,

H

surprising, especially as he regards the thesis ' *esse* is *percipi* ' as the foundation of subjective Idealism. Nor is it surprising that Professor Mackenzie should advise prospective idealists to study Hegel rather than Bradley, since he holds that a true Idealism depends upon the absolute rejection of this principle[1] and on this account replies to Mr. Moore's ' *Refutation of Idealism* ' by a charge of *ignoratio elenchi*. But whether Mr. Moore's arguments are valid or not against the Idealism of Hegel and Professor Mackenzie, they certainly do not miss the point in regard to Mr. Bradley, who is admittedly one of the leading, if not *the* leading figure among British idealists. Accordingly, it will be worth while to examine the Bradleian position that Reality is Sentient Experience, while at the same time bearing in mind that Mr. Bradley's Absolutism may be regarded from another point of view which is more closely related to that of the Objective Idealism of which we shall have to treat in a later chapter.[2]

§ 65. That there is no being or fact which does not ' fall within experience,' or which is outside what we call ' psychical existence,' is a doctrine which Mr. Bradley thinks will, in its general form, be evident at once. The test of it, he says,

lies ready to our hand, and the decision rests in the manner in which it is applied. . . . Find any piece of existence, take up anything that anyone could possibly call a fact, or could in any sense assert to have being, and then judge if it does not consist in sentient experience. Try to discover any sense in which you can still continue to speak of it, when all perception and

[1] *loc. cit. Mind*, N.S. 59, p. 314.
[2] *Vide* chaps. ix., x.

feeling have been removed ; or point out any fragment
of its matter, any aspect of its being, which is not
derived from and is not still relative to this source.
When the experiment is made strictly, I can myself
conceive of nothing else than the experienced. Anything in no sense felt or perceived becomes to me quite
unmeaning. And as I cannot think of it without
realising either that I am not thinking at all, or that
I am thinking of it against my will as being experienced,
I am driven to the conclusion that for me experience is
the same as reality.[1]

§ 66. Two objections may be urged against the
position here set forth. First of all, it may be
questioned whether the results of Mr. Bradley's
introspection are not peculiar to himself, or at any
rate to a few philosophic minds who in their introspection cannot rid themselves of a certain idealistic
prejudice. Secondly, even granted the data which
Mr. Bradley assumes, his conclusion does not seem
to be vouched for by his premises, unless a further
assumption is made, namely, the validity of the
doctrine of Immanence. To deal with the inference
first :—Granting that nothing exists that is not
perceived, what follows ? Not that reality is one
with sentient experience, but that to exist implies
a something or a somebody in whose experience
that existent is perceived, *i.e.*, a percipient something which may or may not be distinct from what is
perceived. The data, even if true, do not warrant
the conclusion that *esse* is *percipi*, still less that it
is *percipere ;* but merely that *esse* implies *percipere.*
Some sort of connection between percipient and
perceived we might infer ; but this, for aught the

---

[1] *Appearance and Reality,* pp. 144, 145.

data have to say upon the matter, might be a causal connection, or a pre-established harmony.

§ 67. I do not think, however, that many psychologists would concede that Mr. Bradley has given a true account of the data of human experience. I certainly cannot agree with him, nor do I think that Professor Mackenzie would do so, in spite of his Idealism. Certainly if you asked the man in the street whether he could conceive of a palm tree growing in the wilds of Africa with nobody there to perceive it, he would answer you in the affirmative ; and I am afraid I am of the same opinion. If anyone was there, of course the tree might chance to be perceived ; but the question is whether it would cease to be there as soon as the visitor went away. I am quite ready to concede that all trees are perceiv*able*. Nay, more, we might say, I think, that every existing being is capable of being experienced, either by perception or by thought. Indeed, I would even go so far as to say that all things *are* 'experienced' by God — whatever 'experience' may mean when predicated of the Divinity ; but I cannot concede, even in this case, that their *esse* is experience. Again, it is a principle with Scholastics that all knowledge is derived, either directly or by inference, from sense-experience ; but this is very different from affirming that it *is* sense-experience. Personally, I can continue to think and speak, and, so it seems to me, quite rationally, about 'facts' and 'beings' and 'pieces of existence' which are not sentient experien*ces*, nor yet experien*ced* by anyone, except —according to my theology—by God.

§ 68. But Mr. Bradley goes further still. Not only are all things sentient experience, but their *given* existence he affirms to be a state of his, *i.e.*, of the experient's soul. Having assured us that his horse and his body are, for him, nothing but experience, he tells us that ' if we push home the question as to their given existence, we can find it nowhere except as a state of his soul.' " When I perceive them, or think of them, there is, so far, no discoverable ' fact ' outside my psychical conditions."[1] Now, either the terms ' fact ' and ' given existence ' here mean ' perception ' as opposed to the object perceived, in which case Mr. Bradley's use of the term ' fact ' is somewhat strained and is hardly consistent with his previous use of it,[2] where he speaks of the want of correspondence which may exist between ' assertion ' and ' fact ' (' fact ' there signifying, not present perception, but objective events which *have* occurred in the past)'; or else Mr. Bradley's account of the perception of a horse and of the body is introspectively incorrect. For the horses and bodies which we perceive are not perceived as states of our own soul ; and the facts about which we think are thought of as other than ourselves. This last point Mr. Bradley apparently is willing to concede. For immediately after affirming that when he perceives or thinks of a horse or of his body, there is no discoverable fact outside his psychical condition, he adds, " But such a ' fact ' is not for me the ' fact ' of my horse, or, again, of my body. Their true existence is not

---

[1] *Appearance and Reality,* p. 301.
[2] *Ibid.* p. 190 and cf. p. 317.

that which is present *in* my mind, but rather, as
perhaps we should say, present *to* it."[1]   What a
world of difference a preposition may make !   The
substitution of ' to ' for ' in ' changes the whole
meaning of Mr. Bradley's assertion, and seems to
convert him from a subjective into an objective
idealist, if not into a realist.   For if objects are
presented *to* consciousness, but are not *in* consciousness, they may not be sentient experience at
all, but something quite different.

§ 69.   Mr. Bradley's theory of judgment, however, saves him from inconsistency.   For though he
admits that objects are present *to*, not in, consciousness, and affirms that the ' true ' existence of
horses and bodies is " a content which works apart
from, and is irreconcilable with, its own psychical
being," this does not mean that the ' true ' existence
of presented objects is not psychical, or that it is
not at bottom identical with sentient experience,
but merely that it is not identical with their
existence as ideas in *my* mind.   Ego and non-egos,
minds and objects, psychical and ' true ' existences
are at bottom one, for in themselves they are mere
abstractions, appearances, thought - distinctions
which have broken out in the background of sentient
experience, and which get their reality therefrom.[2]

In judgment the immediate datum of sense-
experience is analysed into a subject and a predicate, a ' that ' and a ' what,' an ' existence ' and a
' content,' a ' fact ' and an ' idea.'   Predicates,
whats, contents, or ideas work loose from subjects,

---

[1] *Appearance and Reality,* p. 301.
[2] *Ibid.,* p. 301 (italics mine).

thats, existences, facts, and at the same time
transcend them, referring to an Other, to a Beyond,
to something which is not a psychical state of *my*
soul. "The soul *is* not the contents which appear
in its states." "A man is not what he thinks of."
Principles of logic and morality, though they work
in the mind, are not "parts of the mind."[1]   Whether
the predicate "appears not to go beyond its own
subject, or to have been imported divorced from
another fact outside," it is "divorced from its
psychical existence in my head, and is used without
any regard to its being there."[2]   Or, as the realist
would put it, the predicate is not merely an idea,
but a 'quality' which is predicated of reality, and,
except in psychological retrospection, it is always
regarded as a quality and not as an idea.

On the other hand, "the subject is an actual
existence." "No one ever *means* to assert about
anything but reality, and to do anything but qualify
a 'that' by a 'what.'"[3]   Not that the subject is
ever "*mere* reality, or bare existence without
character. The subject, doubtless, has unspecified
content which is not stated in the predicate. For
judgment is the differentiation of a complex whole,
and hence always is analysis and synthesis in one.
It separates an element from, and restores it to,
the concrete basis ; and this basis of necessity
is richer than the mere element by itself." Yet the
subject is neither the mere 'what' of the predicate
nor is it any other mere 'what.' There is in the
subject, whether it be perceived or not, "an aspect
of existence which is absent from the bare pre-

[1] *Ibid.,* p. 302.   [2] *Ibid.,* pp. 163, 164.   [3] *Ibid.,* p. 164.

dicate." Beyond the content of thought there is a
subject (viz., reality) " of which it is true and which
it does not comprehend." " The ' that ' of the
actual subject will for ever give a something which is
not a mere idea, something which is different from
any truth, something which makes such a difference
to your thinking, that without it you have not even
thought completely."[1]   The subject, in short, is
reality presented as ' this.'[2]

§ 70. With this view of the judgment, so far, I
can to a large extent agree. Judgment does
involve an analysis of the data of sentient-experience
into a ' what ' and a ' that,' and the ' what ' is
referred to reality through the ' that ' of which it is
predicated. Thus our ideas about reality are not
merely ideas, but have objective reference and
imply an other than mere thought ; and the reason
of this is that an other than mere thought is ' given '
in sense-experience in which we seem to be brought
into immediate contact with reality. ' Existence '
may, like other elements in the concrete ' this '
or ' that,' become a predicate and so become part
of the content of thought ; but existence, *i.e.*,
objective existence, belongs primarily to the subject of our judgments, for it is given in the data of
experience which we denote by that subject, and
to it the predicate is referred.

Many questions, however, have yet to be settled.
How does existence belong peculiarly to the subject, and in what sense is the latter ' given ' in
sense-perception ? For thought ' existence ' is
objective ; is it also objective for sense-perception ?

---

[1] *Ibid.*, pp. 168, 169.   [2] *Ibid.*, p. 175.

The existence which is predicated in the content of thought is not merely a psychical state of the soul. Is it a mere psychical state of the soul in the subject ? Is it, in fact, psychical at all ? Again, what is this reality that is presented ? Is it the whole of reality or is it a part ? Is it a real '*this*' or is it reality in general presented as a '*this*' ? And lastly, in what sense is the '*this*' presented as a *whole* ? In what sense is it *one*, a felt totality ?

§ 71. It is in the answer to these questions that I find myself at variance with Mr. Bradley ; and as the answers which he gives depend, in part at least, upon his view of the relation of thought to sense-experience, to this we must now turn our attention. Thought can never be equated with experience. Thought-contents cannot — though they try to do so—swallow up reality. The reason is that in sense-experience we have a fact which cannot be conjured away, the fact of sensible experience, of immediate presentation with its colouring of pleasure and pain.[1] This fact for Mr. Bradley contains, or implies, everything, even reality itself. To it he appeals again and again in support both of his doctrine that Reality is Sentient Experience and of his doctrine that Reality is One. Sense experience or presentation is something of which we cannot get rid. It is always there in the background as a 'felt-mass,' a 'felt-totality,' a 'unity below distinction.' It is from this background of sentience that all distinctions and all relations—self and not self, subject and object, psychical and 'true' existence—take their rise, in it

[1] *Appearance and Reality,* p. 170.

that they appear, and through it that they get whatever degree of reality they may possess. By the process of thought the 'felt-totality' of sentient experience is analysed, and from it emerges a system of relational appearance ; but this relational appearance in abstraction from the background of sentient-experience has no reality.

§ 72. It is a fundamental principle with Mr. Bradley that we must not separate product from process, and unless the significance of this principle is understood and its validity admitted the whole force of his argument will be lost. The principle is first introduced in the Chapter on " Relation and Quality," where Mr. Bradley endeavours to prove that qualities are not distinct from relations, and indeed without relations are nothing at all, precisely because " the qualities, as distinct, are made so by an action which is admitted to imply relation ; " . . . " and you cannot ever get your product standing apart from its process." " There is an operation which, removing one part of what is given, presents the other part in abstraction. This result is never to be found anywhere apart from a persisting abstraction. And, if we have no further information, I can find no excuse for setting up the result as being fact without the process. The burden lies wholly on the assertor, and he fails entirely to support it."[1]

The separation of product from process, therefore, in Mr. Bradley's opinion, is indefensible, and, as it cannot be proved, he says, it is 'monstrous' to assume it. Accordingly, Mr Bradley assumes the

[1] *Ibid.*, pp. 27, 28.

contradictory principle, viz., that product and process are *not* separable, but form part of one whole—
a principle which, I suppose, it is not monstrous
to assume. At any rate it *is* assumed, and is
applied to the analysis of sense-presentation with
the following result : Sense-presentation, when
analysed, reveals two aspects—one objective, the
other subjective.

You can certainly abstract from presentation its
character of ' thisness,' or its confused relatedness ; and
you can also abstract the feature of presentation. Of
these you can make ideas, for there is nothing which
you cannot think of. But you find that these ideas
are not the same as the subject of which you must
predicate them. You can think of the subject, but
you cannot get rid of it or substitute mere thought-
content for it.[1]

Hence the ' *thisness* ' or ' *confused relatedness* ' (by
which, I suppose, is meant the objective, though
unanalysed element of presentation—*what* we perceive), and the '*feature of presentation*' (which
clearly refers to the psychical act of perception
itself) are not distinguished in sense-experience or
in reality, but only by abstraction and for thought.
Mr. Bradley's answer, then, to the question whether
objects are presented to the mind or are present in
the mind, is that both objects and presentations
(and also minds themselves, for that matter) are
abstractions due to thought-analysis and construction. They are ideal, not real. Hence, when
we say that objects are presented to a mind, we
must remember that both minds and objects are

[1] *Ibid.*, p. 175.

nothing but appearances which refer us back to
the sentient whole of experience from which and
in which they emerge.

§ 73. The validity of this argument rests upon
the assumption that product and process cannot
be separated—and of this I shall have something
to say in a moment. But even granting this
assumption to be valid, I am not at all convinced
that the argument will hold. On the contrary, it
seems to me that the very assumption upon which
it rests, may be used to refute it.

In thought we distinguish existence from content,
a ' what ' from the ' that.' And this distinction
arises from and emerges in sentient experience, so
that whatever belongs to the ' what ' or content
must also belong to the ' that,' at least in an
unanalysed form. But ' objective existence,' *v.g.*,
the ' true ' existence of the horses and bodies,
forms part of the content of thought and is not to
be identified with the psychical existence of an
idea in the mind.[1] Wherefore it would seem to
follow that objective or ' true ' existence, as opposed
to psychical existence, belongs also to the ' that,' or
to the *subject* of our judgment as given in *sense-
perception*. And if, in reply to this, it be urged
that I have assigned to the subject *before* analysis
what belongs to it only after analysis, I must refer
you to the passage already quoted and to many
other passages in which we are told that reality
belongs in a peculiar manner to the subject of our
judgments, and even that in the subject there is
an aspect of existence which is *absent* in the predi-

---

[1] cf. *Appearance and Reality*, p. 301.

cate. And should it now be said that the existence
which belongs to the subject is not the same as that
which belongs to the predicate ; that whereas the
existence of the subject is psychical, that of the
predicate is ideal, I must ask for proof of this
assertion, for the existence of the subject, in my
judgment, does not appear to be psychical, but
objective and real ; quite as objective, in fact, as
that of the predicate. Moreover, if the existence
of the subject in presentation is psychical, how
comes it that in thought the existence which is
referred to that self-same subject is not psychical
but objective ? This is a mystery, perhaps, which
is due to the nature of thought, whose function it is
to distinguish existences and meanings which, in
reality, are not distinct. But thought, it is
admitted, must work upon the data of experience. If
then, in the product of thought, objective existence
and meaning are distinguished from the psychical
existence of thought itself, it is only reasonable to
infer that objective and psychical existence, not-
self and self, have been distinct throughout the
process, even to its basis in sense-experience itself.

That such a distinction of subject and object is
a datum even of perceptual experience I have
already attempted to show.[1] In perceptual experience we certainly come into immediate contact
with reality, and upon this our knowledge of reality
depends. But the reality which is ' given ' in
perceptual experience is not psychical but objective.
Reality is presented to us, I will not say as material,
but, at any rate, as something quite distinct, quite

[1] cf. § 52.

different, from ' me.' Again, I shall be told that
I am introducing thought-distinctions into my
description of sentient-experience. And it may be
that I am; for thought is involved in all perception.
But if such a fundamental and universal distinction
as this is not to be included in the data of sentient
experience, where are you going to draw the line ?
Sentient experience is not mere feeling, as Mr.
Bradley fully acknowledges, for feeling is itself an
abstraction. But as soon as we get beyond the
stage of mere feeling we find thought-distinction.
Mr. Bradley seems to admit this also, for he speaks
of ' the sensuous infinitude' which belongs to the
'presented subject' in a judgment, by which he
means that it has plurality of features in its content,
the details of which are indefinitely related to something outside.[1] And I take it that it is the subject
as presented in sense-perception that is here referred
to, since it is called a presented subject. In any
case, we are told that in sense-experience there is
a confused relatedness which is not the presentation
itself, *qua* presentation (though why what is presented should be described as ' confused' I do not
understand, since it is usually perfectly clear and
distinct so far as concerns the objects upon which
attention is focussed, and this focussing may be
instantaneous) ; and it would seem that the confused
relatedness and the presentation are not one and
the same thing, even in sense-experience. While
if, in reply, I am told that even this ' confused
relatedness ' is due to abstraction and so to thought-
analysis, then certainly in what is left of sentient-

[1] *Appearance and Reality,* p. 176.

experience there will be no distinction of subject
and object ; but surely it is Mr. Bradley now and
not myself who is guilty of abstraction ; and such
an attenuated fragment of experience is clearly not
identical with presentation, still less with reality,
nor does Mr. Bradley claim that it is.

§ 74. Why, then, is reality identified with
sentient experience ? We have already discussed
one reason, viz., that Mr. Bradley cannot conceive
of an existing object or quality from which all
perception and feeling have been removed. This
reason we found to be inconclusive, since most
people can imagine ' pieces of existence ' and ' facts,'
viz., historical and absent facts, from which all
perception and feeling have been removed. Yet,
though Mr. Bradley's experience would appear to
be abnormal in this respect, ' feeling ' and sense-
perception are undoubtedly very closely connected
with the idea of reality ; and it is upon this fact at
bottom that Mr. Bradley's doctrine seems to be
based. The ' this ' of sense-perception, he says,

brings a sense of superior reality, a sense which is far
from being wholly deceptive and untrue. For all our
knowledge, in the first place, arises from the ' this'.
It is the one source of our experience, and every element
of the world must submit to pass through it. And
the ' this,' secondly, has the genuine feature of ultimate
reality. With however great imperfection and inconsistency it owns an individual character. The ' this '
is real for us in a sense in which nothing else is real.[1]

Now, the ' this ' is defined for us as " the positive
feeling of direct experience." Hence the transition

[1] *Ibid.*, pp. 224, 225.

is easy from the doctrine that this "*feeling* of direct experience" is the source of all knowledge of reality and itself possesses a genuine feature of reality, to the doctrine that, as sentient experience in general, it *is* reality.

Mr. Bradley, to do him justice, does not explicitly make this transition, though I cannot help thinking that he really has made it in his own mind, and that it underlies his general position. At any rate, it will be worth while to discuss how far, and in what sense, the 'this' of sense-perception does possess the genuine feature of reality ; and in order not to misinterpret, let me again quote from *Appearance and Reality*.

Reality is being in which there is no division of content from existence, no loosening of 'what' from 'that.' Reality, in short, means what it stands for, and stands for what it means. And the 'this' possesses to some extent the same wholeness of character. Both the 'this' and reality, we may say, are immediate. But reality is immediate because it includes and is superior to mediation. It develops, and it brings to unity, the distinctions it contains. The 'this' is immediate ... at a level below distinctions. Its elements are but conjoined, and are not connected. And its content, hence, is unstable, and essentially tends to disruption, and by its own nature must pass beyond the being of the 'this'. But every 'this' still shows a passing aspect of un-divided singleness. In the mental background specially such a fused unity remains a constant factor and can never be dissipated. And it is such an unbroken wholeness which gives the sense of individual reality. When we turn from mere ideas to sensations, we experi-ence in the 'this' a revelation of freshness and life. And that revelation, if misleading, is never quite untrue.[1]

[1] p. 225.

The reason, then, why the 'this' seems to bring us into immediate touch with reality is because of its immediacy, its undivided singleness, its fused unity. Unity and immediacy, moreover, apparently mean the same thing, for 'immediacy' is defined as the union or unity of a 'what' and a 'that.' Now the question is, what is meant by this unity of a 'what' and a 'that.' It seems to mean two things between which Mr. Bradley hardly makes any distinction, viz., (1) the unity of subject and predicate before analysis, and (2) the unity of objective meaning and psychical fact.

§ 75. Let us examine this unity first in the sense of a unity between objective meaning and psychical fact. I do not think there can be any doubt that the unity of the 'this' does bear such a signification in Mr. Bradley's mind. For the ' this ' is described *either* as ' the positive feeling of direct experience,' which is clearly something psychical and subjective, *or* it is identified with ' confused relatedness,' the objective aspect in presentation ; and this ' confused relatedness ' and the subjective feature of presentation are, as we know, for Mr. Bradley, one and the same. Again, in a passage already quoted,[1] ' content ' and ' psychical being ' are opposed to one another as a ' what ' and a ' that ; ' while the ideality of the ' what,' since it is attributed precisely to this alienation of content and psychical existence, clearly indicates that in the subject or 'that' content and psychical existence are one.[2] Lastly, the ambiguity of Mr. Bradley's use of the term 'fact'

---

[1] *Ibid.*, p. 301 (cf. *supra*, § 68).
[2] *Ibid.*, cf. pp. 165, 168.

I

points to the same conclusion. 'Existence' is *either* a series of *events or* of *facts ;* facts are either *events* or *what is directly experienced ;* and "any aspect of direct experience, or again of an event, may itself be loosely styled a fact or event, so far as you consider it as a qualifying adjective of one."[1] It is clear, then, that the only kind of 'existence' which Mr. Bradley admits is 'psychical existence,' and that when he speaks of the immediacy of presentation as the unity of a 'what' and a 'that,' or of a 'what' which is not sundered from its 'that,' and turned from fact into truth, he means to say that objective content and psychical existence are one.

Now, many times have I tried to find such a unity about the facts of presentation, but I must confess that I have always signally failed. True, the existence and the content *which belong to what I perceive* are not separated ; and it may be that I do not always distinguish that objective existence from my psychical act ; but, in any case, I do not confuse the two existences, or take them to be one, or discover any sort of unity about them. Either we are conscious of our own psychical existence in an act of perception, or we are not. If we are, it is distinct from the existence which belongs to the object ; and if we are not, there is no question of psychical existence at all but only of objective existence. I may be mistaken in thinking that there is a minimum of distinction between subject and object in sense-perception ; but, whatever else happens, they are certainly not

[1] *Ibid.*, p. 317, n. 1 (cf. *supra*, § 68).

given as one. Still less are they thought of as one in retrospection (except in an idealist theory). Moreover, the 'superior sense of reality' and the peculiar freshness and life which attends sense-perception, seem to belong to the objective and not to the subjective element, for sensation in itself is no more living and real than thought or volition.

The 'genuine feature of reality' which is given in presentation, therefore, provides neither ground for, nor confirmation of, the thesis that Reality *is* Sentient Experience. For that 'feature' belongs to the objective, and not to the 'sentient' aspect of presentation. And if it be said that the two aspects are ultimately one, I must ask on what grounds the assertion is made. If as a datum of experience, I cannot admit it. If, on the other hand, it is affirmed as a metaphysical hypothesis, my answer is that in identifying reality with *sentient* experience, you have identified it with what is, according to your own theory, *a one-sided abstraction*. And this is so whatever interpretation be put upon sentient experience, for sentient experience, as the term 'sentient' implies, and as Mr. Bradley admits, is essentially psychical, and the psychical element in presentation is acknowledged to be but one aspect of the whole.

§ 76. There is, however, another sense in which the unity of a presented 'this' may be understood. It may mean the unity of 'that' and 'what,' or of subject and predicate ; and in this case it is true that in presentation the aspects of 'what' and 'that' are not divorced. What we perceive is a concrete thing, and it is only by thought that we analyse it into subject and predicate. Moreover, in what we perceive, content and *objective* existence are not separated, but form one whole. But, on the other hand, we do not always perceive a single thing. The 'subject' which is given in the 'this' is not always "a single self-subsistent being." It may be a 'garden,' for instance, which, though in a certain sense it has a unity for thought and hence is denoted by a single name, does not seem to be *given as a unity*. In fact, if we keep strictly to sentience and exclude thought, I cannot discover any unity at all about presentation apart from the unity of consciousness which it implies. What is presented is much diversified, especially if the presentation be for sight. The parts of what is presented are 'conjoined,' and may be said to 'co-exist,' but they do not form one integral whole, nor can I find in them any unity below relation and ideas.[1] There is a certain 'togetherness' about them, but that is insufficient. Mr. Bradley requires an indivisible, not merely an undivided, whole, and the object of perception is certainly not given as indivisible even if it be given as one.

True, an *act* of perception is one, *quâ* psychical act, since the possibility of apprehending many things together, even if merely conjoined, pre-supposes a unity, as Kant showed; and, again, the psychical element in presentation—perception itself —is referred to the mind or the self, which we regard as a unity. But this self-reference, like the objective reference to which it is opposed, is admittedly a function of thought, not of sentient

[1] cf. § 29.

experience as such. For me, indeed, the deliverances
of thought are as valid and more valid than those of
sentient-experience ; but for Mr. Bradley this is
not so : thought-content is mere appearance, not
reality. Hence that what we experience at any
given moment should on its psychical side appear as
" a single individual experience " is insufficient for
his purpose ; for what he seeks is a real unity,
which the unities predicated as a result of thought-
abstractions according to his principles can never be.
Moreover, if this unity is to be real, it should come
from the objective and not from the subjective or
psychical side of experience.

§ 77. Mr. Bradley's constant appeal to ' felt
wholes,' therefore, is in vain. For if he means by
the latter what is perceived in external perception,
this is never ' *given* ' as a felt-whole, but rather as
distinct objects accompanied by, but not fused with,
a vague background ; and about such a presentation
there is no unity except for thought. While if what
is meant is a psychical feeling, there is still no felt-
unity or felt-whole which can be clearly recognised
as such *until* we reflect, and when we do reflect the
felt-whole is so indistinguishably mixed up with
reference to the self, that it is impossible to determine
introspectively whether apart from the self there is
any felt-whole at all. Doubtless " all that we suffer,
and do and are at any one time forms a psychical
totality ; " but that totality does not include the
objects about which we think, nor is it recognised
as a totality except by thought. We feel, perhaps,
" the co-existing mass " of sensation which constitutes the bodily ' tone,' but we do not feel directly

the psychical unity which underlies it and which
it presupposes, though belief in such a unity has
instinctively arisen in our minds. Mr. Bradley, in
his psychical analysis of presentation, seems to me
to have read into the introspective data of experience
pre-conceived metaphysical ideas. He has found
in sentient experience what he looked for, felt-wholes
and unities below the level of distinctions ; but he
has found them precisely because he looked for
them, and not because they are really there as clear
and unambiguous data of experience. If the
subject is not *given* as distinct from the object nor
one object as distinct from another, at any rate
they are not given together as one and individual.

§ 78. A similar fallacy seems to characterise
Mr. Bradley's attempt to show that in the immediacy
of the ' this,' reality is present *as a whole*, and in his
further attempt to reconcile the apparent fragmen-
tariness and exclusiveness of a presented ' this '
with the all-inclusive nature of reality itself. I
cannot discover that " sensuous infinitude " of
which he speaks. I admit that the ' this ' has
' ragged edges.' which imply other existences from
which, in a sense, "it has been torn;"[1] but all that
this means for me is *either* that as a rule a number
of things are presented side by side, *or* that it is
difficult to explain any individual thing except by
comparison with other things. Purposes, functions,
transient actions all direct our thoughts from the
individual to something outside, apart from which
they cannot be understood. The ' this ' is self-
transcendent, as Mr. Bradley says. Its inner nature

[1] *Appearance and Reality*, p. 176.

leads our thoughts to pass from it to a 'higher totality' in which it is but a finite element or part. But whether this 'higher totality' is a concrete whole which is identical with reality itself, or whether it is merely a rational plan or design which is manifest in finite and individual existents, is not proved by the mere psychological fact that our thoughts must pass from the 'this' to something outside it and that even then the content of the 'this' is not fully exhausted or explained. Either hypothesis will harmonise so far with the data of experience, and we must have recourse to other considerations in order to decide between the two.

Here, as elsewhere in *Appearance and Reality*, Mr. Bradley seems to beg the whole question by the very form in which he has chosen to describe the facts ; and it is only by interpreting his psychological descriptions in the light of his metaphysical theory that they can possibly be understood, and the apparently gratuitous conclusions which he draws obtain even a semblance of validity. For instance, it is said that the inner nature of the 'this' leads not merely our thoughts, but *it*, (the 'this' itself), to pass outside itself to a higher totality. And this higher totality is *assumed* to be a *real* and not merely an ideal totality, and again not merely a totality but a real and indivisible whole, for we are told that the very exclusiveness of the 'this' involves the reference of itself beyond itself, and *is but a proof of its necessary absorption in the Absolute*.[1]

§ 79. Another instance of the influence of his

[1] *Ibid.*, p. 228.

metaphysics upon his psychology is Mr. Bradley's
psychological (for apparently it is psychological)
dictum that ' product must not be separated from
process.' Taken as a universal proposition, the
principle is false, for whether we can legitimately
separate product and process surely depends upon
whether they are really distinct, as sometimes in the
physical world they are. Of course, assuming the
metaphysical standpoint of *Appearance and Reality*
to be valid, it is clearly illicit to separate the *product*,
appearances, from the psychical *process* by which
they are supposed to be at once differentiated and
re-united in an immanent Ground. But the validity
of this position cannot be taken for granted. Hence
it is manifestly illogical on Mr. Bradley's part to
assume a principle which presupposes the validity
of his metaphysical position, and to use that principle not only to refute the arguments of opponents,
but also to establish the very position upon the
validity of which it depends. Nor is the application
of this principle to the psychology of experience
a success. For, even granting that ' unities below
relations ' and ' felt-wholes ' are among the data of
sentient experience, *we have no direct experience
whatsoever of the process by which the so-called product,
thought-distinctions and relations, arises.* All we
know is that psychoses in which sensation is comparatively predominant, are *succeeded* by psychoses
in which distinctions and relations have taken its
place, and that between the two there is what Professor James calls ' a continuous transition.' To
say that relational appearances emerge within ' the
felt totality ' or that thought-distinctions ' break

out of it,' is to speak metaphorically. Of the process by which sentience is displaced by thought, introspection tells us nothing. Consequently, the Bradleian principle of non-separation between product and process is inapplicable. There are no products and processes to separate, unless we make a gratuitous assumption to the effect that thought-distinctions are evolved from a sentient ground.

§ 80. This being the case, our only alternative is to choose whether we will accept the deliverances of thought or of sentience as more adequate to reveal the nature of reality. Mr. Bradley somewhat in-consistently (for it is the marked Intellectualism of his criterion of truth that has brought down upon him the ire of the pragmatists) seems to prefer the latter, on the ground that sentience gives a superior sense of reality to which the relational form of thought can never be equated and in regard to which it must ever remain a compromise, an un-successful attempt to " unite differences which have broken out in the felt-totality." As against the Hegelian identification of Thought and Reality, Mr. Bradley's argument is probably valid, though it seems to me a pity that he should have identified Reality with *sentient* experience, since he is forced to re-interpret this almost immediately as an ex-perience which is not, but which includes, sentience, as it includes thought and volition and all other forms of psychical reality. But I cannot agree that reality is identical with either thought or with sentient experience, for it seems to me that in both, objective content and *psychical* existence are really distinct. Mr. Bradley assumes throughout that all existence is psychical and that at bottom experience and the experienced, presentation and the presented, are one. But though I grant that in the presentation of a concrete object its ' what ' and its ' that,' its ' meaning ' and its ' existence ' are united, Mr. Bradley's arguments have entirely failed to convince me that the ' existence ' here in question is psychical existence, and not rather the existence which belongs to the object, which is quite distinct from the psychical act of perception in my mind. This being so, the question for me is not whether reality *is* thought or sentient experience, but whether in thought or in sentient experience reality is better known. And of the answer to this question there can be no doubt. For thought is admittedly a higher form of cognition than sentience, which is hardly cognition at all ; and it is precisely on this account that thoughts seem to *take the place of* and to be *preferred instead of*, but not as well as, sensations, whenever it is a question of knowledge. Sentient experience, like anything else, can become the object of thought. Indeed, as Mr. Bradley acknowledges, 'there is nothing which cannot become the object of thought.' And this being so, given a satisfactory criterion of truth, there would seem to be no reason why thought should not be capable of giving us adequate knowledge of reality.

§ 81. My conclusion, then, is that the thesis ' Reality *is* Sentient Experience ' and ' Reality is one and individual' are hypotheses or theories, not introspective facts, nor yet confirmed by introspective facts, which can only be made to harmonise with these theories by reading into them features that are not given and by excluding others that are. Mr. Bradley's account of the psychology of experience is inaccurate ; his assumptions gratuitous ; his terminology ambiguous, and his inferences invalid. The subjective and objective senses of terms such as ' existence ' and ' fact ' are hopelessly confused. What is not *given* as distinct in the first instance is assumed to be identical ; what is not given as divided, to be indivisible and one. Felt-wholes and underlying unities are discovered, though none such are to be found among the data of sentient experience. And, finally, thought-distinctions are declared to be the inseparable product of the evolution of this sentient experience, though for introspection the most we can say is that the latter is the antecedent of the former. These fallacies destroy the conclusiveness of all Mr. Bradley's arguments from psychological data ; while his assumption that in sentient experience *esse* is *percipi*, or that feeling and reality are one, gives to *Appearance and Reality* a subjective tone which is repugnant, not only to realists, but also to more objective idealists, and of this impression it is, as Professor Mackenzie remarks, difficult to get rid. Still *Appearance and Reality* is, after all, not subjective but objective Idealism ; and as a metaphysic of the Absolute is a theory which claims to interpret the universe as a whole, we shall have to examine it in a later chapter from a more metaphysical point of view.

CHAPTER V.

POSTULATION AND THE EXPERIMENTAL THEORY OF KNOWLEDGE.

§ 82. One definition which has been given of Pragmatism is that it is " the thorough recognition that the purposive character of mental life generally must permeate our most remotely cognitive activities."[1] Unlike Absolutism, Pragmatism claims emphatically a psychological foundation, and in essence is little else than the recognition of a particular psychological fact and its application as a general principle to the theory of knowledge. The pragmatist does not go to psychology merely for the data of experience in order to examine their metaphysical conditions. His standpoint is psychological from beginning to end ; and his aim, so he tells us, is to reassert characteristic features of human knowledge which have been hitherto much neglected, but which, nevertheless, are there, and are directly verifiable in human experience. The same may be said of Humanism, which is only Pragmatism stated in a more general form. Pragmatism is the logic of Humanism according to Dr. Schiller, while Humanism, according to Professor James, is Pragmatism applied to the genesis of knowledge. The two terms are practically synonymous, for Humanism is defined by Dr. Schiller as " a philosophical attitude which, without wasting thought upon attempts to

[1] *Humanism*, p. 8.

construct experience *a priori*, is content to take human experience as the clue to the world of human experience." [1] Both the pragmatist and the humanist accept the principle which I have laid down in a previous chapter as that which should guide the epistemologist in the construction of his theory of knowledge. For both profess to start from the standpoint of common-sense, and only in so far as common-sense notions fail to work, do they consider themselves justified in modifying them, and then, only provided sufficient reason can be shown for the modification.

§ 83. The fundamental characteristic of human cognition which the pragmatist claims to have re-discovered is already contained in the definition given above. It is the function of human purposes, which, as expressing human needs, characterise and pervade all human activity. Both human action and human cognition are controlled throughout by purpose. It is our purposes and our needs which prompt us to seek for knowledge ; it is our purposes which guide us in the search ; and it is the satisfaction of our purposes which compel us to accept or reject the various claims to truth which are made by fact and theory alike. [2] The acquisition of human knowledge, according to the pragmatist, always takes the same form. If we are to live, our needs must be satisfied ; hence, in order to satisfy our needs we strive to modify the environment in which we find ourselves. This environment consists of

---

[1] *Ibid.*, Preface.
[2] *Humanism*, p. 10 ; and *Studies in Humanism*, pp. 128, 153–157, and *passim* throughout both books.

sense-experience, and may be modified in two ways
by action and by thought. The 'matter' of sense
experience is characterised by ' a plastic receptivity,'
and upon it thought seeks to impose its own forms
which again may themselves be modified by the
reactions of sense-experience which, as at present
constituted, is not wholly formless, but has already
accepted forms imposed upon it by our ancestors.
Thus postulation and experiment characterise all
human cognition, for in it we demand that experience
shall conform to our pre-conceived ideas, which by
experiment we strive to realise in the concrete.
"Not having a ready-made world presented to us
which we can suck in with a passive receptivity,"
says Dr. Schiller, "we have to make experiments in
order to construct out of the materials we start with,
a harmonious cosmos which will satisfy all our
desires." [1]   These experiments are made under the
control of postulates in which anticipated results are
expressed.   But before a postulate is verified we
have to experiment again and again, and often
enough the postulate gets considerably modified in
the process.   Postulation as expressive of our
needs, and as verified in the concrete by experiments
the results of which satisfy these needs, is, for the
pragmatist, the universal form of human cognition.
There is no other way of acquiring knowledge except
by postulating what our needs demand, and no other
way of verifying these postulates except by experiments in the concrete, the effects of which are to
be judged according to their power to satisfy our
needs.   Postulation is 'universal' and 'necessary;' [2]

[1] '*Axioms as Postulates*' in ' Personal Idealism,' § 5.
[2] *Ibid.*, § 26.

it constitutes "the *nisus formativus* of our whole mental life."[1]

§ 84. Postulation is a principle which all pragmatists admit, though not all are so enthusiastic about it as is Dr. Schiller. "We strive by our efforts to give expression to the ideal postulates of human nature," says M. Blondel. "La Connaissance ne va dans le sens de la vérité qu'en devenant un appel à l'action et en recueillant la réponse de l'action." Postulation, indeed, is admitted in some form or other by almost all philosophers. Positivism, for example, while denying the possibility of Metaphysics, acknowledges the validity of science, and hence concludes in the person of Mr. Spencer that " there must be some principle which, as being the basis of science, cannot be established by science. All reasoned conclusions must rest *on some postulate*,"[2] some widest truth which can be merged in no other, and derived from no other, but which, nevertheless, according to Mr. Spencer, will not be self-evident.

This kind of postulation, however, is more akin to that of Kant than to the pragmatist's. It is used only as a last resource and in regard to an object— in Mr. Spencer's case 'the persistence of force'— which " transcends our knowledge and conception," so that we cannot be said to know, but only to postulate it. Kant also admits postulation only where knowledge fails. The pragmatist, on the other hand, argues somewhat illogically[3] that " the principle, if valid, must be generalised and applied all round to the organising principles of life."[4] This

---

[1] *Ibid.*, § 27.   [2] *First Principles*, p. 192.   (Italics mine.)
[3] cf. *infra*, §§ 88, 89.   [4] *'Axioms as Postulates,'* § 25.

is the chief difference between pragmatic and Kantian postulation; but there are others, and since Pragmatism claims to be the antithesis of Kantian Apriorism[1] upon which Absolutism is largely based, a closer comparison between the two theories in regard to postulation will be instructive.

§ 85.   As Absolutism may be regarded as a development of the first and third *Critiques*, so Pragmatism may in some sense be regarded as a development of the second.   Yet neither is strictly a Kantian theory, for the *Critiques* of Kant go together to form one whole and cannot be thus separated without destroying their meaning.   To adopt the first and reject the second, as Fichte did, or to adopt the second and reject the first as does the pragmatist, is to take up a position essentially different from that of Kant ; and it is only Kant's definition of Criticism as an examination of the presuppositions of knowledge rather than of the presuppositions of faith, that gives the monistic interpreters of Kant a better claim than the pragmatists to be styled Critical philosophers.

Pragmatism, however, does not claim to be a development of Critical Philosophy, nor does the pragmatist always acknowledge his debt to Kant. On the contrary, Professor James scoffs at the mind of the famous author of the *Kritik der reinen Vernunft* as " the rarest and most intricate of ancient bric-a-brac museums," and complains that Kant " has bequeathed to us not one single conception which is both indispensable to philosophy, and which philosophy either did not possess before, or was

[1] *Ibid.*, § 10.

not destined inevitably to acquire after him, through the growth of men's reflection upon the hypothesis by which science interprets nature."[1] Doubtless the latter part of this statement is true, since it is quite conceivable that had not Kant introduced the Copernican revolution into philosophy, it might have been introduced later on by a James or a Schiller. But this is a mere platitude which is equally true of all philosophic conceptions; and the fact remains that many peculiarly pragmatic notions can be traced back to Kant. I do not say that such notions have been deliberately borrowed from Kant; but, since pragmatists are not unfamiliar with Kantian writings, and since in their own Kantian ideas reappear, it is but natural to conclude that, consciously or unconsciously, Pragmatism has been influenced by the mind of that great thinker for which it professes little but contempt. In any case, contemptuous remarks such as these I have just quoted are peculiarly out of place when coming from the pen of a writer whose theory of the soul as a series of thoughts which are born owners and die owned, was forestalled by the Kantian metaphor of elastic balls which are conscious of their own motion and transmit both the motion and the consciousness to other balls in succession till the last ball holds all that the others ever held and realised as their own.[2]

§ 86. Ideas which have reappeared in Pragmatism are to be found even in the first *Critique*. It was as a postulate that Kant assumed that in

---

[1] *Journ. of Phil., Psy. and Sc. Methods*, 1904, p. 687.
[2] cf. James, *Principles of Psychology*, vol. i., p. 337.

J

knowledge the object conforms to the mind ; and it was according to its *working* that he asked that this postulate should be judged.   The pragmatist makes a similar assumption, though for him the object conforms not to *a priori* forms inherent in the structure of mind, but to more plastic postulates constructed gradually under the influence of needs.   Again, there is an affinity between the methodological postulates of Pragmatism and " the Regulative Principles of Pure Reason."   Methodological postulates—such as that of the ' complete plasticity of the world of experience '[1]—are made for the sake of a theory which we would *like* to be true universally ; but as we cannot prove this theory, the function of the postulate is merely regulative. Similarly, " the Regulative Principles of Pure Reason," such, for instance, as the demand that we should think totality present in the object, is not a constitutive principle, but something which our needs force us to postulate, and which guides us in the search for knowledge.

It is, however, not until we come to the second *Critique* that postulation proper is introduced. The attitude of the Practical Reason is essentially different from, though it is the complement of, that of the Pure Reason ; and it is this difference of attitude which makes it possible to regard both Pragmatism and Absolutism as one-sided developments of Criticism.   The two *Critiques* are parallel only in so far as in each reason lays down the laws to which phenomena are to conform.   For, while in the first the conformity of the data of experience

[1] '*Axioms as Postulates,*' § 7.

to the *a priori* element is a condition of the possibility of knowledge ; in the second the material element, hedonistic impulses, not only does not *de facto* conform to the Autonomy of Reason, but is often in marked opposition thereto—a fact which reminds one of the ' resisting something ' in overcoming which, according to Dr. Schiller, intelligence displays itself.[1] So far, however, the principle or law which we seek to impose upon nature, though it expresses human needs, is not strictly a postulate, but an intuitive moral dictate or ' a categorical imperative.' It is the attempt to realise in practice the dictates of our moral nature, which, owing to the opposition of sense, gives rise, according to Kant, to the need of postulation. The moral ideal, implicit within us, must somehow or other be realised : our rational nature demands it. In order, therefore, that this realisation may be possible in spite of sense, we postulate ' freedom ; ' and since its accomplishment will require an indefinite time, we postulate ' immortality ; ' while for the final reconciliation of virtue and happiness and the complete realisation of the highest good, we postulate God.

§ 87. Thus the ideas most closely connected with the pragmatic doctrine of postulation, human needs, human postulates and even human experiments are to be found in the philosophy of Kant. On the other hand, it must be admitted that there is an all-important difference between the Kantian and the pragmatic conception of postulation. Kant's postulates are a last resource aroused by the conflict of reason with our lower nature, and are

[1] *'Axioms as Postulates,'* § 6.

restricted to three transcendental objects. They are also incapable of verification, at least in this life, because *knowledge* of these objects is impossible, there being no perceptions in which, as Professor James would put it, such knowledge can ' terminate.' In Pragmatism, on the contrary, postulation is universal. It is characteristic not only of our belief in a moral Ideal, but of all thought and all cognition without exception. Kantian postulation does not claim to give knowledge but only faith ; whereas by pragmatic postulation it is asserted that we get the only kind of knowledge possible to man.

The validity of a postulate for the pragmatist, as for Kant, depends ultimately upon its power to satisfy human needs, and for neither can that validity ever be completely established. The Kantian postulate never gives more than faith ; and though the satisfactions which ensue from some pragmatic postulates may be both acute and lasting, no postulate is absolute, none completely verified ; even the most stable and the most permanent that have as yet made their appearance are subject to modification and, it may be, to radical change. This being the case, we may well ask what right the pragmatist has to generalise a principle so uncertain in its results. Why does he regard as universal what Kant restricted to faith ? What reason has he for affirming that postulation, which for intro-spection is not the only source of knowledge, is yet the type to which all knowing must and does *de facto* conform.

§ 88. I can find no definite answer to this question in pragmatic writings ; but the real answer would seem to be this, that from whatever point of view Pragmatism is approached, whether it be regarded (1) as a protest against 'pure' intellect which minimises the volitional and emotional side of our nature, or (2) as a return to the methods of science, or again, (3) as "an epistemological method which really describes the facts of actual knowing," it will lead us sooner or later to the Principle of Postulation which stands out clearly as its central doctrine, no matter from what aspect we regard it.

Thus, a 'tender-minded person,' if pragmatically inclined, would probably start from the conviction that the emotional and volitional tendencies of our nature must somehow or other be satisfied, and that what human needs force us to postulate must in the end be realised. A study of Peirce may then persuade him or her that the function of thought is simply to produce belief resulting in action, which action, if satisfactory, tends to strengthen, and if unsatisfactory, to destroy, the belief by which it was prompted. Finally, convinced that all thought is purposive, more or less emotional, and accompanied by conative strivings, he will proceed to apply the principle thus obtained to all our cognitive processes.

A 'tough-minded' person, on the other hand, will be more inclined to take a 'scientific' view of the matter. Fascinated by the apparent security of Physical Science, a belief in which a shallow knowledge of that science is apt to engender, he will seek to apply its method everywhere, even to metaphysics, as did the illustrious Kant ; and, proceeding on these lines, will try to reform, or rather to revolutionise, metaphysics, simply by basing it on science, a procedure which, by the way, was already suggested by Dr. Schiller in his pre-pragmatic *Riddles*.[1] Now the physicist, as a rule, makes use of what has been called 'the Inductive Method,' in which, starting from some provisional hypothesis, he seeks to verify this by observation and experiment. Since, then, argues the would-be pragmatist, this method of science has worked so well, and has proved itself so useful, so satisfactory and so reliable, what need is there of any further and less satisfactory method ? Why not be content with one ? And, lastly, turning from the future to the past, he looks back on the methods that have been used, and finds, as he expected, that in so far as knowledge has been attained, all of them conform to the one type of postulation and verification *viâ* experiment.

But some pragmatists claim to be more psychological, and tell us that they discover in even the simplest cognitive act the form of postulation. All knowledge comes by experience, and experience implies—we are getting less psychological and more critical now—(1) an experimenter, (2) a hypothesis which he doubts and wishes to verify, and (3) the verification-process.[2] This verification-process involves action on our part and reaction on the part of experience ; and the possibility of verification implies that objects always react in the same way, provided we experiment in the same way. Since, therefore, postulation is involved in even the

---

[1] *The Riddles of the Sphinx*, p. 163.
[2] C. S. Peirce, " What Pragmatism is," *The Monist*, 1905, p. 173, and cf. *Studies in Humanism*, p. 185.

simplest act of cognition, *a fortiori* it is involved in more complex acts which are built up of others more simple. Hence postulation occurs in every cognitive act, and is the universal form of all cognition.

§ 89. I am inclined to think that Professor James arrived at the doctrine of Postulation by the first process, and Dr. Schiller by the second ; while the third would seem to be an after-thought, in which the theory itself has suggested what claims to be the result of psychological analysis, and not the analysis the theory. On the other hand, it is by the third process alone that the doctrine of Postulation in its universality can be logically established. The appeal to emotional needs and to the general pur- posiveness of thought fails to validate universal postulation, because, granted that all thought is purposive and that all truth must satisfy our needs, it does not follow that the only way of acquiring truth is by means of postulation and experiment. For, in the first place, all that our needs demand is satisfaction, and so long as satisfaction is obtained, it does not matter, so far as our needs are con- cerned, by what means it is obtained. And secondly, postulation and experiment of themselves are insufficient to account for the satisfaction of cognitive needs. In order to frame a postulate we need some data to go upon. The need which seeks satisfaction cannot itself suggest the means to attain it : it can only guide us in choosing between hy- potheses which have been suggested by objective facts, and these must somehow be known. Again, as all allow, it is the reaction of our environment which ultimately verifies or negatives a postulate, and so satisfies or fails to satisfy our needs. And this implies that we perceive reactions and apprehend their significance, which is, of itself, so much knowledge acquired, but is not postulation.

The second process by which postulation is reached is equally invalid, if offered as a proof. All that a study of the methods of science can do is to suggest universal postulation as a hypothesis. To infer that postulation and experiment are used in all branches of knowledge, because *de facto* they are used in one, would obviously be an illicit induction.

§ 90. The psychological, then, is the only argument which can afford us a valid proof that all knowledge comes by way of postulation and experiment. But is it an introspective datum of experience that all knowledge does come by way of postulation and experiment ? I think not. Indeed, it would be strange if it were, for neither Professor Wundt nor any of our most eminent psychologists have noted the fact, nor does it find mention even in the *Principles of Psychology*. To introspection but few of our cognitive acts partake of the nature of postulation. The facts which we observe and which constitute so large a portion—some would say all— of our knowledge, are not known as verified postulates, but rather seem to be given. This is true in general of all facts, even of those which are used in Science and elsewhere to verify postulates or to test the validity of theories. It is the hypothesis and the theory which are postulates, not the facts.

Axioms, again, as even Dr. Schiller himself admits, *appear* to be immediate judgments, and seem, as it were, to compel our assent to their truth. We may *explain* axioms pragmatically, and affirm that it is our need of them which in reality compels us to assent to their truth, because without them we could not think consistently at all. This, however, is not an introspective fact, but a theory, and quite as much a theory as that which explains axioms as due to the manifestation of the nature of reality to our minds in the act of apprehension or thought. Axioms appear to be self-evident, and there is no trace in our experience of any process of experiment by which we seek to verify them. Put this down to heredity, if you like ; but then, as before, you are theorising, and the fact remains that as soon as we grasp the meaning of an axiom we at once assent to its truth. Ask any lad of thirteen whether fire can be hot and at the same time not be hot. Then ask him in more general terms whether *anything* can be hot and at the same time not be hot. And finally, becoming more abstract still, enquire of him whether anything can be and yet not be whatever it is at one and the self-same time. The result of such an experiment can hardly be doubted. In every case the boy will answer, No ; and if you ask him *why* he accepts with so little hesitation the Principle of Non-Contradiction, he will probably tell you it is obvious (*i.e.*, self-evident). ' Of course things cannot have a quality and at the same time not have that quality.' [1]

---

[1] Doubtless, in order to discover whether two positive qualities (*v.g.*, white and hot) are compatible, we must appeal to experience and ' experiment.' But this is beside the question, for the principle of Contradiction treats of *in*compatibility, not of compatibility. Again, we *may* have to experiment in order to find out whether a quality is really present or not ; but there

Thus, facts and axioms obstinately withstand all efforts to generalise the doctrine of Postulation ; and to these we might add all deductive reasoning and almost all mathematical methods and truths. It must be admitted, therefore, that so far as the data of experience are concerned, psychologists are justified in omitting to mention the postulatory character of all human cognition ; and logicians, too, are justified in not setting postulation down as the one process by which we may arrive at knowledge and truth. The pragmatist who affirms the contrary, must affirm it on theoretical grounds, for he can hardly hope to prove his point by introspection alone.

§ 91.   Various attempts have been made to get rid of the difficulty arising from facts and axioms ; notably two. Professor Dewey, in an article entitled ' The Experimental Theory of Knowledge,'[1] endeavours to get rid of the difficulty in regard to facts by denying that, strictly speaking, facts can be called knowledge at all ; while Dr. Schiller's now famous 'Axioms as Postulates' is an attempt to do the same for Axioms by the simple method of considerably antedating the period of their birth.

Professor Dewey makes a distinction between (1) experience which is mere experience and in no sense knowledge, (2) experience which is *cognitive* only to

is no need to transform the principle, as Dr. Schiller has done, in order thus to apply it.   It is applicable as it stands ; and that in most cases without either postulation or experiment. Nor is the principle of Contradiction verified by being applied. Though abstract, it is true of real things precisely because they are real things ; and therefore is true of every real thing, whether it be applied or not.

[1] *Mind*, N.S. 59 (July, 1906), p. 293.

the outside observer or in reflection, and (3) experience which is properly *cognitional*. These three kinds of experience he illustrates by a single example —our experience of the odour of a rose. In experiences of the 'mere experience' type there appears in consciousness first of all 'just a floating odour, nothing more.' That is succeeded by action ; and finally by the smelling and enjoying of the rose. Here we have a series of three experiences, smell—felt-movement—gratification ; but no knowledge whatsoever, not even of the acquaintance-type, is involved. If, however, we suppose the original smell to persist, and to be still there in consciousness when gratification arrives, the smell now appears under a new form ; it is " represented with a quality, an office, that of having excited activity and thereby having terminated its career in a certain *quale* of gratification."

Here [says Professor Dewey] we have a cognitive, but not a cognitional thing. In saying that the smell is finally experienced as *meaning* gratification (through intervening handling, seeing, etc.), and meaning it not in a hapless way, but in a fashion which operates to effect what is meant, we retrospectively attribute intellectual force and function to the smell—and this is what is signified by 'cognitive.' Yet the smell is not cognitional, because it did not knowingly intend to mean this ; but is found after the event to have meant it.[1]

For knowledge proper something more is required This is obtained when the smell recurs again not as the original smell (the floating odour), nor yet as the

[1] *Ibid.*, p. 277. (N.B.—In what follows, for the sake of clearness, I have replaced the symbols used by Professor Dewey by what they symbolise. Otherwise I have kept as closely as possible to his own words.)

smell *plus* gratification, but as a smell which is
" fated or charged with the sense of the possibility
of a fulfilment " like to the first.   In this latter case,
and in this alone, is experience *cognitional*, for now
for the first time is the smell " contemporaneously
aware that it means something beyond itself."
What it means is not indeed a rose in general, but
simply another experience, viz., the gratification
which it intends to effect by means of an operation
on our part to which it incites us ; but it means it
intentionally and not merely to the outside observer
or in retrospection.   In brief : " *The odour knows
the rose ; the rose is known by the odour ; and the
import of each term is constituted by the relationship
in which it stands to the other*."[1]

Generalising from the last case, Professor Dewey
obtains his definition of knowledge.   Having pointed
out that both the thing meaning (the odour) and
the thing meant (the rose) are present in consciousness, though not in the same way ; one, in fact,
being " present as-*not*-present-in-the-same-way-as-
the-other-is," yet present as " something to be
rendered present in the same way through the
intervention of an operation," he sums up in the
following definition :—

An experience is a knowledge, if in its quale there is
an experienced distinction and connection of the two
elements of the following sort : *one means or intends
the presence of the other in the same fashion in which
itself is already present, while the other is that which,
while not present in the same fashion, must become so
present if the meaning or intention of its companion or
yoke-fellow is to be fulfilled through an operation it sets up*.[2]

---

[1] *Ibid.*, p. 299 (italics *not* mine).   [2] *Ibid.*, p. 301

It is not I, be it noted, who call the above a ' *definition* ' of knowledge, but Professor Dewey ; and complicated as that definition is, it applies only to the simpler kind of knowledge, viz., to knowledge of the acquaintance-type. There is a form of knowledge more complex still. Sometimes intended fulfilments will be realised, sometimes not ; and since we may reflect upon the relations of ' meaning ' to the fulfilments and disappointments which may have resulted in the past, we have also knowledge of a reflective, critical, or scientific type.[1] Fortunately, however, Professor Dewey has not attempted to define this ; and it is with the first type rather than the second that we are now concerned.

§ 92. ' The Experimental Theory of Knowledge,' as explained by Professor Dewey, opens up many problems. Is it, for instance, the smell that knows the rose, or is it I who know the rose by means of its smell ? Can the smell be regarded as a ' thing ' having an intellectual function, or does not this function again belong rather to my mind ? Are these and similar strange-sounding expressions due merely to Professor Dewey's desire to be original and emphatic, or have they a metaphysical significance which implies in the background Radical Empiricism and the Philosophy of Pure Experience ?

The discussion of these questions must be postponed to a later chapter. What at present we wish to find out is whether Professor Dewey has succeeded in establishing the doctrine of universal Postulation. This will depend, of course, upon whether he is

[1] *Ibid.*, cf. pp. 304 to 306.

justified in restricting knowledge to experiences which intend the presence of other objects, in the same way in which they themselves are present through the intervention of action, and which are contemporaneously aware of this their intention. For if, as is asserted, knowledge belongs to these experiences alone, clearly all knowledge begins as a postulate, in the form of an anticipated fulfilment which may or may not be realised when action has intervened. The ' Experimental ' and what we may call the ' Postulatory ' Theory of Knowledge are, I take it, one and the same thing.

Professor Dewey's argument practically amounts to this, that we have only knowledge when we have *actual remembrance* of a past event accompanied by the *anticipation* of some other event with which it has been connected in the past. Now, in reflection, which presupposes memory, knowledge certainly becomes fuller, more adequate, and more systematic ; but knowledge as we ordinarily understand that term is not restricted to remembrance, still less to actual or conscious remembrance, nor does it necessarily imply anticipation.

In the first place, if you restrict knowledge to experiences in which we have *actual* remembrance, you exclude at once all knowledge *per modum habitus*. We know nothing but what is actually present somehow or other in consciousness. Consequently, the scientist knows nothing about the laws which govern the phenomenal world, and the mathematician nothing about the theory of number, except when he is actually thinking of such subjects. This is a strange conclusion, yet it follows from the premises that we know only in so far as ideas function consciously in memory.

§ 93. Let us suppose, however, that Professor Dewey is speaking of actual knowledge, and that he admits as its condition knowledge *per modum habitus*. The question, then, is whether *actual* knowledge can be restricted to thought about absent objects, or to the *memory* of past events. Now, first of all, we think about present as well as about absent objects, and I see no reason why this thinking should not be called cognitional; and, secondly, if memory can be called knowledge, I do not see why the acts by which memory is built up should not be called knowledge, too. Doubtless, mere feelings and sensations, as such, do not constitute knowledge; but then there is something else in perception besides sensation or feeling, namely, thought. When a man goes hunting or botanising, he usually thinks about what he is doing, and so may learn something of the characteristics of horses and dogs and flowers; and this may happen even if, when he set out, he did not do so with the intention of making any systematic observations; for objects, when they present themselves, secure our attention and cause us to think about them quite accidentally, as it were, and without necessarily having any connection with our present purpose or with what for the moment occupies our thoughts. We undoubtedly do think about objects which are present to the senses, and it seems to me quite arbitrary to say that these thoughts do not partake of the nature of knowledge, simply because what we think about, or part of it at least, happens to be there given in the objects before us. Indeed, I can find only one reason for Professor Dewey's denial that what we learn about things from direct observation is knowledge until we happen to reflect upon it ; and that is, that if he admitted such knowledge, he would have to admit that some knowledge at any rate does not come by way of postulation and experiment. Memory is necessary if knowledge is to be of any future use, and if it is to become in any way systematic, but this is quite a different thing from asserting that knowledge exists only in actual remembrance.

§ 94. The inclusion of *anticipation* as one of the essential characteristics of knowledge clearly restricts the latter further still ; yet anticipation, in Professor Dewey's opinion, would appear to be a characteristic of even greater importance than memory. Why this is so, again, it is not easy to understand, unless it be that it is necessary to establish 'the Experimental Theory of Knowledge.' There are innumerable things which ordinarily we say that we know, but of which we have never had direct experience, and probably never shall. I know, for instance, that the arrangement of the streets in Brooklyn is more regular than that of our London streets, yet I have not the slightest anticipation of going to Brooklyn to see those streets for myself. When I walk through the streets of London and they remind me by contrast of what I have heard about Brooklyn, my present experience does not 'intend' another experience which is at all likely to be there in my consciousness in the same way in which *it* is there. Again, if I detect an escape of gas, and think of some flaw in the gaspipes, I do not think of that flaw as 'going to be present in the same fashion as the smell of the gas is present,' for I may be quite content to leave the examination of the pipes to the gas-fitter. Of course, if what we know is an existing sensible object, there is always the abstract possibility of a future experience in which we may actually perceive it. But, then, many things about which we have knowledge are not existing sensible objects, but things of the past, or rational systems and arrangements, physical, social, political ; and of these, as such, we can have no direct experience, but can think only in the abstract. Even when the object of knowledge does happen to belong to the existing sensible order, it is hardly necessary that we should be obliged to contemplate the possibility of experiencing it in order to know it ; still less is it necessary that 'the thing meaning' should incite us to movements for the purpose of realising the 'thing meant.' Everybody has anticipations and ideals which he strives to realise in the concrete ; but that knowledge should be restricted to such anticipations and ideals is an arbitrary distortion of the use of the term 'knowledge,' which is without the slightest foundation in fact.

Professor Dewey's Experimental Theory of Knowledge doubtless describes (though it does not explain) the characteristics of *some* cases of actual cognition. But to generalise from such cases to all cases is illicit, especially when the testimony of experience and of common-sense is against such a generalisation. That Professor Dewey is straining the term knowledge so as to make it harmonise with

K

his preconceived theory is shown by the fact that while declaring that knowledge does not exist till we have ' acquaintance,' he admits that in acquaintance there is 'a little friendliness,' 'a trace of *re*-knowing.'[1] It is a pity that the pragmatist should be so bent upon establishing the universally purposive, postulatory and experimental character of all knowledge, that he should have changed the conventional use of a familiar word in order to force the data of experience into seeming harmony with his theory ; yet such appears to be the case.

§ 95. Dr. Schiller's attempt to make axioms conform to the general doctrine that all knowledge comes through postulation and experiment must now be considered. The *apparent* self-evidence of axioms Dr. Schiller grants, but attributes it, not to the clearness with which the nature of the objects concerned presents itself to our minds, but to a long-established habit of the *race*. Certain principles have been used so long, and have proved themselves so useful and so satisfactory in regard to human needs, that belief in them has become with us a second instinct. Yet all axioms have a history, and all alike began as postulates ; though in some cases their origin as postulates dates back to pre-historic days when the human (?) mind had not yet fully emerged from ' the sentient level of consciousness.' So long ago, indeed, is it since certain of our principles were first postulated, that we have forgotten their postulatory origin, and have come to think of them as if they were axiomatic. This error on our part is due to the extreme usefulness

[1] *loc. cit.*, p. 294.

of these principles in practical life. Axioms as postulates did their work so well, and attempts to impose them on the universe were so seldom resisted, that man has come by force of habit to regard them as immutable and necessary laws, and upon them by tacit mutual consent has been bestowed the honorific name of axioms. Yet, if the truth were told, the tendency to think in these so-called axiomatic forms has been handed down by heredity, much in the same way as tendencies to consumption, drunkenness and imbecility, except that in the first case the tendency has become permanent and universal on account of its utility, while in the second on account of its inutility it is as yet restricted to the few.

Dr. Schiller has kindly sketched for us in brief outline the possible history of several of our more important 'axioms.' Such histories, of course, do not pretend to be a true account of what really occurred; but are rather to be taken as allegories, the purpose of which is to show that axioms could have begun life as postulates, and yet in process of time have acquired an axiomatic character.

§ 96. The origin of the principle of Identity is the case upon which Dr. Schiller bestows the greatest care, and it is quite possible, we might even, I think, say probable, that the principle of Identity, *as he defines it*, did begin life as a postulate which human experience has verified so completely that we are now convinced of its truth. Indeed, so easy is it to verify in experience Dr. Schiller's principle of Identity that it seems to be quite unnecessary to assign it an origin beyond the life of the individual.

True, in a pre-historic age Edwin may have postulated that Angelina of the winter furs was the same as Angelina of the fig-leaves, in spite of the increase of clothing ; but so do we all discover that ' things remain the same ' day after day, in spite of changes in circumstance and accidental qualities. There is no need to call in heredity to explain our belief in ' permanence amid change,' for this principle is so obviously the only interpretation that can be put upon events, that for each of us individually the evidence is sufficient to convince us of its truth. Heredity is only an encumbrance, and gets us at once into difficulties. For it has never been shown that thoughts or ways of thinking can be transmitted by heredity, except in so far as concerns the cerebral dispositions which subserve them as conditions ; and these dispositions can hardly suffice to account for the transmission of axioms, since they do not explain how it is that we come to apprehend the *meaning* of an axiom at all.

Dr. Schiller's argument for the alleged transition of the principle of Identity from a postulatory to an axiomatic stage of existence, is quite beside the point, for the principle whose history he traces is *not* the principle of Identity which logicians claim to be axiomatic, but quite another principle which he has substituted in its place. Dr. Schiller's definition agrees with that given in Mr. Welton's *Logic*, and runs as follows :—" When we say that A is A, we mean that a thing remains itself even amid change, and that a common nature is manifested in different individuals." [1]   Thus the principle

[1] '*Axioms as Postulates*,' p. 98, and cf. Welton, *Logic*, p. 32.

of Identity, A is A, is interpreted to mean 'the persistence of identity through change,' while the complementary principle of Contradiction is transformed into the assertion that "a thing must be capable of excluding whatever threatens (the persistence of) its identity (through change)."[1] But surely no logician of standing has ever claimed self-evidence for assertions such as these. The logical and self-evident principle of Identity is never so enunciated, but affirms merely that "Whatever is, is," or that "A thing is identical with its own nature," no reference whatever being made to the possibility of change. Things may change or cease to be ; the principle of Identity merely states that so long as they exist they are what they are.

§ 97. But lest it be now objected that we have saved the self-evidence of the principle, by making it tautological, and, for my own part, I have always regarded the ' Identity ' formula as simply another way, and not a very lucid way, of putting the principle of Contradiction—let us consider the latter principle. The law of Contradiction, whose mythical history Dr. Schiller has sketched, is, again, not the logical principle of Contradiction, but a creation of his own. The logical principle makes no assertion about the power of things to resist a partial or total transformation. It merely states that "contradictions are incompatible," or that "so long as a thing exists it cannot at the same time not exist, or that, so long as it possesses a certain attribute, to deny that it has that attribute is false." It is difficult to conceive of a principle

[1] *Ibid.*, p. 106.

such as this starting as a postulate to be verified in
experience ; nor can I imagine any inductive process
by which such verification could have been obtained.
On the contrary, the truth of the principle of
Contradiction is presupposed by the possibility of
intelligent thought ; for to affirm that S may be P,
and at the same time not be P (both terms being
used in the same sense in each judgment) is for
thought impossible, and would render predication
meaningless.   As soon as we begin to think at all
we express our thoughts in terms of ' *being* ' and
' *not-being*,' ' *is* ' and ' *isn't*,' which we cannot but
recognise as mutually exclusive.

In his history of the pseudo-principles of Identity
and Contradiction, Dr. Schiller has, I fear, been
guilty of an *ignoratio elenchi ;* and it still remains
for him to show how the real principles of Identity
and Contradiction which are presupposed and
implicitly recognised as true in the very act of
postulation itself, can themselves be merely ' full-
blown ' postulates.

§ 98.   Belief in an external world is more axiomatic, for, at any rate by the realist, the existence
of such a world is admitted as a self-evident truth.
Dr. Schiller's account of the origin of this belief,
however, does not seem to throw much light upon
its nature, or in any way to prove that it was
originally only a postulate. 'Grumps,' a kind of
amœba, so it would appear, gets outside a jagged
flint, and, finding that it hurts, postulates that it is
' external ' to himself.   Now such a postulate, like
all other verified postulates, ought to be extremely
useful.   But it is by no means clear what possible

use it could have been to 'Grumps' to postulate that the offensive flint was 'external' to himself, for *ex hypothesi* he did not know what 'external' meant. Where did this notion of 'externality' come from, and why did not 'Grumps' apply it to his stomach-aches and his other pains, which must have hurt him quite as much as the flint? Dr. Schiller's account of the origin of the notion of 'externality' is extremely vague and inconsistent, for in the example he has chosen, the flint *de facto* was not external at all. This is unfortunate, for had Dr. Schiller's account been more carefully worked out we might have been able to discuss with him the origin of a real axiom.

One statement, however, Dr. Schiller does make, not once, but repeatedly, in regard to the origin of our belief in an external world.

The pragmatically real world [he says] is *not* an original datum of our experience at all, but an elaborate construction, made by man, individually and socially, by a purposive selection of the more efficacious, and a rejection of the less efficacious portions of a 'primary reality' which seems chaotic to begin with, but contains a great deal more than the " external world " extracted from it.[1]

Proof of this statement there is none; and about this most interesting evolutionary miracle Dr. Schiller can tell us nothing except that it is 'obscure.' The whole doctrine, in fact, is merely an assumption, or rather an inference drawn from an assumption, viz., from the fundamental tenet of Pragmatism that all truth and all reality (or at

[1] *Studies in Humanism*, p. 460, and cf. pp. 183, 187, 202, 426.

any rate all our knowledge of reality) comes by way
of postulation and experiment, in which the ' true '
and the ' real ' are gradually separated from the
' false ' and the ' unreal ' on account of their greater
utility.   We begin life with ' primary reality,' which
' includes imaginings, illusions, errors, hallucinations,' and which is ' anterior to the distinction of
appearance and reality ; ' and out of this ' meaningless chaos ' real fact is made ! [1]   Surely it would be
difficult to find a more gratuitous assumption or a
more useless hypothesis, even in Absolutism.   How
do we know that an infant's experience is chaotic,
and that utility is the magic talisman by means of
which he sets it right ?   Doubtless an infant's
experience is very different from ours, and doubtless
also he does not begin life with a full-fledged
concept of the real world or of the self.   But to
affirm that the distinction of self and not-self,
internal and external, is an evolutionary product,
due to the supposed fact that the infant or the
savage appreciates its utility, is just as much an
assumption as to affirm that it is an intuitive
judgment which is made as soon as thought appears
upon the horizon of the infant's human mind.   But
the realist's assumption has this in its favour, that
it is not only more rational, but also more ' useful '
than that of his rival.

It is more rational because it is based on fact,
whereas the pragmatist's assumption is based on
theory.   For it is a fact that in adult life, as a rule,
we intuitively distinguish what is real from what
is unreal.   Dr. Schiller, of course, denies this ; for

[1] *Ibid.*, p. 187.

he, too, has endeavoured to bring ' fact ' within the
all-embracing sphere of postulation. But without
avail. For though we may hesitate to accept the
statement of another in regard to fact, especially if
the alleged fact be extraordinary (*e.g.*, a flying visit
to the North Pole), and occasionally may doubt the
objective reality of our own experiences, ordinarily
we accept them as real on the spot, without experiment or verification. If I see some swans on the
Serpentine I do not need to handle them or to throw
stones at them in order to convince myself of their
real existence. Nor if I visit a friend's rooms do
I need to sit on all his chairs in order to prove that
they are really chairs, as Dr. Schiller suggests.[1] On
the contrary, sometimes the empirical nature of
reality is such that we *can* " argue from one case to
a similar one, which we take to be the same, with
absolute assurance *a priori* "[2] (*i.e.*, without any
active interference on our part) ; and in almost
every case we are at any rate certain ' *a priori* '
that the something we perceive is external and real.
The facts of actual knowing, therefore, are against
Dr. Schiller ; the recognition of external reality is
at present immediate ; and hence, if it is legitimate
to argue from present to past, as Dr. Schiller does,[3]
we must confess that it has always been immediate.

Secondly, the realist's assumption is more ' useful '
than that of the pragmatist. If with the dawn of
intelligence the child is able to distinguish the real
from the unreal, and the external from the internal,
even if it be only in a single case, he has at any rate

[1] *Studies in Humanism*, p. 192.
[2] *Ibid.*, p. 193.   [3] *Ibid.*, p. 196.

a notion of reality and of ' inside ' and ' outside '
upon which to base future judgments, and so to
' build up ' his ' body ' and ' the external world.'
But if he were not blessed with this intuitive insight
into the nature of things, elementary and inadequate
as it is, he could never get to know reality at all.
Utility could not help him, for unless the facts of
his pure, but chaotic, experience differed radically
from one another and fell into two sets, he would
not know which to call useful and which not. While,
if they did differ thus radically from the outset, why
should he not call them real at once ? Nay, further,
if he had not already had experience of ' reality '
and known it as such, a ' claim to reality ' for him
would have no meaning. Hence, no matter how
useful it might be, he would never be able to think
of it as real.[1]

§ 99. When it comes to a question of origin, then
the pragmatic theory breaks down. ' Reality '[2]
cannot be a postulate in the first instance, nor are
our other axioms such. Our needs may prompt us
to postulate, but they are too vague and indefinite
even now to suggest the form which our postulates
must take, and in the beginning of things must
have been still more vague and indefinite. Nor
could postulates have been suggested by things,
for (1) *ex hypothesi* it is we who have to set the
ball rolling by imposing forms on them, and (2) with
their minimum of form and structure they would,
in any case have very little to suggest, and (3) if

---

[1] cf. *supra*, §§ 53-56.
[2] *i.e.*, objective and external, as opposed to subjective or
psychical reality.

the start did come from them we should have knowledge of a kind before we began to postulate, and
thus it would not be true to say that all knowledge
comes *via* postulation and experiment. In fact, if
all knowledge, even to the most rigid of our facts
and to the most ultimate of our axioms, did begin
as a postulate it could never have begun at all !
For postulation—and this Dr. Schiller admits—
' *presupposes a mind which has had some prior
experience and possesses some knowledge already.*'
" It needs a ' platform ' from which to operate
further on a situation which confronts it, in order
to realise some purpose or to satisfy some interest." [1]
As an explanation of how we subsume new things
under old categories, and new events under old
laws, the pragmatic theory is satisfactory enough ;
but it is entirely at a loss to explain how these
categories and laws, these ' initial principles ' and
this ' prior basis of fact,' originated in the first
instance.[2] Doubtless this difficulty confronts alike
all theories of knowledge,[3] but other theories of
knowledge have at least attempted to solve it, and
the *a priori* solution of Kant is at any rate better
than rough guesses, and still more satisfactory than
the cry of ' sour grapes ' upon which Dr. Schiller
at length falls back. For, surely, if the Pragmatic
Method does imply ' a truth and a reality which it
does not make,' it is irrational not to ' conceive them
as valuable,' or to " conceive them only as indicating
limits to our explanations, and not as revealing the
solid foundations upon which they rest." In this

---

[1] *Studies in Humanism,* p. 185.
[2] *Ibid.,* pp. 431, 432.   [3] *Ibid.,* p. 433.

initial reality and this initial truth it is admitted
that all human knowledge began, from it that all
human truth has developed and been made.   Hence,
the value of these ἀρχαί must be inestimably great,
so great, indeed, that it is surprising they have not
crystallised into axioms and so perpetuated
themselves.

Nor is this question of ultimate origin merely an
idle speculation about the beginnings of knowledge
in the race.   It applies also to the individual, whose
mind, active as it may be, and predisposed by its
ancestors to certain forms of thought (or rather
associations and reactions), none the less begins life
as a blank.   This mind also needs a platform of
fact from which to start, and suggestions of truth
out of which to form the claims upon which it is first
to exercise its experimental genius. And these ἀρχαί
certainly cannot come from postulation and
experiment, which *ex hypothesi* have not yet begun.
Where, then, do they come from ?   There would seem
to be but two alternatives.   Either Apriorism or
Aristotelianism.   Either the ideas by which we
represent reality and the relations which we posit
as holding between them are, in the first instance,
derived from the nature of our minds, or they are
suggested by reality to a mind that is capable of
taking the hint.

The pragmatist, though he feels the impossibility
of his present position, has not quite made up his
mind which of these alternatives to choose.   Professor James inclines to the former view, and speaks
of " great systems of logical and mathematical truths
under the respective terms of which the sensible

parts of experience eventually arrange themselves, and which are already true in advance of special verification if we have subsumed our objects rightly." [1] That there is within our minds "a ready-made framework for all sorts of possible objects follows from the very structure of our thinking." Dr. Schiller, on the other hand, to judge from his unconcealed dislike of all things mysterious and *a priori*, would prefer, if a choice must be made, the other alternative. In not a few of Dr. Schiller's theories one can discern an unmistakable undercurrent of Aristotelianism. His theory of 'matter and form,' for instance, and again his theory of 'activity and substance,' has clearly been derived from a study of Aristotle, though his text seems to have suffered from interpolations. And in regard to this very point at present in question he remarks that though "the connection of events which all assume is never a fact of observation," yet to the primitive mind such principles as those we have been discussing "may possibly be suggested by the regularity of phenomena." [2] But if they can be suggested by phenomena, then phenomena must in some way reveal themselves to our intellect ; and since 'regularity' is a relation, relations between phenomena must also reveal themselves. And, if we grant so much, why not go further and say that knowledge presupposes our power to apprehend the nature and relations of the objects that we know, and that,

---

[1] *Pragmatism*, p. 210 (but cf. *Mind*, N.S. 52, p. 460, where an empirical origin is assigned).

[2] '*Axioms as Postulates*.' § 0.

having apprehended the relation between two objects, we at once recognise that the same relation must hold wherever there are given similarly constituted objects. Thus we should have ' universal ' ideas, objectively valid, and yet allowing ample room for postulation, since it would still be necessary to subsume new cases under the old ideas; and often enough recognition and identification is impossible without examination and experiment.

§ 100. Dr. Schiller, then, has failed to establish the postulatory character of axioms, and Professor Dewey has failed to show that it is incorrect to talk of *knowing* facts. The Postulatory or Experimental Theory of Knowledge describes accurately enough a certain class of cognitive processes ; but it is a failure if we try to make it universal, and affirm that postulation and experiment is the only process by which knowledge is acquired, to the exclusion of comparatively passive observation and intellectual apprehension or intuition. Sometimes we apprehend at once the nature of the object which is presented, its colour, size, shape, form and other properties, all of which we recognise may belong in like manner to other objects. At other times we hesitate. We apprehend some qualities only, while for the identification of others, actual handling and purposive experiment must intervene. Especially is this the case when we are dealing with comparatively complex objects, which are known to have many properties but do not seem to manifest them all at once. Could we subsume the object under a general idea, the predication of its properties would follow from previous knowledge ; but often enough presented data are insufficient to admit of immediate and certain subsumption, and it is then we have recourse to postulation. We subsume provisionally, tentatively, and then experiment in order to discover whether properties are really there which ought to be there if our subsumption has been correct. In the sphere of theory and scientific hypothesis postulation and experiment are still more useful. Sometimes we wish to subsume a fact and proceed in much the same way as I have just described. At other times it is a law which we wish to verify, a law which we have found to hold in a given case, but do not know precisely why, because we do not know upon what properties in the concrete thing the law depends. This being so, we postulate that the law depends upon a certain known property, and examine other cases in which this property occurs to see if the law still holds. Or again, it is a theory or a complexus of hypotheses which we wish to verify, and a theory, as we know, is not based directly on inductive reasoning or generalisation from particular cases, but contains an arbitrary element, an arbitrary combination of attributes, or arbitrary assumptions in regard to the inner structure of physical things. Our theory is therefore a postulate, and here, as before, our only means of ascertaining its truth is to experiment in the concrete in order to see how it works.

There is wide scope, then, for postulation even in a theory of knowledge which admits apprehension of the nature of reality, universal ideas, and axiomatic principles. My objection to the Experimental Theory is not that postulation and experiment is not a fact, but that it is not by any means the *only way* to knowledge; and, secondly, that the form in which it is expressed by Professor Dewey and Dr. Schiller seems to imply a Philosophy of Pure Experience which, as I shall endeavour to show, is quite incapable of giving a rational explanation of either knowledge or reality.

CHAPTER VI.

CONCEPTION AND THE COGNITIVE RELATION.

§ 101. In this chapter I propose to discuss two pragmatic doctrines, both of which are closely connected with the Experimental Theory of Knowledge. The first is the pragmatic theory of conception, and the second the view of the relation of the knower and the known set forth by Professors James and Strong. In the Experimental Theory all knowledge comes by way of experiment and experience. By experiment knowledge is made, and by experience it is verified ; and beyond experience there is nothing to be known. From this two consequences follow. First of all, what we make by experiment is usually an instrument by which to manipulate and modify our environment ; and to this rule the concept is no exception. Secondly, the concept and the knower are one, for outside experience there is neither knower nor known.

§ 102. According to the famous ' maxim ' of

Peirce the contents of a concept comprise only the experienced ' effects ' of our actions, or the reactions of an object which have resulted in response to stimulation.[1] We modify experience in order to evoke from it results which will satisfy our needs ; and these results are remembered and grouped together round the nucleus of a word or image, and thus is formed a concept. We remember, for example, that a cat, if stroked, will purr ; if teased, will scratch ; if offered milk, will lap it up ; if left in a room with a canary in an open cage, will be the proximate occasion of the disappearance of that piece of experience which we call a canary. These and other experienced responses to action on our part together form—if I have understood Mr. Peirce aright—our concept of a cat. And, if the maxim of Peirce is to be taken literally, this will be all that a cat means, for these are the differences that it makes to our lives. The term ' cat ' is a name which denotes a certain element or datum of experience which is such that under given conditions it leads to certain practical and sensible effects. Thus concepts denote or ' lead to ' experiences of the sentient type, and their contents, if concrete, consist in the sensory images awakened by the word or symbol, and if abstract, in other words, which must as before " sooner or later reflect you back into sensible realities." [2]

§ 103. The grouping of the experienced effects under names and symbols cannot, however, be

[1] cf. " The Pragmatic Method " (James), *Journ. of Phil., Psy. and Sc. Methods*, 1904, pp. 673, 674.

[2] cf. *Pragmatism*, Sect. iii. and vi., and *The Meaning of Truth*, pp. 82, 104, 105, 133, 140, 141.

L

accounted for in the life-time of a single individual, nor, for that matter, in the life-time of a single generation. Concepts are not the products of an individual's thought - activity, but are largely hereditary, and have gradually been formed as the human mind has evolved from a state of purely sentient experience.[1] Like axioms, they are essentially " tools slowly fashioned by the practical intelligence for the mastery of its experience ; "[2] and the recognition of the instrumental nature of the Concept is, Dr. Schiller tells us, a point of the greatest importance for the theory of knowledge to the neglect of which he attributes the failure of Platonism and Criticism.[2] Concepts do not represent sense-experiences in the copy sense of the term ' to represent.' They are *substituted for* sense-experiences, and of them we form " related systems, corresponding point for point to the systems which the realities form," so that " by letting an ideal term call up its associates systematically, we may be led to a terminus which the corresponding real term would have led to in case we had operated on the real world." [3] Hence their extreme usefulness in the manipulation of experience.

The paths that run through conceptual experiences, that is, through ' thoughts ' or ' ideas ' that ' know ' the things in which they terminate, are highly advantageous paths to follow. Not only do they yield inconceivably rapid transitions ; but, owing to the ' universal ' Character which they frequently possess, and to their capacity for association with one another in

---

[1] *Pragmatism*, p. 170, and *A Pluralistic Universe*, p. 248.
[2] *Studies in Humanism*, p. 64.
[3] *The Meaning of Truth*, p. 119.

great systems, they outstrip the tardy consecutions of the things themselves, and sweep us on towards our ultimate termini in a far more labour-saving way than the following of trains of sensible perception ever could.[1]

§ 104. Thus the *ratio essendi* of the concept is its utility as an instrument for the manipulation of experience. But is it a mere instrument, and is this its only function ? The pragmatist's answer to this question is not quite clear. Both Professor James and Dr. Schiller reject the copy-view of truth, and though this may be due merely to a misunderstanding, viz., to the idea that this view of truth teaches that in knowing we passively mirror reality, it *may* mean that knowledge and truth *in no way* copy or reveal the nature of reality. Professor James, at any rate, speaks of concepts not only as *Denkmittel*, but also as ' tallies,' by which we ' keep tab ' on impressions, and which he likens to the symbols of analytic geometry.[2] He also identifies them with words and images,[3] and tells us that " what the intellect knows clearly is only the word and its steering function." [4] And when we remember that we are expressly admonished to suspect common-sense notions such as 'things,' ' sameness,' ' kinds,' ' minds,' etc.,[5] and that in Radical Empiricism these notions are got rid of altogether as superfluous,[6] it would seem that the concept is, for Professor James, nothing but a

---

[1] *Ibid.*, pp. 112, 113.
[2] *Pragmatism*, pp. 171, 172.
[3] cf. § 107.
[4] *Pragmatism*, p. 185.
[5] *Ibid.*, p. 193, and cf. p. 173, for list of such notions.
[6] " A World of Pure Experience," pp. 534 *et seq.*, and cf. *A Pluralistic Universe*, pp. 290, 291.

useful symbol [1] which we substitute for immediate sense-experiences, and that thus the labour-saving function of the concept is not merely its chief, but its only function. And this view fits in admirably with the philosophy of Pure Experience and with the German philosophy with which Professor James seems to be so closely in touch. The principle of thought-economy is declared by Professor Mach to be the guiding principle of our mental life, and under different forms and various names its merits are extolled by all pragmatic philosophers. Efficiency, Avenarius says, depends upon it; and philosophy is the interpretation of the universe in accordance with it. To this principle and to no other cause is due our attempt to comprehend the many in the one, and to it is due conceptual thought,[2] of which the 'new cuts' and 'short-circuits' through which it leads us account for its high state of development among civilised nations.

§ 105. Now, in this account of the functions of conception there is much truth. Concepts *are* 'tools,' for it is by means of them that we think that we construct great systems of knowledge and that we guide our actions in practical life. Also the more complex of them are 'fashioned by our intelligence,' since they are built up only very gradually and presuppose much experience, both in the individual and in the race, and, it may be, many experiments. Again, concepts are not inaptly compared with hypotheses, for not only have they to be verified in experience, but many of them are plastic and have to be changed from time to time

---

[1] cf. *Humanism*, p. 98, note.　　[2] cf. *Pragmatism*, p. 58.

as experience compels us to adapt them to fresh 'particulars.' This, however, does not apply to all concepts, for some are so simple—*v.g.*, existence, being, reality, sameness, difference—that in the formation of the concept itself, as opposed to its application to particular instances or its relation to other concepts, no constructive activity of the intellect seems to be involved, but rather the concept, vague and undefinable as it may be, is formed directly in immediate experience by an act of intuition or apprehension.[1] This is a point on which there would seem to be a fundamental difference between Pragmatism and Realism, as there is on the question of axioms. But there are others of no less importance. Concepts are, for the most part, and must be, if valid, determined by the objects to which they refer. They are not mere symbols or tallies or names. They have, or at any rate claim to have, real significance, and their primary function is not to aid us in the manipulation of experience, but to reveal to us the nature of what we experience. Here I think that Dr. Schiller will agree with us, for he seems to admit that the end of man is knowledge as well as action, in spite of his rejection of the copy-view of truth and in spite of many assertions which seem to be incompatible with this doctrine. But about Professor James I am

---

[1] Concepts, to have meaning, must always be applicable to reality ; but simple concepts are always applicable to the objects from which they were first derived, and to all other objects like them : hence they always have meaning. Concepts constructed by a more or less arbitrary conjunction of notes, on the other hand, have to be applied *before* we can tell whether they have any real meaning, since they are not derived from immediate experience, and imply a process other than abstraction·

more doubtful. His view of the concept is frankly nominalistic. Concepts, to judge by his description of them, are nothing more than words, images, or useful symbols, the sole function of which is to lead, by continuous transitions, directly or indirectly to sense-experiences.

§ 106. In support of this view Professor James appeals to his own experience. When he thinks of Memorial Hall, his mind, he tells us, may have before it only the name, or it may have a clear image, or it may have a very dim image of the hall, but such intrinsic differences in the image make no difference to its cognitive function.[1] Apparently, therefore, Professor James is able to *think* without the aid of a concept at all. Names and images are all he requires. Yet this I can hardly believe. I do not doubt that images and names may have been used in this particular case, since Memorial Hall is a concrete thing. But surely in Professor James' mind there must have been present something more besides. I can hardly credit the statement that when the name of his favourite hall is mentioned, all that it brings before his mind is an image dim or clear, but without significance or meaning. Surely he knows full well what that name means, even though he does not allow his idea to develop in its details. Even to me, whose ideas have never terminated in a percept of Memorial Hall, it means something—a building designed and constructed by man for a definite purpose and according to a definite plan—and to Professor James, who is fully acquainted with its form, its plan and its purpose,

[1] *The Meaning of Truth*, p. 104.

it ought to mean much more. An image is not a concept, for though it may be a picture more or less detailed and precise of some particular concrete thing, it is wholly incapable of signifying that thing, except to one who has a notion of what it means, *i.e.*, to one who has, beside the image, a concept of that thing. Moreover, when clear images are in question, their very particularity and detail renders them incapable of representing many things at once, except to one who can abstract from that detail and pick out essential features common to all the objects represented, *i.e.*, to one who already has a concept of the things he wants to represent. Generic images are still more inadequate to represent a number of objects, being but a confused blur which can signify nothing in particular and might stand for anything whatsoever. A verbal image is hardly better off. As an image it stands for a word, not a thing, and its meaning, its significance and its function depend wholly upon something else, namely, upon the concept of which it is the outward expression.

§ 107. As I have already discussed the function of the concept so fully in Chapter II., it is hardly necessary to go into the matter more deeply now. Suffice it to say that the evidence of physiological as well as introspective psychology, is, as I there pointed out,[1] decidedly adverse to the Nominalism and Symbolism[2] of Professor James and other

---

[1] cf. §§ 37, 42, 45, 46.
[2] Dr. Schiller repudiates the charge of Symbolism (Cf. *Mind*, N.S. 72, p. 573) ; but, though he does not use the term 'symbol,' so far as I am aware, except in three passages (*Humanism*, p. 98, note 1 ; and pp. 122, 193), the function of a concept in

pragmatists. The laws which govern the combinations of sensory and verbal images are totally inadequate to account for the syntheses and analyses of thought. It is the higher and not the lower centres which are the conditions of thought-activity; and the intricate connections and complex organisations of these higher centres argue a proportionate instability in the direction which nervous impulses may take, an instability which, while accounting readily for the vagaries of association, cannot account for constancy of meaning and definite logical connection between thoughts. Thought, inference and meaning are something more than the psychical aspect of cerebral conditions. Trains of thought and reasoning undoubtedly depend to some extent upon, and are often facilitated, though also at times impeded, by cerebral associations, but the latter are controlled by the selective activity of thought. As Professor Stout, in his *Analytical Psychology*, has clearly proved, thought-processes cannot consist merely in the manipulation of a system of symbols. For in using symbols we think of the symbol and not of what it symbolises, whereas in thought we think of objects, not of the image or name by which they are signified. The image and the name are extrinsic to the meaning we have in mind, and it is meaning with which we are concerned in thinking proper. Words and symbols are not concepts; and to reduce the meaning (say) of Pragmatism, or Humanism to

Pragmatism certainly seems to be to symbolise reality. Cf. *The Meaning of Truth*, pp. 30, 34, 39, 43, 81, 82, where concepts are definitely spoken of as symbols, and conceptual thinking as symbolical.

sensory or verbal images is to destroy the essence
of conceptual thought, and to treat reasoning as
if it were the automatic working of a psychical
machine.

§ 108. But in Professor James' account of conception, one is struck, not only by the absence of
any adequate appreciation of 'meaning,' but also
of 'synthesis.' Concepts are merely parallel with
the experiences for which they are substituted, and
to these experiences they correspond point for point.
Their function is not to synthesise the many in the
one, but to act as a *substitute* for sense-experiences
when the latter are unavailable, and ultimately to
lead us back by continuous felt-transitions to those
same experiences. *This 'principle of substitution'*
is important in Professor James' theory of conception, and has led to a curious result. There must
always be some sense-termini, the place of which is
provisionally taken by the concept or image.
Consequently, Professor James has had to invent
felt-relations, for otherwise thought-relations would
have had no sense-experiences to which to lead.
Now, I must confess that these felt-relations seem to
me to be purely creatures of the imagination and
to have not the slightest foundation in experience.
I have never been able to *feel* a relation yet. I can
apprehend relations, I can conceive them and think
of them, but I cannot feel them. For me, what is
signified by preposition, copula and conjunction is
not a feeling, but a thought. When I see two
objects together, I do not feel their co-existence, I
perceive it and think of it or apprehend it. When
I observe that by the combination of hydrogen and

oxygen and the introduction of a little electricity,
water is produced, I do not *feel* the causal connection : rather it is the object of my thoughts. To
discover any feelings which correspond to ' buts,'
' ifs,' ' becauses,' ' betweens,' ' fors,' is, for me, quite
impossible. I admit that what is signified by
conjunctions and prepositions has foundation in
reality, but I cannot find any ' feelings ' or any
' felt ' objects to which they correspond. ' Feeling,'
it is true, may be used in a loose and metaphorical
sense to denote thought which is not clear and
precise. But ' to feel ' that our economic difficulties
in England will never be solved till we take up
Tariff Reform is quite a different thing from feeling
hot or cold or thirsty. In the latter case ' feeling '
is strictly used and signifies sense-experience : in
the former its use is metaphorical : it does not
imply sensation at all, but apprehension, conception
and thought of a most complex and abstract type,
which cannot possibly be reduced to or represented
by sensational experience. Of course, if *felt*-
relations really mean relations apprehended by
thought, there is an end of the matter ; but I do
not think Professor James can be using terms in
so loose a sense, and, besides, he would then have
a conceptual experience to which no sense-
experiences would be exactly parallel.

§ 109. The doctrine of felt-relations is applied
by Professor James to the cognitive relation itself.
In a couple of articles bearing the significant title
"A World of Pure Experience"[1] he sets forth a new

---

[1] *Journ. of Phil., Psy. and Sc. Methods*, 1904, partly reprinted
in *The Meaning of Truth*, pp. 102, *et seq.*

theory which he calls *Radical Empiricism*, the chief
theses of which are that reality is experience, or
better, perhaps, experiences, and that " the only
function that one experience can perform is to lead
to another experience." [1] The relation of the knower
to the known in this theory is but a particular case
of a felt-relation. Knowledge is a process of leading;
and " either the knower and the known are :

(1) the self-same piece of experience taken twice
over in different contexts ; or they are

(2) two pieces of *actual* experience belonging to
the same subject with definite tracts of conjunctive transitional experience between
them ; or

(3) the known is a *possible* experience, either of
that subject or of another, to which the said
conjunctive transitions *would* lead, if sufficiently prolonged." [2]

Type 1 is " the kind of knowledge called perception." For Professor James, unlike Professor
Dewey, does not wish to exclude facts from the
realm of knowledge. While present, however, all
experiences, whether perceptual or conceptual, are
' pure.' It is only afterwards that their " *naïf*
immediacy is retrospectively split into two parts." [3]
In retrospection we regard our experiences *either* as
part of our personal history, *or* as part of the
physical world ; which means that we take the
same experience twice over, each time regarding it
from a different point of view, and weaving it into
a different system of conceptual ideas.

[1] *Ibid.,* p. 111.
[2] *Ibid.,* p. 103.
[3] *Journ. of Phil., Psy. and Sc. Methods,* p. 564.

Types 2 and 3 are both conceptual experiences, and give ' knowledge about,' as opposed to knowledge of the ' acquaintance' kind, which is that of Type 1. The ' knower' in both types 2 and 3 is an image or word which leads to a sense-terminus. Should the ' knower' actually lead by definite felt-transitions to the percept that is known (type 2, and cf. the *cognitional* experience of Professor Dewey), then we feel it to have been continued in that percept, and in such a felt transition " lies all that the knowing of a percept by an idea can possibly contain or signify." [1]   It is, moreover, only when conceptual experiences do actually terminate in percepts that we can know for certain that they were truly cognitive of such percepts. Otherwise their quality of knowing can still be doubted.[2] Ideas, in this latter case, ' truncated experiences' which are never completely ' nailed down,' lead only to *possible* experiences (type 3) ; and, as a matter of fact, " the greater part of our knowing never gets beyond this virtual stage," for " to continue thinking unchallenged is, ninety-nine times out of a hundred, our practical substitute for knowing in the completest sense." [3]

§ 110. I must confess that when I first read these two articles I could not help a doubt crossing my mind in regard to authenticity. Could the writer who, in language so far removed from that of psychological description, attempts to portray

---

[1] *The Meaning of Truth*, pp. 105, 106.
[2] *Ibid.*, p. 115, but cf. *Pragmatism*, p. 214, where ' unverified' ideas are admitted to be true.
[3] *Ibid.*, p. 116.

the characteristics of human cognition, be the same as the author of the justly famous *Principles of Psychology*? What is said is said vigorously as before, but now it bears the impress of what, if I mistake not, we must describe as metaphysical prejudice. On looking back, however, I remember, even in the *Principles*, a certain empirical tendency which manifested itself, especially in that curious theory of the soul as the stream of its own thoughts, thoughts which become, as it were, little souls themselves for the moment, but only to be absorbed in the thought which succeeds. And then against my will I am forced to believe that the author of the *Principles of Psychology* and the author of the "World of Pure Experience" and similar articles are one and the same.

But is this 'Radical Empiricism' and this 'mosaic philosophy' of Pure Experience intended to be a metaphysic, or is it merely a descriptive psychology of cognition? The existence of 'felt-transitions' and 'felt-relations' is hard to recognise, and it is still harder to believe that in these alone does knowledge consist. Its transitions may be 'functional,' and the concepts from which they start may sometimes lead to sense-experiences and so serve as useful instruments for the manipulation of our future experience. But concepts, at any rate, seem to be more than mere instruments, and knowledge to be more than a mere tool. Yet in a "World of Pure Experience" knowledge is stripped of significance and meaning which is its essential note and universal characteristic. 'Objective reference' is explained as "a mere incident of the fact that so much of our experience comes as insufficient, and is of process and transition." [1] The things which we perceive and the objects about which we think are stolen away : experience is once more confused with the experienced : and the latter being relegated to a world of possibility, experience is left behind dangling in the air. This being so, Radical Empiricism can hardly be regarded as a psychological theory. Rather it would seem to be the forerunner of that metaphysic which Professor James has long promised to the philosophic world.

§ III.   The discussion of the pragmatic theory of the concept has led us away into the realm of metaphysics ; and though this is not the place to treat of Radical Empiricism in so far as it is an attempt to explain the universe, something must be said of the psychological basis of this philosophy of Pure Experience. The question turns, as it usually does, upon perception ; and though Professor James does not admit a conscious subject-object distinction in either perception or conception, it is to the latter alone that he ascribes 'objective reference,' which thus comes to mean simply a reference of our thoughts to absent objects, *i.e.*, experiences. No reason is given for this restriction of objective reference to non-perceptual cognition ; and no arguments are brought forward in support of it. Professor James imagines, I suppose, that all will recognise in what he says an accurate description of the facts. This, however, is far from being the case. To say that perception is simply experience which is retrospectively broken

[1] *Ibid.*, p. 117.

up into a dual aspect is far from satisfactory when considered in the light of introspective data. There being, however, no arguments to discuss, I can only repeat, in regard to Professor James' descriptions, what I have said before.[1] Experience and perception are always experience and perception *of something*. So deeply is the human mind convinced of this that it is embedded in the language which we use, and to this is to be attributed the strangeness with which expressions that presuppose another hypothesis, strike our ears. We never simply perceive, we always perceive an object, and, as a rule, we locate that object. For what does localisation mean if not that we distinguish that object from ourselves or identify it with ourselves, and recognise it either as part of our bodies or else as located at a certain distance from those bodies? And what, again, does this mean if not that some objects are external to ourselves and to one another? It is for the philosopher to determine what externality and objectivity mean, but he cannot get rid of the fact that in perception we perceive objects and perceive them either as external or as part of ourselves, whether or not this is reality or mere appearance.

§ 112. I cannot understand why Professor James and other pragmatists who seem to have adopted as an article of faith that Reality=Experience, should be content merely to state that 'objective reference' applies only to non-perceptual cognition. This is an assumption which is not only incompatible with the data of experience, but begs the whole question.

[1] cf. § 28.

For, granted that objective reference applies only to *absent* objects, the identification of those objects with percepts or sense-experiences, and the further identification of the latter with reality itself follows easily enough. While, on the other hand, if there is objective reference in perception, *i.e.*, if we perceive objects and do not simply experience or simply perceive, the objective reference of ideal thought will be, not to percepts or to sentient experiences, but to the objects perceived. But although English, French and German pragmatists are all inclined to treat experience and reality as convertible terms, among them I have found only one who has attempted to answer the obvious objections which may be urged against such a doctrine on the score of the introspective data of experience. That one is Professor Strong, an able ally of Professor James, and the author of '*Why the Mind has a Body*.' Realising that the rapid spread of 'the New Realism' in both England and America cannot be without significance and foundation, Professor Strong has made an attempt to appreciate the realist's position and, as far as possible, to answer his objections from the psychological point of view. And whether it is that Realism seems to the pragmatist intrinsically absurd, or whether it is that Mr. G. E. Moore in England and Dr. Montague in America are inclined to an Ultra-realism, there is no other pragmatist who can be said to have done so in any adequate way.

§ 113. In an article entitled "The Distinction of Object and Perception,"[1] Professor Strong thus states

[1] Discussion : " Idealism and Realism," *Journ. Phil., Psy. and Sc. Methods*, 1904, pp. 543, etc.

and provisionally answers what he considers to be
the essence of the realist's position. The realist
maintains that the distinction between physical
objects and our consciousness of them are ' two
separate things,' not merely ' two different ways of
regarding the same thing ; ' and is supposed to
urge this point by affirming that we must separate
the quality ' red ' from the sensation of red that
is aware of it, the perception of a tri-dimensional
book from the book itself.[1]

This [says Professor Strong] I have never been able
to do. I quite appreciate that the *conception* of a
quality is a different thing from the *conception* of a
sensation, but it has always seemed to me that what we
conceive in these two ways is the same identical *fact*. *I
can not detect over and above the quality ' red,' any
sensation or consciousness or subject that contemplates
or has it ; but it seems to me that the luminous existence
of that red is the full account of the fact.* Nor can I detect
any perception (though I can detect a certain amount
of thought) over and above the given book. The givenness appears to me to be an inseparable character of
the book, without which it could not exist at all. When
I say, then, that the very same fact or experience can
be thought of in two ways, either as an episode in my
personal history, or as a constituent of a vast continuous
physical world the other part of which I only conceive,
it seems to me that I am giving an account of the
distinction which is idealistic, no doubt, but which
differs from the realistic account in being accurately
true to the facts.[2]

§ 114. Professor Strong, upon reflection, has
come to the conclusion that this is not a sufficient
answer to the realist's difficulties, and proceeds to
make further concessions and distinctions which I

[1] *Ibid.*, p. 547.   [2] *loc. cit.*, p. 547.

M

shall discuss in a moment. But the above answer can hardly be allowed to pass without some comment. In the first place, Professor Strong's appreciation of the realistic position is not so adequate as one might have hoped. The realist does maintain that physical objects are distinct from our consciousness of them. He may also maintain, as I have done, that sometimes, if not always, we are aware of this distinction ; and in doing so he would not be going so far as many idealists who affirm that "we are conscious of objects only in so far as we are self-conscious—a statement which, if taken literally, is incompatible with a fact which the realist fully admits, viz., the fact that self-consciousness and the consciousness of objects usually vary in inverse proportion." Again, it is a fundamental doctrine in Realism that the quality ' red ' is distinct from the sensation by which it is perceived, but few, if any, realists would assert that *in the act of perception this was an introspective fact*.[1] In introspection there is *foundation* for such a distinction, but it is not itself a datum of experience. ' Consciousness ' must not be confused with ' sensation ;' for clearly all consciousness is not sensation. To affirm that what we perceive in external perception is an object distinct from ourselves is not the same thing as to affirm that we perceive it by means of sensation. That sensation is present at all in external perception is known, not directly in the acts of perception, but by inference based upon the gradation between what is perceived as sensation and what is perceived as

[1] cf. § 28,

the quality of an object, and in particular upon cases in which perception may take either form, though never both at once.[1]

§ 115. Are not these data, however, more consistent with the *id quod percipitur* theory of Professor Strong than with the *id quo percipitur* theory of the realist, since it is admitted that sensation sometimes is *id quod percipitur* ? On the contrary, for, while the realist is able to explain the ' how ' of perception (as I shall have occasion to show later on) [2] by his theory that sensation is always *id quo percipitur*, he does not contradict any facts, since he allows that sensation may *also* be, and is, at times, *id quod percipitur*. The idealist, on the other hand, when he asserts that what he perceives is always at bottom a sensation, while explaining nothing at all so far as perception is concerned (since he merely affirms it to be experience) finds himself at once in contradiction with the belief which external perception itself has engendered, namely, that what is perceived in the act of external perception is *not* sensation, but the quality of an object. If physical objects and consciousness (inclusive here of sensation) are not distinct, but merely different aspects of the self-same thing, how comes it about that they appear to be both distinct and different, and are firmly believed so to be by the ordinary man ? How, again, are we to explain the fact that the *conception* of a quality and the *conception* of a sensation are different concepts, if the object conceived in both cases is the same ? Surely there must be some foundation for this

[1] cf. §§ 35, 36.　　　　[2] cf. chap. xiv.

distinction *a parte rei*, for even pragmatic concepts 'correspond' in some sense with their objects. Again, the 'givenness' of what we perceive, what is this, and what does it imply, but some kind of object that 'gives' and which is, therefore, distinct from him to whom it gives? And the 'thought' which Professor Strong detects in perception " over and above the given book," what is this but some kind of self-consciousness which is present, so he would seem to say, in the act of perception itself?

Until these difficulties have been solved, I cannot agree with Professor Strong that " the idealist's account of perception differs from the realist's in being accurately true to the facts." Both accounts belong to theory, but it is the realistic and not the idealistic theory which is at once consistent with and explanatory of the facts.

§ 116. As I have already remarked, however, Professor Strong does not consider that in the passage quoted above he has conceded " to the realist all that he has a right to demand, or, at least," he says, "it does not adequately meet the difficulty in the idealist's position which he feels." Accordingly, he proceeds to grant to us that " thought enters into our perception of objects," and that " *thought* always has an object distinct from itself " (though the latter concession is qualified by the remark that " there is no corresponding principle applying to sensation"). Then comes a distinction.

The realist is therefore so far in the right. But it remains to be determined *in what shape* matter exists independently of the thought of it. Realists jump to the conclusion that it exists as matter-stuff, that their realism is naïve. This in no way necessarily follows from the admission of its independent existence, but the mode of existence still remains to be determined. . . . Realists assume that there is a contradiction between objects being material and independent of thought, and their being composed of sensation ; and they assume this *because they confuse independence of thought with independence of mind.* Now, if it were possible for us to know that objects exist whether perceived or not, we might know them to be independent of the mind, and they could not then be composed of sensation. As it is, we only know them to be independent of thought, and this is perfectly consistent with their being composed of it.[1]

Hence the final conclusion,

thought has an object distinct from itself, but it does not present its object to us as (real) and present ; while sensation presents to us an object that is real and present, but that object is not distinct from the sensation ; [2] . . . . The difficulty between idealists and realists is, therefore, solved in holding that *matter exists independently of the thought of it, but exists in the shape of sensation.*[3]

§ 117. *This* solution of the controversy between idealists and realists will not, I fear, put an end to the strife, for the conclusion at which Professor Strong arrives is neither satisfactory nor logically convincing. ' In perception both thought and sensation are involved, but while thought has an object distinct from itself, sensation has not that good fortune.' Is this an introspective fact or is it a theoretical assumption ? Are we directly conscious of the functioning of either thought or sensation in perception ? Are not both inferences

---

[1] *loc. cit.,* p. 549. (Italics mine.)   [2] *Ibid.*   [3] *Ibid.,* p. 550.

based on the dual fact that we not only perceive
colours and sounds, which *for the psychologist* are
sensations, but also things possessing qualities,
which again for the psychologist implies conception
or apprehension ?   Again, can we distinguish introspectively between sensation and thought in
perception ?   Do they not function together in one
and the self-same act which is directed to one and the
self-same object ?   Psychologically, we may make
the distinction, and it has good foundation.   But if
we separate the two and take sensation by itself,
we no longer have perception.   There can be no
question of sensation having an object external to
itself, if taken in isolation or in abstraction from
perception and thought.   It is only when sensation
functions in perception as the means by which we
apprehend objective qualities, that it can in any
sense be said to have an object, and even then, the
object is not, strictly speaking, an object for sensation, but for perception or for thought with which
sensation functions as a necessary though subordinate factor.

§ 118.   Is there, then, a contradiction in saying
that objects are independent of thought, and yet
are composed of sensation ?   And does the realist,
when he affirms that there is, confuse independence
of thought with independence of mind ?   If by
' mind ' is here meant the mind of the percipient,
and by ' sensation,' sensation which takes place
within the mind (and this is the obvious sense),
there is certainly a contradiction between theory
and fact ; the object of external perception does not
appear to be a sensation, still less a sensation in the

mind of the percipient, but something objective, distinct, external and in no way part of himself. There is no intrinsic contradiction, however, in the statement that the objects of perception are sensations, for we do perceive our own sensations at times. But, if the *normal* object of perception is sensation, perception is an illusion, since what is perceived does not ordinarily appear as a sensation, but as something quite different ; and that it is an illusion is a mere assumption, at once unnecessary and inexplicable. Because the object of perception is *independent* of thought, it does not necessarily follow that it is independent of mind ; but if it is not only independent of thought but also *external* to thought, it must also be external to mind, since mind and thought are one and indivisible ; and, as a matter of fact, it appears to be external to both. In reply, then, to Professor Strong's summing up, I must make several distinctions. That ' thought has an object distinct from itself ' is clear ; but that ' it does not present its object as (real) and present ' I cannot admit ; for in perception the object of thought is both real and present, and though in thought of absent objects the object is obviously not present (*i.e.*, to the senses), it is at any rate real. Again, ' that sensation presents to us an object that is real and present ' is also clear, if sensation here means perception, for sensation of itself does not present an object at all ; but that ' the object (of perception) is not distinct from sensation,' I can in no wise grant, nor has Professor Strong in any way proved that it is.

§ 119. There remains, however, one argument which we have not yet discussed, and though, strictly speaking, it is a metaphysical argument, it will be more convenient to discuss it here. The realist, says Professor Strong, cannot prove the *continuous existence* of material objects when not perceived ; all the knowledge he can legitimately derive from experience is the knowledge of their continuous perceptibility. But, surely, perceptibility cannot exist of itself. To be able *to be perceived* requires a ground and a subject quite as much as to be able *to perceive*. It is not something that hangs loose or is to be found standing on its own legs. Hence, if the *continuous perceptibility* of material objects may be legitimately inferred from the data of experience, the further inference as to their existence would also seem to be legitimate. If material objects are always *perceptible* by existing minds, they cannot belong to the realm of *mere* possibles, but must belong to some existing order of beings, otherwise their perceptibility would be unaccountable, except by a *deus ex machina*. In some way or other their perceptibility implies existence. Hence, either they exist in themselves, or they exist as ' the possibility of sensation ' inherent in the percipient mind. There seems to be no other alternative ; and if, with Mill, we choose the latter we are at once involved in all the difficulties of Subjective Idealism ; the appearance of external reality is declared to be an illusion, and the intercommunication of mind and mind becomes an inexplicable mystery. Again, belief in the existence of an external world which is at once distinct from and independent of ourselves is unquestionably a fact, yet if this belief is illusory its origin becomes inexplicable. Doubtless, the psychological antece-dents of such a belief can, to some extent, be traced, but, as Professor Wundt has pointed out, " in the syntheses of perception properties are found which are not found in its elements or antecedents." [1] The external world in which we believe cannot, therefore, be identified with sensation, because our belief in it arises from sense-experience, for the effect is not only in excess of the cause, but cause and effect would, in that case, be contradictory ; nor can it be argued that all we may legitimately infer from the data of experience is the continual perceptibility of external objects, for continual perceptibility implies something that is continually perceptible. The existence of the external world is presupposed as the condition of our perception of it, and that world does not consist of sensations ; though whether it is material, and, if so, in what sense, is another question, which belongs, not to epistemology, but to metaphysics

CHAPTER VII.

GENETIC PSYCHOLOGY AND THE FACULTIES.

§ 120. Origin, genesis and growth are ideas of primary importance to-day. Evolutionary notions pervade our philosophy and bid fair to drive out the static analyses of traditional methods. To under-stand anything whatsoever nowadays, we think it

[1] cf. §§ 53 to 56, and §§ 98, 99.

necessary to study it in its origin and growth. We are no longer content to take things as they are, we desire above all things else to know how they became ; and unless we know this our knowledge is looked upon with unconcealed suspicion. Historical interpretations are prevalent in every realm of thought, to which the theory of knowledge, and in particular the pragmatic theory of knowledge, is no exception. Thus man is regarded as essentially and above all things else the product of an evolutionary process. He started at the level of dull and undifferentiated sentience, and from this state of uninteresting uniformity have been evolved his so-called faculties. Emotion, volition, and cognition have all arisen by a process of differentiation from a common ground. They are not really distinct. In fact, " all three ' faculties ' are at bottom only labels for describing the activities of what may be called indifferently a unitary personality, or a reacting organism."

§ 121. Doubtless, analytic psychology is inclined at times to carry its analyses too far, and in consequence seems almost to treat the human mind as if it were a bundle of faculties each independent and distinct. Kant, for instance, in his desire to bring together the transcendental unity of apperception and the manifold of sense, freely multiplied human powers of knowing, and marked off the function of inner and outer sense, of imagination, of understanding, of practical and theoretical reason, and of will with such absolute precision that the unity of man seemed lost in the multifarious details of his differences. In contrast with an exaggerated faculty-psychology of this kind the stress which is laid on the unitary character of human personality in Humanism, in Personal Idealism, and more notably still in the psychology of M. Bergson, stands out all the more clearly, and, as an antidote, may serve a useful purpose.

As Dr. Schiller remarks, however, ' attempts at unification are not new.' There has always been a protest against the disintegrating tendencies of Kantian psychology. Kant himself suggested that " the two stems of human knowledge, sensibility and understanding, may perhaps have a common but unknown root ; " and Hegel, too, declared that

the chief aim of a philosophy of mind can only be to re-introduce unity of idea and of principle into the theory of mind. . . . Our sense of the mind's living unity [he says] naturally protests against any attempt to break it up into different faculties, forces, or what comes to the same thing, activities conceived as independent of each other.[1]

§ 122. The notion of independence, true of the faculties as of everything else in its proper degree, may be, and often has been, carried too far. The fact is that there are different kinds of independence, and whereas in regard to the faculties some must be denied, others may be rightly asserted. The faculties are not independent in regard to their ultimate principle. They all belong to and qualify our personality and essential nature. Nor are they independent in the sense that they do not mutually influence one another and work toward a common end. But we recognise introspectively that con-

[1] Hegel, *Phil. of Mind* (Wallace trans.), § 379.

scious processes or activities differ in kind. To feel is not to think, to think is not to will, and to will is not to act. Considered, therefore, as the proximate ground of different mental activities, the faculties are distinct. Moreover, in different psychoses or states of mind, cognition, conation and mere feeling are present in different degrees, and this, as Dr. Stout says in his *Analytic Psychology*, argues a certain kind of independence. Indeed, the very fact that we can speak intelligibly of our emotions controlling our will, or of purpose and volition influencing belief, shows that there is between emotion, volition and belief a difference and also a certain degree of independence as well as inter-dependence. Hence our psychological distinctions cannot be classed as mere ' labels.'

§ 123. A psychology, therefore, which ignores or minimises distinctions is as false as one that exaggerates them or makes them absolute. Nay, of the two, the former error is far more serious in its consequences. A careful analysis of data and a careful distinction in the use of terms is essential to the advance of science and philosophy. Without it classification becomes impossible ; and on classification theory is based. A psychology which obliterates distinctions destroys the very source of knowledge, and leads, not only to laxity of speech, but also to laxity of thought. Terms are used first in one sense and then in another, and theories are founded on the ambiguity which ensues. The result is that often enough a writer so unsystematic does not know himself precisely what he means, and is quite incapable of conveying his meaning to anybody else. Without precision and accuracy intelligible discourse is impossible. And principles, pragmatic or otherwise, which encourage the adoption of a large and loose terminology can only end in hopeless confusion and misunderstanding.

Moreover, as distinctions grow fainter and differences get blurred, it becomes more and more impossible to maintain the balance of power, so to speak, between the faculties. One or other of them is sure to be made supreme, while the rest sink into obscurity. This tendency is well-illustrated in the Hegelian and Neo-Hegelian development of Criticism, in which Monism led first to an identification of other forms of consciousness with thought, and then to the substitution of thought for consciousness in general. True, the monistic idealist points out now and then that ' thought ' embraces something other than thought. Green, for instance, observes that " if thought and reality are identified, thought must be other than discursive activity, other than the particular mode of consciousness which excludes from itself feeling and will." Yet the fact remains that in the metaphysical logics of Absolutism the idea of will is, as a rule, obscured by that of the constructive and formal activity of Thought, and to it no distinctive or adequate function is assigned in the ideal history of the universe.

§ 124. Pragmatism, owing chiefly to its fondness for a genetic psychology, though, in part, also to the philosophy of Pure Experience by which its psychology is supplemented, affords but another illustration of the disastrous consequences of minimising the distinction between the faculties.

As the Hegelian subordinates the will to the intellect, so the pragmatist subordinates the intellect to the will and to the emotions. It is in the strivings of our will and in the vague and quasi-hedonistic impulses of our emotional nature that the nature of man is revealed ; and it is in the satisfaction of these rather than in the satisfaction of intellectual demands that the criteria of truth are to be found. Purposes, expressive largely of emotional needs, dominate all cognition. It is impossible to abstract from them. Cognition without them is a mutilated fragment of mind.

There is no ' pure ' intellect. If ' pure ' intellect does not imply a gross psychological blunder, and this is probably what was too often meant until the conception was challenged, it means an abstraction, an intellect conceived as devoid of function, as not applied to any actual problem, as satisfying no purpose.[1]

Reason is not a faculty. It stands for a group of habits which men (and to some extent animals) have acquired, and which we find extremely useful, nay necessary, for the successful carrying on of life. Among these habits may be mentioned that of inhibiting reaction upon stimulation, *i.e.*, of checking our natural and instinctive tendencies to react, until we have reflected precisely what it is we are dealing with. To determine this latter point we have developed the habit of *analysis*, *i.e.*, of breaking up the confused complex of presentations into ' things ' and their ' attributes,' which are referred to and identified with former similar experiences, and expressed in judgments as to what the situation really is. This enables us to re-arrange the presented connections of attributions, and the whole reasoning process finds its natural issue and test in an action which modifies and beneficially innovates upon the original habit of reaction.[2]

---

[1] *Studies in Humanism,* p. 7.   [2] *Ibid.,* p. 356,

Reason is thus reduced to the common denominator of a couple of habits, only one of which is in any way cognitive (*viz.*, the analysis and rearrangement of presentation), the other being volitional, if not merely physiological. True, Dr. Schiller allows that reasoning may enter into a rational act, and in the next paragraph mentions that thinking or judging, which is one of the habits that make up man's reason, involves the use of concepts, and depends ultimately upon axiomatic principles, which he prefers to call postulates; so that his account of ' reason,' if more fully developed, *might* be made acceptable, even to the ' rationalists.' Still, the haphazard way in which this 'analysis of reason' is carried out, the inclusion of a function which *per se* is certainly not rational in nature, and the substitution of the term ' bundle of habits ' for the time-honoured term ' faculty '—a substitution which is not explained, though it certainly does not suggest the unity and personal character of man—make Dr. Schiller's account of ' reason ' far from satisfactory, especially if we bear in mind that it is an attempt to remedy previous accounts which have hitherto not been conceived with sufficient precision for scientific purposes.

§ 125. Professor James' account of conception also illustrates the baneful influence which an evolutionary pragmatism may have upon psychology. We saw in the last chapter how the concept is reduced to a symbol or an image devoid of meaning and significance; how its contents are made to consist of reactions or practical effects, all of them sensational in nature; how its objective reference is explained, not as a reference to an external and real world, the nature of which it, to some extent, reveals, but as an accident due to the fact that it is prevented from leading us back to the sense-experience for which it stands an inadequate substitute. And, doubtless, there is an element of truth in all this. Thought sometimes does involve images. Concepts are frequently not adequate, and may be at times even symbolic. Knowledge *is* derived ultimately from sense-experience; and our state of mind when we think of absent objects is not the same as when they are present. But when the pragmatist gets hold of a truth like this he spoils it by exaggerating it, generalising it, or insisting on it to the exclusion of all other truths with which it is connected and apart from which it cannot be rightly understood. Recognising that all knowledge is ultimately derived from experience, he infers quite illogically that everything that we know we must be able to feel, and so is led on to invent what he calls felt-relations. Finding that many scientific concepts are more or less symbolic and do not correspond strictly and fully with reality, he generalises this and affirms that all concepts are symbolic. Finding, again, that images and words are used in conceptual thought, he identifies them with the concept itself, and so destroys, or at least is unable to explain their significance, from which he proceeds to the denial of their objective validity. Observing, too, that the content of the concept can sometimes be expressed in terms of sense-perception, he infers that it can always be so expressed, and, hence, affirms that concepts which do not lead back to a percept are no concepts at all, but merely words. And, lastly, the unquestionable truth that concepts are useful and that they serve admirably as instruments by means of which scientists and others are able to secure the control of experience and so promote the advance of civilisation serves only as a pretext for denying that concepts are anything more than instruments, in spite of the fact that their instrumental value depends upon the knowledge they give us of our environment.

§ 126. To judge of everything according to its antecedents, real or imaginary, regardless of the fact that these antecedents may in no way account for, still less be equivalent to, the phenomena to which they give place, must of necessity lead to a theory wholly inadequate if offered as an explanation of the data of actual experience. Yet it is precisely this genetic standpoint which is largely responsible for the symbolic concepts and the emaciated intellect of the pragmatist, as it is responsible for the doctrine of postulation and experiment, which lies at the root of the evil, and which is, as we have seen, in its universal form only another example of illicit generalisation. And it is this same genetic standpoint which accounts for the predominant influence assigned to purpose, which, as better expressing Will and the active side of our nature, has, in Pragmatism, almost completely supplanted the intellect.

Again it is an indisputable fact upon which the pragmatist rests : purpose does play a most important part in the intricate processes of thought-activity. But, as usual, truth is exaggerated. Purpose does not permeate cognition through and

N

through. Its influence is not universal, but is restricted, for the most part, to the intent of thought. Thought's content, when our thinking is accurate and honest, is determined, not by purpose, but by the objects about which we think—objects which otherwise could never be known. Our very purposes themselves, need-expressive as they are, are defined and made precise by the objects with which we have to deal. Nor do the emotions, so closely connected with and dependent upon our purposes and needs, affect directly the content of thought as a rule. Their influence is indirect. Satisfaction and dissatisfaction, interest, monotony, disgust, influence belief by intensifying or inhibiting thought-activity, by keeping it fixed on certain objects or by directing it into other channels. Even when the 'will to believe,' *i.e.*, the emotional satisfaction and volitional striving arising from the contemplation of a proposition as true, seems to be the immediate cause of belief, it never of itself effects a modification in the content of thought, but causes assent to be given without *sufficient* evidence. And here, again, though emotion may influence assent directly, more often than not it does so indirectly by preventing thought from dwelling on those aspects of a problem which are likely to hinder assent or lead to an opposite belief. Satisfaction, moreover, seldom forms part of the purpose which we deliberately strive to realise. On the contrary, the honest enquirer does his best to exclude such subjective influences, and, ordinarily, his efforts are not without success.

§ 127. The *Princip der Denkökonomie* expresses

another human need, the influence of which is much exaggerated by Professor Mach and others. Doubtless, simplicity and unity have a fascination for every thinking mind, but I can hardly believe that the aim of thought is to save ourselves the trouble of thinking any more than we can help, which is practically what the principle of Thought-Economy or Least (mental) Energy amounts to. Thought is itself a pleasure, and the desire to take short cuts in order to bring our journey to an early close, is considerably modified by the pleasures which we meet with by the way, and still more so by the fear that a conclusion too rapidly drawn may be premature and false. Simple hypotheses are preferable, other conditions being the same, not so much because they economise thought, as because a simple hypothesis seems to be more ultimate and to imply that analysis has gone further than in one that is more complex. No one, however, would adopt a hypothesis, however simple, unless there seemed a fair chance of its verification, or, if sincere in his search for truth, would hesitate to reject it were it found to be incompatible with fact. The principle of Thought-Economy is of practically no importance as a criterion of truth ; and, if admitted, is liable to lead to careless inferences and illicit induction. It is said that the power of generalising is an instance of this principle at work; and certainly it may afford an excellent example of its abuse. But there is no proof whatever that universal concepts are due solely to the influence of this principle. Indeed, if they are, the objective validity of subsumption is destroyed ; and, since all knowledge implies universals, it would be advisable to give up the attempt to acquire it and to devote ourselves instead to some more useful occupation.

Considerations such as these the pragmatist is apt to forget. As usual, he has got hold of principles which are true if kept within their proper bounds, and, as usual, so delighted is he at having rediscovered them that he must needs make them universal and apply them to everything upon which he can lay his hands. Just as he reduces everything to sense-experience and explains away conception, and turns the intellect into a machine for the manufacture of meaningless symbols,[1] so now he generalises the influence of purposes, of needs, and of thought-economy regardless of consequences. And, consciously or unconsciously, that which has led him astray is his genetic psychology and the evolutionary principles which are its real foundation. ' Pure ' experience, symbolic concepts, postulation and experiment, a mechanical intellect, purposes, needs and emotional strivings all form part of an evolutionary apparatus. Yet even as an evolutionist, the pragmatist, as we shall see, is not consistent.

§ 128. No one, of course, can rationally object to the study of knowledge from the dynamic or evolutionary point of view, provided the method of study be sound. Some form of development has always been admitted in knowledge. Indeed, the

---

[1] Symbols doubtless have meaning in the pragmatic sense of ' leading to,' or ' working harmoniously with,' reality, but not in the realist's sense of signifying the nature of something real.

transcendental Hegel was a leader in this matter. But if we are to treat knowledge dynamically and to take its development and past history into account, we must select a method by which to proceed ; and our choice in this matter is practically restricted to two alternatives. In general, we must either interpret the past by means of the present, or interpret the present by means of the past. Indirectly the two methods are supplementary ; [1] but as methodological principles they are opposed, and the validity of our conclusions will depend to a large extent upon which principle or method we regard as primary.

Dr. Schiller's first work was a philosophy of evolution,[2] and in it his views or methods were expressed at some length. The ' epistemological ' method he rejects, because it takes no account of evolution. It treats mind, he says, as " a fixed product that can be exhaustively analysed instead of an organically living and developing growth." [3] The ' psychological ' method is dismissed for a similar reason. It studies the actual conditions and laws which govern the human mind as at present constituted ; " whereas the human mind has a history." [4] Two methods remain, the ' historical ' and the ' teleological,' and between them Dr. Schiller has no hesitation in making a choice. He selects the teleological method, and rejects the

---

[1] By this I mean that knowledge of the past may throw light upon our knowledge of the present, as well as *vice versa :* but this use of the historical principle is indirect, since it presupposes that the past has been rightly interpreted.

[2] Entitled *Riddles of the Sphinx.*

[3] *Ibid.,* p. 148.   [4] *Ibid.,* p. 149.

historical, because the latter "supposes that the cause and explanation of a thing is to be found in its past." [1]

This choice is significant. Teleology seeks to explain not by an appeal to past history, but by an appeal to ideals. Lower forms reveal themselves only as they develop; but their *ratio essendi* is to be learned not by looking back, but by looking forward to the higher end toward which they are continuously tending. The past is but the prelude to the future, and only by a study of the future can we hope to understand the past.

§ 129. Here, however, we meet with a difficulty. Future developments and higher forms not yet realised are in themselves unknown. The future, like the past, is an inference drawn from what we know of the present. For this reason Dr. Caird regards the teleological method as essentially 'heuristic.'

All that we can do [he says] is to use the principle that everything has an end or purpose, as suggesting continual enquiries into the relations of the pasts of organisms to each other; and in a secondary way, into the relations of different organisms to each other, and of the organic world to the inorganic. [2]

In this passage the value of teleology seems to me to be somewhat under-rated; but at any rate this is true, that we have no direct knowledge of the future, but can only conjecture what human nature will become by an analytic study of what it is, by a consideration of the progress that has

[1] *Ibid.,* p. 174.
[2] *The Critical Philosophy of Kant,* vol. ii., p. 449.

actually been made, and by a study of ideals and purposes which we set before our minds, and which, prompted by deep-felt needs, we ever strive to realise.

Dr. Schiller is right, then, in saying that lower forms are intelligible only in reference to higher, and that in consequence human nature must be interpreted not historically, but teleologically. Unfortunately, however, he seems at times to forget that the teleological method *presupposes* the psychological, and that in order to know what we were in the past or what we shall be in the future, we must first know, and know well what we *are*. And what is still more unfortunate, in practice Dr. Schiller does not use either the psychological or the teleological method, but that very historical method which he has expressly declared to be fallacious ; and in this he is at one with all pragmatists. Pragmatism is, as Mr. J. M. Baldwin has defined it, " an attempt to construe all reality retrospectively ; " and to this source must be attributed the psychological and epistemological errors which I have enumerated above.

§ 130. The connection of the Postulatory or Experimental Theory of Knowledge with the doctrine of Evolution is obvious. In evolution all psychological changes take the form of what Avenarius has called 'a vital series,' which may be represented physiologically by *disturbance of equilibrium—action—restoration of equilibrium in a modified form*, psychologically by *impulse—striving —satisfaction ;* and in the cognitive order by *postulation — experiment — verified truth.* Now in endeavouring to force axioms into conformity with this hypothetical type of cognitive process, Dr. Schiller, instead of taking axioms for what they are and working backwards, so to speak, begins by assuming that they originated as postulates, and working forwards on these lines, ends by denying that they are axioms at all. His explanation is not teleological but historical. Axioms are not represented as something of a higher nature than mere postulates, but are transformed into postulates which custom and human forgetfulness have permitted to acquire an illusory axiomatic appearance. It is the intuitionist who really explains axioms teleologically ; for he first enquires what axioms are, and what is their function in knowledge, and finding that they are now self-evident and that they serve human purposes better as self-evident truths than as postulates, he is careful in tracing their history not to assign them an origin incompatible with their present ' higher ' form or their present useful function. Axioms were always axioms, but they have had a history because, though implicitly understood and used in all human thought, many attempts have been made to formulate them, and these attempts have not always met with equal success. The pragmatist is hopelessly inconsistent here. His actual method and his methodological principles are in direct contradiction. He lays down as a principle that the lower must be interpreted in the light of the higher. He examines human cognition as it at present exists, and finds that much knowledge is acquired by means of postulation and experiment. So far, so good. But, instead of proceeding with his examination of other 'higher' forms of cognition of which we have direct knowledge in our present experience, he forthwith casts psychology to the winds, and generalising his doctrine of postulation, proceeds to trace the history of knowledge by the aid of this one-sided and partial truth. The result is that the existence of universal and necessary truths is declared to be an illusion, and thus, finding himself in contradiction with the fact that in our experience we recognise such truths, the pragmatist is forced to re-interpret them in a strained, unnatural and 'lower' sense.

§ 131. Let us take as another illustration of the pragmatic attempt to square philosophy with evolution, *viz.*, the doctrine that all knowledge is ultimately reducible to sense-experience, in place of which conceptual thought has substituted images, dim or clear, symbols or words. What has happened? Convinced that the human mind has had a history and has been evolved from some lower form of life, the pragmatist does not study the higher forms of cognition which at present exist, and so discover the presuppositions without which, whatever their origin, present forms could never have come to exist. All he does is to seek about in our experience for some trace of a *lowest* form from which by the aid of a powerful imagination he can *suppose* the rest to have been evolved. And he discovers sentience, or what he calls 'pure experience.' Then, gratuitously assuming that with this the human mind did *de facto* start, he goes on to trace its development, and to show what, on this assumption, conception and intellectual activity really *must* be. Granting him his premises, and the validity of his method, the conclusion he draws is logical enough : concepts cannot be more than images, or, as Hume said, ' faint copies of sensation,' and intellect cannot be other than the habit we have acquired, of substituting these pseudo-concepts for the sense-termini to which they refer. But once again, as a consequence of his method, the pragmatist finds himself in violent contradiction with the facts.

§ 132. This loose and inconsistent psychology is in marked contrast with the careful analysis of Cognition which underlies the Critical Method of Kant. Whatever we may think of the metaphysical conclusions to which that method has led, it began where a true philosophy must always begin—with a study of man as he is. Kant's psychology, when compared with that of the pragmatist, is accurate and precise. He draws a careful distinction between faculty and faculty, function and function. He does not confuse sense and imagination with intellect, or intellect with will. He points out—what the pragmatists are apt to forget—that sensation, in abstraction from the synthetic activity of thought, can give us little more than a series[1] of spatially extended impressions, without unity and without meaning. He recognises that intellect is essential to knowledge : without it, we may have pictures and images, but no cognition either of objects or of their relations. Yet Kant, in spite of his Apriorism, finds room for experience, and insists upon the

[1] A *series* of impressions, *i.e.*, in the sense that the continuity of sentient experience is broken up by the focussing of attention first on one object, then on another.

necessity of ' mediation by experience ' almost as much as the pragmatist himself. Aristotle is more emphatic still. For him, as for Kant, experience is necessary as the condition of thought ; sensation as the means by which thought is brought into contact with reality; while imagination also is admitted as in some sense preparing the way for the syntheses of conception and judgment. But for Aristotle all knowledge is derived from experience, and the knowledge that is so derived is not phenomenal merely, but real. He, too, however, like Kant, affirms that intellectual activity is essential to knowledge, and that without it sensations and images have no significance at all. Truth and falsity do not belong to sensation at all ; for whether an object is present or not, it is only by thinking about it that it comes to have meaning for us.

§ 133. Thus it is in Pragmatism alone, except for an antiquated Empiricism of which it is the latest development, that the function of the intellect is confused in a most un-psychological fashion with the totally different function of volition and sense. Volition, sensation and intellect combine to give us knowledge, but, as Kant says, " because knowledge arises from their united action, this is no reason for confusing the function of one with that of the other." And from this confusion, what does the pragmatist hope to attain ? His aim would seem to be to get a theory of knowledge which shall be consistent with the theory of evolution. Yet even here he fails ; for if thought is simply an economic process, by means of which we seek to adapt

ourselves to our environment, it should, according
to the general law of organic life, tend to become
unconscious in proportion as it has secured that
end, and, as a habit, has become fixed. This,
however, is not the case. Axioms and other habits
of thought, though constant, show no sign of
becoming unconscious. Hence, even on evolutionary principles, the pragmatic account of knowledge breaks down. True, " the progress of action
causes the progress also of thought, as the progress
of thought conditions and determines the progress
of action : " but if the function of thought is *merely*
to determine the progress of action; if, in essence,
it is symbolised sentience and its only function is
to 'lead' thereto ; if, as M. Blondel says, it is but
a 'moment in the general dynamic of life';[1] its
present form, its distinctive features, the consciousness which still attends the most stable of its habits,
becomes a mystery, for it is something wholly
incompatible with the origin assigned.

§ 134. Failure, inconsistency, illicit generalisation, one-sided emphases, conclusions only partially
worked out, meet us everywhere in the pragmatic
Theory of Knowledge ; and the explanation of this
is to be found in the 'thoroughly-genetic psychology' which Pragmatism is determined to secure
regardless of the cost. What the late Dr. Caird
has said of the prevailing method of 'explaining the
world' aptly describes the attitude of Pragmatism
in regard to knowledge. It is " an attempt to level
downwards," *i.e.*, to take the lowest forms (of

[1] Appendix to the *Bulletin de la Société de Philosophie*,
1901–2, p. 190.

thought) as the explanation of those that stand higher in the scale.[1] The true method, on the other hand, recognises that we cannot interpret " even the lowest existence in the world . . . except on principles which are adequate to explain the highest. We must ' level up,' not ' level down.' " [2] We must explain by means of "*le principe supérieur qui en se réalisant suscite les conditions de sa réalisation, que c'est la forme elle-même qui façonne la matière à son usage.*" [3] Yet so eager is the pragmatist in his desire to explain origin and to trace development, that true methods are thrown to the winds. He admits that the teleological method is the true one, that we must ' explain the lower as an imperfect realisation of the higher ' and not explain the higher as a development from what we *imagine* the lower to have been. He acknowledges the necessity of analysing our experience as it is, allowing that " as we ourselves are the highest examples of individuals we know, it is only in exploring the depths of our own nature that the clue to the riddle of the world is to be sought." [4] But when he comes to practical work, he cannot waste time on analytic psychology or on a study of human ideals. Validity is of little consequence, provided origin can be assigned. And should an adversary venture to criticise results or to indicate the illogical character of each procedure, he exposes himself to an onslaught almost mediæval in its fury and in the brilliancy of the epithets bestowed.

[1] *Critical Philosophy of Kant,* vol. i., p. 34.
[2] *Ibid.,* p. 35.
[3] Boutroux, *De l'idée de loi naturelle.*
[4] *Riddles of the Sphinx,* p. 240.

Indeed, to such a pass have matters come of late, that the venerable Peirce, the reputed father of all pragmatists, disgusted with such methods, has felt constrained to disown his own children. Writing in a recent number of the *Hibbert Journal*,[1] he says, "Their avowedly undefinable position, if it be not capable of logical characterisation, seems to me to be characterised by an angry hatred of strict logic, and even some disposition to rate any exact thought which interferes with it as all humbug."[2]

So long as such a practice prevails, it is impossible to hope for satisfactory results from the pragmatist ; and I think we shall find that in the more serious sphere of Metaphysics and of Truth pragmatic methods have not been conducive to the growth of sound philosophy.

[1] October, 1908, p. 112.
[2] Dr. Schiller repudiates the 'paternity' of Peirce, and rightly so, I think, at any rate, so far as Humanism is concerned. All Peirce did was to suggest the general idea of the Pragmatic Method. (Cf. *Pragmatism*, p. 46.)

PART II.

THE METAPHYSICAL CONDITIONS OF KNOWLEDGE.

CHAPTER VIII.

APRIORISM AND ABSOLUTISM.

§ 135. All objects of human enquiry were divided by Hume into ' Relations of ideas ' and ' Matters of fact.' Matters of fact, he said, are learned from experience ; but are particular, disconnected, momentary, and so can give no universal propositions. Relations between ideas, such as those we have in mathematics, are universal ; but they are universal because they belong to the ideal order and are revealed by the operation of thought itself. As, however, Hume could find no bond of connection between ideas and facts, he came to the conclusion that matters of fact alone are real, relations between ideas being merely mental notions without objective validity.

The unsatisfactory nature of Hume's conclusion is obvious. That ideas are merely mental and have no objective validity is admitted neither by pragmatist nor absolutist. Both have found what Hume sought for in vain, a bond of connection between ideas and facts. The pragmatist observes what apparently escaped the notice of Hume, viz., that whether mathematical notions are objectively valid or not, they are certainly applicable in experience ; hence the pragmatic doctrine that such notions are true in so far as they are useful. Kant also took note of this same fact of experience, but observing also that mathematical notions arise first in sense-experiences, was led to a different conclusion. His was a two-fold problem, the problem of origin and the problem of validity. How is it possible, he asked, that we are able to generalise particular perceptive judgments and so obtain laws ? And how is it that these general laws are applicable in experience, and that by them we are able to antici-pate future events ? In order to solve these two problems Kant formulated two hypotheses, first the hypothesis of Apriorism, and secondly that of Immanence.

§ 136. The postulate of Apriorism is made at the very outset of Kant's Critical enquiry, and is made expressly for the purpose of explaining those universal and necessary judgments, the existence of which he recognised as a fact. Let us assume, he says, that in knowledge the object conforms to the mind, and not the mind to the object. Let us assume that there are *a priori* forms within the mind without which the experience of objects would be impossible, and apart from which for us there would be no objects at all. Let us assume that "the sensible object must conform to our faculty of perception " and that in general our mind " deter-mines the nature of objects *a priori*, or before they are actually presented;" just as the mathematician

" in his definitions brings out what was necessarily implied in the conception that he had himself formed *a priori*, and put into the figure," and just as the " physicist, if he is to be successful, must himself lead the way with principles and judgments based upon fixed laws, and force nature to answer his questions." Our only escape from the sceptical empiricism of Hume is to assume that " that which reason has itself put into nature must be its guide to the discovery of all that it can learn from nature." [1]

§ 137. Thus the origin of knowledge in Kant is two-fold. It is partly *a priori* and partly *a posteriori ;* and its validity depends upon its origin. All knowledge is obtained *in* experience and hence is valid only for experience. But because all knowledge ' begins *with* experience ' it by no means follows that it all originates *from* experience.[2] It arises partly from the activity of objects upon our senses, but partly also from " the synthetic activity of our minds which by combining and separating the ideas which have thus arisen, converts the raw material of sensible impressions into that knowledge of objects which is called experience." Principles, such as that of Causality, which are universal and necessary, cannot be wholly due to experience. For experience never bestows on its judgments true or strict universality, but only the assumed or comparative universality of induction ; so that, properly speaking, it merely says that, so far as our observation has gone, there is no exception to the rule. If, therefore, a judgment is thought with strict universality, so that there can be no possible

[1] Preface to the *Critique of Pure Reason* (*passim*).
[2] *Ibid.*, Introduction, p. 1.

O

exception to it, it is not derived from experience, but is absolutely *a priori*. . . . And it is easy to show that in human knowledge there actually are judgments that, in the strictest sense, are universal, and therefore purely *a priori*.[1]

§ 138. Knowledge, then, presupposes as its conditions a certain mental structure on the part of the subject who knows, as well as certain data which come from without and are given in sense-experience. From this dual source Kant obtains three kinds of knowledge properly so-called — *empirical* knowledge, *a priori* knowledge, and *pure a priori* knowledge; together with a fourth kind of knowledge which is not strictly knowledge at all, but only faith.

'*Empirical knowledge*' includes the truths of every-day life and all the applied, as opposed to the abstract, sciences. It is due in part to the object, and in part to the mind. It is expressed in propositions involving time and space, which are the *a priori* forms of perceptual experience. Categories, also, are used in every judgment that we make, and these, again, are *a priori*, and to them the data of sense-experience must conform. Empirical knowledge is objective, since real objects are, for Kant, the cause of our sensations ; but in it we know only objects as they appear, and not things in themselves, which, because of the *a priori* element involved in all human knowledge, must ever remain, for man, unknowable.

In experience the synthesis in which a judgment consists, is mediated by what is given in sense-

[1] Introduction to *Critique of Pure Reason*, p. 3.

perception. The *mind* makes the synthesis, but the content of the synthesis, what is synthesised, is conditioned *a posteriori* by sense data. In *a priori knowledge*, on the other hand, the syntheses which we make are independent of experience, though the ideas between which the synthesis holds are still· conditioned by the data of perception. For instance, " the proposition that ' each change has its own cause ' is *a priori ;* but it is not purely *a priori*, because change is an idea that can be derived only from experience." [1] *Purely a priori knowledge* is entirely independent of experience, both in regard to synthesis and in regard to the ideas that are synthesised, for in it we consider merely the *a priori* forms or categories (under which, in experience, objects are thoughts) in relation to one another.

A priori knowledge in general is derived from a study of the structure and natural functional activity of the mind itself, and, often enough, we possess and use such knowledge without ever having explicitly formulated it. It is only when conflict of opinion arises that we begin to examine the presuppositions upon which respective claims to truth are based, and so come to the knowledge of the ' *a priori* ' forms which all knowledge implies. Thus the conflict of individual judgments in regard to quantity led to an examination of the presuppositions of our knowledge of quantity, and this to

[1] *loc. cit.*, Introduction, p. 3. (On p. 5, Kant calls the principle of causality ' pure *a priori ;* ' but here, I take it, he is speaking either of the synthesis which the principle involves, considered in abstraction from its terms, or he is thinking of the tautological form of the principle, viz., ' every effect must have a cause.')

mathematics and geometry; so that from a critical regress upon the universal implicit in our actual concrete judgments, the principle of number was laid down, and, this accomplished, it became possible to anticipate events and foretell relations which must of necessity be true.

§ 139.   The fourth kind of knowledge (so-called) is quite different from the rest, for it is a knowledge which quits the field of possible experience and claims to extend the range of our judgments beyond its limits by means of conceptions for which no corresponding object can be presented in experience. " It is in this province," says Kant, " that reason carries on those investigations the results of which we regard as more important than all that understanding can discover within the domain of phenomena.   These are the unavoidable problems of God, freedom, and immortality, set by pure reason itself."   Such problems as these belong to metaphysics, a science which men have hitherto built upon knowledge which has come to them " they know not how, and in blind dependence upon principles of which we cannot tell the origin." An examination of the sources of knowledge, however, reveals the fact that knowledge is simply experience determined by *a priori* forms.   Hence knowledge pertains only to objects of experience ; and God, who is not an object of experience, cannot therefore be an object of knowledge strictly so-called, but only of *faith*.   For Kant, as for the pragmatists, the existence of God is a *postulate ;* but Kant is better off than the pragmatists since he can explain both the origin of the notion of God and the reason why we need to postulate His existence. The notion of God arises from a transcendental use of the categories beyond the sphere of their application in experience, and so far the notion is invalid ; but when supplemented by the consideration of human demands for an ultimate harmony and reconciliation, notably between good and evil, the notion of God becomes an idea in the objective validity of which we are forced to believe, even though it be impossible to prove it.

§ 140. Thus the argument by which Kant disproves the objective validity of the Ideas of Pure Reason presupposes the doctrine of Immanence, for it rests upon the assumption that sense-data and *a priori* forms, objective experience and subjective synthesis, are both essential and intrinsic to knowledge, and apart from one another are mere abstractions. Thus object presupposes subject, and subject, object. The unity of the self is the correlate of objective differences. This Kant clearly states in the *Critique of Pure Reason.* " Phenomena," he says, " do not exist apart from forms of synthesis of which the highest is the Transcendental Unity of Apperception." Indeed, the principles of the understanding are expressly called 'immanent,' inasmuch as they are applicable only within the limits of experience.

Modern representatives of Kant, differing as they do in other respects, all agree in holding Immanence essential to Criticism. Mr. Wallace, for instance, tells us that the philosophy of Kant

is an attempt to get at the organism of our fundamental belief—the construction, from the very base, of our conception of reality, of our primary certainty. In technical language he describes our essential nature as a Subject-Object. It is the unity of an ' I am ' which is also ' I know that I am ; ' an ' I will ' which is also ' I am conscious of my will.'[1]

And Dr. Caird declares that

no one has a key to Kant's Logic, who does not see that the result to which it tends [is the view that] that very consciousness of the particular and the contingent, which Hume had turned against the consciousness of ' necessary connection ' is itself dependent upon the ' *a priori* ' it is used to condemn.[2]

§ 141. Unquestionably Immanence is essential to Kant's Apriorism, and unquestionably, too, it *tends* in the direction of Absolutism. But it is, I think, equally certain that Kant stopped short of the ultimate goal. He asserted Immanence, but he asserted it *only in so far as the phenomenal object* was concerned, and so failed to realise, at any rate in its fulness, the first and last axiom of all Absolute philosophies, that the *Universe itself is one and individual*. Kant, in fact, never really transcended the human point of view. Knowledge, for him, was always human knowledge, and, human-like, he could not altogether rid himself of a realistic attitude. He believed in *noumena*, in a real and independent *Ding-an-sich* which was outside the mind and so beyond the reach of human experience. It is from the *Ding-an-sich* that the material element in knowledge is derived, but as it is only this element, viz., sensation, which conforms to the *a priori*

---

[1] Hegel's *Philosophy of Mind*, p. cx.
[2] *The Critical Philosophy of Kant*, vol. i., p. 250.

structure of mind, things in themselves are left without, and, hence, are declared unknowable.

§ 142. The Kantian theory on account of this dualism is not an Absolutism, but rather a compromise between Absolutism and Realism, or at least it may be so regarded in retrospection. And like all compromises it led to endless difficulties. The separation of matter and form, which was due to the realistic admission of a *Ding-an-sich*, necessitated the introduction of numerous intermediaries between the lowest faculty sense, and the highest synthesis of all, the 'Transcendental Unity of Apperception,' in the vain hope of bringing them together. To take a single instance : the transcendental schematism of the imagination is an attempt to explain how the pure conceptions of the understanding can possibly be applied to phenomena. But the result is, as Dr. Caird has pointed out, that we are placed in a dilemma. For either the syntheses of the imagination are independent of the syntheses of the understanding, and in this case their agreement is either fortuitous or due to a pre-established and inexplicable harmony; or the synthesis of conception is the real source and conscious aspect of the synthesis of imagination, in which case the possibility of converting a formless and serial manifold into definite objects is still unexplained.

§ 143. The different sources assigned to the *a priori* and the *a posteriori* elements in knowledge are fatal ; and though Kant tried again and again to overcome this self-imposed dualism, it was always without success. The dialectic in which he discusses the fourth kind of knowledge mentioned above, exhibits clearly the unsatisfactory nature of the synthesis effected between these alien elements. The ' Ideas of Reason '—God, the Universe as a totality, and the Soul—have no objective validity, for " since no phenomena can be found to which they can be applied, they cannot be presented *in concreto* at all." [1] Yet, although we have no perception of the supra-sensuous, it is admitted that the categories have " a wider reach than the perceptions of sense," and that there may be objects independent of sensibility to which, unknown to us, they do in reality apply.[2] Nay, further, reason compels us to transcend the phenomenal and " demands a completeness beyond the reach of all possible knowledge, and a systematic unity with which experience can never be completely harmonised." [3] But this is only an ideal after which we strive, and its function is regulative, not constitutive.   Again, if what Pure Reason demands in order to satisfy itself, is confirmed by the postulates of Practical Reason which are necessary for the realisation of moral ideals, the conclusion is not that these ideals are valid, but that the two reasons are independent and their functions distinct. The result of Kant's endeavour to escape from the dualism with which he started is always the same : instead of transcending it, other dualisms are introduced.

§ 144.   The dualism of the Pure and the Practical Reasons renders necessary a third *Critique* in which

---

[1] *Critique of Pure Reason* (2nd edit.), p. 595.
[2] *Ibid.*, p. 309.   [3] *Ibid.*, p. 596.

the relation between the postulated noumena and
the world of appearances is discussed, and in which
Kant approaches nearer to Absolutism than ever
before. Here, at last, says Dr. Pfleiderer, " Kant
tries to find some connecting link between the
intelligible and the sensible world ; and he seeks
it in a teleology common to them both." [1] The
Critique of Judgment is an attempt to transcend
the point of view of our discursive intellect, and to
look at things from the standpoint of a perceptive
intelligence for which the whole is no longer dependent on the parts, but the parts dependent on
the whole both in their specific nature and in their
interconnection.[2] The universe is conceived as a
teleological whole ; and this whole

> determines the form and combination of all the parts,
> not indeed as cause, but as the ground on which the
> thing is known by the person judging of it, in the
> systematic unity of the form and the combination
> of all its parts ; [while the parts themselves] combine
> in the unity of the whole, and are reciprocally cause
> and effect of each other's form.[3]

The *Critique of Judgment* is undoubtedly an
attempt to reconcile the point of view of the Practical
Reason with that of the Pure Reason, but Kant
seems hardly to have realised the significance of
what he was doing. From the point of view of
Absolutism, the third *Critique* is a higher synthesis
of those which proceed. From Kant's point of view
it was rather a supplement to what had already

[1] *Development of Theology*, bk. I., c. i.
[2] *Critique of Judgment*, pp. 419, 420.
[3] *Ibid.*, p. 385.

been said. His teleological whole was an ideal, a suggestion, but nothing more. Nor does he appear to have seen the connection between this teleology and the doctrine of Immanence. The teleology of the *Critique of Judgment* does not claim to be a development of the doctrine of Immanence. On the contrary, just as Kant never applies the principle of Immanence beyond the sphere of phenomenal objects, but attributes sensation to the causal action of an unknowable *Ding-an-sich*, so he never gets rid of the duality of the determinant and reflective judgments. Since teleological principles are based on the reflective judgment, they are regulative not constitutive, subjective not objective. Hence, "although there are certain peculiarities of our higher faculty of knowledge which it is very natural to transfer as objective predicates to things, they really belong only to ideas." [1] And the final conclusion which Kant reaches, is that, although we may *postulate* a Supreme Being as the ultimate Ground of the Universe of which we are an integral part, yet we can have no *knowledge* of such a Being; for, " to contemplate that Being as he is in himself, the Speculative Reason must assume the form of the determinant judgment, and this is contrary to its very nature." [2]

§ 145. While, then, it may be granted that the thing-in-itself and the dualism which it implies is foreign to the spirit of Criticism, I think that Kant was perfectly sincere and perfectly firm even to the

---

[1] *Critique of Judgment*, p. 417.
[2] *Ibid.*, p. 470, concluding paragraph.

end in his belief in the reality of this dualism.
Fichte has said that it was a concession to Locke
and the Sceptics, but I cannot so regard it, though
it may have been due to the influence of English
Empiricism that Kant did not see further than he
did or realise more fully the significance of his own
philosophy. On the other hand, the human standpoint adopted by Kant undoubtedly has something
to do with the question. It may have been that
Kant foresaw that to deny the existence of things-
in-themselves was to identify knowledge with
reality, and if this was so, it is small wonder that
he should have refused to renounce a dualism which
would have meant Subjectivism and Egoism, since
knowledge for him meant human knowledge. But
whatever his reasons may have been it is certain
that Kant did not transcend the distinction of
noumenal and phenomenal, and that in consequence
he never got further than the half-way house between
Realism and Absolutism. In declining to go further
Kant was doubtless illogical. This blending of a
mutilated Realism with a half-hearted Absolutism
could not but lead, as it did, to many inconsistencies.
It meant failure even in the primary aim for which
Criticism had come into being. For it can hardly
be disputed that, *taken as it stands*, Kantian philosophy tends rather towards, than away from,
Scepticism, precisely because of those realistic
Dinge-an-sich which remain for ever unknowable.
Yet, notwithstanding all this, and notwithstanding
also the fact that within his philosophy were implicitly contained all the principles afterwards
developed by Absolutism, it is evident to me that

Kant remained to the last, and deliberately chose to remain, a dualist.

§ 146. It was obvious, however, that Kant's philosophy could not remain long in the state in which he left it. Fichte saw at once that the dualism of mind and the thing-in-itself was incompatible with transcendental philosophy, and proceeded to apply the remedy which Kant himself had suggested. Things-in-themselves must be abolished once and for all from the realm of philosophy. Fichte always refused to believe that Kant had ever meant to attribute causal action to the *Ding-an-sich*, which would have involved an application of the category of causality beyond the sphere in which alone it had meaning. But, deprived of causal action, things-in-themselves became utterly useless, for their *ratio essendi* thereby ceased to exist. Hence, things-in-themselves were got rid of, and Kant's apparently illogical restriction of Immanence to phenomenal objects in this way removed. The barrier which Kant had placed between the real Subject and the real Object in knowledge having thus been removed, there was no longer any need of mediating links to connect the one with the other. Both real Subject and real Object were henceforth to be regarded as immanent within knowledge, apart from which they were meaningless abstractions. The object could neither be known nor yet exist apart from the subject, nor could the subject exist or become self-conscious apart from the object.

§ 147. Several consequences followed from Fichte's extension of the doctrine of Immanence. From the assumption that the subject and object in knowledge could not *exist* apart, it followed that knowledge and reality must at bottom be one ; and, this being so, knowledge, *quâ* reality, could no longer be regarded as the exclusive possession of human minds. This latter consequence Fichte hardly realised at first, for he identified reality with a system of ' rational egos ; ' though later he changed his view and treated the latter as differences which had broken out in an absolute and wholly ' indifferent ' Ground. Thus, the primary problem which philosophy presented to Fichte was quite different from that which it presented to Kant. He assumed as the first principle of all philosophy that " nothing can exist which transcends self-consciousness." He had to enquire, therefore, not how subject and object, being distinct, can ever come to be united, but how being at bottom one and the same, they can ever come to be for consciousness distinct, or, in other words, how an Ego which is externally identical with itself can ever attain to the consciousness of itself as an ' other.'

This problem which the immanent interpretation of Criticism had introduced, Fichte failed to solve satisfactorily. He attempted to solve it by means of an ' antithesis,' in which the Ego posits a non-Ego in order that it may attain self-consciousness and so realise itself in a higher synthesis where it is determined by, and at the same time determines, the non-Ego it has posited. But this was to reduce ' nature ' to a mere ' moment ' in an eternal act of self-consciousness, to a limit imposed only in order to be transcended. Nay, further, if, as at first conceived, reality is identical with a system of

striving Egos, not only is 'nature' merely the
material in which these finite egos strive to realise
themselves; but the absolute Ego, which in its
infinity embraces all reality and constitutes the term
of self-realisation, is a mere idea, an eternal *Sollen*,
a 'must be' which never wholly is, for, if it were, the
Anstoss would cease and with it consciousness.
Complete self-realisation would thus involve
annihilation.

§ 148. These two defects in Fichte's '*Wissenschaftslehre*' demanded an immediate remedy. For
to reduce nature to a sort of 'spring-board' for the
development of our moral consciousness was to treat
the theories and discoveries of the scientist as so
many illusions ; and to conceive the Absolute as a
mere idea or *telos*, infinite and all-embracing but
never fully itself, was to deprive the universe of that
unity which the new theory thought to give it.
Consequently, Schelling in his *Natur-philosophie*
made nature more real by treating it as the *objective*
expression of an ultimate and rational Ground.
Indeed, Fichte himself in his later writings had
sought to give Reality a metaphysical basis in the
Identity of Subject and Object. This Identity,
however, he conceived in the abstract, as something
which, itself without determination or individuality,
is yet the ground from which all things proceed.
And though Schelling, in his earlier work, gave it
fuller meaning both as the rational, and also as the
dynamical and not merely the teleological, source of
all things ; yet in his *Identitäts-philosophie* he
returned to Fichte's view and regarded the Absolute
as a bare Indifference-point, contentless and mean-

ingless, except in so far as it is the Ground of which
Intelligence and Nature are respectively the subjective and objective aspects.

§ 149. Next came Hegel, who, failing to see how
an empty and undifferentiated abstraction could be
reconciled with, still less account for, the eternal
genesis of the rich variety and manifold differences
of the universe, protested vigorously against this
feature of the philosophy of Fichte and Schelling.
Accordingly, generously returning to the Absolute
all that his predecessors had deprived it of, he
conceived it as at once Ground, organic unity and
final end or term. As Ground or Idea it is the source
whence flow both self and not-self, intelligence and
nature ; as organic unity it is the life of the universe
in which it progressively realises itself ; and as final
end or term, it is self-consciousness in which the
Absolute Idea recognises itself as one and thus
overcomes its own differences.

By thus adopting ' development ' or ' evolution '
as the central idea of his system, Hegel thought to
explain at once the dynamical and the teleological
functions of the Absolute, and at the same time to
preserve it in its full meaning as the real and rational
Ground of a rich and much-differentiated universe.
The evolution, as before, takes place *viâ* thesis,
antithesis and synthesis. Reality—at any rate from
our point of view—is still a never-ending process of
self-realisation and self-development. But the
evolution is real now. It is the Absolute becoming
self-conscious. And the Absolute is not an Indifference-point, nor are nature and spirit collateral or
parallel expressions of an empty abstraction. The

Absolute itself is real, realising and manifesting itself both in nature and in spirit. Nature and spirit, too, are both real; but they have not the same *degree of reality*. Nature is thought in extreme alienation from itself, and though independent of the individual mind, it is *inferior* to it as a manifestation of the Absolute Ground. For in conscious beings, and especially in man, Thought or Spirit manifests itself, first as distinct from the world, then as free, then as an integral part of the world, then as a member of a moral community, till it comes at last to the highest stage of all, in which it knows itself as spirit. Looking back upon the history of mankind, Thought as Spirit recognises there its own self-realisation, and in the history of nature its own self-externalisation ; and at the same time it is conscious that these antitheses are reconciled in itself as in a higher synthesis. The Absolute regarded as ' Ground ' is by Hegel distinguished— relatively of course—from the ' Absolute Idea.' As Ground it is merely the unifying principle of the organic universe, but it is not yet a being *for-itself*. Only when its evolution is regarded as complete can it strictly be called the Absolute, for only then does it exist for itself and recognise itself as the unity in which the dualism of the self and the not-self is overcome.

§ 150. Thus in Fichte, Schelling and Hegel Criticism not only develops, but takes upon itself a new form, passing from a theory of knowledge into a theory of reality. Knowledge is identified with reality. To the categories is attributed a kind of logical development by means of which the structure of the universe is evolved. The ' Transcendental Unity of Apperception ' is transformed into an Absolute, which is at once the Ground and the higher and self-conscious synthesis of all its differences. The Universe is one, individual, systematic, organic, rational. The Absolute is its principle of unity ; nature and thinking beings its differences. All are immanent within the single and individual organism, and the differences apart from their Ground, and the Ground apart from its differences are nothing real, but merely abstractions.

The system of Hegel, as he himself prophesied, underwent much differentiation.

The transformation of the world into objects of consciousness is [says Dr. Wilm] the decisive step of Critical Philosophy. But what, precisely, this consciousness is, from which alone objects have existence, whether it is individual consciousness, the consciousness of the race, or consciousness as such, is a question which admits of a variety of answers, and the particular shade the resulting idealistic system will take on will depend upon whether one or the other of these interpretations be given.[1]

I should have preferred to say that the distinguishing feature of Critical Philosophy was its method ; for the transformation of the world into objects of consciousness is characteristic of any idealism, not exclusive of pragmatic idealisms. The peculiar mark of Absolutism, on the other hand, is the transformation of the world into objects (and subjects) of consciousness *for a single and immanent Ground or Subject*. And here it is true, as Dr. Wilm points out, that the differentiations of Absolutism

[1] Wilm, *Philosophical Review*, May, 1906, p. 349.

P

depend largely upon the view that is taken of the nature of that Ultimate Ground. Hegel lays the emphasis on thought, Schopenhauer on will, the poet-philosopher Schiller on the æsthetic and moral consciousness, and Mr. Bradley on sentience. All these philosophies, however, are Absolutisms. All adopt the doctrine of Immanence. All interpret the Universe as one organic whole, comprising unity of Ground amid structural difference; and all identify the unity of Ground as the Absolute with some form of consciousness. As a rule, too, the method of such philosophers is critical. They argue from the data of experience, and their conditions are presuppositions. But the Critical Method, like Absolutism itself, may take a variety of forms; and of late there has been a tendency to appeal more and more frequently to experience both for data and for confirmation of the theses of Absolutism. This tendency is illustrated in the philosophy of T. H. Green, who, like Mr. Bradley, bases the constructive part of his work on the data of human consciousness. And as the multitudinous differentiations of the philosophy of the Absolute make it impossible to summarise them, I shall content myself with stating in brief the leading characteristics of Green's philosophy as expounded in his *Prolegomena to Ethics*, supplemented by a short sketch of the *metaphysical* standpoint of *Appearance and Reality*.

§ 151. The facts of human consciousness are the data with which Green starts, and the question which he asks himself is, as we should expect, of a critical nature, viz., what do these data presuppose?

What do they imply as the ' conditions ' without which they cannot be explained ? [1] Green, it has been said, starts from the ' Self ' and passes thence to the Cosmos and to God,—a statement which is true, but which must be understood not in the Lockian, but in the *true* psychological sense already explained.[2] In other words, Green begins by enquiring what we can know about human cognition by introspective analysis, and with this as his starting-point he begins to philosophise, *i.e.*, to enquire into its metaphysical conditions.

Analysing, first of all, the object of knowledge, Green finds that it always consists of relations.

Matter and motion, just so far as known, consist in, or are determined by, relations between the objects of that connected consciousness which we call experience. If we take any definition of matter, any account of its ' necessary qualities,' and abstract from it all that consists in a statement of relations between facts in the way of feeling, or between objects that we present to ourselves as sources of feeling, we shall find that there is nothing left.[3]

And, again, if we " exclude from what we have considered real all qualities constituted by relation, we find that none are left. Without relation any simple idea would be undistinguished from other simple ideas, undetermined by its surroundings in the cosmos of experience." [4] The world, then, as conceived by us, consists of relations, and the order of those relations is unalterable. Indeed, " that there *is* an unalterable order of relations, if we could only find it out, is the presupposition of all our enquiries

[1] *Prolegomena to Ethics*, § 14.   [2] *Ibid.*, § 9
[3] *Ibid.*, § 9.   [4] *Ibid.*, § 20.

into the real nature of appearances; and such unalterableness implies their inclusion in one system which leaves nothing outside itself." [1] Thus the only means which we have of deciding " whether any particular event or object is really what it seems to be " is " by testing the unalterableness of the qualities which we ascribe to it, or which form its apparent nature." [2]

§ 152. [Now] experience, in the sense of a consciousness of events as a related series—and in no other sense can it help to account for the knowledge of an order of nature—cannot be explained by any natural history, properly so-called. [For] between the consciousness itself on the one hand, and on the other anything determined by the relations under which a nature is presented to consciousness, no process of development, because no community, can be really traced. Nature, with all that belongs to it, is a process of change. . . . But neither can any process of change yield a consciousness of itself, which, in order to be a consciousness of the change, must be equally present to all stages of the change; nor can any consciousness of the change, since the whole of it must be present at once, be itself a process of change. There may be a change into a state of consciousness of change, and a change out of it, on the part of this man or that; but within the consciousness itself there can be no change, because no relation of before and after, of here and there, between its constituent members.

[Hence] a form of consciousness, which we cannot explain as of natural origin, is necessary to our conceiving an order of nature, an objective world of fact from which illusion may be distinguished.[3] [Further, nature itself implies a spiritual principle. Relation implies the existence of many in one]. Whether we say that a related thing is one in itself, manifold in respect of its relations, or that there is one relation between manifold things . . . . we are equally affirming the

[1] *Ibid.*, § 26.   [2] *Ibid.*, § 24.   [3] *Ibid.*, §§ 18, 19.

unity of the manifold. . . . But a plurality of things cannot of themselves unite in one relation, nor can a single thing of itself bring itself into a multitude of relations. . . . There must, then, be something other than the manifold things themselves, which combines them without effacing their severality.[1]

Now, a system of unalterably related objects is a system of unalterably related objects *in consciousness;* otherwise, there would be no experience of it.[2]

If, therefore, there is such a thing as a connected experience of related objects, there must be operative in consciousness a unifying principle, which not only presents related objects to itself, but at once renders them objects and unites them in relation to each other by this act of presentation. . . . [And] if all possible experience of related objects . . . . forms a single system ; if there can be no such thing as an experience of unrelated objects ; then there must be a corresponding singleness in the principle of consciousness which forms the bond of relation between the objects.[3]

§ 153. Thus the spiritual principle which is implied in our knowledge of a cosmos of related facts is identical with that ‘ single active self-conscious principle,’ which constitutes those facts and is the condition of their existence. A hypothesis which treats the knowable world and the subject capable of knowing it as two independent existences is untenable, for “it renders knowledge, as a fact or reality, inexplicable. It leaves us without an answer to the question how the order of relations, which the mind sets up, comes to reproduce those relations of the material world which are assumed to

[1] *Ibid.*, § 28.   [2] *Ibid*, § 31.   [3] *Ibid.*, § 32.

be of a wholly different origin and nature." [1] The true account of the growth of knowledge is

that the concrete whole, which may be described indifferently as an eternal intelligence realised in the related facts of the world, or as a system of related facts rendered possible by such an intelligence, partially and gradually reproduces itself in us, communicating piece-meal, but in inseparable co-relation, understanding and the facts understood, experience and the experienced world. [2]

How this communication between a human and an eternal consciousness takes place we are not told. Apparently, however, it involves both thought and feeling, for

feeling and thought are inseparable and mutually dependent in the consciousness for which the world of experience exists, inseparable and mutually dependent in the constitution of the facts which form the object of that consciousness [so that] it is one and the same living world of experience which, considered as the manifold object presented by a self-distinguishing subject to itself, may be called feeling, and, considered as the subject presenting such an object to itself, may be called thought. [3]

Doubtless, at times man does not think: he merely feels. " But just in so far as we feel without thinking, no world of phenomena exists for us." [4] Consequently, although we do not thereby cease to be facts, and facts for an eternal consciousness which is the condition of our existence, nevertheless we are not identical with that consciousness in the sense

[1] *Ibid.*, § 34 and cf. § 39.
[2] *Ibid.*, § 36 and cf. § 43.
[3] § 50.   [4] § 49.

that it is reproducing itself in us.   Indeed, precisely because the reproduction has us for its organ,

it is at once progressive and incapable of completion [and] there can never be that actual wholeness of the world for us which there must be for the mind that renders it one. But though the conditions under which the eternal consciousness reproduces itself in our knowledge are thus incompatible with finality in that knowledge, there *is* an element of *identity* between the first stage of intelligent experience—between the simplest beginning of knowledge—and the eternal consciousness reproducing itself in it, which consists in the presentation of the many in one, in the apprehension of facts as related in a single system, in the conception of there being an order of things, whatever that order may turn out to be.[1]

Thus the fact that " the unification of the manifold in the world implies the presence of the manifold to a mind, for which, and through the action of which it is a related whole," [2] together with the fact that that very consciousness of ours, "which holds together successive events as equally present, has itself a history in time . . . can only be explained by supposing that in the growth of our experience, . . . an animal organism, which has a history in time, gradually becomes the vehicle of an eternally complete consciousness."[3]

§ 154. These are, I think, the essential features of the philosophy of T. H. Green, so far as concerns the theory of knowledge ; and between this philosophy and that of Mr. Bradley there are many points of resemblance, and still more perhaps of difference. The differences, however, would seem to be due largely to method, for in his main con-

[1] *Ibid.*, § 72 (italics mine).   [2] *Ibid.*, § 82.   [3] *Ibid.*, §§ 66, 67.

clusions Mr. Bradley is at one with Green. Reality is one and individual, and is to be identified with some form of consciousness. This is the chief thesis of both Absolutisms, in comparison with which it is of small moment whether that form of consciousness be called 'thought' or 'sentient experience,' since for both philosophers the one term includes the other. Nevertheless, the long and intricate process of reasoning by which Mr. Bradley attempts to establish and confirm his conclusions is wholly different from the line of argument adopted by Green ; and of this we must now give some account in order that our sketch of Absolutism may be complete. Fortunately for us, Mr. Bradley frequently sums up his own arguments, and in one place has even devoted a whole chapter to *Recapitulation*, so that by the aid of these summaries it may be possible to give a sketch of his philosophy, which otherwise one might have hesitated to attempt. Accordingly, I shall, as in Green's case, keep as closely as possible to the author's own words in order to avoid misinterpretations, which, judging from the appendices and notes to the Second Edition of *Appearance and Reality*, have already been of somewhat frequent occurrence.

§ 155. In our First Book [says Mr. Bradley] we examined [under the headings *Primary and Secondary Qualities, Substantive and Adjective, Relation and Quality, Space and Time, Change, Causality, Things, the Self*] certain ways of regarding Reality, and we found that each of them contained fatal inconsistency. Upon this we forthwith denied that, as such, they could be real. But upon reflection we perceived that our denial must rest upon positive knowledge. It can only be because we know, that we venture to condemn. Reality, therefore, we are sure, has a positive character, which rejects mere appearance and is incompatible with discord. On the other hand it cannot be something apart, a position qualified in no way save as negative of phenomena. The Reality, therefore, must be One, not as excluding diversity, but as somehow including it in such a way as to transform its character. There is plainly not anything which can fall outside of the Real. That must be qualified by every part of every predicate which it rejects; but it has such qualities as counterbalance one another's defects. It has a superabundance in which all partial discrepancies are resolved and remain as higher concord.[1]

§ 156. The metaphysical proof that Reality is One, rests upon Mr. Bradley's theory of relations. Mr. Bradley does not, as does Green, assert that the cosmos is merely a system of relations to which 'quality,' in inorganic beings at any rate, is ultimately reducible. On the contrary, though qualities imply relations, relations also imply qualities both of which exist upon the same level of appearance. They are never found apart, and separation by abstraction is no proof of real separateness. There are no purely external relations, for all relations make a difference to their terms, and hence must belong to a whole which they qualify. Logically and really, as well as psychologically, "all relations imply a whole to which the terms contribute and by which the terms are qualified."[2] Hence, since all things are distinguished and related,

nothing in the whole and in the end can be external, and everything less than the Universe is an abstraction

---

[1] *Appearance and Reality,* chap. xx., p. 241.
[2] *loc. cit.,* p. 581, cf. chap. iii. and the whole of Note B in the Appendix to the 2nd edition.

from the whole, an abstraction more or less empty, and the more empty the less self-dependent. Relations and qualities are abstractions, and depend for their being always on a whole, a whole which they inadequately express, and which remains always less or more in the background.[1]

The transition from this theory of relations to the doctrine that Reality is one is logical enough. " Reality is one. It must be single, because plurality, taken as real, contradicts itself. Plurality implies relations, and, through its relations, it unwillingly asserts always a superior unity. To suppose the universe plural is therefore to contradict oneself and, after all, to suppose that it is one." [2]

In order to determine the nature of the unity which underlies the universe, Mr. Bradley appeals again to sense-perception. The unity in question cannot be the unity which in thought we contrast with plurality, for this, like plurality itself, is the result of analysis, and is therefore appearance. It is the fact that at any given moment " we may be truly said to feel our whole psychical state as one" that furnishes "the positive idea of unity which we seek." [3] It is true that this unity is given only in " finite centres of experience " (*i.e.*, in the ' this ' and the ' mine '), but none the less,

in our first immediate experience the whole Reality is present. This does not mean that every other centre of experience, as such, is included there. It means that every centre qualifies the Whole, and that the Whole, as a substantive, is present in each of these its adjectives. The self and the world are elements, each separated in, and each contained by experience.

[1] *Ibid.*   [2] *Ibid.*, pp. 519, 520   [3] *Ibid.*, p. 521.

Experience . . . . as a centre of immediate feeling, is not yet either self or not self. . . . Then through its own imperfection it is broken up. Its unity gives way before inner unrest and outer impact in one. And then self and Ego, on one side, are produced by this development, and, on the other side, appear other selves and the world and God. These all appear as the contents of our finite experience, and they are genuinely and actually contained in it. They are contained in it but partially. . . . [Nevertheless] the total universe, presented imperfectly in finite experience, would, if completed, be merely the completion of this experience.[1]

§ 157. In a previous chapter we saw how, by a somewhat similar argument to this last, Mr. Bradley seeks to establish his thesis that Reality is Sentient Experience. It remains now to say something as to the nature of this Sentient Experience, and as to the relation of the Absolute to its appearances.

Again let us quote from the chapter headed 'Recapitulation,' for beyond this in the matter of positive and constructive theory Mr. Bradley makes little advance.

This Absolute is experience, because that is what we really mean when we speak of anything. It is not one-sided experience, as mere volition or mere thought; but it is a whole superior to and embracing all incomplete forms of life. This whole must be immediate like feeling, but not, like feeling, immediate at a level below distinction and relation. The Absolute is immediate as holding and transcending these differences. And because it cannot contradict itself, and does not suffer a division of idea from existence, it has therefore a balance of pleasure over pain.[2]

[1] *Ibid.*, pp. 524, 525.   [2] *Ibid.*, pp. 241, 242.

Thus Mr. Bradley regards the Absolute not only as "immediate," but also as "in every sense perfect." Various forms of the finite all "take a place within this Absolute." "Nothing can be lost," yet "everything must be made good so as to minister to harmony." *How* this takes place is inexplicable, nor is it necessary to explain it since we have a general principle which seems certain. The only question is whether any form of the finite is a negative instance which overthrows this principle.[1]

§ 158. The chapter entitled 'Recapitulation' occurs about half way in *Appearance and Reality*, and the rest of the volume is devoted almost entirely to the enquiry whether there is anything which 'imports discord' when admitted to a place within the Absolute ; for, if not, the Absolute is possible ; and "this is all we need to seek for. For already we have a principle upon which it is necessary ; and therefore it is certain." [2] For the rest, the result of this further enquiry is largely negative. Nothing is found to be contradictory when predicated as an adjective of the Absolute ; yet nothing has reality in itself and apart from the Absolute.

We have found [for instance] that Nature by itself has no reality. . . . It exists only as a form of appearance within the Absolute. . . . It has its being in that process of intestine division, through which the whole world of appearance consists. And in this realm, where aspects fall asunder, where being is distinguished from thought, and the self from the not-self, Nature marks one extreme. It is the aspect most opposed to self-dependence and unity. . . . [It is but] 'one element within the Whole.' [3]

[1] *Ibid.*, p. 242.   [2] *Ibid.*, p. 242.   [3] *Ibid.*, pp. 293, 294.

In the same way " no one aspect of experience, as such, is real. None is primary, or can serve to explain the others or the whole. They are all alike one-sided, and passing away beyond themselves." Hence they are called " appearances," for " anything which comes short when compared with Reality gets the name of appearance." [1] This does not mean, however, that " the thing always itself is an appearance ; " but " that its character is such that it becomes one as soon as we judge it."

This character [of things] . . . is ideality. Appearance consists in a looseness of content from existence ; and, because of this self-estrangement, every finite aspect is called an appearance. And we have found that everywhere throughout the world such ideality prevails. Anything less than the Whole has turned out to be not self-contained. Its being involves in its very essence a relation to the outside, and it is thus inwardly infected by externality. Everywhere the finite is self-transcendent, alienated from itself, and passing away from itself towards another existence. Hence the finite is appearance, because, on the one side, it is an adjective of Reality, and because, on the other side, it is an adjective which itself is not real. [2]

§ 159. In conclusion, then, " All is appearance, and no appearance, or any combination of these is the same as Reality." Yet, on the other hand, " the Absolute *is* its appearances, it really is all and every one of them." " The Absolute is each appearance, and is all, but it is not any one as such. And it is not all equally, but one appearance is more real than another." There are in appearances degrees of reality.

[1] *Ibid.*, p. 485.   [2] *Ibid.*, p. 486,

Everything is essential, yet one thing is worthless in comparison with others. Nothing is perfect, as such, and yet everything in some degree contains a vital function of Perfection. Every attitude of experience, every sphere or level of the world, is a necessary factor in the Absolute. . . . Nowhere is there even a single fact so fragmentary and so poor that to the universe it does not matter. There is truth in every idea however false, there is reality in every existence however slight ; and, where we can point to reality or truth, there is the one undivided life of the Absolute. Appearance without reality would be impossible, for what then could appear ? And reality without appearance would be nothing, for there certainly is nothing outside appearances. But on the other hand reality is not the sum of things. It is the unity in which all things, coming together, are transmuted, in which they are changed all alike, though not changed equally.[1]

It is the unity of the Absolute immanent within the whole, re-uniting and re-absorbing its relational appearances, and giving to each its degree of truth, reality and perfection, which, as such, can belong only to the whole.

CHAPTER IX.

CRITICISM OF APRIORISM.

§ 160. Every Absolutism is not necessarily an Apriorism. The Kantian doctrine that the possibility of experience presupposes not merely thought, but a definite thought-structure or *a priori* schema to which, in knowledge, all objects must conform,

[1] *Ibid.*, pp. 487, 488.

and without which knowledge could not exist, though still upheld in various forms by Dr. Caird and others, is not found in the Absolutism of Green or Mr. Bradley. All allow that the universe is intelligible, that it is built according to a definite plan, and that the relation of part to part and change to change is according to fixed and immutable laws, and again that these laws are logically prior to the details of phenomenal objects ; but Apriorism asserts more than this. It asserts that that thought and cognition generally has a definite structure, which is the necessary and immutable condition of all experience, It maintains that the forms, categories, principles of analysis and synthesis which characterise human cognition are not due to the circumstances in which we find ourselves, nor yet built up by the constructive activity of thought, but belong to the *a priori* nature of mind itself. Forms, categories and principles are all arranged or systematised *a priori* according to a plan or schema, which everyone carries about with him, and which conditions all his thought-activity. The question therefore which I intend to discuss in this chapter is whether there is the slightest evidence for the existence of such a plan or schema of categories and principles as the necessary condition of all experience.

§ 161. Apriorism evokes a vigorous protest from all empiricists, and the pragmatist is not the least loud in his declamation. His favourite charge against Kant and Hegel is that the notions they have introduced into philosophy are ambiguous and futile. ' The conditions of all possible experience,' Dr. Schiller tells us, is an ambiguous phrase, for it may refer to psychical, to logical, or to æsthetic conditions. '*A priori* forms' are ambiguous for they may be the products either of logical or of psychological analysis ; and if the latter, they have a history which Kant has forgotten. 'Universality' and 'necessity' are ambiguous, for whatever meaning may be assigned to them it is ultimately reducible to a psychological and pragmatic necessity.[1]

A charge of ambiguity, however, even if well founded, is clearly insufficient to establish the refutation of any theory ; for ambiguity may easily be remedied by more precise definition, and at once the difficulty vanishes. But is not the ambiguity of Kantism exaggerated by its pragmatic enemies ? Are 'the conditions of all possible experience' really ambiguous ? Will the Kantian theory bear the interpretations suggested for this expression by Dr. Schiller ? Are Dr. Schiller's interpretations exhaustive? Are they mutually exclusive? It seems to me that the conditions of all possible experience in Kant are primarily neither psychological nor logical, nor yet æsthetic, but metaphysical. They may be called psychological if you mean by this that they are supposed to exist *in concreto* in the human mind, and they are also *logical* if you mean by this that the critical method by which they are obtained is a process of logical reasoning ; but strictly they are metaphysical conditions, for though real and existing, according to Kant, they cannot be discovered *as* conditions by any psychological analysis ; and logic, after all, is used in every science. Again, 'universality' and 'necessity' cease to be ambiguous

[1] '*Axioms as Postulates*,' §§ 11–13.

as soon as the conditions of experience are understood. For if no experience can be thought, except under the *a priori* forms by which as experience it is conditioned, clearly the application of those forms to experience both metaphysically and logically *must* be without restriction. Thus the law that each change must have a cause is universal and necessary, because *all* phenomena *must* fall under the category of causality if they are to exist at all as phenomena, *i.e.*, to fall within our experience.

§ 162. The charge that Apriorism asserts mental forms which are static and immutable has better foundation. For though the Kantian and still more so the Hegelian admit and indeed insist upon development, they admit it in a form which is wholly inadequate to satisfy the demands of the pragmatist. Kant allowed that the acquisition of knowledge is gradual ; that it depends upon the growth of experience, and that only in experience can we reflect upon the functioning of the mental forms of which we at first are unconscious. To this Hegel added both his *Dialectic* and also his *Phenomenology ;* which latter may be regarded at once as the story of Absolute consciousness and as the history of his own philosophy in the making.[1] But neither the *Dialectic* nor the *Phenomenology* is capable of satisfying a modern evolutionist ; and the reason is to be found in their Apriorism. It is of the very essence of Apriorism that mind has a structure in which categories and forms of synthesis are involved. Hence for Apriorism the only form of development

---

[1] Wallace, article ' Hegel ' in *Encyclopædia Britannica,*). 618.

Q

which is admissible is one of which the final end is self-consciousness, but in which the self does not really develop but merely becomes known to itself. Development means that the mind acquires a knowledge of objects relatively distinct from itself, and by this means becomes conscious of its own *a priori* structure to which objects conform and under which they are, as it were, subsumed ; while *Absolute Knowledge*, Hegel's *highest* stage of mental development, is realised when spirit, looking back upon the externalisation and manifestation of itself in the world of nature, sees there its own self-conscious evolution, and in so doing comes to know itself as spirit.

Thus mental growth for the Kantian and the Hegelian means the gradual approach toward self-consciousness, or, in other words, the gradual acquisition of knowledge of our own mental structure. But the categories themselves do not grow. Their development in the *Dialectic* is logical, not real. Yet real mental development is a fact, and as a fact it appears to be more than the growth of self-consciousness. As Dr. Schiller says, there is no category which has not had a history, and a history in the individual mind as well as in the race. No one who reflects will deny that his concepts, one and all, become richer and fuller in content and significance as life progresses. Nor will he deny that *some* of them, at any rate, get intrinsically modified. We do not remember the time when we first began to think, and it is useless for our purpose to speculate on the psychology of the infant mind but we can trace the history of some of our concepts such as those of time, or space, or substance, or the self, sufficiently well to know that they have developed. And though the growth of our concepts does not correspond to the growth of the objects about which we think, it is none the less a real growth in which our concepts actually change and become, sometimes in part, sometimes even wholly, other than what they were. Now, if all concepts develop in this way—and I can find none, not even the categories of Aristotle, which do not undergo some kind of development and change, what becomes of the *a priori* structure of the mind which is supposed to function through and in these concepts? Has it changed, too? And if it has, in what sense can it still be said to be *a priori* and to have existed and functioned all along? Again, if the 'forms' under which we think phenomena are *a priori*, how is it that men differ so much in regard even to the most fundamental of principles and the most general of notions, notions and principles which everybody has in his mind and uses day by day? About what have there been more disputes among philosophers than the categories of cause, and substance and thing, and being and existence? Yet these are notions which function in every man's mind and which for everyone have some sort of content. If, then, our concepts, almost without exception, are capable of development and change, and if, in addition to this, and for that matter, because of this, different men have different concepts of the same entities and things, what ground is there for affirming that within the mind of each there is " the general plan for a self-consistent natural system"?[1]   How is it that, if all men carry about with them and constantly use the same *a priori* 'schema' and 'framework,' no one is conscious of it, and no two philosophers have ever agreed as to its structural form ?   How comes it that no one yet has constructed a self-consistent 'natural' system if ready-made within him everyone has its plan ?

§ 163.   It may be said, perhaps, that I have taken this plan or 'schema' too literally and in too Kantian a sense.   It should be restricted to the synthetic and analytic principles which belong to formal Logic or to a Logic such as that of Professor Bosanquet, which is described as the 'Morphology of Knowledge.'   On this point Dr. Caird remarks :

As it is impossible to separate the form from the matter of knowledge, formal Logic is driven upon a curious dilemma.   It has to choose between the alternatives of vanishing into nothing, and of including everything.   If it is to give all the principles of synthesis in judgment, its principles are infinite in number, since *any* conception may be the ground of a synthesis, and, therefore, of the analysis corresponding. And, on the other hand, if it is to give only principles of analysis that are not principles of synthesis, it can discover *no* such principles at all.   The only distinct line that can possibly be drawn between the formal and the material, must be drawn by considering all that is implied in thinking *objects in general* as opposed to any particular objects.[2]

But this consideration does not help us much towards the discovery of an element in knowledge

[1] Caird, *Critical Philosophy of Kant*, pp. 18, 19.
[2] *The Philosophy of Kant*, p. 306.

which is *a priori* in relation to the details of experience and the actual processes of thought. Personally, I can find no other *a priori* condition of rational experience except the power of thinking the many in the one and the one in the many, which presupposes again as its condition the unity of the thinking mind. Exclusive of the power of feeling and the faculty of will, which, in cognition proper, are subordinate to thought, there is nothing else required for thinking except something to think about and thought itself. Another question arises, of course, as soon as we ask where the object of thought comes from ; but we are prescinding from this at present. What we have to discover are what kinds of *a priori* forms and principles of synthesis already exist in the mind before we think, and are, metaphysically as well as logically, prior to thought as its conditions.

§ 164. Let us consider the subject-predicate form in which our judgments are usually expressed. Is this an *a priori* condition of all thought ? It hardly seems to be such. *Most* of our thoughts take this form, and all of them can be and are *de facto* almost without exception *expressed* in a proposition which has both a subject and a predicate. Yet we can think without analysing what we think into a subject and a predicate. In a perception, for instance, in which we subsume instantaneously an object under a universal idea, there seems to me to be no analysis into subject and predicate. The nature of what we perceive and think about in perceiving may be apprehended immediately without any separation of its ' what ' (content) from its

'that' (real existence); and this is especially the
case when an object is familiar. Doubtless, such a
judgment, when expressed in words, must take
some such form as (*v.g.*) 'That is my hat;' but this
does not seem to show that we did not apprehend
without analysis the nature of the object in question.
Again, when one has been thinking long over a
difficult problem, one sometimes seems to get a
grasp of it as a systematic whole, without consciously
determining any part of this system as subject
rather than as predicate. Indeed, thought of this
kind seems to me to be much more common than
one would imagine, for one is apt to overlook this
aspect of thinking, owing to the fact that one
always does try to express one's thoughts and to
express them in subject-predicate form. Yet even
in the verbal expression one may find confirmation
of what I have said, for often it is quite optional
what element in thought's content one takes as
subject and what as predicate, and sometimes it is
not easy to choose. For instance, when predicating
relations, we may say either that 'X is similar to Y,'
or that 'Y is similar to X,' or, again, simply that
'X and Y are similar;' and each of these forms of
expression seems to express equally well the thought
that was in our mind. From which I infer that
while thought implies analysis and synthesis, or
'the power of apprehending the many in the one
and the one in the many,' it need not necessarily
express itself in subject-predicate form, but does so,
as a rule, because we *first* think of an object, *then*
study it in detail, or in its relation to other objects,
and finally refer the result of our analytic exami-

nation back to the object itself, which thus becomes the subject of a proposition.

The subject-predicate form of judgment is due to the fact that objects come to us bit by bit, so to speak ; and again to the fact that our minds are finite and cannot take in things all at once, but have to attend first to one aspect of them and then to another. First of all, we apprehend a thing existing in the concrete, and this becomes our subject, that which we desire to know. Then we observe certain characteristics of that thing or its connection with other things which are near to it or like it. These we predicate of the former either as qualities or relations, since we regard them as belonging to, qualifying, or in some way or other giving us knowledge of, the original thing to which our attention was first directed. Thus predication about a ' subject ' is the natural way in which we express the knowledge we gradually acquire about first one thing and then another ; and all other forms of predication are derivative from this. There is no need, therefore, of any *a priori* structure of mind to account for what is already objectively necessitated by the process in which knowledge of finite objects is gradually acquired by a finite mind.

§ 165. In a similar way may be explained both the ' quality ' and the ' quantity ' of judgment. The affirmative judgment has been explained above. The negative seems to be due to the fact that we try to make an affirmative judgment but cannot. Somebody or something suggests that a certain P belongs to a certain S, but when we examine S, or when we recall it in thought, we find it has no P, and, therefore, we are forced by the objects concerned to assert that S is not P, instead of saying the contrary, as was suggested.[1]

The possibility of negation presupposes finite objects, and the same may be said of ' quantity.' We observe one thing, then a second, then a third, and so on, till finally we decide, arbitrarily or on account of some common characteristic, to put an end to our counting, and to call what we have got a class.[2] The members of this class, taken distributively, then become *all*, and any one or more of them *some*. Once again, therefore, we have no need of *a priori* forms, but only of finite objects presented to a finite mind and presented in a finite way. The multiplication of the finite is of itself sufficient to account for number and quantity, provided there be a mind to which it is presented and which is capable of apprehending the many in the one, and again the one in the many.

§ 166. Lastly, the origin of our notions of both ' *space* ' and ' *time* ' can be explained objectively ; not wholly objectively indeed, for, as usual, they imply a mind which can abstract, but objectively as regards their *fundamentum*. Given a number of finite objects mutually exclusive, and given extension in three dimensions, we have the wherewithal for our concept of space, while another extension of a different kind, viz., duration, provides us with

[1] Cf. an article of mine in *Mind,* July, 1906, entitled ' The Nature of Incompatibility ', where I endeavoured to show that all contradiction and all incompatibility is objectively determined.

[2] This is not an account of the origin of the universal idea, but of ' *quantity* ' in judgment. All ideas are *potentially* universal as soon as they are formed.

data for our notion of time. From the thing-hood
and the qualitative and quantitative differences of
things presented *simul* and side by side we abstract,
and thus are left with extension pure and simple,
which is the *fundamentum* of our concept of space.
Similarly, abstracting from the thing-hood and also
from the qualitative changes of one thing or of a succession of different things we have pure duration,
which is the *fundamentum* of our concept of time.
Pure duration, however, is not time, for in time
measurement is implied. Indeed, measurement is
closely connected both with space and time, for in
b⊃th notions 'dimension' is involved. Yet measurement, though as such it is an act of the mind, is
none the less objectively determined. The only
conditions required are (1) the presentation to a
mind of objects, things or qualities, each of finite
extension or of finite duration and mutually exclusive in regard to its neighbours, and (2) the
arbitrary selection of one of these extensions or
durations as a unit (as the *one*), and its application
to the others (to the *many*) as a measure or basis
by which to compare their respective dimensions.
Thus, for Aristotle, time implied the measurement
of changes by means of a unit of duration, the
extent of which might be fixed by selecting any two
points in the time-series ; and similarly place (*locus*)
implied the measurement of material things *quâ*
movable (*mobile*) by means of space—or distance—
units determined by the superficies of some arbitrarily chosen object. *Tempus est mensura motus*,
says Aquinas, *sicut locus est mensura mobilis*.[1]

[1] Comment. in Aristotle Physics, lib. iv., lec. iv.

The above account of the origin of our notions of space and time, and of the quantity and quality of judgments, does not of course pretend to be in any way adequate. On each of these subjects whole treatises might be, and have been, written. All that I wish to show is that all that our various categories and forms of judgment presuppose, are (1) finite objects, and (2) a mind capable of apprehending the many in the one and the one in the many, or, in other words, capable of analysing, synthesising, abstracting and comparing ; but not necessarily endowed with any *a priori* forms either of analysis or of synthesis. And, in brief, my argument is, that whatever category or form of analysis or synthesis one may take, it can be shown to be explicable *a posteriori*, and to differ from other concepts clearly and admittedly *a posteriori* only in regard to the degree of abstraction or generality involved.

§ 167. Dr. Caird seems to make a similar statement in the passage quoted above, and again when he says " the idea of the discordance of the Logic of thought (formal Logic) and the Logic of reality is a fiction, and the problem of their reconciliation is a self-made difficulty." [1] He points out also that Kant seems to have confused logical with real wholes, for he " overlooked the fact that the combination of species under an abstract genus is just the reverse process to the combination of parts in a concrete or individual whole." [2] There are in fact two ways in which we may combine the many in the one. There is the synthesis of qualities in

---

[1] *The Philosophy of Kant*, p. 313.   [2] *Ibid.*, p. 319.

a concrete thing, and the synthesis of specific differences under a genus ; and these two forms of synthesis are not to my mind equally real. The first implies the apprehension of the many in the one, and the second the apprehension of the one in the many. The first form of synthesis is, I take it, admitted to be a datum forced on us *a posteriori* and is strictly real. The second is a synthesis which has foundation in fact, since the ' one ' apprehended in the many is qualitatively the same ; but *the synthesis* itself neither seems to be *real* nor *a priori*. It is not real, for there is not the slightest evidence for supposing that qualities identical in nature but appearing in different objects are really one. Yet this is frequently assumed, and it would appear that it was upon some such basis as this that Kant hoped to construct the *a priori* form of mind. He seems to have thought that within the mind ideas are arranged according to their generality, the more general embracing the less general and so on.[1] And this is doubtless a fact *for the fully developed mind* as association seems to indicate. But the ' plan ' thus formed is only gradually built up by the experience of the individual, and is not an arrangement which is presupposed by experience, still less a plan of the real structure of the universe. The synthesis again is not *a priori*, as is shown by the fact that the way in which ideas are classified varies from man to man, and by the fact that in no case is the classification complete. In fact, whether we start *a priori* or *a posteriori* it is impossible to construct a plan either of the mind or of

[1] cf. *ibid.*, p. 328.

reality. If we begin with the individual, we find there are an indefinite number of paths by which we may ascend to *genera* and higher *genera* and *summa genera* ; and the road becomes too involved for any human mind to work it out. And if we start from the most abstract concept, ' being,' and work downwards as with Hegel, the result is the same. Each genus comprises an indefinite number of specific differences each of which we ought to select in turn, and so proceed from genus to genus, which would involve an almost endless process. It is true, as Dr. Caird remarks,[1] that " thought always proceeds from the less to the more determinate," and that " in so doing it cannot determine any object positively without determining it negatively ;" but it is not true that thought *proceeding a priori* cannot determine an object negatively (*i.e.*, reject some one species under a certain genus) without determining it positively (*i.e.*, without selecting some other species under the same genus to which it must belong), for the species contained under a given genus may be indefinite in number. To proceed by dichotomy is impossible unless both the *summum genus* and the *infima species* are fixed ; and even then between the *infima species* and the individual concrete object the distance is indefinitely great. To attempt to construct the world *a priori* is acknowledged to be absurd ; and the demand for "a complete and consistent system of categories " seems to me to be scarcely less absurd. At any rate, since such a system of categories has never been constructed, nor does it seem likely that it ever will be

[1] *Ibid.*, p. 313.

constructed, it is perfectly gratuitous to suppose that such a system is "implied in the synthetic process by which the dispersed data of sense are elevated into an organised whole of experience," so long as that process can be accounted for quite as well without such a hypothesis.

§ 168. I find it difficult to reconcile Dr. Caird's admission that the *a priori* principles of synthesis are infinite in number with his tenacious adherence to the doctrine that somehow or other they are systematised and brought to unity in the very nature of thought. We are expressly warned that the Logic of Hegel must not be taken as an attempt to construct the world *a priori;* and yet we are told that Formal Logic, Transcendental Logic, and the Logic of Reality are one and the same. " There is no purely formal logic," says Dr. Caird, " for the process of intelligence is a determination of the object by the categories." " Objects exist only for the conscious self and through the application of the categories," which are " but elements or moments in a truth which is completely stated only in the idea of self-consciousness," or again " stages in a process whose unity the mind is," and between which there is said to be " a logical order, an *order which is immutable and depends on the process of thought.*" [1]

All this seems to indicate that Dr. Caird believed that in thought there was some definite structure or schema, arranged category above category and synthesis above synthesis, a structure to which all knowledge had to conform and which was gradually

[1] ' Hegel ' (Blackwood Series), pp. 157, 187, etc.

brought to consciousness as mind developed. For such a view I can find not the slightest foundation. Hegel's "triadic law of thought" has a meaning when applied to the development of living truth in philosophy or religion, for often enough we do proceed from thesis *via* antithesis to a higher and richer synthesis, but as applied to categories in the way in which Hegel applied it, it seems to me quite meaningless. I cannot even make the first step from being to becoming, for becoming seems to me a notion far lower and less real than the concept of being. Unity in difference, again, is a notion which applies admirably to the concrete living whole, but its application to genera and species is only *per analogiam* and in no way reveals the *real* structure of the universe.

§ 169. A discussion of Hegel's Logic, however, and of other logics of the purely transcendental type belongs to the history of philosophy rather than to problems which press at the present day. I will not say that Apriorism is dead. So long as reality and thought are identified there will still be attempts to discover the *a priori* structure of the latter. But, fortunately, attempts of this kind are becoming less frequent. There is small trace of *Apriorism* in Green, and Mr. Bradley's scornful rejection of the 'bloodless categories' is well known. Transcendental deductions have ceased to be the favourite occupation of Hegelian and absolutist philosophers.

The decline of Apriorism is due largely to the extension of the doctrine of Immanence to cover the noumenal as well as the phenomenal object of knowledge. The Immanence of subject and object in knowledge is now regarded as strictly universal. It embraces all objects and it extends to all minds, bringing them together in the unity of an individual whole. The function of *a priori* forms, therefore, has gone. There is no longer any need of *a priori* categories and principles of synthesis to bring together what is not really distinct. The immediate successors of Kant did not realise this, and for a time philosophy was over-burdened with attempts to construct the universe *a priori*. But the futility of such philosophising has at length been recognised. Gradually it has dawned upon the philosophic mind that to build up a universe out of the variable and indefinite notions framed by human thought is a sheer impossibility, and that, however true it may be that the Absolute thinks in us, it is practically useless to try to look at the universe from the Absolute's point of view until such time as we become the Absolute.

§ 170. The *ratio essendi* of Apriorism has ceased to be. Philosophers now no longer start from a transcendental point of view and argue downwards; they prefer now to start from a more empirical and more human point of view, and, accepting the data of experience as they appear in human consciousness, to argue upwards from these data to the Absolute which alone can make them intelligible. This does not mean that philosophy has renounced the Critical method of Kant. It merely means that it has been found possible to dispense with the inter-mediaries which Kant placed between the ultimate subject and object. Absolutism still enquires into the metaphysical conditions and presuppositions of what is given; and still finds that these conditions take us beyond the human mind, that the theory of human cognition leads us on to a metaphysic of the Absolute, and that even ethics is incomplete without its metaphysical *prolegomena*. With such a *method* I have no fault to find, nor do I wish for one moment to suggest that either ethics or epistemology can be made intelligible apart from metaphysics. On the contrary, I fully agree that they cannot. But it is still open to question whether the Critical method necessarily leads to Absolutism, and whether Absolutism is capable of rendering much service toward the understanding of human cognition, or even toward making the universe intelligible ; and it is to this question that we must now direct our attention.

CHAPTER X.

CRITICISM OF ABSOLUTISM.

§ 171. In this chapter I propose to consider Absolutism from a metaphysical standpoint as a theory which must stand or fall according as it succeeds or fails to explain the universe, and, in particular, the fact of cognition. The cognition with which we are concerned is clearly human cognition ; and the universe which has to be explained *our* universe, the universe which is revealed to us, or which, at any rate, appears to be revealed to us, in the data of our experience. For from these data alone is it possible to make a start, since these alone are immediately given.

That absolutists in general accept this position and this criterion is, I think, clear. Professor Mackenzie remarks that we can only prove a philosophic theory by showing it to be the *only* one which makes the universe intelligible; [1] and Green is of the same opinion. Speaking of his own theory of the immanent presence and activity of God within us, he says:

Proof of such a doctrine, in the ordinary sense of the word, from the nature of the case there cannot be. It is not a truth deducible from other established or conceded truths. It is not a statement of an event or a matter of fact that can be the object of experiment or observation. It represents a conception to which no perceivable or imaginable object can possibly correspond, but one that affords the only means by which, reflecting on our moral and intellectual experience conjointly, taking the world and ourselves into account, we can put the whole thing together, and understand how (not *why*, but *how*) we are and do, what we consciously are and do. [2]

§ 172. Mr. Bradley's view of the function of theory and its relation to fact seems to me to vary somewhat according to whether it is his own or somebody else's theory that is in question. Referring to the doctrine of the reality of the self, he thus addresses his adversaries:

Present your doctrine (whatever it is) in a form which will bear criticism, and which will enable me to understand this confused mass of facts which I encounter on all sides. Do this, and I will follow you, and I will

[1] *Mind*, N.S. 59, p. 323.
[2] *Prolegomena to Ethics*, § 174.

R

worship the source of such a true revelation. But I will not accept nonsense for reality, though it be vouched for by miracle, and proceed from the mouth of a psychological monster.[1]

Observe, however, the change of tone which takes place immediately we get into Book II. Speaking of his own theory, Mr. Bradley says :

We have not to choose between accounting for everything on one side and on the other admitting it as a disproof of our doctrine of the Absolute. Such an alternative is not logical. If you wish to refute a wide theory based on general grounds, it is idle merely to produce facts which upon it are not explained. . . . The facts become an objection only when they are incompatible with some part of it; while, if they merely remain outside, that points to incompleteness in detail and not falsity in principle. A general doctrine is not destroyed by what we fail to understand. It is destroyed only by that which we actually do understand, and can show to be inconsistent and discrepant with the theory adopted.[2]

By this ingenious argument Mr. Bradley has completely reversed the position which he took up in regard to disagreeable doctrines. *He* has not to explain "the confused mass of facts which we encounter on all sides," but just as many or as few of them as suits his convenience. The rest are irrelevant and fall outside as details. Should you produce a 'fact' which seems to be relevant and yet to contradict his theory, he has an answer ready. The fact needs interpretation, and the ordinary and commonly accepted interpretation of it is wrong, or at least inadequate. Mr. Bradley is quite willing to accept any facts which we "really do under-

[1] *Appearance and Reality*, p. 113.   [2] *Ibid.*, pp. 184, 185.

tand ; " but when it comes to the issue there are
none. We assume knowledge where really there is
ignorance. " I maintain," he says, " that we know
nothing of those various forms of the finite which
shows them incompatible with that Absolute, for
he accepting of which we have general ground." [1]

§ 173. Such a position is, of course, practically
unassailable, unless *internal* contradiction can be
proved. But is it logical and rational? What is the
use of a theory unless it is to explain facts? And
how are we to judge whether it explains facts,
unless the facts themselves are understood? Surely
a theory which is consistent with itself may be, as
Dr. Schiller says, wholly irrelevant and useless. If
he metaphysician is to be allowed to disregard facts
at will on the ground that they are never rightly
understood ; if he is to be allowed dogmatically to
assert that no fact can contradict his theory as Mr.
Bradley does when he states that " we cannot know
hat the finite is in collision with the Absolute ; "
if he " can respect no element of experience except on
compulsion," and " can reverence nothing but what
by criticism and denial the more unmistakably
asserts itself," [2] it is small wonder that metaphysics
is treated by other sciences with scant courtesy,
and small wonder either that on these principles
innumerable Absolutisms should have grown up,
each contradictory of the others. I fail to see what
possible use there can be in a metaphysic which is
neither to explain *How* nor *Why*, and yet we are
repeatedly assured by Mr. Bradley that his metaphysic claims to do neither.

[1] *Appearance and Reality,* p. 185.　　[2] *Ibid.* pp. 185, 207.

§ 174. Mr. Bradley will reply that he *does* admit
facts. Has he not told us that " the ' given ' of
course is given ; it must be recognised, and it
cannot be ignored " ? [1] True, this much is conceded, but the sentence in which the concession is
made is surrounded by qualifications. Immediately
before it we are informed that :

It is a mere superstition to suppose that an appeal to
experience can prove reality. That I find something in
existence in the world or in my self, shows that that
something exists, and it cannot show more. Any
deliverance of consciousness — whether original or
acquired—is but a deliverance of consciousness. It is
in no case an oracle and a revelation which we have to
accept.[2]

Now, what possible use there can be in appealing
to consciousness if all that we are going to allow
to the deliverance of consciousness is ' existence,'
I am at a loss to understand. What is the good of
admitting that something exists, if you do not know
anything at all about what that something is ?
And if you are not going to accept the deliverances
of consciousness, content and all, what are you
going to accept ? I quite agree that a deliverance
of consciousness may *sometimes* be an illusion ;
and I agree also that there is ' a very wide interval
between recognising a datum and receiving blindly
(*i.e.*, without careful examination) its content as
reality ; ' but we must accept facts if we are to
reason at all, and to accept a fact as a *mere* datum of
consciousness, while at the same time denying the
reality of what is given as a fact, is surely *not* to
accept it.

[1] *Ibid.*, p. 207.   [2] *Ibid.*, pp. 206, 207.

§ 175. But must we accept facts as reality ? Can they, as Mr. Bradley says, exist without being real ? Most people would say that they cannot. Indeed, were it not that my 'facts' seem to have been surreptitiously removed I should be inclined to assert that Mr. Bradley's denial of the reality of facts is the first point in which his Absolutism conflicts with facts. To me the distinctions he makes between Appearance and Reality and Existence and Reality are invalid, and rest upon a confusion.

Appearances exist and yet are fraught with internal contradiction. The whole of Mr. Bradley's First Book is taken up with attempts to prove the contradictory nature of appearances ; and the whole of his Second Book (after the first two Chapters in which the ' General Nature of Reality ' is established) is taken up with attempts to prove that all appearances, precisely because of their ' self-discrepancy,' transcend themselves and so lead us on to a Reality, which they qualify somehow or other without contradiction. All facts or nearly all facts, for there are one or two exceptions, as we saw in a previous chapter, are for Mr. Bradley, *appearances ;* and the passages quoted above are really part of a protest of his against an appeal to the fact of ' change ' as a disproof of his Absolute.

§ 176. "Change," he says, "is a fact, and, further, this fact, as such, is not reconcilable with the Absolute. And if we could not in any way perceive how the fact can be unreal, we should be placed, I admit, in a hopeless dilemma." [1] The escape from the dilemma is easy, however. " For

[1] *Ibid.,* p. 206.

time has been shown to contradict itself, and so to be appearance. With this, its discord, we see at once, may pass as an element into a wider harmony. And with this, the appeal to fact at once becomes worthless." [1] For the proof that 'time' is a contradiction we are referred back, of course, to Book I, where this is supposed to have been proved. Before discussing this proof, however, there is in the passage quoted above one thing to which I should like to call attention. It is this, that while the *fact* which Mr. Bradley has admitted is the fact of 'change' the appearance which he declares to be contradictory is the appearance of '*time*.' Now I do not wish to quibble about the use of terms, nor do I wish to insinuate that Mr. Bradley's escape from the dilemma is barred by the substitution of 'time' for 'change,' since as a matter of fact change also has been found by him to be self-contradictory; but the transition which Mr. Bradley has made, unquestionably illicit as it stands, is characteristic of many of his attempts to reduce 'facts' to mere appearances. Again and again does he substitute in place of 'facts' philosophical constructions, and it is these constructions, and not the facts, that are shown to be contradictory.

§ 177. His criticism of 'time' itself affords us an illustration of this process, for we are told that "if you take it as a relation between units without duration, then the whole time has no duration, and is not time at all. But, if you give duration to the whole time, then at once the units are found to possess it; and they thus cease to be units." [2] Now, is 'time,' conceived as 'a relation between *units*

without duration,' a *fact* of our experience or a
philosophical construction ?   Clearly it is the latter,
and a bad one at that ; since, as Mr. Bradley says,
it destroys ' duration,' which is the very foundation
upon which that construction is built.   It is duration,
not time, which is a fact ; and it is duration which
has to be proved a contradiction.   The alternative
definition, however, keeps closer to the facts.
Common-sense believes in time and attributes to it
as a whole duration.   Hence, as Mr. Bradley points
out, the units must also have duration.   But why
not ?   Are there no durable units ?   Of course if
you abstract altogether from all the means by
which units can be marked off, you have no units
at all ; but then neither have you got time.   You
have merely an empty abstraction, viz., the unbroken duration of nothing at all.   But concrete,
enduring things are facts, and the duration of some
exists together with change and succession among
others.   Hence we have the means by which to
mark off units of time.   And because these units
themselves have duration, it by no means follows
that they cease to be units, any more than it follows
that the yard-rule which a tailor uses to mark off
his cloth has no length because it is his unit of
length.   That ' time ' as such is not real, I grant,
because it is a philosophic abstraction into which
a human element, viz., measurement, has been introduced ; but I cannot allow that it is not founded
on fact ; nor that, if properly defined, it involves
a contradiction.

§ 178.   Change, however, is more to our purpose,
since upon duration amid change the notion of

time is based, and upon the factual existence of change we are all agreed. But, says Mr. Bradley, change is only appearance, for it involves a contradiction.

Something, A, changes, and therefore it cannot be permanent. On the other hand, if A is not permanent, what is it that changes? It will no longer be A, but something else. In other words, let A be free from change in time, and it does not change. But let it contain change, and at once it becomes A^1, A^2, A^3. Then what becomes of A, and of its change, for we are left with something else? [1]

Now change, as I understand it, is predicable only of the concrete finite thing, a thing consisting of substance and accidents; of unity of ground amid structural differences.[2] Let us, then, substitute for A, a (a, b, c, . . .) (m, n, o, . . .); where a stands for the unity of ground or substance; a, b, c, . . . for the accidents essential to A; and m, n, o . . . for accidents which are not essential. What, then, do we mean when we say that A changes? We mean that one of these unessential accidents or differences is modified or gives place to some other accident or difference; that a (a, b, c . . .) (m, n, o. . .) has become a (a, b, c . . .), (m', n, o. . .). And what do we mean when we say that A is permanent? We mean that the substance a remains the same, and also that the accidents, a, b, c, which are essential to A, remain the same, but nothing more. Of course, if A be taken as a structureless and formless unit, it cannot

---

[1] *Appearance and Reality*, p. 46.
[2] cf. chap. xiv., for a fuller explanation of this.

both be permanent and yet be subject to change. But concrete things are not formless and structureless units ; and, recognising this, when we predicate of them permanence, we do not predicate it of the whole thing, but only of its essential nature ; so that it is still possible to predicate change of the same thing without contradiction, since the predicated changes *ex hypothesi* do not affect its essential nature.[1]

§ 179. If my solution of the difficulty is valid, change does not imply contradiction ; and if change does not imply contradiction, it is *not* appearance ; and if it is not appearance it is reality, in which case Mr. Bradley's Absolute is not the one and only reality. It will be obvious, however, to those who are familiar with *Appearance and Reality* that I have but pushed the difficulty further back ; and I shall be asked to read again the chapters on *Substantive and Adjective, Relation and Quality*. In regard to the argument used in the first of these two chapters, I shall have more to say later ;[2] but I may here remark that if my conception of Substantive and Adjective, or rather Substance and Accident, is intrinsically contradictory, so also is Mr. Bradley's conception of the universe as a ' Unity in difference.' In fact, the Aristotelian conception of Substance and Accident and the Hegelian conception of Unity in difference are one and the same ; but the Aristotelian applies it to the concrete individual thing, while the Hegelian applies it to the universe

[1] For an account of the Aristotelian doctrine of change, *vide* chap. xiii.
[2] *Vide* chap. xiii.

at large.   Hence the real question at issue is whether
the Hegelian is right or wrong in asserting that
Reality is one ; and, as underlying this doctrine in
most modern Absolutisms is a peculiar theory of
relation, to this theory we must now give our
attention.

§ 180.   There is a certain amount of truth in
Green's dictum that all knowledge is knowledge of
relations.   To a large extent definition does consist
in the predication of relations.   Dr. Caird puts the
matter thus :

> The beginning of knowledge is the reference of a
> sensation to an object, of which it is interpreted as the
> quality.   This object is determined merely as object in
> general : it is like all other objects, yet it is conceived
> as completely individual and independent.   The simple
> quality attributed to it, is conceived as belonging to it
> in itself, apart from all relations to other objects.   In
> the advance of knowledge, however, this simple indi-
> vidual object becomes progressively defined and
> determined.   And not only is quality added to quality
> in an indefinite series, but its isolation is taken from
> the object.   It is found that qualities are but relations
> in disguise, and that, therefore, completely to define the
> object in itself, is the same thing as to put it in relation
> to all other objects.[1]

At first sight there seems to be little the matter
with this straightforward description of the growth
of human knowledge.   Yet it requires but a step
to pass from this position to that of Green and
Renouvier, in which the world—or, at any rate, the
inorganic world—is identified with a system of
relations.   Dr. Caird's apparently accurate description, in fact, contains two assumptions—(1) that

[1] *The Philosophy of Kant,* p. 329.

qualities are but relations in disguise, and (2) that
by relations isolation is taken away from the object.

§ 181. The statement that all qualities are at
bottom relations in disguise, if *taken literally*, and
of real qualities, is absurd. For we cannot have a relation unless there is something which it relates; and
that something, since it cannot be a bare identity,
must involve difference and so quality. Relations
presuppose qualities for their very existence. Their
nature depends upon the objects which they relate
or connect, and when those objects are changed,
the relations themselves are changed. It is true
that we often *know* a relation without knowing
precisely the nature of the objects related ; and
this is so particularly when the relation is one of
cause and effect. For in producing an effect many
causes may co-operate, and the re-action of the
object in which the effect is produced, itself may
have played a part. Unless, therefore, we can
analyse the effect and attribute it, part for part, to
the various causes concerned in its production, the
effect tells us little about the causes except that
somehow or other they have been active in relation
to that effect. Nevertheless, each cause has its
own nature, and the relation to which its activity
gives rise depends upon that nature, whether the
latter be known by us or not.

Further, to know a relation implies that we know
something at any rate of the objects or qualities
related. For even if the relation be merely one of
difference, it implies that we know something of
what is different, otherwise we could not know that
it was different. But many relations imply more

than this. We cannot know that one object is bigger than another unless we know what it is to be 'big,' *i.e.*, to have size or quantity. And the fact that mathematics and geometry are possible, presupposes that about the nature of quantity and the nature of figure we have considerable knowledge.

§ 182. While granting, then, that much of our knowledge of qualities comes through a knowledge of their relations, and that sometimes what is predicated as a quality is in truth a relation in disguise, I cannot grant that *all* our knowledge of qualities is at bottom a knowledge of their relations, still less that qualities *in rerum natura* are merely relations in disguise. For if it is true that we sometimes know a relation before we know the precise nature of its terms, it is also true that we often know the terms before we know the relation between them, and that in every case the knowledge of a relation implies some knowledge of the objects related. Hence from the psychology of our knowledge of relations we can draw no conclusion as to the priority of a relation and of the objects it relates.

This fact is of considerable importance; for all absolutist theories of relations seem to be based on psychology, owing, I suppose, to the absolutist doctrine that thought, or at any rate some form of psychical activity, is identical with reality itself. Green, for instance, assumes that relations are prior to, or at least are frequently a condition of, our *knowledge* of the terms. Yet, as I have pointed out, it does not follow, because we often define a term by its relations, that we have no knowledge of that term apart from its relations, for if this be so it is difficult to see how we could define it at all. Again, Dr. Caird's statement that 'completely to define an object is to put it in relation to all other objects' seems to be based upon the psychological fact that our knowledge of an object often consists largely in a knowledge of its relations. But though it is true that, if by 'knowing an object completely' we mean 'knowing *all about it*,' to completely know an object would be to know all its relations, it does not follow that the nature of the thing itself depends upon the nature of its relations, nor yet that an object is unknowable apart from its relations. Indeed, Dr. Caird grants that first of all we conceive simple qualities which belong to objects apart from their relations to other objects; so that not only are the inferences which absolutists draw from the psychology of relations illegitimate, but those inferences are based upon certain psychological facts to the exclusion of other facts which, if taken into consideration, would make a considerable difference to the absolutist theory.

§ 183. This last point may be illustrated from Mr. Bradley's doctrine of relations. He, too, seems to regard the latter from a psychological standpoint; but, observing that the knowledge of a relation and of its terms often seems to arise *simultaneously* in consciousness, he infers not that the relation is prior to its terms, but that the relation and its terms mutually presuppose one another, and at the same time imply in the background a unity or whole from which they have emerged or in which they have broken out. Take, for instance, the following

passage : " Their plurality (*i.e.*, the plurality of
qualities) depends on relations, and without that
relation they are not distinct.   But if not distinct,
then not different, and therefore not qualities." [1]
To what does this passage refer ?   To the distinguishing and relating of qualities by the thinking
mind, or to the qualities themselves which it is said
to distinguish and relate ?   From the context it
would appear that it refers to the act of thought.
But if so, how does the fact (if it is a fact) that
qualities distinguished in consciousness are always
related in consciousness, prove that qualities are
not really distinct in the objective world ?   And,
again, by what kind of logical process can you pass
from the simultaneous appearance of distinction and
relation in consciousness to the objective inter-
dependence of the relation and its terms ?   Mr.
Bradley's argument is valid only provided we grant
(1) that reality and sentient experience are one—
a hypothesis which I have already shown to be
false, and which certainly should not be assumed at
this early stage of the argument—and (2) that in
sentient experience qualities, *afterwards distinguished*, are *really one*—which also is false or at best
is a gratuitous assumption—and (3) that product
(thought distinctions and relations) and process
(unknown, but supposed to connect thought and
sentience) *are not separable*—which adds but one
more to the other assumptions Mr. Bradley has to
make in order to prove his point.[2]

§ 184.   The absolutist theory of relations, then,
cannot be established on the basis of psychological

[1] *Appearance and Reality*, p. 28.   [2] cf. chap. **v.**

fact, and it is to the attempt so to establish it that we must attribute the contradiction which exists between Green's theory and the theory of Mr. Bradley. But when we seek for some more metaphysical foundation for what is obviously a metaphysical theory, it does not seem to be forthcoming. We are told that by its relations the isolation of an object is taken away—a statement which is indisputable if it mean merely that an object conceived in relation to something else is not conceived in isolation, as it is also indisputable if isolation mean isolation from interaction ; but more than this is meant. For the absolutist the negation of isolation means the negation of independent existence, and upon this rests his doctrine that reality is really and substantially one, and not merely one as proceeding from a common source, or one as a systematic logical whole. No proof, however, is given of the statement that relations deprive objects of their ' isolation,' *i.e.*, their individuality or independent existence. We are assured that objects which are held together in an act of thought are really held together by unity of ground *in rerum natura ;* but the validity of this transition from the psychological to the real order has never been demonstrated. We are told that there are no external relations, and that every relation must modify intrinsically both its terms ; but we are not told why this is so. Mr. Bradley, who admits that relations imply qualities, asserts also that qualities imply relations. Relations and qualities are to be found, so to speak, upon the same level of existence. Qualities are no more and no less prior to their terms than terms are prior to their relations, and apart from one another they cannot exist. But except for the psychological argument above discussed, no positive proof of this theory of relations is given, nor does Mr. Bradley tell us definitely what he understands a relation to be. His arguments are almost wholly negative. His aim is to show that the notion of relations and of qualities is contradictory, and that hence relations and qualities are mere appearances which are self-discrepant and lead to something beyond, viz., to an Absolute Ground. But though his discussion of this question in the first part of his book purports to be a criticism of the position of the realist, the theory of relations which he discusses is not that of the realist, or at any rate not that of the Aristotelian realist.

§ 185. The Aristotelian does not conceive a relation as a kind of physical nexus or bond which joins two objects together and so makes them one. A relation is merely a πρός τι σχέσις (an *esse ad aliquid*) which arises from the rational plan or *order* that is manifested in the universe. It is an attribute which is said to belong to an object on account of some one of its qualities (called by the scholastics the *fundamentum* of the relation), but which requires for its existence a ' term ' to which its whole essence as a relation is to refer. That ' term,' if the relation is *real*, ordinarily belongs to some object other than that of which the relation is predicated. But the relation itself does not belong to the two objects at once. If there is only one relation, it belongs to that object which possesses the *fundamentum* on account of which the relation is predicated ; while if the relation is reciprocal or mutual, there are in reality two relations belonging respectively to the two objects related. Hence, while for Mr. Bradley the truth about relations is better expressed by saying that A and B are related, the truth for Aristotle was better expressed by saying that A is related to B, and (if the relation is mutual) that B is related to A.

The arguments upon which Mr. Bradley bases his doctrine that relations and qualities are merely appearances, break down entirely when applied to this theory of relations.

The qualities A and B are to be different from each other, and, if so, that difference must fall somewhere. If it falls, in any degree or to any extent, outside A or B, we have relation at once. But, on the other hand, how can difference and otherness fall inside? If we have in A any such otherness, then inside A we must distinguish its own quality and its otherness. And, if so, then the unsolved problem breaks out inside each quality, and separates each into two qualities in relation.[1]

'A difference must fall somewhere.' What is this difference? Is it an increment in quantity or quality which makes A different from B? If so, the difference itself is an integral part either of A *or* of B, and so falls within one or the other. Or is the nature of A wholly different from the nature of B? If this be so, the difference is A *plus* B, and while part of it coincides with A, the other part coincides with B. Or, again, is this difference simply the '*otherness*' of A in regard to B? If this be what is meant, then '*otherness*' *as such*

[1] *Appearance and Reality*, p. 29.

S

falls only within the mind of the rational percipient, whose judgment on this account is none the less true. For objectively and in fact A has a certain definite nature, and B also ; and the nature of A and the nature of B are *ex hypothesi* not the same. This fact the percipient apprehends, and expresses it by saying that A is different or other than B. To perceive a relation is to apprehend two facts in the same mental act ; and to predicate of one a relation of ' otherness ' in respect of the other is our way of saying that we have apprehended two *different* facts.

§ 186. Mr. Bradley further objects that since qualities are related there must be

a diversity which falls inside each quality. It has a double character, as both supporting and as being made by the relation. It may be taken as at once condition and result, and the question is as to how it can combine this variety. For it must combine the diversity, and yet it fails to do so. . . . [Hence] the diversity is fatal to the internal unity of each (quality); and it demands a new relation, and so on without limit.[1]

Again, Mr. Bradley's objection is based upon a misconception of the nature of a relation. The quality is not *made* by the relation, but the relation arises from the quality as its cause or ground. The relation is the quality considered in respect to something other than itself. And though a relation should always have a *fundamentum in re*, the relation itself may be due merely to our way of considering things, and may not imply any real *ordo* in the

[1] *Ibid.*, p. 31.

quality or object of which the relation is predicated.
Thus Aquinas says :

> Those entities which are called *ad aliquid* signify, accor-
> ding to their proper nature, only a *respectus ad aliud;*
> which *respectus* is sometimes in the nature of things, as
> when certain things are according to their very nature
> ' ordered ' to one another and have a mutual ' inclina-
> tion' toward one another; and relations of this kind
> must be real.   But sometimes the *respectus* signified by
> that which is called *ad aliquid*, is only in the apprehension
> of the intellect which relates (*conferre*) one to another ;
> and then there is a *relatio rationis tantum*.[1]

For instance, whenever one thing is referred to
another on account of some change which has taken
place in it owing to the action of that other thing,
there is a *real* relation, as when an effect is referred
to a cause, or again when a cause is referred to its
effect (*provided* some change takes place in the
object which produces that effect), for in both cases
there is a real *ordo* of one thing to the other.[2]   On
the other hand, the relation of God to His creatures
is not a *real* relation, because the act of creation
implies no change on the part of God ; and similarly
the relation of the knowable to knowledge is not
real, because the knowable does not change by the
fact that it becomes known. Yet both these
relations have a *fundamentum in re*, and, if predicated of the creature and of the knower respectively,
are real, since a real *ordo* is involved.   In neither
case, however, is real diversity introduced into the
quality on account of the relation that is predicated

---

[1] *Summa,* I, 9, 27 @ I.
[2] *De Potentia,* 7 @ 9 and cf. Arist. *Metaph.* Δ. 1021ᵃ 2°, bk. v.
c. 15, § 2.

of it, for the relation itself *nihil est aliud quam ordo unius creaturae ad aliam.*   Hence the relation " *in quantum est accidens, habet quod sit in subjecto ; non autem in quantum est relatio vel ordo ; sed solum quod ad aliud sit quasi in aliud transiens, et quodam-modo rei relatae assistens.   Et ita relatio est aliquid inhaerens licet non ex hoc ipso quod est relatio.*" [1] A relation, then, even when real, is only another aspect of the *fundamentum* which on account of the rational plan of the universe has a certain *ordo ad* other things.   No relation, therefore, is required in order to bring together what are not really distinct. And if you tell me that at any rate the *ordo* and its *fundamentum* are different and so introduce diversity into the thing, my reply is that, though in a certain sense a real relation may be regarded as the ' difference ' of a concrete thing, it does not destroy the individuality or isolation of that thing, any more than the differences of the Absolute destroy its individuality or its isolation, for every concrete thing is essentially a unity amid differences, and the differences are brought together in the unity of the ground.[2]

§ 187.   Two more objections may be briefly discussed.   Mr. Bradley does not believe in merely external relations, and tells us that he cannot understand " the leaving by the terms of one set of relations and their adoption of another fresh set " if relations are merely external and if the result, therefore, makes no difference to the terms.   For, he asks us, if the change of relation does not make a difference to the terms, to what does it make a

[1] *Ibid.*, ad. 7.   [2] cf. chap. xiii.

difference? Professor James' answer to this question is that it makes " a difference to us onlookers at least ; "[1] which is true, but I think we may go further than this. For, if the relations are real, the change of relations implies a real change in some one or other of the qualities which constitute the *fundamenta* of the relations concerned, and it implies also a change in the rational plan of the universe, or in the *ordo* of things one to another. In other words, the relation, in so far as it is real, is not external to the thing of which it is predicated, though it is external to the ' term ' of that relation, and to that other thing to which the term belongs. The absolutist assumes that a change of relation must, in every case, make an intrinsic difference to *both* the objects related, and indirectly to all other objects and all other relations existing in the universe. But this is almost inconceivable; for it is difficult to see how an increase of ·001 inches in my height can possibly affect the height of millions of other people in different parts of the globe. It may be that this is the case ; but if it is, the intrinsic modification which has taken place in them is infinitesimal and can be neglected. Moreover, such a modification, if it really does take place, is certainly not due directly to the change which has taken place in me, or to the change in my relations to other men ; but is brought about by intricate and circuitous paths unknown to either scientist or metaphysician. It is my relation to other men that has changed, because it is in me that the change itself has taken place. It is only *per accidens* that the relations of

[1] *A Pluralistic Universe*, p. 362.

other men to me have changed ; their *real* relations (*i.e.*, their relations to a given standard or unit of height) remaining *ex hypothesi* the same. Thus a change of relation implies a change in the *fundamentum* upon which the relation is based, and so in the *ordo* of the things which exist in the universe ; but no other real change is involved except in so far as other *fundamenta* are affected.

§ 188. Lastly, we are asked how comparison can reveal the truth about things if relations are merely external. In regard to real relations, there is no difficulty on this point, for they are not external to the thing of which they are predicated. And in regard to a *relatio rationis* such as one of mere difference or otherness, comparison may still be valid and true, provided the relation has, as it should have, foundation in reality. For, as I have said, when we perceive or apprehend a difference, what happens is that we perceive in the same mental act two things, one of which has a quality A which the other has not. And provided this is *de facto* the case, the relation of otherness which we predicate on account of our act of perception has, in a real sense, objective validity.

§ 189. Mr. Bradley, then, has failed to show that the Aristotelian theory of relations involves a contradiction, and so has failed to prove that relations and qualities are mere appearances. And as the absolutist theory is acknowledged to be self-contradictory and is based on an illicit transition from the psychological to the real order, the thesis that reality is one and individual certainly cannot be established on these grounds.

On the other hand, the arguments by which Green
seeks to establish that thesis contain much that a
realist would readily grant. He would grant that
the universe consists in a system of relations in the
sense that all created things are related to one
another; and that the order of those relations is
unalterable in that past, present and future are
determinate in nature, whether or not they could
have been or could be other than what they were,
are, or will be ; and, again, that upon the determinate character of these things and their relations
the possibility of knowledge depends, though
whether unalterableness is of much practical utility
as a test of truth might be questioned.[1] Further,
the partial consciousness of the world of ' relations '
implies an intelligence in man which cannot be
accounted for by any natural history, *i.e.*, a spiritual
principle or rational soul which cannot, as such,
have been produced by generation, and which is
simple, inasmuch as it can apprehend the many in
the one. But from this one can hardly infer that
man's intelligence is ' out of time,'[2] for though
different stages of a change must be present at once
to a consciousness of change, and though again that
consciousness, if considered as a single act in
isolation from its antecedents and consequents,
would itself be free from change, it does not follow
that it has no duration, nor yet that consciousness
in man is not subject to change. Indeed, to admit
that man may ' pass into a state of consciousness
of change and pass out of it ' seems to be practically

[1] cf. *supra.* § 151.
[2] cf. *supra,* § 152 and *Prolegomena to Ethics,* § 65.

an admission that man's consciousness does change.
Green's argument here is very far from conclusive.
In fact, the nearer we get to the central doctrine of
his metaphysic the less conclusive and the more
ambiguous do his arguments become, though there
is still much that may be conceded without prejudice
to Realism. 'A plurality of things cannot *of
themselves* unite in one relation, nor can a single
thing of itself bring itself into a multitude of
relations. Hence there must be something other
than the manifold things themselves which combines
them without effacing their severalty.' And, again,
' as the system is one, so must be the principle which
constitutes them and is the condition of their
existence.'

§ 190. So far, so good. But in what way is this
single active self-conscious principle the condition
and source of the cosmos which we know ? Are the
objects which it not only relates, but produces,
objects existing merely in the consciousness of that
being, or have these each their own real, though
dependent, existence ? And is the act by which
these objects are produced better described as an
act of intelligence or an act of creation ? And this
unity which characterises the cosmos. Is it a real
concrete unity like that which is predicable of the
divine principle producing it ? Is the world we
experience one as we ourselves or any other organic
being is one, or is it one only because it proceeds
from a single cause and because its manifold
complexity is ordered to a single end ? In a word,
is God immanent within the cosmos and the cosmos
immanent within God, or is the existence of the

former distinct from, though dependent in all respects upon, the existence of the latter? Here lies the crux of the difficulty. The key to the position of the absolutist lies in the doctrine of Immanence, and yet the doctrine, as interpreted by Absolutism, is a mere assumption, unverifiable in experience and in violent antagonism with common-sense belief. That the content of thought or the object as known is immanent within the mind is obvious; but that the real objects about which we think are immanent is a gratuitous assertion made, in the first instance, by Fichte, with a view to getting rid of noumenal things-in-themselves and so saving the Kantian theory from Subjectivism. And this assertion every absolutist from Hegel to Green and Bradley repeats, but always without proof or confirmation. Doubtless, no object is unrelated to consciousness, otherwise it would be unknowable. And doubtless also, knowledge, in a sense, is only of phenomena, *i.e.*, of things as they appear to us, *scil.*, to our senses and intellect functioning in cognitive harmony. But why assume that real objects, if distinct from ourselves, cannot appear to us as they really are? Green tells us that they cannot, or at least he says that if the knowable world and the subject capable of knowing it are ‘ independent,’ knowledge is inexplicable. But he does not support this statement by an examination of other theories of knowledge which claim to account for the reproduction by mind of relations existing in the outside world. No, the true reason for the doctrine of Immanence is not the bankruptcy of Realism, but the fact that Kant’s Apriorism forced him to postulate noumenal things which, by man, could never be known because their appearances are not manifestations of their nature, are not *their* appearances, but constructions due to the minds which seek to know them. Hence the rational way to reform Kant's error would have been to get rid of unknowable things, not by denying their existence, but by denying their noumenal character. The absolutist, instead of abolishing real and independent things altogether from philosophy, should have abolished Apriorism.

§ 191. Yet this is not the method Absolutism has chosen. Regardless of the consequences of such a procedure, it has extended the doctrine of Immanence so as to include the real as well as the so-called phenomenal object of knowledge. True, in some sort of way Green's theory is an explanation of the origin of human knowledge, but what a cost its acceptance would entail ! The personality of man disappears. In so far as he becomes the vehicle of an eternal consciousness, he is identical with that consciousness, and his human character is gone. His thoughts and actions are not *his* at all, but the thoughts and actions—whether true or false, moral or immoral, it does not matter—of the Supreme Being who, for a longer or shorter time, actuates his so-called organism. And in so far as he is not the vehicle of that consciousness, what is he ? Nothing but a conglomeration of relations which have no existence of their own or of his, but exist merely for some other consciousness. Nor are these merely two ways of regarding the same thing, for it is not the same but a different thing that is regarded.

Man's body and his consciousness or soul in any other theory but Green's are one being, but in Green's theory they are wholly different and unconnected, in so far as things can be different and unconnected in Absolutism. Man's consciousness in so far as it rises above the sentient level is a very partial and inadequate edition of *the* eternal consciousness; but his body and his sensations, in so far as they are not the instruments or objects of his thoughts—and for the most part they are not, are not *his* at all, but are merely " names for substantiated relations between phenomena, relations to which an existence on their own account is fictitiously ascribed, but which, in truth, *only exist for*, or through the action of, *the* unifying and self-distinguishing spiritual subject," [1] and apparently of any other finite self-distinguishing subject which happens momentarily to be conscious of them. Thus not only the personality and humanity, but also the unity of man is destroyed.

§ 192. I have said that Green's theory in some way explains the origin of knowledge. That is an exaggeration. It merely states that knowledge is due to a mysterious reproduction of the Absolute in a finite vehicle. It explains nothing. The manner of this reproduction, its intermittence, its apparent development and growth, are left entirely to the reader's imagination. About the relation of organisms to the eternal consciousness we are told nothing except that they are its ' vehicles.' Whatever judgment, then, we may pass upon the epistemology of Realism, Green's epistemology certainly

[1] *Prolegomena to Ethics,* § 40.

does not explain the growth of knowledge. It does not even explain the ordinary facts which everybody knows; why things appear to be external, individual, distinct from one another and from ourselves, and, except for interaction, independent. Yet that they are so is an ordinary and almost intuitive 'deliver-ance' of every man's consciousness. As I have said before, this may be an illusion, but if it is an illusion it must be proved to be an illusion; and a theory which asserts that it is an illusion must also show how that illusion arises. It would be beside the point here to plead that no theory is bound to take account of all the facts, for these are facts which Absolutism does take account of, since it declares them to be illusory appearances. How, then, are these facts to be explained?

§ 193. T. H. Green makes no attempt to explain 'objectivity' and 'otherness.' Objectivity, in his view, is due to the nature of thought; and this is the solution which is given by all absolutists who identify Reality with Thought—a solution which reminds one of the scholastic who is supposed to have said that engines move because they have *vis locomotiva*. The *ego* posits an *alter ego* because it is its nature so to do. Mr. Bradley finds this simple solution hardly satisfactory, since thought can never equate itself with reality, and so cannot be reality. It is in sentient experience that we meet with and become one with reality, and it is the sensuous infinitude of this which, in his theory, accounts for the otherness of thought

The apparent 'independence' of the external world is also difficult to account for in Absolutism.

In Green's theory it arises, I suppose, from the fact that the eternal consciousness, objectified as the cosmos, is immanent within our minds, and yet is only partly immanent, for we do not know the whole of reality and our efforts to know it are constantly thwarted. In Mr. Bradley's theory also reality is, to some extent, independent (*i.e.*, *relatively* independent) of ' finite centres of experience,' and still more independent, of course, of the ' self ' which is but a construction arising from within these finite centres. The link, however, which connects the ' finite centre of experience ' with reality itself is to be found, not above, as with Green, but below, in the ' this ' in which reality is given, and in which it is on the sentient level one with the centre it produces.

§ 194.   Thus in some sort of way independence and objectivity may be accounted for in Absolutism ; but the independence and objectivity there conceded being essentially relative and to a large extent illusory, it is impossible for Absolutism to explain how it comes about that things appear to be external, individual and material, since they are at bottom immanent, one, and spiritual. The analytic character of thought cannot account for the externality which seems to belong to perceived objects, if, in reality, those objects are one with ourselves and are given as one in the felt-wholes of sentient experience. The relative independence of finite selves and of finite centres of experience cannot account for our belief in their individuality and self-subsistence, if, as Green seems to hold, in so far as we think the same thing we are really not many but one ; or if, as Mr. Bradley affirms, all souls live and move by "real identity of ideal content." 'Degrees of reality,' again, cannot account for the apparent difference between ourselves and what we call the material world, if at bottom that world is the immanent effect of spiritual thought-activity, and, therefore, really spiritual and psychical like thought itself. In short, between the philosophical theory of Absolutism and the facts of our experience there is a contradiction ; and that contradiction is fatal to Absolutism, unless it can be *proved* to be merely apparent, and unless its origin can be satisfactorily explained.

§ 195. In Green's theory there is also internal contradiction. For the thoughts and the rational acts of men are really the thoughts and rational acts of one supreme Intelligence, which is thus responsible for all the errors, illusions, contradictions, false theories, and corrupt moral doctrine and practice of which man has ever been guilty—a hypothesis that is wholly incompatible with the moral rectitude which is held to be the first among the attributes of that supreme and all-wise Intelligence.

Mr. Bradley does his best to escape this contradiction. Indeed, it is a general principle with him from first to last that internal contradictions must be avoided at all costs. But the costs are very serious. Not only are facts completely ignored if it is inconvenient to recognise them ; not only is God, like everything else in which the ordinary man believes, declared to be mere appearance ; but Mr. Bradley's theory is riddled with mysteries and insoluble problems, almost all of his own making,

and is, perhaps, of all Absolutisms the most
inadequate and incomplete. At the end of almost
every chapter Mr. Bradley confesses that he has
failed to explain how appearances are to be reconciled
in the unity of the Absolute to which they are
supposed to belong. Error is a fact; it is not
merely a partial truth, but a positive mistake; yet
we are assured that the Absolute has, without
subtraction

every arrangement which we seem to confer upon it by
our mere mistake. [Even] the one-sided emphasis of
error, its isolation as positive and as not dissoluble in
a wider connection will contribute *we know not how* to
the harmony of the Absolute.[1] [Space again has to be]
absorbed in a non-spatial consummation; [and though]
how in particular this can be, we are unable to lay
down, [we are asked to believe that] our ignorance in
detail is no objection against the general possibility.[2]
The incomplete diversity of various systems, the per-
plexing references of each same feature to many ideal
wholes, and again that positive special feeling [which
is characteristic of the ' this ' and the ' mine '],—all this
detail is not made one in any way which we can verify.[3]

Yet it is made one somehow or other, because
Reality *ex hypothesi* is one, and therefore it must
be so. Good and evil, beauty and ugliness, pleasure
and pain, in spite of their being admittedly contradictions, are all ' to conduce to the ultimate good,
and to be *somehow* reconciled in the unity of the
Absolute.'

§ 196. Mr. Bradley freely acknowledges that he
cannot explain *how* these reconciliations take place;

---

[1] *Appearance and Reality*, pp. 192, 195.   (Italics mine).
[2] *Ibid*, p. 222.   [3] *Ibid.*, p. 239.

for, as we have pointed out, he differs from Green in that he does not consider himself bound to explain either ' *how* ' or ' *why.*' He does claim, however, to have shown that, in general, these reconciliations are not impossible. Yet even in this I cannot admit that his efforts have been successful. As for Green, so for Bradley and for all absolutists, evil and error prove particularly obstinate and impossible to manage, for they seem to make the Absolute contradict itself. It is easy enough to say that error is due to a one-sided and partial point of view ; but if it is the Absolute which differentiates itself and acts through and in finite centres, it is the Absolute which makes mistakes and contradicts its own assertions. It is the Absolute which says that things are what they are not, and that they are real when they only appear ; and these are positive errors which seem to be incompatible with an Absolute which has as another of its differences ' truth.' Again, the explanation of pleasure and pain as counterbalancing or neutralising one another in the Absolute is far from satisfactory ; for apart from the hedonistic tone of this solution, pain, if really neutralised by pleasure, would seem to have ceased to exist altogether. Lastly, the finite and the infinite are, to my mind, wholly incompatible, and cannot be reconciled in any concrete unity or whole. For finites, no matter how many you take or how you arrange them, or harmonise them, or mix them up, are still, in the end, finite as before. And to assert dogmatically that we know so little about the infinite and the finite that we cannot prove them to be contradictory hardly answers this difficulty, since, in that case, they cannot be proved to be one.

It is useless, however, to urge these difficulties further ; for Mr. Bradley acknowledges that they can never be explained by a human mind. Nevertheless, space, time, individuality, personality, evil, error and pain are not details ; and until they *have* been explained Absolutism can hardly be called even a working hypothesis. The thesis that Reality is One and Individual cannot be proved directly, nor can any satisfactory answer be given to the numerous objections that may be urged against it. Hence, though *Appearance and Reality* does not pretend to give " a systematic account of all the regions of appearances, which would be required for 'a genuine proof' of the principles it asserts," it seems to me to have failed even in its primary object of stating consistently 'a general view about Reality' and of answering 'more obvious objections.'

§ 197. Absolutism as a philosophy is essentially incomplete, and whatever form of Absolutism we may consider its incompleteness can hardly escape our notice, especially if we compare it with the philosophy of Kant, which, in spite of its inconsistencies, was comparatively free from those irritating *somehows* which meet us in Absolutism at every turn. Absolutism is a standpoint, not a systematic philosophy ; and as soon as it tries to become systematic, it at once gives rise to divergencies and contradictions, and is forced to declare that most things are insoluble mysteries. There must be some reason for this characteristic incompleteness ; and the explanation is to be found,

T

I think, in the fact that Absolutism tries to work
with too few ideas. The absolutist, like the
pragmatist, gets a firm grasp of one or two conceptions which he attempts to apply everywhere
regardless of consequences. One knows what is the
result of this in the world of common-sense. The
man who is obsessed by a fixed idea loses his balance
of mind. A similar result ensues in the philosophic
world. To allow oneself to be fascinated by one
or two ideas and to try to explain everything by
these alone is to take a one-sided view of the universe
and to lose, so to speak, one's *philosophic* balance of
mind. The point is worth illustrating, perhaps,
for it seems to explain at once the incompleteness
and the inadequacy of Absolutism.

§ 198. The ideas which fascinate the absolutist
are clearly those of ' Immanence,' ' Organic Whole,'
and ' Unity in Difference.' These he regards as
conceptions applicable to all conceivable objects,
and by them all things are to be explained. Now,
that there are such things as ' unities in difference '
and ' organic wholes ' cannot be denied. Both concepts are valid in regard to living things; and it
seems probable, at any rate, that they are valid
also of material things. ' Immanence ' also is valid
when applied to the object of thought as apprehended in a psychical act of the mind. This much
we learn from common-sense and introspection.
The absolutist is right, then, so far in regard to his
facts. His conception of Immanence, of an Organic
Whole, and of Unity in Difference, each has its
foundation in the data of experience. But when
he seeks to apply these concepts to the universe at

large, he is attempting to apply them beyond the sphere within which alone they have validity. With what results ? If the universe is an organism the individuals which were formerly held to constitute its parts now become merely its differences. Hence a contradiction. For the notion of an 'organism' is derived not from a study of the universe as a whole, but from the study of its parts or ' differences.' And it is found in these parts or ' differences ' only in so far as they are real unities having each a nature and existence of its own which does not belong, as such, to the rest of the universe. An organism, it is true, may, and indeed must, 'tself have parts. But its parts are not real organisms (though they may be organic), since their nature and their activities are dominated and controlled by the formal principle of the whole. Hence an organism, being a real unity, is something different from the rest of the universe, so that to apply this notion to the universe at large involves a contradiction, for whatever else the universe is it is certainly not a difference or part of itself. Or, to put the argument in another way, if the universe is a real whole, organisms are among its differences ; but it is illicit to identify the whole with any of its differences ; hence, either the concept organism does not apply to the differences of the universe, and so is invalid (since it is from these differences that the concept has been derived), or else the universe is not an organism.

§ 199. A similar argument may be used, it seems to me, against the doctrine that thought and its real object are immanent within the universe as within a concrete living whole. For the notion of Immanence is, like that of organism, derived from our knowledge of finite living things, *i.e.*, from ourselves and from other rational and individual beings. But if the thoughts of each individual thinker are immanent within his own mind, they are *ex hypothesi* not immanent within the minds of other thinkers. I call my thoughts immanent because they are peculiar and intrinsic to me and are not identical with your thoughts ; and, if they were not really my thoughts but were common to us both, I should certainly have no right to call them immanent in me. Hence either thought is not immanent within the universe, but is centred exclusively in individual minds ; or else, if thought is immanent, there are strictly no individual thinkers, and the fact upon which the notion of immanent thought was based is declared to be an illusion. In other words, everyone is aware that the objects of his thoughts are, *as ideas*, immanent within his own mind, and for that very reason distinguishes his ideas from the objects which are known by those ideas, since no one imagines that the objects of his thoughts, *as realities*, are immanent within his mind. Absolutism, however, in order to apply the doctrine of Immanence to the universe as a whole is forced to deny that there are any realities distinct from ideas. Hence a trilemma. For either (1) my ideas embrace all reality and I as an individual am identical with the universe ; or (2) there are other thinkers besides me of which I know not, and ought not to be able to conceive, in which case the universe becomes an aggregate of individual thinking beings, each of whom has his own world of immanent ideas ; or else (3)—and this is the alternative Absolutism adopts—my mind and your mind are not strictly individual and my thoughts and your thoughts are not strictly immanent within us, but are immanent really within an Absolute which somehow diversifies itself and centres itself in each of us. But on this latter hypothesis there are no longer any individual minds. Hence the data upon which the doctrine of Immanence was based (viz., that the ideas of each one of us are immanent within our own minds) has been cut away beneath our feet and the concept of Immanence thereby rendered invalid.

§ 200. Lastly, the concept of Unity in Difference is, like the rest of our concepts, based upon our knowledge of finite and individual things. In particular, I recognise that I myself am a unity-in-difference, and that my intellect, my will and my emotions are differences of me. Such a conception gives us an excellent idea of the unity of man ; but it can only be applied to the universe at large, provided its applicability to man is denied. For, once again, if man is really a unity, the universe is an aggregate ; while, if the universe is not an aggregate but a unity, man's unity is not real, but only relative, and the foundation of the notion of real unities-in-difference is gone. This difficulty is especially serious for those who assert that all concepts are relative, for the conception of Unity in Difference is itself relative in that case, and so is inapplicable to what is affirmed to be absolute. And, similarly, in Mr. Bradley's theory Unity in

Difference, which is due to thought distinctions, must be mere appearance ; whence it follows that either the notion cannot be applied to the Absolute or else the Absolute, like everything else, is only an appearance.

§ 201. It seems to me that there is only one way of avoiding these difficulties, and that is to hold fast to our finite organisms, to our finite unities-in-difference and to our finite minds in which thought is really immanent, since these alone are known with comparative immediacy and certainty. Then, if our theory of an organic universe can be squared with the facts, well and good. But if it cannot, we must still abide by our facts, and in regard to theories must either attempt a modification or renounce them altogether. For Absolutism to adopt the latter alternative would perhaps be a mistake, since there are many ideas in Absolutism the value of which for human thought is very great. Nevertheless, its theory of the Universe as an Organic Whole cannot stand in its present literal form. It leads not merely to inconsistencies, as I have endeavoured to show ; but it makes error, evil, pain, and man himself a hopeless mystery. It claims to be a regress upon the presuppositions of knowledge ; yet it neglects altogether to take account of some of the most characteristic of our common-sense beliefs, dismissing them without a word of explanation as illusions. We may say of Absolutism, in fact, what Mr. Bradley has said of Phenomenalism : This view " either makes a claim to take account of all the facts, or it makes no such claim ; and in the latter case there is an end of its pretensions." Perhaps we ought to place Absolutism under the second category; but in any case it certainly has not as yet taken account of all the facts, and were it to do so the modifications involved would be very considerable. The bald, bold way in which the characteristics of human cognition are transferred to the Absolute would have to be given up. The concepts of Organic life, Unity in Difference and Immanence would be found to apply only in an analogous, if not merely in a metaphorical, sense to the universe at large. Of the possibility of thus reconciling Absolutism with the data of experience I shall have something to say in the concluding chapter of this volume. We must now consider the rival claims of the philosophy of Pure Experience.

CHAPTER XI.

THE PHILOSOPHY OF PURE EXPERIENCE.

I.—EXPOSITION.

§ 202. In spite of certain remarks of Professor James and Dr. Schiller, to the effect that Pragmatism is compatible with almost any metaphysics, it has, if not its own metaphysics, at least a marked and unmistakable tendency toward the metaphysics of Pure Experience. Professor James' "World of Pure Experience" seems to be metaphysical in character.[1] Avenarius, the philosopher of the German pragma-

[1] cf. *supra*, § 109.

tists, is certainly a metaphysician, and his principal work is entitled *Eine Kritik der reinen Erfahrung*. M. Le Roy in France, Professor Dewey in America, Professor Mach in Germany, and Dr. Schiller in England, all adopt an attitude in regard to metaphysics which closely resembles, if it is not identical with, that which is known as the philosophy of Pure Experience. Pragmatism, in fact, and the philosophy of Pure Experience go hand in hand, and to separate them is to reduce the former to a mere method, which, whatever it was, it certainly is not now. Pragmatism has changed since it parted company with its founder, Dr. Peirce; and however purely methodological *his* intentions may have been, Pragmatism is now a theory of knowledge, and as such it presupposes metaphysics, and must, if it desires to be intelligible, give some account of the relation of the knower to the known.

§ 203. From the psychological standpoint we have already treated of the view taken of this relation by Professors James and Dewey: and sufficient, I think, has already been said to make it clear that the philosophy of Pure Experience is a modern form of Empiricism. There is nothing but experience. Everything is experience; and the only function of one experience is to lead to another experience. There are no objects apart from experience, for objective reference is but an accident incidental to the transitional and truncated nature of many of *our* experiences. Substances, accidents, powers, selves, absolutes are not required. A world of Pure Experience needs no bedding. Such a world is merely an aggregate of experiences which 'hang together by their edges,' and which ' proliferate into one another by transitions;' and these transitions, whether conjunctive or disjunctive, continue the experimental ·tissue and so form part and parcel with experience.[1]

Pure Experience is defined as ' the original flux of life before reflection has categorised it ; '[2] and Professor James is of opinion that we actually get back to pure experience at times ; for he tells us that " the instant field of the present is always experience in its 'pure' state, plain unqualified actuality, a simple *that*, as yet undifferentiated into thing and thought, and only virtually classifiable as objective fact or as some one's opinion about fact."[3] Avenarius, on the other hand (and this is, I think, the view more commonly and also more correctly held) assures us that our experience is never pure. We never get rid of customary forms of representation even in what we call presentation. Whether our experience be that of common-sense, of science,. of religion, or of philosophy, in it we always think under categories; and categories do not belong to pure experience, but have been imposed upon it by our ancestors in the past. The tainted state of our experience is obvious. It is, however, our mis- fortune, not our fault. " Had pure experience," says Professor James, " been always perfectly healthy, there never would have arisen the necessity

---

[1] " A World of Pure Experience," *Journ. of Phil., Psy. and Sc. Methods,* 1904, pp. 533 *et seq.* (*passim*), and cf. *Studies in Humanism,* p. 461.
[2] *A Pluralistic Universe,* p. 348, and cf. *Studies in Humanism,* p. 221.
[3] " A World of Pure Experience," p. 564.

of isolating or verbalising any of its terms. We should just have experienced inarticulately and unintellectually enjoyed." [1] But it was not so. The tendency of 'raw' experience is to 'extinguish the experient himself,' and this tendency " is lessened just in the degree in which the elements in it that have a practical bearing upon life are analysed out of the continuum and verbally fixed and coupled together, so that we may know what is in the wind for us and get ready to react in time."[2]

§ 204. Among the causes which have contributed to the corruption of pure experience and the generation of our own are others besides those of analysis and verbalisation. M. Le Roy, for whom all truth and all reality are due to *l'action-pensée*, emphasises especially the element of choice.

Even in common-sense knowledge, experience has undergone a transformation and is no longer pure owing to reactions which neglect some elements and modify others.... Even in such ordinary notions as the continuity or discontinuity of material objects we exercise choice : we prefer to regard objects which, to sight, are continuous as discontinuous, because it is more convenient ; this, however, is merely a *fiction pratique*.[3]

For the German, Avenarius, on the other hand, physiology seems to be the key alike to psychology and to philosophy. All changes in experience take for him, as we have already seen,[4] the form of a

[1] *A Pluralistic Universe*, p. 350. (These words are attributed to the naturalist, but in the original article in the *Journ. of Phil.*, etc., 1901, p. 35, they were attributed to the pragmatist). Cf. *The Meaning of Truth*, p. 64, and *Studies in Humanism*, pp. 485, 486.
[2] *A Pluralistic Universe*, p. 350.
[3] *Bulletin de la Soc. Française philosophique*, 1902, p. 177. cf. *Studies in Humanism*, pp. 188, 189.
[4] cf. *supra*, § 130.

vital series. Physiological changes begin with some stimulation which disturbs the nervous equilibrium, and finally leads, through reaction, to its restoration. Psychical changes proceed from pain through striving to satisfaction and rest. Thus, when a presentation fails at first to harmonise with previous experience, we invent *Bei-begriffe* — 'mediating notions,' as they are styled by Professor James— and in this way conflict is avoided and harmony, of a kind, restored. The notion of 'incomprehensibility,' for instance, has been invented in order to avoid a conflict between man's free-will and the Omnipotence of God. Our one aim in life is to live in harmony with our environment, and to attain this harmony at the least possible expense. By the *Princip des kleinsten Kraftmasses*, which is but Professor Mach's *Princip der Denkökonomie*[1] stated in a more general form, the whole of life is governed. Under it are classed by the latter two subsidiary principles, the *Princip der Stetigkeit oder Continuität* (Mental action is *secundum habitum*), and the *Princip der zureichenden Bestimmtheit oder der zureichenden Differenzierung*. (Changes from expected recurrence produce in our ideas the smallest possible modification compatible with the assimilation of the new idea). It is the operation of these principles as the dominant laws of our conscious life that has led to the corruption of pure experience by the introduction or super-position of categories and ideas which have gradually become permanent as habits of thought.

§ 205. Professor Simmel also takes physiological

[1] cf. *supra*, § 127.

as the type of psychical processes, but insists more on the anthropomorphic aspect of the development of cognition.

The alternation between rest and motion [he tells us] is not only the physiological condition of our existence, but is also the type of our spiritual life. As we imagine that within ourselves we perceive a psychical being whose existence and character depends only upon itself and is independent of all outside, so we look in the world for substances, magnitudes, forces, whose being and meaning is grounded in themselves alone. As the changeless, the substantial, the fixed, is in our life-content an experience so full of value, so thought seeks amid the fluctuations of the phenomenal for something changeless and sure, and from independence proceeds to the self-sufficient, the self-grounded. Thus we gain fixed points which direct us in the confused jumble of phenomena, and give us the objective counterpart of that which we represent as valuable and definitive within ourselves.[1]

§ 206. The anthropomorphism which is characteristic of Professor Simmel's account of the impurities of our experience finds expression also in '*Axioms as Postulates.*' For in that now famous essay Dr. Schiller, *in the rôle of epistemologist*, re-edits Aristotle's doctrine of matter and form in a new and striking way. Arguing back from existing knowledge to its conditions, he concludes that the latter were originally (1) minds, and (2) a wholly plastic matter, without quality and without determination, but receptive of forms which minds imposed upon it. Thus the world, as it now appears, has been gradually formed by the combined activity of

---

[1] *Philosophie des Geldes*, chap. iii., pp. 58, 59.

many minds.[1] In his advance from the *Grumps* to
the *Edwin and Angelina* stage, and from that to his
present state of rationality, man has imposed on its
plastic receptivity form upon form, category upon
category, with ever-increasing ingenuity and complexity; till at last we have come, by a kind of tacit,
mutual consent, to treat these forms as objective,
and to attribute them, not to the constructive genius
of our ancestors, but to nature itself, which we thus
regard as real and independent. 'Facts,' however,
as well as concepts, are the product of cognitive
functioning.[2] At bottom they are nothing but the
'legacy of past thought,' a 'precipitate' left behind
them by our fore-fathers. We seem, in 'facts,' to
apprehend reality ready made, because *we* did not
make them. But our fore-fathers made them, much
as we now make them when we construct for ourselves new entities such as 'ether' in the hope that
in this way we may somehow satisfy our needs.
Facts, then, are not only relative to man, but are
made by man, evolved, that is, by his experiments
upon the plastic material of his experience.
'Reality' and 'truth' alike are the results of
human experiments based on human hypotheses
and directed to the satisfaction of human needs.[3]

Here we see the result of applying the methods of
science to the theory of knowledge. The transformation of pure into impure experience has been
brought about by postulation and experiment
prompted by human needs, and by this means has

---

[1] cf. *Studies in Humanism,* p. 461.
[2] cf. *ibid.,* pp. 183, 461, and *Humanism,* p. 11 (note) and p. 55.
[3] '*Axioms as Postulates,*' §§ 1-8 (*passim*).

been evolved a pseudo-objective world which now seems to us independent and given, simply because it is not we who, as individuals, have made it. For the thorough-going pragmatist the story of ' reality ' and the story of ' truth ' are one and the same. " What we judge to be 'true,' we take to be 'real,' and accept as a 'fact.' "[1] All three, truth, reality, and fact, arise in like manner from the desire to satisfy the exigencies of our nature, which demand that we should " organise the crude material of experience and transmute it into palatable, manageable and liveable forms." By our experiments we have modified what was once a pure experience, and have imposed upon it forms which by force of habit it seeks to retain. Reality, therefore, *alias* experience, has lost to a large extent its original plasticity. New forms are no longer accepted with the same readiness as of yore. Our efforts to impose them are restricted, and thus experience has acquired a factitious independence and an illusive objectivity which we construe into a real world, distinct from, and external to, ourselves. In reality, however, there is nothing but experience, or, as M. Le Roy puts it, " The mind is never confronted with anything but itself, its degrees and its moments. The world is its work, and itself, so far as it is made, is its work also. In this, Idealism is right, understood in the sense of an idealism of thought-action." [2]

§ 207. It is strange that Pragmatism should have adopted a philosophic attitude in which the principal

---

[1] *Studies in Humanism,* p. 426.
[2] *Bulletin de la Soc, Française philosophique,* 1904, p. 166.

doctrine of the rival and much-despised theory of Absolutism seems to be re-asserted. Yet such is the case. In spite of the philosophic impotence of Hegel and the utter uselessness of Absolute philosophies in general, Pragmatism has borrowed and made its own the fundamental principle of all Hegelians, the doctrine of Immanence. English, French, German and American pragmatists alike tell us that knowledge and reality both live immanent within the tissue of experience. There is no need of any transcendental leap from the knower to the known. " In the very bosom of finite experience every conjunction required to make the (cognitive) relation intelligible is given in full." [1] We have seen how this cognitive relation is explained by Professors James and Dewey ; [2] how they identify the knower with one experience and the known with another, or else with the same experience taken again in a different context ; how Professor Dewey talks of odours which know roses, and of certain elements in experiences which know others and which present them as not-present-in-the-same-way-as-themselves-are-present, but as going to be so present through the intervention of certain operations. " Where are the objects of thought ? " asks Professor James. " We have no ground for saying that they are outside experience. . . . they may be continuous with the present experience itself." [3] For though " the category of trans-perceptual reality is now one of the foundations of

---

[1] *The Meaning of Truth*, pp. 102, 103.
[2] *Vide* chap. vi.
[3] *Mind.*, N.S. 52, p. 563.

our life," we can "speculatively imagine a state of
pure experience before the hypothesis of permanent
objects behind its flux had been framed." [1] Similarly,
Dr. Schiller : " The reality to which truth was said
to correspond, *i.e.*, which it has to know, is *not* a
' fact in its own right, which pre-exists the cognitive
functioning.' It is itself a fact *within* knowing,
immanently deposited or ' precipitated ' by the
functioning of our thought." Hence it is that the
problem of knowledge for the pragmatist is " *not*—
' how can thought engender truth about reality ? '
but, rather, ' how can we best describe the continuous cognitive process which engenders our
systems of ' truth ' and our acceptance of ' reality '
and gradually refines them into more and more
adequate means for the control of our experience ? ' " [2]

Thus Pragmatism and Absolutism are at one in
regard to the all-important doctrine of Immanence ;
but, further than this, they agree neither in
principles, method, nor conclusions. Absolutism
frankly acknowledges that it is a theory devised in
order to explain the universe. Pragmatism, though
it also is a theory, *claims* to be merely describing
what is obviously contained in experience. Absolutism is in the strict sense a metaphysic. Pragmatism,
too, is metaphysical ; [3] but it is so because it cannot
help itself. Its metaphysics are an accident, as it
were, occasioned by its desire to explain cognition
and its consequent attempt to treat of the knower
and the known. Both Absolutism and Pragmatism

---

[1] *The Meaning of Truth*, pp. 64, 63, and 68.
[2] *Studies in Humanism*, p. 426, and cf. pp. 201, 202.
[3] On this point cf. *supra* § 221.

are idealistic ; but while Absolutism is a Rationalism, Pragmatism is a form of Empiricism.

§ 208. The points in which Pragmatism differs
from other empiricisms, will, I think, be clear. The
first is, of course, almost everything that is distinctive of the Postulatory or Experimental Theory
of Knowledge. The second is Professor James'
theory of *Felt*-relations, to which I have already
referred, and on account of which he has given to
his *Weltanschauung* the name of ' Radical Empiricism.' Radical Empiricism, like all empiricisms, is
' a mosaic philosophy,' a ' philosophy of plural
facts ; ' it ' emphasises parts rather than wholes,'
and makes the latter subsidiary and abstract ; and,
like them, it is definitely opposed to Absolutism,
Apriorism, and all forms of mind-stuff theory. But
it differs from Empiricism of Hume and Mill in that
it admits conjunctive and disjunctive relations as
being fully co-ordinate parts of experience. For
Radical Empiricism, *" the relations that connect
experiences must themselves be experienced relations,
and any kind of relations experienced must be accounted
as real* as anything else in the system." [1] We feel
our ' ands,' and ' buts,' and ' ifs,' and ' fors,' just as
we feel other impressions which objects make upon
our senses. " Prepositions, copulas, and conjunctions, ' is,' ' isn't,' ' then,' ' before,' ' in,' ' on,'
' beside,' ' between,' ' next,' ' like,' ' unlike,' ' as,'
' but,' flower out of the stream of pure experience,
the stream of concretes or the sensational stream,
as naturally as nouns and adjectives do." [2] All

[1] " A World of Pure Experience," p. 534.
[2] *A Pluralistic Universe*, p. 349.

U

that is real is sensible; and since relations are real, they, too, must be sensible. The Radical Empiricism of Professor James and the 'new' Empiricism of France both possess the chief characteristic of their predecessors. The fundamental principle of Hume is revived. All ideas that are valid must be verified, or, at least, verifiable, in impressions; they must "lead to the face of directly verifying experiences somewhere." [1]   Both are reactions against a philosophy too much encumbered with *a priori* principles.[2]   But between the Empiricism of Professor James and that of Hume there is a difference. Ideas are still little more than faint copies of sensations, but they include relations, which are as much experiences as anything else. This is the chief reason why Professor James claims that the empirical attitude which Pragmatism takes up is more radical and at the same time less objectionable than any that Empiricism has hitherto assumed.[3]

§ 209. Closely connected with his doctrine of felt-relations is Professor James' doctrine of the Self. The Self is one of those unnecessary notions of which Radical Empiricism is so anxious to get rid, and certainly of the real self in Professor James' explanation very little remains, less even than was conceded to us in the *Principles of Psychology*. Felt-relations, we are informed, are "of various degrees of intimacy." [4]   There is first withness, then nextness, then likeness, then activity (cause and effect), then purpose, and, finally, as the most intimate of all

[1] *Pragmatism*, p. 215.
[2] cf. Le Roy, *Revue Met. et Morale*, 1901, p. 140.
[3] *Pragmatism*, p. 51.
[4] "A World of Pure Experience," p. 535.

relations, but still a relation and nothing more, the Self. If we bear in mind the fundamental thesis of Professor James' "World of Pure Experience," what he means by affirming that the Self is merely a felt-relation at once becomes clear. There is nothing real and existing except experiences and the felt-transitions, themselves experiences, by which we pass from one experience to another. Hence the Self must be either one or the other or both. In fact, it is described as merely a specially intimate felt-relation, or '*co-conscious transition.*' "Personal histories are process of change in time, *and the change itself is one of the things immediately experienced.* 'Change' in this case means continuous as opposed to discontinuous transition. But continuous transition is one sort of a conjunctive relation ; and to be a radical empiricist means to hold fast to this relation of all others, for this is the strategic point, the position through which, if a hole be made, all the corruptions of dialectics and all the metaphysics pour into our philosophy. The holding fast to this relation means taking it at its face value, neither less nor more ; and to take it at its face value means, first of all, to take it just as we feel it." [1] Since, then, "what I do feel simply when a later moment of my experience succeeds an earlier one, is that though they are two moments, the transition from one to the other is *continuous*," [2] it follows that "there is no other *nature*, no other whatness than this absence of break and this sense of continuity in that most intimate of all conjunctive relations, the passing of one experience into another when they

[1] " A World of Pure Experience," p. 536.   [2] *Ibid.*

belong to the same self." [1] Thus "a 'mind' or 'personal consciousness' is the name for a series of experiences run together by definite transitions," just as "an objective reality is a series of similar experiences knit together by different transitions." [2]

§ 210. Now it would seem that if I am a certain series of experiences conjunctively run together, and if you are another such series, we could hardly communicate one with another, since my experiences and yours are mutually exclusive. In spite, however, of his mosaic philosophy, Professor James is able to find something in common between us, and so to establish a means of inter-communication. True, for the most part, my experiences and yours 'float and dangle,' are 'out of sight, irrelevant and unimaginable.' Nevertheless, they terminate in a 'nucleus of common perception.' [3] This does not mean that our experiences ever terminate in numerically the same identical percept; for all percepts, being the experiences of different minds, are somewhat different, at least in their point of view; [4] but it does mean that they terminate in something which is numerically one and the same. That something is space, or, as Professor Strong prefers to call it, *pseudo-space*. Space, then, or place—for the two terms are not distinguished by Professor James—affords a means of inter-communication between mind and mind.

That body of yours which you actuate and feel from within must be in the same spot as the body of yours which I see and touch from without. 'There,' for me

[1] *Ibid.*, p. 537.
[2] *Ibid.*, p. 566. [3] *Ibid.*, pp. 535, 536. [4] *Ibid.*, p. 567.

means where I place my finger. If you do not feel my finger's contact to be 'there' in *my* sense, when I place it on your body, where then do you feel it ? Your inner actuations of your body also meet my finger *there ;* it is *there* that you resist its push, or shrink back, or sweep the finger aside with your hand. . . . In general terms, then, whatever differing contents our minds may fill a place with, the place itself is a numerically identical content of the two minds, a piece of common property in which, through which, and over which they join.[1]

§ 211. This solution of the difficulty of explaining interaction between mind and mind does but involve us in another. For if mind and matter, the knower and the known, are but aspects into which in retrospection we split the unity of an experience, and if our minds "terminate in the same percept, not merely against it ;"[2] if, that is, what is common to you and to me is not merely common but numerically identical and immanent to both of us, then it would seem that we are not different minds at all, but at bottom, and somehow or other, as Mr. Bradley would say, one and the same.

Such a doctrine clearly tends toward Monism. Yet Monism is, by the rigid empiricist, emphatically denied, and many categorical assertions might be found in the writings of Professor James with which it is in direct contradiction.[3] It is certainly incompatible with a pluralistic philosophy, and it is also incompatible with the Personal Idealism toward which so many pragmatists tend (though so, for that matter, is the above inadequate account of the Self). And in any case, it would hardly do for Professor

[1] *Ibid.*, pp. 567, 568.
[2] *Ibid.*, p. 567.   [3] *e.g.*, in *A Pluralistic Universe (passim).*

James, who is at present at war with the Absolute, to borrow a second doctrine from Absolutism in addition to that of Immanence. For the present, therefore, he is content to affirm that

round the nucleus, partly continuous and partly discrete, of what we call the physical world of actual perception, innumerable hosts of thinkers, pursuing their several lines of physically true cogitation trace paths that intersect one another only at discontinuous perceptual points, and the rest of the time are quite incongruent.[1]

Yet Professor James is inclined to adopt some form of Panpsychism, for the 'beyond' in a philosophy of experience, he tells us, must itself be " of an experimental nature ; " and " if not a future experience of our own or a present one of our neighbour, it must be an experience *for* itself." Hence, although " the world is so far forth a pluralism of which the unity is not fully experienced as yet," even Professor James does not deny that ultimately an *Erfahrungseinheit* may be possible.[2]

§ 212. The philosophy of Avenarius is not essentially different in its conclusions from that of Professor James. Avenarius, too, seems to have adopted provisionally a kind of Panpsychism or Personal Idealism, though, like the latter, he thinks that individual minds are tending toward homogeneity, if not toward actual unity. He, too, reduces everything to experience, and distinguishes within it a subjective and an objective aspect. His presentment of his philosophy, however, differs considerably from that of the sketchy style adopted

[1] *Ibid.*, p. 543, and cf. *The Meaning of Truth*, pp. 113, 114.
[2] *loc. cit.*, p. 569, and cf. *A Pluralistic Universe*, p. 328.

in the metaphysical articles of Professor James, though, unfortunately, it is also much encumbered by a new and quite unnecessary terminology. Avenarius' *Empirio-Criticism* is only another name for the philosophy of Pure Experience. We may regard experience either from an absolute or from a relative point of view, *i.e.*, we may either consider the relation of an object (R) to a percept (E), or we may substitute for (E) a brain-state (Cm) (the *Empirio-Critical substitution*) and consider the relation of R to C. In either case our results will be the same ; for the psychical character of an experience and its objective contents are but different aspects of the same entity, experience, and between them there is a functional relation. Hence, for the *independent* vital series, pain—striving—satisfaction, may be substituted the *dependent* vital series, stimulus—reaction—equilibrium ; and this is a law which holds throughout experience. The oscillation of (R), the objective aspect of experience, is always the correlative of (S), the subjective aspect. The magnitude of the oscillations corresponds to the intensity of consciousness ; their direction, according as it is toward or away from equilibrium, means pleasure or pain. A habitual series is the correlative of familiarity and certitude, while a *new* series means a modification of habit in the physiological order and a *Heterotote*, *i.e.*, a modification of knowledge, in the psychical.

§ 213. Character (feeling, perceiving, willing, knowing) may in all experiences be distinguished from content (what is perceived or thought), but it is distinguished only in retrospection, and is perceived immediately and spatially precisely in the same manner as content. (This, by the way, is the *first axiom of Empirio-Criticism*.) Since, then, character, which we ascribe to the self, is just as objective as content, which we ascribe to an objective world, some other difference must be found by which to distinguish the self from the not-self. This difference for Avenarius, as for Professor James, lies in the peculiar intimacy of the relations or transitions which hold within the former.

Other selves or minds are known by the *Empirio-Critical Postulate*, and not by Introjection, which is the method by which common-sense imagines that it attains to this piece of knowledge. In Introjection man first attributes to his likes, feelings and thoughts similar to his own, and in this way distinguishes two worlds, the world of consciousness or minds and the world of material objects. This he sets down as an intuition. But when he comes to reflect, he finds that he cannot explain how the two worlds, if distinct, can interact ; and so comes to the conclusion that his intuition was not an intuition at all, but a very bad inference, which he proceeds to correct by becoming a subjective idealist and denying the existence of any objective world at all. The subjective idealist, however, is fundamentally wrong, for the objective is just as much an aspect of experience as the subjective. And his mistake is due to his having supposed that our knowledge of other minds is an intuition, whereas it is really a postulate. The truth is that we are forced to postulate the existence of other selves in order to account for certain elements in our experience; and so long as our experience retains its dual aspect, this hypothetical element in the *natürliche Weltbegriff* will remain. But should we ever attain to that state in which we 'inarticulately experience' and 'unintellectually enjoy,' this dual aspect will disappear and with it will go those hypothetical other selves which are due to analysis and experiment.

§ 214. The aim of a philosophy of Pure Experience, therefore, is not far to seek. Since so much of our experience is now no longer pure, the philosopher must make it his business to purify it. This he can only do by making a clean sweep of all those notions by which our ancestors strove to facilitate thought, but in fact have only encumbered it. Substance, accident, cause, self, must be done away. We must descend to the purer level again. This process of de-intellectualisation is recommended by Professor James; but it is Avenarius who has given us the most intelligent account of the pure experience to which we must return. By philosophy he understands the interpretation of the universe in accordance with the *Principle of Least Energy* which enjoins upon us that we strive (1) to comprehend the many in the one, and (2) to eliminate all useless ideas (substance, cause, and the like) since they are static, whereas experience is essentially a process and a growth. This done, all that will remain will be impressions. 'Being' must be thought as an impression which presupposes nothing beyond what is apparent to the senses. Impressions are the only real content of experience, while change is the form which experience takes. This is all that the philosopher is concerned with, unless, perhaps, he can complete his work by the discovery of an *Empfindungseinheit*. And as for science, its characteristics, when the ideal of pure experience has been reached, will be the following. It will be purely descriptive, yet simple, exact, complete. Quality will be reduced to quantity ; and laws will treat of quantitative equivalence, not of causal connection or sequence. All values and quantitative relations will be interdependent and mutually deducible one from another. Religion, philosophy and morals also will be characterised by a purely experimental method, and will be regarded from a purely experimental point of view. The vital series will have attained a maximum of simplicity, and the same series will be universal throughout the race. Predispositions, prejudices and individual differences will have disappeared, and their place will be taken by an indefinite variety of minute impressions, leading to reactions of a simple and invariable type. In short, when the ideal of pure experience has been realised, man will have become a mere machine, so that no matter what particular specimen of humanity you may choose, if you press the same lever you will get the same feeling and the same performance will take place.

§ 215. Before proceeding to a discussion of the philosophy described in the chapter, I should like to call attention to what is, to say the least, a somewhat remarkable coincidence. It is this : M. Abel Rey, in a work entitled *La théorie de la Physique chez les physiciens contemporains*, after a careful examination of the theories and methods of

Newton, Rankine, Mach, Ostwald, and Duhem, comes to the conclusion that the philosophy with which physical science is most compatible, even if it does not presuppose it, is a modified form of Positivism which bears a striking resemblance, not only to Pragmatism, but also to the philosophy of Pure Experience.

M. Abel Rey does not profess to be a pragmatist, nor does he acknowledge that he has been influenced by pragmatic ideas. In fact, the only reference which he makes to Pragmatism occurs in a footnote to page 393, where he remarks that certain of his own ideas are analogous to those of Pragmatism, and that Pragmatism for this very reason, provided it abandons the agnosticism toward which it is driven by the fashion of the age, will, like the sceptical criticism of science with which it is connected by numerous bonds, have rendered a service to the experimental rationalism of the future. That this should be the only allusion to Pragmatism in a philosophical treatise of over 400 pages dealing with the theory of knowledge, and with the principles and methods of Mach, Ostwald and Poincaré, all of whom have been claimed as pragmatists, seems to me to be somewhat strange ; and is still more so when we consider that the ideas of M. Rey are not merely analogous to those of Pragmatism, but are as emphatically pragmatic as any held by the most whole-hearted pragmatist or humanist.

§ 216. M. Rey claims to be a positivist or an empiricist, though not of the school of Comte and Stuart Mill, whose Empiricism he rejects because it gives us no satisfactory theory of the categories.

The categories, says M. Rey, are not forms of the mind any more than they are forms of objective reality, but are due to the purposive adaptation of the habitual activities of mind to the demands of objective experience. Nay, more, the opposition of mind and matter is itself strictly relative. Objective experience is not something exterior and independent of mind. " Objective experience and mind are implied one in the other and exist and develop one through the other." [1] Hence, the categories must be treated historically. Since they result from evolution they must have a historical signification. Their nature is psychological and social ; perhaps even biological.[2]

From this point of view M. Rey approaches the question of truth. All truths for him, as for Dr. Schiller, are human truths and have been gradually evolved. They are the result of choice made by man with a view to adapting himself to his environment. Their apparent self-evidence and fixity is due to force of habit. " Little by little our truths have acquired a certain stability like to biological immunity, so that certain ways of thinking have become ours and exclude at the cost of destroying our thinking organism the possibility of becoming other than they are." In this process of adaptation, by which truth has been acquired, moreover, man has been guided throughout by utility and by practical considerations, a criterion which, we are warned, as usual, must be taken not *vulgari modo*, but in a most noble sense. The usual pragmatic conclusion also is drawn. Since all truths have a

[1] *op. cit.*, p. 393.   [2] *Ibid.*, p. 397.

history and are due to the combined product of the mind of man and of his environment, the psychological structure of man must leave an indelible trace even on scientific truths which will ever carry in consequence the mark of human fabrication.

§ 217. In his discussion of the validity of physical theories (Book V.) and of the inferences which may be drawn from science in regard to the theory of knowledge in general, therefore, M. Rey has really given us a brief, but vigorous, exposition of many of the leading doctrines of the pragmatist. Not only this, but by combining his Pragmatism with a philosophy of Pure Experience, he affords but another instance of the marked tendency of Pragmatism toward this philosophy, and at the same time has brought out clearly the difficulties with which Pragmatism is involved if this is in truth the end toward which it inevitably leads. M. Rey believes that his conclusions in regard to truth and reality follow logically from the principles and methods of science. Here I cannot agree with him.[1] Yet by starting from the scientific point of view, M. Rey, though not professedly a pragmatist, seems to throw considerable light upon the metaphysical aspect of the pragmatic theory of knowledge.

The first problem of knowledge, viz., in what does knowledge consist, M. Rey pronounces insoluble. Knowledge for him is a unique and mysterious relation which arises, we know not how, from the adaptation of man to his environment. We cannot say in what precisely knowledge consists. All we

---

[1] cf. chaps. xvii., xviii. on Pragmatism and Realism in Physical Science.

can do is to trace more or less imperfectly its history. It is useless to define knowledge or truth as *adaequatio mentis ad rem*, for mind and its object are essentially relative and must not be treated as if they were independent and distinct. Everything, in fact, is a relation. Experience itself is a relation, a system of relations. Relations are the given, and when we analyse them we do but come across further relations.[1] Terms are only the means by which relations are expressed, and when we try to define them we have to fall back upon relations. Knowledge, experience, reality are ultimately one and the same thing ; they constitute *the* relation, *ce qui est*. But what this is must ever remain a mystery.

The solution of the second problem of knowledge on these lines is simplicity itself. *Ab esse ad posse valet illatio.* Knowledge is possible because it is *ce qui est.* There are no conditions to enquire into, since neither subject nor object can exist apart from the relation from which they arise as co-relative terms. Mind is unintelligible apart from matter. Hence those theories of knowledge—and they are, alas, in the majority—which place matter on the one side and mind on the other as distinct entities, and which then enquire how they can be brought together or how one can come to know the other, are theories which start from an altogether erroneous standpoint and are vitiated throughout by this fundamental fallacy. We may, indeed, speak of knowledge psychologically, regarding it as a complexus of habits ; but further than this we cannot go, for " *L'ensemble de ces habitudes est, dans la*

[1] *op. cit.*, p. 394.

seule langue que nous puissions comprendre, ce qui est." [1]

§ 218. When we consider the relativistic attitude at present adopted by many scientists, it is not very surprising that M. Rey should have arrived at a philosophy in which relation is, as with Renouvier and Green, the Category of categories, and in which the mass of relational appearance which Mr. Bradley holds must somehow qualify the real, is itself identified with the real. But M. Rey has carried his Relativism much further than do the pragmatists, and further, too, than his premises will justify. Science is certainly concerned with relations, since it deals, for the most part, with quantitative changes, and these are strictly relative. It is difficult to understand, however, how the objects which the scientist examines can possibly be *due* to the relations which hold between them. Can the definite and simple ratio which holds between the volumes of combining gases and the volume of the compound gas that results in any way account for the volumes and the gases themselves ? Can ' resemblances,' of themselves, account for the respective functions and organic structures of allied species of animals ? Is it not rather the other way about, that the relations arise from the objects themselves, the equality of volume from the respective volumes of the gases which combine, the specific resemblances from the structure and functions of the animals concerned ? M. Rey, at any rate, is hardly justified in returning to the view of Renouvier and Green without at least giving some further reason for his opinion than the

[1] *Ibid.*, p. 395.

mere fact that science is concerned chiefly with relations.

§ 219. Apart, however, from this exaggerated Relativism, the remarkable similarity between the philosophy of M. Rey and the pragmatic philosophy of Pure Experience, can hardly fail to be noticed. The identification of knowledge with experience and the further identification of experience with *ce qui est* is clearly the principal thesis upon which the philosophy of Pure Experience is built. Even for the Relativism which characterises M. Rey's theory one may find an analogy in Professor James' dual-aspect view of experience in which conjunctive and disjunctive relations play so important a part. And when one reflects that this theory is the logical consequence of M. Rey's pragmatic attitude in regard to the nature of truth, it at any rate suggests that the philosophy of Pure Experience is the natural, if not the necessary, complement of the doctrine that truth consists in a complexus of habits which have acquired a comparative stability on account of the useful consequences to which they lead.

CHAPTER XII.

THE PHILOSOPHY OF PURE EXPERIENCE.

II.—CRITICISM.

§ 220. It is with considerable misgivings that I enter upon a discussion of the philosophy of Pure Experience for fear lest I be told in reply that I have misunderstood. The general standpoint and significance of this philosophy *seems* to me to be clear enough ; but I may be mistaken. And if I am, and have, in consequence, misunderstood what is meant, let me at once apologise to Professor James and to the late Avenarius, at the same time pleading in excuse what Professor James himself has said, viz., that

a philosophy of pure experience . . . presents so many points of difference, both from the common-sense and from the idealism that have made our philosophic language, that it is almost as difficult to state it as it is to think it out clearly, and if it is ever to grow into a respectable system, it will have to be built up by the contributions of many co-operating minds.[1]

Where the author of a new system of philosophy doubts his own power to think that system out, it is rash, perhaps, to attempt to criticise ; yet when a system, while yet inchoate, is offered to the philosophic world, the critic is justified in spite of the difficulty of his task in making the attempt.

§ 221. The real difficulty, however, is not so much in regard to the philosophy of Pure Experience

[1] " A World of Pure Experience," p. 570.

V

itself, as in regard to its connection with Pragmatism and Humanism. The former is unquestionably a metaphysic ; Pragmatism as such is not metaphysical. Yet that so many pragmatists should have adopted a philosophy of Pure Experience, and that the expressions used by pragmatists and humanists when speaking *ex professo* as pragmatists and humanists, should correspond almost word for word with the *dicta* of the philosopher of Pure Experience, indicates that there is, at any rate, a certain harmony and congruity between the two ; and this Professor James admits.[1] On the other hand, Mr. Peirce assures us that " the real world, the system as a whole, is, by definition, outside the sphere of Pragmatism," and that " the genetic account of the origin and selection of truth is not a philosophy of reality." [2] Dr. Schiller, too, protests that '*Axioms as Postulates* ' is "purely epistemological in character," and that " the conception of knowledge as developing by the progressive determination of a relatively indeterminate and plastic matter never pretended to be more than an analysis of knowledge."[3] Against this, however, one has to set the fact that the expressions used in the expositions of these ' epistemological ' doctrines *are* of a metaphysical character. It is, indeed, not easy to determine in what sense such terms as ' matter,' ' form,' ' fact,' ' plasticity,' ' normal objectivity,' ' the making of reality,' are used, if they are not used in a metaphysical sense. And even if they are not meant

---

[1] *Ibid.*, and cf. *The Meaning of Truth*, pp. 124, 128, 132, 215, 220.
[2] Baldwin's *Dictionary of Philosophy*, article, " Pragmatism."
[3] *Studies in Humanism*, p. 17 (note).

metaphysically, but are used in some strange and unnatural signification, they seem to be deliberately chosen ; and this intentional ambiguity suggests that if Pragmatism is not already a metaphysic, it may at any moment become one. In fact, Mr. Peirce, in spite of his declaration to the contrary, which I quoted above, himself tells us that *Synechism*, which, he says, *includes Pragmatism as one of its branches*, is "first shown to be true with mathematical exactitude in the field of Logic, and is thence inferred to hold good metaphysically." [1]

§ 222. May not this be true also of the epistemological theory propounded in '*Axioms as Postulates*'? It is not unlikely. If the statements there made, and oft-times repeated in *Humanism* and *Studies in Humanism*, are not to be interpreted in a metaphysical sense, their value is insignificant. For it is the duty of the epistemologist to assign the conditions of knowledge, and if, instead of assigning its *real* conditions, he assigns fictitious and merely methodological conditions, his theorising is idle and useless, and his speculation sheer waste of time. It is, however, difficult to take the pragmatist's philosophy of experience, even in Dr. Schiller's case, in a non-metaphysical sense. For, in the first place, Dr. Schiller is not a realist. He admits that Realism has 'high pragmatic warrant,' and even a 'high degree of truth,' but, strictly, the real world is merely 'a construction *within* primary reality,' *i.e.*, within a purely chaotic experience which as yet is neither subjective or objective, appearance or

---

[1] Baldwin's *Dictionary of Philosophy*, article, "Pragmatism," and cf. article, "Synechism."

reality.[1] He admits also that "in ordinary life we
assume that we live in an external world, which is
'independent' of us," and that "it would be a great
calamity if any philosophy should feel it its duty to
upset this assumption. For it works splendidly,
and the philosophy which attacked it would only
hurt itself." [2] Nevertheless, Dr. Schiller does attack
it on the very next page, where he tells us that the
pragmatically real world, *i.e.*, the real world as we
know it, is but an elaborate construction composed
of the more efficacious parts of experience which
have been selected by man on account of their
utility and dubbed 'independent' facts, powers,
persons, etc., and which have been 'ejected' and
'extended' from his consciousness and endowed
with an 'independent' existence and 'transcendent'
reality, because he was unwilling to accept
responsibility for them.[3] These 'facts' and these
'realities' are not, however, really independent or
transcendent, but are 'immanent' within the
cognitive process, and live wholly inside the tissue
of experience.[4] Nor are we logically forced to
extrude them. Our motive is emotional and
volitional.[5] "'Truth' and 'reality' are valid, not
because they are 'independent' of us, but because
we have 'made' them, and they are so completely
dependent on us that we can depend on them to
stay 'true' and 'real' independently of us."[6]
Doubtless, reality is not wholly of our making. It
supposes pre-existing fact. But pre-existing fact

---

[1] *Studies in Humanism*, p. 201, and cf. p. 187.
[2] *Ibid.*, p. 459.   [3] *Ibid.*, pp. 470, 471.   [4] *Ibid.*, pp. 426, 460.
[5] *Ibid.*, p. 470.   [6] *Ibid.*, p. 462

does not presuppose the real world of common-sense, but the pre-existence of 'primary reality,' or of chaotic experience.[1] In short, 'reality is experience,'[2] and we might even say 'reality' is 'my' experience, were it not that the statement might lead us into solipsism, whereas, for the present, at any rate, we must admit 'an intimate and plastic correlation between reality and the experient.' Yet times may change, and a more 'child-like attitude may be feasible in heaven,' where our ideals of a *more* 'harmonious universe' may be realised, where experience will become, we may hope, intellectually transparent and continually harmonious, and where, consequently, there will be no 'need to postulate anything beyond our experience to account for it.'[3]

§ 223. But *how* is our experience to be thus transformed ? Chiefly it would appear by the growth of knowledge ; for in knowing we make not only the 'true' but the 'real,'[4] and "the difference wrought by pragmatic verification is as great in the case of reality as it is in that of truth."[5] True, Dr. Schiller is here speaking of the making of 'subjective reality,'[6] or knowledge—though why in that case he should distinguish between reality and truth it is difficult to see ; but he also maintains that in knowing we really alter reality, and cites no less than five ways in which this may take place.[7]

---

[1] *Ibid.*, p. 201. [2] *Ibid.*, p. 463.
[3] *Ibid.*, p. 486, and cf. *supra*, § 214.
[4] cf. *ibid.*, Essay vii., " The Making of Truth," and Essay xix., " The Making of Reality."
[5] *Ibid.*, pp. 431, 432, and cf. pp. 198 *et seq.*
[6] cf. *ibid.*, p. 429. [7] *Ibid.*, pp. 438 *et seq*

(1) " The making of truth," he says, " really alters subjective reality "—a fact which few would dispute, but the real question, of course, is as to reality proper, *i.e.*, objective reality.   (2) " *Our knowledge when applied alters real reality*, and is not real knowledge if it cannot be applied."   This, again, is fairly obvious, but to know and to apply one's knowledge are not the same thing.   Application implies action and experiment which is not, as such, knowledge.   Hence, that knowledge itself alters real reality still remains to be proved.   (3) " *Human beings are affected by the opinions of others*."   Surely, the opinions of others do not affect us directly, but only through their actions and words in which those opinions are expressed.   (4) " *Mere knowing alters reality so far at least as one party to the transaction is concerned*." [1]   Dr. Schiller is here referring to the knower ;   hence this fourth case differs very little from the first.   Moreover, the influence of cognition on the knower is not in question.   (5) The last instance of the ' making of reality ' is the most interesting of all.   Dr. Schiller argues that not only where men and the higher animals are concerned, but " even on the purely physical plane on which our transactions with other bodies are conducted, there is response to our cognitive manipulations which varies with our operation, and so therefore there is real making of reality by us." [2]

§ 224.   Inanimate   things   " respond   to   our

---

[1] *Studies in Humanism*, pp. 438, 439.
[2] *Ibid.*, p. 444. (It should be noted that ' making ' here implies co-operation and reaction. It does not mean ' creating,' though what appears to us as " original and rigid " may be " conceived as having been made by analogous processes.")

cognitive operations on the level on which they apprehend them." Now, ordinarily, by 'cognitive operations,' one would understand either thought or perception, but ' cognitive *manipulation* ' suggests physical action as well. Hence, once again, we are left in doubt as to whether Dr. Schiller is propounding a new doctrine, or whether he is merely affirming again and again an indisputable fact. One thing, however, seems to be clear, and that is that Dr. Schiller is firmly convinced that somehow or other we really do make reality, and make it in a metaphysical sense; for the purpose of his chapter, entitled *The Making of Reality*, is to prove that reality is something which grows up in the process by which truth is made, and to show that this is valid, not only for the theory of knowledge, but also as a ' theory of the Cosmos.' True, he makes a distinction between ' discovering ' and ' making ' reality, and tells us that " to wish for a chair and find one, and to wish for a chair and make one, are experiences which it is not easy to confuse." [1] But we must remember that this distinction for Dr. Schiller is purely pragmatic,[2] and that our only reason for saying that we do not really make the chair which we find is, that " its behaviour is such that it is *practically inconvenient* or impossible to ascribe its reality to our subjective activity : " [3] we do not want to be held responsible for its behaviour, at any rate not just at present, though we may become more lenient and reasonable later on. In

[1] *Studies in Humanism,* p. 430.
[2] *Ibid.,* p. 201.
[3] *Ibid,* p. 430. (Italics mine.)

any case, we alter reality, even if we do not wholly make it. For not only is it irrational to assume

that the Real has a determinate nature which the knowing reveals but does not affect; [but] the *actual* situation is a case of interaction . . . . in which the subject and the object determine each other. . . . . When the mind knows reality both are affected, [just as] when a stone falls to the ground, both it and the earth are attracted; [and just as] in our social relation we frequently put questions which are potent in determining their own answers, and without putting the question would have left the subjects undetermined. [Hence] the 'determinate nature of reality' does not subsist 'outside' or 'beyond' the process of knowing it. . . . . Previous to trial, it is indeterminate, *really* and from every point of view . . . , within limits which it is our business to discover.[1]

§ 225. As a matter of fact, Dr. Schiller never does discover these limits, but this deficiency we must overlook as we have yet to find out *how* reality is altered or 'made' by the knowing of it. Do we impose forms upon the plastic receptivity of matter directly, or do we impose them only through the mediation of action ? If mere cognition imposes them, we can never know the object at all, but only the object *as altered by our knowing it*. Reality as such must for ever remain unknowable. Rather than adopt so sceptical an alternative I prefer to think that Dr. Schiller has merely been reasserting in his own peculiar way what everyone admits, namely that we impose forms on matter through the mediation of action. Thus I take it that when we are said to make reality, what is meant is that by

[1] *Humanism*, pp. 11, 12 (note).

our actions we modify reality. And I am confirmed in this opinion when I reflect upon Dr. Schiller's pronouncements in regard to '*mere knowing.*' It is, he tells us, merely ' an intellectualist abstraction,' " a fragment of a total process, which always ends in an action which tests its truth," and " to establish the bearing on reality of the making of truth we must consider the whole process as completed, *i.e.*, as issuing in action, and as sooner or later altering reality." [1] He then goes on to speak of knowing and of cognitive operations, not in the ordinary and accepted use of the terms, but in his pragmatic sense as *including action ;* and to prove from this that cognitive operations (knowing proper *plus* action) alter reality. The whole force of the argument for ' the making of reality ' rests, therefore, upon this peculiar use of the term knowledge as including the action which sooner or later follows it. And that knowledge *in this sense* produces effects in, and elicits responses or reactions from, even inanimate objects no one will deny. Dr. Schiller's theory that ' knowledge alters reality ' sounds strange to us merely because he is using terms in a strange and unwarranted sense and arbitrarily ignoring a distinction that all psychologists admit, viz., the distinction between cognition and action.

§ 226. If we agree, then, to understand by knowledge, knowledge *plus* action, the thesis that knowledge alters reality becomes painfully obvious. [2] Several difficulties arise, however, as soon as we extend

---

[1] *Ibid.*, p. 440.
[2] That knowledge *always* includes action, as Dr. Schiller assumes and as his theory demands, is contradicted by the facts of experience, cf. *supra*, § 98.

this 'making of reality' to *all* that seems objective.
For if we interpret Dr. Schiller realistically and
regard matter, in spite of its formless and wholly
plastic receptivity as something really distinct from
our minds, not only is it difficult to conceive how it
could have existed in such a state, but it is also
difficult to imagine how its evolution could have
begun.   It is conceivable that our ancestors
might have contrived somehow to endow with forms
the formless receptivity of their environment ; but,
unless they also communicated activity to it, this
wholly plastic matter could not have reacted in
response to these or to any other attempts to
' inform ' it ; and if it did react, then it must have
reacted in a more or less definite manner and so
must have had already a minimum of structure.
In other words, if we suppose matter to have been
independent of mind, and yet to have evolved
solely under the influence of *l'action-pensée*, we are
confronted with a contradiction, for either matter
was wholly formless and plastic, and so could not
react, and consequently could not evolve ; or else
matter could react and so could not have been at
the outset wholly plastic and formless.

§ 227.   Dr. Schiller is not unaware of this
difficulty, for he mentions it on p. 434 of his *Studies*,
and proceeds to answer it by telling us that there
is no answer, for " the whole question is invalid,
because it asks too much.   It demands to know
nothing less than how reality comes to be at all,
how fact is made absolutely.   And this is more than
philosophy can accomplish or need attempt."   But,
surely, this is not the case.   We do not ask how

reality in general began, for clearly, as a whole, reality never could begin. What we want to know is the origin of *contingent* reality, of that reality which we find around us and which is subject to change, and of the knowledge which we, human agents, possess of that reality. Panpsychism, which is but another form of the philosophy of Pure Experience,[1] gives some sort of answer to this question. Indeed, it seems to be, as I have already pointed out, if not the necessary, at least the natural, complement of Pragmatism and Humanism. For while to the collection of psychic experiences in which reality consists, Humanism adds the dynamic element by means of which one series of experiences, *i.e.*, one mind, is able to act upon another series or mind, and thus explains how by interaction and mutual modification the different worlds which each has constructed for himself are gradually brought to unity ; the philosophy of Pure Experience, on its side, gets rid of the inconsistency of a wholly plastic and formless, yet existent, matter by transforming it into rudimentary minds endowed with some activity and at least a modicum of structure. The material universe, in fact, becomes, as M. Bergson puts it, " a kind of consciousness in which everything compensates and neutralises itself." [2]

Toward this solution of the difficulty Dr. Schiller *inclines;*[3] yet it is a solution which one can hardly regard as satisfactory.

---

[1] cf. " A World of Pure Experience," p. 569.
[2] *Matière et Memoire*, p. 262.
[3] *Studies in Humanism*, pp. 443, 446, *et seq.*

The question whence come the forms which we impose upon the quasi-conscious beings-for-themselves, otherwise known as material things, has yet to be answered. But in attempting to answer this question the Pragmatic Method breaks down. It affirms that all categories and principles, and all the forms which we impose upon the plastic receptivity of matter, have had a history. But if everything has had a history, nothing could ever have begun to be at all, and as soon as you assign a beginning to anything, you affirm the existence of something which has not had a history. Thus the pragmatist is compelled to allow that there is an initial basis of reality and truth which has not been made by us; and the question then arises whence that basis with which knowledge began. And, as we have seen,[1] in order to answer this question, the pragmatist is forced to have recourse either to Apriorism or to the theory of Aristotle. In a wholly genetic theory of knowledge the origin of knowledge is not only inexplicable, but impossible; and in a wholly genetic theory of the universe reality could never have come into being at all.

§ 228. Closely connected with this question of the origin of knowledge is another difficulty which confronts the pragmatist when he tries to back up his Pragmatism by a panpsychic version of the philosophy of Pure Experience. In a panpsychic universe all that exists is mind, and all knowledge is about mind, hence the problem is how different minds come to know one another. The metaphysical conditions of knowledge, according to

[1] cf. *supra*, § 99.

Professor James, are (1) a plurality of minds, and (2) a common world which can be known by each. These conditions, however, apply only to our present stage of development, and are expressed in the language of common-sense. Consequently, when used by the philosopher of Pure Experience, they have to be re-interpreted. Thus the 'plurality of minds' becomes "the practically irreversible structure of our consciousness, defining the general forms within which our answers must fall;"[1] while the 'common world' becomes "a most chaotic pure experience which sets us questions," and which at most possesses but a 'minimum of structure;' a chaotic pure experience which belongs, I take it, to psychical beings in an abnormally low stage of development. Now, if knowledge is to make any progress, somehow or other these two sets of psychical beings or experiences must interact. But how is this possible? Professor James has agreed to do without the concept of causation, and he expressly denies that we have any direct apprehension of the nature of other minds. Our thoughts, he says, do not perceptually terminate in other minds, but lead us only to their 'brink,' to their "chromatic fringes, and to the hurtful words and deeds which are their really next effects."[2]   If, then, minds are in themselves unknowable, and if everything is of the nature of mind,

---

[1] Professor James qualifies this statement by adding "that the structure was wrought in us long ago," but this qualification can apply only to some features in the present structure of mind, otherwise we should again be involved in the difficulty of getting knowledge to start.

[2] "A World of Pure Experience," p. 563.

how do we get any knowledge at all ? To say that we postulate other minds is obviously no solution of the difficulty whatsoever, for if we cannot experiment upon other minds, and they cannot react upon ours, there is no possible way in which our postulate can be verified. The universe having been reduced to individual psychical beings, between which no interaction can take place, each individual is shut up within the limits of his own experiences. He cannot communicate them to anybody else. Hence we are driven to Subjective Idealism or Solipsism.

§ 229. Professor James might have got out of the difficulty by admitting some form of monistic Idealism or Absolutism, but that would have been too repugnant to a pluralist ; or he might have admitted, with Dr. Schiller, that mind and matter (*i.e.*, other minds less developed) can interact ; but this would have implied the validity of causation. Accordingly, he has recourse to another experiment, and postulates a common world of space. If we are to be able to communicate one with another, there must be something in common between us, and as our minds do not terminate in the same percepts (since the percepts of different persons are never precisely the same), it is better to say that they terminate in the same place, or space or pseudo-space, or something or other of that kind which is very much like space.

Really I do not see how ' space ' is going to help Professor James out of his difficulty unless he is willing to interpret it realistically. Indeed, it is no easy task to discover what precisely space can mean in a philosophy of Pure Experience. It must be some aspect of experience, however, for *ex hypothesi* there is nothing but experience in existence. Moreover, when a given experience, *per se* pure and simple, has been analysed *post factum* into a dual aspect, we could hardly say that space belonged to the subjective aspect, so that it must belong to the objective. Or, in other words, when two people perceive the same thing, as we say, the objective and spatial aspects of their respective experiences are really identical. Whence it follows that when A and B perceive the same thing, the piece of experience in question, say Memorial Hall, has not only a dual, but a triple aspect, viz., the objective and spatial aspect Memorial Hall and the subjective aspects of A's and B's consciousness respectively. Nay, more, should there happen to be a crowd gathered in front of Memorial Hall, that fortunate piece of experience would thereby obtain an indefinite number of subjective aspects, each of which would be the other side, so to speak, of the same objective experience. But if this given piece of experience is really one and the same, and is really common to all the different minds that perceive it in such a way that they can only be separated from it and regarded as distinct by an abstraction, then minds in reality are not distinct and individual, but are at bottom one. Thus starting from Pure Experience as interpreted by the Personal Idealist or the panpsychist, we arrive at a conclusion which is utterly incompatible with Personal Idealism, and indeed with any species of pluralistic philosophy, a conclusion which ultimately must lead us on to Monism.

On the other hand, if space is interpreted realistically, it is independent and distinct from mind; and experience ceases to be one thing which we retrospectively distinguish into a subjective and an objective aspect, for it is and has been all along dual in that the somebody who experiences is really distinct from the something (viz., space) that is experienced. But if this much is granted, why restrict the common *object* of all perception to space? Why single out an abstraction and make that real, instead of admitting, with common-sense and the realist, that the material world as a whole is real? Common-sense Realism is a much better solution than a half-thought-out philosophy which seems to tear us in pieces and cast some one way, some another.

§ 230. The disruptive tendency of the philosophy of Pure Experience may be further illustrated by the theory that the known in conceptual thought is a "possible experience." When my knowledge does not terminate in an actual percept, it refers, I am told, to a 'possible experience.' What is this 'possible experience,' and to whom does it belong? Is it but another name for Mill's 'possibility of sensation'? Apparently not; for this would mean Subjective Idealism, which we must try to avoid. 'The beyond must be of an experimental nature; and if not a future experience of our own (it cannot be merely a future experience of our own if it really exists) or a present one of our neighbour, it must be a thing in itself, *i.e.*, an experience for itself whose relation to other things we translate into the action of molecules, ether-waves,'[1] etc. So far,

---

[1] " A World of Pure Experience," p. 569.

so good : the possible experience exists, for it is the experience of a psychical something ; and, once again, this ' opens the chapter,' as Professor James says, ' to the relations of Radical Empiricism to Panpsychism.' The 'possible experience' in question, however, is a possible experience *for me*, so that somehow or other I must be able to get at it ; but *how* I cannot conceive. I shall be told, I suppose, that when I move about or take a journey, my experience ' grows by the edges,' and may end by coinciding with the experience of that psychic something which I know. Whether such an account of the way in which we come to perceive objects is adequate I leave it to the reader to judge. Personally, it does not seem to me to *explain* anything at all, for it does not tell me how I am going to appropriate to myself that other experience which, for me, is only possible, and at present belongs to somebody else who is quite distinct from me. The transition from possible to actual experience still remains a mystery. The ' conterminousness of different minds ' and the ' concatenated union ' of different parts of the world of Pure Experience seem to be little more than words, and they certainly cannot help us. Indeed, the very ' termini ' which are supposed to exist between different minds in this hypothesis, serve but to shut each mind up in its own experience and to prevent it from passing from there to other experiences at present belonging to other minds or to psychic things in themselves. Relations of contiguity (nothing between) are equally unavailing, for what is contiguous *ipso facto* does not interpenetrate. Yet I must be able some-

W

how to get from my own to the experiences of
somebody else, otherwise, for me, they are not
possible experiences, and I cannot know them at all.
Hence I am forced to admit a ' transcendental leap,'
or else to postulate a *common something*.   And if I
choose the latter course, again I am driven backwards to the Monism of a previous chapter or
forwards to the Realism of the next.   Either that
common something is inside or it is outside the
minds that experience it.   If it is outside, and we
wish to avoid the *salto mortale*, we must admit
causal interaction and direct apprehension of the
nature of reality ;   if it is inside, we must modify
Personal Idealism and admit the ' through and
through type of union, each in all and all in each,'
which is the characteristic of monistic Idealism.

§ 231.   It is hardly necessary for me to show
that the arguments here used against the philosophy
of Pure Experience as expounded by Professor
James, apply also to the *Empirio-Criticism* of
Avenarius, for I have already shown that the two
philosophies are fundamentally the same.   Subject
and object, character and content, independent and
dependent vital series are but different aspects of
one and the same entity, experience, relatively
distinguished in retrospection, but not really
distinct.   Logical relations between character and
content and functional relations between psychosis
and brain-state are added, but they explain
nothing ;   and the Psycho-physical Parallelism
which they imply cannot be proved to hold except
for sensations and images and those connections and
groupings of images which are classed under the

general heading of Association of Ideas. Hence
the same difficulties arise as before, and similar
alternatives present themselves. Either experiences
are grouped in finite centres or they are not. If
they are, we have Pluralism, and must either admit
causal interaction or else assign a common Ground :
and if they are not, we have Experience left standing
by itself ; without substance, yet giving rise to
differences; without Ground, yet somehow producing
appearances, and from its primary state of undifferentiated purity by some mysterious process,
evolving a conglomeration of ideas, illusory, insignificant, useless, only to return in the end, aided
by the philosopher, to the same dull state of flat
and meaningless monotony.

§ 232. The philosophy of Avenarius suggests
another difficulty which may be urged against the
philosopher of Pure Experience. Avenarius introduces *pro tempore* and by the assistance of his
Empirio-Critical postulate the existence of other
minds. Yet he forgets to tell us how it comes
about that ' character ' is grouped together in these
postulated minds, or how it is that while character
appears to be so grouped content may extend to an
indefinite beyond. No unity of Ground is presupposed as the condition of the grouping of feelings,
thoughts and volitions in these pseudo-real centres
of experience which are eventually to disappear ;
and hence the concept of the self finds no place in
the philosophy of *Empirio-Criticism*.

By Professor James the concept of the self is
treated in like manner, and is emptied of all real
significance. Personality and unity, conceptions

so prominent in Personal Idealism, and so forcibly
thrust upon us by the data of experience are almost
entirely wanting in his mosaic philosophy. Relations
of various degrees of intimacy are much to the fore,
but no unity of Ground is admitted, and consequently for Radical Empiricism there is no real self.
Professor James does not scruple, indeed, to use
realistic terminology. Again and again he speaks
of ' minds ' which think and feel, and which ' *actuate* '
bodies. But neither in his *Principles of Psychology*
nor yet in his metaphysical sketches is a real self to
be found as the result of his careful analyses. The
self for him is merely a system of memories, purposes, strivings, fulfilments or disappointments; an
aggregate of relations intimately cohering together,
co-conscious and somehow leading one into the
other, yet without any unity in the background, or
any substance to explain this fortuitous concourse
of psychical characteristics. What is it holds
together these various items, memories, purposes,
strivings ? What is it forms them into a system ?
How is it that they interpenetrate and suffuse one
another's being while others are left outstanding ?
How are they distinguished from one another and
yet united in synthesis ? What is the significance of
that little word 'my' when I say that *my* experiences
pass continuously from one to the other, yet
never pass directly into the experiences of somebody
else ? What is the significance and what the use of
those purposes, strivings and needs which, together,
determine the ' will to believe,' if they do not belong
to a real person, a real unity, who knows that he
has them and demands that, whatever may happen

to other purposes and needs, *his*, at any rate, must and shall be satisfied ?

§ 233. Pragmatism cannot be reconciled with a Personal Idealism such as has been outlined in the symposium which bears that name, until it assigns to personality a fuller meaning than is assigned to it in Radical Empiricism and in the philosophy of Pure Experience. Purposes, unless they are purposes for somebody, needs, unless they belong to a real self, satisfactions, emotions, will, action, unless they are united and co-ordinated by a living personality, are abstractions quite as empty and meaningless as those of '*pure* intellect' or 'mere knowing.' Faculties and functions which work together for a common end are intelligible only if they are grounded in a real and living unity, and unity and functions alike are abstractions if separated and considered apart. Professor James feels a great repugnance to putting the Kantian 'hurly-burly' of sensations within the soul ; yet sensations are neither more nor less 'chaotic' than memories, strivings, purposes and felt-transitions without a soul. Kant, with his transcendental Unity of Apperception, which is at bottom but another name for the unity of a rational self, is at any rate able to explain the synthesis of the many in the one. But Professor James and the philosophers of Pure Experience not only fail to account for this synthesis, but, neglecting presuppositions, seem to forget that a mosaic is not a mosaic at all, nor a series a series, unless the individuals which compose it somehow form a unity, or are capable of being apprehended by a mind which itself is a unity. The pragmatist cannot be content with such a philosophy. He is pragmatically bound to restore real unities to their proper place in a metaphysic of the universe and in a theory of human knowledge, for without them we are left with a hurly-burly which, in spite of its felt-relations, is more chaotic and more unintelligible than any Kantian manifold, and with a philosophy which is wholly incapable of answering any rational question, of serving any rational purpose, or of satisfying any human need.

§ 234. Supposing, however, that this restitution has been made, that the unities destroyed by Pure Experience and the selves annihilated by Radical Empiricism have been reinstated, and that the philosophy of Pure Experience has been transformed into Personal Idealism, can the pragmatist find here a metaphysic which will satisfy his rational needs? I think not, for Personal Idealism and Panpsychism themselves are incomplete and tend to disruption. The discrepancy which arises when an attempt is made to account for intercommunication between mind and mind we have already pointed out ; but the incompleteness of Personal Idealism may be shown in quite another way. It seems to assume, with Fichte, that the Universe consists of a system of rational, striving Egos. A multiplicity of rational beings, however, cannot be an ultimate fact. This multiplicity must be accounted for, and it cannot be accounted for by saying that each rational ego exists of its own nature, and is necessary independently of its neighbours ; for this would lead to a contradiction. A *necessary* being which is wholly independent of anything else, must be infinite, since,

being independent and distinct, there is nothing
which could limit it. Yet *de facto* it is not infinite
since there are *ex hypothesi* other beings which have
perfections that it does not possess. A multiplicity
of rational beings, then, cannot individually be
necessary. Either they must form a systematic
whole which finds its unity and necessity in an
immanent Ground, in which case their personality
is once more destroyed, for they no longer have any
self which is really distinct from that Ground ; or,
while still retaining their personality and their
mutual independence, they presuppose some Being
who is one, infinite and necessary, and whose
existence and purposive action is the real, though
not the immanent, Ground of theirs.

§ 235. Thus, so far as real and personal unities
and a real and personal God are concerned, we have
come back to Realism. One assumption alone bars
the way to a complete return, and that is the
assumption which is common to all Idealisms, viz.,
that the subject experiencing and the real object
experienced are not distinct. That it is an
assumption is evident ; for the testimony of direct
experience is negative, and the testimony of common-
sense belief is opposed. ' Pure ' experience, if we
have any, tells us nothing whatsoever about real
unities, for though we do not distinguish the self
from the not-self, we certainly do not regard them
as one ; nor do we do so when our experience is
purely objective, as it is said at times to be, for then
there is no *self*-consciousness at all. The fact
remains, therefore, that as soon as reflection super-
venes on an act of direct experience, things and the

conscious self, objects and the psychical acts in which they were known, in a word, what is experienced and we who experience, are held to be really distinct ; and this distinction is referred back by us to the act in which—according to some—it passed unnoticed. It is the denial of this distinction which has led to Absolutism and to the inconsistencies and inexplicable mysteries which are to be found therein. And it is the denial of this distinction which has led to the philosophy of Pure Experience which is even more inconsistent and more mysterious still.

§ 236. But am I right in saying that all Idealisms make the disastrous assumption referred to above ? Perhaps I, too, have exaggerated ? Indeed, it would seem that I have. For I observe a tendency among many idealists, notably *Personal* idealists and possibly Professor Mackenzie, to deny altogether this assumption, and to adopt a philosophy which, in all respects but one, is a Realism. Idealists of this kind admit individual existents and affirm that they interact ; but in order to explain interaction they postulate that the world, which the realist calls material, is at bottom spiritual. This I cannot but regard as a misnomer, for the material world is essentially different from man. On the other hand, between the knower and the known there must be some similarity of nature, and if to the so-called material world we assign a reality less perfect than that which belongs to man, it is largely a question of words perhaps whether we call it spiritual or not. Spirituality, however, connotes intellect and will ; and to predicate those of material things is

neither consistent with facts nor necessary in order
to explain knowledge. Interaction we must postulate ; but interaction is possible even if things are
material, as I shall endeavour to show in the following chapters ; whereas if all things are spiritual, as
the idealist assumes, interaction is simply a mystery
which no one can explain.

In any case this Idealism is not that which the
pragmatist has adopted. It might, indeed, be called
a form of Panpsychism ; but to Panpsychism the
pragmatist adds his doctrine that in every case
reality is really altered by our knowledge of it.
Nothing is more reasonable than to suppose that, if
there be anything personal at the bottom of things,
the way we behave to it must affect "the way it
behaves to us." [1] And, as we have seen, Dr. Schiller
not only does assume this for each and every really
cognitive act, but strives by might and main
to prove it, while at the same time denying
that the contrary hypothesis is capable of rational
defence. Consequently, our knowledge is never
knowledge of reality, but only of modifications
produced in reality by the very act of knowing it ;
and that second factor which must be admitted into
reality, "but is not of our making," [2] must remain
for ever *unknowable*. The pragmatic theory of
knowledge, therefore, if logically carried out, either
drives us back in Kantian Scepticism with its wholly
useless and meaningless *Ding-an-sich ;* or, if interpreted metaphysically, leads us on to a philosophy
of Pure Experience which, of all philosophies, is the

[1] *'Axioms as Postulates,'* § 24.
[2] *Studies in Humanism,* p. 463.

most hopeless, for its power of explaining the universe is absolutely *nil*, and as soon as an intelligent meaning is put upon its atrocious terminology it at once bursts with discrepancy and leaves us no better off than when we started.

CHAPTER XIII.

THE CONDITIONS OF KNOWLEDGE *EX PARTE OBJECTI.*

§ 237. In this and in the two following chapters I do not propose to give a full or in any way an adequate account of the metaphysics of any realistic philosophy, nor do I propose to discuss in detail the various categories of Being. That is a duty which pertains to the metaphysician as a metaphysician, and not to the epistemologist, who is concerned with metaphysics only in so far as he has to treat of the conditions of human knowledge. My intention here is to give merely a brief outline of the metaphysics of Realism and to deal at length only with those of its characteristics which bear directly upon, and are presupposed by, the realist's theory of knowledge.

A not uncommon method in metaphysics is to take its theses one by one, and to endeavour to show that each is self-evident or that it can be inferred from the data of our experience. I have deliberately chosen another course. Not that I disapprove of the older method, or that I think it impossible to establish individually and yet with some degree of conclusiveness the doctrines of metaphysics; but, first of all, because the detailed discussion which this way of proceeding would involve hardly lies within the province of Epistemology; and, secondly, because I feel that, though to a plain man who, like all men, is born a realist, such a method might prove convincing, it could hardly appear so to one who is already persuaded of the truth of his own philosophic position. Every philosopher is a dogmatist in that he believes and affirms his own philosophy to be better than that of anybody else; and unless you can offer him another philosophy which, taken as a whole, is more systematic, more complete, more self-consistent, more compatible with the facts of introspection and common-sense belief, and finally more capable than his own of satisfying his deepest needs, you can hardly hope to convince him of the probability, not to say the truth, of the theory in which you yourself believe. Now the philosophy of Realism, as it was understood by Aristotle, Aquinas, and is still understood by their modern interpreters, the scholastics, to my mind, presents, when compared with either Absolutism or Pragmatism, the characteristics enumerated above. Accordingly, this is the theory which I propose in brief outline to describe. It is a system and not a patchwork mosaic; and as a system I shall present it, and would beg that from this standpoint it be judged. Tear it to pieces, if you will; but remember that in doing so you destroy its significance and will in consequence be only too liable to under-rate its value.

§ 238. Absolutism without the Absolute would be like a city built in the air, and in the same way Scholasticism without God is a philosophy stripped of the central idea which dominates the whole. The limitations, the imperfections, the corruptibility and the changeful nature of the things which surround us, all point to a something beyond, to a Being who is free from the manifest deficiencies of finite things, to whom they owe their existence and whatever degree of reality they possess, yet of whom they are but the imperfect manifestation. And what we find within points in the same direction. On the one hand, our human souls demand with all the authority of a categorical imperative a satisfaction which shall stop at nothing short of the infinite. But, on the other hand, when we reflect on the impotency of human nature, on its finite knowledge, capability and power, on its weakness and inconstancy, its perversity, its proneness to error and disease, on its ideals which are so often frustrated and never realised in full ; when we reflect on these things, I say, we find no guarantee that our needs will ever be satisfied unless indeed it be the obstinate and illogical persistency with which they assert their demands. If, then, these exigencies of our nature are not to be in vain there must be a Being who is capable of satisfying our desires, for their satisfaction cannot come from ourselves or from the finite universe in which we live.

Considerations such as these all point to a supreme and all-powerful Being whose existence and essence are not derived from without, like those of contingent beings, but who exists of Himself, who is what He is because He is, and who cannot, therefore, be other than infinite, since in Him existence and essence are one. Whether the existence of God can be *proved* from these considerations, it is beyond the scope of my subject to discuss. For the purposes of theory I assume the existence of a supreme and infinite Being, because such an assumption is necessary to explain the universe in which we live, and because without such an assumption our theory of knowledge would not be complete.

§ 239. Granted, then, that there is a Being who exists *a se*, it follows that all outside Him must exist in dependence upon Him ; and of these dependent existents something must now be said. They do not exist of themselves, otherwise they would be identical with God ; and they are not infinite, for they could only be infinite if they existed *a se*. Yet they exist, and their existence can only come from God. They are not self-existents, but essentially dependent beings, brought into existence originally by the mere act of God, and sustained in their existence and activity by the Divine power. It is a common mistake to suppose that the scholastic conceives God and the created universe as beings shut off from one another and independent except for the first act of creation by which they came to be. This is an utter misconception. The universe is regarded by scholastics as dependent upon God *almost* as completely as it is in the theory of Absolutism.[1] Finite beings are not mere differences of an Absolute Ground, or mere parts of one organic whole. They have their own existence and their own nature, both of which are distinct from His. Yet they resemble

[1] See Appendix, for precise meaning of 'dependence' and 'independence.'

and manifest God in their own imperfect way, and, though distinct from Him, never for a moment are they independent. So long as they exist, they depend upon Him for what they are and what they do. Divine conservation and divine concursus or co-operation are necessary from beginning to end. In a sense, we may say with truth that God is the Ground of the universe, so completely does it depend upon Him for all that it is. But that Ground is not a Unity amid difference immanent within a concrete individual whole ; for there is not identity, but only a far-off resemblance and a one-sided dependence between created beings and the source from which they ultimately proceed.

§ 240. None the less, in a realist philosophy there is room for the concept of ' unity in difference.' The created universe consists of finite and distinct existents, each having its own nature, each in itself a ' thing ; ' and every ' thing,' for the realist as for the absolutist, implies a unity in difference. This is of the utmost importance ; if it is borne in mind, most of the objections urged against the realist doctrine of ' things ' by Mr. Bradley and others disappear. Each thing has its own existence ; it exists *per se*, and so is a *substance*. Each thing is also a *what*, it has qualities or accidents, in virtue of which it is different from other things, and in virtue of which also it acts and is acted upon. Between substance and accident, existence and essence, the ' this ' and the ' what,' the metaphysician makes what he calls a ' real ' distinction. But it must not be supposed that by this he means to affirm that these entities are separate one from another and exist together in the concrete as an aggregate. He means nothing of the kind. Substances are not accidents, and essence is not existence ; but, in the concrete, substance and accident, essence and existence, form together an integral and real whole ; and if either were taken away there would be no concrete ' thing ' at all. Accidents are the ' differences ' of which substance is the ' ground ; ' to the substance they give quality, in virtue of which it ' appears.' And both accidents and substances are real ; but they do not destroy the unity of the ' thing.'

§ 241. The finite concrete thing always has a certain structure ; and this it has even at the level of substance. A substance is not a bare unity, or ' subject ' of accidents ; nor yet is it merely existence *per se*. In all corporeal things, whether animate or inanimate, it is itself composite, and its differences are called matter and form. The foundation of this distinction is substantial change. None of the ' things ' which we find around us are wholly permanent. They change accidentally and in certain of their outward characteristics ; and they may also cease to be and give place to something else. The most obvious instance of a substantial as opposed to an accidental change is that of death, where what was once a living body ceases to be a living body, and becomes, instead, an aggregate of substances, all of them in a rapid state of decomposition. The ' thing ' is no longer what it was ; its nature has undergone a radical change ; or, rather, the thing has given place to some other thing (or things) whose nature and ' substantial form ' is

essentially different.   Even in a substantial change,
however, there is an element which remains constant
throughout, and that element or principle is metaphysically termed ' matter.'   The matter of the
living organism and of the corpse which is left
behind when death occurs is one and the same.
It is the substantial form alone which has disappeared, and has been supplanted by other
substantial forms.   This will be clearer if we compare more in detail the corpse and the living
organism whose place it has taken.   In the living
organism there is a single principle of life which
dominates the whole structure, which has built it
up from a single cell, which has made it systematic
and organic, which controls all its functions, and
which forms with the matter thus organised one real
and substantial whole.   No part or particle of the
matter of a living organism can be said to have
properties, mechanical or chemical, which are
peculiarly and exclusively its own ; nor can the
cells of which the organism is largely composed be
said to exercise any function in complete independence of the substantial form or principle of life.
With the corpse the case is different.   The matter
of the corpse is the same as that which previously
belonged to the living organism, and it still retains
for a time its organic structure.   But now there is
no single principle which animates the whole.
Many substantial forms have taken its place.   The
chemical and mechanical properties which existed
only *virtually* in each part of the living body have
now become actual.   A substantial change has
taken place, and where formally there existed a

living whole, we now have merely an aggregate of material bodies whose forms are of a distinctly lower type.

§ 242. In the finite concrete thing we have further structural differences at a level above that of its substance. These are its accidents. Accidents do not exist in separation from or independently of the substance, though in their nature they are distinct. On the contrary, they arise directly from the substance itself. " The actuality of an accidental form," says Aquinas, " is caused by the actuality of the subject, in that the subject, in so far as it is *in potentia*, is *susceptive* of the accidental form, but in so far as it is *in actu* is *productive* of it." [1] For this " emanation of essential accidents from the subject takes place by a certain natural *resultance*." [2]

The primary characteristics of all corporeal substances are two-fold. They have quantity, and they have quality. The former follows directly from the material principle in the substance ; and the latter arises from its formal principle. " The primary accidents resulting from a corporeal substance are quantity and quality, and these two correspond to the two essential principles of the substance, *scil.*, its form and its matter ; quantity corresponding to matter, while quality arises from form." [3]

Quantity is the most imperfect of all accidents, and this is one reason why it is said to pertain to the material rather than to the formal principle in a body. But there are other grounds for this assertion. The size of a thing depends upon the

[1] *Summa Theologica*, p. 1, q. 77, a. 6.
[2] *Ibid.*, ad. 3. [3] Aquinas, in IV. Sent, d, 12, q. 1, a. 1.

X

bulk of matter which is united with its substantial form ; and this bulk may to some extent vary. An animal, for example, may grow without losing either his individuality or his species. Now growth implies the acquisition of fresh matter from without in the form of food, which, after being ' proximately disposed ' by the digestive functions of the animal itself, is assimilated and becomes a part of the living organism, whose ' quantity ' is thus increased. That quality arises from the formal principle is also clear ; for figure, shape, internal structure, colour, mechanical and chemical properties, sentience, and the power of action, are the characteristics by which one thing is distinguished from another, and pertain, therefore, to that which makes it what it is, *i.e.*, they are the ' natural result ' of its substantial form.

§ 243. In general, then, it is the substance of the thing which gives rise to and determines the species of its accidents. Their determination in detail, on the other hand, may be due, in part at least, to external causes. Thus while figure, shape and internal structure depend for their general character upon the essential nature of the thing, they may vary considerably in detail according to circumstances. Figure and shape may be altered by action from without. Structure may be modified gradually or violently by external forces. Colour, again, may vary with environment, and action, too, may turn out in effect to be different from what it was apparently intended to be. In short, every individual thing is both passive and active in regard to other things in its immediate neighbourhood. It acts upon them and they act upon it with the result that both are modified. Action and inter-action, therefore, have a good deal to say in respect to the detailed determination of the individual. Prescinding from substantial changes, we may say that in certain respects a thing is permanently *actual*, while in other respects it is always *in potentia*. Accidents in general or the specific qualities and properties of a thing, like the substantial form from which they proceed, are essential and cannot change unless the substantial form and the thing itself ceases to be and gives place to something else. But in regard to the particular determination of its accidents, a thing, though actual at any given moment, is *in potentia* in respect of future modifications. Modifications may take place owing to the action of things outside itself, and similarly the thing itself may produce modifications in other things—and also in itself if it be a living thing capable of immanent action—by virtue of its own activities.

§ 244. Thus activity and passivity, as well as actuality (*actus*) and potentiality (*potentia*) are characteristic of everything that has a finite nature ; and in the higher animals and in man these distinctions, like other structural differences, become more marked. The higher animals possess distinct powers or faculties which, in regard to their objects, may be characteristically active or passive. Thus, sensibility is distinctly a *potentia passiva*, since its function is to receive impressions from without ; whereas the power of bodily movement is distinctly a *potentia activa*, since by this means the animal is able to modify its environment. The actualisation of a *potentia passiva* is due primarily to action *ab extra ;* that of a *potentia activa* is due to, or rather is, action *ab intra.* Sensation primarily is an effect produced by some agent outside the living body, or it may be, by the immanent action of the animal itself. Action is primarily the expression of a conative impulse which arises from within and prompts the animal to action in order to effect some change in itself or in what is external to itself.

These statements, however, apply only to the relation of the *potentia* to its object, and to its mode of actualisation in general. Sensation on its psychical side is an activity, and as with all activities its exercise in any particular form tends to become habitual, and so, according to the general law of all being, to perpetuate itself. Hence even when the object is no longer present, and consequently we have not sensation or perception in the strict sense of those terms, we may have images which are at bottom but faint repetitions of sensations and sensation-complexes. Similarly, action is a particular form of activity and so may become habitual. It is, moreover, closely connected with sensations, perceptions and images, for by them its particular form is largely determined. Habit plays a most important part in all organic life. By it both *potentiæ passivæ* and *potentiæ activæ* are progressively determined and fixed ; and thereby both perception and action are much facilitated. Memory and imagination, too, are accounted for chiefly by habit, and so also are the particular forms of reaction which an animal acquires and which recur immediately a familiar object is perceived.

§ 245. Action is due in part to habit and in par

to preceding sensations and images. It is also due in part to conative impulses, as I mentioned above. These impulses arise from animal needs ; for every sentient organism has an ' end ' or *telos*, for the attainment of which certain conditions must be fulfilled ; and toward the realisation of these con- ditions it is impelled by a vague though conscious striving. Indeed, *every* existing being has an end or *telos*, and in general we may say with Spinoza that its *telos* is *perseverare in esse suo*. Everything, whether it be animate or inanimate, strives to realise its own nature and to maintain itself in existence. If it is legitimate to suppose that there is a being so simple that its sole end and function is to vibrate in a particular way and at a certain rate, it will endeavour, as far as in it lies, to go on vibrating at that particular rate and in that particular way, and will strive to overcome all obstacles which hinder the realisation of that end. The significance of the *telos* in the case of living beings is much greater ; and that they strive to realise their nature and to maintain their own form of existence will hardly be denied. This conative tendency is due to the formal principle by which the matter in a living body is organised and built up into a definite structure, a structure which is necessary for the very existence of the animal and which in consequence it endeavours to maintain.

The striving of the formal principle to persevere in its own being, however, is counteracted by the material principle or body which tends to decay ; and at first sight these seem to conflict with the general law that every being tends to persevere *in esse suo.* But this is not really the case. The ‘ matter ’ of a living organism formerly belonged to material substances having chemical and other properties, and though these substances *as such* no longer exist when they have become part of the living organism, their formal principles still exist *virtually.* Now to exist virtually is not to exist actually nor yet to exist merely *in potentia.* It constitutes a sort of mean between the two, and implies a tendency to exist. Thus, in these virtually existing formal principles—call them chemical atoms and molecules if you prefer—the general law of all being is exemplified, and at the same time by means of this hypothesis several facts may be explained. It explains, for instance, why it is that chemical substances take the place of the living organism immediately after death, not indeed in the original form in which they were first taken up as food, but as re-arranged and reconstituted by the living organism itself. It explains also—at least, so it seems to me—many facts connected with disease and decay ; for it would appear that the parts of the living organism tend to become independent ; and to acquire functions of their own, and so to resist the controlling power and all-pervading influence of the substantial form of the whole. To discuss this point, however, would lead us too far afield. Decay is at any rate a fact which the formal principle of life is ever striving to overcome ; whence it is clear that the end of a living organism is to realise its own nature and to perpetuate its own existence

§ 246. One of the principal ways in which existing things strive to realise their end is by transient action. I refer not merely to those particular actions by which living beings propagate and so perpetuate themselves in their offspring ; but to action *ad extra* of any kind whatsoever. *Omne agens agit propter finem ;* and that *finis* is to produce in some other thing a characteristic belonging to the thing that acts. For—if I may quote again an Aristotelian axiom or *dictum*—*actio sequitur esse ;* a thing can only act according to its nature. And again, *omne agens agit sibi simile ;* the effect must resemble its cause, for one thing can give to another only what itself has got. Hence, in so far as modification produced in one thing is produced therein by the action of another, there is a similarity or an identity of form between the two. As a matter of fact, however, effects are seldom due to a single cause, but to the co-operation of many causes ; and not infrequently the reaction of the relatively passive object may contribute toward that effect. In any given case, therefore, it is difficult to determine what precisely the causes are and to what extent any particular cause is responsible for a given effect. This accounts largely, I think, for the Relativism of many philosophers, especially of those who are scientifically inclined, for in science we know little for certain beyond the fact that, given a certain complexus of phenomena (causes included), another complexus of phenomena will follow. Let us illustrate our principles, therefore, by a comparatively simple example.

A stone is thrown by a small boy and a window-pane broken. The direction and the velocity of the missile were determined by the boy's action, by the

direction in which he moved his hand, and by the
force which he exerted. The stone passed through
the window, and, if its speed was great, the hole in
the window will correspond to the shape of the stone.
In any case our principle, *omne agens agit sibi simile*,
is illustrated. Motion has produced motion ;
direction has determined direction. The reaction
of the objects in which effects are produced is also
illustrated. The air resisted the motion of the stone
and its speed, in consequence, was slackened. The
window-pane resisted it still more, and soon after it
came to a standstill. The stone was thrown against
the force of gravitation, and gravitation in the end
brought it to the ground. The hole made in the
pane of glass, too, will be of the same shape as the
stone only provided the latter struck it with a
velocity approximating to that of a bullet ; otherwise it will be an irregular hole and will be surrounded by cracks due, not to the impact of the
stone alone, but in part to the structure of the glass.
Thus even a rough analysis of a phenomenon of
this kind is sufficient to show that of the many causes
which contributed to produce it, each tended, as
far as possible, to reproduce itself, and had our
analysis been more precise and quantitatively exact
the general principle illustrated would have been
still more apparent.

§ 247. One more example may be taken ;
perhaps not a very good one, but one that is at least
familiar and interesting. What is it that causes
death ? To answer this question we must go back
to the doctrine of matter and form. Every corporeal
whole consists of matter and form, and before the

substantial form can be united with the potentiality
of the matter, it is necessary that the latter should
be 'proximately disposed' for the reception of the
form, and as long as the form exists therein, the
matter must retain the disposition or organisation
requisite for its existence. Hence, if some hostile
agency, violence, or disease of the parasitic type,
or, again, a process of decay, destroys the organic
structure of a living body, the substantial form
which inhabited that body either ceases to be, or,
if it has an existence of its own independently of
the matter with which it is united, it leaves the
body and exists elsewhere. Death, then, in itself,
is a negative rather than a positive effect ; and
considered merely in the negative aspect, it needs
no efficient cause. It is not the production, but
the cessation of existence. It consists in the destruc-
tion of a substantial whole for the existence of which
a certain organisation was the material cause and
the condition *sine qua non*. What the so-called
'cause of death' really does, therefore, is to produce
in that organism a new form, accidental indeed, yet
incompatible with the existence of the principle of
life. This form, moreover, remains when life has
ceased. Hence it is that the 'cause of death'
(*i.e.*, the act which produced the accidental form
that occasioned death) may be discovered by a
medical examination of the corpse. Poison, for
instance, does not act directly upon the formal
principle of a living organism, but upon its matter,
in which (*v.g.*) by hardening certain tissues and
cells, or by causing violent contraction of the
muscles, it produces a condition incompatible with

the performance of its functions as a living body. Hence, the conditions necessary to life being destroyed, life itself ceases to be, and other substances take the place of the living thing. The formal principles of these substances, however, are not an effect produced by the nominal 'cause of death;' but are due to the fact that, being already *virtually* in existence, now that the controlling and unifying influence of the living form is gone, they are able to spring into actual existence toward which they were tending all along.

§ 248. The universe, then, as understood by the realist, consists of a world of finite beings, material, organic, sentient, rational; no one of which is merely a phenomenon nor yet merely a substance; but each a concrete individual whole, each a thing, each existing *per se* and having its own inner structure of substantial ground and accidental differences. And this world of finite beings implies an infinite Being as its ultimate cause or as the condition without which it could neither have begun to be nor yet continue to be. Between God and His creatures there is an intimate connection, for it is to Him that they owe from first to last their existence, their nature, and all their powers. Without His assistance no thing can 'persevere in its being,' and without His concurrence no action can take place. All finite beings are wholly dependent upon the Supreme Being; but they do not proceed from Him as accidents emanate from a substantial ground; nor do they arise within Him as differences within a concrete whole. The relation of God to created existents is unique, and their dependence

upon Him cannot be compared except by analogy
to any kind of dependence that exists within the
finite world. The universe is not an organism, nor
yet a living whole. Indeed, if we consider only the
finite world of creatures, I should prefer to call it a
system, and prescinding from consciousness, to
compare it to a huge machine rather than to a living
being ; for as in a machine so in a finite world, there
are parts distinct from one another, yet adjacent
and interacting, each having its proper function,
and all together forming a systematic whole constructed according to an intelligent plan. Consciousness, however, is a fact, and a fact of supreme
importance, without which the universe would be
meaningless. Hence the above comparison is far
from adequate, as all comparisons must be when
one of their terms is the universe itself. Nevertheless, the universe is better described as a systematic,
than as an organic, whole. For though all its parts
are related, they are real individuals, each having its
own existence ; and though on account of this
relatedness a change in any one part involves a
change in some at least of the others, change as such
pertains to the individual. In essence change is a
transitus de potentia in actum. It presupposes in the
individual an already existing potentiality of
definite nature which is now realised or determined
to ' act ' by the action of an efficient cause. And
since the universe is a system, rational in its design
and its end, all change takes place according to
definite and knowable laws. Did we actually know
these laws in detail, we should know also the nature
of the things upon which they depend, and did we

know the nature of things we should know the laws which govern their interactions. But as yet we know neither adequately nor in detail, and until we do, a complete philosophy of nature is impossible.

§ 249. Of the relation of man to the universe in which he lives, nothing has been said as yet, except in so far as man is included under the general heading of living organisms and finite individual wholes and is endowed with all the characteristics which these possess. I have treated the universe from the objective and not from the human point of view ; and I have done so deliberately, for in this chapter it is with the object of knowledge and with the general metaphysical principles that underlie the theory of knowledge that we are at present concerned. One or two remarks on the general relation of man to the universe, however, must now be added ; and they will, I hope, mitigate somewhat the ire of the humanist at my apparent neglect of the human point of view.

Regarded from the human point of view, everything in the universe is *et unum et verum et bonum*. It is *unum*, for every existing being is an individual comprising unity of ground amid structural difference, and as such may be apprehended by man. It is *verum* (or *cognoscibile*) for the nature and structure of all existing things *is* intelligible, and the object manifesting itself to the intellect is, as we shall see, the foundation and ultimate criterion of all truth. And it is *bonum* (or *appetibile*) ; for everything is capable of becoming an object of human desire, and possesses the power of satisfying, directly or indirectly, a human need. These distinctions, however, do not correspond to real differences in the concrete thing ; but are relative to man. The truth and goodness of a thing are the thing itself and all that is comprised therein, considered as an object of human knowledge and human desire. Indeed, in a sense all things may be said to exist *for* man ; since he alone of all finite existents can know things as they are and as they are distinguished from one another and from himself ; and he alone can rationally appreciate their goodness or value. Other animals can feel the effects which are produced in their sentient organisms by action from without, but not as effects of action from without. And other animals are aware of impulses which prompt them to react in such a way as to satisfy their needs ; but of the meaning and significance of such impulses and needs they know nothing. It is only for man that sensation has meaning, and it is he alone who knows the significance of his impulses and his needs ; for he alone can reflect and is self-conscious. Knowledge in the strict sense of the term and rational action are characteristics peculiar to man ; and for this reason the rest of the world is subordinate to him and, as his knowledge of it advances, steadily becomes more and more subject to his control, more and more subservient to his needs.

§ 250. Our account of the knowable now being complete, we might proceed at once to discuss the knower and the metaphysical theory of the process by which knowledge is obtained, were it not that Mr. Bradley has raised certain objections to the realist's view of the object of knowledge, which must first be disposed of. The objections which concern us most are those which are directed (1) against the doctrine of substance and accident, and (2) against the doctrine of causation.

The doctrine of substance and accident or ' substantive and adjective ' Mr. Bradley finds to be a failure ; and the first reason he gives is that it seems doubtful what the *is* can really mean when we say (*v.g.*) that sugar is white and hard and sweet. " Sugar is obviously not mere whiteness, mere hardness, and mere sweetness ; for its reality lies somehow in its unity." But " we can discover no real unity existing outside these qualities, or, again, existing within them." [1]

What sort of unity is Mr. Bradley looking for here ? A unity apparent to the senses ? One which can be separated from its qualities and perceived in all its nakedness as a unity ? Surely not. Yet, if not, I fail to understand where lies the difficulty. I fear, in fact, that Mr. Bradley is confusing two senses in which the word ' thing ' is popularly used. We may say, as he remarks, either that the thing ' sugar ' *has* certain qualities, or that it *is* white and hard and sweet ; but these two forms of predication are not contradictory, for the term 'thing' is not used in the two cases in precisely the same sense. When we say that a ' thing ' *is* so and so, we speak of the concrete thing, regarded as a whole, complete in itself, and embracing a unity in difference. But when we affirm that a ' thing ' *has* qualities, we no longer regard the thing as a concrete whole ; but, analysing it—mentally, of course—into a unity of ground or

[1] *Appearance and Reality*, p. 19.

substance on the one hand, and differences of structure, accidents or qualities on the other, we say that this unity which we now call by metonymy a 'thing,' *has*, or is the ground of, certain differences. This use of the term 'thing' is liable perhaps to lead to misunderstanding, as it has done apparently in Mr. Bradley's case; but, in spite of the ambiguity thereby introduced, it is a use of the term which is not without justification. For clearly 'thing-ness' belongs in the concrete individual to the unity of ground rather than to the qualitative difference, since it is this unity of ground which makes it a thing.

§ 251. Mr. Bradley urges his difficulty, however, by quoting against us the old dilemma : 'If you predicate what is different, you ascribe to the subject what it is not ; and if you predicate what is not different, you say nothing at all.'

The reply to this sophistical argument really rests upon what logicians call 'the *import* of propositions.' In fact, we have only to distinguish here the use of the term 'subject,' just as we distinguished above the use of the term 'thing' and the difficulty disappears. For if our 'subject' refers to the substantial unity of the thing, we do not contradict ourselves when we say that it has certain differences any more than Mr. Bradley contradicts himself, when he makes a similar predication of the Absolute. While, if the subject be taken to mean the concrete thing as a whole, again there is no contradiction in affirming that it embraces a certain difference, for the universe in Mr. Bradley's philosophy does the same. In other words, if the subject of our judgment is a substance or a unity of ground, we must use the 'has' form of predication, in which case subject and predicate are not the same, nor are they regarded as the same ; whereas if the subject of our sentence be a concrete thing (or, for that matter, a complexus of attributes) then we must use the 'is' type of proposition, in which case we do identify subject and predicate ; but we identify them not on the same level, so to speak, but because and in so far as they imply a unity of ground.

§ 252. Many of the objections which Mr. Bradley raises against the notions which are employed in the metaphysics of Realism are, like his objections to the doctrine of substance and accident, based upon a misconception ; and objections of this kind it is hardly necessary to discuss since they have been met for the most part, I think, by the exposition already given. Others, again—indeed the majority—presuppose his theory of relations which has already been discussed. The difficulties raised in the earlier portion of his chapter on "Causation" are an example of this. Accordingly, I shall pass them over. Toward the end of that chapter, however, an objection of quite a different kind is raised, and this I feel bound to discuss in some detail, not only because it is typical of another type of Mr. Bradley's objections ; but also, and more especially, because the doctrine of causation is of vital importance in the realist's theory of knowledge.

The objection, as usual, is thrown into the form of a dilemma. "*Causation must be continuous ;*" for if it were not, it would not be causation, since we should have the cause " enduring unchanged through a certain number of moments, and then suddenly changing." Yet " *causation cannot be continuous,*" for, if it were, the cause would be entirely without duration. " It would never be itself except in the time occupied by a line drawn across the succession." [1]

§ 253. Now, although Mr. Bradley speaks here of 'continuity,' he seems to me to have a false notion of what a *continuum* really means, or, at any rate, is not clear as to the difference between a *continuum* and a series of mathematical points. No succession of points without extension and without duration can under any conditions give rise to a *continuum,* whether in space or in time. For it is impossible to get extension out of what is unextended, or duration out of a succession of timeless instants, so that a *continuum,* whatever else it is, cannot be made up of contiguous mathematical points, since in that case it would still be a point. If, however, you ask me to define a *continuum,* I confess that I am unable to do so. I might say, perhaps, that to be a *continuum* is to be undivided and yet to have parts outside parts, but this does not help us much, for the parts themselves must have duration and extension, otherwise we shall still be without our *continuum.* The fact is that the notion of a *continuum* is for us an ultimate notion, and to define an ultimate notion is clearly impossible. Because the notion is ultimate, however, and cannot be defined, it is not necessarily invalid. For there must be ultimate notions somewhere, and, if these are necessarily invalid, the whole superstructure

---

[1] *Appearance and Reality,* pp. 60, 61.

Y

falls to the ground ; knowledge becomes an impossibility, and scepticism our only alternative. Did Mr. Bradley admit the validity of the geometrical concepts of points, lines and surfaces, it might have been possible to prove by a regress the validity of the notion of a *continuum* ; for upon that notion the whole of geometry is based, points, lines and surfaces being nothing else but limits or boundaries which mark off one *continuum* from another, which is contiguous but *qualitatively* distinct. Geometrical notions, however, are regarded by Mr. Bradley as fictions, nonentities, useful for some purposes, but none the less fictions.[1] How a nonentity can be useful, or how a *pure* fiction can be of service in dealing with the real world, I am unable to understand ; but if our notions of surfaces, lines, and points have not a valid foundation in reality, it would be illogical under the circumstances for me to argue from their reality to the reality of the *continuum* which is presupposed. Consequently, we must adopt another course.

§ 254. Though a *continuum* cannot be defined, it may be illustrated. And in the first place all consciousness is continuous except for the breaks caused by sleep. Every psychosis has duration and passes gradually and without any actual break of continuity into the next. Secondly, all material things are continuous ; they have extension and they last. Strictly speaking, however, material things do not constitute *one continuum* in the same sense that a spell of consciousness does. For between material things there is a break. They do not pass

[1] *loc. cit.*, p. 61.

into one another, but are individual and distinct.
Nevertheless, there is still a sense in which we may
say that the physical world is a *continuum*. The
extension of the individual in time and in space is
limited and so has boundaries, yet the boundaries
themselves have no extension, but are, as Mr. Bradley
says, limits, in the mathematical sense. While,
then, if we regard the world in the concrete as consisting of many individual things, we must say that
there are many *continua*, contiguous, yet discrete ;
if we abstract from thing-hood and qualitative
differences, we may say with truth that the spatial,
and in like manner the temporal, *continuum* is one.

§ 255. Having thus cleared up our ideas somewhat in regard to what is meant by a *continuum*,
let us return to Mr. Bradley's destructive criticism
of the notion of causation. Is causation continuous ? Certainly ; for, as Mr. Bradley says, if
we were to take a solid slice out of the flow of events,
we should find that it contained elements which
were in process of change. But does it not follow
that a cause is without duration and so cannot be
real ? This will depend entirely upon what we
mean by a cause. If, instead of taking a solid
section out of the flow of events, we bisect it by a
line, and then by another abstraction divide this
line into two aspects one ' before ' and the other
' after,' the ' before ' aspect being our ' cause ' and
the ' after ' aspect our ' effect,' certainly neither
cause nor effect has duration, and both are equally
unreal. But, if we do not make the second of these
two abstractions, but, in so far as our line of section
marks a *difference* in the flow of events, are content

to call whatever comes before it the cause, and whatever comes after it the effect, then we can assign to both cause and effect as much duration as we please, and this time both will be real. Mr. Bradley's argument is based on a fallacy. He *assumes* that causation, though continuous, has no duration, or, in other words, that for a finite cause to produce a finite effect no time is required ; whereas in fact all causal action is a gradual process which may occupy a considerable period of time. That it should do so is, I grant, an imperfection, but so also is change and everything else in this finite world. And if you choose to say that that which is imperfect is *less real* than that which is perfect, again I have no objection to raise. On the contrary, I willingly assent ; and did we know more adequately than we do what is meant by an all-perfect Being, we might define all finite perfections as the negation or limitation of some one of His ; for in some way or other change, time, space imply imperfection and the negation of *tota simul*. But since we cannot adequately conceive the All-perfect, we must be content to start with a knowledge of finite perfections and to infer what God is from our knowledge of them. And though He alone is fully real, it does not follow that finite perfections are unreal, or our notions of them invalid; still less that they are self-contradictory. To much ignorance I confess ; with a doubt I can sympathise ; but a contradiction in philosophy is intolerable.

CHAPTER XIV.

THE CONDITIONS OF KNOWLEDGE
EX PARTE SUBJECTI.

I.—THE SENSES.

§ 256. We have seen that every being in the universe is for the realist *ontologically* true ; it has a nature, a structure, a function, a purpose, all of which are knowable. We have also seen that every being is active, and is capable of producing effects in other things, which in so far as they depend upon it as upon their cause, must resemble it in some one of its characteristics. These are the conditions of knowledge *ex parte objecti*.

Ex parte subjecti we have a human being—for it is with human knowledge alone that we are concerned—and that being is endowed with all the characteristics of a sentient organism, and also with the higher functions of intellect and will. He is a substance, a unity of ground amid structural differences, and all his faculties and functions work together for a common end. He is passive, and in him other things may produce effects like to themselves. He is sentient, and therefore he can feel these effects ; he has an intellect and so can apprehend their meaning. He is also active. Consequently he can move about and so can bring himself into contact with an indefinite variety of things in an indefinite variety of circumstances. He has the power of action, and hence, guided by his reason, can manipulate and experiment upon the objects which make up his environment, and in this way progressively increase both his knowledge of their nature and his control of their activities.

§ 257. What, then, is this knowledge that man possesses, and how does he come to get it ? There are two questions here, and they must not be confused one with the other. I have said above that man is conscious of the effects produced in himself by physical objects ; but, ordinarily, he is not conscious of them as effects. He does not reason within himself ' these are effects due to external objects, but effects must resemble their causes : therefore these effects give me knowledge of objective reality.' *I* am going to argue in this way ; but then I am treating the matter metaphysically, not psychologically, or from the point of view of ordinary common-sense. What are *de facto* sensations the form of which is determined by the causal action of external objects, man spontaneously and naturally apprehends, not as sensations, nor as ' effects,' but as the qualities of natural objects. The *species sensibilis*, therefore, is ordinarily the *id quo percipitur*, not the *id quod percipitur ;* and similarly in regard to the intellect. For, as Aquinas says, " the *species intelligibilis* is to the intellect as the *species sensibilis* is to the sense. But the *species sensibilis* is not *illud quod sentitur*, but rather *id quo sensus sentit.* Hence the *species intelligibilis* is not *id quod intelligitur*, but *id quo intellectus intelligit.*" [1] Ideas,

[1] *Summa Theologica*, p. 1, q. 85 @ 2. *Note :* All scholastics grant that in the idea or concept we know the object immediately, though some prefer to say that the *verbum mentale* or concept is *id in quo res intelligitur* rather than *id quo intelligitur.* And

then, are the means by which we think of objects.
De facto they correspond to the objects about which
we think, for otherwise they could not give us
knowledge of objects ; but we do not first think of
our ideas and then infer an object to correspond;
we think directly of the object through and in the
idea.

Knowledge, therefore, is one thing ; but *how* we
come to know, or what are the metaphysical conditions of knowledge is quite another matter. Yet
to define knowledge, apart from the process by
which it is acquired, is impossible. For knowledge
is an ultimate notion. Everybody knows what it is,
because everybody *knows*. But he cannot define
it unless he also knows its metaphysical conditions.
Knowledge implies a certain peculiar relation
between thought and thing ; or, again, it may be
regarded as an action or a habit of mind which,
being given, that relation arises ; and it will be
better, perhaps, to leave the matter in this vague
form until we have discussed further the conditions
of knowledge.

§ 258. We have, then, on the one side an intelligent
knower and on the other side the knowable, things,
material, organic, sentient, rational and, finally, God.
Of all these we somehow have knowledge. Yet, if
the knowable is distinct from the knower, just as

there is some foundation for this view, since in the thought of
absent objects the idea has a twofold function to perform. It
is (1) the means whereby we think, and (2) in it the object
about which we think is presented to the mind. In other
words, the object of our thoughts, though not actually present
to our senses is none the less present *in idea*. Cf. *supra*, p. 53 ;
and cf. also Aquinas, *De differentia verbi divini et humani*,
and Urraburu, *Psychologia*, Lib. 11, disp. 2, cap. 2, art. 3.

one knower is distinct from another, how are they to be brought together unless we are to admit that abomination of Professor James, a *salto mortale*. The Aristotelian answer is by *interaction*.

Knowledge implies that the *formal* characteristics of the knowable are somehow immanently present to the knower. Consequently, as we have agreed to regard the knower and the known as existentially independent, and since in *our* world the only means by which one thing can influence another is by its actions, for knowledge to be acquired, directly or indirectly the knowable must act upon the knower in such a way as to reproduce in him that characteristic of itself which is known. Things, however, do not act directly upon the mind, but only by way of the body ; and then consciousness is not affected unless they act upon that particular part of the body which we call the terminal organs of sense. Yet when things do act upon the organs of sense, they must—according to our metaphysical principle that the effect resembles the cause—produce therein a modification which is like to themselves *in so far as it is an effect which depends upon their action as upon its cause*. On the other hand, in receiving an effect, the recipient is not merely passive. The effect is received *secundum modum recipientis ;* or, in other words, while the *particular* form which the effect takes is determined by the activity of the cause, its specific nature is determined by the *potentia passiva*, which is thus reduced to *act.* Hence, when effects are produced in a sentient organism, they must in general be *felt ;* not because sensation is something superadded to the modification produced in that organism ; but because the modification itself is a *transitus de potentia ad actum*, which takes place in a *potentia passiva* of a certain specific (*scil.*, sentient) nature. Whenever sensation occurs, it is at once a *species impressa* and a *species expressa*. It is a *species impressa* because it is a modification, the form of which is determined by the action of an object external to the organ of sense ; and it is *expressa* because it is not merely a modification of the bodily organ, but a sensation having a particular quality.[1]

§ 259. The correspondence here affirmed between sensation and its cause may seem to many crude, if not a sheer absurdity. It is, however, essential to Aristotle's theory of knowledge ; and though physiology and physics have made great progress since the days of the famous Greek, it is only the details and not the general principles of his theory that have been affected. As a theory consisting of a complexus of hypotheses and principles, it cannot be established wholly *a posteriori*, nor can it be verified point by point by comparison with the facts ; not, indeed, because these are relevant facts which it cannot account for, but because our ' facts,'

---

[1] The account of the act of perception given in this chapter is based upon the theories of Aristotle and Aquinas ; but, the more adequate knowledge which we now possess of physiological psychology has made it necessary to introduce certain modifications. The *species impressa*, for instance, is not identified by Aquinas with the physiological process that underlies perception ; but is merely the *species sensibilis quâ* an effect. Indeed, the term *species impressa* is not used by him at all; though he admits an *immutatio naturalis* in the organs of sense which resembles the external cause, and which is to sensation as matter to its form ; and similarly, it would appear, in regard to *cerebral* processes that accompany and condition the phantasm, or what we should now call the percept or image.

in physiology especially, are comparatively scanty, and many things which are sometimes asserted as facts belong in truth to physiological theory. I would ask the reader, therefore, to hold whatever prejudices he may have in abeyance. To argue as some do that the ' correspondence notion of truth ' is absurd, because copying is useless, is to beg the whole question. For if copying can give us knowledge and so enable us to increase the control we have of the things around us, and thus to make them more and more subservient to our needs, it certainly is *not* useless. While to affirm as many do, that sensation *cannot* be a copy of its object or cause, is again irrational ; for it assumes that we know what the objective qualities are to which sensations are supposed to correspond, whereas, in fact, we know very little about them, and in some cases, smells and tastes for instance, nothing at all. Let us then suspend judgment until we have examined theories and facts, both physical and physiological, and I think that in the end we shall find there are none with which the Aristotelian theory of knowledge is incompatible.

Our theory affirms that sensation is *like* its object or cause ; and two reasons may be given for this assertion, (1) that it follows logically from the general principle that the effect resembles its cause, and (2) that sensation being the *id quo percipitur*, though not itself either perception or knowledge, must correspond with its object, otherwise it could not be the empirical source whence all knowledge is derived. Were these principles generally recognised as axiomatic, we might leave the matter here ; but a they are not, we must examine in detail the psycho-physical process of sensation, in order to discover how far it resembles what we know—or suppose that we know—of the physical properties of objects.

§ 260. A sensation—or, better, perhaps, a sense-impression—has many characteristics ; but the ' quality ' of sensation is the characteristic in refer-ence to which it is most difficult to establish cor-respondence. In regard to it I shall endeavour to establish two points (1) that what physicists and physiologists have to tell us about the matter tends to confirm rather than to upset our theory ; and (2) that, so far as ' quality ' is concerned, a precise correspondence is not required.

Let us first consider the *species impressa*, which I regard as identical with the nervous processes that are the immediate antecedents or physiological conditions of sensation and perception. Sensation is undoubtedly closely connected with the nervous impulse, and probably arises, so thinks Professor McDougall, as that impulse passes through the synapses that connect one neurone with another. Of the nature of a nervous impulse we know nothing for certain ; but we do know that nervous impulses must differ, because sensations themselves are different. The question is, then, what is the ultimate cause of these differences ? Are they determined objectively by the stimulus, or sub-jectively by the ' specific energy of the nerves ' ? The latter view originated with Professor Müller, and a short time ago was very widely accepted among physiologists. Professor Wundt, however, rejects it in favour of a more objective theory ; and it seems to me that he does so with good reason.

The ' Specific Energy ' theory affirms that the quality of sensation must be due to the structure of the nervous tissues and not to the physical stimulus ; because (1) a specific sensation may be produced by other than 'adequate stimuli,' and also (2) by stimulating the cut end of a nerve ; and (3) the Young-Helmholtz theory of colour-vision, and the Helmholtz theory of audition presuppose this hypothesis.[1] These arguments, however, are by no means conclusive. For (1) the possibility of producing sensations by other than normal stimuli and in cases where the end-organ has been lost or destroyed, may be accounted for in the same way as memory and imagination, viz., by functional differentiation, of the nervous tissue due to habitual activity ; and (2) the Helmholtz theories presuppose not necessarily specific differentiation of the *nerves*, but of the *nerve terminals* in the eye and in the ear. Moreover, there is not the slightest anatomical evidence for original specific difference in the nature of the nerves or of the cells which belong to the various organs of sense ; but *only* in regard to their peripheral *end-organs*. Hence we conclude with Professor Wundt that both centrally and peripherally the general law holds that repeated stimulation of a particular kind changes the nervous substance and gives it a tendency to exhibit a certain specific process in whatever way it may be stimulated ; but that whereas peripherally special-isation of the nervous elements is inherited, centrally it is not, but is acquired during the life-time of the

[1] cf. McDougall, *Physiological Psychology*, pp. 58 *et seq.*

individual. "The central function is that of *combining* and *inhibiting* peripherally excited impulses and only later of reproducing such impressions spontaneously, owing to modifications of the substance of the neurones due to previous excitation." What we inherit cerebrally are "dispositions consisting in neural connections, and hence favouring certain kinds of reaction."[1]

§ 261. Physiologically, then, there is no evidence whatever, so far as the nervous impulse and the quality of sensation are concerned, which can be urged against our metaphysical theory. On the contrary, if, as Professor Wundt says, "functional differentiation of nervous matter is due to special conditions arising from external circumstances and external stimuli," it seems probable that the purpose of peripheral adaptation is that the effect of the stimulus may be the more easily produced. And we are confirmed in this opinion when we take into consideration physical theories in regard to the constitution of the various objects perceived by the senses. If light is a periodic motion in the ether, and colour a property of the molecules in a body in virtue of which certain rays of light are absorbed and others reflected, clearly that a periodic motion of (say) 500 billion vibrations per second should be able to affect the organ of sense requires some special adaptation; and the same may be said of heat-waves which are also periodic, but of considerably greater length, and therefore require a different adaptation in the end organ. Similarly for pressure if it be due to a bombardment of molecules. I do not wish to

[1] Wundt, *Physiological Psychology*, vol. i., p. 320 (Eng. trans.).

suggest, of course, that the rapid vibrations of a hypothetical ether are reproduced in the organ of sight or of temperature precisely in the same manner that they exist in the ether (or in what Aristotle would have called the *Diaphanum*) ; for, colour differences on this hypothesis being quantitative, it would be sufficient if the relative values of the wave-lengths were preserved ; and there are grounds for thinking that the propagation of nervous impulses is periodic.

It is, however, hardly worth while seeking for further analogies between physiological processes and the interpretations put upon the *sensibile proprium* of the various senses by physical theory. The uncertainty of both our physical and our physiological theories makes all speculation of this kind decidedly premature. Nevertheless, what knowledge we have seems to confirm rather than to disprove our contention that an organ of sense is a *potentia passiva*, the actuation of which is due to a stimulus, and ultimately to an object, to which the *species impressa* corresponds.

§ 262. We come now to the *species expressa*, to sensation itself, and here, if our physical theories are correct, there is no correspondence in the literal and punctual sense between the quality of the sensation and the objective quality of the thing. Exact correspondence in every detail, however, is not required ; indeed, if there were a correspondence of this kind sensation would practically be useless for knowledge. Knowledge begins with sense-experience, and what we want first are not minute analyses, but broad distinctions. We do not want to know how many billion times a second there is a vibration in the ether, but what in general are the qualities of an extended thing which we wish to distinguish from some other thing. And for purposes of distinction the ' qualities ' of sensation are extremely efficient. They do not tell us anything about wave-lengths or about the chemical constitution of a molecule, for their function is not to give us a knowledge of details, but to represent them *synthetically* like the mathematician who plots out a curve. And, as a matter of fact, the stimulus itself comes to us in synthesis. Hence, if we did get a distinct sensation corresponding to each element in the stimulus as analysed by the visual substances of the retina or by the basilar membrane in the cochlea, the representative value of sensation, as well as its utility for knowledge, would be far less than what it is. The first condition of all knowledge is the power of discrimination, and the accuracy of the senses in this respect could scarcely be greater than it is. The normal eye never mistakes a wave-length of ·000656 mm. (red) for one of ·000527 mm. (green) ; still less do our senses confuse these shorter wave-lengths of light with the longer ones of heat. Stimuli, whether differing quantitatively or qualitatively, are most accurately distinguished by means of the ' qualities ' of sensations, and are automatically arranged in classes under the general headings of colour, heat, sound, pressure, flavour, odour, etc. Thus, though the quality of sensations tells us nothing of the nature of objects, it tells us a great deal about their differences, and, consequently, is of immense value for knowledge, since thereby we are enabled to distinguish one thing from another and so to make them the objects of further research. Nor can it be said that the senses deceive us by leading us to believe that to be objective which is really subjective. If you ask the plain man what colour is, he will reply that it is a quality in the object, and this is true; for, according to the scientists, it consists in the power of the object to analyse light by absorbing some rays and reflecting others. That the objective quality, colour, is of such a nature, the plain man does not know, for his senses tell him nothing of the nature of colour. But he does know that colour is a quality of objects, and that colours are objectively different; and his knowledge is valid scientifically as well as for common-sense. Even in regard, then, to the quality of sensation, there is a certain correspondence between it and the qualities of objects; and though the correspondence is not precise or detailed, it is sufficient, and were it greater than what it is, the value of sensation as the *id quo percipitur* would be lessened instead of increased.

§ 263. Positive knowledge, however, is derived not so much from the 'quality' of sensation as from other characteristics which correspond to the 'primary' qualities of objects or to *sensibilia communia*, *i.e.*, to qualities of objects perceptible by more senses than one. All sensations seem to have extension or extensity, and in what is presented by *sight* or by *touch*, there is a spatial arrangement of qualitative differences which is the basis of our knowledge of figure, shape, distance, magnitude and

number ; while changes within a presentation and
succession among presentations themselves are data
presupposed by our knowledge of motion and rest,
time, change, duration, etc. Now, between the
extensity and configurations which characterise
sense-presentations, and objective extension and
figure, as we understand it, there is clearly a correspondence ; and this correspondence seems to
apply also to the intermediate link, the *species
impressa*, or the physiological modification produced
in the nervous system. At any rate, it is true in
regard to the *peripheral terminals* of the organs of
sight and touch. The relative positions of different
parts of the retinal image correspond approximately
with the relative positions of objects within the
field of vision.[1] For touch, too, the configuration
of the surface of a body with which we are in
contact corresponds approximately with the configuration of the end-organs of touch in the
part affected ; though the correspondence here
is far less accurate than it is in sight, and depends

[1] That the retinal image should be inverted does not affect
the correspondence theory. All positions are relative. There
is no such thing as an absolute upside-down. The direction
'down' is determined by the force of gravitation as experienced
by touch and by *normal* vision. 'Up' is its correlative.
Tactual space and visual space, moreover, since they reveal to us
identically the same objects, are correlated in experience. Disturb
this correlation (v.g.) by the use of a mask fitted with lenses
that re-invert the retinal image (vide *Psychol. Rev.* iii., 611 f.;
iv., 341 f , 465 f. ; Stratton, *Experimental Psychology and Culture*,
p. 147 f. ; *Mind* N.S. viii., 492 f. ; James' *Prin. of Psychology*,
ii. c. 20, pp. 182, 183). and things will at first appear upside-
down relative to their previous positions as experienced by
normal sight. The relative positions of objects *within* the
visual field, however, remain the same, and a new co-ordination
of tactual with visual space is rapi lly effected,—a fact which
seems to indicate that not only our tactual and visual experiences of relative positions, but also the co-ordination of these
experiences is objectively determined.

Z

largely upon the number of nerve-terminals which are present in the part of our body which is affected. So much so, in fact, that experiment is able to show that an illusion occurs where, for instance, a straight edge (say, the edge of a piece of paper), is applied to a line of terminals in which a distinct bend occurs, for in that case the edge of the paper itself appears to be bent. Nevertheless, even in 'touch,' there is a rough correspondence between the configuration of the object touched and of the nerve-terminals affected.

§ 264. The perception of shape, and especially of distance, is due, however, not merely to touch and sight proper, but also to what is called 'the muscular sense.' A movement of the eye involves sensations arising from the muscles which bring about that movement, from the muscles concerned in the processes of accommodation and convergence, and more especially from the close-fitting socket of the eyeball. A movement of the hand or foot involves sensations arising from the skin, the joints, the muscles, the sinews and the periosteum. In each of these two sets of sensations, not only co-ordination, but also 'fusion' occurs, and the product is a perception of three dimensions by sight or by movement and touch. In what a 'fusion' of sensations consists, or *how* they fuse, it is impossible to say ; hence it is impossible to show precisely how there is 'correspondence' in regard to the sensations involved in the perception of three-dimensional space. But it is clear that such a correspondence is possible, for not only does each element in the complex imply an intensively graduated series of sensations, but many of these elements have spatial values of their own. Thus the sensations arising from the last joints of the fingers, from the wrist, from the elbow, and from the shoulder are each of them capable of giving us a perception of motion in two dimensions. Indeed, since the movements of these respective joints may be made independently one of the other, I do not see why, if there had been a fourth or a fifth dimension, we should not have been able to perceive it. For if these joints and the sensations arising from them are such that each could give us a perception of two dimensions, — a,b, — a',b', — a'',b'', — a''',b''', why should not the a's have fused to give one dimension, while the b's, remaining distinct, each give an additional dimension? In the abstract such a combination seems possible, and had it actually happened, we should have perceived, it would seem, not three, but (in the above case) *five* dimensions. The fusion, however, does not take place in this way, for its product *de facto* is the perception of space in three dimensions. And since we cannot account for this either physiologically or psychologically, it would appear that its cause must be objective. Whence we may infer that *our* space *is* three-dimensional, and that the *combination* of sensations to form a complex in which distance is perceived is itself objectively determined.

§ 265. So far as concerns motion and rest, duration and number, it can hardly be disputed that there is some sort of correspondence between psycho-physical processes and objective reality.

But in regard to the psycho-physical processes which condition the perception of space, exception may be taken to my proof on the ground that it rests upon false assumption. I have endeavoured to show that there is a correspondence between the spatial arrangement of the things we perceive and the impression made by them upon our senses[1]; but this correspondence, it will be said, applies only to the impression made on the peripheral end-organs, and I have no right to assume that these are psycho-physical processes at all.

Two replies may be made to this objection. First of all, the older view that the stimulation of the peripheral end-organs is itself accompanied by consciousness does not seem to have been disproved. In fact, it seems to me probable that the whole afferent process is psycho-physical. The possibility of arousing specific sensations by stimulating the cut-end of a nerve can be explained, as I have said, by the differentiation of cerebral paths arising from their habitual use. The occurrence of hallucinations in a person who has been deprived of some organ of sense may be similarly explained ; for the vividness of the hallucination is sufficiently accounted for by the abnormal condition of the brain in such a case, a condition which implies excessive activity and irritability in certain parts. Again, the lag of sensation may easily be accounted for by inertia in the end-organs themselves. While, on the other hand, if the modification produced in the end-organ is *not* a psycho-physical process, it is difficult to account for the marked difference between a sense-impression and an image.

[1] Cf. *supra*, pp. 384, 385.

Secondly, even if sensation is in the brain and not in the sense-organ itself, it cannot be proved that the spatial arrangement to be found in the sense-organ does not hold also in the cerebral cortex. No physiologist, so far as I am aware, has ever succeeded in tracing an *individual* chain of neurones from its terminal organ to its corresponding centre (if it has one) in the cortex. And even if this could be done, and it should turn out that the chain of neurones do get mixed up, so to speak, ' local signs ' would establish all the correspondence that is necessary. For if each nerve-terminal has a characteristic 'local sign,' it does not much matter where sensation first arises, since that 'local sign' will be quite sufficient to determine the ' place ' of the stimulus.

§ 266. The scholastic *dictum*, then, that *cognitum est in cognoscenti secundum modum cognoscentis*, does not seem so far to have invalidated the general principle that *omnis cognitio fit secundum similitudinem cogniti et cognoscentis*. Sensation is an effect produced in a sentient organism by an objective cause which it resembles ; and that resemblance is not destroyed by the co-operation of the organism in the production of the effect. Before leaving sensation, however, and passing on to intellectual cognition, I should like to point out one characteristic of sense-impressions which seems to offer a striking confirmation of our causal theory. I refer to what is known as ' external projection.' Our sensations, in external perception, are projected outwards as it were. Apart altogether from the fact that *man* perceives through them, *i.e.*, intellectually apprehends in them, the qualities of objects, the latter *appear* at a distance. Distance, in other words, is *felt* as well as perceived. Hence localisation as a mere datum of experience does not imply thought. Yet appearances are localised *not* in the brain or the organ of sense, *nor* yet in the objective medium, *but in their determining cause.* Colour is projected back into the object; sounds are referred to an external source, and in touch when an instrument is used, such as a walking stick, we feel not with the hand, but with the end of the stick. Feelings again are localised in the hair, the beard, and in the teeth, no matter whether the latter be false or real, dead or alive. In short, independently of thought-reference, feelings are localised or projected back into their causes, regardless of medium, of instrument, and of the organ alike. This projection, both normal and 'eccentric,' is, doubtless, a function of the aforesaid 'muscular sense;' but how is it to be accounted for and what is its significance, if not that the form or 'species' of the sense-impression is determined by the objective cause?

From the arguments here adduced it should, I think, be clear that sensation has a representative as well as an affective value. The question, therefore, which now concerns us is how that representative value is, so to speak, converted into knowledge. Sensation, and even sense-perception—*if we abstract from thought*, which in man usually accompanies it— is not knowledge. On the other hand, according to the scholastic, " *nihil est in intellectu quod non fuit prius in sensu.*" How, then, does this transition take place ? How does sensation generate ideas and so acquire a meaning ? This is a question which I shall endeavour to answer *aristotelico modo* in the following chapter.

CHAPTER XV.

THE CONDITIONS OF KNOWLEDGE *EX PARTE SUBJECTI.*

II.—THE INTELLECT.

§ 267. By its functions, its powers of abstraction, of generalisation, of relational judgment and inference, the faculty of intellect is evidently distinct in nature from that of sentience. As a cognitive faculty, if our causal theory is to hold good, it must be, of course, a *potentia passiva*. But it is not merely a *potentia passiva ;* it is in another aspect active, and hence is called an *intellectus agens.* The *intellectus passivus* or *possibilis* is simply the intellect considered as passively receptive of forms or species derived from the phantasm or sense-impression and ultimately from the objects. The functions of the *intellectus agens,* on the other hand, are many. Knowledge is gradually built up by a slow process in which analysis, synthesis, induction and deduction, postulation and verification all play a part. But just as a building cannot be constructed by merely beating the air with hammer and chisel and trowel, but postulates materials as well as tools, so our intellectual activities would be useless unless somehow they could obtain material upon which to work. We must get ideas from somewhere, for it is upon ideas and their relations that the whole superstructure of knowledge is built. Hence, the first intellectual function which we must discuss is that of apprehension or abstraction, for it is by this that our ideas in the first place are formed.

§ 268. Apprehension must not be confused with conception, which is a much more complex process, implying often both judgment and inference. Apprehension is simply the process by which from the phantasm, image or sense-impression, the idea is obtained. Now the phantasm is concrete, particular, complex, and rich with a multifarious detail; whereas the idea is abstract, general, and, in the first instance, simple. The idea, therefore, is something different from the phantasm. Hence, the phantasm does not of itself determine the *actus* of the intellectual *potentia ;* but some process of abstraction is involved in which the universals implicit in sense-impressions are apprehended. It is the individual which is presented in sense-perception ; but the individual, being complex, cannot be known all at once. We have to attend first to one aspect, then to another, all of them simple at first, yet corresponding to some aspect of objective reality, because, though the phantasm does not itself *per se* and *simpliciter* determine the idea, it does so impelled, as it were, by attention and controlled by the selective activity of the intellect.

§ 269. Thus knowledge begins with elementary notions such as existence, being, unity, quality, change, duration, extension, direction, distance, on the objective side ; and psychical existence, thought,

sensation, volition, activity, etc., on the subjective
side. All these notions, and others besides, are both
simple and ultimate for us; by which I mean, not
that they cannot be analysed *metaphysically* or
logically defined, but that in origin they are ultimate,
since they are ideas which we apprehend directly in
experience. Such ideas are often vague at first,
and consequently are regarded by some as bare and
empty. Yet in spite of their alleged bareness and
emptiness, and the unquestionable difficulty there
is in defining them, they are more valuable for
knowledge than any phantasm, for they have something which the phantasm has not, viz., meaning or
objective significance. The phantasm is a picture
which means nothing except to an outside observer.
The idea is significance itself, for in it we know the
object and are aware that we know.

The significance of the idea in a sense is unique
and peculiar to the product of intellectual activity,
which alone has conscious 'objective reference.'
But it presupposes correspondence between the idea
and the objective entity that is signified by that idea.
This correspondence is due to the fact that the idea
is derived from the phantasm. For the phantasm,
as we have seen, corresponds with reality; and in
the phantasm the idea is implied, though it does
not exist there as such, but has to be analysed out,
so to speak, in abstraction. When, therefore, in
an act of intellectual apprehension, the phantasm
determines the idea, it communicates to it that
objectivity which itself unconsciously possesses on
account of its own determination by the object. In
short, the idea has meaning and objective signifi-

cance, because it corresponds with reality ; and it corresponds with reality because through the phantasm it is itself determined by reality.

§ 270. It may seem, perhaps, that in this somewhat complex metaphysical analysis I have been guilty of the Kantian error of splitting up the mind into innumerable water-tight compartments. But this is not so. For, in the first place, my account of cognition is far less complex than (*v.g.*) the physiologist's account of digestion ; and since things *are* complex, and especially Man, complexity is no argument against truth. Secondly, the faculties and functions I have been describing are not contained, like so many pills within a box. On the contrary, they presuppose that the mind is one ; and unless the mind were one, and unless in sense-perception thought and sensation functioned together, no matter how many faculties we had they could not give us knowledge. Some have said that sense-perception is a form of inference ; but I reject this view precisely because it seems to divide sense-perception into two processes, whereas for consciousness it is one. The perception of a complex object implies inference in the past ; and possibly to an outside observer perception itself would appear like an inference, since in it thought formulates what sense-data implicitly contain. But this is not what we ordinarily understand by an inference, nor is it for consciousness an inference at all.

§ 271. There are ideas, however, which are obtained by a process still more analogous to that of inference ; and yet they are ideas which for us are simple and ultimate. Among the simple ideas

which I enumerated above, almost all belonged to
the level of accidents or phenomena, and all were
directly apprehended in the data of experience.
But there are other ideas which seem to involve an
intellectual function which is something more than
mere abstraction. I refer to such ideas as substance, cause, and purpose. Substances, causes and
purposes are implicitly contained in the data of
sense-experience ; but they are not contained in
the same way as quality, change, extension. They
are presupposed as the metaphysical conditions of
the accidents and accidental modifications to which
sense-data directly correspond. It has been suggested, indeed, that the notion of substance is given
in *self*-consciousness, causality in the *influxus* of the
will into action, and purpose in conscious striving
after an ideal. Indeed, it will hardly be disputed
that purpose is revealed directly in the data of our
inner experience. But in regard to substance and
causality the question seems to be more doubtful.
Hume's analysis revealed no ' sensations ' of which
they could be regarded as ' faint copies ; ' and
many since Hume have declared themselves unable
to find any data to which they correspond. On
the other hand, we are certainly conscious of ourselves as real individuals, and again are certainly
conscious of active *processes* as well as mere states
of consciousness. We all know what we mean
by activity, volition, control, self-determination,
responsibility. And that certain ' something ' which
we call self-conscious activity has a dual aspect,
which is *not* adequately expressed by the notion of
antecedent and consequent, but *is* adequately

expressed by the notion of cause and effect. Hence, while in external perception succession is all that is given, self-conscious activity implies something more than mere succession, and it seems to be from this that the notion of causality is derived. But, in any case, we know what is meant by a cause, for, if we did not, it would be impossible to talk rationally of metaphysical conditions and logical presuppositions ; in fact, we could scarcely reason at all. Granted, however, that we have some such notion, it is not difficult to see how causes, substances and purposes alike are implied in the data of objective as well as in subjective experience.

§ 272. Thus, Causality is implied in change, which is a notion derived directly from objective (as well as subjective) experience. Change involves a transition from not-being to being ; and since not-being of itself cannot give rise to being of which it is the negation, we infer a something which causes the change. Change, like incompleteness and limitation, implies a something beyond itself, a something to which that change and that limitation is *due*. Thus far every man goes, for every one talks of causes and seems to talk of them rationally and to understand what they mean. But to determine precisely what is the cause of any particular event, or to determine whether events in general presuppose an ultimate cause *or* an ultimate ground is quite a different matter, and one with which the plain man is hardly concerned.

Substance, too, is a notion which every one possesses and which he uses in almost every judgment that he makes. It is implied in the

' this,' which he takes as the subject of his propositions ; and experience itself forces him to recognise
that the 'this' is one and yet many; that it exists
and is permanent, and yet is subject to change.
All accidents, qualities, appearances, modifications,
when considered in the concrete, are referred to some
individual, either to something outside us or to the
self ; and this predication of accidental differences
of a substantial ground is not an arbitrary process ;
but a process which is forced upon us by experience.
Qualities are given in combination ; and though we
cannot predicate them until we have formed an idea
of each in distinction from the rest and an idea also
of the unity which they presuppose, as soon as these
ideas have been formed, we are constrained by
experience itself to combine them in the way in
which we do. Things qualitatively different and
spatially distinct from their neighbours manifest
within themselves structural differences. They have
many qualities, all of which are localised in the same
objective thing. Experience compels us to affirm
that a thing is a unity in difference, and the concept of
unity in difference is, as we have seen, but another
form of the concept of substance and accident.
Or, again, looking at the matter from a different
point of view, and applying our notion of causality,
we may say that things are one, because they act
as if they were one. And in general this principle
is true. *Actio sequitur esse*, for there is nothing else
from which it can proceed. The actor who successfully impersonates Macbeth can do so only in so far
as he has the same nature as Macbeth, the same
passions, the same love of power, the same hatred

of all that stands in his way; though in ordinary
life he may keep these passions in check. A many-
sided activity proceeding from what is spatially one
implies that it is really and substantially one, or,
in other words, that its activities are held together
by a unity of ground or form. Thus the recognition
of substantial unities, no less than the recognition
of real causes, is forced upon us by experience
itself; and is due to the fact that there *are* real
causes and real substances which determine directly
or indirectly the content of our thoughts.

§ 273. On the other hand, among material
things, it is difficult to distinguish what are substantial unities from what are not; or better,
perhaps, it is difficult to locate the substantial unity.
Is a lump of sugar a substantial unity? Certainly
it is substantial, for it unites within itself sweetness,
hardness, whiteness, and other properties characteristic of carbon compounds. But is it one substance
or many? It would seem that it is many, for it
consists of innumerable particles, cohering together,
yet in reality distinct and individual, and each
possessing the characteristics that belong to what
we call sugar. But it hardly behoves the metaphysician to distinguish between one substantial
unity and another, provided he can show that his
concept of substance is in general valid, and can
state clearly what he understands a substance to be.
A body which consists of parts and possesses
properties relatively distinct and mutually independent, yet held together and controlled by some
one principle or form which makes each and all the
parts different from what they would be, were they

really distinct and separate, and which causes them
to act as one—as in the case of a man, an animal,
a plant, and even an atom as conceived in the
electron theory of J. J. Thompson—is certainly a
substance. But if the parts of a body are really
divided and merely cohere together by mutual
attraction or by some external force, then that body
is not a substantial unity, but an aggregate of substantial unities which interact. It is, however, for
the physicist and the chemist, not the metaphysician,
to draw the line between substantial unities in the
concrete.

§ 274. The ideas of substance, cause, being,
existence, quality and such like simple and ultimate
ideas are, then, objectively valid, and unless they
were valid and were strictly derived from and
determined by objects themselves, through the
mediation of sense-perception, knowledge itself would
be a farce. It is impossible to trace with anything
approaching accuracy or certainty the development
of these ideas, or even to ascertain in what order
they are first derived, for we cannot live again the
period of infancy and youth. Still, in analysing
more complex notions, we arrive finally at simpler
notions which cannot be further analysed, nor yet
defined, but which none the less have meaning and
significance. To define a straight line is impossible,
for it throws us back at once upon direction ; and
direction, though it can be illustrated and pictured,
since it is contained in the data of experience, is for
us an ultimate notion which we understand and are
constantly using, but are unable to define.

§ 275. Every abstract notion, whether ultimate

or not, represents but an aspect of the real thing, and so is incomplete. It has positive content, but it also implies a relation to something else ; and often enough if we wish to define it we can do so only by reference to something else. For the realist, however, this does not mean that ideas and their relations are structural differences or appearances which emerge within the universe as a whole and imply an immanent Ground ; but that the plan or design according to which the universe is constructed and according to which changes in it take place, is rational and intelligible, and may be known by us because it is implied in the finite objects which are presented to our minds in experience. We saw in the last chapter how each individual thing has a purpose ; how action was an attempt to realise this purpose ; how purposes were co-ordinated and subordinated one to another ; how, in short, the universe formed a systematic and teleological, though not an organic, whole. We saw also that this systematisation did not destroy the real unity of the individual thing ; and again that, though all things are inter-related, a relation is not a physical nexus implying an immanent Ground, but rather an *ordo* belonging to the individual things in so far as they imply and express a rational plan, just as a building implies and expresses the plan which existed in the mind of the architect. Now this inter-relatedness and systematic connectedness is a characteristic of all aspects of reality abstract as well as concrete ; and, therefore, is to be found in every science. Not only are things inter-connected and inter-related, but so also are their qualities and attributes when considered in general and apart from their manifestation in this or that object. And what I have said above about relations in the concrete applies here also. The relation is implied in its terms, and as soon as the terms are known the relation is recognised.

§ 276. Let us take Geometry as an example. What is its object ? A number of abstract entities, points, lines, angles, figures, planes, solids, all of them systematically related and inter-connected, yet each having positive content of its own from which its relations arise. An angle is not a line, nor a line an angle ; yet an angle cannot be defined apart from a line, while the line being an ultimate notion cannot be defined at all. A line, you say, is the locus of a moving point ; and an angle (if plane) the space included between two intersecting straight lines. But what is a locus ? What a point ? What intersection ? What motion ? Sooner or later you must come back upon an ultimate notion, the meaning of which you know by a sort of intuition, for you have derived it direct from experience. It does not matter much what notions you call ultimate in geometry, and your choice will depend largely upon your point of view ;[1] but sooner or later your analysis must come to an end, and you will be forced to admit that there are certain notions which you can indicate but cannot define, like the boy who said that a kick was when you hit a man with your foot. Indeed, there is something to be said for the old-fashioned way of defining

---

[1] Compare Staudt *Geometrie der Lage* (or any modern *Geometry*) with the older Euclidian theory.

(*v.g.*) a circle as " When you take a line in a plane such that any point in it is equi-distant from a given fixed point that line is called a circle." Such a definition brings out the fact that we know what a circle is long before we are able to define it, and that our knowledge is derived directly from experience where circles exist, not exactly, but approximately in the configuration of actual bodies. Geometry, like every other science, starts with certain ultimate notions which are obtained direct from experience. These notions have innumerable implications, because there is an indefinite number of other notions to which they are related. But once you have got your notions the relation between them is fixed and determined because it was already implied in the content of the notions themselves.

This, you say, is true, so far as notions are concerned ; but it is true because the notions are arbitrarily defined, and not because they are derived from experience. On the contrary, notions in geometry are never arbitrarily defined, but are always determined in the last instance by experience. You may choose the entities in regard to which you are going to formulate your definition ; but, this done, your definition is fixed and necessary, for it is already implied in the notion itself and in the entity in regard to which you are going to define it. Thus, instead of defining a circle as a line which lies in a plane such that, etc., you may define it as the locus of a moving point, etc., or again as a particular case of an ellipse in which the *foci* coincide, or, again, as a conic such that all its conjugate diameters are at right angles to one another. But whatever

entities you may choose as the ' terms ' in regard
to which your circle is to be defined, the relation
between the circle and those terms is fixed. You
cannot define it as you like, but must define it in
accordance with your pre-conceived, though un-
defined, notion of a circle. Nor does your definition
change or mutilate or intrinsically modify your
pre-conceived notion of a circle. It amplifies it,
if you like ; but it does not alter it or show that it
was self-discrepant. It merely means that you
know more about a circle, and more about
geometrical entities in general, and their relations
one to another.

§ 277. Geometrical science, then, has for its
object a number of entities systematically related.
Our notions of these entities are derived ultimately,
and in many cases directly, from experience, and
the relations between these entities are determined
by the entities themselves ; but not *vice versa*, or,
at least, not in the same rigid sense. For it is no
more true to say that relations react upon and are
intrinsically modified by the nature of the entities
they relate, than it is to say that the nature of a
grain of corn is intrinsically modified by the fact
that it is intended as food for man. Both statements are guilty of a *hysteron proteron*. Nevertheless, geometry is concerned chiefly with relations,
since its aim is to discover the rational plan of the
universe which they express. This, in fact, is the
aim of all science, no matter with what aspect of
reality it is concerned. Every science is an attempt
to discover the rational plan of the real world, in so
far as concerns the particular kind of entity which

it takes as its object. And in every case the entities belonging to this particular kind or class will be extremely numerous and often extremely complex. Hence, as the relations between them will share in their complexity, the general method adopted in order to manifest this rational plan, is again common to all sciences. The physicist, the chemist, the naturalist, and the mathematician alike endeavour to show that the relations between any two entities, no matter how complex, are deducible from a few first principles or general laws in which both entities and relations are comparatively simple, and thus to grasp in synthesis the structure, or plan, of that particular aspect of reality with which they have to deal and the co-ordination of its manifold and intricate parts.

§ 278. But although the aim of all sciences is to know, and to know means to reconstruct a system of ideas which shall correspond to a system of objective entities, different sciences differ considerably not only in the way in which they set about this work of reconstruction, but also in the degree of completeness which as yet they have attained. The reason of this difference is not far to seek. It is simply that some sciences are more abstract than others. I have said that to know the nature of any two entities is to know the relation between them. Whence it follows that the more abstract an entity is the sooner it is known, because in it, if I may say so, there is less to know. The concrete, moreover, includes the abstract, and a knowledge of the concrete implies a knowledge of the abstract ; for, as we have seen, it is by abstraction that all knowledge begins. Hence abstract sciences such as arithmetic, algebra, geometry, not only precede, but are presupposed by more concrete sciences such as mechanics and dynamics, while these in turn precede and are presupposed by the still more concrete physical and natural sciences. The physicist is not concerned merely with configurations which are external and directly apparent to the senses, but with the inner structure of things, with the relations which hold between the various *potentiæ* and qualities that are comprised within the unity of the concrete individual. And he is concerned with these *potentiæ* not as static, but as dynamic and active. "Ever since physical science began in the atomic theories of the Greeks," says Professor Larmor, "its main problem has been that of unravelling the nature of the underlying correlation which binds together the various natural agencies." [1] The physicist has to deal with the complex causes which produce 'quality' of sensation, and 'quality' of sensation does not analyse its object, but presents it in synthesis. He has to deal with phenomena and their transmutations, but those phenomena and their transmutations are particular, detailed, complex, and do not at once reveal their inner nature and their component parts, still less their causes or their presuppositions. In a word, the physicist does not, like the mathematician, take as the object of his enquiry simple entities, the nature of which is at once apparent, but complex entities which have first to be analysed, and which cannot be analysed directly.

[1] *Encyclopædia Britannica*, vol. xxxviii., article " Energetics."

§ 279. From the complex nature of the object of physical science follows an important consequence : the physicist has no axioms. An axiom is a self-evident truth, one which is not only *per se nota quoad se*, but also *per se nota quoad nos*. It is a proposition expressing a relation between two entities, but the nature of the entities in this case, being simple and extremely abstract, it is apprehended at once by the intellect ; for the relation is, according to our theory, implied in its terms and arises immediately the nature of those terms is apprehended.

From the intellectual nature of the soul itself [says Aquinas] it follows that immediately man knows what is a whole and what is a part, he knows that the whole is greater than the part ; and so on for other (axioms). But what a whole is and what a part is, he can only know by means of *species intelligibiles* received from *phantasmata ;* and on this account Aristotle shows (toward the end of the Posterior Analytics), that the knowledge of axioms *(principia)* comes to us *via* the senses.[1]

An axiom, then, comes to us from experience, and, like all knowledge, is determined ultimately by the nature of its object ; but it presupposes that the nature of objects between which an axiomatic relation is seen to hold, be extremely simple : otherwise it could not be *per se nota quoad nos*, but would have to be discovered by means of analysis and inference. This simplicity, therefore, being absent, in the case of physical objects for the reasons above explained, physical science has no axioms of

[1] *Summa Theologica*, I. p. 2, q. 51, ad I. and cf. Maher, *Psychology*, 5th edit., p. 290.

its own, and consequently has to adopt a different method from that of the mathematician. It has no self-evident first principles in regard to the correlation of natural agencies, from which to deduce the systematic structure and interdependence of the objects which constitute the physical world and so to manifest its rational plan. Hence in place of axioms, it substitutes general principles which in origin, at any rate, were ' postulates.'

When we come to treat of the epistemological value of cognition, the ' pragmatic ' attitude which is now so commonly taken up in regard to the methods and presuppositions of physical science will be more fully treated. It will be sufficient, therefore, if I now discuss the foundation of the Newtonian laws upon which the science of Mechanics has been built. Two remarks, however, must be premised in regard to the objective necessity of physical laws in general.

§ 280. In the first place, all the relations between objects existing in the physical world are *necessary*, *i.e.*, given the objects, the relations follow as a necessary consequence, and did we know the nature and structure of the objects we should at once know their relations. But this necessity is only hypothetical, for it is conceivable that physical objects might have been different in structure to what they are and so have been connected by different laws. The *co-existence* of certain attributes, properties, or natural agencies is not a metaphysical necessity, except in so far as one attribute, property or agency is implied in, or presupposes another ; and we have no reason for supposing that this is the case in regard to all physical properties and agencies. There is an element of contingency, therefore, in the physical world. The laws which govern the actions of physical objects are necessary, given the existence of those objects and given the Divine *concursus ;* but the structure of those objects is a *fact* which has to be discovered by experiment and observation, or deduced from provisional hypotheses and postulates which lead to conclusions that correspond with known facts. Secondly, there is no reason *a priori* (so far as I can see) why an object should not tend gradually to increase or decrease, to development or to decay. True, one can hardly suppose that things tend to corruption *of themselves, i.e.,* in virtue of this positive and existential nature, for this would contradict the Spinozistic axiom that every being tends to persevere *in esse suo,* and strives to realise a definite end or purpose. But all finite and contingent beings presuppose Divine conservation and *concursus ;* and we might suppose, I think, that this was gradually withdrawn ; provided always that the withdrawal was regular and according to knowable laws, so that our human demand for knowledge might not be frustrated. On the other hand, the principle of Causality that ' every event must have a cause,'[1] and the further principle that the effect must resemble its cause and be contained in it, either *formaliter* or *eminenter,* is axiomatic, and follows from the very nature of 'being' and of ' change.' In so far, then, as conclusions in Mechanics or in Physical Science are based upon

[1] Or better, perhaps, " Quidquid contingenter existit habet causam sui efficientem."

this principle, they are true *a priori ;* but, as we shall see, the Newtonian laws, though they presuppose the principle of Causality, are in reality based upon another principle less axiomatic, and so have to seek for verification *a posteriori.*

§ 281. The first law of motion states that "every body continues in its state of rest or of uniform motion in a straight line, except in so far as it is compelled by force to change that state." Is this an axiom or a postulate ? Motion is a fact, and so is rest, at least comparative rest; but it does not seem to me to be necessary that motion, once begun, should tend to continue, still less that it should continue in a straight line rather than in a circle or in any other kind of line. If it does so, it is a fact ; but I hardly think that it follows from the nature of motion or from the nature of a moving body. For it is conceivable that things might tend to move progressively faster or slower, given an efficient cause, and yet the laws which governed this motion might be knowable.[1] The law of inertia, as stated above, is, to my mind, not a self-evident truth, but a general physical principle which we know to be true because the conclusions which follow from it have been sufficiently verified in experience.

The second law of motion—"rate of change of momentum is proportional to force and takes place in the straight line in which the force acts "—seems, on the other hand, to be but a particular application

---

[1] If *motion* is a positive quality it must tend, according to Spinoza's axiom, to persevere in its being ; but if it is a *continuous change,* it postulates a continuous cause.

of the law of causality. Change of momentum or of quantity of motion, like every other change, implies a cause, and to attribute motion to a ' force ' is but to give a name to a particular kind of cause, since ' force ' is defined as " whatever changes the state of rest or uniform motion of a body." *Assuming*, then, that the first law of motion is true, *i.e.*, that moving bodies do not of their own accord tend either to increase their speed or to come to a standstill, the second law is a necessary consequence ; the ' change ' in the body's state of motion or rest must be proportional to its cause, and since the force or cause *ex hypothesi* acts in a straight line the change of motion must take place in the same line.

§ 282. It is to be observed, however, that this law says nothing about the nature of force. It may be attractive or repulsive or both or neither. Again, metaphysically, if it produces a real change, it must be something real. But physicists prefer to abstract from the reality of force, and, since they do not know its nature, to define it as the space-rate at which energy is transformed $(F = \frac{1}{2} \ Mv^2/s)$; or the time-rate at which momentum is generated $(F = Mv/t)$. These definitions, however, are not strictly definitions at all. For an equation tells us nothing about the nature of entities, but simply expresses a relation between certain quantities known or unknown. W signifies not the entity 'force,' but the *quantity* of force or the number of units of force. Similarly, if energy is defined as " capacity for doing work" $\frac{1}{2}Mv^2$ is not kinetic energy as such, but *quantity* of kinetic energy expressed in terms of a certain unit. Hence the above equations do not tell us that force *is* a space-rate, but the equation ($W = \frac{1}{2}Mv^2/h$) affirms that the number of units of force (*e.g.*, gravity) is equal to the ratio of two other numbers, viz., the number of units of kinetic energy to the number of distance-units, or the height. Similarly, the equation ($W = Mv/t$) expresses merely a relation of equality between quantity of force on the one hand, and the ratio of momentum (*i.e.*, quantity of motion) to time (*i.e.*, a certain number of time-units) on the other. A mathematical equation, therefore, is not really a definition, but merely a statement that the quantities denoted by certain symbols are equal to certain other quantities denoted by other symbols. Hence, to infer that force and other physical entities are not real because they can be expressed as 'ratios,' 'rates,' or quotients is illogical; for it is not the entity itself which is so expressed or 'defined,' but *the quantitative value of that entity as measured by its effects*. The existence of agencies capable of changing motion is presupposed by the fact that motion is changed; and though as yet we do not know what the agencies are, but only their 'values' as measured by the change they actually produce, it is hardly logical to infer from this that they are not real.

§ 283. The third law of motion—action and reaction are equal and opposite—has also been used as an argument against the reality of force on the ground that it is inconceivable that the objects upon which we act should resist our actions with a force equal in quantity to that which we exercise upon them. This second kind of 'inertia,' however, so far from being inconceivable, seems to be only another example of the more general principle *omne ens perseverare in esse suo*. For if this principle is true, clearly every being will resist force attempting to change its state, and will offer a resistance proportionate to the vigour of the attempt made. In other words, the effect produced in one body will be the measure of the force which has been brought to bear upon it, and the force which was required to produce that effect will be the measure of the resistance or inertia that called it forth.

The doctrine of Conservation of Energy is really implied in the second law of motion, and hence may also be regarded as a particular case of Spinoza's famous axiom. Indeed, we may say that both Mechanics and Physics presuppose the truth of that axiom ; for the first law of motion is a statement to the effect that states of motion and rest tend to persevere. Could we, then, regard Spinoza's axiom as a self-evident truth, it might be possible to show that the fundamental principles of Mechanics are necessary *a priori ;* but, as I have said, Spinoza's axiom is not strictly necessary, except when we consider ' being ' purely in the abstract. It is true that a self-existent being must ' persevere *in esse suo* ; ' and it is true that all beings, whether self-existent or not, *tend* so to persevere in so far as they have being. But it is not true that all being does persevere *in esse suo*, for if it did, not only would the sum of potential and actual energy be constant, but they would be respectively constant, *i.e.*, there would be no transformation of energy nor any other kind of change. Change, in fact, presupposes (1) energies which exist, but are not actual and yet strive to become so ; (2) that these energies are of a different order, or at least of a different degree of strength, such that one energy may be able to realise itself at the expense of another ; (3) that these energies are finite, contingent and essentially dependent upon a supreme Being both for their existence and their activity; and (4) that, being dependent, their sum is not necessarily, though it may be *de facto*, constant. Hence, although the doctrine *omne ens perseverare in esse suo* and the laws of motion in which it is applied to mechanical actions and changes, are true in that they express a tendency which is characteristic of all existent beings, they are not necessarily true ; for a gradual decrease or a progressive increase of motion, force, energy, and dependent ' being ' in general is not metaphysically impossible. As laws, then, which express the co-ordination of physical forces and motions, the mechanical principles formulated by Newton need verification in experience ; a verification which they seem actually to have received, at any rate, in the realm of Astronomy.

§ 284. This need for a verification process in the case of the principles of physical science does not invalidate, but rather confirms our general doctrine ; for scientific induction involves not only judgment and inference, but also apprehension, abstraction, and to some extent at least that intuitive insight by means of which we recognise the relations that hold between abstract notions. In the first place, the notions involved in Newton's laws, motion, rest, uniformity, a straight line, force, action, reaction, etc., are all derived from experience through the phantasm or sense-impression. They are all abstract notions, yet have meaning, and signify entities existing objectively in the real world. True, the notions of force and energy are derived from inner rather than from outer experience ; but just as the intellect apprehends that substance is implied and presupposed by unity in difference, so also it recognises that force and energy are presupposed as the metaphysical conditions of change and motion. And, again, just as we found that it was difficult to 'locate' substance, so to speak, in regard to material and inanimate things ; so also it is difficult to locate a 'force,' if by 'force' is understood the real cause of motion : while neither the notion of force nor that of substance tells us anything in regard to the nature of particular forces or particular substances. Secondly, we found that the first and third laws of motion, as well as the doctrine of Conservation of (material) Energy, might be regarded as particular cases of a more general principle, expressing the relation between two simple entities *ens* and *perseverare*. This relation, however, did not seem to be necessarily valid in regard to an *ens contingens*, but merely to express its natural tendency. Consequently, as Spinoza's axiom, not being itself strictly axiomatic, cannot impart to mechanical principles an axiomatic character, the human intellect is forced to seek for verification elsewhere. This it does by means of deduction and by a careful process of observation,

experimental or otherwise, and generalisation leading to the formulation of empirical laws with which
the conclusions of our deductive reasoning may be
compared.

Of the nature of reasoning little need be said,[1]
except. that, whether syllogistic or not, it is but a
more complex form of that intuitive judgment by
which we recognise the relations that hold between
different entities, the entities here being not ideas,
but other judgments. Doubtless, reasoning often
involves postulation, or rather is a result of postulation. But postulation itself is merely a name for a
complex process which includes the activity both
of intellect and will. Of intellect, because a postulate
is a judgment, uncertain perhaps, as judgments
often are, and possibly abstract, but still a judgment
and therefore an intellectual act. Of will, because
we desire to ascertain the truth of our tentative
judgment ; whether the relation we apprehend really
holds to the concrete. Again, experiment may be
involved ; but experiment is merely perception,
combined with action, and its function is quite
subordinate to the intellectual end we have in view.
So, too, is the will in so far as it co-operates in
cognition. It transforms an idea into a purpose;
it keeps the mind fixed on that purpose ; and directs
all its activities to the realisation of that purpose ;
but beyond this it has no legitimate influence in the
sphere of cognition.

§ 285.   We may now sum up the main character-

[1] For a discussion of the nature of judgment and reasoning
from the Aristotelian point of view cf. Maher, *Psychology,* chap.
xii. and xv. ; and for the logical aspect of the same, Joyce,
Principles of Logic, chap. iii. and xii.

istics of the Aristotelico-Scholastic, or Causal Theory
of Knowledge. *Ex parte objecti* the conditions of
human knowledge are finite individual objects, each
a unity of ground amid structural difference ; each
independent of its neighbours in regard to its
existence, but possessing attributes identical in
nature with theirs ; each forming part of a rational
plan and manifesting in an imperfect way the
attributes of the Deity to whom it owes its existence
and upon whom it depends ; each striving to
realise itself and to bring to act the potentiality of
matter in itself and in other objects ; and thus
capable of producing in them effects like in form to
the activity from which they proceed. *Ex parte
subjecti* the conditions of human knowledge are that
man should be one, organic, sentient, active, and
rational. Through his body he is brought into
contact with external things which manifest their
nature in their activities. The form of the psycho-
physical processes which take place in his brain and
in his organs of sense is determined by the activity
of these objects (or, again, by internal changes
within the organism) and hence the *species sensibilis*
corresponds to some characteristic of the objective
real thing. But knowledge proper is obtained only
in ideas and in the judgments in which these ideas
are combined. The content of an idea, therefore,
must be determined by the object, and this takes
place primarily in simple apprehension, which is one
aspect of human perception. The combination of
these ideas in judgment must also be determined
by the object, and this takes place in the empirical
or *a posteriori* judgment in which relations of

co-existence and sequence are apprehended, and
again in the axiomatic or *a priori* judgment in
which relations between simple entities are apprehended as necessary because implied in the nature of
the entities themselves. But the intellect, besides
apprehending the many in the one, also apprehends
the one in the many and so is able to subsume.
Subsumption is characteristic both of judgment and
of (syllogistic) inference. In judgment a particular
entity is subsumed under a universal idea, and in
the syllogism a particular relation is subsumed under
a general principle or law. The idea corresponds
with some real entity in the objective world or in
the self ; the judgment corresponds with some
relation holding between these entities in that they
imply a rational plan ; systems of ideas, complex
concepts, theories, correspond with the systematic
co-ordination and correlation of real things ; always
*provided and in so far as reality itself is their deter-
mining cause.*

§ 286. *Truth,* then, consists in *a relation of
correspondence* between the idea or judgment and
the thing. It is an *adæquatio intellectus et rei.*
' *Cognition* ' includes all acts whether of the perceptual or purely intellectual order by means of
which this relation is brought about. *Knowledge*
is the possession of true ideas (or systems of ideas),
whether actually functioning in consciousness or
existing only *per modum habitus*. *Error* is a positive
difformity between the idea and the thing, and
we may say in general that it is due to association,
to an *influxus voluntatis,* or to some other subjective
influence which causes assent to be given before the

BB

object has had time or opportunity itself to determine the content of thought. Error will be discussed later in the chapter on the Criteria of Error. It should, however, already be clear that the primary aim of one who seeks for truth should be to allow reality itself to determine the content of thought, and that the primary function of criteria of truth will be to distinguish cases in which the sense impression, the *id quo percipitur*, and the idea or concept, the *id quo intelligitur*, has been objectively determined from cases in which it has not.

PART III.

The Epistemological Value of Cognition.

CHAPTER XVI.

DEVELOPMENT AND VALIDITY.

§ 287. The third problem of the theory of knowledge, the problem of validity, is so intimately bound up with the second problem, the conditions of knowledge, that it is impossible to keep the two distinct. This will become more and more apparent as we proceed. We shall find that Absolutism, because it is Absolutism, has an Absolute theory of truth, a theory in which truth is regarded as an ideal whole, embracing interdependent parts, none of which are true in abstraction from the rest. In Absolutism the doctrine of reality is prior to the doctrine of truth, and both the nature and the criteria of the latter presuppose and are determined by the metaphysical conditions of knowledge. Pragmatism, on the other hand, starts with the criteria of truth, and hence infers, first its nature and then its metaphysical conditions. Consequently, in treating of the philosophy of Pure Experience before we treated of the pragmatic doctrine of truth, we have really been considering the conclusion—at any rate, in the case of Professor James—before we examined the premises. This was necessary owing to the general method we adopted in the beginning, and I do not think it should lead to misunderstanding; for although every theory of knowledge, if it is to be complete, must treat of psychological, metaphysical, as well as epistemological problems, a man may be a pragmatist in method without being a pragmatist in metaphysics.

The strictly epistemological aspect of Realism is no less essentially connected with its metaphysics than is that of Absolutism. The Causal theory, the theory which maintains that all knowledge, in so far as it is in truth knowledge, is determined by its object, is characteristic of Aristotelian Realism from whatever point of view we regard it. Primarily, it is a metaphysical theory; but it pervades also the realist's doctrine of truth, and it characterises also his psychology, whenever the latter is explanatory and not merely descriptive. Nay, even in descriptive psychology we find traces of causality, for causality, as I have already pointed out, seems to be directly revealed in many of the processes of our active conscious life.

§ 288. Having discussed, then, the various theories at present current in regard to the metaphysical conditions of knowledge, we must now proceed to examine how far these theories affect the validity and significance of knowledge, and, incidentally, how far preconceived views in regard to the validity of knowledge have reacted upon and determined metaphysics. It would, however, be

sheer waste of time to discuss the validity of knowledge and the criteria of truth, if knowledge itself
be a nonentity and truth an unattainable ideal.
It would be useless to try to distinguish what is true
from what is false, if everything is false and nothing
true. Unless we have some knowledge and some
truth it is absurd to talk of knowledge and truth at
all. This, in general, is admitted by every philosopher, and is presupposed by the fact that he is a
philosopher. Yet, though no philosopher nowadays
is guilty of so glaring a self-contradiction as to
profess to be an out-and-out sceptic, some philosophers seem to approach dangerously near to this
fatal inconsistency and their philosophies to be im-
pregnated, in consequence, with a suicidal tendency.
No philosopher professes to *know* that knowledge is
impossible, nor does he declare in so many words
that so far we know nothing at all for certain ; yet
this is the logical conclusion which seems to follow
from current theories as to the effect of development
in knowledge upon its validity, just as it follows
from current theories as to the conditions and
ultimate origin of knowledge. To this conclusion
I cannot give my assent, for it seems to destroy
knowledge altogether and to land us at least in
negative, if not in positive, scepticism. I argue,
therefore, that as the conclusion is false there must
be something wrong with the premises. This I
have already endeavoured to show so far as concerns
the origin and conditions of knowledge, and have
also stated in outline an alternative theory which
does not lead to this undesirable conclusion. In the
present chapter I propose to discuss the question

of development in knowledge, and to show that development and validity are not incompatible.

§ 289. Development, we are told, implies an intrinsic and essential modification in knowledge of so radical a nature that what appears to be knowledge may not really be knowledge at all. This view of the development of knowledge may be derived from two sources, either by inference from a theory as to the nature of development in knowledge, or from a study of alleged facts in regard to developments which have actually taken place. In either case the result is the same : knowledge is a fraud and an illusion. But while both the absolutist and the pragmatist seem to adopt this sceptical attitude, the absolutist does so because it is the logical outcome of his theory that all knowledge is a ' reconciliation of antitheses in a higher synthesis,' the pragmatist because he thinks that, knowledge having undergone so many transmutations in the past, there is no reason to suppose that our present knowledge will not be subject to a like corruption. Neither of these methods of establishing the invalidity of human knowledge seem to me themselves to be valid. But while it is comparatively easy to show that the argument of the absolutist is fallacious because it is based on a misconception of the nature of ' reconciliation ; ' it is a very different matter to attempt to answer the arguments adduced by the pragmatist. Indeed, to do so would involve a careful study of the history of every branch of human knowledge. This of course is impossible here, much as such a study is needed. Yet as the pragmatist contents himself with general statements, and as a particular negative is the contradictory of a universal affirmative, I shall be content if I can show that some propositions, and some general laws, and some branches of knowledge have not undergone a change which is radical enough to render them unreliable and uncertain.

§ 290. The principle of 'reconciliation of antitheses in a higher synthesis' is defined by Dr. Caird as "a solution of the antinomy between opposing principles which seem to have an equal or similar claim to our acceptance, by means of a regress upon the ultimate conditions of knowledge or thought— conditions which are presupposed in the controversy itself." So much for the general principle of a 'critical regress.' It is applied, however, not only to divergences in philosophical principles, but also to every kind of divergence and every kind of difference, whether ontological or logical, whether pertaining to categories, propositions, or theories. The doctrine of Unity in Difference and the Dialectic method of reasoning from thesis through antithesis to a higher synthesis is characteristic of every aspect of Kantian and Hegelian philosophy.

We have seen how this principle is applied by Kant. The opposition between physical science and philosophical theory is solved by a distinction of the sphere of the practical from that of the speculative Reason. Materialism and Spiritualism are reconciled by Faith; while the opposition between the speculative and the practical Reason is itself solved in the *Critique of Judgment*, where the universe is regarded teleologically as the mani-

festation of Divine Reason. It is in the third
Critique that the ' principle of reconciliation ' is
especially prominent ; but it is by no means *confined*
to that *Critique.* It appears in the Kantian categories, which are arranged in sets of three, the
' third ' category in each set being the synthesis of
the second with the first. Thus totality is plurality
regarded as unity. Again, Kant defines judgment
as " simply the way in which given ideas are brought
together under the unity of apperception." Thus
we have (1) the thesis or simple assertion of a thing ;
(2) the antithesis or determination of it by distinguishing it from other things—' *omnis deter-
minatio est negatio ;* ' and (3) the synthesis or
"redintegration of the elements thus differentiated
and related." That is to say, objects are "first
determined as things in themselves, then as related
one to another ; and finally as a *system* of distinct
yet inter-related parts within the unity of thought
as their centre." Judgment, therefore, may again
be defined as " at once the distinction of objects
from and their relation to each other, and their
distinction from and relation to the thought for
which they are." [1]

§ 291. Psychologically, the principle of a synthetic reconciliation of differences is well known
under the name of Apperception ; and is admitted
on all sides. Knowledge is a growth. It develops
by differentiation and integration rather than by
mere accretion, for a new truth usually modifies to
some extent our previous knowledge of the subject
to which it pertains. Professor James thus describes

[1] *Critical Philosophy of Kant,* pp. 460–462.

the process by which an individual settles into new opinions:

The individual has a stock of old opinions already, but he meets a new experience that puts them to the strain. Somebody contradicts them ; or in a reflective moment he discovers that they contradict each other ; or he hears of facts with which they are incompatible ; or desires arise in him which they cease to satisfy. The result is inward trouble to which his mind had hitherto been a stranger, and from which he seeks to escape by modifying his previous mass of opinions.[1]

Or, again, in more characteristic language :

Our past apperceives and co-operates ; and in the new equilibrium in which each step forward in the process of learning terminates, it happens relatively seldom that the new fact is added *raw*. More usually it is embedded cooked, as one might say, or stewed down in the sauce of the old. . . . *New truths are thus the resultants of new experiences and of old truths combined and mutually modifying one another.*[2]

Le Roy expresses a similar idea, when he says :— " Progress is a conquest of the obscure, of the unintelligible, almost of the contradictory." And Blondel, " Action is a continuous state of unstable equilibrium, and . . . each attempt to satisfy an actual need reveals further needs *qui s'imposent moralement à l'action.*" [3]

Both Pragmatism and Criticism, then, accept this principle of development as a psychological law ; and Hegel in his History of Philosophy has applied it to the growth of the mind of humanity in general

---

[1] *Pragmatism*, pp. 59, 60.
[2] *Ibid.*, p. 169. (Italics mine.)
[3] *Annales de phil. chrétienne*, 1906, p. 234.

But when we examine this principle more in detail, and try to explain its working and to apply it to the theory of knowledge, we find at once a divergence of opinion.

Pragmatism insists that some *new idea* must "*mediate* between the stock and the new experience." Its function is "to preserve the older stock of truths with a minimum of modification." [1] " Our minds grow in spots; and like grease-spots, the spots spread. But we let them spread as little as possible : we keep unaltered as much of our old knowledge as we can." [2] Hence, for the pragmatist, the ' mediating idea ' does not necessarily lead to a ' higher synthesis.' On the contrary, we prefer usually to ' *patch and timber* ' old prejudices and old beliefs, so as to admit the novelty which is forced upon us. Moreover, these ideas through whose mediation old truth grows, are ' new ' ideas ; we make them ; they did not exist before ; they are *additions* to our former stock. And they are *true* ideas precisely in so far as they perform satisfactorily their function of mediation. " Our thoughts become true in proportion as they successfully exert their go-between function." [3]

§ 292. The pragmatist, then, explains the growth of knowledge by the mediation of *new* ideas or *Denkmittel ;* the Hegelian by the modification and higher synthesis of the old. Let us illustrate this by an example. The idea of radium " paying heat away indefinitely out of its own pocket," seemed, says Professor James, to violate the law of Conservation of Energy. The contradiction was avoided,

---

[1] *Pragmatism*, p. 60.   [2] *Ibid.*, p. 168.   [3] *Ibid.*, p. 66.

however, by supposing that "the radiations were nothing but an escape of unsuspected potential energy, pre-existent inside of the atoms"—an hypothesis confirmed by the discovery of helium as the "radiation's outcome."[1] The new idea —or, in the language of Avenarius, the *Beibegriff* —which mediates here, is the escape of unsuspected potential energy. The Hegelians may object, however, that this is no *new* idea for 'potential energy' was already known, and all we do now is to suppose that it can, as Professor James puts it, 'escape ;' and to this the pragmatist might reply that at any rate the '*possibility of its escape*' is a new idea, and that in this way we have come to know a difference of energy, of which we were formerly ignorant. Certainly the idea of potential energy 'escaping' is new, though, on the other hand, we already had ideas of 'potential energy' and of 'escapings.' Let us, however, substitute for Professor James' picturesque account of radio-activity the scientific explanation, and see what kind of modification it has introduced into previous theories.

Radio-activity is supposed to be due—so I understand — to the disintegration of the relatively complex atom of radium into the less complex atom of helium, in which process the internal energy of the former is transformed into electrical and thermal energy ; hence the 'rays' and the rise of temperature. The argument is one from experienced effects (electrical, photographic, luminescent, chemical, and even physiological) to presupposition or cause (internal disintegration of the atoms)—a type of argument that we have met

[1] *Ibid.*, pp. 62, 63.

with before. But the question which is of interest
for us is whether the Electron theory—for it is this
which has been modified, if any—has been so
modified by this postulated disintegration of the
atom of radium as to render previous accounts of
it not only inadequate but false. It would not
matter much, perhaps, if this were so, since the
atomic structure of material substances is a hypothesis and not an established truth. But, as a
matter of fact, it is not so. The idea of atomic
disintegration is not only compatible with, but,
according to Sir Oliver Lodge, was already potentially contained in the theory of Lorentz, Larmor,
and J. J. Thomson, which affirms that the atom is
a positively charged sphere inside which are
grouped relatively small and negatively charged
electrons. Whether the doctrine of Conservation is
saved by this ' regress ' will depend, of course, upon
the validity of the Electron theory. But, at any
rate, we have here a regress which reconciles *pro
tempore* an apparent contradiction, not by showing
that both the antitheses were false and reuniting
them in higher synthesis, but by denying one of
them altogether (viz., the assertion that in radio-
activity *new* energy comes into being) and re-
affirming the other (that energy is merely transformed).

§ 293. This kind of reconciliation is typical of
the way in which theories develop. The growth of
knowledge does not necessarily involve the negation
of a previous thesis, but rather its amplification ;
and when this is the case, as it often is, I can find
no sense in which the reconciliation effected can be
called a ' higher ' synthesis, unless all syntheses are

to be called ' higher ' which make knowledge fuller and more complete.

The ' higher synthesis ' of the Hegelian, however, means more than this. It means a synthesis in which all the differences remain and yet are intrinsically changed in some mysterious manner by the synthesis. Unfortunately, the Hegelian is not fond of illustrating his doctrine of ' reconciliation in a higher synthesis,' and perhaps I have misinterpreted its meaning in my application of it to the above example of a scientific regress. But I do not think that I have. The general doctrine and its consequences seem to be clear enough ; and though it is applied primarily to the universe as a whole, we know that for the Hegelian thought and reality are one. In all forms of Absolutism, the endeavour of human thought is to equate itself with reality, and when this has been accomplished the logical principle of ' reconciliation in a higher synthesis ' will be identical with the ontological principle of Unity in Difference. The function of reason, according to Kant, is to guide the understanding in its search for a full and adequate knowledge, of which the final aim is an " absolute totality of syntheses on *the side of conditions*." And Fichte, starting with the ultimate condition of conditions, the Ego, obtained by a process of analysis and synthesis a logic and a phenomenology or pragmatic (*sic*) history of consciousness. The rational procedure of the human intellect was thus interpreted, by Fichte statically and by Hegel dynamically, as revealing the inner structure of the universe. And this as a general principle is still characteristic of the attitude of the absolutist. Hence, whatever can be predicated of the inner structure and processes of the universe can be predicated of the structure and processes of thought. As, therefore, the differences which are *somehow* reconciled in the Absolute undergo an essential modification in the process, it follows that in the synthetic reconciliations which will have to take place in human thought before it is completely identical with the universe, modifications of the most wholesale, radical and indefinite kind will surely occur. Hence the conclusion that human knowledge, which at present is certainly far from adequate or complete, is not strictly knowledge at all, but a construction in which truth and error are inseparably blended and mixed.

The significance of this doctrine will be clearer when we come to treat of Absolute truth, but its sceptical tendency is evident. If human knowledge contains an element of truth, but an element which cannot be distinguished from error, we might as well be without truth altogether, for to possess truth and yet to be ignorant of what it is, is certainly not what we mean by possessing truth. To affirm that all and every part of human knowledge is liable to modification is to affirm that we cannot be certain of anything; and if this is not scepticism, it is something very like it. The Hegelian theory of the development of knowledge follows logically from its metaphysical theory of the universe; and just as the metaphysical theory is inconsistent with facts, so also is the epistemological theory, as we shall see presently. But first I wish to point out that the pragmatist, though approaching the matter from a different point of view, has arrived at the same sceptical conclusion.

§ 294. In Baldwin's *Dictionary of Philosophy*,[1] we are informed by Mr. C. S. Peirce that Pragmatism is part of a larger doctrine which he calls Synechism. Synechism is " that tendency of philosophic thought which insists upon the idea of continuity as of prime importance in philosophy." [2] " Metaphysically "— though Synechism professes not to be metaphysical— " a *continuum* is something whose possibilities of determination no multitude of individuals can exhaust," while epistemologically it is a conception of the universe of thinking beings as gradually approximating to, but never attaining systematic truth. Man is ever striving toward a more rational and more complete interpretation of the universe, but his knowledge at present is so incomplete and so disjointed that he can never tell how far any one of his theories or even of his propositions about reality may have to be modified in the future. Gradually, however, through the intercourse of many minds, his knowledge is becoming more coherent, and, perhaps, more adequate, and " the becoming continuous, the becoming governed by laws, the becoming instinct with general ideas, are but phases of one and the same process, the growth of reasonableness." [3] All hypotheses must be regarded as ' continuous,' *i.e.*, as subject to further determination, which for us can never be exhausted.[4] Truth grows and will continue to grow. It has had a

[1] Baldwin's *Dictionary of Philosophy*, article, " Pragmatism."
[2] *Ibid.*, article, " Synechism."
[3] *Ibid.*, article, " Pragmatism."
[4] cf. *Studies in Humanism*, p. 195.

'career,' and therefore is going to have a career in the future.

This is obvious enough ; but the problem is as to *how far* future truths have " the power of retrospective legislation." How far will our theories, physical and metaphysical, be modified ? How far our axioms ? Will it be beyond all recognition ? And will the modification be so radical as to extend even to our 'truest formulæ ' ? Pragmatism, in spite of its admission that we strive to retain old theories with a minimum of change, thinks that it may be so ; and Absolutism, in the person of Mr. Joachim, is of the same opinion. Professor James writes :

The enormously rapid multiplication of theories in these latter days has well-nigh upset the notion of any one of them being a more literally objective kind of thing than another. There are so many geometries, so many logics, so many physical and chemical hypotheses, so many classifications, each one of them good for so much and yet not good for everything, *that the notion that even the truest formulæ may be a human device and not a literal transcript* has dawned upon us.[1]

Nay, has more than 'dawned upon us,' has led Pragmatism to adopt as a fundamental tenet that our solutions must be imperfect, and that human knowledge is throughout only an approximation to truth.[2] And this must be so, *if* thought and action are really one, and *if* our only justification for admitting a proposition or a theory is that it enables us to ' think clearly and act efficiently.'[3]

[1] *The Meaning of Truth*, p. 58. (Italics mine.)
[2] *Riddles of the Sphinx*, p. 9.
[3] cf. Albee, " Methodological Principles," *Amer. Phil. Review*, 1906.

§ 295. Professor James, indeed, seems at times to be struggling against this sceptical current in the pragmatic stream. He speaks of relations betw?en our ideas, which are irreversible, and of questio..s to which there can only be one answer.[1] He acknowledges, too, that it is Dr. Schiller who leads the way in this genetic view of truth, though, at the same time, he declares himself a staunch supporter of the English leader.

Surely Professor James has need to hesitate before adopting an attitude so avowedly sceptical. A cursory view of current philosophy and current science may suggest a hopeless confusion ; but to a more careful observer there will appear much harmony amid the strife, and much that is true amid what is erroneous or doubtful. There may be *two* geometries ; but meta-geometry is confessedly based on the denial of a postulate which the three-dimensional world of our experience necessitates. There may be several logics; but the logic of Hegel should rather be classed as a metaphysic, and the logic of Pragmatism as a very one-sided aspect of psychology. There may be many hypotheses, chemical and physical ; but most do not conflict, and of those which do the majority are based on theories so well-established that upon them further speculation rests as upon an accepted fact. And as for classifications, these are confessedly pragmatic, having utility as their end, and seldom claiming to be more than provisional. Let us, however, examine the matter a little more closely and see whether development does involve a radical

---

[1] *Pragmatism*, pp. 244, 245, and *The Meaning of Truth*, p. 69.

CC

change in past belief ; whether our knowledge, such
as it is, does contradict the claims to truth our
ancestors asserted ; or whether it is not rather that
development adds to truth, enriches it, renders it
more adequate and more complete.

§ 296. By far the most important sphere of
knowledge which it is necessary to rescue from the
corrosive influence of Scepticism is that body of
common-sense truths, which, as M. Duhem remarks,
are " in the last analysis the source whence flows all
truth and all scientific certitude."[1] These truths are
not static ; they develop. They are not a treasure
buried in the ground, but a treasure which everyone
shares, which he needs in order to perform the
actions of his daily life, and to which he is ever
adding by fresh discovery and research. The truths
of common-sense grow, and in growing are modified.
But the question is whether these modifications
affect the main body of truth or only its excrescences.
Certainly, if we exclude interpretations of a theoretical kind, legendary stories and local traditions
as to the nature and number of the gods, the
identification of tribal heroes on account of prodigies
long since forgotten and in consequence exaggerated,
and the superstitious attributing of natural events
to unseen spirits of a superhuman or diabolical
character, there remains a vast number of truths
which men believe in now and always have
believed in. Our environment is much the same
as it was two thousand years ago ; and the events
which occur in that environment are perceived in
much the same way and under almost precisely the

[1] *La Théorie Physique*, chap. vii., § 5.

same categories as they were in bygone ages. We understand perfectly what Herodotus means when he says of the Borysthenes (Dnieper) that:

It has upon its banks the loveliest and most excellent pasturages for cattle ; it contains abundance of the most delicious fish ; its water is most pleasant to the taste ; its stream is limpid, while all the other rivers near it are muddy ; the richest harvests spring up along its course, and where the ground is not sown, the heaviest crops of grass ; while salt forms in great plenty about its mouth and large fish are taken in it of the sort called Antacei (sturgeon) without any prickly bones, and good for pickling.[1]

Moreover, Herodotus' account of the general features of Scythia is remarkably accurate ; so much so that

it might pass [says Rawlinson] for an account of the same country at the present day. The rivers are still as large as before, and their fish are still abundant. The sturgeon of the Dnieper are still celebrated and the natural salt which is found near its mouth is still of the greatest value. Again, the steppes through which the Dnieper flows are still a corn-growing country, while to the east cattle are even now produced in great abundance.[2]

The knowledge our forefathers possessed of the general sequence of events and of the results which inevitably follow from certain lines of action also was reliable ; though, owing to the lack of *detailed* information, and the absence of any scientific method of induction, they were unable to distinguish the real causes of the sequences they observed, and of

---

[1] *History,* chap. iv., § 53 (Rawlinson's trans., vol. iii., p. 40).
[2] Rawlinson's *Herodotus,* iii., pp. 171, 172, and cf. p. 40.

their unscientific surmises Herodotus gives us
innumerable examples.

§ 297. But perhaps it will be said that I have
no right to exclude all that we now call superstition
and rash theoretical speculation from the general
head of knowledge and then to claim that common-
sense truths have developed without any essential
or intrinsic change. For it may be contended, in
the first place, that the residue is 'mere fact,' and
that facts are not knowledge; and, in the second
place, that the beliefs of our ancestors, though
superstitions, were none the less 'beliefs,' and
therefore claims to knowledge.

I have already given reasons for the inclusion of
facts under the head of knowledge. Everybody
does call acquaintance with facts real knowledge;
and whatever else facts are they are certainly not
'pure experiences,' for in that case it would be
absurd to talk of their getting 'made' and
're-made.' Facts imply to some extent interpretation; but they differ from theoretical interpretations
in that they are more direct, more vague, more
haphazard, and at the outset are neither systematised
nor co-ordinated. Yet facts do claim to belong to
what is generally understood by the term knowledge;
while, on the other hand, beliefs of a religious
character, as a rule, do not. The superstitious and
contradictory beliefs of the ancients were not inferences based upon the data of experience, but were
due to ignorance, tradition, or blind and unreasoning
faith. Moreover, they have no claim whatsoever
to be called *common-sense* truths, for they were not

---

[1] *Studies in Humanism*, p. 189.

common to humanity at large, but varied from tribe
to tribe ; and were frequently looked upon with
considerable suspicion by thinking men. The great
variety of opinions and beliefs which existed among
the Greeks and Romans in regard to the nature,
the number, the character and the legendary
history of the 'gods,' and the sceptical view of these
myths which was taken by Socrates and other
philosophers, needs no comment. But observe, too,
how in the interpretation even of natural events
opinion was tentative, uncertain and varied. Take,
for instance, the causes which were suggested in
order to account for the madness and death of
Cleomenes.

> The Argives [says Herodotus][1] declare that Cleomenes
> lost his senses and died so miserably on account of these
> doings (sacrilege and massacre). But his own country-
> men say that his madness arose, not from any super-
> natural cause at all, but from the habit of drinking wine
> unmixed with water, a habit which he learned from the
> Scythians ; . . . while, for my own part, I believe that
> his death was a judgment on him for wronging
> Demaratus.

Observe, again, how cautious Herodotus is in
accepting the legendary histories of tribal heroes
and gods ; how, for example, while not rejecting
altogether the story of Zelmoxis, he does not put
" entire faith in it, and even doubts whether there
ever really was a man of that name ; " [2] and, lastly,
how when himself endeavouring to account for
natural phenomena by natural causes, he seldom
claims positive knowledge; but uses, again and
again, some such expression as δοκέει δέ μοι.

---

[1] *History*, Book vi., § 84.   [2] *Ibid.*, iv., § 95.

I maintain, then, that the reversals which have occurred as common-sense knowledge has developed, have for the most part affected only (1) traditional and irrational beliefs which were by no means universal, and (2) hypothetical interpretations of natural events which were little more, and as a rule claimed to be little more, than rough guesses. The complexus of common-sense truths has grown rather by increment than by higher syntheses, and the main body of such truths is still left intact. Modern research confirms instead of invalidating the general knowledge which our forefathers possessed of the geographical features of the countries in which they lived, of the periodicity of the seasons, the phases of the moon and the tides, of the species of plants and animals of which no less than five hundred are enumerated by Aristotle in his 'Researches,' of minerals and some of their properties, of the habits and characteristics of man : in a word, of the co-existences and sequences which in general characterised their environment. Nay, further, their very belief in supernatural agencies testifies to their recognition of the principle of causality ; while the ready credence which they gave to the existence of a region of preternatural phenomena is not without foundation, if we may credit the accounts which are given of that region in the Proceedings of the Society for Psychical Research.

§ 298. The general impression which one gets from a study of 'factual' knowledge is adverse, therefore, to the sceptical view of development. Can we say the same in regard to theory ? In discussing this question, we must remember that theory is at present, owing to the stupendous advance which has been made in scientific appliances, instruments and methods, on quite a different footing from what it was three hundred years ago. The telescope and the microscope alone have revealed a vast complexus of data of which our ancestors never dreamt, and, thanks to modern metrical instruments, measurement and detail is incomparably more exact than ever it was in the past. The Greeks and Romans, the Schoolmen, the astrologers and the alchemists of the Middle Ages had no data upon which to build a scientific theory worthy of the name. Hence, that reversals should have occurred in the realm of theoretical speculation is not surprising. Indeed, the possibility of it was recognised by theorists themselves much more fully, I think, than we are apt to imagine. They appear, moreover, to have distinguished between different parts in a theory, some of which they regarded as of greater probability than others. Thus, according to Aquinas,

there are two ways of arguing. The first way is to bring forward reasons in order *sufficiently* to prove a certain principle ; as in natural science reasons are given sufficient to prove that the motion of celestial bodies is of uniform velocity. The second way is to bring forward reasons which do not sufficiently prove a principle, but which show that with a principle already postulated the consequent effects agree ; as in Astronomy the principle of eccentrics and epicycles is postulated in order that on this hypothesis sensible appearances [1] in regard to celestial

---

[1] *v.g.* the apparent increase of speed when the sun and earth approach.

motions may be saved ; but this reason is not sufficient proof, because it may be that on some other hypothesis they can be saved.[1]

The difference between a verified truth and a mere ' claim to truth ' was recognised, then, even by one who is generally regarded as a typical dogmatist. And the fact that such a distinction should have been made by the theorists of former ages is of considerable import in the problem of development and validity ; for, as a rule, it is in the less essential parts of a theory or system that reversals occur.

§ 299. The one striking exception to this rule in the sphere of scientific research is the Copernican revolution in Astronomy, in which the Ptolemaic system was literally turned inside out by the denial of its fundamental hypothesis. I do not intend to attempt to explain this reversal away, for although Aquinas apparently suspected that there was something wrong somewhere, it can hardly be doubted that most astronomers believed that the heavens really moved round the earth. Being led astray by appearances, they came gradually to regard as a fact what was really an interpretation of a fact, and an interpretation which was not the only one possible, as even the ancients might have inferred

---

[1] I. q. 32, a. 1 and 2. " Ad secundum dicendum, quod ad aliquam rem dupliciter inducitur ratio ; uno modo ad probandum sufficienter aliquam radicem ; sicut in scientia naturali inducitur ratio sufficiens ad probandum quod motus cœli semper sit uniformis velocitatis. Alio modo inducitur ratio non quæ sufficienter probet radicem, sed quæ radici jam positæ ostendat congruere consequentes effectus; sicut in astrologia ponitur ratio excentricorum et epicyclorum ex hoc quod hac positione facta possunt salvari apparentia sensibilia circa motus cœlestes ; non tamen ratio hæc est sufficienter probans, quia etiam forte alia positione facta salvari possent."

from their knowledge that motion through space is relative. The Copernican revolution, therefore, was unquestionably a reversal of an essential principle in previous theory.

In saying this, however, we must bear in mind that this reversal by no means invalidated all the astronomical knowledge that had hitherto been acquired. The precession of the equinox and many other truths were left intact. And it is curious, too, that the principle of uniform ' velocity ' mentioned by Aquinas as ' sufficiently proved ' should have reappeared in a somewhat different form in the 'first law of motion.'[1] Moreover, the Ptolemaic system, *as a system*, can hardly have been regarded as proved, for its explanations were inadequate and hard to reconcile with facts. Indeed, the epicycles and eccentrics which are essential to it, were, as we have seen, regarded only as probable and tentative by Aquinas. Lastly, the reversal introduced by Copernicus, Kepler and Galileo, was not a ' higher synthesis of previous hypotheses,' but a flat contradiction of what had hitherto been regarded as a fact.

§ 300. The negative element in Newton's theory of Gravitation is much less prominent. The law of inverse squares was not previously known ; but that heavy bodies tend towards a centre of gravity had already been asserted by the Greeks, notably by Aristotle, and was, in fact, generally held ; though as to the nature of gravity, again, there was no

---

[1] ' Uniform velocity ' in the Ptolemaic system is supposed actually to exist ; in the Newtonian theory it is a tendency. In the Ptolemaic system bodies move in a *circular* orbit ; according to Newton's law they tend to move in a straight line.

commonly accepted theory and no certain knowledge. Consequently, Newton's discovery was not
a reversal of established truths, but rather a new
truth which at once supplemented and systematised
the old.

§ 301. The theory of chemical elements, on the
other hand, as at present held, seems directly to
contradict the more ancient theory that the elements
were four, if we take that theory to be a bare statement that fire, air, earth and water are the ultimate
constituents of all material things. But this is not
what was meant. For, in the first place, the four
so-called elements were not regarded, by Aristotle
at any rate, as ultimate; but as due to the combination of an active hot-cold principle with a
passive wet-dry principle. And, secondly, the
essence of Aristotle's theory lay not in his assertion
that the ultimate principles were 'hot-cold' and
'wet-dry'—an error which was due to the almost
complete absence of scientific data—but in his
assertion that the principles were active and passive,
for this he deduced *a priori* from his metaphysics.
Now, that the ultimate principles of things are
active and passive, positive and negative, actual
and potential, is a doctrine which is fundamental in
modern theories of the nature of matter. Again,
that there are "solid massy, hard, impenetrable,
moveable particles of such size and figure and with
such and such properties," is a view held not only
by Newton and Dalton in modern times, and by
Democritus and Leucippus of old, but still held and
indeed widely recognised as true, though 'atoms'
are no longer regarded as ultimate and indivisible.

Indeed, the transmutation of the elements, which was a belief that prompted so much research in mediæval times, does not seem so utterly impossible now that radium converts itself into helium. Looking back, therefore, upon the various theories which have been held in regard to the constitution of matter, so far from finding grounds for scepticism, we seem, on the contrary, to find good reason to trust that knowledge is gradually advancing, and that in its advance what was essential and fundamental in past theories will be preserved, the accidental and the subsidiary alone being sacrificed.

§ 302. Modern theories of light and heat do not tend to destroy this optimistic view. Many physicists have given up the Emission theory. Its minute corpuscles and the transmitted species of the Greeks have been interpreted as motions in the ether. But that light is a something which is propagated by vibration in luminous bodies, that its propagation is rectilinear, and that it comes to us through a medium which reminds one forcibly of the media so characteristic of Aristotelian Physics is still maintained. The theory that heat is a ' caloric ' or highly elastic fluid permeating the interstices of substances has also been abandoned ; but we still believe with the Greeks that it may be due to the highly repellant and rapid movements of particles, and with the Calorics that it is connected with an entity which is elastic and which interpenetrates all material things, though this entity is now regarded as the medium for the propagation of heat and not as its source.

§ 303. One more point, and I have finished this

brief review of the effect of development on validity. Has the older geometry of Euclid been invalidated by meta-geometries and the geometry of a fourth dimension ? Dr. Schiller thinks that it is nonsense to enquire whether our space is Euclidian or not. Conceptual space is valid, he says, in so far as it is useful, but it is never real.[1] But can this assertion be proved ? The notion of space seems to be valid, not merely because it is useful, but because it has a *fundamentum in re ;* because the ideas and relations of which it is made up are derived directly from the data of objective experience ; and because they adequately express the relations which hold between the configurations of objects in the real world, in so far as those configurations conform to the precise notions of geometry, which they do approximately. The idea of a fourth dimension may be got at in several ways, but it seems to me that it owes its origin really to the algebraical theory of indices. As, however, it is generally admitted that *our* space has only three dimensions, and as I have already given one reason for thinking that this is so, I shall not say more on this matter. In fact, if we are mistaken here, the error is negative, not positive ; so that it is of no consequence from our present point of view.

§ 304. On the other hand, the meta-geometries of Riemann and Lowatchewski are of consequence, for at first sight they seem to contradict the Geometry of Euclid, and also to contradict one another ; and yet in spite of this to be each of them self-consistent. Both Lowatchewski and Riemann deny Euclid's assumption that a straight line is determined by any

[1] *'Axioms as Postulates,'* p. 115.

two points, and both deny Euclid's axiom that
through a given point in the same plane one, and
only one, straight line can be drawn parallel to a
given straight line ; but while Riemann postulates
that through a given point in the same plane no
line can be drawn such that it will never meet a
given line, Lowatchewski postulates that not one
but an indefinite number of such lines can be drawn.
Similarly, the sum of the angles of a triangle for
Euclid is equal to two right angles, for Riemann
greater than two right angles, and for Lowatchewski
less than two right angles. Now, if you imagine
straight lines and parallels and triangles to be drawn,
not on an Euclidian plane, but on the outside surface
of an immense sphere, you have straight lines which
are not determined by two points, parallels all of
which must meet, and triangles the angles of which
are greater than two right angles. In other words,
your space is spherical and your plane has a positive
curvature. And if now you could imagine the
contradictory opposite of all this—which I confess
I cannot do, for the inside of a spherical or
ellipsoidal surface is obviously not what is needed—
you would have planes with a negative curvature
upon which you might construct the geometrical
figures of Lowatchewski. What has really
happened, then, is this: both Riemann and
Lowatchewski have been working with spaces and
planes which are not Euclidian spaces and planes,
but imaginary entities constructed by themselves.
In place of the Euclidian notion of a straight line
they have substituted notions of their own. It is
impossible to *prove* the validity of Euclid's notion of

a straight line having invariable direction, for the notion is, as I have said, ultimate. Nevertheless, we have such a notion and know what it means; whereas a *solid* body in which straight lines are not straight lines at all, but positive or negative curves, is inconceivable.

Modern meta-geometries, therefore, do not contradict Euclidian geometry. On the contrary, they presuppose it; for they are in reality an Euclidian spherical geometry or its inverse conceived as a pseudo-plane geometry of two dimensions. That this is so is proved by the fact that the theorems of Riemann and Lowatchewski may be translated into Euclidian theorems by the aid of analytical geometry. While that the Euclidian notion of a straight line alone is valid, is, at any rate, confirmed by the fact that, when applied in the concrete, meta-geometries will not work.

§ 305. Our conclusion is, therefore, that neither a study of the changes that have actually taken place as knowledge has developed, nor a study of the principles which have governed those changes, justifies us in adopting a sceptical attitude in regard to present knowledge, whether theoretical or factual. In the realm of facts there have been but few reversals. Our knowledge of facts grows not by intrinsic modifications, but by an increase in the number, the detail, and the accuracy of our observations. In the realm of theory, on the other hand, there have been many reversals; yet these have seldom, if ever, entirely destroyed the validity of those interpretations we now stigmatise as false. On the contrary, the tendency has been to distinguish in previous theories principles which have led to error from those which led to truth, and while rejecting the former to retain the latter and embody them in a more adequate theory. Moreover, the principles which have been retained are in general those which were most essential in previous theories and which were recognised as such at the time that those theories were framed. Apperception by the individual and apperception, if I may so call it, by the race adds to the old stock of truths, and at the same time gives them a fuller significance ; but it does not destroy either the facts or the more fundamental principles upon which those truths were based. Our conception of things and their relations grows more and more systematic ; but the facts upon which it is based and the principles which guide us in the search for truth alike remain constant throughout.

§ 306. The Hegelian theory of Apperception likewise affords no ground for scepticism. In the theoretical developments, briefly outlined above, I can find no trace of reconciliation by higher syntheses in the Hegelian sense of that term. Rather, development has consisted in the explicit negation of certain principles in a previous theory and the reassertion of others supplemented by an element which was new. There is some truth in the statement that development is a sort of critical regress in which the universal implicit in divergent views is analysed out and reasserted. But the differences between divergent views are seldom reconciled in a ' higher ' synthesis. In fact, often enough they are not reconciled at all, but one is denied and the other established. And if a reconciliation is effected, it is effected by a *distinction in the differences* rather than by a synthesis of them wholesale and *vago modo*. The result of the regress in this case is that the differences are taken in analysis and some part of one or both rejected. For so long as either of the antitheses contains positive error, a synthesis is impossible. The error must first be removed, and then, since all theories, however divergent, contain an element of truth, they may be combined to form a system of truth more adequate, and in this sense higher than before. This kind of synthesis, indeed, it is the aim of the French philosophy of Immanence to bring about. Led by the author of *L'Action* it seeks to reconcile conflicting opinions in religious matters by a regress which shall draw forth from error the truth that is immanent within it. No need is more urgent than the need of getting rid of contradictions. It is felt alike by pragmatist, absolutist, and realist. But while the pragmatist says ' take your choice of either alternative according as you feel yourself prompted by emotional desires ; ' and the absolutist says, ' No, don't choose, but wait, the antitheses will some day be reconciled in higher but misty synthesis ; ' the realist of the Scholastic frame of mind says, ' First distinguish, then choose ; but choose on rational, not on emotional, grounds ; and thus by separating truth from error, you will be able, without waiting long, to obtain a synthesis which shall include past truths, and at the same time be a basis from which to proceed to further truth.' And the latter, it seems to me, is the best answer of the three.

CHAPTER XVII.

PRAGMATISM AND PHYSICAL SCIENCE.

§ 307. Science not infrequently protests against the encroachments of the philosopher who wishes to interpret its theories in a metaphysical sense. ' You keep to your province and I will keep to mine,' it says to the metaphysician; 'I am concerned only with phenomena, their sequences and their quantitative relations : you are concerned with substance and accident, matter and form, cause and effect ; in a word, with reality itself. Let us be content to leave one another alone and to keep our provinces distinct.'

This principle might work very well, provided the province of science *could* be completely shut off from the realm of philosophy, and provided neither philosophers nor scientists were anxious to scale the dividing wall. Unfortunately, neither condition is completely fulfilled. The respective provinces of science and of philosophy coincide in two points. In the first place, the phenomena whose variations are measured, classified, and to some extent explained by the scientist, are precisely the same as those whose *ratio essendi* and *ratio cognoscendi* the philosopher seeks to discover ; while the methods which the scientist uses presuppose the principles of sound logic, a discussion of which clearly lies within the sphere of the philosopher, *quâ* logician. And in the second place, often enough the scientist

DD

is not content to keep to his science. He insists upon his right to speculate metaphysically on the validity of scientific theories and on the ultimate nature of the phenomena with which he has to deal, and it is by no means uncommon to find that he mingles his metaphysical assumptions with the methods and principles of his science.

Now, if a particular scientist wishes to indulge in metaphysical speculations it is not for the philosopher to say him nay. It is only natural that one who devotes himself to the study of the laws which govern the phenomenal world should desire to know what phenomena are, and should form for himself a metaphysical theory of the universe. But if the scientist constructs a metaphysical theory, he can hardly complain should the philosopher criticise that theory which is not the less metaphysical because it comes from the pen of a scientist. Physicists such as M. Duhem place themselves beyond the reach of the metaphysician by denying that their theories have in any sense a metaphysical import ; but there are others who, in discussing the methods of science and the validity of its laws, have taken up a definite metaphysical position, which, they tell us, is more compatible with, if it is not actually presupposed by, the principles of science. This attitude, which is becoming more and more prevalent both in Germany and in France, is closely connected with the pragmatic movement. The pragmatic method claims to be based on that of science, and not a few scientists seem in return much inclined to adopt as their own the pragmatic theory of knowledge-in-general and the philosophy of Pure Experience with which it is so intimately bound up. Science has given up the naïve, uncritical and often materialistic Realism which was formerly its customary attitude, and in its stead many of the devotees have taken up, not the non-metaphysical position of M. Duhem, but the position of Empirical Idealism.

§ 308. Fifty years ago every scientist started from the common-sense point of view, assuming with his less educated brethren, that material things really exist independently of the exercise of mental activity. He took it for granted that his thoughts *about* the universe did not affect the nature of the 'facts' with which he had to deal. He did not trouble about the possibility of there being any *a priori* forms of the mind to which experience, consciously or unconsciously, had to conform; nor did he dream that in observing facts he was in reality making them. The aim of scientific research was to give an explanation, not only of the relations holding between phenomena, but also of the nature of the universe itself. Both mechanists and dynamists hoped to find an interpretation of the objective, real world at least in so far as it is material. Their atoms and molecules and their centres of force were real entities constitutive of material things and giving rise to those phenomena which we perceive by the senses. In fact, the complaint which the mechanist found with the dynamist was that the latter introduced into reality an unknown entity 'force,' which could neither be imagined nor defined.

Nowadays the position is changed. By many of

our leading scientists the older metaphysics has been discarded and an Empirical Idealism or Pragmatic Sensationalism substituted in its stead. Mind and matter, relatively independent, are no longer the metaphysical conditions of scientific knowledge. For matter has been substituted sensation, and instead of knowledge arising through the manifestation of objective reality to a relatively passive mind, knowledge is now said to be due for the most part to the constructive activity of thought, to "*l'action pensée*," to ideas due, in part at least, to the creative power of mind, and striving to realise themselves in the field of sense-experience. The data of modern science are sensations ; its aim is to discover the relations which hold between them ; the means by which it seeks to acquire this knowledge is first of all sense-experience, in which experiment plays an important part, and, secondly, a mental activity of a higher order in which spontaneity and choice are conspicuous. Through the senses we have experience of relations between phenomena or sensation-complexes, and through the instrumentality of definitions and hypotheses created by thought we endeavour to arrange and classify these relations, to subsume them under general forms, and, if possible, to reduce them to unity by the discovery, or better, perhaps, the invention of some primary relation which holds throughout.

§ 309. Two names stand out prominently as representative of this attitude, at once metaphysical and epistemological, in regard to the scope of science. They are those of Mach and Karl Pearson ; and to

these we may add a third, chosen from the more
sceptical school of the *Philosophie de la Contingence*, M. Le Roy. M. Poincaré, on the other hand
must be placed in a different category, for he admits
the 'objectivity' of fact, and even to 'laws' assigns
a certain 'normal objectivity,' though in certain
passages he seems to speak as if he were a sensationalist like Mach.[1]

Mach distinguishes three stages in scientific procedure, the *experimental* stage, in which we are in
immediate contact with reality, *i.e.*, with sensation,
and merely tabulate the results of experiment and
observation ; the *deductive* stage, in which we
substitute mental images for facts, as in Mechanical
Physics ; and the *formal* stage, in which our terms
consist of algebraical symbols, and our aim is to
construct by their means the most convenient and
most uniform synopsis of results. Similarly
Poincaré distinguishes three kinds of hypotheses,
(1) hypotheses suggested by facts and verified at
least *à peu près* in experience, (2) 'indifferent hypotheses,' which are useful in that they express under
images and figures relations between phenomena,
but which are neither true nor false ; and (3)
'mathematical conventions,' which consist of
definitions more or less arbitrary, and which are
independent of experience.[2] Poincaré's 'indifferent
hypotheses ' correspond to Mach's second stage in
the development of science, and manifest a tendency
eventually to disappear. Already Mach himself

[1] Cf. *La Valeur de la Science,* chap. xi., especially p. 266.
[2] *La Science et L'Hypothèse,* Introduction, p. 2, and cf.
pp. 180, 181.

prefers to dispense with their service as rather encumbering than facilitating thought ; while Poincaré, though he considers them still indispensable *for the moment*, holds them to be devoid of real significance.

§ 310. Thus the second stage of scientific procedure in this view is of secondary importance. It is the experimental and mathematical stages that really constitute science. By observation and experiment we are brought into contact with reality ; not indeed with the material world, for no such entity is supposed to exist ; nor even with the world of sensible appearances strictly so-called— for an appearance implies something that appears,— but with *sensations*. The objective condition of scientific knowledge, the reality which in science we desire to know, is sensation. The data of experience are sensations. Mach, in his *Analyse der Empfindungen und das Verhältniss des Physischen zum Psychischen*, has developed this view at considerable length. Sensations and sensation-complexes— these, he says, are reality. All science consists in the analysis of sensations. Nature is composed of elements given by the senses. From these we choose those which are most important for practical purposes and call them ' objects ' or ' things.' But ' things ' are really abstractions, and a name is a symbol for a complex of sensations whose variations we neglect. There are no things-in-themselves, nor are sensations symbols of things, but what we call things are symbols of sensation-complexes of relative stability. Colours, sounds, pressures, spaces, durations, these are the real things. All thought is governed by the principle of Thought-Economy.

We are ever trying to save ourselves trouble. Hence we have acquired the habit of grouping sensations together in a lump and calling them by a single name. One group of sensations we call 'water,' another ' a leaf,' another ' a stone.' Smaller groups, again, are combined to form larger ones. The group 'leaf' is joined to the groups 'branch,' 'stem,' etc., and the whole, being vaguely or generically pictured, becomes a 'plant.' These larger groups, again, are included in others larger still. What we call 'the external world' comprises all those sensation-complexes which are relatively constant, *i.e.*, which repeat themselves again and again in the same sort of way and are not subject to the control of our will: whereas 'the self' comprises that other very extensive group of sensation-complexes, some of which are always present in consciousness, though ever varying in tone, while others can be produced at any time if we so desire, and thus are directly under our control.[1]

In the external group the relations between sensation-complexes are constant, *i.e.*, the complexes follow one another in the same order. Thus the sensation-complex (water) is juxta-posed in a certain way to another complex (bunsen-burner), and *always* after a certain time the bright transparency of the former complex gives place to a dull whiteness of another considerably greater in extent. Ordinarily, however, we prefer—according to the *Princip der Denkökonomie*—to use names to denote our sensation-complexes, as it saves us the time and trouble of

---

[1] *La Mécanique*, pp. 450 *et seq.* (The examples here given are my own).

describing them. The usual account that one would give of the above phenomenon, for instance, would be that when we heat water over a bunsen-burner, after a time it begins to boil. Indeed, it would be very awkward for the sensationalist, if he often had to carry out Pascal's principle of substituting the definition for the thing defined.

§ 311. The physicist selects the above class of sensations, which are characterised by greater stability, greater regularity, and are common to mankind, as the data of his scientific researches; while the psychologist treats of these in another way, and also of other sensations which are less stable, more subject to the control of the will, and, hence, often peculiar to the individual. But the standpoint of Mach is really psychological throughout. Both psychologist and physicist treat of the same class of objects from different points of view.

All that we can know of the world is necessarily reduced to sense-perception : and all that we can wish to know is given in the solution of a mathematical problem, in the knowledge of the functional dependence which exists between sense-elements. This exhausts the sources of the knowable.[1]

Professor Mach has given up the apparently hopeless task of reducing things to indefinitely small and ultimate elements. Both he and Poincaré prefer to regard atoms and such like as hypotheses, as mere picturesque fictions of greater or less utility, but of no objective value; and for things Mach substitutes sensations. Scientifically, indeed, sensation is regarded as a form of

[1] Mach, *op. cit.*, p. 287.

energy, the differences of which are probably quantitative. But in course of time, says Mach, we shall discover that the sense of hunger is not so very different from the action of sulphuric acid on zinc, and that our will is not so very different from the pressure of stone on its support, and so we shall get nearer nature. Thus, for Energetics, everything is reducible to energy, *alias* sensation, and the final aim of physical science is to demonstrate the truth of this assertion.

§ 312. Both Mach and Poincaré speak of the sense-data of science as if they were uninfluenced by the subjective factor in cognition. They regard them as relatively stable, independent of the individual, and therefore objective. But even in the objects of scientific knowledge, philosophers such as M. Le Roy would admit an element of ' contingency.' Sensations are not given in isolation, but are grouped together in complexes and integrated into percepts ; and in the construction of our percepts there may enter an element of caprice. We are influenced by our *point de vue choisi d'avance*, practical utility in some cases, the exigencies of scientific theory in others. Hence we introduce into our percepts just what suits our convenience and leave out the rest. This follows logically from the philosophy of Pure Experience, a philosophy which is practically identical with the metaphysical standpoint of MM. Karl Pearson and Mach. For if, as M. Le Roy says, " nothing is put before the mind, except what is put by the mind ; " if, in other words, we do not copy reality, but construct it, as Dr. Schiller affirms ; then all is due to " hypothesis and fabrication " either by the individual or by the race, *i.e.*, we construct our percepts as well as our concepts. Again, racial development takes place by individual variation, and this is possible in the sphere of experience only if thought exercises purposive control over the data of sense, in which case even in this, the lowest stage of human knowledge, we must admit that there is an element of caprice. Hence, all scientific laws are unverifiable, to put the matter rigorously, first because they are the instrument with which we make in the continuity of the primitive datum the indispensable parcelling out (*morcelage*) without which thought remains powerless and shut in, and again because they constitute the criterion itself with which we judge the apparatus and methods which it is necessary to use in order to subject them to an examination, the accuracy of which may be able to surpass all assignable limits.[1]

§ 313.   Contingency and choice in the sphere of experimental science is emphatically denied by Poincaré. "All that the scientist creates in a fact," he says, " is the language in which he expresses it." We do not interfere with facts, except in so far as we select those which are relevant to our purpose. In experience relations are determined, not by experiment, but by inexorable laws which govern the succession of our sensation-complexes. ' We do not copy reality '—that is true ; but the laws which govern the sequences and combinations of sensations are fixed *for* us, and not by us. They are something which we experience as a datum, not something we arbitrarily construct ; and these laws may be known by us at least *à peu près*.

[1] Le Roy, *Revue Métaph. et Morale*, 1901, p. 140.

This view, though doubtless the correct one, is hardly consistent with the doctrine that sensations and not material objects are the data of science. If it be the mind that groups sensations together and so forms sensation-complexes or *objects*, then, as M. Le Roy and Dr. Schiller affirm, such groupings may not always be precisely identical. Not only may modification and even mutilation of fact have occurred during the long process in which habits of perception have been built up and have become common to the race, but such modifications are still possible since habits are only relatively constant and only approximately common to the race. Moreover, the significance of M. Poincaré's assertion that all we create in a fact is the language in which we express it, is considerably modified when we compare it with another statement to the effect that 'language is strewn with preconceived ideas ; ' for the latter, since their influence is unconscious, are far more dangerous than those which we deliberately formulate and make use of in hypotheses.

M. Le Roy's statement, therefore, that scientific laws are unverifiable because they are the instruments by means of which we parcel out the primitive datum of experience would seem to be valid in a pragmatic and evolutionary theory of knowledge. His second argument (granting the validity of his premises) is no less conclusive. When the correspondence-notion of truth is rejected, our only criteria of truth are utility and consistency, both of which are determined by the development and systematisation of science itself. Scientific laws, as M. Duhem has pointed out, mutually involve and

imply each other's truth. Hence, if in no individual
case we can eliminate the subjective element and so
prove that a law has arisen from the manifestation
of reality itself to our minds, we have no right to
assume one law to prove another ; all laws, whether
empirical or not, will be equally unverifiable in the
pragmatic and pseudo-scientific theory of knowledge.

The unrestricted jurisdiction of the *Princip der
Denkökonomie* points to the same conclusion ; for,
according to Professor Mach, this principle is not
confined to the realm of physical theory, but is a
general principle applicable to all forms of cognition
alike. It governs the construction of the percepts
and concepts of common-sense, just as it directs the
scientist in the formulation of definitions and
physical hypotheses. Efficiency depends upon
economy, and efficiency, adaptation to environment
and practical utility for the control of sense-
experience is the final aim, not only of physical
theory, but of all human cognition.

§ 314. The Pragmatism and Sensationalism of
Mach and Karl Pearson, which is really a *philosophical* theory of knowledge, must be carefully
distinguished from the view that in *Physical Theory*
definitions and laws are merely symbolic formulæ
useful for the classification, co-ordination and
systematisation of scientific fact : for this view is
held by many who, except on this point, are in no
sense pragmatists either in regard to science or
philosophy. A pragmatic interpretation of physical
theory is, in fact, quite compatible with metaphysical Realism.

For instance, M. Duhem is a realist in regard to

the notions of common-sense, yet he tells us that
the aim of physical theory is "to construct a
symbolic representation of what our senses, aided
by instruments, make us know, in order to render
easier, more rapid, and more sure, reasoning about
experimental knowledge." Concepts for him as for
MM. Poincaré and Mach are means to this end. Their
function is symbolic. As definitions they are
arbitrary, and in no way represent reality or reveal
its inner rational structure. 'Masses' are "co-
efficients which it is convenient to introduce into our
calculations." 'Energy' must not be confused
with the force exerted by a horse in drawing a cart ;
it is merely "a function of the state of a system
whose total differential in every elementary modification is equal to the excess of work over heat set free."[1]
Concepts as definitions form the basis of scientific
deduction, but they do not reveal the nature of
objective facts. The most they can do is to indicate
certain experiences, and so enable us to verify the
phenomenal relations which we have deduced by
means of mathematical reasoning in which these
symbolic definitions function as terms.

Some have endeavoured to find a similarity
between M. Duhem's theory of chemical combination and the scholastic doctrine of matter and
form. This, however, as he informs us in his work
entitled *Le Mixte et la combinaison chimique*, in
which his views on that subject are developed, is
merely an analogy, and nothing more. 'Forms,' as
conceived by the chemist and the physicist, are
quantitative, not qualitative ; whereas quality is

[1] *Le Mixte et la Combinaison chimique*, pp. 202-205.

of the essence of things, the nature of which it is the business of the metaphysician and not of the scientist to determine. Nevertheless, in spite of this denial that ' forms ' in chemistry and in physics are comparable with the metaphysical forms of Aristotle, M. Duhem's standpoint is quite compatible with Realism ; and it is so precisely because he relegates all questions as to the nature of quality and essence to Metaphysics.

§ 315. The standpoint of M. Duhem differs essentially, therefore, from that of Karl Pearson and Mach ; for, while carefully distinguishing physical theory from physical fact, M. Duhem does not identify the latter with sensation, but leaves it to the metaphysician to determine the ultimate nature of the data of experience. Again, it is only in Theory that postulation and symbolism are admitted by M. Duhem, and that we are allowed to construct and modify definitions at will. Mathematical Physics in the course of its development is independent of Experimental Physics, and uses a different method. In the latter we are bound down by empirical facts, whereas Mathematical Physics is free to disregard all facts till theory is complete, when it must be verified as a whole by comparing the conclusions which have been mathematically deduced with the complexus of experimental data. "In the course of its development a physical theory is free to choose whatever way it pleases, provided it avoids all logical contradiction ; in particular, it is free to disregard the facts of experience." [1]

[1] Duhem, *La Théorie Physique*, vi., § 7.

On the other hand, for Professor Mach, and apparently for M. Poincaré also, symbolism, postulation and the principle of Thought-economy apply to theory and fact alike. The experimental differs from the mathematical stage only in this respect, that in the former we group under one name sensations which are actually present in consciousness, and our grouping is more or less spontaneous ; whereas in the latter we arbitrarily combine symbols denoting sensation-complexes already grouped, and postulate that the new symbol shall denote actual groupings which have never as yet been given in consciousness.

The real difference, then, between Karl Pearson and Mach on the one hand and Duhem on the other is in regard to their philosophic standpoint. Both Karl Pearson and Mach, and, to some extent, Poincaré also, philosophise on the data of experience and on the development of knowledge in general ; and their philosophy is pragmatic. M. Duhem declines to philosophise, and, if a pragmatist at all, is a pragmatist only in regard to the methodology of physical theory, an attitude which is quite consistent with philosophic Realism.

§ 316. There is also a further difference between the views of M. Poincaré and M. Duhem in regard to the relation of Mathematical to Experimental Physics. M. Poincaré admits " truths founded on experience and verified almost exactly so far as concerns systems which are practically isolated ; " and these truths, he says, when generalised beyond the limits within which experience verifies them, become " postulates, applicable to the whole universe and *regarded as rigorously true*." [1] "*Mais, le principe désormais crystallisé, pour ainsi dire, n'est plus soumis au contrôle de l'expérience. Il n'est pas vrai ou faux, il est commode.*" Thus such principles as Newton's Laws of Inertia and of the Equality of Action and Reaction, Lavoisier's Conservation of Mass, Mayer's Conservation of Energy, and Carnot's Degradation of Energy are axiomatic, though not *a priori*. They are suggested by facts, but are unverifiable, because in their absolute form they are mere conventions ; and our right to postulate them lies precisely in this, that experience can never contradict them.

Mathematical Physics, on the other hand, for M. Duhem *is entirely independent of experience throughout the whole process of its development. No* hypothesis whatever can be verified till the theory of Physics is complete in every detail, for every physical law is " a symbolic relation the application of which to concrete reality supposes that one accepts quite a system of other laws." [2] No individual, physical law is, properly speaking, either true or false, but only approximate, and on that account provisional. Sufficiently approximate to-day, the time will come when it will no longer satisfy our demand for accuracy. [3] Principles, therefore, which MM. Milhaud, Le Roy and Poincaré alike place *beyond the control of experience* are, says M. Duhem, either not physical laws at all (since every physical law must retain its meaning when we insert the words *à peu près*, which these do not) or else, when their

[1] *Revue Métaph. et Morale*, 1902.   (Italics mine).
[2] *op. cit.*, ix., § 1.   [3] *Ibid.*, §§ 2, 3.

consequences have been fully deduced, they must be rigorously subjected to the test of experience in the theory to which they belong, and with that theory stand or fall.[1] In other words, Poincaré, admitting the existence of relatively isolated systems of experimental facts, thinks that it is possible to apply the process of verification to a physical theory in the course of its development ; while Duhem, convinced that all physical laws are intimately connected, prefers to formulate a complete and self-consistent system of hypotheses before attempting to compare the consequences of any one of these hypotheses with experimental fact. A similar difference is manifest in regard to the method of teaching Physics. Poincaré prefers the inductive and experimental method. Duhem holds that physical theory should be presented to those who are capable of receiving it, *in toto*, and that experiments should serve merely as illustrations of different stages in its development.

§ 317. This difference between two of our most eminent physicists, though great at first sight, can, I think, to some extent, be explained. M. Duhem insists that all hypotheses must be verifiable *à peu près* if they are to have physical significance : consequently, there can be no laws in physical theory, when complete, which are not at least approximately true. On the other hand, the use of purely conventional hypotheses in the construction of a theory is allowable, provided they are ultimately verifiable in their systematic completeness. M. Poincaré points out that such conventional

[1] *Ibid.*, vi., §§ 8, 9.

EE

hypotheses are often experimental laws generalised beyond the limits within which they are verifiable, and so worded that they cannot, as such, be contradicted by experience. That in their most general form, as applicable to the whole universe, universal postulates of this kind cannot be verified directly, is obvious ; for not only are they universal, but they are expressed in symbolic terms, such as energy and inertia, terms which it is almost impossible to translate into their corresponding sensations (if such there be). Yet, inasmuch as such postulates lead to particular conclusions about less abstract realities of which we can have immediate experience, inasmuch as their function is to guide us in the construction of hypotheses which are verifiable *à peu près*, and so have a physical sense, it may be said that even the most abstract laws and the most general principles can be verified indirectly through their consequences.

§ 318. Thus the divergent views taken by M. Poincaré and M. Duhem respectively in regard to physical 'axioms' are apparently reconciled. Yet the divergence has, I am inclined to think, a deeper root. M. Duhem's reason for affirming that physical laws are not as yet either true or false, but simply useful, is that they have not been and cannot as yet be completely verified, and hence are only provisional. But when they have been completely verified in the physical theory to which they belong they will become, together with the principles upon which that theory is founded, not only useful but true in the realistic sense of that term. M. Poincaré, on the other hand, can easily find room for ' axioms '

which are already 'regarded as true,' because truth
for him, as for the pragmatist, is apparently one
with utility, though, as we shall see, it is not
merely utility.   Truth and objectivity, in the sense
in which they were understood by Aristotle, by the
Scholastics, and in which they are still understood
by common-sense, do not exist for those scientists
who are prone pragmatically to philosophise.
Objects being identified with sensations,[1] objectivity
acquires a new sense ; for the objective value of
science is, according to M. Poincaré, the same as our
belief in external objects.   Granted that nothing is
put before the mind except what is put by the mind,
granted that " all that is not thought is pure nothing
since we can think only thought, and the words we
use in speaking of things can only be expressions of
our thoughts," granted that " to say that there is
anything besides thought is a statement that can
have no meaning," [2] it would seem to follow that
physics is merely a branch of psychology, and that
in studying things we are really studying the work
of our own minds.

§ 319.   What sense, then, can be given to the term
objective truth ?   How can there be anything really
objective or really true, if sensations and the laws
which determine their relations proceed from the
nature of the mind itself and refer to nothing
beyond ?   Pragmatists attempt to solve the difficulty by distinguishing between what is peculiar to

---

[1] M. Poincaré is not always consistent on this point.   Sometimes he seems to speak as if he were a realist, as in chap. x.
of *La Valeur de la Science*, where he attacks M. Le Roy ; sometimes as a sensationalist (chap. xi., and cf. *infra*).

[2] *La Valeur de la Science*, p. 276.

the individual and what is common to the race.
Doubtless the relations between sensations " could
not be conceived outside a mind which conceives
them or which feels them, but they are, nevertheless,
' objective,' because they are, will become, or will
remain common to all thinking beings." [1] Some
sensations " *nous apparaissent comme unies entres
elles par je ne sais quel ciment indestructible et non
par un hasard d'un jour.*" [2]   These are the sensations
which are common to all thinking beings, and which
in this sense may be said to be objective.   From
these premises the nature of truth and the criterion
of truth may easily be deduced.   That will be true
which the individual holds in common with his
fellow-men, that false which he holds in isolation ;
and the function of truth-criteria will be to distinguish what is held collectively from what is
peculiar to the individual.   The *Philosophie de la
Contingence*, realising this, has defined truth as that
which is ' normal ' enough to be accepted by anyone
of sound mind.

§ 320. The connection between the conception
of truth as that which is useful, fruitful, *commode*,
and the conception of it as 'normal objectivity' is
clear.   In the first place, the relation of intellect to
sense is in this view regarded as merely ' functional.'
Intellect symbolises and relates sense-data solely
with a view to controlling them, manipulating them,
and adapting them to the needs of human nature.
In so far as the hypotheses which we formulate fulfil
this end, they perform their function well, and are
useful.   The needs of humanity, however, and

[1] *Ibid.*, p. 271.   [2] *Ibid.*, p. 270.

consequently the reactions which will satisfy those needs are more or less constant ; hence there will be a certain degree of harmony in our judgments of what does satisfy our needs, *i.e.*, we shall have a kind of ' normal objectivity ' based on common consent as to the usefulness of certain hypotheses. Secondly, science, like all other knowledge, is in process of evolution. Mind interacts on mind through social intercourse. The thought-habits of the individual get modified and become more like those of his neighbour. Thus needs-for-knowledge and the processes by which we strive to acquire that knowledge have, in course of time, become more or less identical throughout the race. The Newtonian laws, says Mach, are the result of a long process of observation and experiment, of scientific evolution, in the race. Ideas, not found in sense-data, and whose working is often unconscious, guide the development of science. *Now* the psychological factor in cognition has obtained a fuller recognition, and the naïve Realism of Mechanical Physics is being displaced by Energetics. We find now that what we took to be true, in the copy sense of the word, is merely useful ; useful, not because it satisfies the needs of the individual, but because it satisfies the needs of humanity at large, because it conforms to our preformed habits of thought, and enables us to go on adapting ourselves to our environment. It is however, only a pragmatic truth, this utility ; a truth based on common needs, but always incomplete, always changing, never absolute ; always provisional and approximate, subject to continual modification as human needs and human environments advance together on the wave of evolution.

§ 321. The doctrines of Poincaré, Mach and Le Roy, since they deal with truth, knowledge and objectivity in general, not merely with the scientific use of these terms, do not belong to physics, or, at any rate, not to physics alone, but to the theory of knowledge. They are philosophical doctrines which bear clearly the impress of Pragmatism ; and will be discussed together with other pragmatic theories in the chapters entitled "Pragmatic Truth." It would be an error, however, to attribute the Pragmatism of Poincaré, Mach and Le Roy to the influence of Professor James and Dr. Schiller, though it can hardly be doubted that the world-wide reputation and the vigorous polemics of the latter have had their effect. The Pragmatism of the philosophising scientist has arisen from quite another source. It is, in fact, but a development of the doctrine that the definitions and laws which belong to Physical Theory are only symbolic formulæ, figured hypotheses, postulates which are useful, but not true. And this doctrine can only be called 'pragmatic' retrospectively, for it existed before Pragmatism proper was invented, and by it—at least in Dr. Schiller's case—the general epistemological theory of Pragmatism appears to have been suggested.

§ 322. The origin of scientific Pragmatism—if such a term is permissible—arises apparently from the feeling of hopelessness aroused in the scientific mind by the multiform variety of physical theories at present existing, theories which, if taken as they stand, are mutually incompatible. Contradiction is so violently repugnant to the human mind that we are ready to take almost any means to escape it. And to many scientists, anxious to solve the mystery presented by a daily-increasing multitude of conflicting and seemingly irreconcilable hypotheses, only two alternatives seemed to offer themselves, either Scepticism or a kind of provisional Pragmatism. Believing themselves confronted with a choice such as this, many have adopted the latter alternative, *i.e.*, rather than give up truth altogether, they prefer to regard it in Physical Science as a ' value.' Provisionally, at any rate, truth is not something which corresponds with reality or reveals its inner nature, but something which enables us the better to manipulate and control our environment. The reason of this choice is, I think, not the intrinsic reasonableness of the pragmatic position, but rather the reluctance which is felt towards the sceptical alternative. Scepticism would not satisfy our practical needs. It would involve the surrender of laws in practice extremely useful, and theoretically, at any rate possible, and sometimes probable. It would deny even *approximate* truth, and would destroy the *possibility* of certitude ; and so would take away all motive for further research, rendering science both futile and meaningless. In the face of such an alternative, the scientist prefers to take up a position which admits of at least some degree of certitude, and gives, at any rate, some meaning to the notions of truth, validity and objectivity.

§ 323. But the adoption of a pragmatic attitude in regard to the function of physical theory, whether it be merely provisional or not, by no means implies the adoption of Pragmatism in general, with its idealistic interpretation of the universe, its theory of *universal* postulation, and its man-made truths which at bottom are no truths at all, but merely 'values.' Scientific Pragmatism is, as I have said, quite consistent with philosophic Realism, and the two are not infrequently found together, and were so found before philosophical Pragmatism had been conceived. One may be permitted to ask, therefore —and the question is both interesting and instructive from the epistemological point of view—whether some form of Realism is not still compatible with Physical Science itself ; whether, for instance, the physicist in his aim should not be a realist after all ; nay, more, whether some physical principles and some branches of physical theory do not already admit the predicate 'true' in the correspondence sense of that term. It would be strange, indeed, if in one of the most extensive, most important, most fruitful spheres of human research, to which for centuries many of the keenest human intellects have devoted themselves, we should have, as yet, obtained no knowledge whatsoever of objective reality. One can scarcely credit the assertions of those who maintain that the whole complexus of physical hypotheses and laws is merely a working instrument, a useful calculating machine. Fortunately, how- ever, Realism in Physical Science is not yet extinct. Not only were scientists of ancient and world-wide fame, such as Newton, Huyghens, Bernoulli, Lagrange and Laplace, realists, but realists survive to the present day. Nor is their survival an anomaly. They do not exist in spite of their failure to adapt themselves to an idealistic environment. On the contrary, the Realism of English science has proved one of the chief obstacles to the advance of Anglo-German Absolutism. Most scientists who do not philosophise adopt a realistic attitude in regard to facts ; and many who do, find it extremely difficult, if not impossible, to eliminate realistic expressions and ideas. And if Realism is compatible with Physical Science, it certainly gives to it a fuller, a more consistent and a more satisfactory meaning than can be got from Pragmatism. It is worth while considering, therefore, whether a moderate form of Realism may not yet be upheld in regard to Physics, in spite of the manifold diversity of its hypotheses ; and, accordingly, to this question I propose to devote the following chapter.

CHAPTER XVIII

REALISM AND PHYSICAL SCIENCE.

§ 324. Realism interprets truth as ' correspondence ' between our concepts and judgments on the one hand, and objective reality on the other, though in true knowledge the nature of objects is revealed to our minds, not completely, but in part. A true concept represents, or, better, in a true concept we know, some real object in some one or more of its aspects or of its relations. Hence, truth must be determined objectively, not by our needs, but by objects themselves, if it is to be truth at all. In perception, in conception, and in judgment, purposes and needs have their proper function, as psychology shows ; but their influence, in the main, is restricted to the intent, as opposed to the content, of thought. Certainly we may frame hypotheses in which we provisionally determine the content of thought by our own constructive powers, but a concept so formed is not true unless it is confirmed or verified by reference to the object.

§ 325. Is this position compatible with the standpoint adopted in Physical Science ? In general it seems to me that it is. For the majority of physicists admit that determination of the mind by its object is the only possible means of attaining truth ; though they hesitate when asked how far physical concepts and laws have been so determined, and sometimes seem to doubt whether they will ever be more than symbolic and useful. Nevertheless, in her aim and in her practice science is almost always objective. The aim of the physicist is to force nature to reveal her inner workings and ' the correlations of natural agencies.' Facts are regarded as something independent of mind and our knowledge of them as objectively determined. Purpose is allowed to determine, not facts themselves, but only what facts are relevant to the problem in hand. Guided by purpose, the scientist selects his facts, taking note of what is relevant and neglecting the rest. But in the sphere of observation and experiment, never, if he can help it, does he allow purpose to determine *content*. Abnormal cases occur, cases in which associations or the 'will to believe' is exceptionally strong; but the careful observer—and the scientist is, or should be, a careful observer—will suspect such influences, if present, and will hesitate to trust his conclusions in such a case until they are confirmed by independent evidence. It is only in the framing of hypotheses that the constructive activity of mind plays a part. But a hypothesis is not a law; it is a question, a postulate which we ask nature to answer or confirm. We apprehend some relation as holding between concrete realities—for even in its interrogative form a hypothesis is suggested by facts; we modify that relation and try whether it still holds in nature; or we postulate that the relation holds in other and different cases, and experiment to discover whether it is so. Should reality persistently answer our question in the affirmative, our hypothesis then becomes a law, true approximately and under the given conditions for all cases. Throughout the experimental stage of science it is the aim of the scientist to get the object itself to determine the answer to his questions, as it determines, in part at least, the questions themselves. He wants to know reality as it is. His whole endeavour is, therefore, to exclude subjective considerations and pre-conceived ideas, so that he may read aright the answer that nature gives. He tries more than anyone else to keep in subjection his 'will to believe,' knowing that, if this is impossible, he may as well relinquish all attempts to discover the laws which govern the universe.

§ 326. The scientist, then, fully admits that if

scientific concepts and laws are to be verified, they must be determined by their objects, and by their objects alone ; and the aim of experiment is to place conditions precisely in order that such a determination may take place. The problem which we have to solve, then, is how far the concepts and laws of physical science in its present stage of development have been *de facto* determined by objective reality, for upon this will depend their power to give us true knowledge of objective reality.

Science, which as a rule is non-assertive on this point, is apt to appear somewhat sceptical on account of its fondness for such terms as symbolic,[1] conventional, probable, approximate, useful. M. Duhem, for instance, tells us that all concepts in Physical Science are symbolic, and all laws approximate, and that hence, strictly speaking, they cannot be said to be either true or false. For this reason he distinguishes common-sense laws from scientific laws, because of the former we may predicate truth and falsity, notions which are inapplicable in science. The reason is, he says, that common-sense laws " simply extract what is common in each particular case to which the law applies, so that in each of those cases to which we apply the law, we shall find concrete objects in which these abstract ideas are realised ; " whereas scientific notions, mass, temperature, pressure, are " not only abstract, but symbolic, and have meaning only thanks to physical theories."[2] And from the approximate character or indetermination of the

[1] *La Théorie Physique*, chap. v., § 2.
[2] *Ibid.*, § 1.

symbol follows the indeterminate and approximate nature of the law.

Common-sense laws are very true, but on condition that the general terms between which they establish a connection be abstractions arising spontaneously from the concrete, abstractions unanalysed, taken *en bloc*, like the general idea of a carriage or of a horse.[1] . . . A physical law possesses a certitude much less immediate and much more difficult to appreciate than a law of common-sense, though it surpasses the latter in the minute and detailed precision of its predictions.[2]

§ 327. Let us examine a scientific definition and then a scientific law in order to see for ourselves how far its genesis and its precision affect its truth. " The words hot and cold, or hotness and coldness," says Professor Preston, in sketching the development of the notion of Temperature, " refer to the state of a body as judged by the sense of heat," a hot body being " regarded as the source of an influence which affects the sense of heat."[3] We begin, then, with sense-perception. Hotness is some property of objects in virtue of which they affect our temperature-sense, as psychologists sometimes call it. And this, we may note in passing, is probably at bottom what many who belong to the new school of Energetics mean when they say that the data of science are sensations. Ostwald, for instance, who is more objective than Mach, says that all sensations are due to a difference of energy between the organ of sense and the medium which surrounds it. At any rate, the common-sense notion of hotness, like

[1] *Ibid.*, chap. viii., § 5.
[2] *Ibid.*, chap. v., § 5.
[3] *Theory of Heat*, p. 12.

those of sound, light, pressure, is at first objective. True, in the beginning, such notions are denotative rather than connotative ; but their connotation is not zero. We know enough to be able to distinguish hotness from other qualities of the same, or of different objects ; and are thus able to enquire what is its cause, what its nature, what its relations to other properties of matter.

§ 328. It is in the course of this enquiry that the notion of temperature comes to be scientifically defined ; for the scientific definition of temperature presupposes the common-sense notion of hotness. Finding that several pieces of the same substance can be arranged in a series by the sense of heat alone according as one is hotter or colder than another, " we are hence led," says Professor Preston, " to the idea of a *scale of hotness*, and to enquire how much one body is hotter than another." The estimation of hotness implies some scale or standard of measurement, and when this is chosen

we may speak scientifically of the hotness of a body, and for this purpose the word *temperature* is employed. The word *temperature* thus means simply *the degree of hotness of a body measured according to some arbitrarily chosen scale*. It is a *scientific* term, and contains all the meaning of the primitive word hotness, as well as the idea of a measure of hotness.[1]

Observing that " one of the most general effects of change of temperature or hotness in a body is change of bulk, or expansion by heat," and that, in the case of certain bodies, their bulk increases

[1] *Theory of Heat*, p. 13. (Italics mine.)

continuously in proportion to their hotness,[1] science has selected this change as the basis of a method of indicating temperature. But "the mode by which the change of temperature is indicated by the change of volume remains, of course, a matter of choice, as well as the particular substance employed." [2] For instance, we can measure change of volume directly through expansion indicated by the rise of a liquid, mercury or spirits of wine, in a tube divided into parts of equal or known capacities ; or we may allow the liquid to overflow and determine the volume of the overflow, and hence the expansion of that which remains in the tube, by weighing.[3] Again, we may take a gas, air, hydrogen, or nitrogen, as our thermometric substance, in which case temperature may be measured either by "change of volume while the pressure is kept constant, or by change of pressure while the volume is kept constant." [4] Thus, not only is the scale itself arbitrary, but so also is our choice of a thermometric substance, of the property of that substance which we take as a basis of measurement, and of the means by which that measurement is effected.

Is, then, our definition of temperature arbitrary ? Strictly speaking, it is not. It is in deciding what particular fact or class of facts the term 'temperature' is to denote that we exercise choice. We find that degrees of hotness may in general be indicated by changes of volume, and we therefore decide to use the term 'temperature' to signify

[1] For a thermometric substance the law of the increase of bulk must be one of simple proportion, and this law will hold only within certain limits, exclusive of change of phase.
[2] *Op. cit.*, p. 14.   [3] *Ibid.*, p. 112.   [4] *Ibid.*, p. 116.

degrees of hotness *as indicated* in that particular
way. It is the choice of the thing to be defined
that is arbitrary, not the definition of it ; for the
definition merely expresses a fact or relation which
has been found to hold in nature itself.

§ 329. The question, then, really is whether our
definition of temperature expresses an objective fact
or not. Do changes of volume and changes of
pressure really indicate changes in degree of hotness ? If so, our definition is objectively valid; if
not, it is merely a creation of the mind.

Now, theoretically, two phenomena which vary
concomitantly must be in some way ' causally connected,' in which case changes in the one phenomenon will correspond to changes in the other, in
so far as that phenomenon which we may call the
effect depends upon the other phenomenon as upon
its cause. Hence we may say that *in so far as* change
of volume ' varies continuously ' with change of
hotness, there is a causal connection between the
two, so that change of volume indicates and may
be used in order to measure change of hotness. But
the statement that change of volume varies continuously with change of hotness applies only to
certain cases and even then is not exact. Changes
of volume may be due also to changes of pressure,
surface-tension, etc., and, in addition to this, there
are apparent changes arising from variation in the
solid envelope in which the thermometric substance,
whether a liquid or a gas, is enclosed. These *other*
causes of variation or of apparent variation the
scientist must eliminate or allow for, if his measure_
ments are to be exact ; and since he can do neither

completely, there will always be some slight error
in his results. The personal equation, too, is a
source of error, for it varies somewhat; and the
lines which indicate the sub-divisions of the thermometric scale have always a certain thickness.
Hence the degree of hotness of a body as measured
by some chosen scale is not the degree of hotness as
it objectively exists. There is always some error; and
though of errors in general we may take an average
or mean, the result will never be more than approximate. Hence the scientific definition of
temperature itself is approximate : it does not
correspond exactly with the object defined ; or
rather it implies an impossibility, viz., that changes
of hotness can be measured with absolute accuracy
by an arbitrary scale ; whereas measurement, since
it implies quantity or degree, owing to the
'*faiblesse de notre esprit*' can never be precisely
determined.

§ 330. Ought we, then, to refuse to apply the
predicates ' true ' and ' false ' to scientific definitions
on account of their approximate character ? By
no means. A scientific definition does not *claim*
to be exact, and it is only about its ' claim to truth '
that the logician has to judge. The scientist, indeed,
does not introduce the term ' approximate ' into his
definitions, but it is always understood. Approximation is all we can get when, as in science, quantity
is involved. But although it implies that knowledge
is as yet *incomplete*, it does not destroy its truth.
We do not say that a statistical statement—*v.g.*, a
statement with regard to the population of a
country—is untrue because it is approximate, nor

FF

yet do we say that it is neither true nor false. Such
statements, like scientific laws and definitions, do
not claim to correspond exactly with objective fact,
nor is such exactitude required in order for them to
be true. That is true which corresponds with fact
in so far as correspondence is claimed. We know
that all quantitative laws imply a ' margin of error ; '
but provided we know also that this margin of error
is relatively small in comparison with the quantities
involved, our statement is what it claims to be,
approximate, and in this sense may correspond
with reality, and be true. A ' margin of error ' is
not strictly a margin of *error*, but rather a margin
within which the quantities involved in a statement are known to be invariable. Moreover, not
only does the scientist know, when he says that his
law is approximate, that such variations are
relatively small with respect to the quantities concerned, but he can also determine the limits of these
variations. He can tell us, for instance, that his
quantities are certainly exact, say, to the fourth
decimal place, and probably to the fifth ; so that he
can also determine the degree of approximation
within which any further deduction he may make
from the original law will be true.

§ 331. Strictly speaking, then, we cannot say
that a scientific definition as such is either arbitrary,
symbolic or invalid. The most serious charge we
can bring against it is that it is only approximate,
and this does not destroy its objective validity. To
call a scientific definition such as that of temperature,
arbitrary or symbolic, seems to me to be, to say the
least, inaccurate and misleading. For a symbol is

either a purely arbitrary sign chosen to denote some
object, *or* it is a sign chosen by convention to
represent some object *on account of* a supposed
resemblance between that object and the symbol
used ; and in neither of these senses is the definition
of temperature which we have been considering a
symbol. What we have defined is not ' *degree of
hotness* ' simply, but ' the degree of hotness of a
substance considered in relation to the concomitant
variations in magnitude of certain other substances.'
This is the particular fact or class of facts which the
term ' temperature ' denotes. True, we *choose* this
particular fact and agree to call it ' temperature ; '
but this done, we cannot define ' temperature ' as
we will : its definition is determined by the facts.
The denotation of ' temperature,' like that of other
terms, is chosen arbitrarily or by convention ; but
once the denotation is fixed, the connotation will
depend upon the facts to which the term is applied.
When we say that temperature is ' degree of hotness
as indicated by an arbitrarily chosen scale,' we are
describing something objective and real. The
' degree of hotness ' is objective and real, and so is
the ' chosen scale,' for by it we mean the thermometric substances whose variations in magnitude
are causally connected with and therefore indicate
degrees of hotness. The introduction of the term
' arbitrary ' into our definition is a little inaccurate,
perhaps ; for, though the selection of a thermometric substance is to some extent arbitrary,
choice is restricted to those substances which really
indicate changes in degrees of hotness. But what
is meant is that, *provided this condition is fulfilled*, it

is matter of indifference what substance we choose, or what units we take as a basis of our scale ; and this also is an objective fact, since there are many substances whose magnitude varies concomitantly with their degree of hotness, or with the degree of hotness of some other substance. What we choose is not the definition, but the thing to be defined ; and when the thing defined determines the definition, as it should do and usually does, there is between the two, not merely a symbolic resemblance, but something more ; for the definition—so far as it goes— expresses true knowledge of a certain class of objective facts.

§ 332. Our definition of ' temperature ' is not symbolic, then, if by temperature we mean ' degree of hotness ' considered in relation to changes of volume or weight.

Yet there is a sense in which that definition may be said to be symbolic. For ' temperature ' may be regarded as a quality of an object, as ' degree of hotness ' *simpliciter*. In fact, it is *hotness* which the scientist really wishes to define ; but instead of defining it, he finds that all he can do is to indicate its changes in degree by certain other changes of a different nature. What the nature of hotness or the nature of temperature is he does not know, but he does know that variations in magnitude correspond to degrees of hotness. Hence he uses variations in magnitude (volume or weight) to signify or *symbolise* degrees of hotness. The definition of Temperature, therefore, though not itself symbolic, contains a symbolic element, since variations in magnitude in no way reveal to us the nature of temperature, if by temperature we mean degrees of hotness. Yet even this symbolism is symbolism in the less rigid sense of that term. For the variations in magnitude by which we symbolise 'temperature' are not arbitrarily chosen, nor are they chosen by mere convention, but on account of a certain 'resemblance' between the symbol and that which it symbolises. And that 'resemblance' is not merely *supposed* to exist; but is known to exist and to consist in concomitant variations which imply either a direct causal connection or, at least, a common cause. Our definition, then, though it does not tell us what the nature of 'temperature' is, nevertheless expresses real knowledge *about* temperature. To call such a definition 'symbolic,' therefore, though true in a certain sense, is somewhat misleading, for a symbol *usually* means a purely arbitrary sign, and does not necessarily imply any kind of resemblance. Moreover, if we use the term 'temperature' in the strict sense of degree of hotness, *quâ* measured, our definition is not symbolic at all, as we have seen.

§ 333. We may, of course, substitute in place of the above definition of temperature the formula $V - V_0 = v\theta$, or $V = V_0 (1 + a\theta)$ where $a = v/V_0$. Obviously a definition of this kind is *in form* strictly symbolic, since its terms are now purely arbitrary or conventional signs. In reality, however, it is as objective as the real definition for which it is substituted. Its symbols refer to names, and through names to concepts which correspond to objective fact. We might re-write the definition in the form $\theta = (V - V_0)/v$, which would mean that the number of degrees or scale-units of temperature in a given body or in the thermometric substance is equal to the ratio of $V - V_0$, (the difference between the actual volume of the thermometric substance at θ and the volume which the same substance had at the zero of the scale), to v, (the degree-measure, or increase in volume of that substance for one degree).[1] Now v is *by definition* the same all along the scale, hence in the formula $V = V_0 (1 + a\ \theta)$, $a\ [= v/\ V_0]$—*the co-efficient of expansion* or the expansion per unit volume of the thermometric substance in changing its temperature from $0°$ to $1°$,' should also be the same all along the scale. Yet this, in fact, is not the case. Not only does ' a ' vary for different substances, but for most substances it is greater when we measure it between (say) $70°$ and $71°$ than it is between $0°$ and $1°$. ' v ' and ' a,' then, as soon as we come to deal with an actual case, are approximate, and so also, for that matter, are V and V_0, which are supposed to be constant. Yet our definition is not thereby invalidated, for though the statement $V = V_0 (1 + a\ \theta)$ in *form* is exact, it does not claim to be really exact. We are quite aware that in reality it is approximate, and that we must allow for a margin of error in any particular case to which we may apply it.

§ 334. Hitherto we have been discussing the definition of temperature only in so far as it is based on experimental data ; and have found that, though only approximate and in a sense symbolic, it nevertheless gives us true knowledge about objective

[1] Preston, p. 19.

reality. Physical science, however, is not content with this. It wishes to get at the real nature of temperature, and for this purpose frames hypotheses which, taken together, constitute the theory of Heat. Heat is regarded as ' the molecular energy of matter,' and temperature thus becomes ' the molecular energy of matter as measured by some chosen scale.' Here, then, we have a definition which, as M. Duhem says, is not only ' due to a slow and complex process of elaboration,' but which ' gets its whole meaning from physical theory.' And that theory is not established. It involves numerous hypotheses about the constitution of matter, and the nature of different forms of energy, none of which can as yet be treated as objectively valid and certain. Hence the definition of temperature which is based on such a theory, though useful, cannot be said to be ' true.' Again, it is a symbolic definition that is pictured in terms of mechanical imagery. A ' hot ' substance is symbolised as an indefinite number of minute particles of matter all moving about with greater or less rapidity, and behaving according to known mechanical laws. A symbol of this kind corresponds to some extent with objective fact, for particles of matter certainly have mechanical properties. But how far it corresponds, or what other properties of matter are also manifested in the phenomenon of heat we cannot say. By treating heat *as if* it were the molecular energy of matter, many phenomena may be explained and many experimental laws co-ordinated ; but there are phenomena which the theory fails to explain, and cases in which it breaks down completely. At present, then, the molecular theory of heat is neither true nor false. It contains an element of truth, as other theories have done before it; but indefinite modifications will have to be introduced before it can be established, and what precise effects those modifications will have upon the various hypotheses and definitions of which the theory is made up, it is impossible to say. The theoretical definition is symbolic, because though it ' corresponds ' with the facts, we cannot say how far it corresponds, or how far it fails so to do. It embraces both an element of truth and an element of error, and between the two it is impossible for us at present to draw the dividing line.

§ 335. Definitions which belong to the theory of physics must be distinguished, therefore, from those which are based directly on experimental facts; and a similar distinction must be made between experimental laws and theoretical hypotheses. The latter are symbolic, provisional, and, strictly speaking, neither true nor false; the former are approximate, but none the less objectively valid. Boyle's or Mariotte's law may be taken as an example of an experimental or empirical law. It is a generalisation based directly on experiment and observation, and states that " at the same temperature, the volumes occupied by the same mass of gas are in inverse proportion to the pressure to which it is subject." This law, M. Duhem tells us, is a " symbolic relation whose application to concrete reality implies that one knows quite a system of theories."[1] Neverthe-

---

[1] Duhem, *La Théorie Physique*, chap. v., § 1.

less, I think that we are justified in regarding it as
objectively valid. But let us examine its significance more closely and see for ourselves whether
this is the case.

That Boyle's law merely expresses a *relation*
between temperature, volume, pressure and mass,
yet does not tell us anything of the intrinsic nature
of those entities is clear ; and the same may be said
of almost all experimental laws. They express
relations, sequences, causal connections, not essences.
Nevertheless, they may give us true knowledge, and
if ' *actio sequitur esse*,' they tell us something *about*
the nature of the entities concerned (in this particular case, the properties of a gas), even if they
do not tell us what that nature is. If we wish to
explain the law or to discover *why* the relation
arises, we must have recourse to theory. But
considered merely from the experimental point of
view, Boyle's law and any other empirical relation
of this kind can be established independently of
theory, unless, indeed, we apply that term to
the complexus of experimental laws themselves.
General statements of facts, however, are certainly
not what we mean by theory ; but, on the contrary,
are the data by means of which theory is ultimately
to be established or condemned.

§ 336. Boyle's law, then, expresses a relation
which can experimentally be shown to hold between
certain entities, of the intrinsic nature of which we
know little or nothing for certain. And if on this
account you choose to call the relation symbolic,
well and good ; though the expression is liable to
mislead, because it suggests that the law does not

express real knowledge. And this is not true, for all the terms denote objective facts. Temperature and mass cannot be defined in their essential nature, but only by means of their relations to other properties, *v.g.*, to volume or to motion and weight. Yet mass, like temperature, signifies an objective fact, and our concept of it is true so far as it goes. For even if mass be ultimately reducible to electromagnetic inertia, it is still true that material bodies have some property in virtue of which, in varying but measurable degree, they tend to keep their state of motion and resist all influences tending to change it, whether in quantity or direction. Doubtless this correspondence can be established in a concrete case only by the use of instruments and by means of measurements and calculations which are often long and complicated. But, as we have seen in regard to temperature, the approximate nature of measurement does not detract from its truth, nor does a long and complicated calculation lead to inaccurate results, for when once our margins of error are known, it is possible to determine with mathematical precision the accuracy of our conclusion.

Boyle's law is inaccurate when stated, as generally it is, in the form which M. Duhem has given, but it is inaccurate because it was proved to hold *only* for *certain* gases when subject to *moderate* pressures, and not because its terms are symbolic or its measurements inexact. For moderate pressures and for the so-called permanent gases, oxygen, hydrogen, and air, the formula ($PV =$ constant) will hold with a margin of error that is comparatively small; but for most gases PV gradually diminishes up to a certain point as the pressure is increased, and after this point is passed it begins to increase; and again its variations are different according to the particular gas which is being examined, and according to the temperature at which the experiment is performed. Yet, while still keeping clear of molecular and other hypotheses in regard to the nature of matter, it is possible to devise more complicated formulæ which shall take account of these facts, and which will therefore be applicable in cases where the simple formulæ failed. These more complicated formulæ will, in a certain sense, be *more* true than those which they supersede, since they will contain a smaller margin of error. Nor does there seem to be any reason for supposing that certitude diminishes as a law becomes more precise, for it will still be possible to construct formulæ such that all possible variations from any of the quantities involved will be small in comparison with the quantities themselves.

§ 337. There is, however, a limit to the precision with which experimental science can at present determine the magnitudes it wishes to measure, and if this limit is passed certitude gives place to proba bility. In proportion as the scientist endeavours to make his measurements more exact, errors due to observation, to the instruments he uses, and to the impurity of the substances upon which he experiments, become of greater importance, till finally the observed discrepancies he has to allow for, counterbalance the degree of accuracy which he seeks to obtain. It is then that he invokes the aid of theory. Assuming general principles which apply unreservedly to all material objects, he constructs hypotheses, assigning a definite structure to minute particles of matter upon which it is impossible to experiment individually, and of whose existence he has no immediate experience. From these hypotheses he deduces conclusions whose precision can be as minute and detailed as he wishes to make it, and whose accuracy is unquestionable, granting that his premises are true. But when he comes to apply such conclusions to experimental data he finds that in some cases they are confirmed and in others they are not, and he discovers also that for any individual case there is more than one theoretical formula which will satisfy the experimental conditions. Consequently, he is in doubt as to which to choose, and in such a dilemma, other considerations being of equal value, the simplest is usually selected. But now it is necessary to explain why the formula selected should not exactly or under all conditions fit the facts. But this is impossible, for we do not know how far theoretical definitions have an objective counterpart or how far they are merely symbolic ; and when a particular formula fails to apply in a given case, we do not know where the error lies, since all theoretical formulæ and definitions pre-suppose an indefinite number of hypotheses of which the validity is uncertain.

§ 338. Clearly, then, the region of theory in Physics differs essentially from that of experimental law. Experimental laws are true so far as they go, or they are false. If qualitative merely, they are true in so far as they establish relations between real

properties of matter ; false, if supposed adequately
to express its whole nature. If quantitative, they
are true, provided the limits within which the
quantities may vary are known to be relatively
small ; false, if the quantities involved pretend to
be other than approximate. Of theoretical hypotheses, on the other hand, we cannot say definitely
that they are true, nor yet that they are false, until
they have been verified ; and they can only be
verified by comparing them with experimental laws
already established. Hence the possibility of ever
being able to establish a physical theory presupposes that experimental laws are already true ;
for " *le seul contrôle expérimental de la théorie physique
qui ne soit pas illogique consiste à comparer le système
entier de la théorie physique à tout l'ensemble des lois
expérimentales et à apprécier si celui-ci est représenté
par celui-là d'une manière satisfaisante.*" [1]

In the experimental stage of physics the scientist
may work with symbols, as when he regards the sun
as an ideal sphere, whose matter can be treated as
if it were massed at its centre ; but he knows in this
case that, owing to the distance of the sun from the
earth and planets, the error he has deliberately
introduced cannot affect the degree of accuracy
which he wishes to obtain in the deductions he is
going to make. The theorist in physics is in a
different case. When experience refuses to verify
his symbolic formulæ, he cannot say where the error
lies. It may be in some symbol he is using, or it
may be in some hypothesis which is presupposed ;
he cannot tell. He has no means of comparing his

[1] *La Théorie Physique*, chap. vi., § 5.

symbols with the object to which they are supposed
to correspond. All he can say for certain is that
something is wrong somewhere. Such being the
case, when the theorist has no means of locating
the error, his only alternative is, as M. Duhem says,

to keep rigidly to the signification of symbols when once
they have been fixed, regardless of experimental facts,
but to use absolute freedom in the matter of postulation
and hypothesis, provided no contradiction is involved
and provided, ultimately, all hypotheses be subjected
to the test of experience when once a theory is complete.[1]

§ 339. What function, then, is to be assigned to
physical theory? Various answers have been given
to this question. It co-ordinates and systematises
experimental laws; it synopsises and condenses
them in accordance with economy of thought; it
enables us to classify what is known and to predict
what is unknown; it suggests questions and guides
as well as prompts future research. At any rate,
then, its function is useful; but is it anything more?
M. Le Roy would answer in the negative. The
symbolic relations which we postulate and express
in mathematical language are merely instruments,
more or less convenient, useful, suitable for the
purpose of connecting and systematising experimental laws with a view of bringing them under
human control and rendering them more manageable.
Like M. Boutroux, he regards science as " a collection
of methods for the assimilation of things to our
intellect *in order to bend them to our will*." M.
Duhem takes a more objective view, but even he
declares that physical theories do not pretend to be

[1] *Ibid.*, chap. v., §§ 7, 9.

explanations of the nature of material things. They are independent of all metaphysical systems. [1]

The question, however, may be raised, whether it is justifiable thus to separate the useful and the true. Whether, in other words, 'symbolic representation' can render more easy, more rapid, and more sure our reasoning about 'what our senses, aided by instruments, make us know' without in some way corresponding to those same data of experience ; or whether, again, it is possible to devise methods for assimilating things to our intellect in order to bend them to our will, unless those methods are based on *true* principles and are capable of giving knowledge of reality. Can a thing be useful without being in some sense true ? I do not see how it can.

§ 340. Theories are not like machines which work automatically, or like physical instruments which may be brought to some degree of perfection by the haphazard process of chopping and changing them at random till they suit the practical purpose we have in view. In science we are dealing with *knowledge* from first to last. Our 'manipulations of experiences' in their primary purpose are not practical but theoretical, and consist in classification, co-ordination, systematisation and explanation. Verification, too, does not consist in the realisation of a practical end, nor in the successful performance of some physical action ; but in a certain identity between the detailed inferences drawn from our theories and given physical facts. With a view to discovering the general principles or laws which

[1] *Ibid.*, chap. vii., § 1.

underlie these facts, the physicist frames a theory comprising many hypotheses logically connected together, and expressed either in mathematical symbols or in images of particles endowed with some form of energy. These symbols and images, however, are not mere pictures, but concepts. They signify things the existence of which we postulate, and which we suppose to obey known laws, mechanical, dynamical, or electro-magnetic. These laws form the basis of theoretical deduction. From them the physicist infers that under given conditions certain phenomena should occur, and his inferences are often confirmed by fact. What conclusion, then, ought we to draw in regard to the objective significance of these symbols and images, and the laws that govern their relations? Are they, in the strict sense, objectively valid, *i.e.*, do they represent adequately the nature of that for which they stand substitute? No; for in many cases the conclusions deduced from them are not confirmed by experience. Ought we to say, then, that they are neither true nor false? Clearly they are not wholly true, otherwise the conclusions deduced would always be verified; neither, on the other hand, can they be wholly false, for, then, the conclusions ought never to be verified unless *per accidens*, and in a few cases here and there only. They must contain at least an element of truth, and represent, at any rate, an aspect of reality.

§ 341. Again, the concepts which are involved when we think of facts are of a similar nature to those which we use when we think of hypotheses or laws, which seems to show that facts and hypotheses are not entities of a wholly different order. That on December 28th, 1908, many people were killed in Messina by falling buildings is a fact. That the buildings were shattered owing to an earthquake is also a fact. On the other hand, that the buildings fell to the earth is supposed to have been due to gravity, which is a hypothesis. And that the earth moves round the sun is another hypothesis, itself also accounted for by the further hypothesis of gravitation. Now the concepts which function in our minds when we think of the earth moving round the sun are to a large extent the same as those which we use when we think of buildings falling to the ground, viz., concepts of motion and direction ; and we may say the same, I think, of the concepts involved in the Law of Gravitation, viz., distance, mass and force, except that mass is a complex concept involving volume and density, while force can only be conceived as the cause of change from rest or uniform linear motion. Why, then, should we regard hypotheses and facts as entities of wholly different order ? If these were really so, it is difficult to see how verification could take place. But if not, why should we make this forced separation between what is useful and what is true? We cannot say that a hypothesis *is* true until it is verified ; yet I can see no reason whatsoever why we should not admit that it may be found to be true later on. All hypotheses seem to me to possess the potentiality of becoming true. And if this is so, it is irrational to deny that hypotheses may contain an element of truth, even though we cannot distinguish what is true in them

GG

from what is false, and so cannot tell how far they are true until they have been completely verified.

§ 342. Or, again, to put the same argument in another form : if the so-called 'symbols' and 'images' of Physical Theory contain no element of truth, how are we to explain the coincidence of experimental fact with theoretical deduction? A precisely similar effect can be produced only by a precisely similar cause ; for the nature of the effect proceeds from that of the cause, in which it must be already potentially contained, otherwise it could not get into the effect. The cause may comprise many other properties besides that of producing this particular effect ; but, in so far as an effect does proceed from a given cause, the nature of the effect must be already there implicitly in the cause. Now, the particular conclusions that are deduced in physical theory are based upon hypotheses in which things having certain mechanical or electro-magnetic properties are supposed to exist. Hence, in our ideal physical world it is from the nature of these hypothetical entities that certain effects, the phenomena that we anticipate, proceed. Similarly in the real world actual phenomena or events proceed from and are dependent upon the nature of existing entities and their properties. If, then, and in so far as, we find that the phenomena which we anticipate are realised in the concrete, the anticipated and the actual phenomena must proceed from a similar cause ; or, in other words, the nature of the entities which we conceive as causes in a verified hypothesis and the nature of real things must be one and the same.

If facts are true, then, the hypothesis which explains them must also be true, and, in so far as our anticipations are realised, the concepts which they presuppose must be objectively valid. Unfortunately, however, our anticipations are never precisely realised as they are constructed in theory, and often enough they are negatived by concrete experience. Until, therefore, we can localise the source of error and rectify our theoretical constructions, it is impossible to say more than that theories contain an element of truth, the degree of which will depend largely upon the precision and the extent of its confirmation by experimental facts.

§ 343. But can we ever distinguish what is true in a theory from what is false ? Can we localise error and affirm that it lies in one hypothesis rather than in another ? Are there any physical theories or any hypotheses which we know for certain to be true ? M. Duhem, as we have seen, holds that the parts of a physical theory are so intimately bound up together that no one hypothesis can be verified apart from the rest. Nothing can be regarded as objectively valid until it is complete, and has been verified as a whole by comparison with the complexus of physical facts. M. Poincaré, on the other hand, takes a different view, and thinks that some hypotheses or laws, if not more certain, are at any rate more probable than others ; and this seems the more reasonable view to take, though it by no means follows that there are strictly physical laws, however universal, which can be regarded as certain *a priori*, or as self-evident.

M. Duhem's argument that the law of inertia is

not self-evident because it was not recognised as such by the Greeks is hardly conclusive ; for a self-evident truth must be understood before its self-evidence can be recognised,[1] and it is quite conceivable that there are truths which would be self-evident if anybody thought about them, but which are not so, because no one as yet has thought of them at all.[2] I see no ground, however, for regarding the law of inertia as self-evident. Development is a fact, and so is decay ; and, as I have already pointed out, there seems to be no reason *a priori* why things should not tend constantly to develop or increase in some way or other, or why, on the other hand, they should not tend continuously to diminish and decay. Yet few people would question the truth of the law of inertia now, nor indeed any of Newton's three laws of motion. Why is this ? It is precisely because on the three laws of motion, together with that of Gravity, the whole system of Astronomy is based. I know not whether M. Duhem would treat astronomical theory as part of the theory of Physics, or whether he would regard it as a theory sufficiently distinct and sufficiently complete to be verifiable apart from the rest. Astronomers, at any rate, seem to have no doubt as to the validity of the law of Inverse Squares or of the laws of Motion, laws which have led to conclusions completely verified by fact, except for a slight margin of error, which can, in most cases, easily be accounted for by the personal equation or by instrumental

---

[1] Compare the scholastic distinction between truths which are *per se nota quoad se*, and *per se nota quoad nos*.
[2] cf. chap. xv. *re* Self-Evident Truths.

defects. The law of Gravitation is, at any rate, approximately true if we express it in the form— between two material bodies there is an attractive force which varies directly as the product of their masses and inversely as the square of their distances ; but whether that force is an ultimate property of all material bodies, or whether it is due to a *vis a tergo*, we do not know. Our knowledge is limited. We know for certain that a relation which we call Gravitation holds between all material bodies, but we do not know whence that relation arises.

§ 344. Let us take another physical theory, the Undulatory Theory of Light. Here, again, we can distinguish what is true in that theory from what is doubtful and possibly false. The theory, taken as a whole, explains nearly all the phenomena of light. In particular, the characteristic hypothesis from which it gets its name affords us the most satisfactory explanation of refraction and interference phenomena which seem to show conclusively that the propagation of light is by means of *undulatory motion in which there is some form of periodic change transverse to the line of propagation*. The *subsidiary* hypothesis of an ' ether,' which we seem forced to postulate as a medium for the transmission of light, presents certain difficulties. For the properties of this ' ether ' approximate at once to those of a solid and to those of a perfect gas. Nor is this difficulty entirely overcome, though it is relieved somewhat, by stating it in a more accurate form, as when we say the ratio between the elasticity of the ether and its density must be very large. Another difficulty arises, too, from Michelson's experiment, which apparently shows that no relative motion exists between the ether and the earth, whereas a relative motion between the two must be postulated in order to explain the aberration of light. It has been suggested that this latter difficulty may be obviated by supposing that moving bodies contract in the direction of movement ; but this hypothesis, though not impossible, cannot be experimentally proved. Further discussion of the difficulties connected with the Undulatory Theory of Light, however, would be beyond the scope of my present purpose. Doubtless, that theory contains an element of error as well as an element of truth. Yet the source of the error can be located, I think, in the postulate of 'ether,' and the essential hypothesis of the theory as stated above does not seem thereby to be affected, and so may be regarded as true.

§ 345. This view of the applicability of truth to scientific theories is not altogether foreign to the minds of physicists whose expressions—as far as physical theory is concerned—are often pragmatic in tone. M. Duhem seems to imply that when physical theory is complete and when it has been completely verified it will become not only useful, but true, and true in the realist sense. M. Poincaré is even more emphatic. Science, he says, is not merely a rule for action—it gives us knowledge of objects. Its utility lies in its power to enable us to foresee events, but foresight implies sight, and the value of prediction depends upon the accuracy with which events have previously been represented.

The symbols or figured concepts, which in mathematical physics form the terms between which
relations hold, may vary, but the equations to which
they lead are the same. Mass and energy cannot
as yet be accurately defined, but conservation of
mass and conservation of energy point at least to
something which in reality is constant throughout.
Even the famous postulate of Simplicity or Thought-
economy is, in the opinion of M. Poincaré, not
wholly subjective. Simple laws are verified *à peu
près ;* and this cannot be due to chance. There
must be some cause for it in the nature of objective
reality. Finally, he points out that, though
Mechanism is distrusted on account of its tendency
to Realism, yet one of the chief conclusions to be
drawn from Maxwell's work is that we can always
give to the material universe a mechanical explanation if we wish. Nor will such an interpretation be
altogether symbolic, for electric oscillations, the
movements of a pendulum, and all periodic
phenomena manifest " *une parenté intime qui
correspond à une realité profonde.*"

§ 346. The significance of statements such as
these seems to point to something more than a
parallelism between the logical connections of a
physical theory and the system of experimental
laws upon which it is based. Moreover, this
' parallelism '—which, in the opinion of Hertz, is
the term that best expresses the relation of theory
to fact—itself requires explanation. If the concepts which are used in physical theory, are merely
ideal constructions logically connected together,
how comes it about that they correspond symboli-

cally, point for point and connection for connection, with the facts to which they are applied ? The epistemology of physical theory cannot rest content without some further explanation. Parallelism cannot be ultimate, but, like concomitant variations, seems to postulate some causal connection. The concepts of physical theory are ultimately derived from experience, and the conclusions of physical theory bring us back again to concrete experience in which more or less completely they are realised. In neither case is the coalescence whole and entire : yet contact with reality is thereby established, whence it would seem to follow that between logical connections on the one hand, and physical relations on the other, there must also be some form of correspondence, the nature of which the term parallelism is hardly adequate to express.

The possibility of parallelism, of useful symbolism, and of predicating and controlling events by means of calculations based on theoretical assumptions can be explained only on the further assumption that the concepts which physical theory employs have some kind of objective truth. These concepts may not be wholly true, still less adequately express the nature of objective reality ; but they are not mere symbols or mere picturesque representations. They give us at any rate some knowledge of our material environment. Most hypotheses, even when verified, tell us little of the inner nature of things. The knowledge which they give concerns for the most part their operations and the relations one to another. Still ' *actio sequitur esse* ' and the nature of a relation depends upon the objects it relates. Mechanism is an attempt to penetrate deeper into the nature of material things, and though it has failed to reduce everything to matter and motion or to show that no properties exist besides the mechanical, it represents a true, if a one-sided and partial, aspect of the material world.

It is not irrational, therefore, to interpret the aim of physical science in a realistic sense, or even to say that some of the hypotheses which belong to physical theory give us real knowledge of the laws which govern the universe in which we live. Realism is not incompatible with physical science. On the contrary, it gives to its speculations a richer meaning and a fuller significance than any that Pragmatism affords ; and it raises within us a rational hope that the realistic terminology of which the scientist, whether deliberately or from force of habit makes use, will in the end turn out to be something more than mere metaphor ; for, as M. Duhem remarks, " *Au fur et à mesure que les methodes expérimentales progressent, l'indétermination du symbole abstract que l'expérience physique fait correspondre au fait concret va en diminuant.*" [1]

[1] *La Théorie Physique,* chap. v., § 3.

CHAPTER XIX.

ABSOLUTE TRUTH.

§ 347. In the chapter on " Development and Validity" we saw that an absolutist of the Hegelian type regarded all development as a reconciliation of differences in a higher synthesis, and hence inferred that, until the complete and total synthesis of all differences is realised, knowledge is not only imperfect, but is subject to indefinite modification. Truth consists in a totality of syntheses ; it is the complete harmony and unification of every part of knowledge. What we strive to know is Reality itself, and Reality is a system in which each part is related to all the rest and cannot be understood in isolation from the rest. It is a coherent, organised whole, an individual whole, a whole which is essentially intelligible ; and as such it is at once the Object which we seek to know, the Ideal towards which our knowledge tends, and the Criterion by which it must be judged. Truth, therefore, is only another aspect of Reality itself, and is defined by Dr. Joachim as " the systematic coherence of a significant whole."

On this point there is substantial agreement among all absolutists, though in regard to points of secondary importance they differ. The Hegelian, for instance, identifies Reality and Thought, whereas Mr. Bradley maintains that Thought is only a fundamental ' difference ' of Reality. Thought, he says, can never equate itself with Reality ; for in thought content and existence are essentially distinct, whereas in the Absolute they are one. Nevertheless, as it is the Experience of the Absolute which constitutes Reality, so it is the manifestation of that Experience in finite centres, where it is broken up by analysis and reunited in synthesis, that constitutes human truth, a truth which is ever approaching but never attains the systematic coherence of an individual whole. It is essential to truth, says Dr. Joachim, to " manifest itself in the thinking of finite subjects." [1] The Absolute somehow reveals itself in us, and our human thinking is thus in some way or other the reproduction of the one eternal consciousness, " in respect, at least, of its attribute of self-origination and unification of the manifold." [2] So says T. H. Green ; and again : " Finite experiences are rooted in the Ideal. They share its actuality and draw from it whatever being and conservability they possess." " Perfection of truth and of reality has in the end," Mr. Bradley tells us, " the same character. It consists in positive, self-subsisting individuality."

Less or more [our judgments] actually possess the character and type of absolute truth and reality. They can take the place of the Real to various extents, because containing in themselves less or more of its nature. They are its representatives, worse or better, in proportion as they present us with truth affected by greater or less derangement. Human truths are true according as it would take less or more to convert them into reality.[3]

[1] *The Nature of Truth*, p. 163 and cf. p. 20.
[2] Green, *Prolegomena to Ethics*, § 77.
[3] *Appearance and Reality*, pp. 362, 363.

And again, Professor Bosanquet declares that "for Logic, at all events, it is a postulate that 'the truth is the whole.' The forms of thought have the relation which is their truth in their power to constitute a totality." [1]

§ 348. Three doctrines underlie this Absolute theory of Truth : the doctrine (1) that relations intrinsically modify their terms ; (2) that all parts and single judgments get their meaning from the whole ; and (3) that the part played by the mind in the making or finding of truth is essential and intrinsic. That this is so should, I think, be clear from what has already been said of the general standpoint of Absolutism in previous chapters. Hence I shall merely quote one or two passages from Dr. Joachim's *Nature of Truth* to illustrate the point.

Dr. Joachim rejects the correspondence-notion of truth precisely because and precisely in so far as it contradicts the three fundamental doctrines of Absolutism mentioned above. "There is no correspondence," he says, "between two simple entities, nor between elements of wholes considered as simple beings, *i.e.*, without respect to the systematisation of their wholes." [2] " If we identify, distinguish, or in any way relate A and B—two simple entities—we have *eo ipso* retracted their simplicity ; and their simplicity never existed, if their nature justified our proceedings." A purely external relation is meaningless, and would be " a third independent entity which in no intelligible

---

[1] *Logic*, i., p. 3.
[2] *The Nature of Truth*, p. 10.

sense relates the first two." Every relation qualifies and modifies intrinsically its terms.[1]

§ 349. Correspondence, indeed, is admitted as a 'symptom of truth,' but this correspondence depends primarily on something which itself conditions the being and the nature of the correspondence.[2]

Correspondence, when attributed to wholes, is simply a name for identity of purpose expressed through materially different constituents as an identical structure, plan, or cycle of functions ; and, when attributed to the parts, it means identity of function contributed mainly by materially different constituents towards the main-tenance of the identical plan or purpose.[3]

Even the unity of the elements is derived from the whole. Hence, " correspondence, as a con-stitutive condition of truth, sinks more and more into the background," and instead " truth is seen to depend on the nature of the idea expressing itself in the inner structure of the corresponding wholes." And this idea acquires its own significance, its fulness of meaning and its power to constitute truth, from " a larger significant system to which it contributes." [4]

§ 350. Again, " truth is not truth unless it is recognised." The finding of truth as a historical process in my mind is irrelevant to the nature of truth, yet truth must be for some mind if it is to exist at all.[5] The real factor in knowledge cannot be external to mind or unrelated to consciousness. Truth is independent of this or that mind, *quâ* this or that mind, and to its stubborn and independent

[1] *Ibid.*, p. 11, and cf. pp. 43 *et seq.* 49.
[2] *Ibid.*, p. 16.   [3] *Ibid.*, p. 10.   [4] *Ibid.*, p. 16.   [5] *Ibid.*, p. 14.

nature all thinking must conform under pain of error ; yet ' this independent truth lives and moves and has its being in the judgments of finite minds.' It is essential to it to be expressed, and it is expressed as a system of knowledge which constitutes and is constituted by the intellectual individualities of many finite thinkers.[1]   If the truth of my judgments be regarded as the correspondence between two factors in knowledge, the *one* vague, imperfectly articulate, and more or less unmediated feeling, *i.e.*, the common environment which is the world, the *other* a reflective judgment, a distinctly conceived synthesis of Thing and Property, then my judgment is true only if, as a whole of parts, it exhibits an inner structure identical in structure with the real factor, or some subordinate whole within the real factor.   Yet the two factors are not independent. The ' real ' factor is ' uniquely tinged with our respective individualities,' and the mental factor is communicable and so not purely personal.   The correspondence cannot be one of structure only, the difference being merely ' material ; ' for a purely external relation is impossible.   The matter of the ' felt-whole ' and of ' thought-whole ' must affect their respective forms.   They cannot consist of elements together with a scheme of relations.[2] Facts, again, if regarded as objects of possible sensations or judgments, are not independent ; but are essentially related to sensating and thinking. They are only a partial factor, dependent for its being and nature upon another factor, and incapable of being in itself or independent.[3]

[1] *Ibid.*, pp. 20, 22.   [2] *Ibid.*, pp. 23, 24.   [3] *Ibid.*, p. 41.

For Absolutism, then, there is no hard and fast
separation between knowledge and reality. Knowledge is an attempt to express reality, to think it ;
and in so far as our knowledge approximates to
reality itself it is true.

> Anything is true [says Dr. Joachim] which can be
> conceived (!), [and] to conceive means to think out
> clearly and logically, to hold many elements together
> in a connection necessitated by their several contents;
> [while] ' the conceivable ' is a significant whole, a whole
> possessed of meaning for thought, [a whole] such that
> all its constituent elements reciprocally determine one
> another's being as contributory features in a single
> concrete meaning.[1]

§ 351. Several important corollaries are deduced
from this ' Coherence-notion ' of truth. First of all
' necessity ' is hypothetical. Strictly speaking,
there are no ' necessary truths.'

> Necessity [says Professor Bosanquet] is a character
> attaching to parts or differences inter-related within
> wholes, universals or identities. If there were any
> totality such that it could not be set over against
> something else as a part or difference within a further
> system, such a totality could not be known under an
> aspect of necessity.[2]

Necessity is thus dependent on the Whole. It
may be used synonymously with ' self-evidence ' and
'propriety' to express the fact that in knowledge
" we are not free, but are under a constraint
exercised upon us by the content of knowledge
itself, such that some judgments have to be accepted
and others to be rejected." [3] But the ' content of
knowledge ' in this case is a more or less clear

---

[1] p. 66.   [2] *Logic*, vol. ii., p. 235.   [3] *Ibid.*, p. 232.

apprehension of some whole (space, for example), but ultimately of the Whole or of Reality itself.

As a consequence of this doctrine, Professor Bosanquet is forced to find some other name for the Laws of Thought. He cannot call them ' necessary truths,' since, concerned as they are with the nature of being itself, they cannot be regarded as dependent on any whole less than Reality itself. Hence Professor Bosanquet treats them as postulates.

I call these principles by the name of Postulates [he says] because when presented to me as abstract reflective ideas they operate as guides to knowledge which lead to their subsequent substantiation in a concrete form. As reflective conceptions, then, they are postulates, *i.e.*, principles which we use because we need them.[1]

Thus, the absolutist, having set up the systematic coherence of a significant whole as the sole criterion of truth is forced to take an almost pragmatic view of the fundamental laws of being and of thought.

§ 352. Another corollary to the Coherence-notion of Truth is the doctrine that truth cannot be predicated of any single judgment in isolation.[2] Dr. Joachim rejects the view that "what is true is *eo ipso* absolutely true." Partial truths are not 'true about a part of the matter, but false when taken as equivalent to the whole.' Nor do we add to them or supplement them by further determination. Such a view "would make it impossible to show that the truth of true judgments is essentially the truth of a system of knowledge ; and it would make it equally impossible to show

---

[1] *Ibid.*, p. 206,   [2] *Ibid.*, p. 92,

that the truth of systems of knowledge is borrowed from the Ideal experience, which is struggling for self-fulfilment in them." [1] The judgment that a triangle with equal angles has also equal sides, or that $3^2 = 9$ is not true at all, if taken in isolation ; for in isolation such judgments are practically meaningless. Every judgment is "a piece of concrete thinking which occurs in a particular context, issues from a special background, concentrates in itself various degrees of knowledge ; and by these determining factors its meaning is coloured." A judgment is the inseparable unity of thinking and of the object thought ; so that to the boy who is learning the multiplication table, the judgment $3^2 = 9$ possesses probably a minimum of meaning ; while to the arithmetician it is perhaps a symbol for the whole science of Arithmetic.[2] The numerical system in its fundamental features is assumed in every judgment that anyone makes about numbers. And similarly in Science no universal judgment can be violated without destroying its determinate meaning ; and, therefore, in isolation such a judgment cannot be absolutely true.[3] Isolated judgments are at best mutilated fragments, caricatures, faint shadows of truth.[4]

§ 353. Absolute truth, then, is an Ideal ; it is not something which actually exists. It is an organised individual experience, self-fulfilling and self-fulfilled, but its organisation is the process of its self-fulfilment and the concrete manifestation of its individuality. The whole *is* not, if 'is' implies that its nature is a finished product prior or posterior to the process, or in any sense apart from it.

[1] *loc. cit.*, pp. 87-89.   [2] pp. 92, 93.   [3] pp. 97 *et seq.*   [4] p. 102.

HH

Human knowledge—not merely *my* knowledge and yours, but the best and fullest knowledge in the world at any stage of its development—is clearly not the significant whole in the ideally complete and individual sense. Hence truth is, from the point of view of the human intellect, an ideal, and an ideal which can never *as such* or in its completeness be actual as human experience.[1] Human knowledge may have degrees of truth in proportion as it contains more or less of the nature of the Real,[2] and its degree of truth will depend upon its completeness and its systematic coherence ; but human knowledge can never attain the ideal of Absolute truth which is the completely individual, self-sustained, significant whole, the articulate connectedness of which demands discursive experience in a system of judgments.[3] All human knowledge, therefore, is wanting, not only in completeness, but also in certainty. No portion of knowledge is certain, says Dr. Mellone, until all portions have been so developed that they may be seen to form an all-inclusive whole. And as this would be omniscience, it is impossible for man so long as he remains finite. Thus, human knowledge is only an approximation, as yet very inadequate and far removed from the ideal ; and therefore, except within the bare facts of our sensations and mental images, it is uncertain, and may have to be completely transformed.[4]

§ 354. The doctrine of Absolute Truth which I have briefly outlined above, chiefly in the words of

[1] *Ibid.*, pp. 76, 79.
[2] *Appearance and Reality*, p. 162 (but cf. whole of chap. xxiv.).
[3] *The Nature of Truth*, pp. 113, 114.
[4] *Essays in Phil, Criticism and Construction*, Introduction.

Dr. Joachim, its principal exponent, itself undoubtedly contains much that is true ; and yet also much that, to my mind, seems false. It is based on assumptions which I cannot admit ; and it leads to consequences which, to a seeker after knowledge and truth, are, on account of the scepticism they imply, extremely repugnant. The assumptions upon which it is founded have already been discussed, with the result that they proved to be not only unnecessary and useless as an explanation of the data of experience, but also self-contradictory. Relations presuppose qualities, and modifications in relations arise from modifications in the qualities. But the relation is not a link between the qualities except in so far as the objects related are apprehended in a single mental act ; and if a relation exist objectively at all, it exists as an attribute of each object, not of the two taken together. When I apprehend the nature of a simple entity to be A and the nature of another simple entity to be B, and then combine these two judgments in one and say A is different from B, I do not see why ' either the simplicity of A and B is destroyed *or* else my judgment is unfounded.' Again, granted that the correspondence between two wholes is due to identity of structure or identity of function in the parts, and that this presupposes a universal idea which is expressed in each, it by no means follows that the universal is *really* one, or that it is the ground of a *real* whole. The ' correspondence ' is sufficiently accounted for by the logical unity of the universal under which are apprehended the structural similarities of the objects that correspond

And a logical unity gives us, not a real whole, but a logical whole, a whole for thought. That logical and teleological wholes imply a Divine mind which apprehends them and has constructed them according to a rational plan which they imperfectly realise, may be granted; but this rational plan is expressed in substantial real unities or individuals, co-existing and interacting, but not necessarily postulating an immanent ground. And, lastly, if the real factor in knowledge does get a unique tinge from the mental factor, that 'tinge' must vitiate the objectivity of knowledge and the alleged independence of truth, unless, indeed, it can be distinguished from the real and objective factor which would thus be left untinged.

Dr. Joachim's novel definition of truth as the "systematic coherence of a significant whole," if interpreted in the sense in which he interprets it, seems to me an unwarrantable assumption. Human knowledge does become more coherent and more systematic as it advances, and on this account is more adequate to represent Reality; but truth can hardly be identified with this 'coherence,' which is only one of its properties. Nor is coherence of much practical use as a criterion of truth, for it is extremely difficult, if not impossible, to compare two theories in regard to their degree of systematisation and coherence.

§ 355. The sceptical consequences which follow from this doctrine of absolute truth are disastrous for human truth. Professor Bosanquet's view of necessity as essentially dependent on the whole, if taken in combination with the doctrine that a part is unintelligible in abstraction from the whole, destroys the axiomatic character of all 'necessary truths.' But, in the first place, why should necessity be restricted to the parts and be denied of the whole ? The whole, it is admitted, exists of itself, for itself, and through itself ; and so may surely be said to necessitate itself, or to constitute a factual necessity. And, secondly, why may not a part manifest, without mutilating, some character or aspect of the whole ? If it does, the laws of thought may still be necessary truths, though in this view only hypothetically necessary ; but, if it does not, they are reduced to the status of postulates, and the certainty of human knowledge is taken away. For if the laws of thought are merely postulates, all human knowledge is a postulate ; since the validity of the laws of thought is presupposed in every judgment that we make. And if these postulates are due merely to human needs, human knowledge ceases to be objectively valid until we can prove that what human needs force us to postulate is itself objectively valid ; and this we cannot do without assuming the validity of the laws of thought.

At first sight, Mr. Bradley's Intellectualism seems to be irreconcilable with the pragmatic position adopted by Professor Bosanquet in regard to the Laws of Thought. " In all cases," says the former, " that alone is valid for the intellect which in a calm moment it is incapable of doubting ;" and in the next sentence the intrinsic necessity of axioms seems to be admitted, for we read : " It is only that which for thought is compulsory and irresistible—only that which thought must assert in attempting to deny it—which is a valid foundation for metaphysical truth." [1] But Mr. Bradley's concession that "the theoretical axiom is the statement of an impulse to act in a certain manner" destroys the force of his intellectual criterion and seems to make it as subjective as that of Professor Bosanquet and the pragmatists. For, though theoretical needs are distinguished from practical needs, and though we are told that "thinking is the attempt to satisfy a special impulse," it is still a subjective and a psychological impulse that prompts us to think ; and though the attempt to think " implies an assumption about reality " which becomes ' our intellectual standard or axiom,' that assumption about reality *is* an assumption, the objective validity of which cannot be known, but is merely postulated.

§ 356. The subjectivity of axioms in Absolutism may be traced back to the Copernican Revolution of Kant. There are but two alternatives. Either the content of thought is determined by the object or it is determined by the structure of the mind ; and in the latter case it is subjective. And though the identification of Thought and Reality once more restores a certain objectivity to the content of our axiomatic principles as to the content of other thoughts ; it does so only again to deprive us of it by the doctrine that no truth short of the whole truth is really true. Axioms, like other single and isolated judgments, are but ' mutilated shreds of knowledge,' torn from a larger whole and liable to indefinite modification before they can be joined

[1] *Appearance and Reality,* p. 151.

up in the coherent system of Absolute Truth. Dr. Joachim acknowledges that this view is inconsistent with the ' obvious ' interpretation which we put upon ' true judgments,' and that the ordinary doctrine that what is once true is always true seems at first sight unanswerable. But, he urges, if this view of isolated judgments is false, it would be impossible to show that all partial truths are derived from the truth of the whole ; hence isolated judgments must be sacrificed. Personally, I should prefer to sacrifice the doctrine that truth is a whole, rather than have to mutilate my premisses in order to make them lead to the conclusion which I might desire to deduce. Dr. Joachim, however, has elected to hold fast to the Coherence-notion of truth at all costs, and so has sought about for some means of reconciling the doctrine that no isolated judgment can be true with the apparent fact that such judgments are true and persist in remaining true in spite of growth and development. Hence, he has discovered that isolated judgments on examination turn out to be practically meaningless.[1]

This I cannot admit. I am quite willing to grant, of course, that the proposition ' three threes are nine ' for the boy who is only just learning the multiplication table has only a ' minimum of meaning,' in the sense that he knows little of its *relations* to other arithmetical propositions of a more complex nature. Still the proposition has meaning and very definite meaning even for a small boy in a Preparatory School, provided he has been properly

[1] *Nature of Truth,* pp. 87 *et seq.*

taught, and has not merely learnt his tables like a parrot. It implies that he already knows something of the way in which numbers may be grouped and combined. Nor do I think that as the boy develops into a mathematician the proposition 'three threes are nine' undergoes any intrinsic modification. It is still the same item of knowledge that it always was, though the arithmetician knows *more about it*, because he knows its relation to other items of knowledge and its place in the general science of Arithmetic.

The doctrine that every item of knowledge is related to every other item of knowledge is true ; but to suppose that each item is *intrinsically* affected by its relations to other items, and, in consequence, changes as these other items become known, seems to lead to absurdity. It is difficult, for instance, to see how one's knowledge (*v.g.*) of the Constitution of Sparta can be affected by one's knowledge of the Law of Specific Gravity, or how one's knowledge of the multiplication table can be modified by what one learns later of the anatomy of the Amphioxus. No one dreams that 'isolated' judgments express the whole truth about reality, nor does anyone deny that as knowledge grows in any particular branch of science the judgments in which it is expressed acquire fuller significance. But this is very different from asserting that isolated judgments are *intrinsically* modified as knowledge grows, and is quite compatible with the facts of actual knowing, which the Coherence-theory is not. It is useless, however, to discuss the matter further, for it rests entirely upon the view that one takes of relations. If relations are a kind of physical nexus binding objects together and arising simultaneously and on the same level within an organic whole, then it is doubtless impossible to know an object without knowing its relations; but if the relations are essentially dependent upon the nature of the objects related, though not *vice versa* as well, then it *is* possible to know an object without knowing its relations; and, as those relations become known, one's previous notion of the object will not necessarily have to be changed, but will merely become larger, fuller and more significant.

§ 357. Closely connected with the Absolute theory of Truth is the absolute theory of Error. Error is defined by Mr. Bradley as " the qualification of Reality in such a way that in the result it has an inconsistent content; "[1] and by Dr. Joachim as " that form of ignorance which poses, to itself and to others, as indubitable knowledge, or that form of false thinking which unhesitatingly claims to be true, and in so claiming substantiates or completes its falsity."[2] There are no judgments which are false as such, says Dr. Joachim. The judgment '2 + 3 = 6' is no more false, as such, than a road is wrong *per se*. It is false because its meaning is part of a context of meaning, and a part which collides with other parts. The judgment is really 2 + 3 conceived under the conditions of the numerical system = 6.[3]

How the judgment 2 + 3 = 6 or any other judgment involving numbers can be conceived, or can have

---

[1] *Appearance and Reality*, p. 189.
[2] *The Nature of Truth*, p. 142.   [3] *Ibid.*, p. 143.

any meaning whatsoever apart from the numerical system, is more than I can understand. If such a judgment is made intelligibly and means anything at all it implies that the notions of 'units,' 'addition of units,' 'sums of units,' and 'equality' are already understood; and when these are understood (*i.e.*, as soon as it is possible to make the judgment at all) the assertion that $2+3=6$ at once becomes false; and false as such, so it seems to me, because between the notions which it involves there is an obvious contradiction.

§ 358. Mr. Bradley's view of error is somewhat less sceptical. He admits that " every judgment, whether positive or negative, and however frivolous in character, makes an assertion about Reality ; " and that " the content asserted cannot be altogether an error ; " though he adds that " its ultimate truth may quite transform its original meaning." [1] The expression 'quite transform its original meaning,' however, is clearly an exaggeration. The original meaning will have to be transformed *only in so far as it is erroneous*. This is implied in the doctrine of degrees of Truth and of Reality ; for we are distinctly told that " of two given appearances the one more wide or more harmonious is more real (and more true). It approaches nearer to a single, all-containing individuality. *To remedy its imperfections*, in other words, *we should have to make a smaller alteration*." [2]

But the real question is whether in a given claim to truth or in a system of such claims

[1] *Appearance and Reality*, p. 366.
[2] *Ibid.*, p. 364. (Italics mine.)

we can distinguish parts which will have to be modified from parts which will not ; or, in other words, whether we can locate our errors. And upon this question Realism and Absolutism are in violent antagonism. The absolutist with his theory that Reality is one organic whole in which each part is essentially dependent upon the rest, denies that any one part can be truly known until the whole is known, and so is forced to take up a sceptical attitude in regard to human knowledge and human truth. The realist, on the other hand, while admitting that the universe is a logical whole, or a whole such that each of its parts is systematically related to all the rest and would be apprehended as such by an intelligence which should be capable of understanding the whole universe, affirms that each part and each aspect of the universe expresses truly, though inadequately and incompletely, the systematic plan of the whole. He affirms that, were our knowledge complete, the relation between 3^2 and 9 would still be one of equality, and that the circumference of a circle would still be π times its diameter. And he does so on good grounds. For not only is there no evidence that any intrinsic change has taken place, or is likely to take place, in regard to judgments such as these ; but the absolutist in order to establish the contrary doctrine which is implied in the Coherence-notion, would have to prove that every relation of every object so modified *each and all its other relations* that unless every one of them was fully known, our knowledge of the rest would not only be inadequate and partial, but false ; and this he cannot do. New experience does sometimes render erroneous what was formerly taken to be true ; but this cannot be said to be a general rule, nor can we say that an increase of knowledge entirely destroys the validity of those interpretations we stigmatise as false. Often enough, as we have seen in a previous chapter, within a theory we can distinguish what may possibly be false from what is certainly true ; and in general, as our conception of things and their relations grows more and more systematic, we find that axioms and first principles, as well as facts, remain for the most part, unchanged, subordinate hypotheses and explanations the scope of which is comparatively narrow, alone being subject to modifications and reversals.

§ 359. But apart from the testimony of experience there is an *impasse* in Dr. Joachim's theory of truth, which, as we saw when discussing Absolutism from the metaphysical point of view,[1] no ingenuity on the part of absolutist has been able to eliminate or overcome. I refer to the difficulty, or, rather, the impossibility, of explaining metaphysically the relation of finite centres of experience to the Absolute Ground upon which they depend. In what way does the Absolute manifest itself in finite centres, and how, if our thoughts are wholly a manifestation of the Experience of the Absolute, can we reconcile human error with Absolute Truth ? We do make mistakes. We affirm that S is P when it is not P ; and to say that the error is removed when P is referred to a larger whole does not get rid of the falsity of our previous statement, a falsity which is

[1] cf. § 195.

inconceivable if the absolute is really responsible for
our thoughts. Indeed, Dr. Joachim frankly confesses that 'the reconciliation of the *modal* nature
of finite subjects with this self-assertive independence,' and 'the conception of the individuality
of the significant whole as a life timelessly self-
fulfilled through the opposition which it creates,
and in creating overcomes' are mysteries, and
mysteries which he does not attempt to solve. But
neither he nor any other absolutist seems to recognise that between the 'modal' nature of the finite
subject and its 'self-assertive independence,' between
a life timelessly self-fulfilled and lives which are
contingent and temporal, and between the creation
of something opposed and different and the overcoming of that opposition and difference, there is a
flat contradiction which can be solved only by
denying the fundamental assumptions upon which
it rests. This objection is, in my opinion, fatal to
Absolutism, and shows that the idea which it
endeavours to express is one-sided and full of
inconsistency. Absolutism has this in its favour,
that it appeals to our love of unity and to our desire
for union with the Divine ; and for this reason has
elicited the sympathy even of an analytic mind
such as that of the late Professor Sidgwick. But it
is vague and indefinite, and it fails to explain just
that which we all of us desire most to know—the
relation which holds between God and man. Its
failure, too, is not merely one of ignorance, but of
positive error. The conception of the finite mind
as a vehicle of the Eternal Consciousness, in which
the latter is ever trying in vain to realise and express

itself, seems to merge the individual in the Absolute. Man becomes merely a particular collection or synthesis of the thoughts of an Eternal Ego, a 'finite centre of experience' entirely dependent upon the Ground for its nature, its character, and even its individuality. Personality and Freedom are thus declared to be illusions, arising from the human point of view, instead of fundamental truths which every human mind is forced to recognise in the data of his experience ; while human knowledge, ever tinged by ' the confused mass of idiosyncrasies which distinguish this mind from that,' is, and is destined to remain, incomplete, and to an unascertainable extent erroneous.

CHAPTER XX.

THE NATURE OF PRAGMATIC TRUTH.

§ 360. Some time ago my attention was called to the writings of Georg Simmel, who, though his energies have been devoted, for the most part, to the study of Economics and to the history of philosophy, is justly regarded as one of Germany's leading pragmatists.[1] Between economical values and logical values Herr Simmel finds a resemblance which is not merely external, but deep-rooted in the very nature of value, and for this reason in the third chapter of his *Philosophie des Geldes,* he gives us a sketch of his views on truth, a sketch which is

[1] cf, *The Meaning of Truth,* p. 66,

extremely useful for our purposes, (because it provides us with a connecting link between the Relativism implicit in absolute truth and the Humanism which is the chief characteristic of pragmatic truth.) Indeed, Herr Simmel has given to pragmatic truth a philosophic setting which seems to present it in its true light, and to give one an appreciation of its real meaning, such as is difficult to obtain from the somewhat disconnected and more rhetorical utterances of Anglo-american pragmatists.

§ 361. Herr Simmel's standpoint is essentially physiological and anthropomorphic.[1] Like Dr. Schiller, he believes that *our* 'world' is due to a process whereby we attribute to objective reality forms that we find within our psycho-physical organism, in which an alternation between rest and motion, between anabolism and katabolism is the primary condition of life.[2]

(Then only do we think that we are qualified to enter as part of the universe, provided its form corresponds with the forms of our own inner nature.) Accordingly, we organise the irregular co-existences and sequences of our first impressions, in that we distinguish in an object its permanent and essential substance from its motions, colourings and changes whose comings and goings leave the constancy of its essence unchanged. Just as we believe that we perceive within ourselves a psychical being whose existence and character depends upon itself

[1] cf. *supra*, § 205.
[2] The following paragraphs have been translated from the third chapter of Herr Simmel's *Philosophie des Geldes*, pp. 58 *et seq.* The aim of the translator has been to give the sense, rather than an exact literal rendering, of the author; and many phrases and passages of minor importance have, of course, been omitted.

alone, and distinguish this from those thoughts, occurrences, and developments which are what they are only through reference to others ; so we look in the world for substances, magnitudes, and forces whose being and meaning is grounded in themselves alone, and distinguish these from all relative determinations which are what they are only through comparison, contact, or reaction with others. . . . [Thus grows up the distinction between *absolute* and *relative*.] And though in our psycho-physical being, motion and rest, activity *ad extra* and aggregation *ad intra* are bound together in such a way that they find in one another their actuality and their meaning, yet it is the ' rest ' and the ' substantial ' that we find peculiarly full of value. Hence in the objective world also we look for the self-sufficient and the self-grounded, for substances, spirits, things in themselves, and in this way gain fixed points which direct us in the confused jumble of phenomena and give us the objective counterpart of that which we represent in ourselves as our values and definitives.[1]

This search for an absolute, however, is only a preliminary stage which must be got over by thinking. [Thus] it is a fundamental characteristic of modern science that it understands phenomena no longer through and as special substances, but as movements whose grounds move further and further away into propertylessness ; that it seeks to express the qualities attached to things as quantitative, and therefore as relatively defined ; that it teaches instead of organic, physical, ethical and social forms, a restless evolution in which each element acquires a place confined and determinable only through its relation with its before and its after; that it renounces the actual essence of things as such, and contents itself with the establishing of relations which appear between ' things ' and our minds, as seen from the standpoint of the latter.[2]

§ 362. On the other hand, all this seems to postulate a fixed point, an absolute truth. . . . The flux and relativity of physical processes must not affect the pre-

---

[1] pp. 58, 59. cf. *The Meaning of Truth*, pp. 61 *et seq.*   [2] p. 60,

suppositions and rules according to which we first decide whether our actual knowledge really bears this or another character. The purely psychological origin into which all objective knowledge has to be analysed, needs fixed axioms which themselves cannot have a purely psychological significance. . . . The truth of any proposition can be known only by reason of criteria which draw their legitimation from yet higher ones, so that there is built up a series of items of knowledge one above the other, each of which is valid only on condition of another. Yet these series—lest they hang in the air, or rather in order to be possible at all—must somewhere have an ultimate ground, a highest court of appeal, which shall give legitimation to all the following links in the chain without needing such itself. This is the *schema* under which all actual knowledge can be co-ordinated. But what this absolute knowledge is, we can never know, for the process of analysis into higher principles can never come to an end. There is always the possibility of discovering that what we have taken to be an ultimate proposition is really conditioned by another, as the history of knowledge has shown times without number.[1] We certainly have axioms which cannot be proved and upon which all derivative proofs depend ; but thought stops with these only until it can get beyond to something higher which on its side shall prove the hitherto axiomatic.[2]

Again, if one pursues the proof of a proposition into its grounds, and these again into theirs, one often finds that the proof is possible only provided one assumes the first proposition which was to be proved, as already proved. . . . [And] if we do not want to stop dogmatically and once for all at a truth which needs no proof, we had better take this *reciprocity of mutual proof* as *the fundamental form of thought* and of completed knowledge. Thus knowledge is a process which hangs freely in the air, so to speak, and of which the elements determine reciprocally their positions, just as masses of matter do theirs in virtue of their weight. And this is

[1] pp. 60, 61. [2] p. 63.

II

no mere coincidence, but a necessity peculiar to our minds, which know truth through proof, and so must either put off its knowability indefinitely, or twist it round in a circle. For one proposition is true only in relation to another, which other is true ultimately only in relation to the first. Thus the whole of knowledge is as little true as the whole of matter is heavy. It is only of the relations of the parts among themselves that these properties are valid. Of the whole they cannot be predicated without a contradiction.[1]

§ 363. Starting from a physiological point of view, Herr Simmel has led us on to a doctrine of truth which is very similar to the Coherence-theory of Dr. Joachim, except that he lays the chief emphasis on the relativity of the parts rather than on the unity of the whole. But Herr Simmel does not stop here. He finds that the relativity which exists between the inner elements of knowledge is but part of a wider relativity which embraces both the theoretical and the practical interests of life. (In knowing we do not copy reality, but all presentation is a function of a special psycho-physical organisation.)

From the vast difference which is to be found between the *weltbilder* of the insect with its facet-eyes, of the eagle with a power of sight the keenness of which is inconceivable, of the *proteus anguinus* with eyes scarce developed at all, of ourselves and of countless others, we are forced to conclude that no one copies the outer world in its objectively existing form. Our representations are *directive* of our practical life, of actions through which we place ourselves in connection with the world as it stands relatively independent of our subjectively determined ideas. [And similarly for animals], though their actions are determined by very different forms of the same world. [In both cases] actions undertaken

---

[1] pp. 63, 64.

by reason of ideas which certainly in no way resemble objectively existing beings, obtain from the latter results of such a calculability, purposiveness, certainty, that it could not be greater even if we possessed a knowledge of objective relations as they are in themselves ; whilst other actions, viz., those which result from ' false ' ideas, result only in real injury.[1]

What, then, can truth mean [asks Herr Simmel], which is wholly different for the animals and for us, which in no way corresponds with objective reality, and which nevertheless leads to the desired results as surely as if this were the case ?[2] [His reply is :] Each species has an organisation suited to its special purpose in life. Hence whether an action prompted by a presentation will lead to useful consequences cannot be determined by the content of that presentation ; but will depend upon the result to which the presentation leads as a real process within the organism acting in co-operation with the rest of its psycho-physical powers and in reference to the special life-exigencies of each. If, then, we say that man performs actions which support and further life on the basis of true ideas, and actions which are destructive of life on the basis of false ideas, *truth, which is different for each species endowed with consciousness and for none is a mirror of the thing in itself, can only mean that idea which in connection with the entire and specific organism its faculties and its needs, leads to useful results.* Originally an idea is not useful because it is true ; but we give the honourable name of ' true ' to those ideas which, working in us as real forces or processes, lead to useful conduct. Hence there are, in the main, as many specifically distinct truths as there are specifically distinct organisations and life exigencies. The sense-form which for the insect is ' truth,' would clearly not be so for the eagle ; since that very sense-form on the basis of which the insect in connection with his inner and outer constellations acts usefully, would for the eagle in connection with his lead to wholly meaningless and destructive actions.[3]

[1] p. 64.   [2] p. 64.   [3] pp. 65, 66.

§ 364. That man now has an aggregate of fixed and normative truths is due to his having always exercised a choice in regard to the countless ideas which arise psychologically within him, according to whether the actions which they prompted led to useful or harmful consequences. He has no other criterion of truth except that it leads to the desired consequences. But inasmuch as by means of this process of selection there has been bred within him certain permanently useful ways of perceiving, these together form a *kingdom of the theoretical*, which now acts as an inner criterion determining the relevance of all fresh ideas. Thus individual items of knowledge reciprocally support one another [*v.g.*, in Geometry] in that norms and facts, once fixed, serve as a proof for others. . . . But the whole itself has validity only in relation to determinate psycho-physical organisms, to their conditions of life, and to the useful nature of their actions.[1]

This notion of truth as the relation of ideas to one another, but as belonging to none as an absolute quality, applies also to the idea of a single object. Kant was right when he said that out of the chaotic manifold of our sense-impressions we pick out individual impressions as belonging to one another and group them into units, which we describe as ' objects.' An object is nothing but a totality of impressions gathered into a unity, and its unity is nothing but the functional inter-connection, inter-relation, and inter-dependence of the individual impressions and perception-materials. . . . As the unity of a social body means the forces of interaction and cohesion exercised by the individuals which compose it, or, in other words, the dynamical relation between them ; so the mental realisation of the unity of an object implies nothing more than interaction between the elements which go to form the percept of it. In knowledge, just as in art, isolated elements are neither true nor false in themselves, for they do not copy reality ; but their truth consists in the relation of the elements one to another.[2]

[1] p. 66.   [2] p. 67.

§ 365. One may formulate Relativism in respect to the principles of knowledge thus : Constitutive axioms expressing once and for all the being of things must be transformed into regulative norms which are merely landmarks for advancing knowledge. The highest and most ultimate abstractions, unifications and integrations of thought must give up their dogmatic claim to final knowledge. Instead of saying things *are* so and so, we should rather say knowledge works *as if* things were so and so. And in this way it is possible to express the mode and manner of the relation of our knowledge to the world. For the constitutive assertions which attempt to fix the being of things having been changed into heuristic principles which only profess to determine our ways of knowing, clearly it is possible for contradictory principles to be valid at one and the same time, since we may use each methodologically just as we may use either the inductive or the deductive method. Thus dogmatic fixity must give place to the living, flowing process of knowledge. Only if we regard ultimate principles not as limits mutually contradictory, but as ways to knowledge, inter-related, inter-dependent, and mutually completing one another, can we ever attain unity in knowledge.[1]

Of the relativity of ultimate principles Herr Simmel gives many examples :

Our thought is so constructed that it must strive after unity, . . . but as soon as this unity is reached, as in the Substance of Spinoza, it is at once apparent that we cannot use it for the understanding of the world without a second principle. Monism thus passes beyond itself into Dualism and Pluralism, and so we proceed from the many to the one and from the one to the many. Neither principle can be regarded as dogmatic or constitutive ; both are heuristic, relative and mutually complementary. The monistic principle bids us unify every manifold *as if* we were going to end in absolute Monism ; the pluralistic

[1] pp. 68, 69.

principle bids us *not* stop with unity, but analyse it into simpler elements and generating pairs of forces *as if* the end were to be a pluralistic one.[1]

Similarly, in political, social and religious sciences we can only understand the present through a knowledge and understanding of the past ; while the past of which only fragments, dumb witnesses, and more or less uncertain reports and traditions have come down to us, will be intelligible and living only through the experience of the immediate present.[2] Again, in Psychology the knowledge of the Ego is our only means of knowing the soul that lies behind mere sound-producing and gesticulating automata ; while our knowledge of the Ego, and in particular our distinction of it into an observing and an observed part, is due to our knowledge of other things.[3] And in like manner the antithesis between the *a priori* and experience, and in Economics the antithesis between the *a priori* method and the historical method, will be solved if we regard both as heuristic principles in the application of which each seeks its ultimate ground in the other.[4] (This interactive self-dependence and inter-dependence of opposite pairs of principles is not a mere compromise, but rather opens up to each principle an unlimited sphere of action.) And though of these principles each remains somewhat subjective, by means of the relativity of their application is expressed the objective meaning of things. Elements of which each is in content subjective, obtain or determine by means of this reciprocal reference what we call objectivity. Single objects by the cohesion and inter-action of sense-impressions, ' personality ' by reciprocal associations and apperceptions, ' right ' by the counterbalancing of the subjective interests of the individual, all acquire their objective value. Thus the methods of knowledge may be only subjective and heuristic, and yet inasmuch as each finds in the other its complement and through this its legitimation, they approximate gradually to the ideal of objective truth.[5]

(Truth, then, consists in a relation of reciprocity within

[1] p. 69. [2] p. 70. [3] p. 70. [4] p. 71. [5] p. 72.

a complexus of ideas which are mutually demonstrable one by means of the other.) . . . The truth of the greater number of our ideas is at any given moment taken for granted, and the decision we come to in regard to the truth of a new idea will depend upon whether it harmonises with or contradicts the ideas already possessed ; and, again, one of the ideas belonging to this complex may become questionable and over it the majority will decide. . . . (The reason why we do not notice the relativity of truth is because of the immense quantitative disproportion between the actually questionable and the mass of ideas which we regard as true,) just as for a long time the attraction of the apple for the earth passed unnoticed and all that we observed was the attraction of the earth for the apple. . . . (Nevertheless] relativity is of the very essence of truth.) . . . It is not a patchwork, nor yet an added determination which weakens the notion of truth otherwise determined ; but it is the specific property in virtue of which objects of desire become valuable. (Truth exists in spite of its being a relation. Indeed it exists precisely because it is one.[1])

§ 366. The view of truth set forth in the preceding paragraphs does not differ essentially from the doctrine of other pragmatists. Herr Simmel's point of view and consequently the general tone and emphases of his doctrine may be different ; but, apart from this personal tinge, his theory of truth is fundamentally the same as that of the Anglo-american pragmatist. Ideas are set over against reality, and to them alone the property of truth belongs. But truth does not copy reality. Rather it is a mental function which has proved itself useful in dealing with an objective environment, and has thus become habitual. This latter point—truth

[1] pp. 72, 73.

conceived as a way of thinking or perceiving which has become habitual on account of its utility—is hardly noticed in the essentially psychological account of truth given by Professor James, though we have already come across it in the thoroughly pragmatic philosophy of M. Abel Rey, and shall find that it is also characteristic of Dr. Schiller's view. So, too, is the relativity of truth, though on this point some divergence of opinion is manifest. In any case, both these characteristics of Herr Simmel's theory may, I think, justly be regarded as corollaries to the general pragmatic doctrine ; and in other respects Herr Simmel is, as Professor James has said, a genuine pragmatist. It will be well, however, to consider more in detail the leading characteristics of truth as conceived by the leaders of the pragmatic movement in America and England.

§ 367. Professor James has again and again assured us that epistemologically he is a realist. " Our beliefs are in realities, and if no realities are there our beliefs are false." [1] Consequently he starts from the standpoint of Dualism.[2] On the one side we have objective facts, on the other side claims ; on the one side ideas and judgments, on the other side reality ; and truth is, as common-sense regards it, a peculiar sort of relation between these two poles.[3] But in a philosophy of Pure Experience reality is identical with experience. Hence, although Professor James postulates " a standing reality independent of the idea that knows it," [4] we find him frequently substituting ior

---

[1] *The Meaning of Truth*, pp. 241, 242. [2] *Ibid.*, p. 217.
[3] *Ibid.*, Preface, p. xix., and p. 163. [4] *Ibid.*, p. 158.

" reality " some form of sense-experience—sensations or a percept.[1] Thus, speaking of the humanistic development of Pragmatism, he says that " by ' reality ' Humanism means nothing more than the other conceptual or perceptual experiences (including of course any amount of empirical reality independent of the knower) with which a given present experience may find itself in point of fact mixed up."[2] And it is only on this hypothesis of the identity of reality and experience that he is able to get rid of the *salto mortale* of the common-sense realist, and to maintain his thesis that " the truth of our mental operations must always be an intra-experiential affair."[3] Experiences know one another and represent one another. They do not know or represent realities outside of ' consciousness.' In experiences of the acquaintance-type " object and subject *fuse* in the fact of ' presentation ' or sense-perception."[4] And though the philosopher gets beyond this stage—which Professor James calls (wrongly, I think) the stage of common-sense—and ' interpolates ' or ' extrapolates ' his realities, if a humanist, he still regards them as experiences of some kind or other, actual or possible.[5] Experiences of the acquaintance-type are ultimate *thats* or facts of being, and to these it is the function of conceptual experiences to lead. Truth thus means, says Professor James, " the relation of less fixed parts of experience (predicates) to other relatively more fixed parts (subjects) ; and we are not required to seek it in a relation of experience, as such, to anything

---

[1] *Ibid.*, p. 81.   [2] *Ibid.*, p. 100.   [3] *Ibid.*, p. 133.
[4] *Ibid.*, pp. 127, 128, and cf. p. 103.   [5] *Ibid.*, pp. 129 *et seq.*

beyond itself." [1]   It is "a relation, not of our ideas
to non-human realities, but of conceptual parts of
our experience to sensational parts;" [2]   while
"cognition, whenever we take it concretely, means
determinate 'ambulation,' through intermediaries
(*i.e.*, intervening experiences) from a *terminus a quo*
to a *terminus ad quem*." [3]   In a similar sense must be
understood the following remark of Professor
Dewey :

> Truth and falsity are not properties of any experience
> or thing, in and of itself or in its first intention ; *but of
> things where the problem of assurance consciously enters
> in. Truth and falsity* present themselves as significant
> facts only in situations in which specific meanings and
> their already experienced fulfilments and non-fulfil-
> ments are intentionally compared and contrasted with
> reference to the question of worth, as to the reliability
> of meaning or class of meanings. [4]

§ 368.   What Professor James calls an 'ambu-
latory' process from idea through definite tracts of
experience to some other experience, actual or
possible, is of the very essence of pragmatic truth. [5]
And from this two important consequences follow.
First, truth can be both defined and described in
terms of experience. [6]   It is a process.   Truth is
made. [7]   Secondly, that process is a *particular* one,
and varies with the particular case in hand.   Verity
in act means *verifications* (in the plural). [8]

To the description of the process by which truth
is made and in which, for the pragmatist, its nature

---

[1] *Ibid.*, p. 70.   [2] *Ibid.*, p. 82.   [3] *Ibid.*, p. 142.
[4] *Mind*, N.S. 59, p. 305.   [5] *The Meaning of Truth*, p. 234.
[6] *Ibid.*, pp. 234, 235, 142, 143, and Preface, p. xiv.
[7] *Ibid.*, p. 235, and *Pragmatism*, pp. 201, 218.
[8] *Ibid.*, pp. 212, 235.

consists, Professor James has devoted a very considerable portion both of *Pragmatism* and of *The Meaning of Truth*. Yet the very particularity of the process makes the task of the *psychological* epistemologist an extremely difficult one ; and, despite his valiant attempts, Professor James' descriptions are considerably bewildering and, at times, decidedly vague. He defines truth, in the first place, as property of ideas, in virtue of which they are said to ' agree ' with reality.[1] But ' agreement ' does not always mean ' copying.' It is only our ideas of sensible things that copy reality.[2] And even here not always, but only when the ' idea ' in question is an image. Copying is not essential to truth.[3] " In strict theory the mental terms themselves need not answer to the real terms in the sense of severally copying them, symbolic terms being enough, if only the real dates and places be copied." Indeed, " much even of common descriptive truth is couched in verbal symbols." And " if our symbols *fit* the world, in the sense of determining our expectations rightly, they may even be the better for not copying its terms." [4] But if, in the realm of phenomenal fact, there is no need of copying in every case, still less is there any need of assuming archetypes in the abstract spheres of Geometry and Logic. Their objects can be better interpreted as being created step by step by men, as fast as they successively conceive them. Triangles and genera are of our own production. They are improvised

[1] *Pragmatism*, p. 198.
[2] *Ibid.*, p. 199.
[3] *Ibid.*, pp. 213, 235, and *The Meaning of Truth*, pp.79 *et seq.*
[4] *The Meaning of Truth*, p. 82.

human ' artefacts ; ' and precisely because they are so, their relations are eternal ; we can keep them invariant if we choose.[1]

§ 369. A true idea, then, for Professor James, is not necessarily one that copies reality. A symbol which *fits* the world, a substitute which works practically, an abstract concept which enlarges mentally our momentary experiences by *adding* to them the consequences conceived, a thought which gets in ' touch ' with reality by innumerable paths of verification,[2] even a name, may be true.[3] In each individual case " the ' workableness ' which ideas must have, in order to be true, means particular workings, physical or intellectual, actual or possible, which they may set up from next to next inside of concrete experience." [4] And this working, in which the truth of an idea *consists*, is essentially " a concrete working in the actual experience of human beings, among their ideas, feelings, perceptions, beliefs and acts, as well as among the physical things of their environment, and the relations must be understood as being possible as well as actual." [5] Consequently the familiar terms, which common-sense and the intellectualist apply to the truth-relation, have to be re-translated and re-interpreted by the pragmatist in an experiential sense. We ' correspond ' in *some* way, says Professor James, with anything with which we enter into any relation at all, whether it be a thing of which we produce an

---

[1] *Ibid.*, pp. 82, 83, and cf. *Pragmatism*, pp. 209 *et seq.*
[2] *Ibid.*, pp. 208, 218, 248, 214.
[3] *Pragmatism*, p. 213.
[4] *The Meaning of Truth*, Preface, p. xiv.
[5] *Ibid.*, p. 262.

exact copy, or which we feel as an existent in a
certain place ; a demand which we obey without
knowing anything more about it than its push; a
proposition which we let pass without contradicting
it ; a relation between two things, upon the first of
which we act so as to bring ourselves out where the
second will be ; or something inaccessible, for which
we substitute a hypothetical object, having the
same consequences and therefore enabling us to
cipher out real results.¹ / To ' represent ' reality,
again, means *either* to be substitutable for it in our
thinking, because the experience that represents leads
to the same associates ; *or* to ' point to it ' through
a chain of other experiences that either intervene or
may intervene.²) While to ' agree ' with a reality
means " to be guided either straight up to it or into
its surroundings, or to be put into such working
touch with it as to handle either it or something
connected with it better than if we disagreed—
better, either intellectually or practically." ³

Actual verification, however, is not necessary in
every case. " Indirectly verifying processes may be
true as well as full verification-processes." ⁴

That on innumerable occasions men do substitute
truth *in posse* or verifiability for verification or truth in
act, is a fact to which no one attributes more importance
than the pragmatist : he emphasises the practical utility of
such a habit. But he does not on that account consider
truth *in posse*,—truth not alive enough ever to have
been asserted or questioned or contradicted,—to be the
metaphysically prior thing, to which truths in act are
tributary and subsidiary.⁵

¹ *Ibid.*, p. 67.   ² *Ibid.*, p. 132.   ³ *Pragmatism*, pp. 212, 213.
⁴ *Ibid.*, pp. 208, 209.   ⁵ *The Meaning of Truth*, p. 205.

For one truth-process completed there are a million in our lives that function in this state of nascency ; [that] turn us *towards* direct verification ; [that] lead us into the *surroundings* of the objects they invisage ; and then, if everything runs on harmoniously, we are so sure that verification is possible that we omit it, and are usually justified by all that happens. Truth lives, in fact, for the most part on a credit system. Our thoughts and beliefs ' pass,' so long as nothing challenges them, just as bank-notes pass so long as nobody refuses them. . . . You accept my verification of one thing, I yours of another. . . . But beliefs verified concretely by *some-body* are the posts of the whole superstructure.[1]

Truth-processes are also useful. In *The Meaning of Truth* ' utility ' is not so prominent as it is in the writings of other pragmatists, though Professor James by no means overlooks this aspect of pragmatic truth. In *Pragmatism*, forinstance, he tells us that " the possession of true thoughts means everywhere the possession of invaluable instruments of action." [2]   " True is the name for whatever idea starts the verification process, useful is the name for its completed function in experience." [3]   " Primarily, and on the common-sense level, the truth of a state of mind means this function of *a leading that is worth while.*" [4]   " ' *The true,*' *to put it very briefly, is only the expedient in the way of our thinking, just as ' the right ' is only the expedient in our way of behaving.*" [5]   But in *The Meaning of Truth* Professor James carefully points out that in saying that ' the meaning of any proposition can always be brought down to some particular consequence in our future practical experience, whether passive or active,' the

[1] *Pragmatism*, pp. 207, 208.   [2] *Ibid.*, p. 202.
[3] *Ibid.*, p. 204.   [4] *Ibid.*, p. 205.   [5] *Ibid.*, p. 222.

point of the statement lies " rather in the fact that
the experience must be particular than in the fact
that it must be ' active,'—by ' active ' meaning
here ' practical ' in the narrow literal sense. Particular consequences may be of a theoretical nature."[1]
Hence the ' cash-value ' of truth in experiential terms
is that :

*True ideas are those that we can assimilate, validate,
corroborate and verify. False ideas are those that we can
not.* That is the practical difference it makes to us to
have true ideas ; that, therefore, is the meaning of
truth, for it is all that truth is known-as. [2]

§ 370. Dr. Schiller takes a wider view of truth
than that set forth by Professor James. He
considers it in its historic setting. Consequently his
emphases are somewhat different, and more akin to
those of Herr Simmel's exposition of the doctrine
of truth. *The Riddles of the Sphinx* is a philosophy
of Evolution, and evolutionary ideas permeate and
affect the whole of Dr. Schiller's epistemological
speculations. Applying these ideas in *Axioms as
Postulates* to the fundamental principles of human
thought, he concludes that these are not axiomatic,
but postulatory in character. Generalising the
doctrine in *Humanism,* Dr. Schiller applies it to
every sphere of human knowledge, to Logic, to
Metaphysics, to Ethics, and to Religion. In all
these spheres of human thought, he says, the method
is the same, viz., the postulation of hypotheses and
their verification in experience, differences being due
chiefly to variations in the mode and extent of the
verification.[3]

[1] *The Meaning of Truth,* p. 210.
[2] *Pragmatism,* p. 201.   [3] cf. Preface to *Humanism,*

Now, in the evolution of life, and still more so in the evolution of human experience and human modes of thought, the supreme idea which governs the whole is not that of the ' real ' or of the ' true,' but of the ' good.' All life is purposive. It is purpose that prompts man to postulate ; guided by it that he experiments ; under its influence that he evaluates results. Pure reason is a pure figment : the practical use which has developed it must have stamped itself upon its inmost structure, even if it has not moulded it out of pre-rational instincts. And this being so, we must bear in mind that all our realities are related to the ends of our *practical* life ; that " human valuations hold sway over every region of our experience, and cannot validly be eliminated from the contemplation of any reality that we know." " Our knowing is driven and guided at every step by our subjective interests, our desires, our needs and our ends. Hence our effort, determined by our powers and will to know, enters as a necessary and irradicable factor into whatever revelation of reality we can attain." " That the ' real ' has a determinate nature which the knowing reveals but does not affect, is a gratuitous assumption incapable of rational defence." [1]

From this humanistic and evolutionary view of knowledge, it follows (1) that theory is subordinate to practice, the ' true ' to the ' good ; ' and (2) that the ' true' is identical with the ' useful.' In both these respects it seems to me that Dr. Schiller goes further than his colleague, Professor James. He does not ignore theory or deny its value ; but that

---

[1] *Humanism*, pp. 1-11.

value in the end is practical. His position is, as he himself has pointed out, the reverse of the Platonic view that action presupposes knowledge, and that the ' true ' is the source of the ' good.' He makes action primary ; knowledge is always derivative, secondary, subservient, useful. It is not sufficient to say that θεωρία is πράξις, in the sense that it is a characteristic of human activity. The true is the true for us *as practical* beings.[1] In the second of Dr. Schiller's essays in *Humanism*, the practical aspect of truth is even more prominent. There he endeavours to establish the thesis that ' whatever is true is useful ;' and all exceptions are ruled out of court on the ground that either the utility of the apparent truth has not yet been discovered, or else it is really useless knowledge, and therefore no truth at all.

Utility, therefore, is of the essence of the truth-relation for Dr. Schiller, as it is for Herr Simmel. He is also equally explicit in his rejection of the copy-view of truth ; though he rejects it on different grounds.[2] Unlike Professor James, he does not even accept *provisionally* the Dualism of Common-sense, but starts from a ' chaotic experience ' or '*primary* reality,' in which, as yet, there is no distinction of ' appearance ' and ' reality,' but from which, as from ' the raw material of the cosmos,' ' real fact ' and ' true reality ' are, in course of time, experimentally evolved.[3] ' Reality,' as we ordinarily

[1] *Ibid.*, p. 30.
[2] cf. *Ibid.*, pp. 45, 46 ; *Studies in Humanism*, p. 425 ; and *Mind*, N.S. 72, p. 573.
[3] *Ibid.*, pp. 186, 187 ; cf. pp. 428 *et seq.* ; and *The Meaning of Truth*, p. 242.

JJ

understand it, ' does not pre-exist the cognitive functioning,' but is a fact within knowing, immanently deposited or ' precipitated ' by thought.[1] Both Dr. Schiller and Professor James regard truth from the standpoint of experience, in which it and its object alike are immanent. For both, the aim of the pragmatist is to describe as best he can ' the continuous cognitive process,' to trace out the actual ' making of truth,' and thence to derive ' the method of determining the nature of truth.' [2] But, for Dr. Schiller, the *ratio essendi* of the cognitive process is not merely to engender systems of truth and of reality, but " to refine them into more and more adequate means *for the control of our experience.*" [3] He does not under-estimate the particularity and the experiential character of truth; but, owing, I think, chiefly to his essentially genetic standpoint, he lays still more stress upon the active and practical aspect of the making of truth, or, in other words, upon its utility. The consequences by which truth-claims are validated, he insists, must be both ' practical ' and ' good : ' ' practical ' in that sooner or later they affect our action ; ' good ' in that they further our interests and satisfy our purpose.[4] Truth, in short, is that peculiar kind of utility which belongs to an idea, or results from the functioning of an idea.

§ 371. The emphasis thus laid on the practical value of truth influences Dr. Schiller's views on abstract truth, which he seems to treat with somewhat less courtesy than Professor James. An

---

[1] *Ibid.*, p. 426, and cf. pp. 182, 183.
[2] *Ibid.*, p. 5. [3] *Ibid.*, p. 426, [4] *Ibid.*, pp. 6, 7.

abstract truth, until it is applied, is a mere claim which "must always be regarded with suspicion ; and if it will not (or cannot) submit to verification, is not properly true at all. Its truth is at best potential, its meaning null or unintelligible, or at most conjectural and dependent on an unfulfilled condition." "Truths must be *used* to become true, and (in the end) to stay true." A purely formal logic is little more than "solemn trifling ; " and even the truths of arithmetic and geometry are not fully true until they are applied ; and they will not apply in every case. The honourable predicate of ' true ' should be "reserved for what has victoriously sustained its claim." "*Real* truths must have shown themselves to be *useful ;* they must have been applied to some problem of actual knowing, by usefulness in which they were tested and verified." [1] Dr. Schiller does not, of course, deny, any more than does Herr Simmel, either the value or the validity of abstract systems of truth ; but, regarding such systems from an evolutionary and pragmatic stand-point as products of human thought slowly evolved to the end that man may more easily and more successfully deal with his environment, his tendency is to make both their value and their validity depend upon the practically useful purposes which they serve.

Closely connected with this point is another on which Dr. Schiller's views coincide to a large extent with those of the German pragmatist. We cannot determine the utility of a truth without examination,

[1] *Ibid.*, pp. 8, 9 ; 112, 113 ; 144, 145. (Italics, where used, are mine.)

just as we cannot at once decide upon the expediency of a certain line of conduct. We must first select our truth, whether it be a general doctrine, a principle, or a fact, and then test it by experiment.[1] A claim to truth, whether it be on the level of perception or on the higher level of thought, must be allowed to work ; for only thus can it be validated. It is only when a mode of perception or of thought has become more or less habitual, only when it has, by a long series of successful experiments, proved itself a useful instrument enabling us to act more easily and more rapidly in the way best suited to the furtherance of life, that it becomes a *true* mode of perceiving or thinking. Regarded from this point of view, we may say, I think, that truth is for Dr. Schiller, as for other pragmatists, a useful habit. Human knowledge and human truth consist in certain habits of perception and of thought, which are, as M. Rey puts it, *les résultantes nécessaires et les seules possibles des conditions dans lesquelles elles ont été contractées—la science, c'est nous.*[2]

It is clear, however, that one of the fundamental needs of our nature is that we should be able to communicate with our fellow-men ; and, to do this, we must perceive and think and live more or less in the same way as they do. Hence the social factor plays no small part in the building up of habit and in the making of truth. Society exercises a severe control over the intellectual and the perceptual, as

---

[1] ' *Axioms as Postulates,*' §§ 1, 2 and 24 ; *Studies in Humanism,* pp. 186, 187.
[2] *La Théorie de la Physique,* p. 395.

well as the moral, eccentricities of its members.
Only some of the truths which we, as individuals,
deem valuable come to be recognised by society,
and so to be regarded as ‘ objective.’ Similarly, in
the lower sphere of sense-experience, those who
have managed to perceive things in practically the
same way, have prospered at the expense of those
who could not ; and hence certain ways of perceiving
have become habitual and more or less common
throughout the race. As our experience grows, we
adapt ourselves to our environment and to one
another ; but the process is none the less practical,
useful and teleological throughout. Whether our
adaptation be objective or intra-subjective, the
determining factor of survival and permanence is
that it should lead to useful, practical consequences.[1]

§ 372. One other point in regard to the relation of
Dr. Schiller’s views to those of Herr Simmel is
deserving of mention. Both are agreed that truth
is relative to our faculties. Dr. Schiller, in fact,
frankly adopts the Protagorean principle that man
is the measure of all things ; a principle which is
capable, he says, of a two-fold interpretation. In
the individual sense it means that “ Whatever
appears to each, that really is for him ; ” and in the
generic sense it means that “ reality for us is relative
to our faculties.” [2] But Dr. Schiller says little or
nothing of that other aspect of truth’s relativity,
upon which Herr Simmel insists so much, viz., the
relativity of truths *inter se*. True, in a chapter [3]

---

[1] cf. *Humanism*, pp. 31 *et seq. ; Studies in Humanism*, p. 153.
[2] *Studies in Humanism*, pp. 33, 34.
[3] *Ibid.*, chap. xviii.

dealing with the relation of the postulate of Freedom
to that of complete Determinism, he treats these
principles as to some extent reciprocal and complementary.[1]   But this is the only place, so far as I am
aware, where the reciprocity of truth is touched
upon.   To Herr Simmel, then, belongs the honour of
having discovered this aspect of pragmatic truth ;
though it is, I think, a corollary to the doctrine that
truth is a value, and that its value is primarily
useful or practical.

CHAPTER XXI.

THE VALUE OF PRAGMATIC TRUTH.

§ 373.   The account of truth given in the last
chapter may be regarded from two points of view.
We may regard it as an account of the psychological
processes and habits which underlie the ' making ' of
truth, or we may regard it as an account of the
nature of truth.   Herr Simmel has described in his
own way many of the psychological characteristics
of knowledge.   We do seek in objective experience
for fixed points round which we group qualities and
relations, for in order to acquire knowledge we must
attend first to one object and then to another.   And,
again, we analyse and synthesise ; we seek for unity,
and within the unity look for multiplicity.   Axioms,
too, and other habits of mind function in the acquisition of fresh knowledge.   We subsume under

---

[1] cf. Professor James' treatment of Unity and Plurality.
Pragmatism, pp. 129 *et seq.*

general ideas and general laws, and we apply principles and criteria almost automatically. We exercise selection in the apperception of new ideas. We assent to fresh truths when they harmonise with the old; and we reject ideas and propositions which fail thus to harmonise with previous knowledge. We are reluctant to admit more than a minimum of modification in what we already know ; and when a truth which we accept is called in question we refuse to sacrifice it, because it is implied in what we still hold to be certain. And, lastly, we apply our knowledge to practical purposes ; we use it in order to adapt ourselves to our environment and to promote the advance of civilisation. All these are psychological facts. But the question is whether we have here the clue to the essential nature of truth, to its real significance. Are these processes of the very essence of truth, or are they merely its psychological conditions and its practical consequences ? When we say that truth is " an idea which in connection with the entire and specific organism, its faculties and needs, leads to useful results," are we describing the nature of truth, or merely its relations and its properties ? The question is of vital importance for the theory of knowledge, for if we must answer with the pragmatist that truth is a useful habit and nothing more than a useful habit, knowledge, in the strict sense of that term has ceased to exist, and in its place we have something which is largely subjective and which in no way reveals to us the nature of reality.

§ 374. Herr Simmel rejects the ' mirror ' view of truth, and with it Realism. So apparently do

pragmatists in general. But when one examines
the arguments which have led to this renunciation
—that is, if the pragmatist has renounced Realism
and not merely mutilated it and made it obscure
and ambiguous—one finds that for the most part
they are reducible to the stock objections already
discussed in Chapter XIV. To these, however,
Herr Simmel adds one of his own. ⟨Animals perceive
things differently from what we do ; hence they
cannot be said to mirror reality in their percepts,
but the latter must be regarded as the products of
their special psycho-physical organisms the habits
of which are gradually formed by the repetition of
actions and processes which have led to beneficial
results.

This argument hardly disproves the correspondence-notion of truth. In the first place, animals do
not appear to make ' judgments,' and so present no
' claims ' to truth. Secondly, we know nothing
whatsoever of the psychoses which accompany or
follow the retinal impressions of eagles, insects, and
amphibia ; and so cannot tell for certain whether
they do or do not correspond with the objects
perceived. ⟩ But if it is legitimate to argue from the
retinal impressions themselves, animals, in spite of
their optical peculiarities, do seem to ' mirror ' the
real world in a way similar to our own, though
sometimes more and sometimes less accurately.
The difference between our own visual perception
(*quâ* sensation-complexes) and the visual perceptions of the eagle on the one hand and the *proteus
anguinis* on the other, apart from variations due to
objective conditions, would seem to be chiefly one of

degree in the distinctness with which details and
minutiæ are perceived. The *proteus anguinus*, like
the owl, cannot perceive things accurately in the
light. Still, the dark-adapted eyes of the former
do not prevent them from ' mirroring ' things with
sufficient accuracy, given the requisite conditions.
Again, the many-faceted eye of the insect does not
represent things falsely, any more than a many-
faceted mirror does ; though we cannot say what
precisely is the function of these peculiarly-con-
structed visual organs or how the impressions
produced by each facet are combined to form a
percept. While, lastly, if we wish to decide whether
other eyes, shaped differently to our own, are or are
not capable of mirroring reality, we must assume
that our eyes *do* mirror reality, and that our
' optics ' have a value which is more than merely
normative.

§ 375. The facts, brought forward by Herr
Simmel, therefore, do not force us to the conclusion
that differences in the structure of the organs of
sense-perception are incompatible with the perception of things, their qualities and their spatial
relations, as they are *in rerum natura*. All we can
infer from them is that the organs of sense which
are to be found in different species of animals are
peculiarly adapted for the perception (and probably
the ' true ' perception) of certain kinds of objects
under certain circumstances and conditions of life,
just as are the various senses to be found in man.
While on the other hand, the further fact which
Herr Simmel remarks, viz., that 'actions undertaken
by reason of these percepts lead to results of such a

calculability, purposiveness and certainty, that they could not be greater even with a *knowledge* of objective relations as they are in themselves,' *cannot be accounted for unless* we suppose that these percepts correspond approximately with reality, and thus for us give, as they claim to give, real knowledge. In the chapters on Physical Science, I have already endeavoured to show that truth as utility presupposes truth as correspondence. The utility of our ideas is inexplicable, nay more, impossible, unless they have representative value. To summarise briefly the arguments there used : The utility of our ideas depends upon the consequences to which they lead through the mediation of action. Hence there must be *either* a symbolic parallelism *or* a real correspondence between the logical connections of ideas and the real connections of objects. But a symbolic parallelism is inadequate to account for these ' useful leadings.' For (1) it is impossible to explain how symbols become attached and remain attached to particular objects, if the symbol is purely arbitrary and if there is no kind of identity between symbol and thing ; and (2) our ideas are not merely symbolic but have objective meaning upon which our inferences are based, and it is impossible to explain why these inferences should coincide approximately with empirical facts unless the idea has a real and not merely a symbolic meaning. We conclude, therefore, with M. Poincaré, that " the fact that we see the conclusions of science verified before our eyes would not be possible if it did not reveal to us something of the nature of reality."[1]

---

[1] Preface to *Science and Hypothesis*.

It is not merely that our thoughts are 'added' to reality, and that reality 'suffers the addition.'[1] Our thoughts must be determined by reality itself in and through sense-perception; and thus may we gain real knowledge, which, because it *is* real knowledge, is capable of leading to useful results.

§ 376. Truth cannot be merely utility, for utility is the consequence of truth; and similarly axioms cannot be merely regulative, for the possibility of their exercising a regulative function in regard to objective experience presupposes their objective validity. Axioms are not 'universal' and 'necessary' because they satisfy our needs; but they satisfy our needs because they are 'universal' and 'necessary.' It is true that postulates may be universal, if we choose to make them so;[2] but the question is whether we have any right to make them so, and, if so, what right. It is also true that necessary principles are 'a means to human ends,' but the question is whether they could be useful as a means to human ends, if their necessity is psychological and if the 'psychical feeling of *having to*' is merely 'the emotional accompaniment of the purposive search for means.' It seems to me, in fact, that in treating necessary truth, and indeed all truth, from an exclusively teleological point of view, and again in distinguishing the accompanying emotional feeling from the intellectual apprehension of a principle and identifying the 'necessity' of the principle with the former only, Dr. Schiller has been guilty of an 'abstractionism' quite as vicious as that of a 'pure' intellectualist.

[1] *The Meaning of Truth*, p. 67. [2] '*Axioms as Postulates*,' § 10.

Other arguments by which Dr. Schiller attempts to disprove ' intrinsic ' necessity are no more success- ful. He tells us that "no one *needs* to add two and two as four, unless he needs to add, i.e., *wills* to add them, because he needs arithmetic." [1] This is obvious ; but the question is why, when we do need to add, we must needs add two and two as four. He maintains also that "*the ' truth ' of an assertion depends on its application ;* " and in support of this urges that " the abstract statement, *e.g.*, that ' two and two make four,' is always incomplete." It needs to be applied, and " its application is quite limited." " It would not be true of lions and lambs nor of drops of water, nor of pleasures and pains." [2] Of course it would not, if the statement were *wrongly* applied ; but it is always true that two lions and two lambs, *quâ* units or animals, make four units or four animals ; that two drops of water *plus* two other drops make four drops, provided they remain distinct ; and that two pleasures and two pains make four hedonic experiences, provided those experiences take place at different times, or belong to different individuals. (It is not the principle that is shown to be false, when it is wrongly applied ; but merely that particular way of applying it.) If the lions in question ate the lambs, or the drops of water intermingled, or the pleasures and pains *per impossibile* existed in the same individual at the same time, *there would neither be two and two nor four.*

§ 377. I have already indicated that there appears to be some divergence of opinion between Professor James and Dr. Schiller in regard to this

[1] *Ibid.*   [2] *Studies in Humanism,* p. 9.

question of abstract truth.[1] Professor James conceives abstract truth very much as the intellectualist conceives it. He admits "relations between
purely mental ideas," which are *absolute, unconditional, eternal,* and which are also "perceptually
(I should prefer to say intellectually) obvious at a
glance." These relations, again, though they may
not exist "effectually *in rebus,*" and though "nobody may experience them," have yet their own
reality in the ideal order ; they exist *in posse* or
virtually. So real are they, in fact, that "they
coerce us ; we must treat them consistently whether
or not we like the results." "Our ideas must agree
with realities, be such realities concrete or abstract,
be they facts or be they principles, under penalty of
endless inconsistency and frustration." The only
difficulty is in regard to the *application* of abstract
propositions. The abstract truths themselves are
eternal, and in their application they are also true
*in advance of special verification, if we have subsumed
our objects rightly.*[2]

If you can find a concrete thing anywhere that is ' one '
or ' white ' or ' gray ' or an ' effect,' then your principles
will everlastingly apply to it. It is but a case of
ascertaining the kind, and then applying the law of its
kind to the particular object. You are sure to get
truth if you can but name the kind rightly, for your
mental relations hold good of everything of that kind
without exception. If you then, nevertheless, failed
to get truth concretely, you would say that you had
classed the objects wrongly.[3]

[1] cf. *supra,* § 371.
[2] *Pragmatism,* pp. 209-211 ; *The Meaning of Truth,* p. 203,
and cf. p. 247.
[3] *Pragmatism,* p. 210.

Professor James neither protests against the validity, nor against the utility,[1] of abstract truths. What he contends for, against a 'vicious abstractionism,' is (1) that an abstract truth is "less real, not more real, than the verified article "[2] (*i.e.*, than abstract truth when applied), and (2) that abstract concepts are often "made a means of diminishing the original experience by *denying* (implicitly or explicitly) all its features save the one specially abstracted to conceive it by."[3]

§ 378. With such a view no sober-minded intellectualist could reasonably find fault; and I am also far from denying that "*the viciously privative employment of abstract characters and class names* is one of the original sins (better, perhaps, 'tendencies') of the rationalistic mind." To abstract, and then to forget or deny the other attributes of the concrete thing from which abstraction has been made, or to assume that the abstract concept or principle applies in every case, is a fault into which not only rationalists, but also pragmatists, not infrequently fall. But what the intellectualist, on his side, finds fault with, is the statement that "*the truth of an assertion depends on its application.*" As he understands it, to say this is *not* to say, *in other words*, that "'abstract' truths are not *fully* truths at all." Doubtless they "crave for incarnation in the concrete;" but they are not useless or unemployed, nor are they meaningless or necessarily ambiguous. Doubtless, again, they may *also* be used as 'rules for action;' but they are not *merely*

---

[1] *The Meaning of Truth*, p. 246.
[2] *Ibid.*, p. 205.   [3] *Ibid.*, p. 248.

rules for action. Hence, they do not ' mean nothing,' when not employed, nor does their meaning ' depend on their application.' [1]

It is not, then, against the general pragmatic doctrine in regard to abstract truth that I venture to enter a protest—except in so far as the pragmatist denies that abstract truth corresponds in the strict sense with reality ; but against the exaggerated form in which that doctrine appears in the writings of Dr. Schiller. I am quite ready to grant that abstract truths are less real than concrete truths ; that, in order for their significance to be fully realised, they must be constantly applied to concrete cases ; and that unless they are thus applicable in the concrete, directly or indirectly, they can have very little meaning and still less utility. But what I maintain is that an abstract concept always refers to reality—to the concrete thing from which it was abstracted, at least implicitly, and potentially to all objects like it ; and that, in like manner, an abstract truth, whether it be arrived at by inductive generalisation (for even empirical truths are always more or less abstract) or by the intuitive apprehension of a relation necessarily holding between the entities concerned, always has reference to reality, and therefore is true of reality whether we apply it to individual cases or not. Thus the principle of Contradiction applies to every ' real being,' and the principle of Causality to every ' contingent being.' Similarly, a geometrical proposition about a circle applies to every concrete real thing in so far as its shape approximates to that of a

[1] *Studies in Humanism*, pp. 8, 9.

circle, and the arithmetical relations of one number to other numbers apply to all objects that are numerable. Abstract truths, in short, are true objectively, because they express relations between notions that refer to and have been derived from reality ; they are true necessarily, and apart from special verification, because the relations they express are implied in the notions themselves, and, as Professor James says, are obvious at a glance ; they are true universally and apart from any special application, because to be true ' universally ' means simply to be true of every object or every system of objects to which the notions apply and in so far as they apply.

§ 379. Clearly, if we wish to know how far an abstract truth holds in any concrete case, we must apply it. But to apply a truth and to verify it are not the same thing. In applying the truth, what we wish to discover is whether a particular case can be subsumed under our abstract law, *i.e.*, whether the notions involved in our law are or are not realised in *this* case. We already know what the ' consequences ' of our law are, our present business —again to quote Professor James—is to find out whether we can *add* these consequences in this particular case.[1] Dr. Schiller does not seem to me to have grasped this, to my mind, very obvious distinction. He confuses application with verification, and hence gives as one of his reasons for denying the universality and necessity of abstract truths, that they will not apply to every case or that in applying them we sometimes make mistakes. But,

[1] cf. *The Meaning of Truth*, p. 248.

surely, to verify or prove a mathematical statement
and to apply it are two altogether different processes. To verify a statement in *pure* mathematics
is to show that it is deducible from other statements
which are either already proved or self-evident (*i.e.*,
'obvious at a glance' when rightly understood).
The application of mathematical statement, on the
other hand, involves analysis, identification and
measurement, all of which may go wrong, and, being
quantitative, are never absolutely accurate, so that
at best our results will only be approximate.

The case is very different when we are dealing
with an empirical law, a scientific hypothesis, or a
principle in dynamics. For here we are dealing with
entities or with relations of the nature of which we
know little *a priori*. Hence we cannot establish
necessary relations, but must proceed either by
postulating that an empirically known relation holds
under other than the observed conditions, or by
postulating that the nature of physical objects is
(*v.g.*) mechanical and then deducing particular
conclusions from this hypothesis. Whichever
method we adopt the validity of our postulate can
be established only by experiment. In other words,
while abstract truths are true *a priori* and independently of their application, empirical truths
cannot be established apart from their application.

Dr. Schiller, on the other hand, assuming that
all knowledge comes *via* postulation, hence infers
that *no* proposition is really true until it has been
subjected to a process of experimental verification
to which no term or limit can be assigned. Such a
position is surely untenable. Not only does it fail

KK

to take cognisance of the distinction between empirical generalisations and necessary principles, or between truths which require to be verified in experience and truths which are true in advance of such special verification, but, as its logical consequence, it forces us to declare that what appear to be most certain truths are not really more than probabilities, since we cannot be sure that at some future date we may not, in applying them, meet with reverse. This sceptical tendency in Pragmatism we have already met with in a previous chapter ; [1] and that it is the necessary outcome of a wholly ' experimental ' theory of knowledge is clear. For in such a theory all truth starts as a claim or a postulate, and

all postulates, whether axiomatic or not, have the same origin. They differ only in the scope of their usefulness and in the amount and character of their confirmation. Some are held *faute de mieux*, and even full-blown axioms may be conceived as becoming otiose under changed conditions ; though practically the possibility of modifying them is one that may be safely neglected, for it would be gratuitous to suppose a revolution in our experience sufficient to upset them.[2]

§ 380. The next question which demands our attention is the very important one of how truth should be defined. This question the pragmatist claims to have solved in a *new* way, and its solution is of the very essence of Pragmatism. All other problems, metaphysical or epistemological, which have arisen out of Pragmatism, are secondary and accidental.

[1] chap. xvi.   [2] '*Axioms as Postulates,*' § 26.

Of the multitudinous and extremely varied definitions of truth given by Professor James and other pragmatists, I shall have something to say in the next chapter, when we shall consider them as embodying pragmatic criteria of truth ; but here it will be sufficient if we confine our attention to two types of such definitions only. ⎛The first is that in which truth is identified with the verification process or with its workings ; the second, that in which the essence of this verification-process is said to be that it should lead to consequences *practically useful.* ⎞

⎛Truth, for Professor James, is essentially a process of leading which starts from an image, concept or symbolic term and terminates either in other ideas or in percepts, but ultimately in the latter.⎞ It is a relation between an idea, on the one hand, and perceptual experiences (*or* reality) on the other, and the essence of the relation *consists in* certain processes or workings (or at any rate ' functional *possibilities* ') which *make* the idea true, and are capable both of being experienced and described. There is nothing transcendent about the truth-relation in Pragmatism. It is something that lies wholly within experience. Both its *terminus a quo* and its *terminus ad quem,* and the intermediary links which constitute the workings of the ' true ' idea, are one and all experiences.

There is nothing ambiguous about pragmatic truth so far, and had the pragmatist always made his meaning as clear as Professor James has done in the last few chapters of *The Meaning of Truth,* much misunderstanding and many futile disputes

might have been avoided. But is the pragmatist
right? Certainly the pragmatist's view of truth is
neither the common-sense nor the traditional view,
and Professor James would, I think, be the first
to acknowledge this. The ordinary unsophisticated
individual does not understand by 'agreement' a
process of working in which our ideas lead us, or
tend to lead us, to reality in the sense of adapting
us to it so that we may handle it better than if we
disagreed. *That*, he would say, is a consequence
of truth, not its essential nature. (Agreement for
common-sense, when applied to truth, means that
our ideas copy, resemble, correspond to reality in
such a way that the nature of what is known is
reproduced in our minds, not *really* or physically
of course, as it exists in the outside world, but
ideally, mentally by our thoughts.) And the
philosopher of common-sense explains this as
arising from the fact that in knowledge the *content*
of our thoughts is determined, directly or indirectly,
by their objects, to which accordingly they *conform*.
(The pragmatist, he would allow, is perfectly correct
in saying that 'truth is made by its consequences,' if
he mean by this that it is only by the functional
workings of truth in many cases that we come to
know that our ideas (or, better, our judgments) are
true. But the 'consequences' or 'workings' of
truth are not truth itself, as is evident from the
fact that we speak of *truth*'s workings or *truth*'s
consequences; thereby implying that truth is one
thing and its 'workings' or 'consequences' something else which is not identical with it, but belongs to
it, or follows from it, and is therefore predicable of it.

§ 381. We have not yet settled the question, however; for if truth does not consist in correspondence, the pragmatist is fully justified in looking for something else in which it does consist ; for it cannot be an incomprehensible or meaningless entity. Nor do I see that *prima facie* the absolutist has anything to complain of, since he himself identifies truth with ' consistency,' which is itself *one* of truth's workings. The real question is, then, (1) whether the pragmatist has entirely given up the view that truth consists in correspondence with reality, opprobriously styled the copy-view of truth; and, if so (2) whether he is warranted in substituting in its place his own view that truth consists in its workings.

The first question need not detain us long. There can be no doubt that Dr. Schiller has entirely renounced the ' copy-view ' of truth : the only point that remains dubitable is whether Professor James has also accomplished this feat. He certainly clings to the idea that images ' copy ' reality, and images in his theory can be true. He also affirms that the truth of ' relations between ideas ' is ' perceptually obvious at a glance,' and it is difficult to see how, in such cases, there can be any time or space for ' workings.' Again, he allows that of a given event " only one sort of possible account can ever be true ; " yet surely many different ' accounts ' may be ' true ' of an event if all they have to do is to ' work ' with it agreeably and profitably. Nor do I see how " the truth about any such event is already generically predetermined by the events of nature," and thus " virtually pre-exists," [1] unless the event

The Meaning of Truth, p. 289.

itself somehow determines our thoughts about it, and so brings them into conformity with, and causes them to resemble, itself. I am unaware of any kind of determining action which does not tend in some way to reproduce itself, or any kind of passivity which is not receptive of forms, which, at bottom, resemble the activity from which they proceed. Still more difficult is it to conceive how reality can be such that some of our questions " can be answered in only one way," or how " mirrored matter " can give " cognitive lustre " to our ideas,[1] unless our ideas somehow correspond to reality and are determined by it. Doubtless such expressions can be squared with the pragmatic view ; but they seem to me to be relics of a ' copy-view ' not entirely given up. And if this is so, the ' workings ' of truth are not its essence, but its consequence ; in which case it would be better to give them some other name, such as ' truth - function,' rather than to offer them as the definition of truth.[2]

§ 382. Supposing, however, that the ' copy-view ' of truth has been given up by *all* pragmatists, and that truth is, for them, nothing but its ' workings ' or ' consequences,' we have next to enquire whether this transformation of the common-sense view is justifiable. One way to show that it is not justifiable would be to re-establish the so-called ' copy-view ' of truth, which I have already attempted to do in other chapters. Here, therefore,

---

[1] *Ibid.*, pp. 69, 93.
[2] cf. *ibid.*, p. 224.   ' Truthful '-ness is certainly not an adequate term to describe this function, especially as it already has a definite significance in morals.

I shall content myself with endeavouring to trace the consequences which follow from the pragmatic view, consequences which I propose to 'value' pragmatically by their power of satisfying our human needs. Now, 'workings' may mean either practical workings which lead to *useful* results, or theoretical workings which lead to consistency and harmony amongst our ideas. The pragmatic use of the term will bear both meanings. But as 'theoretical workings,' if they do not lead to a correspondence between our ideas and reality, can hardly be themselves of very great value, except in so far as they satisfy an idle desire to play with symbols and ideas, and as both Dr. Schiller and Herr Simmel subordinate theory to practice, probably, in part at least, for this very reason, it will be as well to kill two birds with one stone by examining at once what is the logical result of identifying truth with its *practically* useful consequences. There can be no doubt that Herr Simmel actually makes this identification, and little doubt, I think, that for Dr. Schiller also the 'logical-value' of truth is ultimately practical in character. A similar tendency may be noted in Professor James, when, for instance, he interprets 'agreement' as "a process of leading which puts us in working touch with reality, enabling us to manipulate and control it better than we should otherwise have been able to do," [1] and again in the words of a French pragmatist who says "*La science ne reproduit pas la réalité, elle ne tend qu'à nous représenter les choses d'une façon commode et pratique pour l'usage que nous avons à en*

[1] *Pragmatism*, p. 212 ; and cf. *supra*, § 370.

faire." The utility-view of truth is, in fact, the logical outcome of the rejection of the copy-view in a thoroughly genetic and voluntaristic philosophy.

§ 383. One consequence of this is that truth may be regarded as a habit ; but as the primary question is not *whether* true modes of thinking and perceiving tend to survive (a fact which can hardly be disputed), but rather *why* they tend to survive, this aspect of pragmatic truth may be passed over as of secondary importance. A far more significant consequence of the pragmatic view is the doctrine of the *relativity* of truth. For Dr. Schiller this means that truth is relative to our faculties and is essentially a *human* product. For Herr Simmel it means both this *and* that truth-values are relative *inter se ;* that no idea is true of itself any more than a body is heavy in itself ; and hence that the whole of knowledge is no more true than the whole of matter is heavy.

What precisely is the connection between the relativity of true ideas and the utility in which their truth primarily consists, Herr Simmel does not tell us. When he says that the truth-value of ideas is relative, however, he seems to mean that ideas are true *or* useful only in connection with other ideas.[1] An idea is for him a means to a practical end—the progressive adaptation of man to his environment ; but an idea, taken in isolation, so far from promoting adaptation, tends to check it, and by becoming ' fixed ' or abnormally predominant, to destroy it altogether. Hence no idea is useful *per se :* ideas

---

[1] cf. *Pragmatism,* pp. 59, 60, 169; (quoted above § 291) ; 210.

are only true, *i.e.*, useful, when they operate in conjunction with one another and reciprocally determine one another's function, for thus only can they be of service as means enabling man to control and manipulate his experience. It may be doubted whether Herr Simmel, in denying that ideas are useful *per se*, has not carried the doctrine of relativity too far, since each idea has its own sphere of objective reference, and in that sphere is useful irrespective of other ideas, though the latter may vastly increase its utility if they function in harmony with it. But if ' relativity ' mean merely the need of consistency, harmony and mutual corroboration among our ideas, it is again a point of secondary importance, and to it the realist would readily assent.

Relativity or reciprocity as applied to the normative aspect of leading principles of thought is also a doctrine to which no realist would demur ; and Herr Simmel is undoubtedly right in saying that certain of our more fundamental conceptions, regarded as regulative principles, can only lead to truth if they be treated as reciprocal and complementary, just as in the physiological order the furtherance of life is conditioned by the dual process of anabolism and katabolism. One of the most striking examples of a pair of complementary principles which may thus be regulatively used is that of Unity and Plurality. Thus the Plurality-Norm says : Do not imagine that the universe is one, its differences mere seeming. Do not identify everything. Allow their full and proper value to distinctions, differences, individuals, persons, things. Do not delude yourself with the vain and idle fancy that you can reduce all this to mere appearance and force it back into the boundless capacity of an imaginary Ground in which it is absorbed and its own peculiar reality taken away. To this the Unity-Norm replies : On the contrary, what you have most to guard against is the splitting things up into individual existents, isolated, independent, unconnected, unrelated. Unions are as real as disjunctions, unities as real as differences. The universe *is* one, and if you forget it, your facility in making distinctions will lead you hopelessly astray. Both norms are right ; both of inestimable value. Each has its function and its own proper sphere of operation ; and only by the conjunction, the alternation, the co-operation of both, is it possible to arrive at truth.

But are the norms merely regulative ? Are they merely norms ? Have they not real objective value, real significance, real meaning ? Could they be norms at all in the sphere of knowledge if they had not ? Is it not an abuse of that very principle of reciprocity that they illustrate to say that they have not ? That is a question which Herr Simmel does not touch. It is manifest that unity must not be sacrificed to plurality, freedom to necessity, matter to mind, the will to the intellect, the objective to the subjective, nor *vice versa ;* and that it is only by assigning to each principle or concept its proper place and sphere of application that truth can be attained. But neither pluralist nor monist, libertarian nor determinist, materialist nor spiritualist, think that the question at issue between them is as to the best means of manipulating their experience and so furthering life. When the pluralist says that existents are many and distinct, he means that they are really many and really distinct, just as he thinks them to be ; and when the monist says the universe is one he means that it is really one, and that his thought about it is in the ideal order what the universe is in the real order. (It is primarily a question of the truth of knowledge, not of the utility of action to which knowledge may lead. And as I have already endeavoured to show,[1] the *practical* value of knowledge is, even in science, essentially dependent upon its validity. Accordingly, I shall not re-open the question here, but shall content myself with pointing out that, while Herr Simmel is undoubtedly justified in affirming that ultimate principles are complementary and must be taken in conjunction, not in isolation, we may question whether, in emphasising reciprocity to the neglect of positive value, and utility to the neglect of real significance, he has not violated his own principle of reciprocity and relativity ; whether, in other words, by ignoring the positive and representative aspect of truth, he has not made it as one-sided a conception as the most exaggerated Monism or the most thorough-going Determinism or Intellectualism. (The real significance of the reciprocity of truth seems to me, to be that no ideas and no principles *which are contradictory* can give us true knowledge about the universe when taken in isolation and made to apply universally, but only when reconciled by means of distinction and re-united in what the Hegelian calls a ' higher ' synthesis.)

[1] *supra*, § 378, and §§ 339 *et seq.*

§ 384. We now come to the sense in which Dr.
Schiller says that truth is ' relative,' viz., in relation
to the knowing mind, its faculties, its purposes, its
interests, its needs, or, in a word, to its "entire and
specific organism." This, again, is a consequence
of the doctrine that truth is a process which leads
to useful consequences, for the consequences, though
in themselves they may be objective, can only be
useful as a means to an end which must be more
or less subjective, and which will vary, if not with
the individual, at least with the specific organism.
Hence, although it is a dangerous thing to assert
that Pragmatism leads to Subjectivism, yet if Herr
Simmel's theory of truth be really pragmatic,
Subjectivism seems to be its logical result. And the
same may be said of Pragmatism as "worked in a
humanistic way " by Dr. Schiller, though I would
not go so far as Professor James and say that
Humanism " is compatible with Solipsism." [1] Let
me explain, however, what I mean here by Subjectivism. I do *not* mean Solipsism, nor do I that
the pragmatist, *alias* the humanist, *denies* the
existence of all objective reality ' outside ' our
human minds. What I mean is that, if we interpret
the expressions used by Dr. Schiller, Herr Simmel
and other pragmatists, as philosophical expressions
should be interpreted, viz., literally, the logical
conclusion to which we are forced is that the pragmatic or humanistic theory of truth is equivalent
to a denial of the possibility of *knowing* the nature
of objective reality. It is a *sceptical* Subjectivism,
a subjectivism that makes knowledge so human

[1] *The Meaning of Truth*, p. 215.

that it ceases to be real knowledge.[1] I am quite
aware that Humanism does not admit its own
subjective tendency, and that we have been fore-
warned by Dr. Schiller that to accuse Humanism
of denying that truth is objective is " to put upon it
the silliest of possible meanings, and is nothing
short of an ' impudent slander.' " Nevertheless,
reluctant as I am to slander anyone, and fully
conscious that I am again exposing myself to the
charge of having misunderstood,[2] I still maintain
that Humanism does tend logically to Subjectivism,
and shall forthwith proceed to prove the truth of
this statement.

§ 385. First of all, Humanism is, we are told, a
revised form of Protagoreanism, which means
(1) that ' whatever appears to each, that really is
for him,' and (2) that ' reality is, for us, relative to
our faculties.'[3] Now that whatever appears to each
is for him *psychologically* a fact, no one can deny.
But when Protagoras asserted that ' man is the
measure of all things,' he certainly did not mean

[1] That this is the ordinary sense of the term ' Subjectivism '
is borne out by the definitions given in the new *Standard
Dictionary*, where it is defined as " the doctrine (1) that knowledge is merely subjective and relative, (2) that we know directly
no external object, (3) that there is no objective measure of
truth." And, again, by the definition in Eisler's *Philosophisches
Wörterbuch :* " The view that all knowledge and thought is
subjective, expressing, not the essence (being) of things, but
only the subjective manner of reacting to the action (*einwirken*)
of things, or, indeed, just the conditions and modifications of
the subject ; that there exists only subjective truth. ' Baldwin's
Dictionary defines Subjectivism as " The theory which denies
the possibility of objective knowledge ; " but identifies this with
Subjective Idealism (wrongly, I think).

[2] cf. an article of mine in *Mind*, N.S. 67, entitled " Martineau
and the Humanists ; " and the discussion which ensued between
Dr. Schiller and myself in *Mind*, N.S. 69, 71 *et seq.*

[3] *Studies in Humanism*, p. 38.

merely that appearances were psychological facts. He meant that man's way of looking at things intrinsically modified his perception and his knowledge of them. And this Dr. Schiller realises, for he tells us in another place [1] that a man's personal "idiosyncrasy must colour and pervade whatever he experiences." Not only his knowledge in general, but even his metaphysics "*must* have this personal tinge;" so that not only *ought* not two men with different fortunes, histories, and temperaments, "to arrive at the same metaphysic," but they *cannot honestly do so*, for a metaphysic "always *takes its final form* from an idiosyncrasy"!

Such language bears the unmistakable impress of Subjectivism. Metaphysics to be modified to suit our idiosyncrasies! Metaphysics to differ with differences of temperament! Dr. Schiller surely cannot be in earnest. He is only trying, as pragmatists are wont, to shock his enemy, the intellectualist. He cannot be serious when he proposes so drastic a means of avoiding a "monstrous uniformity." No; for he confesses his exaggeration, and saves himself to some extent by admitting that, though "a valid metaphysic need not show itself cogent to all," at least "it must make itself acceptable to reasonable men, willing to give a trial to its general principles," [2] and reasonable men are not reasonable in so far as they give way to idiosyncrasies. Yet this admission, consoling as it is, does not entirely get rid of Subjectivism, for a certain amount of personal tinge will still survive, even when most of our eccentricities have been rubbed away by contact

[1] *Ibid.*, p. 18.   [2] *Ibid.*, p. 20.

with our fellow-men. And if this tinge must affect
all our knowledge, if personal idiosyncrasy " must
colour and pervade whatever we experience," it will
modify, not only our metaphysic, *but also our opinion
as to how far our metaphysic has been or ought to be
acceptable to reasonable men.* We shall require,
therefore, some rule by which to eliminate in knowledge the effect of our subjective point of view.
But such a rule is not as yet forthcoming.

§ 386. The second formulation of the Protagorean principle informs us that knowledge is
' relative to our faculties ; ' and this, too, as interpreted by the humanist, involves Subjectivism.
The meaning of the term ' faculties ' is in Pragmatism not quite clear, for the existence of faculties as
such is denied. But if we take the principle to mean
that knowledge is modified by our human way of
looking at things—taking human here in the generic
sense, as Dr. Schiller says—we shall not, I think,
be very far wrong. Now the human way of looking
at things is, according to the humanist, dependent
upon needs which are common to the race. And
needs are subjective. Hence, as the humanist in
this matter makes no distinction between the
content and intent of thought, all truth is modified
by this subjective point of view. It may or it may
not reveal to us the nature of reality. We at any
rate have no means of finding out how far it does so,
and consequently no right to assume that such
a revelation *de facto* takes place. For it is meaningless to enquire into the nature of reality as it is in
itself, if human evaluations pervade our whole
experience and affect whatever ' fact ' and what-

ever 'knowledge' we consent to recognise.[1] The
subjective element in cognition cannot be got rid
of, for " selective attention and purposive manipulation are essential and *all-pervasive* influences in the
construction of the 'real' world, and even the
fundamental axioms . . . are now shown to
originate in *subjective* demands." [2]   " Independent
facts which we have merely to acknowledge are a
figure of speech. The growth of experience is ever
transfiguring our facts for us, and it is only by an
ex post facto fiction that we declare them to have been
all along what they have come to mean for us." [3]
Hence " that the real has a determinate nature
which the knowing reveals but does not affect, so
that our knowing makes no difference to it, is one of
those sheer assumptions which are incapable not
only of proof, but even of rational defence."   " The
actual situation is a case of interaction, a process of
cognition in which the 'subject' and the 'object'
determine each other, and both 'we' and 'reality'
are involved, and, we might add, evolved." [4]

If, then, " when the mind 'knows' reality, both
are affected," [5] if there are no independent facts, but
all facts are 'transfigured' and distorted [6] by our
apperception of them, if purpose, subjective demand,
and idiosyncrasy influence and pervade all our
experience so that " the determinate nature of
reality does not subsist 'outside' or 'beyond'

---

[1] *Humanism*, p. 10 and pp. 11, 12 (note).
[2] *Studies in Humanism*, pp. 467, 468.   (Italics mine.)
[3] ' *Axioms as Postulates*,' § 24 (italics mine), and cf.
Pragmatism, pp. 248, 249.
[4] *Humanism*, pp. 11, 12 (note).
[5] *Ibid.*, p. 11.
[6] ' *Axioms as Postulates*,' *loc. cit.*

the process of knowing it," [1] but the world, as it now appears, is but "the reflexion of our interests in life," [2] *truth for us is not objective in the ordinary sense of that term*. It does not give us knowledge of reality, but at most of reality *as modified by our cognitive functioning, our purposes and needs*. It is ' objective ' only in that it leads to practically useful results in our dealings with what we call objective experience. Its objectivity comes from the valida-tion process. " True ideas are those which we can assimilate, validate, corroborate, verify." [3] But ' assimilation ' is a purely subjective process ; and ' corroboration,' if it means the avoiding of contra-diction between ideas and experiences, is also subjective ; *unless*, indeed, the ideas and ex-periences have themselves objective value, and agree with reality. While ' verification,' if all it does is to " put us in *working* touch with reality" and to guide us to beneficial interaction with sensible particulars as they occur, [4] does not give any real objectivity to truth. For ' working contact ' and ' beneficial interaction ' are possible without any knowledge at all, and are sometimes the better for being without it, otherwise acquired habits would not tend to become unconscious, and the instincts of birds, butterflies, and bees would never have attained a perfection so complex and yet so admirably adapted to their environment. Indeed, we are expressly told that " the ' objective control ' of our subjective freedom to predicate is not effected by some un-

---

[1] *Humanism*, p. 11.
[2] *Studies in Humanism*, p. 200.
[3] *Pragmatism*, p. 201.   [4] *Ibid.*, pp. 205, 213.

LL

comprehended pre-existing fact : it comes *in the consequences of acting out the predication*." [1] And these consequences are to be judged according as they satisfy or thwart a purpose, assist or hinder the building up of a science. Consequences, in short, are ' good ' if they forward, ' bad ' if they baffle, our interests.

To determine, therefore, whether an answer to any question is ' true ' or ' false,' we have *merely* to note its *effect* upon the inquiry in which we are interested, and in relation to which it has arisen. And if these effects are favourable, the answer is ' true ' and ' good ' for our purpose, and ' useful ' as a means to the end we pursue. [2]

Consequences, therefore, though they may be objective in themselves, considered as determinants of truth-values, are subjective and relative, their value *as consequences* being itself determined by subjective interests and purposes.

§ 387. Again, consequences belong to the ' sensational parts of experience,' which, for Professor James, *are* reality. And as both these and the ' conceptual parts ' are, as parts of experience, subjective, the relation between them, in which truth consists, must also be subjective. Even if by ' sensational parts of experience ' Professor James means what in another place he has called ' facts,' the substitution of this term does not make much difference. For ' facts ' for the humanist mean either (1) sensations, which are subjective psychological facts ; or (2) facts which " do not pre-exist the

---

[1] *Studies in Humanism*, p. 192.
[2] *Ibid.*, p. 154.   (Italics mine.)

cognitive functioning," but are "immanently
deposited within it," and so are still subjective ;
or (3) facts which "simply are," *i.e.*, experiences
which have not yet been analysed into a subject and
an object, or classified as appearance or reality, and
which, when they are split up by our own reflective
act into aspects relatively distinct, still leave us
without any *really* objective reality to which the
' conceptual parts of our experience ' can lead.

Similarly, the interpretation which Humanism
puts upon the objectivity, independence, absoluteness, invariability, eternity, universality and
necessity of truth clearly manifest its subjective
tendency. (The ' *objectivity* ' of truth means for
the humanist that experiences ' demand to be kept
with a minimum of change, and that they interfere
with one another : it has nothing to do with representative value.') The ' *independence* ' of truth is
merely a description of that selective valuation by
which we discriminate more precious experiences
from those which are of inferior value. It depends,
therefore, upon subjective needs and conditions.
The ' *absoluteness* ' of truth is but our conception of
an ideal state in which all our needs shall be
satisfied. The ' *invariability* ' and ' *eternity* ' of
truth signify that, since truth is our own production,
we can keep it invariable if we choose, and can apply
it at whatever time we will.[1] Similarly, truths are
universal if we choose to make them so, and their
necessity is a psychological feeling of ' having to,'
which arises from the practical impossibility of
thinking otherwise than we do think in the matter of

[1] *Studies in Humanism*, p. 69, and cf. p. 461.

certain so-called axiomatic principles.[1] As, however, this impossibility is merely due to force of
habit, and as the force of habit is due primarily to
the exigencies of our nature which have gradually
adapted themselves to their environment, necessity
is largely, if not wholly, subjective.

§ 388. In brief, truth, since it is human truth,
must always bear ' the mark of human fabrication
and the impress of human needs.' It always has a
' personal tinge ' and the influence of need-expressive
purposes permeates it through and through. All
knowledge is relative to our faculties. In the
perception of facts, facts themselves get distorted
by our human points of view, and since in order to
know we must always act, the making of truth
implies the making of reality. (Hence arises the
following dilemma ; either we can or we cannot
distinguish in the content of our thoughts that
which is determined by the object from that which
is due to human fabrication, to the personal tinge,
to idiosyncrasy, to the influence of our points of
view, our manipulation, our purposes, and our
needs. If we can make this distinction, then all
and every part of our knowledge has *not* a personal
tinge, is *not* made by us, and is *not* intrinsically
modified and transfigured by our faculties, our
purposes and needs ; in which case Humanism is
false as it stands, and if it is to hold at all, must be
considerably toned down. While if we cannot
make this distinction, then what we know is not
reality, but reality *as modified and mutilated and in
part made by us*. In other words, our knowledge

[1] ' *Axioms as Postulates,*' § 10.

is subjective ; of its objective significance and meaning we are ignorant, and so must console ourselves with the belief that at any rate it is useful.

§ 389. Humanists and pragmatists reject with scorn this accusation of Subjectivism, and various attempts have been made to escape it. These attempts may be summarised under four heads. The first asserts that pragmatic truth is not subjective because in the making of it we are controlled to a large extent by our environment ; the second appeals to 'normal objectivity ; ' the third introduces a new version of the doctrine of Immanence ; and the fourth maintains that we have 'quite as much objective validity as we need.'

In the first place, then, it is urged that in the making of pragmatic truth we are controlled by objective experience. We cannot make it how we please. We cannot elicit any answer we like to our experimental questions ; but must take the answer that comes. We 'add' our thoughts to reality ; but reality does not always welcome the addition. Sometimes our theories will not work.

In saying, however, that pragmatic truth is subjective, I do not mean to imply that the pragmatist denies all real control over the working of our thoughts. What I mean is that the representative function which it claims to possess is in the humanistic theory impossible. The 'working' of our thoughts may be controlled by real objects, but they can have no strictly cognitive significance if their origin is subjective, their value determined by interest and purpose, and if they do nothing more than enable us to manipulate experience. The

objectivity of truth can be proved, not by *any* kind
of control which reality may have over us, but only
by a particular control, that by which it determines
the content of our thought. We must, moreover,
be able to distinguish between cases in which this
control is operative, and cases in which it is not, and
must attribute truth only where it is clear to our
mind that such control has been exercised. But
this is not what Pragmatism does. It judges
thoughts to be true not when they are determined
by the object, but when they satisfy a subjective
purpose or need, when they prove themselves useful
and worth our while. To assert that the pragmatist and the humanist deny that reality exercises
any control over our thoughts would certainly be to
misinterpret and misunderstand, for application
and verification are nowhere more insisted on than
they are in the pragmatic and humanistic account
of truth. It is the interpretation that is put upon
application and verification that makes the latter
subjective.[1] It is admitted that reality determines
the answers to our questions ; but for the humanist
this means, not that reality determines the content
of thought, but that it produces, or rather helps to
produce, in our psycho-physical organism certain
experiences which satisfy our needs. It is upon its
consequences for *us*, upon the satisfaction it gives
us, that truth depends, not upon its objective
determination or its correspondence ; so much so
that the existence of the latter is usually denied.
Since, then, in the effects produced upon our
psycho-physical organism by the reaction of objects

[1] *Studies in Humanism*, pp. 192, 154 (cited above, § 386).

the subjective factor co-operates and cannot be distinguished or allowed for, and since the final determinant of truth is the satisfaction of subjective purposes and needs, truth in Humanism cannot have real objective significance and meaning in the ordinary sense of those terms.

§ 390. Many pragmatists, especially those of France, appreciating the force of this argument, have sought an escape from Subjectivism in ' normal objectivity.' In place of objectivity in the ordinary sense of ' correspondence with reality ' they have substituted an objectivity which is said to arise from common consent. Thus Simmel, Milhaud, Le Roy, Abel Rey, etc. *La science, c'est nous,* says M. Rey, yet it does not depend upon *my* taste, *my* turn of mind, *my* will, *my* choice ; but rather upon conditions common to all intelligences alike, con- ditions which are humanly necessary and humanly universal. Anthropomorphism in human knowledge is inevitable ; but it must proceed from the race, not from the individual. Science is the measure of *our* mind, not of the mind of each individual nor even of each society. Individual truths are deter- mined by individual needs, yet they admit of a ' selective valuation ' by means of which " individual judgments become recognised universally as valid," and " a truth which cannot win recognition is not a truth at all, for it has failed in its purpose." [1]

This appeal to ' normal objectivity,' however, cannot save the pragmatist from Subjectivism ; for

[1] Abel Rey, *La Théorie Physique*, p. 381 ; Le Roy, *Revue Métaph. et Morale*, 1899, p. 560 ; Schiller, *Humanism*, pp. 55-59 ; *Studies in Humanism*, p. 70 ; and Poincaré, *La Valeur de la Science*, p. 265.

normal objectivity is not real objectivity, but merely
a something which by common consent we agree
to regard *as if* it were objective. The ' objectivity '
of truth here is not due to the object any more than
it was before, but is ultimately determined by the
satisfaction of human needs ; and needs, whether
peculiar to the individual or common to the race,
are still subjective. The analogy of economical
values, urged by Herr Simmel, is not to the point,
for the ' objectivity ' which is given to individual
evaluation by common consent *is recognised as
being still subjective*, whereas truth-values are held
to be objective in quite a different sense.

§ 391. The third appeal is to Immanence as
interpreted in the philosophy of Pure Experience.
We have no ground for saying that facts lie outside
experience ; the objects about which we think may
be immanent within or continuous with the present
experience itself.

The category of transperceptual reality is now one of
the foundations of our life, [yet] we may speculatively
imagine a state of pure experience before the hypothesis
of permanent objects behind its flux had been framed.[1]
The ' independence ' ascribed to certain realities does not
really transcend the cognitive process. It only means
that *in* our experience there are certain features which
it is convenient to describe as ' independent ' facts,
powers, persons, etc., by reason of the peculiarity of
their behaviour. . . . The whole is an intra-experiential affair.[2]

The whole is an intra-experiential affair ! This
is the fundamental note of Pragmatism and

[1] *The Meaning of Truth*, pp. 64, 63.
[2] *Studies in Humanism*, p. 461.

Humanism. This is why Dr. Schiller affirms that the problem of knowledge is not how we get to know reality, but how the cognitive process engenders means for the control of our experience. True, the humanist does not absolutely *deny* an ' other,' to the structure of which our predicates may perhaps correspond ; but " *for us,* at any rate, reality is an accumulation of our own intellectual inventions," into which we try to " work new nouns and adjectives, while altering as little as possible the old." [1] Yet to admit the *possibility* of such a reality is worse than to deny it altogether. For Dr. Schiller emphatically asserts that we can never *know* this reality *as it is in itself ;* [2] and this relic of an ancient and dogmatic idealism is, I am convinced, one of the two stumbling-blocks that has caused the pragmatist to fall into Scepticism.

But why is it irrational to enquire into the nature of reality as it is in itself ? Undoubtedly we can only " know the real as it is when we know it," *i.e.,* as it appears to us in our cognitive acts. But why *gratuitously assume* that reality does not appear to us as it really is ? Certainly the reality we know cannot be shut off from us, isolated, unconnected with our purposes and needs ; for *our* experience is the means and *our* purposes and needs the guiding principle and the motive force that conditions human knowledge. But why should not what we know be reality itself ? Dr. Schiller is forced to admit that " the acceptance of fact leaves us with a *surd quâ* the fact." [3] Why, then, should not these pre-

---

[1] *The Meaning of Truth,* p. 65.
[2] *Humanism,* note to pp. 11, 12.   [3] *Studies in Humanism,* p. 200.

existent facts belong to the real world of common-
sense, instead of to a mysterious ' primary reality ' ?
There can only be one reason for all this—a deep-
rooted idealistic prejudice. Yet Idealism, Immani-
ence, and a philosophy of Pure Experience, apart
from the inconsistencies to which they lead and the
violence they do to common-sense, are powerless to
save the pragmatist and the humanist from the
sceptical Subjectivism implied in his assumption
that reality, as known, is not reality as it is, but
reality as modified and transfigured by his own
subjective interests.   For if this reality be immanent
within us, and in large part the product of our own
cognitive acts, the knowledge of it is not the knowledge which the human mind desires.   It is not
knowledge of something other than ourselves, but
merely knowledge of our own objective aspect,
relatively distinguished and split off from ourselves,
as it were, by our own thoughts.   The ' category of
transperceptual reality ' is thus declared to be
invalid, and ' one of the foundations of our life '
thereby 'destroyed'—a result which, even for the
pragmatist, should be sufficient irrevocably to
condemn the philosophy of Immanence and Pure
Experience.

§ 392.   One last plea is offered in extenuation of
the Subjectivism from which the pragmatist can
find no effective escape.   Truth, it is acknowledged,
is relative ; yet at any rate it is related to man.   It
is subjective ; yet at any rate it is something he can
possess.   It is only probable ; yet probability is at
any rate better than an impossible ideal.   It has
not ' objective validity ' in the realist's sense ; yet

at least it has quite as much ' objective validity '
as we need or it needs, if it is to be progressive.[1]

Thus, with a cry of ' sour grapes,' the pragmatist
makes one last attempt to escape Subjectivism, if
it can be called an attempt to escape and not rather
an admission that the charge is well-founded. That
pragmatic truth is something we can possess, that
it is related to us, is probable, and progressive,
cannot be questioned ; but it is not the truth which
we, as rational human beings, yearn for and strive
to obtain. What man wants, whether he be
philosopher, scientist, or only one in a crowd, is a
truth which shall tell him what reality is, truth
which shall ' copy ' or ' resemble ' reality. Professor James admits that this is the way knowledge
and truth are conceived by common-sense ; and I
maintain that nothing short of this can fully
satisfy the purposive cravings of our intellect and
the rational strivings of our will. Again, Professor
James is really on my side. Not only does he
describe truth at the common-sense level in terms
of his own philosophy as the confluence or identity
or fusion of idea and reality ; but he affirms that
" *the maximal conceivable truth* of an idea would
seem to be that it should lead to an actual merging
of ourselves with the object, to an utter mutual confluence and identification." [2]   In short, correspondence, *alias* identity or confluence, is the ideal
of the pragmatist and the philosopher of Pure
Experience, just as it is the ideal of the realist !
Ideas may ' fit ' reality, lead to it, agree with it,

[1] *Mind*, N.S. 69, p. 127.
[2] *The Meaning of Truth*, p. 156.

work with it, enable us to manipulate it better, and modify it to suit our practical needs, but they will never satisfy us theoretically *until* they correspond with it in the full and literal sense of that term. This is the aim of science ; this the purpose of philosophy ; and unless it is in fact an aim which *is being progressively realised*, it must be confessed that the primary *ratio essendi* of both science and philosophy is a futile fancy, an illusory will o' the wisp. Pragmatic truth is pragmatically a failure. It may satisfy our practical needs, but it cannot satisfy our need for real knowledge, which is one of the most imperative needs of our nature. Like an exaggerated Intellectualism, it makes man a one-sided monstrosity, demanding to know that which is unknowable, and striving to attain that which must remain for ever beyond his reach. Pragmatism is but a humanised form of Scepticism, and Humanism is Subjectivism attuned to pragmatic ideas. In the end both are unworkable, because the elements of truth that lie within them are exaggerated beyond all endurance. Hence Pragmatism to the anti-pragmatist seems ridiculous and useless as a theory of the *nature* of truth. It remains, however, to consider whether it has provided us with anything useful in the way of *criteria* of truth.

CHAPTER XXII.

PRAGMATIC CRITERIA OF TRUTH.

§ 393. It is not a little consoling to find that Professor James has set down, as the *sixth misunderstanding* of Pragmatism, the statement that " *Pragmatism explains not what truth is, but only how it is arrived at ;* " [1] for so much beside the point do pragmatic definitions of truth seem to me, that I have often wondered whether the pragmatist ever really intended to *define* truth at all. But although the discussion in the last chapter thus appears not to have been mere waste of words, there is no doubt that the question, ' How is truth validated ? ' is of supreme importance in the eyes of the pragmatist. In fact, the nature of truth and the validation-process are for him one and the same. Truth is *that which makes it !* But here we must consider the pragmatist's ' definitions ' of truth as statements of truth's criteria.

In Dr. Schiller's opinion, there is no more momentous distinction than that between a truth and a mere claim to truth, and no distinction, he says, which it is more difficult to get the formal logician to recognise. Granted, then, that we start with mere claims, how does a claim get converted into a real truth according to the pragmatist ? By its consequences, we are told. That is obvious : there can be no other way, if no truths are self-evident.

---

[1] *The Meaning of Truth*, p. 200.

But what are the consequences of truth ? They
are, says the pragmatist, consequences which are
practically useful, relative to a human purpose and
in the furtherance of human life. But from the
very particularity of the truth-process it follows
that these consequences are many and varied, as
varied as the definition of truth itself. Hence if we
wish, like good pragmatists, to treat of the criteria
of truth *in the concrete*, we must perforce consider
these consequences one by one.

The first characteristic of truth, then, which
Pragmatism has selected as one of the most valuable
of its criteria, is that *truth must make a difference to
action*. Thought is purposive ; its function is to
generate belief ; and belief results in action. Hence
different beliefs should lead to different actions, in
reference to which the validity of the belief may be
judged. This is the central doctrine of the " Pragmaticism " of Mr. Peirce, and is a corollary of his now-
famous dictum that " our conception of the practical
bearings or effects of an object constitutes the whole
of our conception of that object." [1]

If this be a mere statement of the psychological
fact that ideas tend to find for themselves outward
expression, and that sooner or later and directly *or
indirectly* an idea will result in a modification of
action ; or, again, if this doctrine be applied in a
hortatory sense to moral and religious truths, it can
hardly be denied that truth often does, and, in the
latter case, certainly should, make a difference to
action. Moral truths must be ' living truths.'

[1] cf. James, " The Pragmatic Method," *Journ. of Phil., Psy.
and Sc. Methods*, 1904, p. 673 ; and *Studies in Humanism*, p. 6.

They must make a difference to our lives ; and to
' live a truth ' consists " in making it an object of
the interior life, in which one believes, by which one
is nourished, and which one carries out in practice." [1]
But if the doctrine means that *all* truths, scientific
and theoretical as well as religious and moral, must,
if they are to be true at all, directly influence conduct, exceptions to the rule are far too numerous and
too striking for us to allow it any general applicability
or even to concede that it is a *rule* at all.   What
practical difference, for instance, can it make to the
actions of the ordinary man whether the earth is
round or flat, or whether it is the sun that circum-
navigates the earth or the earth that revolves on
its own axis while the sun is relatively stationary ?
Yet, I suppose that the ordinary man, in spite of his
' passivity ' in this respect, and even if he has not
the use of a laboratory or a telescope, is at liberty
to form his own opinion on this ' claim to truth ' if
he chooses to do so.

One is hardly surprised, therefore, that Professor
James should have amended the phrase ' difference
to action,' and interpreted it as ("particular consequences, in our future practical experience, whether
active or passive ; the point lying rather in the fact
that the experience must be particular than in the
fact that it must be active." [2]) Truth must make a
difference *to our* experiences, active or passive,
practical or theoretical.

Thus, if no future detail of experience or conduct is
to be deduced from our hypothesis, the debate between

[1] Le Roy, *Revue Métaph. et Morale*, 1901, p. 327.
[2] *loc. cit.*, p. 674 ; and cf. *The Meaning of Truth*. p. 210,

Materialism and Theism becomes quite idle and insignificant. Matter and God, in that event, mean exactly
the same thing—the power, namely, neither more nor
less, that can make just this mixed, imperfect, yet
completed world—and a wise man is he who, in such a
case, would turn his back on such a supererogatory
discussion.[1]

If theoretical consequences are to count, the
wisdom of Professor James's ' wise man ' may, I
think, be called in question. Nevertheless, it is
undoubtedly true that with the ' hypothesis ' of a
God " the actually experienced details of fact . . .
grow solid, warm, and altogether full of real significance." But surely the point of such a criterion
lies in the *kind* of difference that it makes to our
lives. If ' practical bearings ' mean *any* particular
experiences that may result from a hypothesis or
claim, ' practical bearings ' do not provide us with
a very useful criterion of truth ; for truth and error
alike make a difference to experience. Some further
criterion is needed, therefore, in order to distinguish
between different kinds of ' differences to experience,' and it has been suggested that only
beneficial differences should be regarded as a sign
of truth.

§ 394. ' Beneficial differences ' are in general
those which satisfy our human needs ; but ' differences ' are to be taken as ' differences for me ' and
only those which are beneficial to me, which satisfy
my purposes and needs, are to be regarded as
validating claims to truth. Truth is a " function
of agreeable leading," a " function of *a leading that*

[1] *Ibid.*, p. 676.

is worth while." The consequence of a true idea is
that by it we are enabled to *handle* reality "*better
than if we disagreed.*" [1]

Now one way of judging whether we are better
for something that has happened to us, is to ask
ourselves whether we *feel* the better for it, or, in
other words, whether we are satisfied emotionally.
In *The Will to Believe*, Professor James assigned to
emotional grounds for belief a definite value in cases
where the intellect failed to provide a sufficient
reason for assenting to doctrines of a religious
character, and where it was imperative that some
decision should be come to. Pragmatism has taken
up this idea and made it a fundamental doctrine
applicable to all truth. Indeed, it seemed at one
time as if the claims of our ' passional ' nature were
going to drive out intellectual and logical claims
altogether and to constitute themselves the sole
pragmatic criterion of truth. The protests of
intellectualists, however, have obtained certain concessions on this point. Professor James grants that
intellectual claims must be admitted as of equal
importance with those of the emotional side of our
nature ; and Dr. Schiller insists that truth is not
merely a value, but a ' logical value,' in the estimation of which the intellect has, at any rate, something to say.

The question may be raised, however, whether the
satisfaction of emotional needs has *any claim at all*
to be regarded as a criterion of truth. Have we any

---

[1] *Pragmatism,* pp. 202, 205, 213 ; cf. *The Meaning of Truth,*
pp. 80, 82 ; *Humanism,* Essay I ; and *Studies in Humanism,* pp. 6,
152, 153 ; 187, 188.

right to appeal to the emotions in order to settle whether a theory is true or is not true ? Certainly if by an appeal to the emotions is meant an appeal to mere feeling or sentiment ; if it merely signifies that the theory in question is *pleasant* to contemplate, and stirs us up to enthusiasm, without appealing also to our more rational nature, such a criterion is irrational and of little value. For, after all, it is the intellect which must judge and give the final assent, and to subordinate it to mere feeling, to an ' epi-phenomenon,' to a bye-product, as it were, of a confused mass of sensations, of vague and half-formed judgments, and of moods which largely depend on the state of our bodily health, is clearly to degrade it and pervert it from its natural purpose. The emotions are peculiarly unstable ; they vary from moment to moment, sometimes filling us with exuberant hope and joy, sometimes plunging us into despair. How, then, if our criterion itself is variable, can it possibly help us to determine truth ? *When* are we to form our judgment about (*v.g.*) a future life beyond the grave ? When we are in an optimistic mood and such a prospect seems bright, attractive and full of promise, or when we are gloomy and dejected and a future life seems impossible, illusory, incapable of realisation ? If we choose in a brighter moment, the promise of a future existence will seem to hold good. But it will hold good only so long as our mood lasts. When the mood passes, our criterion itself has gone, and the doctrine of a future life, unproved and unprovable according to the pragmatist if emotional grounds for belief are excluded, is no longer able to satisfy us. When

despondent or distressed we *need* the doctrine of a
future life in order to succour our failing energies ;
but such a doctrine is powerless to help us unless
we already believe in its truth. The mere *will* to
believe is of no avail in such a contingency unless
assent has already been given on more rational
grounds. The emotions and the ' will to believe '
may prepare the way for belief ; they may even
directly influence assent in some cases, and so lead
often enough to error ; but they cannot generate a
permanent assent to the doctrines (*v.g.*) of a future
life or of the existence of God, because the emotions
which we experience when contemplating such
doctrines *will depend upon whether we believe in them
or not*.

Again, by whose emotions and by whose needs
is a claim to truth to be judged ? Is each one to
judge for himself ? If so, we shall have contradictory verdicts, for each one will declare that to be
true which seems to him to satisfy *his* needs. The
selfish and carnal who desire only to do as they
please and to satisfy their craving for pleasures,
regardless of consequences to anyone else, will
declare that Naturalism is valid because it gets rid
of God and so removes all cause for conscientious
scruple or supernatural fear. The upright man,
on the other hand, will declare for Theism, because
it promises him that some day the mystery of evil
and pain will be solved and the good will receive their
deserts.[1]

An appeal to the emotions as such, then, has

---

[1] cf. an article of mine, entitled " Truth and Toleration," in
the *Irish Theological Quarterly* for Jan., 1910.

little, if any, value as a criterion of truth ; for, as
Newman has said, the strength which the emotions
seem to give to assent is " adventitious and accidental ; it may come, it may go ; it does not (or
at any rate it should not) interfere with the genuine-
ness and perfection of the act of assent." [1]

§ 395. But we may interpret an appeal to the
emotions quite differently. In the emotions the
fundamental needs of our nature are expressed ;
and an appeal to them may mean that after a careful
consideration of the fundamental demands of our
nature, of its psychological structure, its functions
and its purposes, we have come to the conclusion
that unless these demands are satisfied, our nature
will be meaningless, futile, inexplicable ; and if this
is what is meant, then our argument may be valid.
For now we are no longer allowing our judgment
to be determined by the emotions or by our felt
needs ; but we are rationally considering those
needs, distinguishing the fundamental from the
accidental, separating those which are peculiar to
the individual from those which are common to
human nature ; in a word, judging rationally and
intellectually of the significance and purpose of
man.

Such an appeal as this is of quite a different
nature from that which is merely emotional ; and
the value of ' psychological ' arguments of this kind
was recognised long before any pragmatist ever
thought of taking them up. Even so thorough an
intellectualist as Mr. Bradley, though insisting
that the will and the emotions have no right ' to

[1] *Grammar of Assent*, p. 185.

dictate to the intellect,'[1] yet admits that "the realisation of any aspect of human nature should— to speak in general—be limited by due regard to the whole." [2] Truth, for Mr. Bradley, is, as it should be, primarily an affair of the intellect, and the aim of metaphysics is 'to find a general view which will satisfy the intellect ; ' yet he also affirms that "truth is harmony, and harmony is attended with an emotional accompaniment. Hence the absence of the latter is an indication that something is wrong." [3] Intellectualists, then, are not loth to admit that it is legitimate to base arguments on the rational demands of our nature ; but this, they maintain, is a very different thing from allowing our emotions to influence beliefs, without previously considering whether they express a fundamental need or whether they are quasi-hysterical and wholly irrational feelings dependent on we know not what. Yet the pragmatist hardly seems to have grasped this distinction, vital as it is to the right evaluation of truth-claims.

§ 396. Emotional criteria, however, no matter what interpretation we put upon them, are applicable in comparatively few cases. The scientist is not helped much by his emotions in deciding whether he will accept or reject the principle of the Conservation of Mass ; nor are emotional considerations of great account when it is a question of determining the probable effects of Fiscal Reform on English commerce, or of a rise in the value of certain stocks

---

[1] *Appearance and Reality*, p. 150.
[2] *Mind*, N.S. 51, p. 321.
[3] *Appearance and Reality*, p. 155.

upon market prices in general. Hence the pragmatist has to look for a further test of truth, and he finds it in that other aspect of a 'beneficial difference,' *utility*, or the value of truth as a *means of manipulating reality*.

> To agree with reality in the widest sense [says Professor James], can only mean to be guided straight up to it or its surroundings, or to be put in such working touch with it as to handle either it or something connected with it better than if we disagreed.[1]

Now utility ordinarily means that which satisfies some practical need as opposed to a theoretical or moral need ; and in this sense all *things* are useful more or less, for all things are, as the scholastic puts it, *et unum et bonum et verum*. Chairs, tables, walking-sticks, aeroplanes, flowers, fields, fresh air, indeed the majority of the things which we find around us, are useful to somebody or to something, though they may not be useful *to me*. Utility, however, cannot be taken in this ontological sense, if it is to serve as a criterion of logical truth ; for otherwise things themselves would be logically true. Clearly, then, the utility which is to be our criterion must be an *experienced utility ;* and hence arises the question, *utility for whom ?*

This question is not easy to answer. For if you reply *utility for anybody*, I must then point out first that the earthquake in Messina and such like catastrophes are apparently not useful to anybody ; and, secondly, that you need some criterion by which to tell when things are really useful to other people, for it is *you* who must judge of their utility.

[1] *Pragmatism*, pp. 212, 213.

And if you reply, ' useful ' means *useful for me*, I must enquire of what use it is to you that someone should have broken a pane of glass in your conservatory, or that your neighbour should insist upon playing ' Home, sweet Home ' on a badly-tuned piano. It is useful, you tell me, *to know* that the pane of glass has been broken, because you can then have it repaired ; and it is useful *to know* that your neighbour is not a musician, because then you may try to persuade him to give up practising, or may take up your abode elsewhere. But it may be questioned whether these consequences are really useful, especially in the latter case, for if your persuasion fails to take effect, you will be put to considerable expense. And even if the ultimate consequences are useful, they will be useful only *provided your knowledge of the original facts was true.* For if the facts were not real but illusory, your endeavour to escape their immediate consequences has been so much waste of time. The utility or uselessness of *particular* consequences, therefore, does not show whether what you take to be fact is or is not really fact. What you perceive may be useful, and yet be fact as mutilated by your perception of it ; and conversely it may be quite useless, and yet be real fact.

But, you tell me, it is useful to regard as objectively real whatever is perceived in a particular way (*i.e.*, by external perception) ; and if what is perceived in this way is in general to be regarded as objectively real, we must not make arbitrary exceptions. Doubtless this is true. The question is, however, not whether we are to make arbitrary exceptions, but whether we are to allow any exceptions at all, and, if so, under what circumstances. If the objective reality of facts is *not* self-evident, as the pragmatist asserts, we need some criterion by which to decide whether a fact that *claims* to be real is *really* real, and for this purpose the criterion of utility is, to say the least, inadequate. When applied to ' facts ' it breaks down completely. There are innumerable ' facts ' observed by us every day, of which many are not of the slightest utility to us personally, and some are distinctly harmful and unpleasant ; yet we do not for this reason regard them as pragmatically false. And conversely there are many facts which would be extremely useful to us, could we regard them as ' really ' facts ; but which cannot be so regarded because their claims to truth are *obviously* unfounded. The pragmatic criterion of utility, therefore, is not of the least value when it is a question of distinguishing between facts which are ' *really real*,' and facts which only claim to be real ; yet this is a distinction which we must make, and actually do make, on innumerable occasions in the course of a single day ; and, further, it is a distinction upon which the possibility of all higher kinds of knowledge depends. I do not mean to say, of course, that to be able to distinguish between facts which are ' really real ' and those which are illusory, is not something of the greatest practical value. I willingly grant that all knowledge has a practical value greater or less in degree and extent ; but I maintain that in deciding upon a claim to factual reality we never do use the criterion of utility, nor would it prove of any service to us if we were to try so to do.

§ 397. Still keeping to the ordinary sense of the term ' utility ' (viz., that which satisfies a practical need), we may apply it now to theory. Theory, we are told, enables us to ' deal efficiently with reality ; ' which may mean either that it *determines our expectations rightly*, or that *it enables us to control the course of events by inventions and appliances of various descriptions in such a way as to make them subservient to the practical needs of life*. In either case the theory is useful ; but can its utility be employed as a test of its truth ? Is it not rather a consequence of truth already established ? Of course, if by saying that a theory is useful in that it determines our expectations rightly, you merely mean that particular consequences deduced from the theory harmonise approximately with empirical facts, there can be no question that ' utility ' in this sense is a criterion of truth ; but this is not the sense in which the term utility is ordinarily used. Moreover, we need *other* criteria, (1) by which to distinguish the particular hypothesis from which our consequences have been deduced from the rest of the theory ; (2) by which to decide whether that hypothesis really does lead to these consequences ; (3) by which to know whether these are the only consequences to which it can lead : and ' utility ' for these purposes is of no avail.

It is not utility, then, in the ordinary sense of that term, which is used by the scientist as a criterion by which he tests the truth of his theories. Nor do I think that the fact that truth leads to ' inventions '

which can be applied to useful practical purposes,
can be of any use as a criterion of truth. Can we
regard the *utility* of the Forth Bridge, for instance,
as testifying to the truth of mechanical principles ?
The *existence* of the Forth Bridge and the fact that
it carries the weights that it was intended to carry,
undoubtedly testifies to the truth of the principles
which guided the architect in its construction. But
this is not quite the same thing as to say that the
Forth Bridge is useful for purposes of actual transit.
The truth of the mechanical principles in question
would be verified just as well by shunting train-loads
of sand backwards and forwards from one end of the
bridge to the other, as by the actual use of the bridge
in practical life as a means of getting from Edinburgh
to Perth.

In so far, then, as a theory determines our expectations rightly, it is true ; but the ' utility ' of the
theory seems to depend rather upon the possibility
of applying it to practical purposes, which is an
afterthought, as it were, and is not essential to the
truth of the theory ; though inasmuch as it is a
particular case of expectations which have been
rightly determined, it goes to confirm the theory
itself. The right determination of our expectations
again, is doubtless itself useful ; but it is useful
because it is ' right,' not ' right ' because it is useful.
Hence, to call this right determination of our expectations ' utility ' is misleading ; for in ' utility '
we seem to have a *new* criterion of truth, whereas the
criterion of conformity of fact with expectation, to
which it is reducible, is as old as science itself.

§ 398.   It is important that the point of the above

argument should be clearly grasped, for what I have
said applies also to the next criterion which we have
to discuss. I am *not* trying to prove that the
pragmatist ignores the theoretic interest, which,
as Professor James remarks, would be ' simply
idiotic.' What I wish to show is (1) that many of the
criteria of truth which Pragmatism offers us are as
old as truth itself, and were recognised as ' consequences ' of truth which might be used in order to
verify it long before Pragmatism was invented ;
and (2) that the pragmatist has no right to identify
these consequences, directly or indirectly, with the
practical utility of truth.

Now Professor James frequently insists that an idea
is a ' substitute ' for some sentient experience, and
that in order to be true it must ultimately lead to the
sense-experience for which it has been substituted.
" A conception," he says, " is reckoned true by
common-sense when it can be made to lead to a
sensation." " Our ideas and concepts and scientific
theories pass for true only so far as they harmoniously lead us back to the world of sense ; " [1]
and " such simple and fully verified leadings
are the originals and prototypes of the truth-
process." [2]

Here, once again, we have a very old criterion of
truth rehabilitated in pragmatic dress. Apparently
there is nothing new about this criterion, except the
form in which it is expressed. Everyone will admit
that scientific hypotheses and theories, to be true,
must lead to conclusions which harmonise, coalesce,

[1] *The Meaning of Truth*, pp. 132—136.
[2] *Pragmatism*, p. 206.

or agree with empirical facts. The only questions
are (1) What does the pragmatist mean when he
says that truth must lead us to reality, put us in
working touch with it, and enable us to deal with
it beneficially and satisfactorily ; and (2) is this
criterion the only criterion of truth, the original or
prototype of all truth-processes ?

Now 'handling,' 'controlling,' 'manipulating,'
'getting into working touch with' reality or with
sensation, all suggest 'practical utility.' (Hence one
is inclined to think that in using such expressions
the pragmatist is really trying to bring the old and
well-established criterion of 'verification by the
senses' into line with his pragmatic doctrine that
truth is ultimately verified by its *practical* consequences.) And if this is so, it is necessary again to
point out that it is by the coincidence of fact with
particular conclusions deduced from hypothesis or
theory that the latter are verified, and not by any
practically useful results that may ensue. But
perhaps the second question is the more important
one in this connection.

Is 'verification by the senses' really the fundamental form of all verification ? Is there no other
criteria of which this is not the prototype ? What
about 'relations between ideas,' the propositions of
mathematics and geometry, statements about events
in the past, and the validity of deductive processes
of reasoning ? Here it is that, according to Professor
James, "indirectly or only potentially verifying
processes" [1] come in ; yet these, although they do
not lead *directly* to sense-termini, do so indirectly,

---

[1] *Ibid.*, pp. 208, 209

and hence conform to the prototype of all truth-processes.

True ideas lead us into useful verbal and conceptual quarters as well as up to useful sensible termini. They lead to consistency, stability and flowing human intercourse. They lead away from eccentricity and isolation, from foiled and barren thinking. The untrammelled flowing of the leading-process, its general freedom from clash and contradiction, passes for its indirect verification ; but all roads lead to Rome, and in the end, and eventually, all true processes lead to the face of directly verifying sensible experiences *somewhere*, which somebody's ideas have copied.[1]

Professor James admits that this is a "large loose way" of speaking. Nevertheless it describes more or less accurately what happens in regard to the verification of some truths of the conceptual order ; but does it apply to all ? Sometimes we hold a proposition in mathematics or geometry to be true, because it leads to, or follows from, other truths already established ; and, again, we verify a process of reasoning by examining whether it conforms to logical rules. But how do we test our ultimate principles, our mathematical axioms and our logical rules ? And how do we know that our reasoning conforms to these rules ? Intuition has to be called in here, and Professor James does not hesitate to invoke it. As we have seen, he admits that sometimes truths are "perceptually obvious at a glance ; " but in his anxiety to reduce all truth-processes to one pragmatic prototype, he forgets this. Yet intuition is needed as the very foundation of conceptual truth. ' Relations between

[1] *Ibid.*, p. 215.

ideas ' do, indeed, lead us at times to the face of sensible experiences ; but that process of leading is a process of application, not of verification. The relations themselves are true eternally, in advance of any such special application to objects in the concrete. Moreover, it is difficult to see how ideas of past events can lead even indirectly to sense-termini ; while facts, on the other hand, may be truly as we apprehend them, yet do not *lead* to immediate experience, since it is in immediate experience that they are given. We are forced to conclude, therefore, that the criterion of sense-verification is neither applicable nor necessary in every case, and so cannot be the original or prototype of all truth-processes.

§ 399. From what has been said above, it is clear that Professor James holds the satisfaction of theoretical needs to be of very great importance, even if ultimately theoretical are subordinate to practical needs. Truth, especially when it leads into conceptual quarters, must lead to consistency and flowing human intercourse. New truth " must derange common-sense and previous belief as little as possible." Even " that past time itself was, is guaranteed by its coherence with everything that's present." [1] In short, the demand for consistency, coherence, agreement between subjects and predicates, accord between process and process, object and object, is so imperative for a highly organised intellect that " so long as such an accord is denied us, whatever collateral profits may seem to inure from what we believe in, are but as dust in the balance." [2]

[1] *Pragmatism*, pp. 216, 215.　　[2] *The Meaning of Truth*, pp. 98, 99.

Dr. Schiller's views on this subject, though less emphatically expressed, are no less clear than those of Professor James. In spite of his vigorous attack on the Absolutist position (that consistency or coherence is the *sole* test of truth, he admits that truths must be compatible with one another, and that a self-contradictory proposition is wholly meaningless.[1] He points out that the getting rid of contradictions is by no means the easiest or most logical point from which to begin our attempt to harmonise experience ; but admits that the getting rid of contradictions is *one* aspect of the attempt to secure greater harmony therein.[2] And there can be no doubt, I think, that Dr. Schiller is right here. The principle of Contradiction is both valid and valuable ; but its value is chiefly negative. Contradiction proves error, but the absence of contradiction does not necessarily prove truth. Doubtless it is highly improbable that a *complex* theory should be self-consistent, and yet be false. Still such a contingency is conceivable. Whence it follows that consistency and the ' absence of frustration ' is, if taken by itself, inadequate as a criterion of truth.

But the real question is, Wnence arises tne value of this criterion of consistency ? Is it due to the fact that the universe proceeds from a common Cause or Ground which itself is one and consistent, or is it due to human habits which are now so fixed and constant that they will not allow themselves to be thwarted ? Is the principle of Contradiction

---

[1] *Studies in Humanism*, p. 111.
[2] *Ibid.*, p. 239, and cf. *The Meaning of Truth*, pp. 99, 100.

'necessary' because things are so constituted that they are what they are and not otherwise, and hence force our thinking to conform to the order of nature ; or is its necessity psychological, the result of a human need ? We have already discussed this question,[1] and have seen that the pragmatic view leads to a sceptical Subjectivism. If the demand for consistency be due merely to a mental habit, or arise merely from a human need, the value of consistency or non-contradiction as a criterion of objective truth is destroyed. Nor does the fact that reality has played a part in the building up of this habit[2] affect our conclusion, unless, in the formation of the habit, reality does not merely control, but determines the content of thought. But if our abstract concepts are merely 'man-made products' or 'artificial mental things,'[3] which, when they are consistent, lead to, or are terminated by, sense-experiences, and so give satisfaction, our real criterion of truth is not 'consistency,' but the satisfaction that ensues from reactions terminated as we wish them to be terminated, reactions which can be most readily brought about by consistent conceptual thinking. Thus the criterion of 'consistency,' as interpreted by the pragmatist, is a *subjective* criterion, for it is reducible to the satisfaction, and apparently to the *felt*-satisfaction, of our needs ; and this is clearly something subjective.

§ 400. The idea of habit as a sign of truth may, however, be worked out on somewhat different lines. Habit, in fact, may be taken as the sole criterion of

---

[1] cf. *supra* §§ 97, 376, 387.
[2] cf. *The Meaning of Truth*, pp. 97 *et seq.*   [3] *Ibid.*, p. 85.

truth ; and this would seem to be the actual conclusion to which M. Rey's Pragmatism has led him. M. Rey, like other pragmatists, speaks of truths being verified by ' useful consequences,' understood, of course, " in a most noble sense." But realising that it takes a very long time to discover whether a truth is really useful, and also that it is impossible without considerable experience to determine how far consequences which are apparently useless, unworkable, *incommode*, should be allowed to depreciate the value of an otherwise useful hypothesis, M. Rey is driven to the conclusion that only those forms of perception and thought are true which have become habitual. Truth arises from habits that are practically irreversible and biologically immune from change. Its ' necessity ' is not intrinsic, but psychological. It is the necessity of mental habits which are the combined product of thought-activity and objective experience, and which in course of time have become so fixed that nothing short of a radical disruption of the structure of the human mind could change them.[1]

This doctrine, as we have already seen, is the logical consequence of the pragmatic or humanistic theory that knowledge is the product of an evolutionary process in which the mind progressively adapts itself to its environment. Hence it would seem that Pragmatism, if pushed to its logical consequences, brings us back to that old and venerable criterion of truth, ' necessity,' or the ' impossibility of conceiving the contrary.' But in explaining how this ' necessity ' arises, there is a

---

[1] cf. *Humanism,* pp. 52 *et seq.* ; and *'Axioms as Postulates,'* § 10.

NN

fundamental difference between the traditional and the pragmatic theory. That certain ways of perceiving and thinking have only gradually become habitual can hardly be denied. Nor can it be denied that felt-satisfaction arising from consistency and abhorrence of all that is contradictory and inconsistent also grows stronger as the intellectual side of our nature becomes more highly developed. It is stronger, for instance, in a scientist than in a schoolboy, and stronger, again, in a European than in an Oriental mind. So far both traditionalist and pragmatist are agreed. But while the former starts from the principle that knowledge is possible, and hence infers that all forms of thought and perception which are natural, normal, and habitual, must *per se* be capable of giving truth, and as the condition of this lays down that the content of cognitive acts must be determined by their respective objects ; the pragmatist, on the other hand, starts with the assumption that ideas—at least in part—are man-made products which in no case present at the outset more than a claim to truth, but may *become* true, should they in the long run lead to useful results. Hence, as ideas or modes of cognitive reaction which lead to useful results do become habitual, and would not become habitual unless they did prove useful, he is logically bound to accept M. Rey's criterion of the ' psychologically necessary ' or ' biologically constant,' as his only sure test of pragmatic truth. Verification in experience, as pragmatically interpreted, is ultimately reducible to this, for verification is complete only when adaptation is complete and habits, perceptual

and intellectual, have become so fixed that their
reversal is practically impossible, since it would
involve a radical change in our mental structure.

§ 401. Putting aside the scepticism involved in
the view that cognition is only a peculiar way of
reacting upon our environment, when we attempt
to apply in practice the above criterion of truth,
we are at once confronted with a very serious
difficulty. It is easy enough to apply the test of
'psychological necessity' to axioms and first
principles, but it is not so easy, indeed it may be
questioned whether it is possible at all, to apply it to
theories; and it is *certainly* impossible to apply it to
any kind of truth *in the making*, for then our habits
of thought are *ex hypothesi* not fixed. Yet it is
precisely in this latter case that we most need a
criterion of truth. Apart from axioms and the
general facts of every day life, almost all truths are
in process of making; and it is surely for these truths,
or rather for these claims to truth, that a criterion
is most urgently needed. If, however, as seems to
be the case, 'psychological necessity' is the only
pragmatic criterion that can give us certainty, it
follows that we have no criterion at all for truth
in the making, but must always wait until it is made.
And if in reply to this argument you tell me that in
regard to many objects habits of perception and
thought have already been formed, and that new
objects are accepted as true, or rejected as false,
according to whether they can be apperceived or not
by the former—which is practically the criterion
suggested by Avenarius and Simmel[1]—I must ask

[1] cf. *Studies in Humanism*, pp. 157, 158.

in what this ' apperception ' can consist, if you deny
that we have any apprehension of the nature of
objects. We can hardly apprehend the compatibility or incompatibility of that the nature of which
we are ignorant. True, we may invent or postulate
a mysterious *vis apperceptiva* in obedience to whose
autonomous dictates relations of compatibility and
incompatibility ' flower out ' of the stream of experience ; but this is not only to declare apperception
inexplicable, it also means that the pragmatist has
had to fall back upon an intellectualist criterion just
precisely in those cases for which his original pragmatic criterion was introduced, viz., in cases where
truth is yet in process of making.

§ 402. (A further difficulty might be raised against
the doctrine that psychological necessity arising from
habit is our only criterion of truth, on the ground
that habits vary considerably with individuals.)
And I know not whether it is in order to avoid this
difficulty, or whether it is merely in order to supplement and complete the general doctrine that truth
is relative to our needs, (but certainly pragmatists
seem more and more inclined to appeal to common
consent or to the consent of experts as one of their
chief criteria of truth.) This tendency is especially
characteristic of French Pragmatism.[1] M. Poincaré
insists much on the importance of social agreement,
and M. Milhaud bases truth on the harmonious
working of a collective mind. The mind, he says,
is like an instrument in which harmony is produced
by *normal* vibrations ; and when this is so, one mind
agrees with another and we have both truth and

[1] cf. *supra* §§ 319, 320.

objectivity. Hence *that* assertion and *that* theory
is true and valid which is " normal enough to be
accepted by every man of sound mind." [1]

Dr. Schiller, on the other hand, has been accused
of making the individual criterion ultimate. Truth
is that which is good for *me*, that which satisfies
my needs and enables *me* to live in harmony with
my environment. Consequently Mr. Hoernlé, in
criticising Dr. Schiller's view, has pointed out that
though none of us submit tamely to the opinions of
our age, but claim each of us for his own hypotheses
universal validity, a truth-finder is of necessity a
truth-teacher, and hence our individual world must
somehow be bound up with the common world.
He suggests, therefore, as a 'universal' criterion of
truth, the *Arbeitswelt* of Professor Eucken, which is
" to comprise the whole of human life in its
theoretical and practical aspects." [2]

Dr. Schiller, however, though he certainly emphasises the personal character of truth, by no
means ignores the importance of collective criteria.
In fact, it is to social recognition that he, like Herr
Simmel and the French pragmatists, attributes the
' objectivity ' of Truth. In *Studies in Humanism* [3]
for instance, he tells us that " whatever individuals
may recognise and value as ' true,' the ' truths '
which *de facto* prevail and are recognised as objective
will only be a *selection* from those which we are
subjectively tempted to recognise." And in his
earlier work, *Humanism*, [4] he had already warned us

---

[1] *Etudes sur la pensée scientifique*, p. 10 ; and cf. (Poincaré)
La Valeur de la Science, pp. 264–271.
[2] *Mind*, N.S. 56, p. 476. [3] p. 153. [4] p. 58.

that " truth, to be really safe, must be more than an individual valuation ; it has to win social recognition, to transform itself into common property "—a doctrine which is completely in harmony with his general position that truth and reality (as we know it) are the product of the combined activity of the human race in reaction upon its environment.

But, however useful a collective criterion of truth may be as a check upon individual vagaries, it cannot be ultimate ;) and Dr. Schiller is undoubtedly right in regarding truth as in this sense a personal matter. If truth is valued by our needs, it must be in the last resort by our own needs. My needs may in general be the same as those of the rest of mankind, and what satisfies these common needs will be *pro tanto* more true. But, after all, truths are truths for *me*, and it is *I* who have to judge in the last instance whether other people's needs are satisfied, as they seem to be. Everyone recognises that expert opinion is credible provided it agree, for experts are supposed to know all the facts of the case, and to understand how far their theories apply and what relation they bear to other theories and accepted truths. The opinion of the expert, there-fore, under such circumstances, has clearly a special value such as that of an amateur can never possess. Still, at best, the agreement of experts is only a subordinate criterion, for it presupposes belief in the capacity and trustworthiness of witnesses, to test which another criterion is needed.

§ 403. Thus we are driven back upon individual criteria. Neither a consensus of opinion among

experts nor the common consent of mankind at
large can be our ultimate criterion of truth, and
for that matter at most they give us only moral
certitude. Habit or psychological necessity is also
inadequate, since, like the social criterion, it will
apply to but few cases. It is seldom, if ever, that a
mental act is due solely to habit. Objective experience, or the nature of the objects about which
we think, is almost always a conditioning factor
in any judgment we may make. Nor will the other
criteria suggested by the pragmatist be found to
work any better. ' Difference to action,' ' difference
to experience,' and ' utility,' all take into account
objective conditions ; but ' difference to action ' and
' utility ' are too narrow, while ' difference to
experience ' is too wide to be of any practical use.
Where, then, are we to look for a suitable working
criterion whereby to test the validity of claims to
truth made by our minds both at the common-sense
and at the higher scientific or philosophic level of
intelligence ? Either, it would seem, we must fall
back upon that time-honoured criterion, ' evidence,'
or we must adopt what seems to be very like
its emotional counterpart, ' satisfaction.'

Both Professor James and Dr. Schiller have
chosen the latter alternative. Having pointed out
that " emotion accompanies actual cognition as a
shadow does light," but with effects not always
salutary, Dr. Schiller, nevertheless, affirms that
" if a feeling of satisfaction did not occur in cognitive
processes the attainment of truth would not be felt
to have value."[1] Without it, logical ' necessity,'

---

[1] *Studies in Humanism,* pp. 82—84.

'cogency,' 'insight,' and 'certainty' are meaningless words. We judge reasoning to be *pro tanto* good,
results *right*, operations *valid*, conceptions and
predications *true, when the results or consequences of
our experiments are satisfactory.*[1] Consistency tends
to the same end. It is but the reacting of one
portion of our beliefs on another " so as to yield the
most satisfactory total state of mind." [2]   Similarly
" truth in science is what gives us the maximum
possible sum of satisfactions," in which taste is
included, but of which consistency is " the most
imperious claimant." [3]   In fine, though to be
' satisfactory ' is a term that admits of no definition,
so many are the ways in which it can be practically
worked out,[4]

yet at each and every concrete moment, truth for each
man is what that man ' troweth ' at the moment with
the maximum of satisfaction to himself ; and similarly,
abstract truth, truth verified by the long-run, and
abstract satisfactoriness, long-run satisfactoriness,
coincide. If, in short, we compare concrete with
concrete and abstract with abstract, the true and the
satisfactory do mean the same thing.[5]

The vagueness and ambiguity of ' satisfaction,'
or a ' sum of satisfactions,' as a criterion of truth,
needs little comment. Satisfaction not only varies
in quality, tone, and intensity with the individual,
but also with the particular truth-claim in question.
Satisfactions, like pleasures, can neither be defined
nor measured, except by a multitude of standards

---

[1] *Ibid.*, p. 185.
[2] *The Meaning of Truth*, p. 88.
[3] *Pragmatism*, p. 217.
[4] *The Meaning of Truth*, p. 101.   [5] *Ibid.*, p. 89.

which do not admit of comparison and cannot be
tabulated or scaled. One man prefers one kind of
satisfaction, another another, according to his
temperament, education, general mode of life. With
Professor James the satisfactions arising from consistency seem to prevail ; with Dr. Schiller those
which are due to the fulfilment of purpose and the
furtherance of interest ; with others those which
arise from utility or expediency in a less noble sense.

So long, then, as the pragmatist is unable to tell
us what satisfactoriness is, we can hardly discuss
further its value as a criterion of truth. It has
occurred to me more than once, however, that
satisfactoriness may be nothing more than the
emotional accompaniment of what Newman would
call a judgment of the Illative Sense, what I should
call ' evidence.' [1] And if this is so, the only fault I
have to find with the pragmatist in this respect is
that he has selected the more variable, and therefore
the less valuable, aspect of what we all acknowledge
must be the final test of truth. He admits that
truth is ' a property of an idea,' yet he has chosen as
his criterion its emotional accompaniment. He
allows that ' the making of truth ' must be controlled by reality and that consequences are in part
determined by reality ; but instead of simply stating
that truth ' happens ' or is recognised, when it is
' evident ' that reality has controlled and determined
thought, he bases his valuation of truth on the
affective tone of this evidence, which is distinctly
subjective. Did this emotional accompaniment of
the apprehension of truth run parallel with, or were

[1] cf. *infra,* §§ 418 *et seq.*

it exactly proportionate to. the evidence upon
which judgment is based, it would not perhaps
matter much whether we took satisfactoriness or
evidence itself as our criterion. (But since satisfaction depends largely upon volition,) and upon
purpose, interest, and general tone of body and mind,
it matters a great deal; (for it makes our criterion,
so far as we can tell, in any concrete case, subjective
to an almost indefinite extent, and so destroys almost
entirely its value as a criterion.) Truth must satisfy
us, and it will do so in the long run if it is evident ;
but a feeling of satisfaction may arise from other
causes besides objective evidence, and when this is
the case, it cannot but lead us astray if we use it as
a criterion of truth.

§ 404. The pragmatist's view of truth's criteria,
therefore, is, like his doctrine of the nature of truth,
more than tinged with Subjectivism—a consequence
which is due partly to Humanism and Protagorean
principles, which exaggerate the subjective element
in cognition and ascribe to purposes, interests and
needs an all-pervading and all-permeating influence ;
partly to disgust with Intuitionism, which has led to
the opposite extreme, to the belief that no value
can be intuitively recognised and that the experienced consequences of truth must therefore
be evaluated by their subjective emotional effects ;
but chiefly, I think, to the substitution of ' utility '
for ' correspondence ' in the definition of the relation
of truth to reality. If truth can in no intelligible
sense be said to ' copy,' ' correspond with,' or
' represent ' reality, what other relation can it have
to reality except that of leading to useful results ?

And if these results are never experienced as they are objectively, but only as modified by purpose, why should they not be judged by the total state of satisfaction or dissatisfaction to which they give rise ? The whole question turns upon one point : Is the true subordinate to the useful and the good ? Does the seeker after truth *merely* aim at satisfying a purpose and gratifying a need ? Does science exist merely that it may be used to harmonise our experience ? Is the whole function and motive of all theoretical constructions from the highest to the most elementary and simple, directed in the end to the furtherance of human control over reality, and the transformation of it to suit our human needs ? If it is, the criteria of truth that Pragmatism has offered us are probably the best we can get. But if it is not, utility and satisfactoriness are certainly inadequate and of very little value for either practical or theoretical purposes wherever the question of truth comes in. As a last example of this, and at the same time as an illustration of our main contention that ' utility ' presupposes truth already established, we may instance the variety of opinions that exist in regard to practical matters where knowledge is wanting. What precisely is the effect of exercise on the body and particularly on the brain ? We do not know, and hence eminent doctors will give contradictory advice and will even go to the length of writing articles, some recommending more, some less exercise, on the sole ground of utility. Again, in regard to food (than which no question could be more practical) the advice of experts is contradictory. Some recommend ample food, others a minimum. Some forbid animal food, others advise it. Some say alcohol is injurious, others that it is beneficial. Most advise regular food ; but some say eat when you like and more or less what you like, while one authority on the subject of ' vitality ' has recently published a large volume in which he advises a perpetual fast ! [1] Then, too, in educational matters, the utility of compulsory Greek has for a long time been a burning question. Nay more, in respect of elementary education, if we may judge by the Report of the Poor Law Commissioners, the experience of half a century seems likely to be reversed, since they tell us that the studies and the methods at present in vogue are not of a kind likely to be useful to the children in after life. And why all this contradiction in practical matters ? (It is due to the fact that, lacking knowledge, we are forced to base our judgments upon the utility of consequences, and about the utility of consequences it is impossible to secure agreement even among experts.) Unless, then, truth be utility and nothing more, it is irrational to use utility as our criterion of truth ; for judgments about value or utility are almost as variable as judgments in regard to beauty or taste, especially when they are not based on recognised truth, but have to rely solely on experience.

[1] " Vitality, Fasting and Nutrition," by Hereward Carrington, cf. Review in *Nature,* for Nov. 1908, p. 68.

CHAPTER XXIII.

CRITERIA OF ERROR IN REALISM.

§ 405. A realist, whether he explain human knowledge by means of a causal interaction between object and subject or not, must at least admit that somehow or other the object determines the content of thought, and that between percepts, concepts and judgments on the one hand, and real entities on the other, there is a correspondence or resemblance. So vital is this idea of correspondence to the theory of knowledge and truth that neither the absolutist nor the pragmatist is able quite to get rid of it. Kant, though rejecting correspondence in the realist's sense, retains it in another form. In the *Critique of Pure Reason* the syntheses of the imagination anticipate and correspond to those of conception. The structure of the rational mind, which is so minutely analysed by Kant, also corresponds to a type ; and it is precisely because of this correspondence and its universality that ' objective ' knowledge is possible. This idea of truth as conformity with a type or ideal is further developed by the Critical and Neo-Critical writers of to-day. In their view, Reality is a systematic whole, a coherent organised unity, constituted by the experience of the Absolute ; and this Reality, considered as significant and intelligible, is Truth— what the scholastic would call Ontological Truth. Ontological Truth, or Reality considered as intelligible, is the foundation of Logical Truth. Logical truth consists, therefore, in the conformity of the individual and finite mind with Reality itself ; for it is essential to Truth " to manifest itself in the thinking of finite subjects." And precisely in proportion as this Ideal or Absolute Truth is realised in us, we possess knowledge or logical truth. Indeed, Dr. Joachim acknowledges that we can never rise above the level of knowledge which at the best attains to the truth of correspondence, since all human discursive knowledge must ever remain thought about another.[1] The pragmatist, too, admits, as we have seen, *at least provisionally*, that truth consists in ' agreement with reality.' So that the correspondence-notion has, at any rate, an excellent claim to our attention, since it would appear that after all there must be some kind of correspondence between the mind of the knower and the object which he knows.

§ 406. Assuming, then, with the realist, that truth consists in an *adæquatio intellectus et rei*, and that *this adæquatio* or correspondence is due to the determination of the content of thought by the object, in order to ascertain the validity of any particular claim to truth, we need criteria by which to decide whether this correspondence exists, *i.e.*, whether our thoughts have been objectively determined or not. This does not mean that *per impossibile* we must be able to *compare* our thoughts and our percepts with real things as with something outside of thought and perception, since clearly it is only by means of thoughts and percepts that

[1] *Nature of Truth*, p. 73.

things are known. The only comparison possible for us is a comparison between things as thought and as perceived. The realist asks for no ' miraculous second-sight ' by means of which to detect the agreement or disagreement of copy and original, of idea and reality.[1] Truth is correspondence of thought and reality, but this correspondence can be established without comparison, provided we can answer the question : ' When has thought been determined by the object and when has it not ? '

§ 407. Now there are two ways of attacking this problem. We may start from methodical doubt, or we may start from what I may call, perhaps, methodical and rational assurance. Granting that the function of thought is to give us knowledge of reality, we may begin by assuming that our thoughts as a rule go wrong, in which case we shall require criteria of truth by which to decide when they have *not* gone wrong. Or we may begin by assuming, not that perception and thought are psychological monstrosities, but that, in general, they perform well the function they are obviously intended by nature to perform ; in which case we shall need, primarily, not criteria of truth, but criteria of error by which to determine when *per accidens* a function has gone wrong. This difference of standpoint is no mere verbal question such as whether we are to cut off a slice and keep the apple or to cut off the apple and throw away the slice ; it is one of the utmost consequence in making up our

---

[1] cf. Wallace, *Hegel's Philosophy of Mind ;* and *Humanism*, pp. 45, 46. This objection is simply absurd, since it totally mis represents the realist's doctrine.

minds in regard to the epistemological value of human cognition. If we begin by doubting everything and affirm that *no* proposition has more than a claim to truth until it is validated, we can never get at truth at all, for *ex hypothesi* our criteria of truth themselves have only a claim to truth, and so has the validation-process ; and so, also, for that matter, has our original statement that no proposition has more than a claim to truth until it is validated. Scepticism is just as much the inevitable outcome of a doctrine which begins by asserting that no truth is more than a claim till its validity has been tested, as it is of the doctrine which makes truth an absolute and impossible ideal. On the other hand, if we begin by assuming—what in reality is not an assumption at all, but a self-evident truth—that *ordinarily* and *per se* perception, conception and judgment, when functioning normally, are capable of giving us knowledge, then we have something positive and definite with which to start, and can proceed to establish criteria by means of which to eliminate abnormal functionings which are likely to lead to error.

§ 408. The latter standpoint is that of the realist. The first principle of his theory of knowledge is that knowledge is possible, and that his cognitive faculties are capable of attaining to truth, which is the purpose and end of their existence. His aim, then, as a logician, is not to devise criteria of truth, but rather criteria of error. Error is a fact; but it is not a sufficient reason for us to distrust altogether the deliverances of our faculties. For, being a fact, it must have a cause, and we may be

able to discover this cause and so to eliminate error
by distinguishing from the rest those circumstances
in which the deliverances of our faculties are *not*
to be trusted.

We have said that truth consists in conformity
between the content of thought and the nature of
the object or system of objects to which it is referred.
And conversely error consists in a positive disconformity between the two. In other words, truth is
the reference of the content of thought to an object
to which it corresponds ; while error is the reference
of the content of thought to an object to which it
does not correspond. Now the correspondence in
which truth consists arises when the content of
thought has been determined by the object to which
it is referred. Error, on the other hand, since it
consists in positive disconformity, implies that
thought has been determined by something other
than the object to which it is referred. In order to
decide, therefore, under what circumstances the
deliverances of our cognitive faculties are *not* to be
trusted, we must know what other causes may
determine the content of thought besides the object
to which it is referred.

There are several causes which may determine the
content of thought. It may be determined (1) by
the object of sense-perception through the mediation
of the phantasm ; (2) by habit or association of
ideas, and (3) by the constructive activity of
thought itself guided by some purpose which it
seeks to realise. And each of these determining
causes may *per accidens,* and under certain circumstances, lead to error. Error, however, will not

occur until a false objective reference has been made, for in abstraction from objective reference neither sense-impressions nor ideas are either true or false. Hence the causes of error which we are about to consider are material rather than formal causes ; they account for the disconformity between thought and thing, not for the false objective reference, which, as we shall see, is due to quite another cause.

§ 409. All that the senses give us as such (*i.e.*, abstracting from any intellectual function that may co-operate in human sense-perception) are the external *appearances* of things ; and appearances cannot, in themselves, be false, though they may be misleading ; which is, I take it, what we mean when we speak of ' false appearances.' Now ' false ' appearances may be due either to objective or to subjective conditions. The bent appearance of a straight stick when it is partly in and partly out of water is an instance of the first, for the optical illusion in this case is due to the refraction of the rays of light which have to pass through the water in order to affect the eye of the observer. Again, the Muller-Lyer illusion is due to objective conditions. A straight line appears shorter if it is terminated by arrow-heads which are turned inwards, and longer if the arrow-heads are turned outwards ; the reason being that in the first case the motion of the eye by which the length of the line is estimated, is checked, and in the second case increased, by the arrow-heads. The ' false ' appearance in both these examples is due to the determination of the sense-impression by something else besides the object

upon which attention is focussed. It is not merely
the stick and the straight line which determine the
' form ' which the percept takes, but the stick and
the straight line *in certain circumstances*. Neither
case, however, is strictly normal, for ordinarily we
do not perceive things through water, nor do
we require to judge by the senses, alone and unaided,
of the length of lines in more or less complicated
figures. And though in neither case can we get
rid of the optical illusion, it need not lead to false
judgment, provided we take account of the circumstances. For in both cases the tendency to error
can be counteracted, in the first by handling and
in the second by measurement. Nevertheless, the
examples given may serve to establish two useful
criteria in regard to sense-perception. First, we
must be careful to take account of the circumstances
under which perception takes place, and, if abnormal,
must experiment in order to discover whether the
special circumstances make any difference to what
we perceive. And, secondly, if accuracy as to detail
is required, we must make use of instruments which
place the senses in conditions in which they are
known to be reliable.

§ 410. False appearances are sometimes due to
subjective conditions, to the inaccuracy of the
senses or to their abnormal state. The sense-
impression does not always correspond exactly with
the objective stimulus. For instance, a straight
edge of paper may, as has already been pointed out,
be perceived as bent if applied to a line of nerve-
terminals which itself is bent. And though the
circumstances in this case, being those of a psycho-

logical experiment, are clearly abnormal, in no case can the senses be relied on for more than a certain degree of accuracy. In respect of accuracy, however, the senses vary considerably, so that the inaccuracies of one sense acting under certain conditions may be counteracted by employing the same or another sense under different conditions, or again, and more especially, by the use of instruments.

Other errors, v.g., illusions and hallucinations, may be due to the abnormal conditions of the senses or of the brain. Giddiness may cause an apparent motion of the room in which one stands ; paralysis in one of the muscles of the eye may cause the stone-mason to strike his hand instead of his chisel ; while abnormal sensibility in any organ may lead, not only to exaggerated perception, but to the perception of what is not real at all, but merely subjective. It is clear, then, that the senses are trustworthy only so long as they are in their normal condition ; otherwise they are likely to lead us astray.

§ 411. The ' relativity ' of sensation seems to present a more serious difficulty. But this is not really so ; for in all cases the illusion due to the relativity of sensation may be counteracted by varying its circumstances or its antecedents. If we want to judge of colour accurately, we must judge of it in various lights and with various backgrounds ; though in ordinary life we do not need this exceptional accuracy, for colour is only one among many qualities by means of which we distinguish objects. Moreover, contrast seldom effects a total change in the colour of an object, and since it is by differences of colour for the most part that we distinguish objects, and since differences are not toned down but exaggerated by contrast, it is probable that the latter assists rather than hinders the true perception of real things. The ' relativity ' of sensation is also quantitative. Two objects of the same weight but of different size are perceived as of different weight if one is lifted immediately after the other. But here, again, if we want accuracy we do not trust the unaided senses, but have recourse to instruments. Fechner's law, perhaps, might be cited as an instance of quantitative illusions due to relativity ; but to me it seems that to perceive differences proportionately is a more accurate way of perceiving them than to perceive them by addition and subtraction.

One more illusion illustrating a relativity of a different kind. When seated in a railway train the fields and hedgerows seem to rush past us as we proceed ; whereas, in reality, they are motionless. The cause of this illusion is that when we are unconscious of our own motion, movement, if any, appears to belong to the object. The alleged ' apparent ' motion of the sun round the earth is due to a similar cause, though here there does not seem to be an illusion strictly so called. For we do not perceive an actual motion in the sun ; all we perceive is that its position relative to our point of observation changes from hour to hour. There is no ' false ' appearance ; but the error of the older astronomers was due to a gratuitous assumption leading to a false inference. Illusions due to the relativity of motion, however, rarely lead to error, and need never occur provided we are careful to ascertain whether the object or system of objects relative to which another object is said to move, is itself really stationary.

Ordinarily, then, appearances are to be trusted ; but (1) we must exclude those cases in which the condition of the senses is abnormal ; (2) when the circumstances are abnormal we must ascertain whether they make any difference to the percept ; and (3) if accuracy is required, we must employ objective methods of measurement which place the senses in such circumstances that they are reliable even in regard to details.

§ 412. Habit also determines the content of thought ; and again *per se* it is not a cause of error. For a habit is but a tendency to repeat an act already elicited, and assuming that the previous act corresponded with its object, so also will its repetition. Habit, however, depends largely upon physiological conditions, particularly upon cerebral connections ; and the same set of neurones may function on many different occasions not only in the experiencing of fact, but also in reading and conversation. Hence the course which the nervous impulse takes when free from intellectual control is somewhat haphazard, so to speak, and thus arise dreams and the play of fancy. It is clear, however, that neither dreams nor the play of fancy lead to error under normal conditions ; for, although both have 'false' appearance of objectivity, there is, strictly speaking, no objective reference. Hallucinations and 'fixed' ideas, too, are clearly due to abnormal and pathological conditions, and, if continued, lead eventually to madness. With these cases, therefore, we are not concerned ; but there are two cognitive processes in which habit is operative, both of which are of considerable importance from our point of view. I refer to memory and to the subsumption of particular cases under general ideas and laws.

In memory we definitely set ourselves to recall some past event, something which we have seen, or heard, or read ; so that the cerebral processes which in part at least condition memory are not free to function according to the law of least resistance, but are subject to intellectual control. In what this control consists we do not know, for in spite of much modern research on the subject memory is still a mystery. Nevertheless, it is clear that the course which the nervous impulse takes *is* controlled in memory, and that in consequence ideas tend to revive in the order in which they occurred on the occasion which we are trying to recall. To me, indeed, this seems to imply not merely intellectual control, but an intellectual memory, the activity of which is conditioned physiologically, but as a habit is independent. At any rate, this would account for the fact that the intellect accepts or rejects ideas suggested by physiological associations according as the events we are trying to remember do or do not seem to us to be therein correctly recalled—a fact which is not fully accounted for by internal consistency or inconsistency in what we remember. In any case, we do remember, and in so far as we have *certain*

remembrance, our memory is ordinarily trustworthy, and if we wish for greater certainty we may
appeal to written records and other objective criteria.

§ 413. The functioning of habit in perception
occurs both at the sensory and at the intellectual
level. The integration of the percept itself is due
partly to habit, and the subsumption of the percept
under a general idea or category is also due partly
to habit. In both cases, however, the functioning
of habit is controlled by objective conditions, and
as the habit itself has been built up by previous
perceptual and conceptual activities, themselves
objectively determined, the correspondence of
percept and concept is not destroyed, but rather
facilitated and made more accurate. Thus, the
perception of distance and of the third dimension is
largely due to habit ; but, though in the perception
of long distances error may occur, and illusions of
' reversible perspective ' are familiar to the experimental psychologist, here as before the senses are
reliable except in special circumstances, and here
as before their deficiencies may be easily remedied.
Similarly in regard to subsumption. A few characteristics suffice whereby to recognise an object and
to cause a certain concept to function in the mind.
A few strokes of the pen are sufficient to suggest a
soldier, a wheel-barrow, a bird, or any of the
common objects with which we are familiar. And
in the same way real objects are instantaneously
subsumed, and usually correctly subsumed, under a
general idea by force of habit, and without any
careful examination of their characteristics. But
sometimes the idea suggested by habitual association

may be wrong, and the predicates which are contained within that idea may turn out to be incompatible with this particular concrete instance, as in the case of Madame Tussaud's policeman who is found to be not a policeman at all, but a wax figure incapable of movement. Seldom, however, when formal and deliberate assent accompanies subsumption, does error occur ; for unless the object is familiar and the subsumption obvious, we hesitate, and only subsume after a more or less careful examination of the characteristics of the object in question. In most cases certainty is possible if we require it ; and if we do not require it, we are content with probability, and so do not give a full and complete assent.

The influence of one's ' point of view ' and of expectancy in perception and subsumption are particular cases of the influence of habit. The plain man and the artist admire the sturdy grandeur of a venerable oak ; the botanist examines its peculiar structure and estimates its age ; the builder laconically remarks that it is a fine piece of timber and would cut into a number of valuable planks. Each has considered the oak from a different point of view, yet neither has been thereby led to make a false judgment. Again, expectancy is seldom the cause of error. It may lead to a momentary illusion, but this is usually corrected spontaneously and immediately. Only in abnormal cases does expectancy lead to a false judgment, as in pathological cases, and in pre-perception, where the conditions are those placed by the experimental psychologist.

§ 414. Habit, then, though it is more or less concerned in almost all cognitive activity, seldom, if ever, leads to error, provided due care is exercised in any particular case, whether it be one of memory, of perception, or of subsumption under general ideas. There remains, then, what I have called— for want of a better name, which should be equally comprehensive—the constructive activity of thought. Under this head I include any kind of purposive enquiry, inference and postulation, since all these cognitive processes may be regarded as constructive. That purpose functions in almost all cognition can hardly be questioned ; but since, as I have already shown in a previous chapter,[1] purposes do not affect the content of thought, but only its intent, *i.e.*, the questions which we ask, the influence of purpose is not ordinarily, nor need it ever be, a cause of error. That *de facto* purpose does sometimes lead to error, I grant ; and as to why it does so I shall have something to say in a moment ; but it is not because facts are ' selected ' and ' accepted ' according to our purposes, even though selection is ' immensely arbitrary,' and many facts are ' allowed to drop out and so to become unreal.' All who wish to explain or to theorise choose those facts which are relevant to the purpose in hand ; but an honest enquirer will ' accept ' indifferently facts which confirm, and facts which militate against, the hypothesis which is to be proved ; while only those which are irrelevant will be neglected. Why purpose should be supposed to ' make ' or to ' distort ' fact I cannot understand. It makes us generally alert and

[1] cf. *supra*, § 47.

observant ; it determines the relevance of fact ; it causes us to ' accept ' certain facts and neglect others, and to consider those we do accept in relation to our hypothesis and to neglect other relations and significances which the same facts may have, but which are irrelevant. In short, it determines what Professor Stout has called the ' *intent* ' of thought. But the accepted facts are facts for all that ; and their *content* is not affected by our choice of them in preference to others.[1]

Almost all the difficulties which the pragmatist finds in the ' rigidity ' and ' coerciveness ' of fact arise from a confusion between content and intent. Take, for instance, the following dilemma in which Dr. Schiller sums up his arguments against the realist's position on this point :

If our choice, selection, and *congé d'élire* does not affect the rigidity of fact, it is an illusion which ought not even to seem to exist, and we certainly have no right to talk about it : if, on the other hand, there really is ' selection,' will it not stultify the assumption of a rigid fact, introduce a possible arbitrary manipulation, aud lead to alternative constructions of reality ? [2]

In reply to the first horn of this dilemma, we may grant that the *congé d'élire* exists and is no illusion, but really determines the intent of thought, *i.e.*, it settles what facts are to be admitted as relevant : but in reply to the second horn of the dilemma, we must deny that the rigidity of fact is stultified by our selection, since its content and nature is not affected. Nor can we admit that selection intro-

---

[1] cf. Professor Stout's excellent essay on ' Error ' in *Personal Idealism*, with which I find myself almost wholly in agreement.
[2] *Studies in Humanism*, p. 125.

duces arbitrary manipulations, since it is the facts
themselves which must determine our manipulation
of them if we are seeking truth ; or that it necessarily
leads to alternative constructions, since alternative
constructions imply ignorance or neglect of relevant
facts, and this is precisely what selection is intended
to avoid.

§ 415.   There seems to be no reason, then, why
purposive selection or any other kind of purposive
activity should lead to error.   On the contrary,
since, like habit, it facilitates both perception and
conception by defining the point at issue and
excluding irrelevant matter, it seems to tend rather
the other way and to be, in fact, a function of the
greatest service in the acquisition of truth.   No
intellectual function of itself can lead us astray.
Abstraction is trustworthy, for in it we consider
entities, which, though they do not exist as such
a parte rei, nevertheless exist as aspects of reality,
and by reality indirectly through the phantasm the
intellect is determined to act.   Abstraction is not
falsification, unless we assume with the Hegelian
that all aspects of reality intrinsically modify one
another, or with the pragmatist that selection
implies transformation : both of which assumptions
are wholly gratuitous and unwarranted, and lead
inevitably to Scepticism.   Judgment, too, is trustworthy.   For, if *a posteriori* and contingent, the
conjunction of subject and predicate in a certain
relation is directly determined by facts ; and, if
necessary, the predicated relation is implied in the
abstract entities the nature of which the intellect
has apprehended.   In like manner, inference is

trustworthy, for we apprehend explicitly what is already contained implicitly in the premisses, as when by means of the syllogism we apply a general law to a particular concrete case. We have no reason, then, for distrusting the results of our intellectual operations, which *per se* are reliable *provided and in so far as they claim our assent.*

But intellectual operations do not always claim an unconditional assent. Not infrequently judgment and inference is tentative, hesitating, doubtful. We are not sure that we have apprehended things correctly or that the conclusions we are inclined to draw are really contained in the premisses. This is the case not only in regard to inferences based on a complexus of hypotheses or principles, all inter-related and inter-dependent ; but it is true also of those immediate judgments in which we apprehend a relation as holding universally and necessarily between subject and predicate. On this point Aquinas remarks that the recognition of the truth of principles varies according to the intellectual capacity of each individual.[1] Sometimes our immediate judgments and our inferences are certain, as when the entities or laws with which we are dealing are comparatively simple ; but sometimes they are doubtful and present only a claim to truth which requires verification. Now a doubtful judgment, a doubtful inference, or a mere postulate is not an error, since, in so far as it is doubtful, it is not accompanied by assent. The activity of thought, therefore, even when inferential and constructive, is

[1] *Summa Theologica*, 2. 2, q. 5, a. 4, ad 3.

not *per se* a cause of error, though it may be so *per accidens*, as I shall now proceed to explain.

§ 416. When the pragmatist asserts that the function of the will and of the emotions is of the greatest importance in cognition, he is perfectly correct. Not only is almost all cognition governed by purposes which we strive to realise ; but the will may also directly affect assent, provided we have that to which assent may be given.

A rational act [says Aquinas] can be considered in two ways ; first *in reference to the exercise of the act ;* and regarded from this aspect a rational act is always under the *imperium* of the will ; and, secondly, *in reference to the object,* in respect of which there are two rational acts to be considered. The first is the apprehension of the truth about anything ; and in this the intellect is not under our control. For it takes place by virtue of some natural or supernatural light. Hence in this respect the intellect is not under our control, nor is it under the *imperium* of the will. There is another rational act, however, in which the intellect assents to what it apprehends. If, therefore, what is apprehended is such that the intellect naturally assents to it (as in the case of first principles) such assent or dissent is not under our control, but pertains to the order of nature, and so, properly speaking, is subject to the imperium of nature. There are, however, certain things which we apprehend, which do not compel the intellect to assent or to dissent, or, at any rate, do not prevent it from withholding assent or dissent for some reason ; and in such cases assent or dissent is under our control, and is subject to the imperium of the will.[1]

It lies in our power, therefore, not only to think or not to think, but also to give or to withhold our

[1] *Summa Theologica,* I. 2, q. 17, a. 6.

assent in a doubtful case, *i.e.*, in a case where the evidence *ex parte objecti* is insufficient to establish more than a claim to truth ; and if assent is given in such a case error is the *probable*, though not the necessary, result.

§ 417. There are various ways in which the will may influence assent. We may be unwilling to take the trouble to examine facts carefully or to think a difficult problem out. We may be in too great a hurry to pay due attention to the observation of facts and their circumstances, or too impatient in our desire to arrive at a solution to consider carefully the *pros* and *cons*. Or, again, we may be anxious to prove that we are right and somebody else is in the wrong. Many, indeed, and varied are the motives which may impel us to give a premature assent or dissent to a matter that has only been half thought out. Errors due to inadvertence and carelessness, to a kind of mental inertia, are the most common of all. Facts, inferences and postulates, though recognised as doubtful at first, tend to become ' true ' by force of habit, if we do not examine and reject their claims. For what is constantly before the mind and yet is never examined comes to be regarded as part of the body of truths which have already been established and validated. Errors due to the emotions and to the ' will to believe ' are also not uncommon, especially in cases where personal judgments are concerned, and where in consequence there is more scope for emotional likes and dislikes. We are inclined to believe what is derogatory to the character of an enemy and to disbelieve what is derogatory to the character of a friend. Again, if the object of our affection or dislike is a class or an institution, it is easy to generalise what we have found to the credit or to the discredit of one or two individuals, and to extend it to the whole. More-over, errors due to the influence of these and other emotions tend to accumulate and so to form a system of erroneous beliefs which hang together and mutually support one another, and which, acting as bias or prejudice, prevent the apperception of what has in reality a valid claim to our assent. There can be no question but that there are systems of error as well as systems of truth ; and systems of error are peculiarly difficult to get rid of ; for though they must inevitably lead to contradiction some-where, either internally or with facts, the emotions backed up by the system itself may be sufficiently powerful to cause us to slur over the contra-diction, or, if it is a question of fact, to deny the fact that threatens to destroy our cherished beliefs.

It is needless, however, to develop further the unfortunate effect of the *influxus voluntatis* in the matter of truth. It is the formal cause of most, I think we may say of all, error ; for strictly the dis-conformity between thought and reality in which error consists does not exist until the content of thought has been definitely referred to some object. The material causes of error account for the dis-conformity, but they do not account for the assent that accompanies it. We know that under abnormal conditions perception is unreliable, and we are also aware that doubtful inferences and hypothetical constructions may or may not correspond with their objects. In such cases, therefore, assent implies either inadvertence and carelessness—a negative *influxus* of the will, as it were—or else it is conditioned directly by emotional influences and the ' will to believe.'

§ 418. Nevertheless, the cognitive faculties *per se* and when functioning under normal conditions, are trustworthy ; and in so far as this is the case their deliverances do not present merely a claim to truth, but they *are* true, since they are under these circumstances determined by the object itself. The criterion of truth here, therefore, is nothing more nor less than *objective evidence*. We assent because we are forced so to do by the object itself ; because it is the object itself and not some other object or cause which seems to have determined the content of our thoughts, and so to have manifested itself to our mind. We assent because that to which we assent is ' *obvious* ' and we cannot help assenting. Ridiculous and empty as this criterion of truth may seem to some, it is nevertheless the only criterion which the ordinary man uses, and the *only ultimate criterion that there is*. There are many *negative* criteria : we must not assent if we have reason for doubting the normal condition of the senses, if the formal laws of logic have been violated, or if we have contravened the norms of scientific method. But these criteria are criteria of error rather than of truth. Moreover, their value as means by which error may be detected presupposes the validity of the methods to which they pertain ; and this we can only know because the truth of the principles on which they are based is objectively evident in the sense and under the conditions above explained.

§ 419. What has been said above of the trust-worthiness of human faculties in general applies to my neighbours' as well as to my own. Consequently, although information gained from others, whether by word of mouth or by reading, at first presents only a claim to truth, we are justified in accepting the testimony of others in regard to facts, provided we have reason to believe that their observations were made with due care, and provided we have no reason to suspect any motive which would have led them to state what they knew to be false.

The theoretical constructions and explanations of others are in a different case ; for in the construction of theory the possibility of error is so great that we cannot accept as authoritative the testimony of one of the workings of whose mind we are ignorant. We must examine the evidence for ourselves, and if we can detect no error, and both data and inferences seem to us 'objectively evident,' then we have rational grounds for giving our assent. We may apply as many negative criteria as we like, but in the end we shall come back to objective evidence, and shall ask ourselves is it or is it not clear to my mind that the reasonings of this author or this lecturer are valid, that his data are accurate, his inferences logical, his conclusions consistent with facts ; in a word, is it obvious to me that the theory there before me is indirectly reality itself manifesting its nature to my mind, or does there seem to be mingled with it something subjective, something personal, something due *merely* to the constructive activity of the thinker who propounds the theory which claims my assent ?

§ 420. The case is not very different when it is a question of verifying our own deductions or theoretical constructions. When we have taken due care to avoid mistakes, when the ordinary logical criteria and the special criteria and methods of the particular science with which we are concerned, have been applied, we are forced back finally upon objective evidence. Is it or is it not clear to my mind that the content of my thoughts has been determined by the object ? Is the evidence sufficient to justify assent ? Do my theoretical conclusions and the complexus of experimental facts harmonise sufficiently to justify me in giving my assent to the truth of the former, or have I still reasonable ground for doubt ? These are the questions which I ask myself when judging of the truth of physical and other scientific theories, and according to the answer which the evidence compels me to make, I give or withhold my assent. The evidence in such a case is not, nor can it be, complete. The human mind is finite. It cannot analyse a theory into a complete system of propositions logically connected together and arranged in order of generality. It cannot deduce from each proposition all possible conclusions ; nor can it discover all the facts with which these conclusions must coincide if the theory is to be a complete and adequate explanation. We cannot hope that any construction of ours shall in this sense be verified and validated, for that would imply omniscience. Nevertheless, granted that ab-

straction is not falsification and that systems of fact
may be considered in comparative isolation without
destroying their nature, we are justified in holding
that theoretical constructions are true, provided
the *system* of theoretical inferences coincides approximately with the *system* of known facts and
nowhere leads to contradiction : and truth here is
real truth in spite of its approximate character and
its incompleteness. For an approximate truth is
not one that is subject to indefinite modification,
but one that is permanently true within known
limits of error. Such a truth expresses laws which
really govern the operation of real things, and which
really belong to the structure and plan of the
universe, though there may be other laws which
co-operate with these of the nature of which we are
ignorant. Evidence, then, without being complete
may be sufficient to justify assent, provided it is
objective. And it is objective in the case of theoretical
constructions, even though the latter may have
begun as postulates due in part to the activity of
mind. For our facts are objectively valid and our
principle that like effects presuppose *formaliter* or
eminenter a similar cause is also objectively valid.
Hence in so far as our ideal laws are expressed in
particular conclusions, the real laws which express
themselves in particular facts that correspond to
these conclusions must be in nature one and the
same.

§ 421. In metaphysical theory our ultimate
criterion is the same. Our last appeal is always to
objective evidence. Many of the principles upon
which metaphysics is based are, or should be,

necessarily true. They should, as Mr. Bradley says, be such that in denying them we implicitly affirm their truth. Yet the test of necessary truth is not the psychological impossibility of thinking the contradictory, for we may still ask why this should be a test of truth. The final criterion is self-evidence, the self-manifestation of the nature of the object to a rational mind. From self-evident principles and from others that are less clearly self-evident we make deductions, which we may test by the laws of formal logic. But the validity of the laws of formal logic itself demands a criterion, and that can only be self-evidence. Finally, comparing principle with principle and deduction with deduction we ask whether they are consistent; or applying our theory in the concrete we enquire how far it explains or fails to explain or contradicts the data of experience. Should it manifest self-discrepancy or prove incompatible with facts we pronounce it erroneous; should it merely fail to explain we pronounce it inadequate and incomplete. But our criteria are not ultimate. Contradiction certainly shows that somewhere there is error. Indeed, contradiction is our only *certain* test of error, for inadvertence and the influence of subjective conditions do not necessarily invalidate a theory : they merely render it doubtful. But, on the other hand, the absence of contradiction does not establish truth. We cannot say that a thing is true simply because it is coherent; unless we take coherence in a very wide sense as including harmony with facts. And even then our criterion is not ultimate, for we may still ask (1) how we recognise facts ; (2) how we recognise that a theory is coherent and does harmonise with facts ; and (3) how we know that reality must be consistent and coherent and must *not* be contradictory and self-discrepant. And to all these questions our final answer must be the same, it is obvious or evident.

We have said that if a metaphysical theory is incoherent or incompatible with facts it must contain error. Can we say conversely that it is true if it *is* coherent and *does* harmonise with facts ? This will depend upon what we understand by a metaphysical theory. If we understand by it a theory which shall explain all facts and co-ordinate all sciences, clearly there is no such theory. But if we understand by it a certain complexus of doctrines which explain facts in general, then these may be established as true. From the general fact of finite existence we may argue to the infinite, from the contingent to the necessary, from the caused to the uncaused or self-existent, and from the existence of a rational plan in the universe to an intellect which constructed and devised it. These arguments, I shall be told, are old-fashioned and at best only probable. That they are old-fashioned I admit ; but that they are only probable I cannot grant, for to me their validity is evident. To discuss this question, however, would take us outside the theory of knowledge. What I wish here to point out, is that even if the arguments by which the existence of God is commonly proved are, when taken individually, only probable, they may yet be valid when taken together, for then they form not merely a sum of probabilities, but, as the Hegelian would say, a coherent whole. The universe is a coherent system of inter-related parts, and the only condition which can satisfy this fact, the only 'hypothesis' that can explain it, is the doctrine of the existence of a necessary Being from whom it proceeds by an unchanging yet creative act.

§ 422. What I have said above of objective evidence as the ultimate and in many cases the only criterion of truth is in substance what Newman has said in his *Grammar of Assent* of what he calls the sanction of the Illative Sense. "The course of inference," he says, "is ever more or less obscure, while assent is ever distinct and definite, and yet what is in its nature thus absolute does, in fact, follow upon what in outward manifestation is thus complex, indirect, and recondite." Hence he infers that we must take things as they are, and "instead of devising, what cannot be, some sufficient science of reasoning which may compel certitude in *concrete* conclusions, must confess that there is no ultimate test of truth *besides the testimony born to truth by the mind itself.*" [1] Newman treats the subject of truth psychologically, whereas I have treated it epistemologically. He does not ask ' how comes it about that we can be certain ; ' [2] he accepts certitude as a fact and then enquires what is its nature, what its conditions, what the processes that lead up to it *as a psychical act of the mind.* Consequently he does not base certitude on objective evidence as I have done, but rather on the trustworthiness of the faculty of reason. Nevertheless, Newman maintains the certainty of knowledge and the real objective

---

[1] *Grammar of Assent*, p. 350. (Italics mine.)   [2] *Ibid.*, p. 344.

validity of knowledge as earnestly as does any
realist. Certitude is a natural and normal state of
the mind. It is not something to hide away and be
ashamed of. Our very possession of certitude is a
proof that it is not a weakness nor an absurdity to be
certain.[1] And the object of certitude and assent
is something real, something the nature of which we
apprehend ; it is not a mere notion or symbol or
word, the product of abstract and formal reasoning
which is out of touch with reality.

§ 423. There is scarcely a single doctrine now
upheld by the pragmatists which is not to be found
verbally stated in the *Grammar of Assent ;* yet
Newman was not a pragmatist. His standpoint is
psychological and human ; nay, more, he acknowledges the personal element in truth ; yet his
standpoint is perfectly compatible with Realism
because the results of his psychological analyses are
not exaggerated. The real nature of truth is not
confused with its pragmatic value. Product is not
confused with process, content with intent, the
various processes and methods by means of which
truth is attained with the real objective validity of
truth itself. He had as great a horror of verbal
arguments as any pragmatist, yet he insists that
certitude must follow on investigation and proof.[2]
He admits that certitude is accompanied by intellectual satisfaction and repose ; yet any
additional strength given to it by the emotions he
regards as adventitious and accidental. He shows
how knowledge is a growth, how in knowing a truth
we are active, and how in order to understand and

[1] *loc. cit.,* pp. 344, 209.   [2] *Ibid.,* p. 258.

appreciate a truth we must live it ; but the active recognition of propositions as true must be exercised *at the bidding of reason ; and reason never bids us be certain except on absolute proof.*[1] No merely formal or verbal argument is valid for Newman. And while, with Simmel, he acknowledges that in a series of reflex judgments each in turn may exercise a critical function towards those of the series that precede it ; yet the certitude which results from this series of proofs when taken in the concrete—not as a sum, but as a systematic whole—is certitude, indefectible and irreversible.[2] Lastly, everyone who reasons is his own centre, and no expedient for attaining a common measure of minds can reverse this truth, yet the personal action of the ratiocinative faculty, the perfection of which is called the Illative Sense, is capable of pronouncing a final judgment on the validity of inference in concrete matters such as may warrant that certitude is rightly elicited in favour of a proposition we infer.[3]

§ 424. For Newman, as for all realists, there is only one ultimate and universal criterion of truth, the evidence which results from a careful examination and study of that which we wish to know ; and as to the sufficiency of that evidence we are forced to trust and may rightly trust the deliverance of reason itself. Other criteria of error and of truth are useful and have methodological validity, but taken singly and in isolation from the living process of reasoning about objective real things, they are inadequate criteria. " Our enquiries," he says, " spontaneously fall into scientific sequence, and we think in logic

---

[1] *Ibid.*, p. 345.   [2] *Ibid.*, p. 255.   [3] *Ibid.*, p. 345.

as we talk in prose, without aiming at doing so."
But such a tangible defence of what we hold, though
it so fortifies and illustrates our holdings that it
acts as a vivid apprehension acts, giving them
luminousness and force, yet considered as an analysis
of our ratiocination in its length and breadth, is
necessarily inadequate.[1] " Thought is too keen and
manifold, its path too personal, delicate, and
circuitous, its subject-matter too various and
intricate, to admit of the trammels of any language,
of whatever subtlety and of whatever compass."[2]
And precisely because thought is so subtle and
intricate and personal, the human mind is capable
of attaining truth and yet is incapable of proving
the truth of what it holds by formal arguments to
another who fails to appreciate the concrete evidence
upon which that truth is based, and the concrete
and intricate process of reasoning by which it has
been established.

[1] *Ibid.*, pp. 286, 287.   [2] *Ibid.*, p. 284.

CONCLUDING CHAPTER.

§ 425. By a 'higher synthesis,' I understand, a synthesis in which antitheses are reconciled by means of distinctions which, while eliminating that which is false in the differences, retain what is true and reunite it in a truth that is higher because it is fuller and more significant. And at the outset of this essay in cognition, I boldly ventured to claim that Realism, if properly understood, is a higher synthesis of Absolutism and Pragmatism. It now remains for me to resume the chief points which I have endeavoured to make in this somewhat lengthy discussion, and to show that my main contention is valid.

The Critical Philosophy of Kant assumes as its first principle that in knowledge the object conforms to the mind, and this is the direct contradictory of the first principle of Aristotelian Realism. Absolutism and Pragmatism may be regarded as differences of Kantian Criticism ; not that they do not contain many ideas that are new, nor yet that they are opposed on every point ; but that in general they are antitheses of which the fundamental principles were enunciated more or less clearly by the author of the *Critiques of Reason and Judgment*. Both retain the fundamental assumption of the Copernican revolution, and both attribute know-ledge, and to some extent reality, to the con-structive activity of mind ; but the 'forms' which in knowledge are imposed upon the receptivity of matter are in Absolutism constitutive principles arising from the nature of thought as such, while in Pragmatism they are practical forms expressive of human needs and directive of human actions. Both seek to re-establish metaphysics on a sounder basis, but while Absolutism seeks that basis in the doctrines of the first *Critique*—Apriorism and Immanence, Pragmatism seeks it in the second *Critique*, in postulation and the experimental activity by which we seek to realise our postulates in the concrete and so to satisfy our needs. The standpoint of Absolutism is theoretical : it emphasises the functions of the intellect against Sensationalism. The standpoint of Pragmatism is empirical and practical : it emphasises the function of the will against Intellectualism. Consequently, Absolutism tends to Monism, while Pragmatism has a pronounced metaphysical inclination toward Pluralism, and toward a philosophy of Pure Experience which shall ultimately resolve itself in Personal Idealism. Finally, Truth for the absolutist is an Ideal Whole, and its test is coherence ; while for the pragmatist it is utility, and its test is its practical consequences for man. What Kant says of Rational Psychology, the pragmatist applies to all knowledge. It is merely a

'salutary discipline,' and its manifest contradictions show that the nature of the self (and the nature of things) cannot be known by the speculative intellect, and thus we are prevented from giving ourselves up to a mystic spiritualism that has lost its hold of actual life. The refusal of reason to answer our curious questions as to a life beyond the present we ought to interpret as a hint to apply our self-knowledge to fruitful, practical ends and to turn away from fruitless and transcendant speculations.[1]

Pragmatism, then, is the antithesis of Absolutism, for what the one asserts the other for the most part denies. Yet, although Absolutism and Pragmatism are differentiations of Criticism which have taken a diametrically opposite direction, both attempt to transcend the fundamental principle of the Kantian revolution and to reintroduce into knowledge, either from above or from below, some form of objective determination. In other words, both tend to return to a more realistic attitude in which the principle of Kant is practically denied. And it is, I maintain, only by following out this tendency that the absolutist and the pragmatist can hope to find an adequate solution of the problems of reality and of knowledge in which their differences, psychological, metaphysical and epistemological, may finally be reconciled.

§ 426. In Absolutism psychology is almost completely absorbed and overshadowed by metaphysics. Psychological questions are discussed for the most part only in so far as they seem to lend support to metaphysical theory. Hegel's *Phenomenology* and Dr. Joachim's *Nature of Truth* are in a sense psychological, genetic and human. So, too, is the standpoint adopted by Professor Bosanquet in his *Logic ;* for his analysis of the functions of thought, and his theory of the development of the hypothetical and universal from the individual judgment, are based on a study of the human mind ;

[1] Kant, *Werke*, vol. iii., p. 694,

chiefly, one would suppose, of his own. Nevertheless, the tendency of Absolutism is to regard knowledge from the Absolute and not from the human point of view ; to treat of knowledge in general, and then to predicate it, not of a human, but of a supra-human intelligence, which manifests and realises itself in finite centres. Consequently, human knowledge is at bottom an illusion ; its development is not real but apparent. The psychology of Absolutism does not reveal a dynamic process in time, but is rather a static analysis of what eternally *is*, into the organic differences of an underlying ground.

Pragmatism seeks to counteract the exaggerations of this static, lifeless Intellectualism by going to the other extreme. Nothing is ; everything becomes. Knowledge is a process without presuppositions or grounds ; and it is above all things an active, living, psychological, human process. There is nothing static about it ; nothing which has not had a history, and is still destined to have a history ; nothing which did not begin as a postulate to some extent unverified and liable to change, and which must ever so remain. All knowledge is human knowledge ; springing from human needs, expressing itself in human actions, leading to consequences the value of which depends upon their power to satisfy human needs. The pragmatist claims to have found as the result of his analysis of the process of human cognition, not *a priori* forms, but postulates and experiments. The postulatory or experimental theory of knowledge is a psychological theory. It does not enquire with the absolutist ' how knowledge is possible,' but rather what happens when we know or think that we know.

The psychological analyses upon which Pragmatism is based, however, are somewhat scanty and far from adequate; and to make up for this deficiency the pragmatist does in psychology what the absolutist does in metaphysics; he generalises categories beyond the limits within which they are applicable. Kant analysed experience and assumed that the categories he found there belonged to the subject ; Fichte analysed self-consciousness, and assumed that in so doing he had discovered the structure of Reality : the pragmatist analyses cognition, and, finding that we sometimes postulate, assumes that we do so always and in every case. Absolutism overcomes the Subjectivism of Kant, by making the Eternal Ego the subject of all consciousness and by transferring to Him (or It) the *a priori* forms through which Reality is constructed. Humanism gets rid of the fallacy of attributing to the Absolute the processes of human cognition by making psychology once more a human science ; but in so doing, it goes *too* far, and returns once more to a Subjectivism similar to Kant's, except that in place of *a priori* forms we now have human needs and purposes.

§ 427. The realist, on the other hand, is able to assign to psychology its due place in the theory of knowledge without finding himself impelled toward Subjectivism, and without having to invoke a psychology of the Absolute, of which he knows little or nothing, in order to save himself from it. His psychology is as human as that of the pragmatist.

He grants that all thought is purposive, and tends to satisfy human needs ; yet by restricting purpose to the intent of thought and regarding satisfaction as the consequence rather than as the essence of truth he is able to find room in knowledge for objective determination and real objective meaning. He grants that action is essential to knowledge, and that concepts are useful tools which help us in the manipulation of experience ; but, on the other hand, he insists that action is subordinate to knowledge *quâ* knowledge, and that, though by action knowledge is acquired and in it is expressed, knowledge and action must not be confused or identified. And thus the realist, without reducing the intellect to a mere machine for the manufacture of useful symbols, can justly claim that knowledge is living, and, though he does not attribute it to the mere unaided intellect, can truly claim that it is real.

Again, to the pragmatist the realist concedes that axioms are useful as regulative principles and that they are derived from and may be applied in concrete experience, but he denies that axioms are merely regulative or merely useful, or that their truth depends upon their application. While to the absolutist he grants that axiomatic principles are constitutive of knowledge, and that their objective counterparts are constitutive of reality ; but he refuses to identify knowledge and reality or to assign to axioms an *a priori* birth. Thus in Realism the necessity and objectivity of axioms is reconciled with their empirical origin, and their utility as practical norms is found to be compatible with, nay more, to depend upon, their objective significance.

Again, the empirical origin which is assigned to all
knowledge in Realism makes it possible for knowledge to have a real and not merely an apparent
development, and at the same time allows full scope
for experiment and for the constructive activity of
thought ; but since the realist acknowledges also
the power of the intellect to apprehend to some
extent the nature of real entities and the relations
which in some cases hold of necessity between them,
he is not forced to explain away self-evidence nor
to invent mythical stories in order to explain how
what is clearly not a postulate might possibly have
been so in its origin.

§ 428. It is difficult to compare Pragmatism
and Absolutism metaphysically : for while Absolutism is essentially metaphysical, Pragmatism
professes to be unattached ; and the philosophy of
Pure Experience with which it harmonises best,
itself tends to disruption, leading us on either to
Monism or to some form of Panpsychism or Personal
Idealism. Pragmatism, however, like Absolutism,
is idealistic in so far as it denies that the object of
perception and thought is independent of and
external to the mind in the realist's sense ; but
this does not seem to be essential to Pragmatism.
And though the pragmatist is inclined to adopt the
doctrine of Immanence, his philosophy does not
stand or fall with that doctrine. Rather, it is an
excrescence, a supplementary theory, a confession
of ignorance as to the metaphysical relation which
holds between mind and mind, between thought and
reality. Yet on one point there is clearly a resemblance, viz., between Fichte's idea of a system of

QQ

rational egos which eternally strive to realise themselves, and the Personal Idealism of those pragmatists who conceive the universe as an aggregate of rational, purposive minds, interacting one with another, and each striving to satisfy its needs by forcing a thoroughly plastic and formless matter to conform to its preconceived notions and hypotheses. The later philosophy of Fichte also suggests a comparison ; for his Personal Idealism eventually gave place to an Absolutism which was more like a philosophy of Pure Experience than what we now understand by Absolutism. Compare, for instance, Fichte's assertion that the Life of Knowledge is everything, that it alone exists, and exists of itself, requiring no subject in which to inhere, with the Radical Empiricism of Professor James in which substances and selves are done away and there is left only the cognitive process, the series of present thoughts or experiences which succeed one another and pass one into the other by continuous transitions, out of which are engendered in reflection both subject and object, thought and reality.

In spite of these similarities, however, Pragmatism as a theory of knowledge is radically different from and opposed to Absolutism. It denies that the universe is really one, and insists that both methodologically and epistemologically it must be regarded as plural. The universe for the pragmatist is not an organism, but rather a flat mosaic of which the parts, though inter-related, are yet distinct. And if he sometimes seems to identify reality with experience, he identifies it not with the experience of the Absolute, but with his own experience and with the experiences of other minds, human or incipiently human. Reality may be the product of mind, but it is the product not of a single all-embracing Mind, but of the combined activity of many minds, past, present, and in respect of future realities yet to be evolved. Facts, if they are immanent at all, are immanent within finite human experiences, and not within the experience of a self-sufficient and eternal consciousness. The pragmatist laughs at an Absolute which is a higher synthesis of God and the devil ; and of all kinds of knowledge, that which he singles out as most useless, is the knowledge which Absolutism claims to give.

§ 429. The realist does not go so far as this in his opposition to Absolutism. He admits that both Absolutism and Pragmatism contain much that is true, and that of the two from a metaphysical standpoint Absolutism is more satisfactory since it is less ambiguous, more consistent and more complete. Nevertheless, he cannot accept Absolutism as it stands, for the assumptions upon which it is based seem to him wholly unfounded, and the conclusions to which it leads he finds to be incompatible with facts. The fundamental theses of Absolutism have no foundation in the data of experience, but on the contrary, contradict many such data, a contradiction which Absolutism is neither able to explain nor yet to explain away. All idealists affirm that we cannot think of objects except as experienced, nor continue to speak of a piece of existence from which all perception and feeling have been removed. And this statement, if rightly interpreted, is true ; but if rightly inter-

preted, it does not lead to Idealism. For if by a
' piece of existence ' is meant a corporeal thing, and
by the ' removal of all perception and feeling,' that
it is possible to know that thing otherwise than by
means of sense-perception, then it is true that ' we
cannot find any piece of existence of which we can
still continue to speak when all perception and
feeling have been removed, or any fragment of
its matter, any aspect of its being, which is not
derived from, and is not still relative to this source ; '
but it does not follow from this that an object does
not *exist* independently of our perception of it or
that we cannot think of it except as actually being
perceived. Again, psychological introspection does
not reveal those felt-wholes of which Mr. Bradley
speaks and from which relational appearances are
supposed not merely psychologically but really to
emerge. What we perceive is a felt-whole, if by a
felt-whole you mean that what is perceived is perceived all together and in a single act. But what
we perceive is perceived neither as one nor yet as
many until we think about it, and then it may become
either one *or* many, and not until it has become
either one *or* many do we regard it as revealing to
us the nature of what we perceive. On the other
hand, it is a datum of our experience that what we
perceive is external, independent and material, and
until the idealist can explain this he is not justified
in treating as an illusion a belief which is both
natural and universal and apparently has been so
for all time.

Realism, then, has at any rate this advantage,
that it is consistent with facts which Absolutism

seems to deny. But I will go further than this, and will endeavour to show that as an explanation of the Universe Realism is more adequate and more consistent than Absolutism precisely in regard to those points where the demand of the human mind for an explanation is most urgent and peremptory. As, however, the metaphysics of Absolutism is so intimately bound up with its theory of relations, it is necessary first to sum up briefly the results of our previous discussion of this matter.

§ 430. Almost all philosophers now admit that relations are real. Even the empiricist has at length been forced to acknowledge this truth, though, being unable to explain *how* relations are real, he affirms that they are real because we feel them, which we certainly do not. Neither the absolutist nor the realist is content with so superficial a view. Both attempt to explain the nature of relations and the connection of relations with what they relate. But the absolutist, assuming that thought (or experience) and reality are one, prefers to treat the matter psychologically, since for him what is true of our knowledge of relations must be true of relations *in rerum natura*. The result is that he has given us two theories which are mutually contradictory ; for while Green, observing that our knowledge of relations is often prior to our knowledge of the objects they relate, infers that objects are *really* subsequent to and dependent on their relations ; Mr. Bradley, observing that our knowledge of relations is often simultaneous with our knowledge of their terms, infers that relations and their terms are interdependent and mutually presupposed one by the other. But the fact is that our knowledge of relations may be *either* prior to, *or* simultaneous with, *or* subsequent to our knowledge of the objects related ; hence a psychological theory must inevitably lead to contradiction if applied to *real* relations. Moreover, common-sense invariably regards a relation as arising from and as dependent on its terms, irrespective of the order in which our knowledge of relations and objects has developed; and this fact the Absolutist neglects altogether, as he also neglects the fact that relations may be predicated as an attribute, and in most cases as a real attribute, of *either* of the objects related. The realist alone takes account of all these facts, for in his theory alone are relations regarded as entities belonging to individual objects and conditioned by qualities in those objects which have a real *ordo* in regard to other objects, an *ordo* which is implied in and is dependent upon the rational plan of the universe. The realist's theory is more adequate than that of the absolutist, and it is so because, as usual, where the absolutist makes general statements of somewhat vague import, the realist inserts a distinction, and so makes the statement at once more precise and more consistent with facts. Instead of affirming that relations and their terms are int rdependent, he affirms that the terms give rise to the relations and the relations presuppose the terms ; and instead of asserting that ' relations intrinsically modify their terms,' he asserts that real relations *imply* a modification in *at least one* of the objects they relate, and thus is able to avoid the somewhat absurd and decidedly sceptical conclusion that every little bit of additional knowledge we acquire involves an intrinsic modification of every particle of the knowledge we already possess.

§ 431. The absolute theory of relations accounts largely for the unmistakably pantheistic tone of many of the theses of Absolutism ; while that ambiguity which characterises the conception of a relation as a something which *somehow* connects, and *somehow* intrinsically modifies, and *somehow* arises from and in and together with its terms, also characterises almost all the leading doctrines of the absolutist. And it is these mysterious ' somehows ' which meet us at every turn and are not only unexplained but are declared to be inexplicable, that more than anything else arouses the anger and provokes the scorn of the pragmatist. Yet it is possible by the aid of distinctions to reinterpret these doctrines, almost without exception, in a realistic sense, and so not only to render them more precise and more compatible with facts and with common-sense, but also to rid them of that dangerous pantheistic character which seems to destroy that which is most valuable to man, his freedom and his personality. Thus it is true that

the unification of the manifold of the world (of human knowledge) implies the presence of the manifold to a (human) mind, for which and through the action of which it is a related whole[1] (in the *logical*, but not in the *real* sense of that term). (And, again, it is true that) the unification of the manifold of the (real) world implies the presence of the manifold to a (divine) mind, for which, and through the action of which, it exists

[1] *Prolegomena to Ethics*, § 82.

as a system of inter-related and inter-active beings, constructed according to a rational plan in which each being has its proper place.

It is true also that the universe is a logical whole and a teleological whole, but not that it is a real whole ; and again that it implies a unity of Ground, and that a number of absolutely independent co-existing reals is impossible, but not that this unifying Ground is immanent, though the co-existing reals are present to It, and exist for It, and are sustained in their being by It. For the realist, each existing being is one and individual and has its own existence and its own nature, though it is wholly and essentially dependent upon the Divine Being for that existence and that nature, and may also in a different sense be dependent on another finite being for its existence and its nature, since it may have been by the action of that finite being as a secondary cause that it was brought into existence in time.

§ 432. Realism, it has been said, conceives God anthropomorphically ; but in Absolutism the conception of the universe is more anthropomorphic still. The absolutist, finding that man is one, individual, organic, and that his thoughts and actions are immanent within him, applies this conception to the universe itself ; but he forgets that human attributes can be predicable of God only in an analogous sense, and he forgets also that man's thoughts are not merely immanent, but refer to a something other and beyond, and that his actions are transient as well as immanent. Nor can it be said that the realist is guilty of a similar illicit use of a category when he says that God is the First

Cause of the Universe ; for he does not predicate causality of God in the same sense that he predicates it of finite agents. A finite cause cannot act without intrinsic modification, and is itself caused, being in fact but one among a series of causes, finite in power, extent and duration. God acts without intrinsic modification, is the Cause of all things without Himself being caused, and does not belong to the finite series of causes at all, but exists of Himself, is omnipotent, omnipresent, and eternal.

The relation between God and the universe is a mystery, and creation does not fully explain it ; but the difference between Absolutism and Realism in this respect is that while the former makes the relation between God and man a hopeless mystery and describes it in terms which, to say the least, sound pantheistic, the latter at any rate attempts to solve the mystery ; and though recognising that the human mind is incapable of comprehending it and that human language is powerless adequately to express it, is careful not only to point out that terms are not used in the same sense when predicated of God and of His creatures, but also to indicate as clearly as is possible in what sense they are used. And thus by clear conception and a correspondingly precise use of language, he is able to save himself from even the imputation of Pantheism and at the same time to reconcile Monism with Pluralism. For Realism the universe is one and it is also many ; and in a certain sense it is also one in many. It is one because it proceeds from and is sustained in its being by one divine Source ; and it is many because it consists of many individuals really distinct and really having a nature of their own. It is also many in one, because God is ' immanent ' within the universe, not anyhow nor yet in the same way that my thoughts are immanent within me, but "est *in* omnibus per potentiam, in quantum omnia ejus potestati subduntur ; est per præsentiam in omnibus in quantum omnia nuda sunt et aperta oculis ejus ; est in omnibus per essentiam, in quantum adest omnibus ut causa essendi." [1]

§ 433. Realism does not destroy Absolutism by thus distinguishing within its vague but suggestive theses a sense in which they are true from a sense in which they are not. The reality of the Absolute Ground is still preserved, and so, too, is the reality of the process by which from that Ground finite beings proceed, and the reality of their dependence upon it. Finite beings are really ' differences ' and ' ap-pearances ' of the Absolute, since they manifest in different ways, though always imperfectly, its attributes. But they are not mere appearances nor mere differences, nor do they proceed from that Ground by emanation. Finite beings, though essentially dependent upon the Divinity, are yet distinct, having each their own nature and finite contingent existence ; while the Divinity itself, precisely because it is the Ground or Cause of all things, and yet is distinct, is not merely an abstract Ground, but a living Personality having in an infinite degree all that is manifested in the finite beings that are due to Its creative act.

So closely at times does Absolutism seem to approach to the metaphysic of Realism that the

[1] *Summa Theologica*, i. q. 8, a. 3.

insertion or the omission of a few distinctions would
be sufficient to change the one into the other. By
Professor Mackenzie and in a certain sense by Hegel
and even by Mr. Bradley, the real existence of the
so-called 'material' world is granted. "The
idealist," says Professor Mackenzie, "does not seek
to rob anyone of his sun and planets, nor even of
his cups and saucers. To say that something is
more than what it seems is not to say that it is not
what it seems." [1] And, in truth, if it be granted
that 'material' things are 'less real' than strictly
spiritual beings, *i.e.*, that they have the properties
that we predicate of them physically, but have
neither intelligence, will, nor sentience, even on
this point there is not much difference between
Realism and Objective Idealism, save that the
realist objects to calling material things 'spiritual'
on the ground that it is a misuse of terms. The
realist holds with Kant "that what lies at the back
of phenomena is the thing-in-itself which may not
be heterogeneous." Indeed, he would go further,
and say that if the thing-in-itself here means God,
as it seems to do, it *cannot* be *wholly* heterogeneous,
since if God has created the universe he must have
created it like to Himself. And though the realist
would not grant that the material world may be but
another aspect of the Divinity, he would certainly
acknowledge the existence of "a thinking being,
the signs of whose thoughts in phenomena we can
perceive." [2]

Thus the difference between Realism and

[1] *Mind*, N.S. 59, p. 325.
[2] *Werke*, iii., p. 694.

Absolutism in regard to metaphysics is not insuperable, and yet it is sufficient for Realism to be able to claim that it retains all that is of vital importance to the metaphysics of Pragmatism. The unity, the changelessness, and the absolute reality of the universe are realised in the Divine Being who is one, eternal, and who alone has reality *a se*. Yet real personality, real activity, and real development exist in the created universe of finite and contingent beings ; and this is what the pragmatist demands. He demands, too, a ' world of plural facts ; ' and this also is to be found in Realism, though the realist's world of plural facts and plural beings is not a mosaic, but rather a system created and maintained in its being according to a definite and rational design which it manifests. Upon more than this the pragmatist does not insist, and it is little use re-discussing or trying to reconcile the hopeless ambiguities and obvious discrepancies of an incomplete philosophy of Pure Experience.

§ 434. In regard to Truth there are many points upon which Realism may be said to reconcile the differences of Absolutism and Pragmatism. In the first place, almost all of what is positive in that which the pragmatist contends for may be granted. Truth is empirically determined, and yet is due in large measure to the activity of the human mind. It is not static ; it develops ; and in its development postulation, experiment and purposive selection each play a part. And truth, when 'made', is regulative of human actions, leads to useful consequences and satisfies human needs. All this may be granted as psychological fact ; but in granting it we must make certain reservations. Truth in the process of ' making ' is not a passive ' mirroring ' of fact, but truth, when made, does correspond with and reveal the nature of reality. Postulation and purposive selection are of the greatest importance in the acquisition of truth ; but all truth is not obtained by postulation, nor does selection necessarily mutilate truth, or purpose modify its content. All truth is normative, useful and satisfactory ; but it is not merely normative nor merely useful, nor is it determined as truth by its power of giving satisfaction.

The realist, finding himself in agreement with the pragmatist on so many points in regard to the characteristics and growth of human truth, must to some extent find himself at variance with the absolutist in so far as the latter denies and does not merely neglect these points. Thus he cannot admit that human truth is due to the immanence of the Absolute within our finite minds. Indeed, it is inconceivable that the Absolute should be thinking in us, since error is a fact and in it our thoughts go wrong. Nevertheless, Realism holds that human truth, in so far as it is truth, really manifests the thoughts of the Absolute as expressed in concrete facts, and really reveals in part that systematic and coherent Truth which the absolutist calls Ideal and the realist ontological, but which both grant to be at bottom identical with reality itself. The realist, again, maintains as firmly as the absolutist that the concepts by means of which we think have real meaning and are not mere symbols or norms, and that the relations which hold between these concepts at any rate correspond even if they are not identical with relations and laws that hold in the real world. Lastly, Cognition in Realism as in Absolutism is properly a function of the intellect to which in this matter other faculties are subordinate.

§ 435. Thus in Truth, as understood by Realism, are brought together the chief characteristics of both Absolute and pragmatic truth, but in regard to the criteria of truth and in regard to its approximate character the realist finds himself at variance with both. ' Useful consequences ' and ' the satisfaction of needs ' as such do not seem to him to be criteria of truth at all, but rather the result of truth already established. On the other hand, the necessity of application and verification in experience he grants ; as also he grants the necessity of ' coherence.' But neither criterion for him is either universal or ultimate. The only criterion which at once possesses both these characteristics is that evidence which comes from the object, and which the mind, conscious that it has not been influenced by subjective conditions, has carefully examined, and so has come to recognise for what it is, a true manifestation of objective reality. The approximate nature of human truth is also granted, and not merely granted, but insisted upon by the realist ; yet he also insists that this approximation does not destroy truth, and that to be approximate is quite a different thing from being subject to indefinite and intrinsic modification. Here he dissents from both absolutist and pragmatist. Convinced that knowledge is possible, he

infers that the means or instruments by which
knowledge is acquired, viz., the human faculties of
cognition, must be veracious. Hence, when by a
process of reasoning which, as Newman says, it is
impossible completely to analyse or adequately
to express in words, reason (or the ' Illative Sense ')
pronounces a proposition or a doctrine to be true, the
realist prefers to accept this dictum of his intellect
rather than fall into Scepticism.

§ 436. Pragmatist and absolutist, on the other
hand, though the one derives the doctrine from his
Postulatory theory of knowledge and the other from
his Coherence-notion of Truth, both affirm that
knowledge is liable to indefinite modifications and
may become some day completely transformed.
But in spite of Dr. Schiller's assertion to the contrary, it is Pragmatism and not Absolutism that is
most infected by this Scepticism. The absolutist
is an intellectualist, and an intellectualist can hardly
be a sceptic. He may admit that human knowledge evolves ; but he is not as a rule so fascinated
by the idea of evolution that he must needs extend
evolution to all truths, even to those which in denying we implicitly affirm, nor does he feel bound to
reduce all knowledge to a process which could never
have had a beginning and will never have an end.
On the contrary, he has a metaphysic in which
apparently he believes, and with his view of truth
a ' Corridor-theory ' is incompatible. Not so the
pragmatist, as witness Le Roy and Papini. Le
Roy exhorts us not to reject Aristotle and Aquinas
any more than we reject Plato, Descartes or Kant.
Each theory is to be taken as an experience of

thought, a moment in its progressive life, in which
the claim to rest there would engender immediately
error, but in which the truth would appear, on the
contrary, in its dynamic tendency.[1]   And Papini,
too, has shown that the pragmatic method is
consistent with any philosophy.   By it theories and
beliefs are rendered plastic, which, for the Florentine
school, is equivalent to saying that we may believe
what suits us best, and may change our beliefs
according to our present needs.   All that Pragmatism excludes is the useless and the verbal.   It may
be used to establish any metaphysic ; and Professor
James himself has offered it as a means of reconciling
the religious demands of Rationalism with the
empiricist's love of facts.

That such a reconciliation is desirable no one will
deny.   Indeed, it is somewhat similar to that
which I myself have attempted.   And a method so
broad and so comprehensive as to embrace standpoints so thoroughly opposed would indeed be
valuable, *if* it could effect the reconciliation without
destroying the validity of knowledge and the
objectivity of truth.   But a pragmatic harmony
can be brought about only by the sacrifice of these,
and in effect is not a harmony at all.   Pragmatism
does not reconcile Rationalism with Empiricism ;
it flatly denies that Rationalism has any ground to
stand on, as Professor James himself has again and
again assured us.   Nor does it preserve that
' richest intimacy with facts,' which is acknowledged
to be the aim of all genuine Empiricism.   On the

[1] *Revue de Philosophie*, v. 19. 6, p. 419.   Reprint from the
Matin, 15th June, 1906,

contrary, in order to maintain its theory of universal postulation, it is forced to ignore a fact which introspection reveals, viz., that knowledge is based on self-evident first principles, which cannot be explained away except by a violation of the fundamental law of teleological interpretation, that the lower must be explained by the higher and not the higher by the lower.

§ 437. A pragmatic reconciliation in fact, like Pragmatism itself, is based on ambiguity ; and, if possible at all, is possible only because Pragmatism deliberately refuses to define its terms or to determine precisely the meaning of its statements. Pragmatism which began as a method for ' making our ideas clear,' has ended by offering us a theory of knowledge which is more ambiguous than any that ever existed before, so ambiguous, indeed, that its founder has renounced it and changed the name of his own more intelligible and more practical method to Pragmaticism. Truth in Pragmatism is said to ' happen ' to an idea under certain circumstances, a statement which tells us nothing about the nature of truth, but leaves us in doubt as to whether it is or is not to be identified with utility. We are said to ' make ' truth, which may mean either that ideas are the products of psychological processes or that truth has no objective counterpart. Finally, we are said to ' make ' reality, where reality would ordinarily be interpreted as objective reality, but apparently may also signify knowledge. Nor is this ambiguity merely incidental to the pragmatic method. Its ' large, loose way of speaking ' and of reasoning is one of its essential characteristics.

RR

M. Le Roy insists not only that what is clear is uninteresting, but that "*raisonnements sourds, sans paroles ni divisions, sont les seuls féconds.*" No wonder, then, that Pragmatism can retain, not merely the aim, but more than half the cardinal principles of Kantian Criticism, its doctrines of Postulation and of Reconciliation in Synthesis, its theory of the Constructive Activity of Thought and its principle of Immanence, and yet despise the mind of its author as a ' bric-a-brac museum,' which has given to philosophy no idea of value that it did not already possess,[1] and scornfully describe his most eminent successor as a philosopher who, " leaving to his disciples a glittering legacy of magniloquent but meaningless phrases, vanishes into thin air before he can be caught and questioned about the meaning of his enchantments."[2]

§ 438. If we are to judge Pragmatism by the purpose which it claims as its *ratio essendi*, Pragmatism is a failure. So far from increasing the clearness of philosophic language and ideas, it has by its exaggerations increased the confusion already existing. So far from establishing metaphysics on a sounder and more scientific basis, it has not yet made up its mind what metaphysic is to be established. And instead of removing from human knowledge the taint of Scepticism, it has provided the sceptic with a further argument against its validity by informing him that our faculties were never meant to give us real knowledge, but only to lead to useful, practical results. Criticism as a

---

[1] James, *Journ. of Phil., Psy. and Sc. Methods*, 1904, p. 687.
[2] Schiller, *Riddles of the Sphinx*, p. 158.

method and Absolutism as a theory of reality are at any rate more capable of satisfying our needs than the useless norms and ambiguous dicta of the pragmatist. For Absolutism, despite its inconsistency, its vagueness, and its fondness for hypostatising psychological abstractions and converting logical notions into metaphysical realities, at any rate does not explain away knowledge, nor minimise the intellect, nor destroy entirely our notions of truth, nor even glory in its own ambiguity. Moreover, it has a metaphysic to offer us which the pragmatist has not. Yet Pragmatism has its function in the economy of philosophic life and the development of philosophic thought. As the antithesis of Absolutism, it exaggerates precisely those characteristics of knowledge and reality which Absolutism neglects, and thus, by bringing us back to the human point of view, it saves us from falling into errors to which the Absolute position is liable, and at the same time emphasises truths which are of the greatest value to man and of the greatest importance both in the theoretical and in the practical affairs of human life.

§ 439. In Pragmatism and Absolutism Herr Simmel's doctrine of dual heuristic principles or standpoints is illustrated. But neither Absolutism nor Pragmatism nor any other philosophical antitheses are merely heuristic. They each have a certain objective validity and are capable of being united in a synthesis which shall reveal more fully the real nature of the Universe than either does if taken apart from the other. But in order thus to reconcile antitheses we must distinguish. To recon-

cile what is contradictory is impossible : for con-
tradictories as such are incompatible. Yet no
philosophical antitheses are merely contradictory ;
they are also complementary. Each takes up a
different point of view, and emphasises a different
aspect of reality. And different aspects and
different points of view are not necessarily either
contradictory or incompatible. Hence by distinguishing the different senses which assertions on
either side may bear, we may be able to bring about
a reconciliation which shall be not a synthesis of
contradictions—for that is impossible—but a synthesis of differences which are due to the different
points of view from which, as human beings, we
may regard the same eternal truths.

This is what I have attempted to do in regard to
Absolutism and Pragmatism. I may have succeeded,
or I may have failed ; but, at any rate, I have shown
that the fundamental theses of the two philosophies
are retained in Realism with distinctions and
reservations. The realist is fond of distinctions,
and though this tendency may at times lead to a
' *subtilitas affectata nimis et inutilis*,' and to
' *præcisiones mentales et varia alia mentis otiosa
deliria*,' it has its proper function in philosophy,
and is necessary as a preliminary to any kind of
' higher ' synthesis. By distinguishing matter from
form the Aristotelian is able to maintain without
contradiction the reality of both, and yet to explain
matter as the imperfect manifestation and inadequate expression of mind. The distinction which
he asserts between the faculties of the human mind
enables him to avoid those fallacies which result

from the identification of intellect with will, or will with intellect, or intellect with sense ; and yet to retain the unity and integrity of man and the reality of human personality. While the distinction between God and the created Universe enables him to reconcile unity with plurality, necessity with contingency, the infinite with the finite ; and yet to maintain that all alike are real. Lastly, his theory that in cognition the object determines the mind explains both the certainty of knowledge and the objectivity of truth, and at the same time is consistent with a teleological and genetic psychology, allows for the growth of knowledge, admits the constructive activity of thought, and acknowledges the limitations that are due to our human ways of knowing and to our human points of view.

§ 440. Realism, too, is consistent with facts and with the data of human experience. It is a philosophy which recognises the laws of common-sense as in the last analysis the source whence flows all certitude and truth. Science and philosophy are but the work of common-sense carried to greater perfection. The difference between the philosopher or the scientist and the man-in-the-street is chiefly one of degree. The intellectual activity of the former has attained a maximum ; that of the latter is spasmodic, and in intensity and in concentration is comparatively feeble. But the thinking of both is based on experience and is governed by the same laws and subject to the same criteria. Philosophy, science and common-sense must stand or fall together. If we cannot trust the quasi-instinctive beliefs of the one, we cannot rely upon the more

delicate and intricate reasonings of the other. If in
the ordinary exercise of our faculties we may err in
regard to fundamental truths, whose acceptance is
universal, what guarantee have we that when
applied to more difficult and more theoretical
problems those same faculties are reliable ? Either,
then, common-sense deceives us, and in that case
both philosophy and science are impossible, or the
scientist and the philosopher should join with the
man-in-the-street in adopting the standpoint of the
realist. For common-sense belief in objective
reality and in the existence of a world that is independent of the thinking self, arises spontaneously
and naturally within the mind of each one of us,
and has so arisen from time immemorial. If, then,
common-sense has erred in this, the most universal
and most natural of all its beliefs, neither scientific
reasoning nor philosophical speculation can be
regarded as reliable in any matter whatsoever. Our
only alternative is Scepticism. We must declare all
knowledge impossible, and the quest of it waste of
time ; we must pronounce the problems of life insoluble, and so must acknowledge that one of the
most urgent needs of human nature is a source of
illusion, a spring of action which will never be
satisfied, a purposive striving that can never attain
its end. But this conclusion is incompatible with
the existence of such a need and destroys the very
notion of a rational and intelligible universe.

§ 441. Whether, then, Realism is or is not a
higher synthesis of Absolutism and Pragmatism, it
is certain that Realism is the only philosophy which
is self-consistent, and at the same time consistent

with facts. And that it is possible seriously to offer Realism as a reconciliation of two positions so antagonistic as those of Pragmatism and Absolutism, is itself a proof that Realism is not a static theory, devoid of life, incapable of development, and always some hundreds of years behind the times. The philosophy of Aristotle and Aquinas has developed and still contains the potentiality of future life. Latent within it are many ideas which yet remain to be broken up into differences and reunited in higher syntheses. If we take it as it was, we shall find that the principles which a critical regress on more modern positions will reveal, are there set forth ; while if we take it as it is, it can still claim to be the only philosophy which can show " what are the universal conditions which must be satisfied by anything of which we can say that it is or that it happens."

APPENDIX

THE INDEPENDENCE OF REALITY

I AM not aware that I have used the term 'independence' in any loose or ambiguous sense; yet my meaning does not seem to have made itself clear to some of my critics. I take this opportunity, therefore, of attempting to clear up any misunderstanding that may have occurred.

THE NOTION OF INDEPENDENCE. There is a tendency among idealists to use the term 'independent' in an exclusive or absolute sense, sometimes even to employ it as the equivalent of 'out of relation.' This is unfortunate, for to be independent of anything is by no means the same as to be unrelated to it. Nor is independence in a finite world *ever* absolute. B is *dependent* upon A when (1) A is the cause of the whole being of B, or (2) when A is the cause of certain modifications in B, or again (3) is the condition *sine qua non* of certain of B's activities. And conversely B is *independent* of A when, and in so far as, any of these relations are wanting. But B will not be wholly independent of A, unless all are wanting; and this never happens. In predicating independence, therefore, the sense in which it is understood should be stated, and this I have throughout been careful to do.

THE INDEPENDENCE OF FINITE BEINGS *inter se.* I assume, so I am told by one critic,[1]

[1] *Hibbert Journal*, October, 1910.

" a plurality of independent finite substances,"
and this assumption is inconsistent with my
theory that finite substances form a system
governed by universal laws, that they are complex,
that they grow by assimilation of 'material' from
without, and that they are active as well as passive.
How my critic extracts the above assumption from
such a theory, I am at a loss to understand. I
certainly hold that finite substances are 'distinct'
in that each has its own nature and its own
existence ;[1] but for its existence each substance
depends not only upon God,[2] but also upon
the act of another finite substance in the
order of time,[3] and again for its *continued* existence
upon the simultaneous activity of other substances
which condition its own.[4] Finite substances are
independent of one another only in so far as
(1) their continued existence is not *caused* by the
action of other finite substances, and (2) the
specific character of their activities is determined
ab intra and directed (consciously or unconsciously) to the end for which they exist.

INDEPENDENCE AND INDIVIDUALITY. It is
further urged (*loc. cit.*) that upon the alleged
assumption of independence among finite substances rests my theory of their individuality.
Since, however, I do not assert independence
except in the sense above explained, this can
hardly be the case. Individuality certainly implies
the distinction of one complex whole from another,
but it does not connote their absolute independence.
A being is individual when it is *one* in that

[1] Pp. 350, 362.   [2] P. 349.   [3] P. 351 *f*.   [4] P. 355 *f*.

(1) its existence, its nature, and its attributes are its own, and (2) in that its activities, however diverse, proceed from within, from a single principle, and are directed by that principle toward the development (or perseverance) of the whole. A quality is not individual. It belongs to, and is dependent upon, that which it qualifies, and its whole function is to qualify that to which it belongs. Nor is a part individual ; for a part is subordinate to the whole, and whatever functions may pertain to it are dominated by, and subservient to, the purpose of the whole. A part may have definite character distinguishing it from other parts. It may also be possible in some cases to separate it from the whole without destroying its essential character. But this can happen only in wholes which are less highly organised, and therefore less perfect both in themselves and in their parts. It is surely a mistake to suppose that the *individuality* of the part is more perfect in proportion as its relation to other parts, and again to the whole, is more intimate. Its *character* may be more perfect, and its functions more definitely specialised. But if this is so, it is due not to the part, but to the active principle which dominates the whole and makes it one. The more perfect the character of the parts, the more completely are they subordinated to the purpose of the whole, determined by it as to their structure, and controlled by it in their functions. When this is so, the individuality of the whole is undoubtedly greater, but precisely for this very reason the individuality of the parts is less. Cut off from

a substance thus highly organised one of its parts, and at once the character of that part is radically changed. Its functions cease, and its organisation is rapidly dissolved. Why so ? Surely it is because the part has no individuality of its own. In a perfect organism a part is what it is only through the whole to which it belongs. Its character and its organisation are completely dominated by the active principle of the whole, and apart from this whole have neither purpose nor meaning.

INDIVIDUALITY AND THE ABSOLUTE. Apply this conclusion, which experience seems to force upon us, to the doctrine that Reality is one and we see at once that the individuality of non-rational substances and the personality of man is utterly destroyed by the absolute and all-embracing individuality of the perfect whole to which they are alleged to belong. Man is just a function of the Absolute, nothing more. He has neither being nor purpose of his own. As part of a Universe which is absolutely one and perfect in its organization, he is completely dominated, subordinated, nay more, constituted by its purposive activity;—and this is a far truer sense than his hand or his foot can be said to be dominated by that less perfect organism, himself. Consequently, his individuality, his liberty, his responsibility, in a word everything that he can call his own disappears. He owns nothing, and *is* nothing, in abstraction from the Absolute to which he belongs as an integral function or part.

Because this is so, and because it is at the same time so utterly repugnant to rational experience

and common sense, I have preferred—*abstracting
from consciousness* (my critic omits these important words)—to compare the universe to a machine
rather than to an organism.[1] The universe is
not a machine, for its operations and connections
are more than merely mechanical ; but still less
is it an organism, for its parts have real individuality, real unity. Though dependent upon
the Supreme Being whence all proceed, and
though dependent also in a lesser degree upon
finite beings other than itself, each created thing
has in a true sense its own existence, its own
nature, its own functions and activities determined
from within, its own end ; and therefore may
truly be said to be one and individual.

THE INDEPENDENCE OF KNOWER AND KNOWN.
I have been asked[2] to define what I mean by the
' independence ' of reality in respect of the knowing mind. This I have already done in a note
to p. 48 so far as concerns the object of external
perception ; but in order to make the matter
clearer some further statement seems desirable.
In the first place, then, the ' independence ' of
reality is predicable only in respect of finite
knowers, not in respect of God. The created
universe is ' distinct ' from, *i.e.*, other than, God ;
but its existence pre-supposes His knowledge of
it. Indeed, the divine Intelligence is, as St. Thomas
says, the cause of all things that exist.[3] But of
all *finite* knowers reality is independent in that
(1) it does not need to enter into any finite experi-

---

[1] P. 363.   [2] *Mind* N.S. 76, p. 569.
[3] *Summa Theol.* i. q. 22. a. 1.

ence in order to exist, nor yet (2) in order to
'find its true being,' nor (3) when it does so enter
is it (reality) in any way modified. Knowledge
does not directly affect reality as such, still less
constitute it. If it is to make a difference to
reality, it can do so only through action, not
through perception or thought. Strictly speaking,
it is in my view incorrect to say that reality
' enters ' experience. It may enter the field of
observation and so become an object of experience, but it does not ' enter,' *i.e.*, become an
integral part or aspect of experience as such.
Reality *as experienced*, i.e., the content of perception
or thought, which we refer to objective reality as a
predicate, is in part the product of that reality and
in part the product of our minds (*vide infra*). Our
experience of reality, therefore, may be very considerably modified by our cognitive activities. But
the modification thus effected by abortive strivings
after knowledge, does not affect the objective
reality which we seek to know. It affects only
subjective reality, or reality as experienced, a
reality which as such exists only within our minds.
Its consequence, moreover, is error, not truth or
knowledge properly so called.

The relation of the known to the knower, therefore, is not in the Scholastic sense a ' real '
relation : it does not intrinsically affect or modify
that which it relates. The relation of the
knower to the known, on the other hand, is, as I
have endeavoured to show in the preceding pages,
a very real relation, implying, as it does, a causal
dependence, whereby is produced in the mind of

the knower a modification that *de facto* corresponds
with, or resembles, that to which it is referred.

But in what consists, I am asked, this correspondence, the presence of which is truth, its absence
ignorance, and its distortion error. Speaking from
the point of view of the epistemologist who has
before him both knower and known, not from the
point of view of the knower himself to whom
(except in reflection) is present only the known ;
we may define correspondence as a relation of like
to like. But how, you now ask, can immaterial
ideas resemble material things ? An analogy
drawn from action and its effects may help us
here. One knows from one's own experience that
it is possible to form in one's mind a plan or
design in which various objects of definite structure
and with definite properties and functions are
connected together by certain laws in accordance
with which they interact. It is also possible to
give expression to such a plan or design, to realise
it in the concrete. Suppose that this has been
done ; suppose that (*v.g.*) an architect has constructed a cathedral or an engineer a bridge. The
cathedral and bridge express and embody the design
of him who conceived and constructed them.
That design is realised in them and lives in them,
for it is this that makes them what they are.
The design now exists, therefore, in the real as
well as in the ideal order, and between the two
orders there is thus a correspondence. Bring on to
the scene a student of architecture or of engineer-
ing, and once more the ideal plan of cathedral or
bridge will reproduce itself. Through the instru-

mentality of the concrete real objects, there will
arise in the mind of the student an idea which
corresponds with that conceived by architect or
engineer and embodied in the objects they ' create.'
And the correspondence is in both cases twofold.
The architect does not merely conceive a cathedral built according to certain laws, he imagines
(or pictures) it so built, and his cathedral realises
both image and concept. So too with the student,
who not only sees a sensible object which he calls
a cathedral, but also understands the idea which
it expresses, the idea which, objectively realised,
makes it what it is.

So it is with all knowledge. The universe and
every finite being within the universe, is the
expression, the realisation, the concrete embodi-
ment of an idea conceived in the mind of God,
and in so far as the universe and things within it
are known by us, that idea reproduces itself in
our mind through the instrumentality of the
objects in which it is embodied. There is in both
cases, therefore, correspondence between idea and
reality ; but in the first case it is the reality that
is created like the idea, and in the second it is the
idea in our mind which is determined through the
object in its own image. Knowledge is thus
the converse of action or ' creation.' In ' creation '
the idea (itself existent in a mind) pre-exists reality ;
in knowledge it is reality that pre-exists and is
reproduced in mind. It need hardly here be
pointed out that this view does not mean that our
cognitive faculties are purely passive *potentiae*.
On the contrary our mind itself constructs plans

or theories by which it seeks to explain phenomena. In our search for truth we both ' invent ' and ' interfere.' Interference is necessary in order that the objects in which we are interested and no others may be allowed to act upon our senses. Invention is necessary because our data are incomplete. But if we are to know truly, neither our inventions nor our interference must modify those facts we seek to know and explain. The purpose of our interference is merely to render the facts more˙manifest ; and these same facts must in the end be the criterion whence we judge of the validity of theoretical constructions. Conclusions deduced from theory must coincide or correspond with the observed facts which it is the aim of theory to explain,—and the existence of correspondence in this case must be proved. Observed facts, too, as subjectively apprehended, must correspond with facts as they are in reality ; but here no proof is either possible or necessary, for the correspondence of facts *quâ* observations and *quâ* realities is not itself a fact of observation, but rather a condition of the true observation of fact. Only on this condition can truth be attained, and our theories about the universe approach nearer and nearer to that ideal plan or design which exists in the mind of God and is embodied in the reality He has created.

INDEX

Abbreviations:—c.s.=common-sense; f=and following page or pages; kn=knowledge; Metaph.=metaphysics; n=note; Phil. P. E.=Philosophy of Pure Experience; prin= principle; *sec.*=*secundum*; sc.=science; *v.*=*vide*.

STONYHURST PHILOSOPHICAL SERIES.

EDITED BY RICHARD F. CLARKE, S.J.

Extract from a Letter of His Holiness the Pope to the Bishop of Salford, on the Philosophical Course at Stonyhurst.

" You will easily understand, Venerable Brother, the pleasure We felt in what you reported to Us about the College of Stonyhurst in your diocese, namely, that by the efforts of the Superiors of this College, an excellent course of the exact sciences has been successfully set on foot, by establishing professorships, and by publishing in the vernacular for their students text-books of Philosophy, following the principles of St. Thomas Aquinas. On this work We earnestly congratulate the Superiors and teachers of the College, and by letter We wish affectionately to express Our good-will towards them."

1. Logic. By RICHARD F. CLARKE, S.J., formerly Fellow and Tutor of St. John's College, Oxford. New Impression. Price 5s.

"An excellent text-book of Aristotelian logic, interesting, vivid, sometimes almost racy in its illustrations, while from first to last it never, so far as we have noticed, diverges from Aristotelian orthodoxy."—*The Guardian.*

"Though Father Clarke mainly concerns himself with Formal Logic, he occasionally, for the sake of edification, makes excursions into wider fields. Adopting the standpoint of 'moderate realism,' he directs his chief attack against the limitation of the Principle of Contradiction, the nominalist statement of the Principle of Identity, and the theory of conception set forth by Mill. The arguments usually employed in these time-honoured controversies are marshalled with much vigour. . . . The uncontroversial portions of the book are extremely clear, and the descriptions of the various forms of syllogism as little dry as their subject matter permits."— *Saturday Review.*

2. First Principles of Knowledge. By JOHN RICKABY, S.J., late Professor of Logic and General Metaphysics at St. Mary's Hall, Stonyhurst. Fourth Edition. Price 5s.

" In the two volumes named below (*First Principles of Knowledge* and *Logic*), we have set forth in clear and vigorous English the doctrine of knowledge and the principles of reasoning taught by the learned and subtle Aquinas in the thirteenth century, but adapted to the needs of students and controversialists of the nineteenth century by teachers who, like St. Thomas himself, are able to discuss doubts without doubting, to hold converse with sceptics of every school, and still to hold to the faith. . . . To those who would like to know exactly the form that philosophy takes when she enters the service of 'The Church' the volumes may be commended."—*Inquirer*

3. Moral Philosophy (Ethics and Natural Law).
By JOSEPH RICKABY, S.J., M.A. Lond.; late Professor of Ethics at St. Mary's Hall, Stonyhurst. New Impression. Price 5s.

"The style of the book is bright and easy, and the English (as we need not say) extremely good. . . . The manual will be welcome on all sides as a sound, original, and fairly complete English treatise on the groundwork of morality."—*Dublin Review.*

"The style is popular and easily intelligible; the principles are fully illustrated by concrete examples."—*Church Quarterly Review.*

4. Natural Theology. By BERNARD BOEDDER, S.J.,
Professor of Natural Theology at St. Mary's Hall, Stonyhurst. Second Edition. Price 6s. 6d.

"This volume considerably increases the debt which English-speaking Catholics owe to the Jesuit Fathers who have brought out the 'Stonyhurst Series' of philosophical manuals. It is really a treatise *de Deo* dealing with the proofs of the existence of God, the Divine attributes, and the relation of God to the world—in plain intelligible English, and adapted to the difficulties raised in our own country at the present day. The author is evidently well acquainted with Mill, Spencer, Huxley, and other contemporary writers; they are quoted freely and clearly answered."—*Dublin Review.*

5. Psychology: Empirical and Rational. By
MICHAEL MAHER, S.J., D.Lit.; M.A. Lond. Sixth Edition. Twentieth to Twenty-Second Thousand. Price 6s. 6d.

"Father Maher's admirable volume has reached its fourth edition. It has been re-written and considerably enlarged. Already regarded as one of the best handbooks on the subjects, in its revised and enlarged form it will not fail to approve itself still more to the teacher and the student. . . It deserves all the success it has met with."—*Scottish Review.*

6. General Metaphysics. By JOHN RICKABY, S.J.
Third Edition (1898) Re-issue. Price 5s.

"*Metaphysics* is not a popular study, but Father Rickaby has done his best to popularize it. He expounds the idea of Being with its nature, existence, and attributes, and other notions less general, as substance, causality, space, and time. He ought to succeed in dissipating the common prejudice that metaphysics is mere cobweb spinning."—*Bombay Advertiser.*

Old Criticism and New Pragmatism. By J. M. O'SULLIVAN, M.A. (R.U.I.) ; D.Ph. (Heidelberg) ; Fellow of the Royal University of Ireland. 8vo, 7s. 6d. net.

The Individual and Reality: an Essay touching the First Principles of Metaphysics. By EDWARD DOUGLAS FAWCETT. Medium 8vo, 12s. 6d. net.

The Science of Ethics. By Rev. MICHAEL CRONIN, M.A., D.D., Ex-Fellow, Royal University of Ireland, Professor Clonliffe College, Dublin. Vol. I., General Ethics. 8vo, 12s. 6d. net.

The Mystery of Existence in the Light of an Optimistic Philosophy. By C. W. ARMSTRONG. Crown 8vo, 2s. 6d. net.

The Approach to Philosophy. By RALPH BARTON PERRY. Crown 8vo, 6s. net.

Synthetica : being Meditations Epistemological and Ontological ; comprising the Edinburgh Gifford Lectures of 1905-6. By S. S. LAURIE. 2 vols. (Vol. I., Book I., On Knowledge, Vol. II., Book 2, On God and Man). 8vo, 21s. net.

Intuitive Suggestion: a New Theory of the Evolution of Mind. By J. W. THOMAS. Crown 8vo, 3s. 6d. net.

The Origin and Growth of the Moral Instinct. By ALEXANDER SUTHERLAND, M.A. 2 vols. 8vo, 28s.

Government or Human Evolution. By EDMOND KELLY, M.A., F.G.S. Vol. I. Justice. Crown 8vo, gilt top, 7s. 6d. net. Vol. II. Individualism and Collectivism. Crown 8vo, gilt top, 10s. 6d. net.

The History of English Rationalism in the Nineteenth Century. By ALFRED W. BENN. 2 vols. 8vo, 21s. net.

LONGMANS, GREEN, AND CO.

39 PATERNOSTER ROW, LONDON

NEW YORK, BOMBAY, AND CALCUTTA